STRATEGY | *2008-2009*

David J. Ketchen, Jr.
Auburn University

Alan B. Eisner
Pace University

Gregory G. Dess
University of Texas at Dallas

G. T. Lumpkin
Texas Tech University

D1399860

McGraw-Hill Irwin

Boston   Burr Ridge, IL   Dubuque, IA   New York   San Francisco   St. Louis
Bangkok   Bogotá   Caracas   Kuala Lumpur   Lisbon   London   Madrid   Mexico City
Milan   Montreal   New Delhi   Santiago   Seoul   Singapore   Sydney   Taipei   Toronto

McGraw-Hill
Irwin

STRATEGY: 2008–2009

Published by McGraw-Hill/Irwin, a business unit of The McGraw-Hill Companies, Inc., 1221 Avenue of the Americas, New York, NY, 10020. Copyright © 2009 by The McGraw-Hill Companies, Inc. All rights reserved. No part of this publication may be reproduced or distributed in any form or by any means, or stored in a database or retrieval system, without the prior written consent of The McGraw-Hill Companies, Inc., including, but not limited to, in any network or other electronic storage or transmission, or broadcast for distance learning.

Some ancillaries, including electronic and print components, may not be available to customers outside the United States.

This book is printed on acid-free paper.

1 2 3 4 5 6 7 8 9 0 WCK/WCK 0 9 8

ISBN 978-0-07-338128-2
MHID 0-07-338128-4
ISSN 1937-9072

Executive editor: *Doug Hughes*
Senior sponsoring editor: *Michael Ablassmeir*
Developmental editor: *Laura Griffin*
Senior marketing manager: *Anke Braun Weekes*
Senior project manager: *Harvey Yep*
Production supervisor: *Gina Hangos*
Lead designer: *Matthew Baldwin*
Senior photo research coordinator: *Jeremy Cheshareck*
Lead media project manager: *Cathy L. Tepper*
Cover design: *Kay Lieberherr*
Interior design: *Artemio Ortiz*
Cover image: © *Corbis Images*
Typeface: *10/12 Times Roman*
Compositor: Laserwords Private Limited
Printer: *Quebecor World Versailles Inc.*

Photo Credits—page 18, Royalty-Free/CORBIS; **page 30,** David Zurick; **page 44,** Royalty-Free/CORBIS; **page 62,** The McGraw-Hill Companies, Inc./Lars A. Niki, photographer; **page 69,** Digital Vision/PunchStock; **page 80,** Getty Images; **page 100,** The McGraw-Hill Companies, Inc./John Flournoy, photographer; **page 112,** The McGraw-Hill Companies, Inc./Christopher Kerrigan, photographer; **page 122,** B. Drake/PhotoLink/Getty Images; **page 140,** The McGraw-Hill Companies, Inc./John Flournoy, photographer; **page 144,** The McGraw-Hill Companies, Inc./Andrew Resek, photographer; **page 162,** Flying Colours Ltd/Getty Images; **page 165,** The McGraw-Hill Companies, Inc./Jill Braaten, photographer; **page 181,** The McGraw-Hill Companies, Inc./Jill Braaten, photographer; **page 186,** The McGraw-Hill Companies, Inc./John Flournoy, photographer; **page 203,** Digital Vision/Getty Images; **page 279,** The McGraw-Hill Companies, Inc./Jill Braaten, photographer

Dedication

To Bill Brashers and Mark Sharfman
DAVE

*To my family, Helaine,
Rachel, and Jacob*
ALAN

About the Authors

David J. Ketchen, Jr. serves as Lowder Eminent Scholar and Professor of Management at Auburn University. He earned his PhD at the Pennsylvania State University. His research interests include entrepreneurship and franchising, methodological issues in organizational research, strategic supply chain management, and the determinants of superior organizational performance. His work has been published in outlets such as the *Academy of Management Journal, Strategic Management Journal,* the *Academy of Management Executive, Journal of Operations Management,* and *Journal of Management,* among others. He is currently an associate editor for the *Academy of Management Journal* and he has completed terms as an associate editor for the *Journal of Management, Organizational Research Methods, Journal of Operations Management,* and *Journal of International Business Studies.* He is co-founder of HultKetchen International Group LLC, a consultancy.

Alan B. Eisner is Professor of Management and Graduate Management Program Chair at the Lubin School of Business, Pace University. He received his PhD in management from the Stern School of Business, New York University. His primary research interests are in strategic management, technology management, organizational learning, and managerial decision making. He has published research articles and cases in journals such as *Advances in Strategic Management, International Journal of Electronic Commerce, International Journal of Technology Management, American Business Review, Journal of Behavioral and Applied Management,* and *Journal of the International Academy for Case Studies.* He is the Associate Editor of the Case Association's peer reviewed journal. *The CASE Journal.*

Preface

Every good book has a good story behind it. *Strategy 2008–2009* is no exception. In the spring of 2006, McGraw-Hill/Irwin brought together an outstanding group of strategic management teachers for a symposium on teaching. One task of this group was to design a textbook that would meet a rapidly growing market need for a book that would address the core issues within strategic management and do so in a rigorous yet engaging way. Drawing on their conversation with colleagues, these professors called for a book that concentrated on key strategic management topics, addressed these topics by building on both real-life examples and academic research, and did so at a price point attractive to students. Over the course of two days, the group discussed and debated what an ideal book for meeting these criteria would look like and include. The group recognized that outstanding raw material for such a book was available from Dess, Lumpkin, and Eisner's *Strategic Management, Text and Cases.* By the time the symposium ended, a clear plan for delivering a market leading book was in place. The book you hold in your hands is the product of the group's collective insights and wisdom.

The Dess author team realized there were already some good strategy books on the market. However, they felt there was a need for a text that students would find not only readable and relevant but also challenging. In essence, their tagline is: "Strong enough for the professor, but made for the student."

In their text, the Dess team has endeavored to use an engaging writing style free of unnecessary jargon, to cover all the traditional bases, and to integrate some central themes throughout the book that are vital to understanding strategic management in today's global economy. Among these themes are globalization, technology, ethics, and entrepreneurship. The authors bring concepts to life with short examples from business practice to illustrate virtually every strategy concept in the book as well as more detailed examples to drive home key points. In addition, they provide an excellent set of cases to help students analyze, integrate, and apply strategic management concepts.

The Dess team was also closely involved with the creation a variety of supplements to aid instructors with class preparation and delivery. Key features that have been consistent throughout all editions remain the same. However, a hallmark of the Dess text (consistent with the strategy concept) is value added. The authors repeatedly asked themselves what new features would add value to the process of teaching and learning.

For example, the chapter notes in the Instructor's Manual, prepared by the Dess team, do not simply summarize the material. Instead, numerous discussion questions and boxed examples supplement material in the text. They also prepared the Test Bank themselves. These authors feel so strongly about providing a supplements package that makes classes relevant, rigorous, and rewarding for instructors and students alike that they developed almost all of these materials themselves. They firmly believe that this enables them to ensure a high level of quality and consistency.

We would like to thank Greg Dess and Tom Lumpkin for allowing us to use their text and supplements as the launching point for this book. We also thank the following symposium participants, who gave so much of their creativity and teaching experience to help shape this book:

David Flint, *Utah Valley State College*

Scott Latham, *Bentley College*

Hun Lee, *George Mason University*

Jim Marshall, *Cal Poly Pomona*

Kathryn Martell, *Montclair State University*

Richard Mpoyi, *Middle Tennessee State University*

Don Neubaum, *Oregon State University*

David A. Page, *Robert Morris University*

Doug Polley, *St. Cloud State University*

Annette Ranft, *Florida State University*

Gary Roberts, *Kennesaw State University*

Phillip Stoeberl, *St. Louis University*

Ray Van Ness, *State University of New York at Albany*

Page West, *Wake Forest University*

So what else makes this book special? First, *Strategy 2008–2009* makes its way through the core concepts in shorter chapters. Decisions on what to include in each chapter were driven by the results of a questionnaire distributed to scores of leading strategic management professors. The result is a truly market-driven book. Not only is the material current, but it is also free of superfluous detail, allowing instructors and students time to opt for a more flexible format either by further discussing relevant selected case studies or taking advantage of using a simulation like BSG or GLO-BUS in the classroom. The survey also made clear the importance of examples to enhance student learning. Despite the relative brevity of the chapters, each chapter includes a wide variety of intriguing examples to illustrate ideas, providing ample raw material for stimulating classroom discussions.

Second, the approach taken to two of today's most vital issues sets this book apart. Following an overview of the strategic management process (Chapter 1), Chapter 2 focuses on the two key contextual features that today's managers must keep in mind as they make strategic decisions: the international dimensions of strategy and the ethical dimensions of strategy. This approach was strongly recommended by symposium participants.

Best-selling author John Naisbitt uses the term "megatrends" to describe dominant directions that shape the world. For today's managers, globalization and ethics provide a context within which strategy is pursued. By examining these two factors in Chapter 2, instructors can make it clear to students how important they are. In Chapters 3 through 8, this idea is reinforced through tying the topics presented (such as internal analysis, external analysis, and strategy selection) to globalization and ethics. The expectation is that students will exit their strategic management class at the end of the semester with a greater understanding of strategy in general and globalization and ethics in particular than if another textbook had been used.

The third feature that makes this book special is the engaging content and the writing style that avoids unnecessary jargon and uses a conversational tone that students will appreciate. An extensive set of examples illustrates critical concepts. Incidents of both success and failure are presented, because both are vital to learning and mastery. Emphasis is on industries that students find interesting to ensure that they remain engaged.

The fourth special feature is the approach to case selection. The symposium participants made it clear that they preferred medium-length cases closely tied to the issues covered in a strategy course. Asking undergraduate students to navigate a 30-page case is asking a lot, and just as much pedagogical value can be offered in a 10-page case as in a much longer one. Drawing on his vast experience as a case author, Alan Eisner has assembled an outstanding set of cases profiling well-known companies that will enrich the classroom experience including Enron, QVC, JetBlue Airways, Johnson & Johnson, Yahoo!, World Wrestling Entertainment, The Casino Industry, Claire's Stores, Nintendo's Wii, and Ford Motor Company.

In closing, we would like to thank the excellent McGraw-Hill team that brought this book to completion. McGraw-Hill/Irwin former Editorial Director John Biernat, former Sponsoring Editor Ryan Blankenship, former Development Editor Natalie Ruffatto, Executive Editor Doug Hughes, Senior Sponsoring Editor Michael Ablassmeir, Senior Marketing Manager Anke Braun Weekes, Development Editor Laura Griffin, and Senior Project Manager Harvey Yep all provided vital support.

David J. Ketchen, Jr.
Auburn University

Alan B. Eisner
Pace University

STUDENT RESOURCES

ONLINE LEARNING CENTER (OLC)

The following resources are available to students via the publisher's OLC at **www.mhhe
.com/ketchen:**

- Chapter quizzes students can take to gauge their understanding of material covered in each chapter.
- A selection of PowerPoint slides for each chapter.
- Case Web Links with supplementary Internet reading and suggestions for further discussion.
- Links to strategy simulations the Business Strategy Game & GLO-BUS. Both provide a powerful and constructive way of connecting students to the subject matter of the course with a competition among classmates on campus and around the world.

Purchasing access to our premium learning resources right on the OLC Web site provides students with the following value-added resources:

- A selection of case-related videos.
- Self-Assessments and Test Your Knowledge Exercises available at the chapter level that include a wide variety of self-assessment activities and class group projects.

INSTRUCTOR RESOURCES

INSTRUCTOR'S RESOURCE CD-ROM

All instructor supplements are available in this one-stop multimedia resource, which includes the Instructor's Manual, Test Bank, PowerPoint Presentations, and Case Study Teaching Notes.

INSTRUCTOR'S MANUAL (IM)

Annette Ranft of Florida State University adapted the Instructor Manual composed by textbook authors Greg Dess and Tom Lumpkin to support this text with summary/objectives, lecture/discussion outlines, discussion questions, extra examples not included in the text, teaching tips, experiential exercises, and more.

TEST BANK

Carol Johnson of the University of Denver adapted the test bank originally created by textbook authors Greg Dess and Tom Lumpkin. It contains approximately 800 true/false, multiple-choice, and essay questions. It has been tagged with learning objectives, level of difficulty, Bloom's Taxonomy, and AACSB criteria. The AACSB tags allow instructors to sort questions by the various standards and create reports to help give assurance that they are including recommended learning experiences in their curricula.

ASSURANCE OF LEARNING

Many educational institutions today are focused on the notion of assurance of learning, an important element of some accreditation standards. *Strategy 2008–2009* is designed specifically to support your assurance of learning initiatives with a simple, yet powerful solution. Each test bank question for *Strategy 2008–2009* maps to a specific chapter learning outcome/objective listed in the text.

AACSB STATEMENT

McGraw-Hill Companies is a proud corporate member of AACSB International. Recognizing the importance and value of AACSB accreditation, the authors of *Strategy 2008–2009* have sought to recognize the curricula guidelines detailed in AACSB standards for business accreditation by connecting selected questions in the book to the general knowledge and skill guidelines found in the AACSB standards. It is important to note that the statements contained *Strategy 2008–2009* are provided only as a guide for the users of this text. The AACSB leaves content coverage and assessment clearly within the realm and control of individual schools, the mission of the school, and the faculty. The AACSB does also charge schools with the obligation of doing assessment against their own content and learning goals. While this book and its teaching package make no claim of any specific AACSB qualification or evaluation, the authors have labeled selected questions according to the six general knowledge and skills areas. There are of course, many more within the test bank, the text, and the teaching package which might be used as a standard for your course. However, the labeled questions are suggested for your consideration.

McGraw-Hill's flexible and easy-to-use electronic testing program **EZ Test** allows instructors to create tests from book-specific items. It accommodates a wide range of question types, and instructors may add their own questions. Multiple versions of the text can be created, and any test can be exported for use with course management systems such as WebCT or BlackBoard.

COMPUTERIZED TEST BANK ONLINE

A comprehensive bank of test questions is provided within a computerized test bank powered by McGraw-Hill's flexible electronic testing program EZ Test Online (**www. eztestonline.com**). EZ Test Online allows you to create paper and online tests or quizzes in this easy to use program!

Imagine being able to create and access your test or quiz anywhere, at any time without installing the testing software. Now, with EZ Test Online, instructors can select questions from multiple McGraw-Hill test banks or author their own, and then either print the test for paper distribution or give it online.

Test Creation

- Author/edit questions online using the 14 different question type templates
- Create printed tests or deliver online to get instant scoring and feedback
- Create questions pools to offer multiple versions online—great for practice

- Export your tests for use in WebCT, Blackboard, PageOut and Apple's iQuiz
- Compatible with EZ Test Desktop tests you've already created
- Sharing tests with colleagues, adjuncts, TAs is easy

Online Test Management

- Set availability dates and time limits for your quiz or test
- Control how your test will be presented
- Assign points by question or question type with drop-down menu
- Provide immediate feedback to students or delay until all finish the test
- Create practice tests online to enable student mastery
- Your roster can be uploaded to enable student self-registration

Online Scoring and Reporting

- Automated scoring for most of EZ Test's numerous question types
- Allows manual scoring for essay and other open response questions
- Manual re-scoring and feedback is also available
- EZ Test's grade book is designed to easily export to your grade book
- View basic statistical reports

Support and Help

- User's Guide and built-in page-specific help
- Flash tutorials for getting started on the support site
- Support Web site—**www.mhhe.com/eztest**
- Product specialist available at 1-800-331-5094
- Online Training: **http://auth.mhhe.com/mpss/workshops/**

PowerPoint Presentations prepared by Amit Shah of Frostburg State University consist of more than 300 slides incorporating an outline for the chapters tied to learning objectives. Also included are multiple choice and discussion Classroom Performance System (CPS) questions as well as additional examples outside of the text. And Case Study PowerPoint slides are available to facilitate case study coverage.

CASE VIDEOS

A set of videos related to selected cases accompanies the text to support your classroom. Videos are available for nine of the 10 cases including Enron, QVC, JetBlue Airways, Johnson & Johnson, Yahoo!, World Wrestling Entertainment, The Casino Industry, Nintendo's Wii, and Ford Motor Company. These thought-provoking video clips are available on our instructor DVD upon adoption of this text. Selected videos will be available for students on the Online Learning Center.

ONLINE LEARNING CENTER (OLC)

In addition to the student resources, the instructor section of **www.mhhe.com/ketchen** also includes the Instructor's Manual, Case Study Teaching Notes, expanded PowerPoint Presentations, and Case Study PowerPoint Presentations as well as additional resources.

Standard Cartridge is included in the price of the textbook. It includes all of the material that is contained in the OLC, but in a format ready for Blackboard, WebCT, and so on.

THE BUSINESS STRATEGY GAME AND GLO-BUS ONLINE SIMULATIONS

Both allow teams of students to manage companies in a head-to-head contest for global market leadership. These simulations give students the immediate opportunity to experiment with various strategy options and to gain proficiency in applying the concepts and tools they have been reading about in the chapters: **www.mhhe.com/thompsonsims**

ADDITIONAL RESOURCES

McGRAW-HILL/PRIMIS CUSTOM PUBLISHING

You can customize this text. McGraw-Hill/Primis Online's digital database offers you the flexibility to customize your course including material from the largest online collection of textbooks, readings, and cases. Primis leads the way in customized eBooks with hundreds of titles available at prices that save your students over 20 percent off bookstore prices: **www.primisonline.com/ketchen or (800) 228-0634**

KETCHEN IN EBOOK FORMAT

Real Texts—Real Savings! If instructors are interested in giving students the option to access the textbook contents digitally, with interactive, dynamic features, in order to save students money, they should consider eBooks, which are *identical* to the printed textbooks but *cost about half as much.* Students will be able to search, highlight, bookmark, annotate, and print the eBook. McGraw-Hill Higher Education's eBooks can be viewed online on any computer with an Internet connection *or* downloaded to an individual's computer.

BUSINESSWEEK EDITION

Students can subscribe to *BusinessWeek* for a special rate of $8.25, in addition to the price of this text, when instructors order the *BusinessWeek* edition. Students will receive a pass code card shrink-wrapped with their new text. The card directs students to a Web site where they enter the code and then gain access to *BusinessWeek*'s registration page to enter address information and set up their subscription. Students can now choose from receiving their subscription in print copy or digital format.

STANDARD & POOR'S EDUCATIONAL VERSION OF MARKET INSIGHT

McGraw-Hill/Irwin is proud to partner with Standard & Poor's Market Insight.© This rich online resource provides six years of financial data, key ratio summary reports, and S&P's exclusive "Industry Surveys" that offer an in-depth look at industry trends, projections, and competitive analysis for 500 top U.S. companies in the renowned COMPUSTAT® database. The password-protected Web site is the perfect way to bring real data into today's classroom for use in case analysis, industry analysis, and research for team and individual projects: **www.mhhe.com/edumarketinsight**

Brief Contents

Contents

STRATEGY | *2008-2009*

What Is Strategic Management?

After reading this chapter, you should have a good understanding of:

LO 1 The definition of strategic management and its four key attributes.

LO 2 The strategic management process and its three interrelated and principal activities.

LO 3 The resource-based view of the firm and the different types of tangible and intangible resources, as well as organizational capabilities.

LO 4 The four attributes that a firm's resources must possess to maintain a sustainable advantage.

We define strategic management as *consisting of the analyses, decisions, and actions an organization undertakes in order to create and sustain competitive advantages.* At the heart of strategic management is the question: How and why do some firms outperform others? Thus, the challenge to managers is to decide on strategies that provide advantages that can be sustained over time. There are four key attributes of strategic management. It is directed at overall organizational goals, includes multiple stakeholders, incorporates short-term as well as long-term perspectives, and recognizes trade-offs between effectiveness and efficiency. We discuss the above definition and the four key attributes in the first section of this chapter.

The second section addresses the strategic management process. The three major processes are strategy analysis, strategy formulation, and strategy implementation. These three components parallel the analyses, decisions, and actions in the above definition. We discuss how each of the nine chapters addresses these three processes.

The third and final section examines the resource-based view, which is a very popular way for managers to think about strategic management. The resource-based view focuses on a firm's tangible and intangibles resources, as well as its capabilities. Advantages that tend to be sustainable over time typically arise from creating *bundles* of resources and capabilities that satisfy four criteria: they are valuable, rare, difficult to imitate, and difficult to substitute.

LEARNING FROM MISTAKES

One of the things that makes the study of strategic management so interesting is that struggling firms can become stars, while high flyers can become earthbound very rapidly. For example, consider Ford Motor Company. As they begin the second century of its existence, this pioneer of the auto industry is struggling for answers to a variety of problems.[1]

Ford Motor Company's losses for the year 2006 alone were a staggering $12.7 billion! And even by the company's own projections, they do not see a return to profitability until at least 2009. Along with continuing losses, the company is also experiencing shrinking market share and a stock price that has not risen above single digit levels in many years. According to analysts at Morgan Stanley, Renault-Nissan may overtake Ford as the world's No. 3 automaker as early as 2007. As the company struggles to avoid drowning in a sea of red ink, one cannot but help wonder how this pioneer of the auto industry went into a downward financial spiral after years of comfortable profits and innovative products. While a number of errors may have contributed to this decline, nothing illustrates their poor strategy and mismanagement more compellingly than the decision to discontinue the production of the popular Taurus sedan.

Introduced in 1985, the Taurus won acclaim as a symbol of American automotive renaissance. It was admired for its sleek aerodynamic design, which was revolutionary for its time. Often referred to as a "jellybean" or a "flying potato" for its futuristic styling, the car was an instant hit, selling 263,000 units in its first year of production. The designers at Ford had spotted an interesting trend among North American car buyers: They were moving away from big, cushy American cars to better handling European models. They catered to this trend by offering a car with stiffer suspension, more interior room, firmer seats, better ergonomics, and more trunk space. They also added a number of "surprise and delight" features such as a cargo net to hold grocery bags in the trunk, rear seat head rests, and heat ducts. In 1989, the Taurus SHO (Super High Output) model was introduced.

After a very successful six-year run, the car was revamped for the 1992 model year, maintaining the overall oval shape, but adding new body panels, slimmer headlights, and smoothed-out body sides. The result was a less controversial, more refined design, which catapulted Taurus to the position of the highest selling passenger car in the United States with sales of nearly half a million units that year. From 1992 to 1996, Taurus was America's best selling car, instilling a sense of pride in American manufacturers that they could indeed compete with their Japanese rivals and win. It also reversed Ford's financial losses of the early 1980s, contributing immensely to its profitability.

The signs of the decline of Taurus began in the late 1990s. In 1997, Toyota Camry edged out Taurus for the No.1 spot in the passenger car segment. By 2006, the Camry was outselling Taurus 2 to 1 and Taurus sales had slid below 200,000 annual units. By October 2006, after 21 years and sales of 7.5 million cars (not counting its sibling Mercury Sable), Ford announced the decision to discontinue production of the Taurus.

The obvious question in the minds of millions of loyal customers was: How did the proudest brand of the last two decades come to such an inglorious end? "It didn't keep pace. That's the whole story in four words," claims Joel Pitcoff, Taurus' marketing manager of the mid-1990s. For nearly a decade, Ford treated the Taurus strictly as a cash cow, leaving the car virtually unchanged and with little advertising support. Instead, the company's focus was on high margin products such as big trucks and sport utility vehicles. Meanwhile, competitors had copied and refined many of the attractive features of the Taurus. While the increasingly sophisticated American customers who had plenty of choice in the overcrowded passenger sedan market walked away from the product, Ford focused mainly on the volume-intensive but less demanding fleet sales to rental car companies. When the sudden spike in oil prices in mid-2005 sent customers scurrying for more fuel-efficient vehicles, Ford was caught flat-footed with virtually no desirable product to offer. "They put no money into the product for the last several years," said Jack Telnack, Taurus's original chief designer, who retired in 1998. "They just let it wither on the vine. It's criminal. The car had a great reputation, a good name. I don't understand what they were waiting for."

While all the financial woes of Ford cannot be attributed to the demise of the Taurus, it is symptomatic of the many ills that have brought this once proud company to the brink of losing the industry leader position it has enjoyed for decades. Some of the causes of their problems are external in nature such as the high retiree health benefit costs, the saturation of American markets by numerous producers from Japan and Korea, and the sudden doubling of oil prices. But in the final analysis, many of Ford's wounds are self-inflicted. Their excessive reliance on trucks and SUVs for profits showed that they had forgotten all the lessons they learned from the oil price increases of the early 1980s. Ford spent $5 billion in the late 1990s in their ill-conceived effort to introduce a "world car." Introduced as Ford Contour and its sibling Mercury Mystique, the cars were an instant flop. To starve a successful brand that had captured the imagination of the public and contributed to the resurgence of the company was perhaps the biggest mistake of all.

Responding to the public uproar in the aftermath of the discontinuation of the Taurus brand, the company announced in early 2007 that they would reintroduce the brand by renaming the Ford Five Hundred as Taurus. Only time will tell how customers will respond to this reincarnated Taurus.

Today's leaders, such as those at Ford, face a large number of complex challenges in the global marketplace. In considering how much credit (or blame) they deserve, two perspectives of leadership come immediately to mind: the "romantic" and "external control" perspectives.[2] First, let's look at the romantic view of leadership. Here, the implicit assumption is that the leader is the key force in determining an organization's success—or lack thereof.[3] This view dominates the popular press in business magazines such as *Fortune, Business-Week,* and *Forbes,* wherein the CEO is either lauded for his or her firm's success or chided for the organization's demise. Consider, for example, the credit that has been bestowed on leaders such as Jack Welch, Andrew Grove, and Herb Kelleher for the tremendous accomplishments of their firms, General Electric, Intel, and Southwest Airlines, respectively.

More recently, Carlos Ghosn has been lionized in the business press for turning around Nissan's fortunes in the worldwide automobile industry. He transformed huge losses into a $7 billion profit, eliminated $23 billion of debt, and made Nissan the world's most profitable volume producer.[4] And in the world of sports, managers and coaches, such as Bill Belichick of the New England Patriots in the National Football League, get a lot of credit for their teams' success on the field.

On the other hand, when things don't go well, much of the failure of an organization can also, rightfully, be attributed to the leader. For example, when Carly Fiorina was fired as CEO of Hewlett Packard, the firm enjoyed an immediate increase in its stock price of 7 percent—hardly a strong endorsement of her leadership! The failure of Ford's top management to halt their continuing losses and market erosion finally led the company's board to hire an industry outsider—Boeing's Alan Mulally.

However, this reflects only part of the picture. Consider another perspective of leadership called "external control." Here, rather than making the implicit assumption that the leader is the most important factor in determining organizational outcomes, the focus is on external factors that may positively or negatively affect a firm's success. We don't have to look far to support this perspective. For example, Ford Motor Company's decline can be partly attributed to a number of external factors. The rising health care costs in the United States and the company's pension obligations make it practically impossible to make a profit. Further, the sudden increase in the cost of gasoline after years of steady or declining prices caused a sudden reversal of consumer preferences from high margin SUVs to more efficient vehicles. These developments had serious negative effects not just on Ford, but also on General Motors and Chrysler.

The point, of course, is that, while neither the romantic nor the external control perspective is entirely correct, we must acknowledge both in the study of strategic management. Our premise is that leaders can make a difference, but they must be constantly aware of the opportunities and threats that they face in the external environment and have a thorough understanding of their firm's resources and capabilities.

THE NATURE OF STRATEGIC MANAGEMENT

LO1 The definition of strategic management and its four key attributes.

Given the many challenges and opportunities in the global marketplace, today's managers must do more than set long-term strategies and hope for the best.[5] They must go beyond what some have called "incremental management," whereby they view their job as making a series of small, minor changes to improve the efficiency of their firm's operations.[6] That is fine if your firm is competing in a very stable, simple, and unchanging industry. But there aren't many of those left. As we shall discuss in this chapter and throughout the book, the pace of change is accelerating, and the pressure on managers to make both major and minor changes in a firm's strategic direction is increasing.

Rather than seeing their role as merely custodians of the status quo, today's leaders must be proactive, anticipate change, and continually refine and, when necessary, make dramatic changes to their strategies. The strategic management of the organization must become both a process and a way of thinking throughout the organization.

DEFINING STRATEGIC MANAGEMENT

Strategic management consists of the analyses, decisions, and actions an organization undertakes in order to create and sustain competitive advantages. This definition captures two main elements that go to the heart of the field of strategic management.

First, the strategic management of an organization entails three ongoing processes: *analyses, decisions,* and *actions.* That is, strategic management is concerned with the *analysis* of strategic goals (vision, mission, and strategic objectives) along with the analysis of the internal and external environment of the organization. Next, leaders must make strategic decisions. These *decisions,* broadly speaking, address two basic questions: What industries should we compete in? How should we compete in those industries? These questions also often involve an organization's domestic as well as its international operations. And last are the *actions* that must be taken. Decisions are of little use, of course, unless they are acted on. Firms must take the necessary actions to implement their strategies. This requires leaders to allocate the necessary resources and to design the organization to bring the intended strategies to reality. As we will see in the next section, this is an ongoing, evolving process that requires a great deal of interaction among these three processes.

Second, the essence of strategic management is the study of why some firms outperform others.[7] Thus, managers need to determine how a firm is to compete so that it can obtain advantages that are sustainable over a lengthy period of time. That means focusing on two fundamental questions. First, *How should we compete in order to create competitive advantages in the marketplace?* For example, managers need to determine if the firm should position itself as the low-cost producer, develop products and services that are unique and will enable the firm to charge premium prices, or some combination of both.

Second, managers must ask how to make such advantages sustainable, instead of highly temporary, in the marketplace. That is, *How can we create competitive advantages in the marketplace that are not only unique and valuable but also difficult for competitors to copy or substitute?*[8,9]

Ideas that work are almost always copied by rivals immediately. In the 1980s, American Airlines tried to establish a competitive advantage by introducing the frequent flyer program. Within weeks, all the airlines did the same thing. Overnight, frequent flyer programs became a necessary tool for competitive parity instead of a competitive advantage. The challenge, therefore, is to create competitive advantages that are sustainable.

Michael Porter argues that sustainable competitive advantage cannot be achieved through operational effectiveness alone.[10] Most of the popular management innovations of the last two decades—total quality, just-in-time, benchmarking, business process reengineering, outsourcing—all are about operational effectiveness. Operational effectiveness means performing similar activities better than rivals. Each of these is important, but none lead to sustainable competitive advantage for the simple reason that everyone is doing them. Strategy is all about being different from everyone else. Sustainable competitive advantage is possible only through performing different activities from rivals or performing similar activities in different ways. Companies such as Wal-Mart, Southwest Airlines, and IKEA have developed unique, internally consistent, and difficult-to-imitate activity systems that have provided them with sustained competitive advantages. A company with a good strategy must make clear choices about what it wants to accomplish. Trying to do everything that your rivals do eventually leads to mutually destructive price competition, not long-term advantage.

EXHIBIT 1.1

Strategic Management Concepts

Definition: Strategic management consists of the analyses, decisions, and actions an organization undertakes in order to create and sustain competitive advantages.

Key Attributes of Strategic Management

- Directs the organization toward overall goals and objectives.
- Includes multiple stakeholders in decision making.
- Needs to incorporate short-term and long-term perspectives.
- Recognizes trade-offs between efficiency and effectiveness.

THE FOUR KEY ATTRIBUTES OF STRATEGIC MANAGEMENT

Before discussing the strategic management process in more detail, let's briefly talk about four attributes of strategic management.[11] In doing so, it will become clear how this course differs from other courses that you have had in functional areas, such as accounting, marketing, operations, and finance. Exhibit 1.1 provides a definition and the four attributes of strategic management.

First, strategic management is *directed toward overall organizational goals and objectives.* That is, effort must be directed at what is best for the total organization, not just a single functional area. Some authors have referred to this perspective as "organizational versus individual rationality."[12] That is, what might look "rational" or most appropriate for one functional area, such as operations, may not be in the best interest of the overall firm. For example, operations may decide to schedule long production runs of similar products in order to lower unit costs. However, the standardized output may be counter to what the marketing department needs in order to appeal to a sophisticated and demanding target market. Similarly, research and development may "overengineer" the product in order to develop a far superior offering, but the design may make the product so expensive that market demand is minimal. Therefore, in this course you will look at cases and strategic issues from the perspective of the organization rather than that of the functional area(s) in which you have had the most training and experience.

Second, strategic management *includes multiple stakeholders in decision making.* Managers must incorporate the demands of many stakeholders when making decisions.[13] Stakeholders are those individuals, groups, and organizations who have a "stake" in the success of the organization, including owners (shareholders in a publicly held corporation), employees, customers, suppliers, the community at large, and so on. We'll discuss this in more detail later in this chapter. Managers will not be successful if they continually focus on a single stakeholder. For example, if the overwhelming emphasis is on generating profits for the owners, employees may become alienated, customer service may suffer, and the suppliers may become resentful of continual demands for pricing concessions. As we will see, however, many organizations have been able to satisfy multiple stakeholder needs simultaneously. For example, financial performance may actually be greater because employees who are satisfied with their jobs make a greater effort to enhance customer satisfaction, thus leading to higher profits.

Third, strategic management *requires incorporating both short-term and long-term perspectives.* Peter Senge, a leading strategic management author at the Massachusetts Institute of Technology, has referred to this need as a "creative tension."[14] That is, managers must maintain both a vision for the future of the organization as well as a focus on its present operating needs. However, financial markets can exert significant pressures on executives to meet short-term performance targets. Studies have shown that corporate leaders often take a short-term approach to the detriment of creating long-term shareholder value. Consider:[15]

> According to recent studies, only 59% of financial executives say they would pursue a positive net present value project if it meant missing the quarter's consensus earnings per-share estimate. Worse, 78% say they would sacrifice value—often a great deal of value—to smooth earnings. Similarly, managers are more likely to cut R&D to reverse an earning slide if a significant amount of the company's equity is owned by institutions with high portfolio turnover. Many companies have the same philosophy about long-term investments such as infrastructure and employee training.

Fourth, strategic management *involves the recognition of trade-offs between effectiveness and efficiency.* Closely related to the third point above, this recognition means being aware of the need for organizations to strive to act effectively and efficiently. Some authors have referred to this as the difference between "doing the right thing" (effectiveness) and "doing things right" (efficiency).[16] While managers must allocate and use resources wisely, they must still direct their efforts toward the attainment of overall organizational objectives. Managers who are totally focused on meeting short-term budgets and targets may fail to attain the broader goals of the organization. Consider the following amusing story told by Norman Augustine, former CEO of defense giant, Martin Marietta (now Lockheed Martin):

> I am reminded of an article I once read in a British newspaper which described a problem with the local bus service between the towns of Bagnall and Greenfields. It seemed that, to the great annoyance of customers, drivers had been passing long queues of would-be passengers with a smile and a wave of the hand. This practice was, however, clarified by a bus company official who explained, "It is impossible for the drivers to keep their timetables if they must stop for passengers."[17]

Clearly, the drivers who were trying to stay on schedule had ignored the overall mission. As Augustine noted, "Impeccable logic but something seems to be missing!"

Successful managers must make many trade-offs. It is central to the practice of strategic management. At times, managers must focus on the short term and efficiency; at other times the emphasis is on the long term and expanding a firm's product-market scope in order to anticipate opportunities in the competitive environment. For example, consider Kevin Sharer's perspective. He is CEO of Amgen, the giant $12 billion biotechnology firm:[18]

> A CEO must always be switching between what I call different altitudes—tasks of different levels of abstraction and specificity. At the highest altitude you're asking the big questions: What are the company's mission and strategy? Do people understand and believe in these aims? Are decisions consistent with them? At the lowest altitude, you're looking at on-the-ground operations: Did we make that sale? What was the yield on that last lot in the factory? How many days of inventory do we have for a particular drug? And then there's everything in between: How many chemists do we need to hire this quarter? What should we pay for a small biotech company that has a promising new drug? Is our production capacity adequate to roll out a product in a new market?

LO2 The strategic management process and its three interrelated and principal activities.

THE STRATEGIC MANAGEMENT PROCESS

We've identified three ongoing processes—analyses, decisions, and actions—that are central to strategic management. In practice, these three processes—often referred to as strategy analysis, strategy formulation, and strategy implementation—are highly interdependent. Further, these three processes do not take place one after the other in a sequential fashion in most companies.

INTENDED VERSUS REALIZED STRATEGIES

Henry Mintzberg, a very influential management scholar at McGill University, argues that conceptualizing the strategic management process as one in which analysis is followed

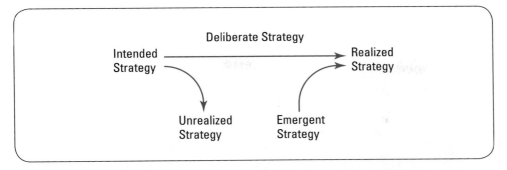

EXHIBIT 1.2   **Realized Strategy and Intended Strategy: Usually Not the Same**

Source: From Mintzberg, H. & Waters, J. A., "Of Strategies: Deliberate and Emergent," *Strategic Management Journal*, Vol. 6, 1985, pp. 257–272. Copyright © John Wiley & Sons Limited. Reproduced with permission.

by optimal decisions and their subsequent meticulous implementation neither describes the strategic management process accurately nor prescribes ideal practice.[19] In his view, the business environment is far from predictable, thus limiting our ability for analysis. Further, decisions in an organization are seldom based on optimal rationality alone, given the political processes that occur in all organizations.

Taking into consideration the limitations discussed above, Mintzberg proposed an alternative model of strategy development. As depicted in Exhibit 1.2 , decisions following from analysis, in this model, constitute the *intended* strategy of the firm. For a variety of reasons, the intended strategy rarely survives in its original form. Unforeseen environmental developments, unanticipated resource constraints, or changes in managerial preferences may result in at least some parts of the intended strategy remaining *unrealized.* On the other hand, good managers will want to take advantage of a new opportunity presented by the environment, even if it was not part of the original set of intentions. For example, consider the wind energy industry.[20] In September 2004 the United States Congress renewed the wind tax credit. Legislation in 19 states now requires that electricity providers offer a certain percentage of "green" (i.e., renewable) energy. Such legislation, combined with falling clean energy costs and rising prices for coal, oil, and gas, have created a surge in demand for competitors such as GE Wind Energy, which makes large turbines and fan blades. Not surprisingly, such businesses have increased hiring and research and development, as well as revenue and profit forecasts. The final *realized* strategy of any firm is thus a combination of *deliberate* and *emergent* strategies.

Next, we will address each of the three key strategic management processes: strategy analysis, strategy formulation, and strategy implementation. Exhibit 1.3 depicts the strategic management process and indicates how it ties into the chapters in the book.

Strategy analysis may be looked upon as the starting point of the strategic management process. It consists of the "advance work" that must be done in order to effectively formulate and implement strategies. Many strategies fail because managers may want to formulate and implement strategies without a careful analysis of the overarching goals of the organization and without a thorough analysis of its external and internal environment. Our examination of strategy analysis includes three chapters. Chapter 2, "The Context of Strategic Management," focuses on the two dominant trends shaping business today—globalization and corporate ethics. When considering any strategic situation, executives need to carefully consider the role of international and ethics issues.

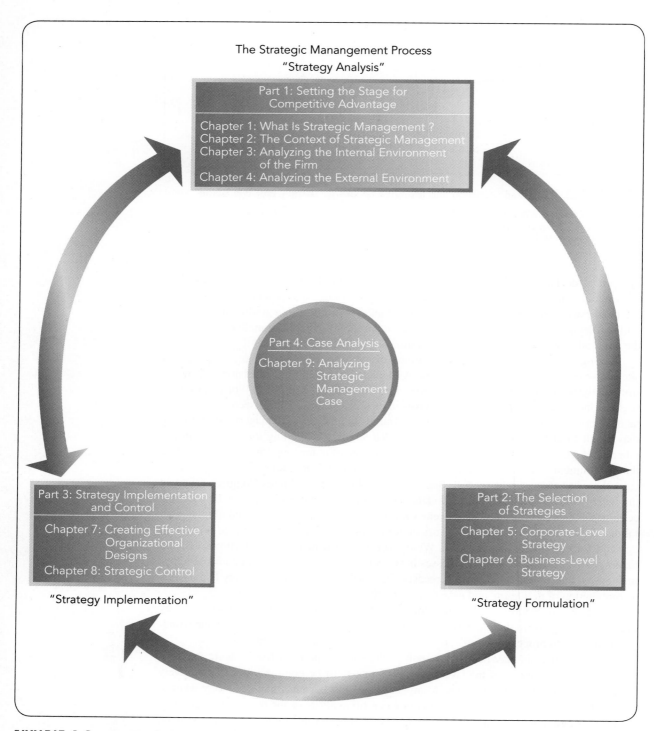

The Strategic Manangement Process
"Strategy Analysis"

Part 1: Setting the Stage for
Competitive Advantage

Chapter 1: What Is Strategic Management ?
Chapter 2: The Context of Strategic Management
Chapter 3: Analyzing the Internal Environment
of the Firm
Chapter 4: Analyzing the External Environment

Part 4: Case Analysis

Chapter 9: Analyzing
Strategic
Management
Case

Part 3: Strategy Implementation
and Control

Chapter 7: Creating Effective
Organizational
Designs
Chapter 8: Strategic Control

"Strategy Implementation"

Part 2: The Selection
of Strategies

Chapter 5: Corporate-Level
Strategy
Chapter 6: Business-Level
Strategy

"Strategy Formulation"

EXHIBIT 1.3   **The Strategic Management Process**

Chapter 3, "Analyzing the Internal Environment of the Firm," covers organizations' goals and the value chain. An organization must establish three types of goals—vision, mission, and strategic objectives—in order to channel the efforts of people throughout the organization in a desired direction. The value chain charts how organizations add value to their products and services through various functional areas such as operations, marketing, and human resource management. Analysis of an organization's strengths and weaknesses along the value chain reveals potential sources of competitive advantage as well as areas that competitors can attack.

Within Chapter 4, "Analyzing the External Environment," two frameworks are provided. First, the general environment consists of several elements, such as demographic, technological, and economic segments, from which key trends and events can have a dramatic impact on the firm. Second, the industry environment consists of competitors and other organizations that may threaten the success a firm's products and services. Within this chapter, we also discuss the value to executives of the strategic groups concepts and SWOT (strengths, weaknesses, opportunities, and threats) analysis.

Strategy formulation involves making strategic decisions that are intended to help a firm become more successful. Strategy formulation centers on two key questions. Each of these questions is the basis for a chapter in this section of the book. The first question is, in what business or business should we compete? Ways to answer this question are presented in Chapter 5, "Corporate-Level Strategy." This chapter considers how firms manage their portfolio of businesses and try to create synergies among the businesses. The second question is, how should we compete in our chosen business or businesses? Ways to answer this question are presented in Chapter 6, "Business-Level Strategy." This chapter discusses how firms compete with their rivals based on cost leadership, differentiation, or both.

Sound strategies are of no value if they are not properly implemented. Strategy implementation involves ensuring that the corporate and business-level strategies that executives devise are actually put into practice. The section of the book on implementation includes two chapters. Chapter 7, "Creating Effective Organizational Designs," explains that in order to be successful, a firm must have a structure that is consistent with its strategies. Chapter 8, "Strategic Control," describes how executives attempt to monitor activities within organizations to ensure that strategies are being pursued effectively and goals are being met.

We've discussed the strategic management process. Our ninth and final chapter, "Analyzing Strategic Management Cases," provides guidelines and suggestions on how to evaluate cases. Through case analysis, the concepts and techniques discussed in the first eight chapters can be applied to actual organizations.

RESOURCE-BASED VIEW OF THE FIRM

LO3   The resource-based view of the firm and the different types of tangible and intangible resources, as well as organizational capabilities.

The resource-based view of the firm is a very helpful perspective for understanding strategic management and the activities that make up the strategic management process. The **resource-based view** (RBV) of the firm combines two perspectives: (1) the internal analysis of phenomena within a company and (2) an external analysis of the industry and its competitive environment.[21] It goes beyond the traditional SWOT (strengths, weaknesses, opportunities, threats) analysis by integrating internal and external perspectives. The ability of a firm's resources to confer competitive advantage(s) cannot be determined without taking into consideration the broader competitive context. That is, a firm's resources must be evaluated in terms of how valuable, rare, and hard they are for competitors to duplicate. Otherwise, at best, the firm would be able to attain only competitive parity. A firm's strengths and capabilities—no matter how unique or impressive—do not necessarily lead

resource-based view of the firm Perspective that firm's competitive advantages are due to their endowment of strategic resources that are valuable, rare, costly to imitate, and costly to substitute.

EXHIBIT 1.4

The Resource-Based View of the Firm: Resources and Capabilities

---

Tangible Resources

Financial	• Firm's cash account and cash equivalents.
	• Firm's capacity to raise equity.
	• Firm's borrowing capacity.
Physical	• Modern plant and facilities.
	• Favorable manufacturing locations.
	• State-of-the-art machinery and equipment.
Technological	• Trade secrets.
	• Innovative production processes.
	• Patents, copyrights, trademarks.
Organizational	• Effective strategic planning processes.
	• Excellent evaluation and control systems.

Intangible Resources

Human	• Experience and capabilities of employees.
	• Trust.
	• Managerial skills.
	• Firm-specific practices and procedures.
Innovation and creativity	• Technical and scientific skills.
	• Innovation capacities.
Reputation	• Brand name.
	• Reputation with customers for quality and reliability.
	• Reputation with suppliers for fairness, non–zero-sum relationships.

Organizational Capabilities

- Firm competencies or skills the firm employs to transfer inputs to outputs.
- Capacity to combine tangible and intangible resources, using organizational processes to attain desired end.

EXAMPLES:

- Outstanding customer service.
- Excellent product development capabilities.
- Innovativeness of products and services.
- Ability to hire, motivate, and retain human capital.

Source: Adapted from Barney, J. B. 1991. Firm resources and sustained competitive advantage. *Journal of Management:* 17: 101; Grant, R. M. 1991. *Contemporary Strategy Analysis:* 100–102. Cambridge England: Blackwell Business and Hitt, M. A., Ireland, R. D., & Hoskisson, R. E. 2001. *Strategic management: Competitiveness and globalization* (4th ed.). Cincinnati: South-Western College Publishing.

---

to competitive advantages in the marketplace. The criteria for whether advantages are created and whether or not they can be sustained over time will be addressed later in this section. Thus, the RBV is a very useful framework for gaining insights as to why some competitors are more profitable than others.

In the two sections that follow, we will discuss the three key types of resources that firms possess (summarized in Exhibit 1.4): tangible resources, intangible resources, and organizational capabilities. Then we will address the conditions under which such assets and capabilities can enable a firm to attain a sustainable competitive advantage.[22]

It is important to note that resources by themselves typically do not yield a competitive advantage. Even if a basketball team recruited an all-star center, there would be little chance of victory if the other members of the team were continually outplayed by their opponents or if the coach's attitude was so negative that everyone, including the center, became unwilling to put forth their best efforts. Although the all-star center is unquestionably a valuable resource he would *not* enable the organization to attain advantages under these circumstances.

TYPES OF FIRM RESOURCES

We define firm resources to include all assets, capabilities, organizational processes, information, knowledge, and so forth, controlled by a firm that enable it to develop and implement value-creating strategies.

Tangible Resources   **Tangible resources** are assets that are relatively easy to identify. They include the physical and financial assets that an organization uses to create value for its customers. Among them are financial resources (e.g., a firm's cash, accounts receivables, and its ability to borrow funds); physical resources (e.g., the company's plant, equipment, and machinery as well as its proximity to customers and suppliers); organizational resources (e.g., the company's strategic planning process and its employee development, evaluation, and reward systems); and technological resources (e.g., trade secrets, patents, and copyrights).

> **tangible resources**
> Organizational assets that are relatively easy to identify, including physical assets, financial resources, organizational resources, and technological resources.

Many firms are finding that high-tech, computerized training has dual benefits: It develops more effective employees and reduces costs at the same time. Employees at FedEx take computer-based job competency tests every 6 to 12 months.[23] The 90-minute computer-based tests identify areas of individual weakness and provide input to a computer database of employee skills—information the firm uses in promotion decisions.

Intangible Resources   Much more difficult for competitors (and, for that matter, a firm's own managers) to account for or imitate are **intangible resources,** which are typically embedded in unique routines and practices that have evolved and accumulated over time. These include human resources (e.g., experience and capability of employees, trust, effectiveness of work teams, managerial skills), innovation resources (e.g., technical and scientific expertise, ideas), and reputation resources (e.g., brand name, reputation with suppliers for fairness and with customers for reliability and product quality). A firm's culture may also be a resource that provides competitive advantage.[24]

> **intangible resources**
> Organizational assets that are difficult to identify and account for and are typically embedded in unique routines and practices, including human resources, innovation resources, and reputation resources.

For example, you might not think that motorcycles, clothes, toys, and restaurants have much in common. Yet Harley-Davidson has entered all of these product and service markets by capitalizing on its strong brand image—a valuable intangible resource.[25] It has used that image to sell accessories, clothing, and toys, and it has licensed the Harley-Davidson Café in New York City to provide further exposure for its brand name and products.

Organizational Capabilities   **Organizational capabilities** are not specific tangible or intangible assets, but rather the competencies or skills that a firm employs to transform inputs into outputs.[26] In short, they refer to an organization's capacity to deploy tangible and intangible resources over time and generally in combination, and to leverage those capabilities to bring about a desired end.[27] Examples of organizational capabilities are outstanding customer service, excellent product development capabilities, superb innovation processes, and flexibility in manufacturing processes.[28]

> **organizational capabilities**
> The competencies and skills that a firm employs to transform inputs into outputs.

Gillette's capability to combine several technologies has been one of the keys to its unparalleled success in the wet-shaving industry. Key technologies include its expertise concerning the physiology of facial hair and skin, the metallurgy of blade strength and

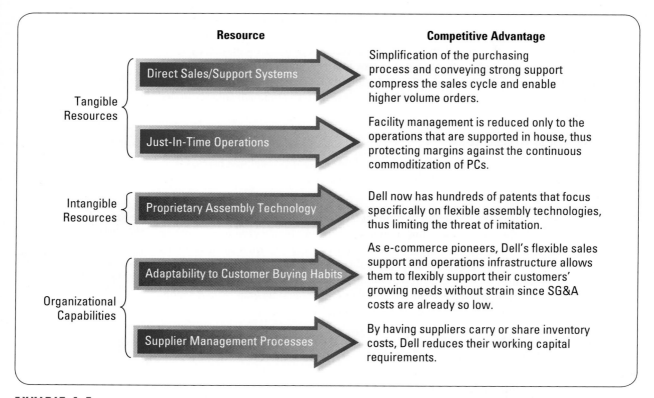

EXHIBIT 1.5 **Dell's Tangible Resources, Intangible Resources, and Organizational Capabilities**

sharpness, the dynamics of a cartridge moving across skin, and the physics of a razor blade severing the hair—highly specialized areas for which Gillette has unique capabilities. Combining these technologies has helped the company to develop innovative products such as the Excel, Sensor Excel, MACH 3, and Fusion shaving systems.

In 1984, Michael Dell started his company in a University of Texas dorm room with an investment of $1,000. By 2006, Dell had attained annual revenues of $56 billion and net income of $3.5 billion. Dell achieved this meteoric growth by differentiating itself through the direct sales approach that it pioneered. Its user-configurable products enabled it to satisfy the diverse needs of its corporate and institutional customer base. Exhibit 1.5 summarizes the Dell recipe for its remarkable success through integrating its tangible resources, intangible resources, and organizational capabilities.

Dell has continued to maintain this competitive advantage by further strengthening its value-chain activities and interrelationships that are critical to satisfying the largest market opportunities. They achieved this by (1) implementing e-commerce direct sales and support processes that accounted for the sophisticated buying habits of the largest markets and (2) matching their operations to the purchase options by adopting flexible assembly processes, while leaving inventory management to its extensive supplier network. Dell has sustained these advantages by investing in intangible resources such as proprietary assembly methods and packaging configurations that help to protect against the threat of imitation. Dell recognizes that the PC is a complex product with components sourced from several different technologies and manufacturers. Thus, in working backwards from the customer's purchasing habits, Dell saw that they could build valuable solutions by organizing their resources and capabilities around the build-to-specification tastes, making both the sales and integration processes flexible, and passing on overhead expenses to their suppliers. As the PC industry has become further commoditized, Dell has been one of the few competitors that has retained solid margins. They have accomplished this by adapting their manufacturing and assembly capabilities to match the PC market's trend toward user compatibility.

FIRM RESOURCES AND SUSTAINABLE COMPETITIVE ADVANTAGES

As we have mentioned, resources alone are not a basis for competitive advantages, nor are advantages sustainable over time. In some cases, a resource or capability helps a firm to increase its revenues or to lower costs but the firm derives only a temporary advantage because competitors quickly imitate or substitute for it. Many e-commerce businesses in the early 2000s have seen their profits seriously eroded because new (or existing) competitors easily duplicated their business model. For example, Priceline.com expanded its offerings from enabling customers to place bids online for airline tickets to a wide variety of other products. However, it was easy for competitors (e.g., a consortium of major airlines) to duplicate Priceline's products and services. Ultimately, its market capitalization had plummeted roughly 98 percent from its all-time high.

For a resource to provide a firm with the potential for a sustainable competitive advantage, it must have four attributes.[29] First, the resource must be valuable in the sense that it exploits opportunities and/or neutralizes threats in the firm's environment. Second, it must be rare among the firm's current and potential competitors. Third, the resource must be difficult for competitors to imitate. Fourth, the resource must have no strategically equivalent substitutes. These criteria are summarized in Exhibit 1.6. We will now discuss each of these criteria. Then, we will examine how Dell's competitive advantage, which seemed secure just a few years ago, has eroded.

Is the Resource Valuable?   Organizational resources can be a source of competitive advantage only when they are valuable. Resources are valuable when they enable a firm to formulate and implement strategies that improve its efficiency or effectiveness. The SWOT framework suggests that firms improve their performance only when they exploit opportunities or neutralize (or minimize) threats.

The fact that firm attributes must be valuable in order to be considered resources (as well as potential sources of competitive advantage) reveals an important complementary

L04   The four attributes that a firm's resources must possess to maintain a sustainable advantage.

EXHIBIT 1.6

Four Criteria for Assessing Sustainability of Resources and Capabilities

Is the resource or capability . . .	Implications
Valuable?	• Neutralize threats and exploit opportunities
Rare?	• Not many firms possess
Difficult to imitate?	• Physically unique
	• Path dependency (how accumulated over time)
	• Causal ambiguity (difficult to disentangle what it is or how it could be re-created)
	• Social complexity (trust, interpersonal relationships, culture, reputation)
Difficult to substitute?	• No equivalent strategic resources or capabilities

relationship among environmental models (e.g., SWOT and five-forces analyses) and the resource-based model. Environmental models isolate those firm attributes that exploit opportunities and/or neutralize threats. Thus, they specify what firm attributes may be considered as resources. The resource-based model then suggests what additional characteristics these resources must possess if they are to develop a sustained competitive advantage.

Is the Resource Rare?   If competitors or potential competitors also possess the same valuable resource, it is not a source of a competitive advantage because all of these firms have the capability to exploit that resource in the same way. Common strategies based on such a resource would give no one firm an advantage. For a resource to provide competitive advantages, it must be uncommon, that is, rare relative to other competitors.

This argument can apply to bundles of valuable firm resources that are used to formulate and develop strategies. Some strategies require a mix of multiple types of resources—tangible assets, intangible assets, and organizational capabilities. If a particular bundle of firm resources is not rare, then relatively large numbers of firms will be able to conceive of and implement the strategies in question. Thus, such strategies will not be a source of competitive advantage, even if the resource in question is valuable.

Can the Resource Be Imitated Easily?   Inimitability (difficulty in imitating) is a key to value creation because it constrains competition.[30] If a resource is inimitable, then any profits generated are more likely to be sustainable. Having a resource that competitors can easily copy generates only temporary value. This has important implications. Since managers often fail to apply this test, they tend to base long-term strategies on resources that are imitable. IBP (Iowa Beef Processors) became the first meatpacking company in the United States to modernize by building a set of assets (automated plants located in cattle-producing states) and capabilities (low-cost "disassembly" of carcasses) that earned returns on assets of 1.3 percent in the 1970s. By the late 1980s, however, ConAgra and Cargill had imitated these resources, and IBP's profitability fell by nearly 70 percent, to 0.4 percent.

Monster.com entered the executive recruiting market by providing, in essence, a substitute for traditional bricks-and-mortar headhunting firms. Although Monster.com's resources are rare and valuable, they are subject to imitation by new rivals—other dot-com firms. Why? There are very low entry barriers for firms wanting to try their hand at recruitment. For example, many job search dot-coms have emerged in recent years, including jobsearch.com, headhunter.com, nationjob.com, and hotjobs.com. In all, there are approximately 30,000 online job boards available to job seekers. It would be most difficult for a firm to attain a sustainable advantage in this industry.

Clearly, an advantage based on inimitability won't last forever. Competitors will eventually discover a way to copy most valuable resources. However, managers can forestall them and sustain profits for a while by developing strategies around resources that have at least one of the following four characteristics.[31]

Physical Uniqueness   The first source of inimitability is physical uniqueness, which by definition is inherently difficult to copy. A beautiful resort location, mineral rights, or Pfizer's pharmaceutical patents simply cannot be imitated. Many managers believe that several of their resources may fall into this category, but on close inspection, few do.

Path Dependency   A greater number of resources cannot be imitated because of what economists refer to as **path dependency.** This simply means that resources are unique and therefore scarce because of all that has happened along the path followed in their development and/or accumulation. Competitors cannot go out and buy these resources quickly and easily; they must be built up over time in ways that are difficult to accelerate.

path dependency
A characteristic of resources that are developed and/or accumulated through a unique series of events.

The Gerber Products Co. brand name for baby food is an example of a resource that is potentially inimitable. Re-creating Gerber's brand loyalty would be a time-consuming process that competitors could not expedite, even with expensive marketing campaigns. Similarly, the loyalty and trust that Southwest Airlines employees feel toward their firm and its cofounder, Herb Kelleher, are resources that have been built up over a long period of time. Also, a crash R&D program generally cannot replicate a successful technology when research findings cumulate. Clearly, these path-dependent conditions build protection for the original resource. The benefits from experience and learning through trial and error cannot be duplicated overnight.

Causal Ambiguity   The third source of inimitability is termed **causal ambiguity.** This means that would-be competitors may be thwarted because it is impossible to disentangle the causes (or possible explanations) of either what the valuable resource is or how it can be re-created. What is the root of 3M's innovation process? You can study it and draw up a list of possible factors. But it is a complex, unfolding (or folding) process that is hard to understand and would be hard to imitate.

causal ambiguity
A characteristic of a firm's resources that are costly to imitate because a competitor cannot determine what the resource is and/or how it can be re-created.

Often, causally ambiguous resources are organizational capabilities, involving a complex web of social interactions that may even depend on particular individuals. When Continental and United tried to mimic the successful low-cost strategy of Southwest Airlines, the planes, routes, and fast gate turnarounds were not the most difficult aspects for them to copy. Those were all rather easy to observe and, at least in principle, easy to duplicate. However, they could not replicate Southwest's culture of fun, family, frugality, and focus since no one can clearly specify exactly what that culture is or how it came to be.

Social Complexity   A firm's resources may be imperfectly inimitable because they reflect a high level of **social complexity.** Such phenomena are typically beyond the ability of firms to systematically manage or influence. When competitive advantages are based on social complexity, it is difficult for other firms to imitate them.

social complexity
A characteristic of a firm's resources that are costly to imitate because the social engineering required is beyond the capability of competitors, including interpersonal relations among managers, organizational culture, and reputation with suppliers and customers.

A wide variety of firm resources may be considered socially complex. Examples include interpersonal relations among the managers in a firm, its culture, and its reputation with its suppliers and customers. In many of these cases, it is easy to specify how these socially complex resources add value to a firm. Hence, there is little or no causal ambiguity surrounding the link between them and competitive advantage. But an understanding that certain firm attributes, such as quality relations among managers, can improve a firm's efficiency does not necessarily lead to systematic efforts to imitate them. Such social engineering efforts are beyond the capabilities of most firms.

Although complex physical technology is not included in this category of sources of imperfect inimitability, the exploitation of physical technology in a firm typically involves the use of socially complex resources. That is, several firms may possess the same physical technology, but only one of them may have the social relations, culture, group norms, and so on to fully exploit the technology in implementing its strategies. If such complex social resources are not subject to imitation (and assuming they are valuable and rare and no substitutes exist), this firm may obtain a sustained competitive advantage from exploiting its physical technology more effectively than other firms.

Are Substitutes Readily Available?   The fourth requirement for a firm resource to be a source of sustainable competitive advantage is that there must be no strategically equivalent valuable resources that are themselves not rare or inimitable. Two valuable firm resources (or two bundles of resources) are strategically equivalent when each one can be exploited separately to implement the same strategies.

Dell's competitive position in personal computers—including desktops and laptops—has eroded in recent years.

Substitutability may take at least two forms. First, though it may be impossible for a firm to imitate exactly another firm's resource, it may be able to substitute a similar resource that enables it to develop and implement the same strategy. Clearly, a firm seeking to imitate another firm's high-quality top management team would be unable to copy the team exactly. However, it might be able to develop its own unique management team. Though these two teams would have different ages, functional backgrounds, experience, and so on, they could be strategically equivalent and thus substitutes for one another.

Second, very different firm resources can become strategic substitutes. For example, Internet booksellers such as Amazon.com compete as substitutes for bricks-and-mortar booksellers such as B. Dalton. The result is that resources such as premier retail locations become less valuable. In a similar vein, several pharmaceutical firms have seen the value of patent protection erode in the face of new drugs that are based on different production processes and act in different ways, but can be used in similar treatment regimes. The coming years will likely see even more radical change in the pharmaceutical industry as the substitution of genetic therapies eliminates certain uses of chemotherapy.[32]

To recap this section, recall that resources and capabilities must be rare and valuable as well as difficult to imitate or substitute in order for a firm to attain competitive advantages that are sustainable over time.[33] Exhibit 1.7 illustrates the relationship among the four criteria of sustainability and shows the competitive implications.

In firms represented by the first row of Exhibit 1.7, managers are in a difficult situation. When their resources and capabilities do not meet any of the four criteria, it would be difficult to develop any type of competitive advantage, in the short or long term. The resources and capabilities they possess enable the firm neither to exploit environmental opportunities nor neutralize environmental threats. In the second and third rows, firms have resources and capabilities that are valuable as well as rare, respectively. However,

EXHIBIT 1.7

Criteria for Sustainable Competitive Advantage and Strategic Implications

Is a resource or capability . . .				
Valuable?	Rare?	Difficult to Imitate?	Without Substitutes?	Implications for Competitiveness
No	No	No	No	Competitive disadvantage
Yes	No	No	No	Competitive parity
Yes	Yes	No	No	Temporary competitive advantage
Yes	Yes	Yes	Yes	Sustainable competitive advantage

Source: Adapted from Barney, J. B. 1991. Firm resources and sustained competitive advantage. *Journal of Management,* 17: 99–120.

in both cases the resources and capabilities are not difficult for competitors to imitate or substitute. Here, the firms could attain some level of competitive parity. They could perform on par with equally endowed rivals or attain a temporary competitive advantage. But their advantages would be easy for competitors to match. It is only in the fourth row, where all four criteria are satisfied, that competitive advantages can be sustained over time.

Revisiting Dell   For many years, it looked as if Dell's competitive advantage over its rivals would be sustainable for a very long period of time. However, by early 2007, Dell was falling behind its rivals in market share. This led to a significant decline in its stock price—followed by a complete shake-up of the top management team. But what led to Dell's competitive decline in the first place?[34]

- Dell had become so focused on cost that it failed to pay attention to the design of the brand. Customers increasingly began to see the product as a commodity.

- Much of the growth in the PC industry today is in laptops. Customers demand a sleeker, better-designed machine instead of just the cheapest laptop. Also, they often want to see the laptop before they buy it.

- When Dell outsourced its customer service function to foreign locations, it led to a decline in customer support. This eroded Dell's brand value.

- Dell's efforts to replicate its made-to-order, no-middleman strategy to other products such as printers and storage devices proved to be a failure because customers saw very little need for customization of these products. Meanwhile, rivals such as Hewlett-Packard have been improving their product design and reducing their costs. Thus, they now have cost parity with Dell, while enjoying a better brand image and the support of an extensive dealer network.

. . . .

We began this introductory chapter by defining strategic management and articulating some of its key attributes. Strategic management is defined as "consisting of the analyses, decisions, and actions an organization undertakes to create and sustain competitive advantages." The issue of how and why some firms outperform others in the marketplace is central to the study of strategic management. Strategic management has four key attributes: It is directed at overall organizational goals, includes multiple stakeholders, incorporates both short-term and long-term perspectives, and incorporates trade-offs between efficiency and effectiveness.   **LO1**

The second section discussed the strategic management process. Here, we paralleled the above definition of strategic management and focused on three core activities in the strategic management process—strategy analysis, strategy formulation, and strategy implementation. We noted how each of these activities is highly interrelated to and interdependent on the others. We also discussed how each of the nine chapters in this text fits into the three core activities.   **LO2**

In the final section, we discussed a very useful perspective for considering strategic management. The resource-based view of the firm considers the firm as a bundle of resources: tangible resources, intangible resources, and organizational capabilities. Competitive advantages that are sustainable over time generally arise from the creation of bundles of resources and capabilities. For advantages to be sustainable, four criteria must be satisfied: value, rarity, difficulty in imitation, and difficulty in substitution. Such an evaluation requires a sound knowledge of the competitive context in which the firm exists.   **LO3, LO4**

SUMMARY

1. How is "strategic management" defined in the text, and what are its four key attributes?
2. Briefly discuss the three key activities in the strategic management process. Why is it important for managers to recognize the interdependent nature of these activities?
3. What four attributes must a resource have to create a sustained competitive advantage?
4. Why do firms need to have a greater strategic management perspective and empowerment in the strategic management process throughout the firm?

resource-based view
  of the firm 11
tangible resources 13

intangible resources 13
organizational capabilities 13
path dependency 16

causal ambiguity 17
social complexity 17

1. Can you think of a company that possesses a unique bundle of resources? How does the company build advantages from the resources?
2. Apple dominates the music player business with the iPod. What competitive advantage does Apple possess that helps the firm do so well?
3. General Motors and Ford have struggled in the automobile industry in recent years. What might they do strategically to better compete with strong competitors such as Honda and Toyota?
4. Think of a strategic decision you will have to make, such as the selection of a job. How could the ideas on strategic management offered in the chapter help you make a good decision?

1. This section draws from the following articles: Maynard, M. 2006. Gone but not forgotten. *New York Times.* October 28: C1; McCracken, J. 2007. Big three face new obstacles in restructuring. *Wall Street Journal.* January 26: A1 & A8; Edmondson, G. 2007. Putting ford in the rearview mirror. *BusinessWeek,* February 12: 44; and, McClellan, B. 2006. The Ford Taurus is dead, but what an amazing run. *Ward's Dealer Business.* December 1, np.

2. For a discussion of the "romantic" versus "external control" perspective, refer to Meindl, J. R. 1987. The romance of leadership and the evaluation of organizational performance. *Academy of Management Journal* 30: 92–109; and Pfeffer, J., & Salancik, G. R. 1978. *The external control of organizations: A resource dependence perspective.* New York: Harper & Row.

3. A recent perspective on the "romantic view" of leadership is provided by Mintzberg, H. 2004. Leadership and management development: An afterword. *Academy of Management Executive,* 18(3): 140–142.

4. Anonymous. 2005. Face value: The 10 billion dollar man. *The Economist.* February 26: 66. Interestingly, this article speculated that Mr. Ghosn could add approximately $10 billion to the market value of Ford or General Motors if he were to sign on as Chief Executive Officer. Such a perspective is clearly consistent with the "romantic view" of leadership. For an insightful perspective on the challenges faced by Mr. Ghosn as he assumes the roles of CEO for both Nissan and Renault (which owns 44 percent of Nissan), refer to: Edmondson, G. 2005. What Ghosn will do with Renault. *BusinessWeek,* April 25: 54.

5. For an interesting perspective on the need for strategists to maintain a global mind-set, refer to Begley, T. M., & Boyd, D. P. 2003. The need for a global mind-set. *MIT Sloan Management Review* 44(2): 25–32.

6. Porter, M. E. 1996. What is strategy? *Harvard Business Review* 74(6): 61–78.

7. See, for example, Barney, J. B., & Arikan, A. M. 2001. The resource-based view: Origins and implications. In Hitt, M. A., Freeman, R. E., & Harrison, J. S. (Eds.), *Handbook of strategic management:* 124–189. Malden, MA: Blackwell.

8. Barney, J. 1991. Firm resources and sustained competitive advantage. *Journal of Management,* 17(1): 99–120.

9. Much of Gary Hamel's work advocates the importance of not focusing on incremental change. For example, refer to Hamel, G., & Prahalad, C. K. 1994. *Competing for the future.* Boston: Harvard Business School Press; see also Christensen, C. M. 2001. The past and future of competitive advantage. *Sloan Management Review,* 42(3): 105–109.

10. Porter, M. E. 1996. What is strategy? *Harvard Business Review,* 74(6): 61–78; and Hammonds, K. H. 2001. Michael Porter's big ideas. *Fast Company,* March: 55–56.

11. This section draws upon Dess, G. G., & Miller, A. 1993. *Strategic management.* New York: McGraw-Hill.

12. See, for example, Hrebiniak, L. G., & Joyce, W. F. 1986. The strategic importance of managing myopia. *Sloan Management Review,* 28(1): 5–14.

13. For an insightful discussion on how to manage diverse stakeholder groups, refer to Rondinelli, D. A., & London, T. 2003. How corporations and environmental groups cooperate: Assessing cross-sector alliances and collaborations. *Academy of Management Executive,* 17(1): 61–76.

14. Senge, P. 1996. Leading learning organizations: The bold, the powerful, and the invisible. In Hesselbein, F., Goldsmith, M., & Beckhard, R. (Eds.), *The leader of the future:* 41–58. San Francisco: Jossey-Bass.

15. Samuelson, J. 2006. A critical mass for the long term. *Harvard Business Review,* 84(2): 62, 64; and, Anonymous. 2007. Power play. *The Economist,* January 20: 10–12.

16. Loeb, M. 1994. Where leaders come from. *Fortune,* September 19: 241 (quoting Warren Bennis).

17. Address by Norman R. Augustine at the Crummer Business School, Rollins College, Winter Park, FL, October 20, 1989.

18. Hemp, P. 2004. An Interview with CEO Kevin Sharer. *Harvard Business Review,* 82: 7/8: 66–74.

19. Mintzberg, H. 1985. Of strategies: Deliberate and emergent. *Strategic Management Journal,* 6: 257–272.

20. Carey, J. 2005. Tax credits put wind in the sails of renewables. *BusinessWeek.* January 10: 94.

21. Collis, D. J., & Montgomery, C. A. 1995. Competing on resources: Strategy in the 1990's. *Harvard Business Review,* 73(4): 119–128; and Barney, J. 1991. Firm resources and sustained competitive advantage. *Journal of Management,* 17(1): 99–120.

22. For recent critiques of the resource-based view of the firm, refer to: Sirmon, D. G., Hitt, M. A., & Ireland, R. D. 2007. Managing firm resources in dynamic environments to create value: Looking inside the black box. *Academy of Management Review,* 32(1): 273–292; and Newbert, S. L. Empirical research on the resource-based view of the firm: An assessment and suggestions for future research. *Strategic Management Journal,* 28(2): 121–146.

23. Henkoff, R. 1993. Companies that train the best. *Fortune,* March 22: 83; and Dess & Picken, *Beyond productivity,* p. 98.

24. Barney, J. B. 1986. Types of competition and the theory of strategy: Towards an integrative framework. *Academy of Management Review,* 11(4): 791–800.

25. Harley-Davidson. 1993. Annual report.

26. For a rigorous, academic treatment of the origin of capabilities, refer to Ethiraj, S. K., Kale, P., Krishnan, M. S., & Singh, J. V. 2005. Where do capabilities come from and how do they matter? A study of the software services industry. *Strategic Management Journal,* 26(1): 25–46.

27. For an academic discussion on methods associated with organizational capabilities, refer to Dutta, S., Narasimhan, O., & Rajiv, S. 2005. Conceptualizing and measuring capabilities: Methodology and empirical application. *Strategic Management Journal,* 26(3): 277–286.

28. Lorenzoni, G., & Lipparini, A. 1999. The leveraging of interfirm relationships as a distinctive organizational capability: A longitudinal study. *Strategic Management Journal,* 20: 317–338.

29. Barney, J. 1991. Firm resources and sustained competitive advantage. *Journal of Management,* 17(1): 99–120.

30. Barney, 1986, op. cit. Our discussion of inimitability and substitution draws upon this source.

31. Deephouse, D. L. 1999. To be different, or to be the same? It's a question (and theory) of strategic balance. *Strategic Management Journal,* 20: 147–166.

32. Yeoh, P. L., & Roth, K. 1999. An empirical analysis of sustained advantage in the U.S. pharmaceutical industry: Impact of firm resources and capabilities. *Strategic Management Journal,* 20: 637–653.

33. Robins, J. A., & Wiersema, M. F. 2000. Strategies for unstructured competitive environments: Using scarce resources to create new markets. In Bresser, R. F., et al., (Eds.), *Winning strategies in a deconstructing world:* 201–220. New York: John Wiley.

34. Byrnes, N., & Burrows, P. 2007. Where Dell went wrong. *BusinessWeek,* February 18: 62–63; and Smith, A. D. 2007. Dell's moves create buzz. *Dallas Morning News.* Februrary 21: D1.

The Context of Strategic Management

chapter objectives

After reading this chapter, you should have a good understanding of:

LO 1 The effects of globalization and business ethics on today's organizations and on the nature of competition.

LO 2 The sources of national advantage; that is, why an industry in a given country is more (or less) successful than the same industry in another country.

LO 3 The potential benefits and risks of international expansion.

LO 4 The vital role of corporate governance and stakeholder management as well as how "symbiosis" can be achieved among an organization's stakeholders.

LO 5 The importance of social responsibility including environmental sustainability.

Globalization and business ethics are two pervasive factors that play important roles in all organizations' strategic management activities. The global marketplace provides many opportunities for firms to increase their profits, but it also presents potential pitfalls that firms must avoid. Meanwhile, firms face considerable pressure to conduct their activities in ways that meet high moral standards. Globalization and business ethics have accelerated the rate of change that executives face, making it essential that executives understand key aspects of both in order to maximize their chances of leading their firms toward success. Together, these two factors create a context within which the strategic management process takes place.

After some introductory comments on the global economy, we address the question: What explains the level of success of a given industry in a given country? To provide a framework for analysis, we draw on Michael Porter's "diamond of national advantage," in which he identified four factors that help to explain performance differences across national borders.

In the second section of the chapter, we shift our focus to the level of the firm and discuss some of the major motivations and risks associated with international expansion. Recognizing these potential benefits and risks enables executives to better assess the growth and profit potential in a given country. We also address important issues associated with a topic of growing interest in the international arena—offshoring and outsourcing.

Next, we consider three key aspects of business ethics: corporate governance, stakeholder management, and social responsibility. Corporate governance addresses the issue of who "governs" the corporation and determines its direction. It consists of three primary participants: stockholders (a firm's owners), executives (led by the chief executive officer), and the board of directors (elected by stockholders to monitor executives). Stakeholder management recognizes that the interests of various stakeholders such as owners, customers, and employees can conflict and create decision-making dilemmas. However, we discuss how some firms have been able to achieve "symbiosis" among stakeholders wherein their interests are considered interdependent and can be served simultaneously. We also discuss the importance of social responsibility, including the need for firms to incorporate environmental sustainability in their strategic actions.

LEARNING FROM MISTAKES

Wal-Mart, the world's largest retailer, certainly didn't have a good year in 2006.[1] There were executive turnover problems—such as the resignation of Sam's Clubs marketing head Mark Goodman and the embarrassing firing of Julie Roehm, the young advertising whiz whom Wal-Mart had hired away from DaimlerChrysler. Also, there were ongoing legal problems—a Philadelphia jury ordered Wal-Mart to pay $78 million to a class of 185,000 workers who had claimed that they were denied breaks and forced to work off the clock.

There were also business setbacks: same-store sales were up only 1.6 percent (while those of Costco and Target were up 9 percent and 4.1 percent, respectively). Wal-Mart's stock was flat in an otherwise strong year for equities. In fact, from the period of January 2000 (when Lee Scott took over for David Glass as CEO) to early 2007, the stock had fallen 22 percent.

The company had also had its share of setbacks overseas. Wal-Mart took a $900 million charge after its forays into Germany and South Korea failed. Let's take a closer look at what might explain its 2006 exit from South Korea—a market it entered in 1998.

Wal-Mart was never successful in South Korea. They were slow in opening stores—failing not only in winning customers but also in building enough market share to press suppliers on pricing. The core of their problem was an inability to adapt to local markets. As noted by Na Hong Seok, an analyst in Seoul: "Wal-Mart is a typical example of a global giant who has failed to localize its operations in South Korea."

Wal-Mart put off South Korean consumers by sticking to Western marketing strategies that concentrated on dry goods, from electronics to clothing. Their rivals, on the other hand, focused on food and beverages, the segment that specialists say attracts South Koreans to hypermarkets. In South Korea, fresh, quality food is a key ingredient of success. It typically generates half of a store's revenues. To make matters worse, one of Wal-Mart's competitors, E-Mart, even owned its own farms that supplied its stores.

Wal-Mart also ran into problems with a membership approach that was similar to the one used by its Sam's warehouses. According to Song Kye-Hyon, a financial analyst: "It turned out to be a strategic flaw of Wal-Mart when it first adopted the Western policy of the membership where customers were required to pay a membership fee for shopping privileges."

Further, Wal-Mart had difficulty overcoming some of the mechanisms that some of its rivals had developed to create greater customer loyalty. Some employed green-capped young men who helped bring the shopping carts to the customers' cars in the parking lot. Further, rivals operated shuttle buses to go through neighborhoods to pick up customers and drop them off at their homes after they completed their shopping. Simply put, Wal-Mart did not adapt to the local market conditions by investing the resources necessary to achieve some level of parity on such customer service initiatives.

In the end, Wal-Mart continued to flounder until it sold all 16 of its South Korean outlets in May 2006 to Shinsgae, a local retailer. Consistent with its long-term problems in the South Korean market, Wal-Mart lost $10.4 million on revenues of $787 million in 2005—its last full year of operations. Wal-Mart's vice chairman, Michael Duke, summed up the situation quite well: "As we continue to focus our efforts where we have the greatest impact on our growth strategy, it became increasingly clear that in South Korea's environment it would be difficult for us to reach the scale we desired."

In this chapter we discuss how firms can create value and achieve competitive advantage in the global marketplace. We also discuss how firms can avoid pitfalls such as those experienced by Wal-Mart in South Korea and by other firms such as Tyco and Enron, which have stumbled in dealing with ethical issues. In our view, globalization and business ethics provide an important "context" that shapes how well firms perform in today's economy.

LO1   The effects of globalization and business ethics on today's organizations and on the nature of competition.

 ## THE GLOBAL ECONOMY: A BRIEF OVERVIEW

Managers face many opportunities and risks when they diversify abroad.[2] The trade among nations has increased dramatically in recent years and it is estimated that by 2015, the trade *across* nations will exceed the trade within nations. In a variety of industries such as semiconductors, automobiles, commercial aircraft, telecommunications, computers, and consumer electronics, it is almost impossible to survive unless firms scan the world for competitors, customers, human resources, suppliers, and technology.[3]

GE's wind energy business illustrates the benefits of tapping into talent around the world. The firm has built research centers in China, Germany, India, and the United States.

"We did it," says CEO Jeffrey Immelt, "to access the best brains everywhere in the world." All four centers have played a key role in GE's development of huge 92-ton turbines. How did each contribute?[4]

* Chinese researchers in Shanghai design the microprocessors that control the pitch of the blade.

* Mechanical engineers from India (Bangladore) devise mathematical models to maximize the efficiency of materials in the turbine.

* Power-systems experts in the United States (Niskayuna, New York—which has researchers from 55 countries) do the design work.

* Technicians in Munich, Germany, have created a "smart" turbine that can calculate wind speeds and signal sensors in other turbines to pitch their blades to produce maximum electricity.

The rise of globalization—meaning the rise of market capitalism around the world—has undeniably contributed to the economic boom in America's New Economy, where knowledge is the key source of competitive advantage and value creation. It is estimated that it has brought phone service to about 300 million households in developing nations and a transfer of nearly $2 trillion from rich countries to poor countries through equity, bond investments, and commercial loans.[5]

Without doubt, there have been extremes in the effect of global capitalism on national economies and poverty levels around the world.[6] Clearly, the economies of East Asia have attained rapid growth, but there has been comparatively little progress in other areas of the world. For example, income in Latin America grew by only 6 percent in the past two decades when the continent was opening up to global capitalism. Average incomes in sub-Saharan Africa and the old Eastern European bloc have actually declined. Indeed, the World Bank estimates that the number of people living on $1 per day has *increased* to 1.3 billion over the past decade.

Such disparities in wealth among nations raise an important question: Why do some countries and their citizens enjoy the fruits of global capitalism while others remain or become more deeply mired in poverty? Or, why do some governments make the best use of inflows of foreign investment and know-how and others do not? There are many explanations. Among these are the need of governments to have track records of business-friendly policies to attract multinationals and local entrepreneurs to train workers, invest in modern technology, and nurture local suppliers and managers. Also, it means carefully managing the broader economic factors in an economy, such as interest rates, inflation, and unemployment, as well as a good legal system that protects property rights, strong educational systems, and a society where prosperity is widely shared.

The above policies are the type that East Asia—in locations such as Hong Kong, Taiwan, South Korea, and Singapore—has employed to evolve from the sweatshop economies of the 1960s and 1970s to industrial powers today. On the other hand, many countries have moved in the other direction. For example, in Guatemala only 52.0 percent of males complete fifth grade and an astonishing 39.8 percent of the population subsists on less than $1 per day.[7] (By comparison, the corresponding numbers for South Korea are 98 percent and less than 2 percent, respectively.)

Focus on Strategy 2.1 provides an interesting perspective on global trade—marketing to the "bottom of the pyramid." This refers to the practice of a multinational firm targeting its goods and services to the nearly 5 billion poor people in the world who inhabit developing countries. Collectively, this represents a very large market with $14 trillion in purchasing power.

Marketing to the "Bottom of the Pyramid"

Many executives wrongly believe that profitable opportunities to sell consumer goods exist only in countries where income levels are high. Even when they expand internationally, they often tend to limit their marketing to only the affluent segments within the developing countries. Such narrow conceptualizations of the market cause them to ignore the vast opportunities that exist at "the bottom of the pyramid," according to University of Michigan professor C. K. Prahalad. The *bottom of the pyramid* refers to the nearly 5 billion poor people who inhabit the developing countries. Surprisingly, they represent $14 trillion in purchasing power! And they are looking for products and services that can improve the quality of their lives such as clean energy, personal-care products, lighting, and medicines. Multinationals are missing out on growth opportunities if they ignore this vast segment of the market.

Innovative firms have found creative ways to serve the poor and still make a profit. Grameen Bank in Bangladesh is very different from the money center banks of London or New York. Pioneers of the concept of micro-credit, Grameen Bank (whose founder, Muhammad Yunus, won the 2006 Nobel Peace Prize) extends small loans—sometimes as small as $20—to thousands of struggling micro-entrepreneurs who have no collateral to offer. (The value of microcredit loans soared from $4 million to $1.3 billion between 1996 and 2006.) Not only are their loan recovery rates comparable to big banks, but they are also changing the lives of thousands of people while making a profit as well. Casas Bahias, the Brazilian retailer, has built a $2.5 billion-a-year chain selling to the poor who live in the *favelas,* the illegal shanty towns. Another amazing example is Aravind Eye Care, an Indian hospital that specializes in cataract surgeries. Today, they are the largest eye care facility in the world, performing more than 200,000 surgeries per year. The secret of their volume: The surgeries cost only about $25! A comparable surgery in the West costs $3,000. And best of all, Aravind has a return on equity of more than 75 percent!

As the above examples demonstrate, in order to sell to the bottom of the pyramid, managers must rethink their costs, quality, scale of operations, and even their use of capital. What prevents managers from selling to this vast market? Often they are victims of their own false assumptions. First, they think that the poor have no purchasing power. But $14 trillion can buy a lot. Second, they assume that poor people have no need for new technologies. We only have to see the demand for cell phones from entrepreneurs who run microbusinesses in villages in India to dispel this myth. Third, they assume that the poor have no use for their products and services. Shampoo, detergents, and banking satisfy universal needs, not just the needs of the rich. Fourth, they assume that managers may not be excited about working in these markets. Recent experience shows that this may be a more exciting environment than dogs fighting for fractions of market shares in the mature markets of the developed countries.

No one is helped by viewing the poor as the wretched of the earth. Instead, they are the latest frontier of opportunity for those who can meet their needs. A vast market that is barely tapped, the bottom of the pyramid offers enormous opportunities.

Sources: Miller, C. C. 2006. Easy money. *Forbes* November 27: 134–138; Prahalad, C. K. 2004. Why selling to the poor makes for good business. *Fortune,* 150(9): 32–33; Overholt, A. 2005. A new path to profit. *Fast Company,* January: 25–26; and Prahalad, C. K. 2005. *The fortune at the bottom of the pyramid: Eradicating poverty through profits.* Philadelphia: Wharton School Publishing.

Next, we will address in more detail the question of why some nations and their industries are more competitive. This establishes an important context or setting for the remainder of the chapter. After we discuss why some *nations and their industries* outperform others, we will be better able to address the various strategies that *firms* can take to create competitive advantage when they expand internationally.

LO2 The sources of national advantage; that is, why an industry in a given country is more (or less) successful than the same industry in another country.

FACTORS AFFECTING A NATION'S COMPETITIVENESS

Michael Porter of Harvard University conducted a four-year study in which he and a team of 30 researchers looked at the patterns of competitive success in 10 leading trading nations. He concluded that there are four broad attributes of nations that individually, and as a system, constitute what is termed "the diamond of national advantage." In effect, these attributes jointly determine the playing field that each nation establishes and operates for its industries. These factors are:

- *Factor conditions.* The nation's position in factors of production, such as skilled labor or infrastructure, necessary to compete in a given industry.
- *Demand conditions.* The nature of home-market demand for the industry's product or service.
- *Related and supporting industries.* The presence or absence in the nation of supplier industries and other related industries that are internationally competitive.
- *Firm strategy, structure, and rivalry.* The conditions in the nation governing how companies are created, organized, and managed, as well as the nature of domestic rivalry.

We will now briefly discuss each of these factors.[8] Then we will provide an integrative example—the Indian software industry—to demonstrate how these attributes interact to explain India's high level of competitiveness in this industry.

FACTOR CONDITIONS[9]

Classical economics suggests that **factor conditions**—factors of production such as land, labor, and capital—are the building blocks that create usable consumer goods and services.[10] But this tells only part of the story when we consider the global aspects of economic growth. Companies in advanced nations seeking competitive advantage over firms in other nations *create* many of the factors of production. For example, a country or industry dependent on scientific innovation must have a skilled human resource pool to draw upon. This resource pool is not inherited; it is created through investment in industry-specific knowledge and talent. The supporting infrastructure of a country—that is, its transportation and communication systems as well as its banking system—are also critical.

To achieve competitive advantage, factors of production must be developed that are industry and firm specific. In addition, the pool of resources a firm or a country has at its disposal is less important than the speed and efficiency with which these resources are deployed. Thus, firm-specific knowledge and skills created within a country that are rare, valuable, difficult to imitate, and rapidly and efficiently deployed are the factors of production that ultimately lead to a nation's competitive advantage.

For example, the island nation of Japan has little land mass, making the warehouse space needed to store inventory prohibitively expensive. But by pioneering just-in-time inventory management, Japanese companies managed to create a resource from which they gained advantage over companies in other nations that spent large sums to warehouse inventory.

DEMAND CONDITIONS

Demand conditions refer to the demands that consumers place on an industry for goods and services. Consumers who demand highly specific, sophisticated products and services force firms to create innovative, advanced products and services to meet the demand. This consumer pressure presents challenges to a country's industries. But in response to these challenges, improvements to existing goods and services often result, creating conditions necessary for competitive advantage over firms in other countries.

Demanding consumers push firms to move ahead of companies in other countries where consumers are less demanding and more complacent. Countries with demanding consumers drive firms in that country to meet high standards, upgrade existing products and services, and create innovative products and services. Thus, the conditions of

factor conditions
A nation's position in factors of production.

demand conditions
The nature of home-market demand for the industry's product or service.

India and the Diamond of National Advantage

Consider the following facts:

- SAP, the German software company, has developed new applications for notebook PCs at its 500-engineer Bangalore facility.
- General Electric plans to invest $100 million and hire 2,600 scientists to create the world's largest research and development lab in Bangalore, India.
- Microsoft plans to invest $400 million in new research partnerships in India.
- Over one-fifth of Fortune 1000 companies outsource their software requirements to firms in India.
- McKinsey & Co. projects that the Indian software and services industry will be an $87 billion business by 2008; $50 billion of this will be exported.
- For the past decade, the Indian software industry has grown at a 50 percent annual rate.
- More than 800 firms in India are involved in software services as their primary activity.
- Software and information technology firms in India are projected to employ 2.2 million people by 2008.

What is causing such global interest in India's software services industry? Porter's diamond of national advantage helps clarify this question. See Exhibit 2.1.

First, *factor conditions* are conducive to the rise of India's software industry. Through investment in human resource development with a focus on industry-specific knowledge, India's universities and software firms have literally created this essential factor of production. For example, India produces the second largest annual output of scientists and engineers in the world, behind only the United States. In a knowledge-intensive industry such as software, development of human resources is fundamental to both domestic and global success.

Second, *demand conditions* require that software firms stay on the cutting edge of technological innovation. India has already moved toward globalization of its software industry; consumer demand conditions in developed nations such as Germany, Denmark, parts of Southeast Asia, and the United States created the consumer demand necessary to propel India's software makers toward sophisticated software solutions.*

Third, India has the *supplier base as well as the related industries* needed to drive competitive rivalry and enhance

(continued)

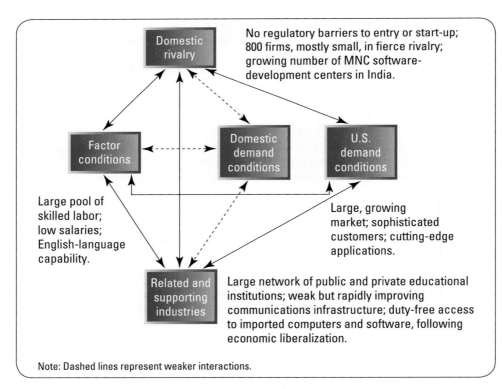

No regulatory barriers to entry or start-up; 800 firms, mostly small, in fierce rivalry; growing number of MNC software-development centers in India.

Large pool of skilled labor; low salaries; English-language capability.

Large, growing market; sophisticated customers; cutting-edge applications.

Large network of public and private educational institutions; weak but rapidly improving communications infrastructure; duty-free access to imported computers and software, following economic liberalization.

Note: Dashed lines represent weaker interactions.

EXHIBIT 2.1   India's Diamond in Software

Source: From Kampur D. and Ramamurti R., "India's Emerging Competition Advantage in Services," *Academy of Management Executive: The Thinking Manager's Source.* Copyright © 2001 by Academy of Management. Reproduced with permission of Academy of Management via Copyright Clearance Center.

(continued)

competitiveness. In particular, information technology (IT) hardware prices declined rapidly in the 1990s. Furthermore, rapid technological change in IT hardware meant that late-comers like India were not locked into older-generation technologies. Thus, both the IT hardware and software industries could "leapfrog" older technologies. In addition, relationships among knowledge workers in these IT hardware and software industries offer the social structure for ongoing knowledge exchange, promoting further enhancement of existing products. Further infrastructure improvements are occurring rapidly.

Fourth, with over 800 firms in the software services industry in India, *intense rivalry forces firms to develop competitive strategies and structures*. Although firms like TCS, Infosys, and Wipro have become large, they were quite small only five years ago. And dozens of small and midsized companies are aspiring to catch up. This intense rivalry is one of the primary factors driving Indian software firms to develop overseas distribution channels, as predicted by Porter's diamond of national advantage.

*Although India's success cannot be explained in terms of its home market demand (according to Porter's model), the nature of the industry enables software to be transferred among different locations simultaneously by way of communications links. Thus, competitiveness of markets outside India can be enhanced without a physical presence in those markets.

Sources: Kripalani, M. 2002. Calling Bangalore: Multinationals are making it a hub for high-tech research *BusinessWeek*, November 25: 52–54; Kapur, D., & Ramamurti, R. 2001. India's emerging competitive advantage in services. 2001. *Academy of Management Executive*, 15(2): 20–33; World Bank. *World development report*: 6. New York: Oxford University Press; Reuters. 2001. Oracle in India push, taps software talent. *Washington Post Online*, July 3.

consumer demand influence how firms view a market, with more demanding consumers stimulating advances in products and services. This, in turn, helps a nation's industries to better anticipate future global demand conditions and proactively respond to product and service requirements.

Denmark, for instance, is known for its environmental awareness. Demand from consumers for environmentally safe products has spurred Danish manufacturers to become leaders in water pollution control equipment—products it successfully exported.

RELATED AND SUPPORTING INDUSTRIES

Related and supporting industries enable firms to manage inputs more effectively. For example, countries with a strong supplier base benefit by adding efficiency to downstream activities. A competitive supplier base helps a firm obtain inputs using cost-effective, timely methods, thus reducing manufacturing costs. Also, close working relationships with suppliers provide the potential to develop competitive advantages through joint research and development and the ongoing exchange of knowledge.

related and supporting industries
The presence, absence, and quality in the nation of supplier industries and other related industries that supply services, support, or technology to firms in the industry value chain.

Related industries offer similar opportunities through joint efforts among firms. In addition, related industries create the probability that new companies will enter the market, increasing competition and forcing existing firms to become more competitive through efforts such as cost control, product innovation, and novel approaches to distribution. Combined, these give the home country's industries a source of competitive advantage.

In the Italian footwear industry the supporting industries show how they can lead to national competitive advantage. In Italy, shoe manufacturers are geographically located near their suppliers. The manufacturers have ongoing interactions with leather suppliers and learn about new textures, colors, and manufacturing techniques while a shoe is still in the prototype stage. The manufacturers are able to project future demand and gear their factories for new products long before companies in other nations become aware of the new styles. Similarly, geographic proximity of industries related to the pharmaceutical industry (e.g., the dye industry) in Switzerland has given that nation a leadership position in this market, with firms such as Novartis, Hoffman LaRoche, and Sandoz using dyes from local manufacturers in many pharmaceutical products.

Starbucks, based in Seattle, Washington, has aggressively expanded its international operations. By 2007, it had several thousand coffeehouses in 36 countries outside of the United States. Above is one of its coffeehouses in Bangkok, Thailand.

FIRM STRATEGY, STRUCTURE, AND RIVALRY

firm strategy, structure, and rivalry
The conditions in the nation governing how companies are created, organized, and managed, as well as the nature of domestic rivalry.

Rivalry is particularly intense in nations with conditions of strong consumer demand, strong supplier bases, and high new entrant potential from related industries. This competitive rivalry in turn increases the efficiency with which firms develop, market, and distribute products and services within the home country. Domestic rivalry thus provides a strong impetus for firms to innovate and find new sources of competitive advantage.

Interestingly, this intense rivalry forces firms to look outside their national boundaries for new markets, setting up the conditions necessary for global competitiveness. Among all the points on Porter's diamond of national advantage, domestic rivalry is perhaps the strongest indicator of global competitive success. Firms that have experienced intense domestic competition are more likely to have designed strategies and structures that allow them to successfully compete in world markets.

In the United States, for example, intense rivalry has spurred companies such as Dell Computer to find innovative ways to produce and distribute its products. This is largely a result of competition from IBM and Hewlett-Packard.

Focus on Strategy 2.2 on page 28 discusses India's software industry. It provides an integrative example of how Porter's "diamond" can help to explain the relative degree of success of an industry in a given country. Exhibit 2.1 illustrates India's "software diamond."

CONCLUDING COMMENT ON FACTORS AFFECTING A NATION'S COMPETITIVENESS

Porter drew his conclusions based on case histories of firms in more than 100 industries. Despite the differences in strategies employed by successful global competitors, a common theme emerged: Firms that succeeded in global markets had first succeeded in intensely competitive home markets. We can conclude that competitive advantage for global firms typically grows out of relentless, continuing improvement, and innovation.

Now that we have talked about the important role that nations play in international strategy, let's turn to the level of the individual firm.[11] In the next section, we will discuss a company's motivations and the risks associated with international expansion.

LO3 The potential benefits and risks of international expansion.

● INTERNATIONAL EXPANSION: A COMPANY'S MOTIVATIONS AND RISKS

MOTIVATIONS FOR INTERNATIONAL EXPANSION

There are many motivations for a company to pursue international expansion. The most obvious one is to *increase the size of potential markets* for a firm's products and services.[12] By early 2007, the world's population exceeded 6.5 billion, with the United States

EXHIBIT 2.2

Populations of Selected Nations and the World

Country	March 2007 (in millions) (estimated)
China	1,320
India	1,107
United States	300
Japan	127
Germany	82
World Total	6,580

Source: www.geohive.com/global/pop_data2.php.

representing less than 5 percent. Exhibit 2.2 lists the population of the United States compared to other major markets abroad.

Many multinational firms are intensifying their efforts to market their products and services to countries such as India and China as the ranks of their middle classes have increased over the past decade. These include Procter & Gamble's success in achieving a 50 percent share in China's shampoo market as well as PepsiCo's impressive inroads in the Indian soft-drink market.[13] Let's take a brief look at China's emerging middle class:[14]

- China's middle class has finally attained a critical mass—between 35 million and 200 million people, depending on what definition is used. The larger number is preferred by Fan Gong, director of China's National Economic Research Institute, who fixes the lower boundary of "middle" as a family income of $10,000.
- The central government's emphasis on science and technology has boosted the rapid development of higher education, which is the incubator of the middle class.
- China may be viewed as a new example of economies of scale. Many American companies already have factories in China exporting goods. Now that there is a domestic market to go along with the export market, those factories can increase their output with little additional cost. That is one reason why many foreign companies' profits in China have been so strong in recent years.

Expanding a firm's global presence also automatically increases its scale of operations, providing it with a larger revenue and asset base. Such an increase in revenues and asset base potentially enables a firm to *attain economies of scale.* This provides multiple benefits. One advantage is the spreading of fixed costs such as research and development over a larger volume of production. Examples include the sale of Boeing's commercial aircraft and Microsoft's operating systems in many foreign countries.

A second advantage would be *reducing the costs of research and development as well as operating costs.* Recall Microsoft's software development operations and other firms in talent-rich India (see Strategy Spotlight 2.2). A final advantage would be the attainment of greater purchasing power by pooling purchases. For example, as McDonald's increases the number of outlets it has all over the world, it can place larger orders for equipment and supplies, thus increasing its bargaining power with suppliers.

International expansion can also *extend the life cycle of a product* that is in its maturity stage in a firm's home country but that has greater demand potential elsewhere. Products (and industries) generally go through a four-stage life cycle of introduction, growth, maturity, and decline. In recent decades, U.S. soft-drink producers such as Coca-Cola and PepsiCo have aggressively pursued international markets to attain levels of growth that simply would not be available in the United States. Similarly, personal computer manufacturers such as Dell and Hewlett-Packard have sought out foreign markets to offset the growing saturation in the U.S. market.

Finally, international expansion can enable a firm to *optimize the physical location for every activity in its value chain.* The value chain, which we will discuss in detail in Chapter 3, represents the various activities in which all firms must engage to produce products and services. They include primary activities, such as inbound logistics, operations, and marketing, as well as support activities, such as procurement, research and development, and human resource management. All firms have to make critical decisions as to where each activity will take place.[15] Optimizing the location for every activity in the value chain can yield one or more of three strategic advantages: performance enhancement, cost reduction, and risk reduction. We will now discuss each of these.

Performance Enhancement   Microsoft's decision to establish a corporate research laboratory in Cambridge, England, is an example of a location decision that was guided mainly by the goal of building and sustaining world-class excellence in selected value-creating activities.[16] This strategic decision provided Microsoft with access to outstanding technical and professional talent. Location decisions can affect the quality with which any activity is performed in terms of the availability of needed talent, speed of learning, and the quality of external and internal coordination.

Cost Reduction   Two location decisions founded largely on cost-reduction considerations are (1) Nike's decision to source the manufacture of athletic shoes from Asian countries such as China, Vietnam, and Indonesia, and (2) the decision of many multinational companies to set up production operations just south of the United States–Mexico border to access lower-cost labor. These operations are called *maquiladoras.* Such location decisions can affect the cost structure in terms of local manpower and other resources, transportation and logistics, and government incentives and the local tax structure.

Managing across borders can lead to challenging ethical dilemmas. One issue that has received a good deal of attention in the recent business press is the issue of child labor. Focus on Strategy 2.3 discusses how two multinational companies have taken different approaches to address this issue.

Risk Reduction   Given the erratic swings in the exchange ratios between the U.S. dollar and the Japanese yen (in relation to each other as well as other major currencies), an important basis for cost competition between Ford and Toyota has been their relative ingenuity at managing currency risks. One of the ways for such competitors to manage currency risks has been to spread the high-cost elements of their manufacturing operations across a few select and carefully chosen locations around the world. Location decisions such as these can affect the overall risk profile of the firm with respect to currency, economic, and political risks.[17]

POTENTIAL RISKS OF INTERNATIONAL EXPANSION

When a company expands its international operations, it does so to increase its profits or revenues. As with any other investment, however, there are also potential risks.[18] To help companies assess the risk of entering foreign markets, rating systems have been developed to evaluate political, economic, and financial and credit risks.[19] *Euromoney* magazine publishes a semiannual "Country Risk Rating" that evaluates political, economic, and other risks that entrants potentially face. Exhibit 2.3 depicts a sample of country risk ratings, published by the World Bank, from the 178 countries that *Euromoney* evaluates. Note that the lower the score, the higher the country's expected level of risk.

Next we will discuss the four main types of risk: political risk, economic risk, currency risk, and management risk.

Child Labor: How Two Companies Have Addressed This Issue

It is interesting to consider how multinational companies have taken different approaches to address the issue of child labor in their overseas operations. Nike, for example, has revised its code of conduct a few times since 1992, including increasing the minimum age from 14 to 18 years for footwear factory workers and from 14 to 16 for equipment and apparel, which is quite a bit higher than other company codes and the International Labor Organization's (ILO) convention. The company also has started an internal compliance program, supplemented with external monitoring. However, this does not seem to have silenced the staunchest critics. Nike's Web site reflects the way in which the company tries to openly address this critique, providing ample information about the monitoring of facilities and the dilemmas the company faces after the introduction of its latest code.

Chiquita Banana almost completely follows the SA 8000 standard, including all references to international conventions, but with a few modifications, primarily to take account of workplace issues specific to agriculture. (The SA 8000 standard is developed by the Council on Economic Priorities Accreditation Agency and is widely recognized and accepted. It is based on ILO and United Nations conventions.) The company's strict child labor provisions do not apply to family farms or to small-scale holdings in the seasonal, nonbanana business, which do not regularly employ hired workers. This is also meant to allow for employment of a farmer's own children in seasonal activities. In line with its standard, Chiquita Banana tries to address the problem associated with children found to be working in supplying factories by giving "adequate support to enable such children to attend and remain in school until no longer a child."

Source: Kolk, A., & Tulder, R. V. 2004. Ethics in international business: Multinational approaches to child labor. *Journal of World Business,* 39: 49–60.

Political and Economic Risk   Generally speaking, the business climate in the United States is very favorable. However, some countries around the globe may be hazardous to the health of corporate initiatives because of **political risk.**[20] Forces such as social unrest, military turmoil, demonstrations, and even violent conflict and terrorism can pose serious threats.[21] Consider, for example, the ongoing tension and violence in the Middle East between Israelis and Palestinians, and the social and political unrest in Indonesia.[22] Because such conditions increase the likelihood of destruction of property and disruption of operations as well as nonpayment for goods and services, countries that are viewed as

political risk
Potential threat to a firm's operations in a country due to ineffectiveness of the domestic political system.

EXHIBIT 2.3

A Sample of International Country Risk Rankings

Rank	Country	Total Risk Assessment	Economic Performance	Political Risk	Total of Debt Indicators	Total of Credit and Access to Finance Indicators
1	Luxembourg	99.51	25.00	24.51	20.00	30.00
2	Switzerland	98.84	23.84	25.00	20.00	30.00
3	United States	98.37	23.96	24.41	20.00	30.00
40	China	71.27	18.93	16.87	19.73	15.74
55	Poland	57.12	18.56	13.97	9.36	15.23
63	Vietnam	52.04	14.80	11.91	18.51	6.82
86	Russia	42.62	11.47	8.33	17.99	4.83
114	Albania	34.23	8.48	5.04	19.62	1.09
161	Mozambique	21.71	3.28	2.75	13.85	1.83
178	Afghanistan	3.92	0.00	3.04	0.00	0.88

Source: Adapted from worldbank.org/html/prddr/trans/so96/art7.htm.

high risk are less attractive for most types of business. Typical exceptions include providers of munitions and counterintelligence services.

The laws, and the enforcement of laws, associated with the protection of intellectual property rights can be a major potential **economic risk** in entering new countries. Microsoft, for example, has lost billions of dollars in potential revenue through piracy of its software products in many countries, including China. Other areas of the globe, such as the former Soviet Union and some eastern European nations, have piracy problems as well. Firms rich in intellectual property have encountered financial losses as imitations of their products have grown due to a lack of law enforcement of intellectual property rights.[23]

Focus on Strategy 2.4 discusses an ethical problem that presents a severe threat to global trade—piracy. As we will see, estimates are that counterfeiting accounts for between 5 percent and 7 percent of global merchandise trade—the equivalent of as much as $512 billion a year. And the potential corrosive effects include health and safety, not just economic, damage.

Currency Risks Currency fluctuations can pose substantial risks. A company with operations in several countries must constantly monitor the exchange rate between its own currency and that of the host country to minimize **currency risks.** Even a small change in the exchange rate can result in a significant difference in the cost of production or net profit when doing business overseas. When the U.S. dollar appreciates against other currencies, for example, U.S. goods can be more expensive to consumers in foreign countries. At the same time, however, appreciation of the U.S. dollar can have negative implications for American companies that have branch operations overseas. The reason for this is that profits from abroad must be exchanged for dollars at a more expensive rate of exchange, reducing the amount of profit when measured in dollars. For example, consider an American firm doing business in Italy. If this firm had a 20 percent profit in euros at its Italian center of operations, this profit would be totally wiped out when converted into U.S. dollars if the euro had depreciated 20 percent against the U.S. dollar. (U.S. multinationals typically engage in sophisticated "hedging strategies" to minimize currency risk. The discussion of this is beyond the scope of this section.)

Management Risks **Management risks** may be considered the challenges and risks that managers face when they must respond to the inevitable differences that they encounter in foreign markets (as was the case in our opening example of Volkswagen). These take a variety of forms: culture, customs, language, income levels, customer preferences, distribution systems, and so on.[24] As we will note later in the chapter, even in the case of apparently standard products, some degree of local adaptation will become necessary.

Differences in cultures across countries can also pose unique challenges for managers.[25] Cultural symbols can evoke deep feelings.[26] For example, in a series of advertisements aimed at Italian vacationers, Coca-Cola executives turned the Eiffel Tower, Empire State Building, and the Tower of Pisa into the familiar Coke bottle. So far, so good. However, when the white marble columns of the Parthenon that crowns the Acropolis in Athens were turned into Coke bottles, Greeks became outraged. Why? Greeks refer to the Acropolis as the "holy rock," and a government official said the Parthenon is an "international symbol of excellence" and that "whoever insults the Parthenon insults international culture." Coca-Cola apologized for the ad. Below are a few examples of how culture varies across nations and some of the implications for business.[27]

- (Ecuador) Dinners at Ecuadorian homes last for many hours. Expect drinks and appetizers around 8:00 p.m., with dinner not served until 11:00 p.m. or midnight. You will dismay your hosts if you leave as early as 1:00 a.m. A party at an Ecuadorian home

economic risk
Potential threat to a firm's operations in a country due to economic policies and conditions, including property rights laws and enforcement of those laws.

currency risk
Potential threat to a firm's operations in a country due to fluctuations in the local currency's exchange rate.

management risk
Potential threat to a firm's operations in a country due to the problems that managers have making decisions in the context of foreign markets.

Piracy: A Key Threat to World Trade

Counterfeiting has grown to become a major threat to multinational corporations. "We've seen a massive increase in the last five years, and there is a risk that it will spiral out of control," claims Anthony Simon, marketing chief of Unilever Bestfoods. "It is no longer a cottage industry."

The figures are astounding. The World Customs Organization estimates that counterfeiting accounts for about 5 percent to 7 percent of global merchandise trade—equivalent to as much as $512 billion. Seizures of fakes by United States customs jumped 46 percent last year as counterfeiters boosted exports to Western markets. Unilever Groups says that knockoffs of its shampoos, soaps, and teas are growing at a rate of 30 percent annually.

Such counterfeiting can also have health and safety implications. The World Health Organization says up to 10 percent of medicines worldwide are counterfeit—a deadly hazard that could be costing the pharmaceutical industry $46 billion a year. "You won't die from purchasing a pair of counterfeit blue jeans or a counterfeit golf club. You can die from taking counterfeit pharmaceutical products. And there's no doubt that people have died in China from bad medicine," says John Theirault, head of global security for American pharmaceutical giant, Pfizer. And, sadly, cases like the one in China, where fake baby formula recently killed 60 infants, have investigators stepping up enforcement at U.S. ports. Injuries from overheating counterfeit cell phone batteries purchased right on Verizon store shelves sparked a recall. According to Hal Stratton, of the Consumer Product Safety Commission, "We know of at least one apartment fire that's occurred. We know of at least one burn situation of someone's face that's occurred." And bogus car parts are a $12 billion market worldwide. "Counterfeiting has gone from a local nuisance to a global threat," says Hanns Glatz, DaimlerChrysler's point man on intellectual property.

China is the key to any solution. Given the country's economic power, its counterfeiting is turning into quite the problem itself, accounting for nearly two-thirds of all fake and pirated goods worldwide. Dan Chow, a law professor at Ohio State University who specializes in Chinese counterfeiting provides some perspective: "We have never seen a problem of this size and magnitude in world history. There's more counterfeiting going on in China now than we've ever seen anywhere. We know that 15 to 20 percent of all goods in China are counterfeit."

Source: Engardio, P. & Yang, C. 2006. The runaway trade giant. *BusinessWeek*. April 24: 30–32; Letzing, J. 2007. Antipiracy group makes list of worst-offendor nations. www.marketwatch. February 12: np. Balfour, F. 2005. Fake! *BusinessWeek*, February 7: 54–64; Anonymous. 2005. Editorial. *BusinessWeek*, February 7: 96; and Simon, B. 2004. The world's greatest fakes. www.cbsnews. com, August 8.

will begin late and end around 4:00 a.m. or 5:00 a.m. Late guests may sometimes be served breakfast before they leave.

- (France) Words in French and English may have the same roots but different meanings or connotations. For example, a French person might "demand" something because demander in French means "to ask."

- (Hong Kong) Negotiations occur over cups of tea. Always accept an offer of tea whether you want it or not. When you are served, wait for the host to drink first.

- (Singapore) Singaporeans associate all of the following with funerals—do not give them as gifts: straw sandals, clocks, a stork or crane, handkerchiefs, or gifts or wrapping paper where the predominant color is white, black, or blue.

We have addressed several of the motivations and risks associated with international expansion. A major recent trend has been the dispersion of the value chains of multinational corporations across different countries; that is, the various activities that constitute the value chain of a firm are now spread across several countries and continents. Such dispersion of value occurs mainly through increasing offshoring and outsourcing. We now address some of the primary associated benefits and costs.

GLOBAL DISPERSION OF VALUE CHAINS: OUTSOURCING AND OFFSHORING

A report issued by the World Trade Organization describes the production of a particular U.S. car as follows: "30 percent of the car's value goes to Korea for assembly, 17.5 percent to Japan for components and advanced technology, 7.5 percent to Germany for design, 4 percent to Taiwan and Singapore for minor parts, 2.5 percent to U.K. for advertising and marketing services, and 1.5 percent to Ireland and Barbados for data processing. This means that only 37 percent of the production value is generated in the U.S."[28] Similarly, in the production of a Barbie doll, Mattel purchases plastic and hair from Taiwan and Japan, the molds from the United States, the doll clothing from China, and paint from the United States and assembles the product in Indonesia and Malaysia for sales worldwide. In today's economy these are not isolated examples. Instead, we are increasingly witnessing two interrelated trends: *outsourcing and offshoring.*

outsourcing
Using other firms to perform value-creating activities that were previously performed in-house.

Outsourcing occurs when a firm decides to utilize other firms to perform value-creating activities that were previously performed in-house.[29] In some cases, it may be a new activity that the firm is perfectly capable of doing, but it still chooses to have someone else perform the function for cost or quality reasons. Outsourcing can be to either a domestic company or a foreign firm.

offshoring
Shifting a value-creating activity from a domestic location to a foreign location.

Offshoring takes place when a firm decides to shift an activity that they were previously performing in a domestic location to a foreign location. For example, both Microsoft and Intel now have R&D facilities in India, employing a large number of Indian scientists and engineers. In many cases, offshoring and outsourcing go together; that is, a firm may outsource an activity to a foreign supplier, thereby causing the work to be offshored as well.

Spending on offshore information technology will nearly triple between 2004 and 2010 to $60 billion, according to research firm Gartner.[30] And offshore employment in information technology (IT), banking, and six other areas will double to 1.2 million (from 2003 to 2008), says the McKinsey Global Institute.

The recent explosion in the volume of outsourcing and offshoring is due to a variety of factors. Up until the 1960s, for most companies, the entire value chain was in one location. Further, the production took place close to where the customers were in order to keep transportation costs under control. In the case of service industries, it was generally believed that offshoring was not possible because the producer and consumer had to be present at the same place at the same time. After all, a haircut could not be performed if the barber and the client were separated!

In the case of manufacturing industries, the rapid decline in transportation and coordination costs has enabled firms to disperse their value chains over different locations. For example, Nike's R&D takes place in the United States, raw materials are procured from a multitude of countries, actual manufacturing takes place in China or Indonesia, advertising is produced in the United States, and sales and service take place in practically all the countries. Each value-creating activity is performed in the location where the cost is the lowest or the quality is the best. Without finding optimal locations for each activity and the resultant dispersion of the value chain, Nike could not have attained its position as the world's largest shoe company.

The experience of the manufacturing sector was repeated in the service sector as well by the mid-1990s. A trend that began with the outsourcing of low-level programming and data entry work to countries such as India and Ireland suddenly grew manyfold, encompassing a variety of white collar and professional activities ranging from call-centers to R&D. Now, the technical support lines of a large number of U.S. firms are answered from call centers in faraway locations. The cost of a long distance call from the United States to India has decreased from about $3 to $0.03 in the last 20 years, thereby making it possible to have call centers located in countries like India where a combination of low labor costs and English proficiency presents an ideal mix of factor conditions. Bangalore, India, in recent years, has emerged as a location where more and more U.S. tax returns are prepared.

In India, U.S.–trained and licensed radiologists interpret chest X-rays and CT scans from U.S. hospitals for half the cost. The advantages from offshoring go beyond mere cost savings today. In many specialized occupations in science and engineering, there is a shortage of qualified professionals in developed countries whereas countries like India, China, and Singapore have what seems like an inexhaustible supply.[31]

For most of the 20th century, domestic companies catered to the needs of local populations. However, with the increasing homogenization of customer needs around the world and the institutionalization of free trade and investment as a global ideology (especially after the creation of the WTO), competition has become truly global. Each company has to keep its costs low in order to survive. They also must find the best suppliers and the most skilled workers as well as locate each stage of the value chain in places where factor conditions are most conducive.

Next, we turn our attention to the second key contextual factor facing executives: business ethics. We first discuss corporate governance and stakeholder management. We then examine the need for social responsibility.

CORPORATE GOVERNANCE AND STAKEHOLDER MANAGEMENT

Most business enterprises that employ more than a few dozen people are organized as corporations. As you recall from your finance classes, the overall purpose of a corporation is to maximize the long-term return to the owners (shareholders). Thus, we may ask: Who is really responsible for fulfilling this purpose? Robert Monks and Neil Minow, in addressing this issue, provide a useful definition of **corporate governance** as "the relationship among various participants in determining the direction and performance of corporations. The primary participants are (1) the shareholders, (2) the management (led by the chief executive officer), and (3) the board of directors."[32] This relationship is illustrated in Exhibit 2.4.

The board of directors (BOD) are the elected representatives of the shareholders. They are charged with ensuring that the interests and motives of management are aligned with those of the owners (i.e., shareholders). In many cases, the BOD is diligent in fulfilling its purpose. For example, Intel Corporation, the giant $35 billion maker of microprocessor

LO1 The effects of globalization and business ethics on today's organizations and on the nature of competition.

LO4 The vital role of corporate governance and stakeholder management as well as how "symbiosis" can be achieved among an organization's stakeholders.

corporate governance
The relationship among various participants in determining the direction and performance of corporations. The primary participants are (1) the shareholders, (2) the management, and (3) the board of directors.

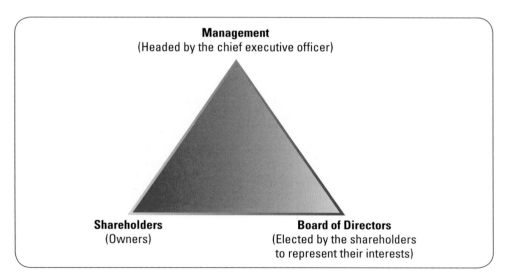

Management
(Headed by the chief executive officer)

Shareholders
(Owners)

Board of Directors
(Elected by the shareholders to represent their interests)

EXHIBIT 2.4   The Key Elements of Corporate Governance

chips, is widely recognized as an excellent example of sound governance practices. Its BOD has established guidelines to ensure that its members are independent (i.e., not members of the executive management team and do not have close personal ties to top executives) so that they can provide proper oversight, it has explicit guidelines on the selection of director candidates (to avoid "cronyism"), and it provides detailed procedures for formal evaluations of both directors and the firm's top officers.[33] Such guidelines serve to ensure that management is acting in the best interests of shareholders.[34]

Recently, there has been much criticism as well as cynicism by both citizens and the business press about the poor job that management and the BODs of large corporations are doing. We only have to look at the recent scandals at firms such as Arthur Andersen, WorldCom, Enron, Tyco, and ImClone Systems.[35] Such malfeasance has led to an erosion of the public's trust in the governance of corporations. For example, a recent Gallup poll found that 90 percent of Americans felt that people leading corporations could not be trusted to look after the interests of their employees, and only 18 percent thought that corporations looked after their shareholders. Forty-three percent, in fact, believed that senior executives were in it only for themselves. In Britain, that figure, according to another poll, was an astonishing 95 percent.[36] Perhaps worst of all, in another study, 60 percent of directors (the very people who decide how much executives should earn) felt that executives were "dramatically overpaid"![37]

Concerns about corporate governance led the U.S. Congress to pass the Sarbanes-Oxley Act in 2002. The legislation was an effort to restore investor confidence in how publicly traded companies are managed and how they report financial information. It requires U.S. corporations to abide by many stringent measures, including:

- CEOs and chief financial officers must fully reveal off-balance-sheet finances and vouch for the accuracy of the information provided.

- Executives must promptly reveal the sale of shares in firms they manage and are not allowed to sell shares when other employees cannot.

- Corporate lawyers must report to senior managers any violations of securities laws within the organization.

Although the Sarbanes-Oxley Act has improved investor confidence, the costs of meeting its requirements are substantial. Large corporations are estimated to spend an average of $35 million a year on compliance, while medium-sized firms spend an average of $3.1 million. Small firms find compliance particularly burdensome because they have a smaller revenue base to pay the needed costs.[38]

Next we examine how governance mechanisms can solve these problems.

GOVERNANCE MECHANISMS: ALIGNING THE INTERESTS OF OWNERS AND MANAGERS

A key characteristic of the modern corporation is the separation of ownership from control. To minimize the potential for managers to act in their own self-interest, or "opportunistically," the owners can implement some governance mechanisms.[39] There are two primary means of monitoring the behavior of managers. These include (1) a committed and involved *board of directors* that acts in the best interests of the shareholders to create long-term value and (2) *shareholder activism,* wherein the owners view themselves as share *owners* instead of share *holders* and become actively engaged in the governance of the corporation. As we will see later in this section, shareholder activism has increased dramatically in recent years. Finally, there are managerial incentives, sometimes called "contract-based outcomes," which consist of *reward and compensation agreements.* Here the goal is to carefully craft managerial incentive packages to align the interests of management with those of the stockholders.

A Committed and Involved Board of Directors The **board of directors** acts as a fulcrum between the owners and controllers of a corporation. In effect, they are the intermediaries who provide a balance between a small group of key managers in the firm based at the corporate headquarters and a sometimes vast group of shareholders. In the United States, the law imposes on the board a strict and absolute fiduciary duty to ensure that a company is run consistently with the long-term interests of the owners—the shareholders. The reality, as we have seen, is somewhat more ambiguous.[40]

board of directors
A group that has a fiduciary duty to ensure that the company is run consistently with the long-term interests of the owners, or shareholders, of a corporation and that acts as an intermediary between the shareholders and management.

The Business Roundtable, representing the largest U.S. corporations, describes the duties of the board as follows:

1. Select, regularly evaluate, and, if necessary, replace the chief executive officer. Determine management compensation. Review succession planning.

2. Review and, where appropriate, approve the financial objectives, major strategies, and plans of the corporation.

3. Provide advice and counsel to top management.

4. Select and recommend to shareholders for election an appropriate slate of candidates for the board of directors; evaluate board processes and performance.

5. Review the adequacy of the systems to comply with all applicable laws/regulations.[41]

Given these principles, what makes for a good board of directors? According to the Business Roundtable, the most important quality is a board of directors who are active, critical participants in determining a company's strategies.[42] That does not mean board members should micromanage or circumvent the CEO. Rather, they should provide strong oversight going beyond simply approving the CEO's plans. A board's primary responsibilities are to ensure that strategic plans undergo rigorous scrutiny, evaluate managers against high performance standards, and take control of the succession process.

Although boards in the past were often dismissed as CEOs' rubber stamps, increasingly they are playing a more active role by forcing out CEOs who cannot deliver on performance. According to a recent study by the consulting firm Booz Allen Hamilton, the rate of CEO departures for performance reasons has more than tripled, from 1.3 percent to 4.2 percent, between 1995 and 2002.[43] And the trend has continued. In 2006, turnover among CEOs increased 30 percent over the previous year.[44] Well-known CEOs like Gerald M. Levin of AOL Time Warner and Jack M. Greenberg of McDonald's paid the price for poor financial performance by being forced to leave. Others, such as Bernard Ebbers of WorldCom, Inc., and Dennis Kozlowski of Tyco International, lost their jobs due to scandals. "Deliver or depart" is clearly the new message from the boards.

Another key component of top-ranked boards is director independence.[45] Governance experts believe that a majority of directors should be free of all ties to either the CEO or the company. That means a minimum of "insiders" (past or present members of the management team) should serve on the board, and that directors and their firms should be barred from doing consulting, legal, or other work for the company.[46] Interlocking directorships—in which CEOs and other top managers serve on each other's boards—are not desirable. But perhaps the best guarantee that directors act in the best interests of shareholders is the simplest: Most good companies now insist that directors own significant stock in the company they oversee.[47]

Exhibit 2.5 provides some suggestions for how boards of directors can improve their practices.

EXHIBIT 2.5

Best Practice Ideas: The New Rules for Directors

Issue	Suggestion
Pay	**Know the math**
Companies will disclose full details of CEO payouts for the first time in their 2007 SEC filings. Activist investors are already drawing up hit lists of companies where CEO paychecks are out of step with performance.	Before okaying any financial package, directors must make sure they can explain the numbers. They need to adopt the mind-set of an activist investor and ask, "What's the harshest criticism someone could make about this package?"
Strategy	**Make It a Priority**
Boards have been so focused on compliance that duties like strategy and leadership oversight too often get short shrift. Only 59% of directors in a recent study rated their board favorably on setting strategy.	To avoid spending too much time on compliance issues, strategy has to move up to the beginning of the meeting. Annual one-, two- or three-day off-site meetings on strategy alone are becoming standard for good boards.
Financials	**Put in the Time**
Although 95% of directors in the recent study said they were doing a good job of monitoring financials, the number of earnings restatements hit a new high in 2006, after breaking records in 2004 and 2005.	Even nonfinancial board members need to monitor the numbers and keep a close eye on cash flows. Audit committee members: Prepare to spend 300 hours a year on committee responsibilities.
Crisis Management	**Dig in**
Some 120 companies are under scrutiny for options backdating, and the 100 largest companies have replaced 56 CEOs in the past five years, nearly double the terminations in the prior five years.	The increased scrutiny on boards means that a perfunctory review will not suffice if a scandal strikes. Directors can no longer afford to defer to management in a crisis. They must roll up their sleeves and move into watchdog mode.

Source: From Byrnes, N., & Sassen, J. 2007. Board of hard knocks. *BusinessWeek.* January 22: 36–39. Reproduced with permission.

Shareholder Activism As a practical matter, there are so many owners of the largest American corporations that it makes little sense to refer to them as "owners" in the sense of individuals becoming informed and involved in corporate affairs. However, even an individual shareholder has several rights, including (1) the right to sell the stock, (2) the right to vote the proxy (which includes the election of board members), (3) the right to bring suit for damages if the corporation's directors or managers fail to meet their obligations, (4) the right to certain information from the company, and (5) certain residual rights following the company's liquidation (or its filing for reorganization under bankruptcy laws), once creditors and other claimants are paid off.[48]

Collectively, shareholders have the power to direct the course of corporations.[49] This may involve acts such as being party to shareholder action suits and demanding that key issues be brought up for proxy votes at annual board meetings. In addition, the power of shareholders has intensified in recent years because of the increasing influence of large institutional investors such as mutual funds (e.g., T. Rowe Price and Fidelity Investments) and retirement systems such as TIAA-CREF (for university faculty members and school administrative staff).[50] Institutional investors hold approximately 50 percent of all listed corporate stock in the United States.

Shareholder activism refers to actions by large shareholders, both institutions and individuals, to protect their interests when they feel that managerial actions diverge from shareholder value maximization.

shareholder activism
Actions by large stockholders to protect their interests when they feel that managerial actions of a corporation diverge from shareholder value maximization.

Many institutional investors are aggressive in protecting and enhancing their investments. In effect, they are shifting from traders to owners. They are assuming the role of permanent shareholders and rigorously analyzing issues of corporate governance. In the process they are reinventing systems of corporate monitoring and accountability.[51]

Managerial Rewards and Incentives One of the most critical roles of the board of directors is to create incentives that align the interests of the CEO and top executives with the interests of owners of the corporation—long-term shareholder returns.[52] After all, shareholders rely on CEOs to adopt policies and strategies that maximize the value of their shares.[53] A combination of three basic policies may create the right monetary incentives for CEOs to maximize the value of their companies:

1. Boards can require that the CEOs become substantial owners of company stock.

2. Salaries, bonuses, and stock options can be structured so as to provide rewards for superior performance and penalties for poor performance.

3. Threat of dismissal for poor performance can be a realistic outcome.

ZERO SUM OR SYMBIOSIS? TWO ALTERNATE PERSPECTIVES OF STAKEHOLDER MANAGEMENT

Generating long-term returns for the shareholders is the primary goal of a publicly held corporation. As noted by former Chrysler vice chairman Robert Lutz, "We are here to serve the shareholder and create shareholder value. I insist that the only person who owns the company is the person who paid good money for it."[54]

Despite the primacy of generating shareholder value, managers who focus solely on the interests of the owners of the business will often make poor decisions that lead to negative, unanticipated outcomes. For example, decisions such as mass layoffs to increase profits, ignoring issues related to conservation of the natural environment to save money, and exerting excessive pressure on suppliers to lower prices can certainly harm the firm in the long run. Such actions would likely lead to negative outcomes such as alienated employees, increased governmental oversight and fines, and disloyal suppliers.

Clearly, in addition to *shareholders,* there are other *stakeholders* (e.g. suppliers, customers) who must be explicitly taken into account in the strategic management process.[55] A stakeholder can be defined as an individual or group, inside or outside the company, that has a stake in and can influence an organization's performance. Each stakeholder group makes various claims on the company. Exhibit 2.6 provides a list of major stakeholder groups and the nature of their claims on the company.

There are two opposing ways of looking at the role of stakeholder management in the strategic management process.[56] The first one can be termed "zero sum." In this view, the role of management is to look upon the various stakeholders as competing for the organization's resources. In essence, the gain of one individual or group is the loss of another individual or group. For example, employees want higher wages (which drive down profits), suppliers want higher prices for their inputs and slower, more flexible delivery times (which drive up costs), customers want fast deliveries and higher quality (which drive up costs), the community at large wants charitable contributions (which take money from company goals), and so on. This zero-sum thinking is rooted, in part, in the traditional conflict between workers and management, leading to the formation of

Stakeholder Group	Nature of Claim
Stockholders	Dividends, capital appreciation
Employees	Wages, benefits, safe working environment, job security
Suppliers	Payment on time, assurance of continued relationship
Creditors	Payment of interest, repayment of principal
Customers	Value, warranties
Government	Taxes, compliance with regulation
Communities	Good citizenship behavior such as charities, employment, nonpollution

unions and sometimes ending in adversarial union–management negotiations and long, bitter strikes.

Although there will always be some conflicting demands, there is value in exploring how the organization can achieve mutual benefit through *stakeholder symbiosis,* which recognizes that stakeholders are dependent upon each other for their success and well-being.[57] That is, managers acknowledge the interdependence among employees, suppliers, customers, shareholders, and the community at large. Consider Outback Steakhouse:[58]

> Outback Steakhouse asked their employees to identify on a six-point scale how strongly they agreed or disagreed that Outback's principles and beliefs (P&Bs) were practiced in their particular restaurants. The turnover rate of the hourly employees in the group most strongly agreeing that the P&Bs were their stores' guiding ethos was half what it was in the group most strongly disagreeing. Five times as many customers in the strongly agreeing group indicated that they were likely to return. Further, at the strongly agreeing group's restaurants, revenues were 8.9% higher, cash flow was 27% higher, and pretax profit was 48% higher. Not surprisingly, the survey is now mandatory for Outback managers.

LO5 The importance of social responsibility including environmental sustainability.

SOCIAL RESPONSIBILITY AND ENVIRONMENTAL SUSTAINABILITY: MOVING BEYOND THE IMMEDIATE STAKEHOLDERS

Organizations cannot ignore the interests and demands of stakeholders such as citizens and society in general that are beyond its immediate constituencies—customers, owners, suppliers, and employees. That is, they must consider the needs of the broader community at large and act in a socially responsible manner.[59]

Social responsibility is the expectation that businesses or individuals will strive to improve the overall welfare of society.[60] From the perspective of a business, this means that managers must take active steps to make society better by virtue of the business being in existence.[61] Similar to norms and values, actions that constitute socially responsible behavior tend to change over time. In the 1970s affirmative action was a high priority and during the 1990s and up to the present time, the public has been concerned about environmental quality. Many firms have responded to this by engaging in recycling and reducing waste. And in the wake of the 2001 terrorist attacks on New York City and the Pentagon, as well as the continuing threat from terrorists worldwide, a new kind of priority has arisen: the need to be vigilant concerning public safety.

Today, demands for greater corporate responsibility have accelerated.[62] These include corporate critics, social investors, activists, and, increasingly, customers who claim to

American Express: Using Cause-Related Marketing Effectively

American Express has benefited in terms of favorable public relations as well as financially from its cause-related marketing initiatives. Back in 1983, in connection with the restoration of the Statue of Liberty project, it promised that it would contribute to this initiative a portion of the amount that consumers charged on their American Express cards. The resulting campaign made marketing history. AmEx eventually donated $1.7 million to the cause. AmEx card use increased 28 percent and new card applications increased 17 percent. Cause-related marketing has grown significantly, from $125 million in 1990 to $991 million in 2004, and the figure is expected to continue to increase.

According to a recent Cone Corporate Citizenship Study, cause-related marketing can both reinforce consumer relationships as well as strengthen employee morale. For example, 84% of respondents said they would likely switch brands to one associated with a good cause and 92% of Americans said that they have a more positive image of companies and products that support causes. Similarly, 57% of employees wish that their company would do more to support a social issue and 75% of Americans would consider a company's commitment to social issues when deciding where to work.

Sources: Vogel, D. J. 2005. Is there a market for virtue? The business case for corporate social responsibility. *California Management Review,* 47 (4): 19–36; and 2002 Cone Corporate Citizenship Study Cone, Inc.

---

assess corporate responsibility when making purchasing decisions. Such demands go well beyond product and service quality.[63] They include a focus on issues such as labor standards, environmental sustainability, financial and accounting reporting, procurement, and environmental practices. At times, a firm's reputation can be tarnished by exceedingly poor judgment on the part of one of its managers.[64]

> In 2006, Judith Regan, a publisher at HarperCollins, was set to publish a book, *If I Did It,* with O. J. Simpson detailing how he would have committed the 1995 murder of his ex-wife Nicole Brown Simpson and her friend, Ron Goldman. The book was characterized by Regan as his "confession," and it earned the world's outrage as an "evil sweeps stunt" that will likely be remembered as a low point in American culture. Regan's boss, News Corporation Chairman Rupert Murdoch, cancelled the book and the TV special that was also planned. But this was not before preorders for *If I Did It* cracked the Top 20 on Amazon.com. Not surprisingly, Judith Regan was fired.

A key stakeholder group that appears to be particularly susceptible to corporate social responsibility (CSR) initiatives is its customers.[65] Surveys indicate a strong positive relationship between CSR behaviors and consumers' reactions to a firm's products and services. For example:

- Corporate Citizenship's poll conducted by Cone Communications found that "84 percent of Americans say they would be likely to switch brands to one associated with a good cause, if price and quality are similar."[66]
- Hill & Knowlton/Harris's Interactive poll reveals that "79 percent of Americans take corporate citizenship into account when deciding whether to buy a particular company's product and 37 percent consider corporate citizenship an important factor when making purchasing decisions."[67]

Such findings are consistent with a large body of research that confirms the positive influence of CSR on consumers' company evaluations and product purchase intentions across a broad range of product categories.

Cause-related marketing is another example of the growing link between corporate social responsibility and financial objectives. Such marketing generally features promotions in which a portion of the purchase price of a product or service is donated to a social

Solar cells can be organized into arrays, such as this one to provide electric power for industrial, commercial, and residential customers. Solar power is a more sustainable, environmentally friendly option than nuclear power plants or coal- and oil-fired power plants.

cause: It essentially links marketing and corporate philanthropy. Focus on Strategy 2.5 discusses how American Express became one of the pioneers of this emerging trend and significantly benefited.

The Triple Bottom Line: Incorporating Financial as well as Environmental and Social Costs Many companies are now measuring what has been called a "triple bottom line," which involves assessing financial, social, and environmental performance. Shell, NEC, and Procter & Gamble, among other corporations, have recognized that failing to account for the environmental and social costs of doing business poses risks to the company and its community.[68]

The environmental revolution has been almost four decades in the making.[69] It has changed forever how companies do business. In the 1960s and 1970s, companies were in a state of denial regarding their firms' impact on the natural environment. However, a series of visible ecological problems created a groundswell for strict governmental regulation. In the United States, Lake Erie was "dead," and in Japan, people were dying of mercury poisoning. Clearly, the effects of global warming are being felt throughout the world. Some other examples are:[70]

- Ice roads are melting, so Canadian diamond miners must airlift equipment at great cost instead of trucking it in.
- More severe storms and rising seas mean oil companies must build stronger rigs, and cities must build higher seawalls.
- The loss of permafrost and protective sea ice may force villages like Alaska's Shismaref to relocate.
- Yukon River salmon—and fisheries—are threatened by a surge of parasites associated with a jump in water temperature.
- Later winters have let beetles spread in British Columbia killing 22 million acres of pine forests, an area the size of Maine.
- In the country of Mali, in Africa, crops are threatened. The rainy season is now too short for rice, and the dry season is too hot for potatoes.

Stuart Hart, writing in the *Harvard Business Review,* addresses the magnitude of problems and challenges associated with the natural environment:

How Adobe Systems Benefits from "Being Green"

In June 2006, Adobe Systems, the $2 billion software maker, became the first firm to receive a platinum award from the nonprofit U.S. Green Building Council. Platinum certification of Adobe's buildings was based on ratings in six categories: sustainability; water efficiency; energy efficiency and atmospheric quality; use of materials and resources; indoor environmental quality; and innovations in upgrades, operations, and maintenance.

Thus, Adobe's San Jose headquarters is the greenest corporate site on record in the United States. What is more impressive is that Adobe earned the honor by retrofitting its two existing office towers (approximately 1 million square feet); most of the 151 buildings that have received the council's gold ratings (a "step down" from platinum) are new structures.

By installing everything from motion detectors to waterless urinals, the firm has reduced its electricity use by 35% and its gas consumption by 41% since 2001. In addition, it conserves 295,000 gallons of water each month. And during this time, headcount has shot up 80%!

Adobe is proving that building "green" isn't just good citizenship—it is profitable. Adobe has invested approximately $650,000 for energy and environmental retrofits since 2001. The retrofits on the two office towers have resulted in approximately $720,000 savings to date, for a total return on investment of approximately 115 percent. Randy Knox III, Adobe's director of real estate, facilities, and security, comments: "This isn't some pie-in-the-sky kind of thing the enviros are pushing. It really works."

Sources: Nachtigal, J. 2006. It's easy and cheap being green. *BusinessWeek*, October 16: 53; Warner, J. 2006. Adobe headquarters awarded highest honors from U.S. green building council. December 6: *Adobe Press Release*; and Juran, K. 2006. Adobe wins top California flex your power! Award for energy efficiency. July 3: *Adobe Press Release*.

The challenge is to develop a *sustainable global economy:* an economy that the planet is capable of supporting indefinitely. Although we may be approaching ecological recovery in the developed world, the planet as a whole remains on an unsustainable course. Increasingly, the scourges of the late twentieth century—depleted farmland, fisheries, and forests; choking urban pollution; poverty; infectious disease; and migration—are spilling over geopolitical borders. The simple fact is this: in meeting our needs, we are destroying the ability of future generations to meet theirs . . . corporations are the only organizations with the resources, the technology, the global reach, and, ultimately, the motivation to achieve sustainability.[71]

Environmental sustainability is now a value embraced by the most competitive and successful multinational companies.[72] The McKinsey Corporation's survey of more than 400 senior executives of companies around the world found that 92 percent agreed with former Sony President Akio Morita's contention that the environmental challenge will be one of the central issues in the 21st century.[73] Virtually all executives acknowledged their firm's responsibility to control pollution, and 83 percent agreed that corporations have an environmental responsibility for their products even after they are sold.

For many successful firms, environmental values are now becoming a central part of their cultures and management processes. And, as noted earlier, environmental impacts are being audited and accounted for as the "third bottom line." According to one 2004 corporate report, "If we aren't good corporate citizens as reflected in a Triple Bottom Line that takes into account social and environmental responsibilities along with financial ones—eventually our stock price, our profits, and our entire business could suffer."[74] And according to a KPMG study of 350 firms: "More big multinational firms are seeing the benefits of improving their environmental performance . . . Firms are saving money and boosting share performance by taking a close look at how their operations impact the environment. . . . Companies see that they can make money as well." Focus on Strategy 2.6 discusses how Adobe Systems benefits financially from its environmental initiatives.

SUMMARY

We live in a highly interconnected global community. Two of the dominant features of this context are that many of the best opportunities for profits lie beyond the boundaries of a firm's home country and that there are increased pressures for firms to act in ways that outsiders view as ethical. In essence, globalization and business ethics provide a context within which the strategic management process takes place.

LO1, LO2   The first section of the chapter addressed the factors that determine a nation's competitiveness in a particular industry. The framework was developed by Professor Michael Porter. He identified four dimensions—factor conditions, demand characteristics, related and supporting industries, and firm strategy, structure, and rivalry—that collectively shape the competitive process in the international arena.

LO3   Next, we discussed the potential benefits and risks associated with a firm's overseas expansion efforts. The benefits include increasing the size of a firm's customer base, achieving economies of scale, extending a product's life cycle, and optimizing the location of activities within a firm's value chain. Key potential pitfalls include political and economic risks, currency risks, and management risks. We also addressed some of the challenges and opportunities associated with offshoring and outsourcing.

LO1, LO4   We then turned our attention to business ethics. We began this section by introducing the concepts of corporate governance and stakeholder management. Governance refers to efforts by a firm's owners to ensure that executives act appropriately in their role as leaders of the firm. Stakeholders are groups such as owners, customers, suppliers, employees, and society at large for whom the firm is important. Successful firms go beyond an overriding focus on just satisfying owners. Instead, they recognize the inherent conflicts among stakeholders' interests and work to develop "symbiosis"—that is, interdependence and mutual benefit—among them.

LO5   In the final section, we noted that executives must also recognize the need to act in a socially responsible manner. They also should address issues related to environmental sustainability in their strategic actions. Overall, globalization and business ethics must be taken into account throughout the strategic management process.

KEY TERMS

factor conditions 27
demand conditions 27
related and supporting industries (national advantage) 29
firm strategy, structure, and
  vivalry (national advantage) 30

political risk 33
economic risk 34
currency risk 34
management risk 34
outsourcing 36

offshoring 36
corporate governance 37
board of directors 39
shareholder activism 41

SUMMARY REVIEW QUESTIONS

1.   What is national advantage, and what are its sources?

2.   What is globalization, and why does it matter to companies?

3.   What is corporate governance? What are its three key elements and how can it be improved?

4.   How can "symbiosis" be achieved among a firm's stakeholders?

1. What national advantages do firms based in the United States enjoy? How do these advantages provide an edge in the international arena?

2. Many companies choose to have their goods manufactured overseas, where labor costs are low. Is this just good strategic thinking, or are there ethical issues involved as well?

3. Select a company that interests you. Using the Internet, what are some recent demands that stakeholders have placed on this company? Can you find examples of how the company is trying to develop symbiosis among its stakeholders?

4. Some critics believe that executives engage in social responsibility in an effort to manage impressions, while others believe that executives who pursue social responsibility sincerely want to improve society. With which side do you agree, and why? More generally, does it matter why good is being done?

1. Birger, J. 2007. The unending woes of Lee Scott. *Fortune.* January 27: 118; 122; Berner, R. 2007. My year at Wal-Mart. *BusinessWeek,* February 12: 70–74; Anonymous. 2006. Wal-Mart in Japan sees losses. www.sptimes.com. August 23; and Mi-Young, A. 2000. Wal-Mart has to adapt to the South Korean customer. *Deutsche-Presse-agentur.* November 8: 1–3.

2. For a recent discussion on globalization by one of international business's most respected authors, read Ohmae, K. 2005. *The next global stage: Challenges and opportunities in our borderless world.* Philadelphia: Wharton School Publishing.

3. Our discussion of globalization draws upon Engardio, P., & Belton, C. 2000. Global capitalism: Can it be made to work better? *Business-Week,* November 6: 72–98.

4. Sellers, P. 2005. Blowing in the wind. *Fortune,* July 25: 63.

5. Engardio & Belton, op. cit.

6. For insightful perspectives on strategy in emerging economies, refer to the article entitled: Strategy research in emerging economies: Challenging the conventional wisdom in the January 2005 issue of *Journal of Management Studies,* 42(1).

7. The above discussion draws on Clifford, M. L., Engardio, P., Malkin, E., Roberts, D., & Echikson, W. 2000. Up the ladder. *BusinessWeek,* November 6: 78–84.

8. For another interesting discussion on a country perspective, refer to Makino, S. 1999. MITI Minister Kaora Yosano on reviving Japan's competitive advantages. *Academy of Management Executive,* 13(4): 8–28.

9. The following discussion draws heavily upon Porter, M. E. 1990. The competitive advantage of nations. *Harvard Business Review,* March–April: 73–93.

10. Landes, D. S. 1998. *The wealth and poverty of nations.* New York: W. W. Norton.

11. A recent study that investigates the relationship between international diversification and firm performance is Lu, J. W., & Beamish, P. W. 2004. International diversification and firm performance: The s-curve hypothesis. *Academy of Management Journal,* 47(4): 598–609.

12. Part of our discussion of the motivations and risks of international expansion draws upon Gregg, F. M. 1999. International strategy. In Helms, M. M. (Ed.). *Encyclopedia of management:* 434–438. Detroit: Gale Group.

13. These two examples are discussed, respectively, in Dawar, N., & Frost, T. 1999. Competing with giants: Survival strategies for local companies in emerging markets. *Harvard Business Review,* 77(2): 119–129; and Prahalad, C. K., & Lieberthal, K. 1998. The end of corporate imperialism. *Harvard Business Review,* 76(4): 68–79.

14. Meredith, R. 2004. Middle kingdom, middle class. *Forbes,* November 15: 188–192; and Anonymous. 2004. Middle class becomes rising power in China. www.Chinadaily.com, November 6.

15. This discussion draws upon Gupta, A. K., & Govindarajan, V. 2001. Converting global presence into global competitive advantage. *Academy of Management Executive,* 15(2): 45–56.

16. Stross, R. E. 1997. Mr. Gates builds his brain trust. *Fortune,* December 8: 84–98.

17. For a good summary of the benefits and risks of international expansion, refer to Bartlett, C. A., & Ghoshal, S. 1987. Managing across borders: New strategic responses. *Sloan Management Review,* 28(5): 45–53; and Brown, R. H. 1994. *Competing to win in a global economy.* Washington, DC: U.S. Department of Commerce.

18. For an interesting insight into rivalry in global markets, refer to MacMillan, I. C., van Putten, A. B., & McGrath, R. G. 2003. Global gamesmanship. *Harvard Business Review,* 81(5): 62–73.

19. It is important for firms to spread their foreign operations and outsourcing relationships with a broad, well-balanced mix of regions and countries to reduce risk and increase potential reward. For example, refer to Vestring, T., Rouse, T., & Reinert, U. 2005. Hedge your offshoring bets. *MIT Sloan Management Review,* 46(3): 27–29.

REFERENCES

20. For a discussion of some of the challenges associated with government corruption regarding entry strategies in foreign markets, read Rodriguez, P., Uhlenbruck, K., & Eden, L. 2005. Government corruption and entry strategies of multinationals. *Academy of Management Review,* 30(2): 383–396.

21. For a discussion of the political risks in China for United States companies, refer to Garten, J. E. 1998. Opening the doors for business in China. *Harvard Business Review,* 76(3): 167–175.

22. Shari, M. 2001. Is a holy war brewing in Indonesia? *BusinessWeek,* October 15: 62.

23. Gikkas, N. S. 1996. International licensing of intellectual property: The promise and the peril. *Journal of Technology Law & Policy,* 1(1): 1–26.

24. For an excellent theoretical discussion of how cultural factors can affect knowledge transfer across national boundaries, refer to Bhagat, R. S., Kedia, B. L., Harveston, P. D., & Triandis, H. C. 2002. Cultural variations in the cross-border transfer of organizational knowledge: An integrative framework. *Academy of Management Review,* 27(2): 204–221.

25. To gain insights on the role of national and regional cultures on knowledge management models and frameworks, read Pauleen, D. J., & Murphy, P. 2005. In praise of cultural bias. *MIT Sloan Management Review,* 46(2): 21–22.

26. Berkowitz, E. N. 2000. *Marketing* (6th ed.). New York: McGraw-Hill.

27. Morrison, T., Conaway, W. & Borden, G. 1994. *Kiss, bow, or shake hands.* Avon, MA: Adams Media; and www.executiveplanet.com/business-culture.

28. World Trade Organization. *Annual Report 1998.* Geneva: World Trade Organization.

29. Lei, D. 2005. Outsourcing. In Hitt, M. A., & Ireland, R. D. (Eds.). *The Blackwell encyclopedia of management.* Entrepreneurship: 196–199. Malden, MA: Blackwell.

30. Dolan, K. A. 2006. Offshoring the offshorers. *Forbes.* April 17: 74–78.

31. The discussion above draws from Colvin, J. 2004. Think your job can't be sent to India? Just watch. *Fortune,* December 13: 80; Schwartz, N. D. 2004. Down and out in white collar America. *Fortune,* June 23: 321–325; Hagel, J. 2004. Outsourcing is not just about cost cutting. *The Wall Street Journal,* March 18: A3.

32. Monks, R., & Minow, N. 2001. *Corporate governance* (2nd ed.). Malden, MA: Blackwell.

33. Intel Corp. 2007. www.intel.com/intel/finance/corp_gov.html.

34. Jones, T. J., Felps, W. & Bigley, G. A. 2007. Ethical theory and stakeholder-related decisions: The role of stakeholder culture. *Academy of Management Review,* 32(1): 137–155.

35. For example, see The best (& worst) managers of the year, 2003. *BusinessWeek,* January 13: 58–92; and Lavelle, M. 2003. Rogues of the year. *Time,* January 6: 33–45.

36. Handy, C. 2002. What's a business for? *Harvard Business Review,* 80(12): 49–55.

37. Anonymous, 2007. In the money. *Economist.* January 20: 3–6.

38. Brown, E. 2006. London calling. *Forbes,* May 8: 51–52; Henry, D. 2005. Death, taxes, and Sarbanes-Oxley? *BusinessWeek,* January 17: 28–31.

39. For an insightful, recent discussion of the academic research on corporate governance, and in particular the role of boards of directors,

refer to Chatterjee, S., & Harrison, J. S. 2001. Corporate governance. In Hitt, M. A., Freeman, R. E., & Harrison, J. S. (Eds.). *Handbook of strategic management:* 543–563. Malden, MA: Blackwell.

40. This opening discussion draws on Monks & Minow, op. cit. 164, 169.

41. Business Roundtable. 1990. *Corporate governance and American competitiveness,* March: 7.

42. Byrne, J. A., Grover, R., & Melcher, R. A. 1997. The best and worst boards. *BusinessWeek,* November 26: 35–47. The three key roles of boards of directors are monitoring the actions of executives, providing advice, and providing links to the external environment to provide resources. See Johnson, J. L., Daily, C. M., & Ellstrand, A. E. 1996. Boards of directors: A review and research agenda. *Academy of Management Review,* 37: 409–438.

43. McGeehan, P. 2003. More chief executives shown the door, study says. *New York Times,* May 12: C2.

44. Gerdes, L. 2007. Hello, goodbye. *BusinessWeek.* January 22: 16.

45. For an analysis of the effects of outside director's compensation on acquisition decisions, refer to: Deutsch, T., Keil, T., & Laamanen, T. 2007. Decision making in acquisitions: The effect of outside directors' compensation on acquisition patterns. *Journal of Management,* 33(1): 30–56.

46. There are benefits, of course, to having some insiders on the board of directors. Inside directors would be more aware of the firm's strategies. Additionally, outsiders may rely too often on financial performance indicators because of information asymmetries. For an interesting discussion, see Baysinger, B. D., & Hoskisson, R. E. 1990. The composition of boards of directors and strategic control: Effects on corporate strategy. *Academy of Management Review,* 15: 72–87.

47. Hambrick, D. C., & Jackson, E. M. 2000. Outside directors with a stake: The linchpin in improving governance. *California Management Review,* 42(4): 108–127.

48. Monks and Minow, op. cit.: 93.

49. A discussion of the factors that lead to shareholder activism is found in Ryan, L. V., & Schneider, M. 2002. The antecedents of institutional investor activism. *Academy of Management Review,* 27(4): 554–573.

50. There is strong research support for the idea that the presence of large block shareholders is associated with value-maximizing decisions. For example, refer to Johnson, R. A., Hoskisson, R. E., & Hitt, M. A. 1993. Board of director involvement in restructuring: The effects of board versus managerial controls and characteristics. *Strategic Management Journal,* 14: 33–50.

51. For an interesting perspective on the impact of institutional ownership on a firm's innovation strategies, see Hoskisson, R. E., Hitt, M. A., Johnson, R. A., & Grossman, W. 2002. *Academy of Management Journal,* 45(4): 697–716.

52. Jensen, M. C., & Murphy, K. J. 1990. CEO incentives—It's not how much you pay, but how. *Harvard Business Review,* 68(3): 138–149.

53. For a perspective on the relative advantages and disadvantages of "duality"—that is, one individual serving as both Chief Executive Officer and Chairman of the Board, see Lorsch, J. W., & Zelleke, A. 2005. Should the CEO be the chairman? *MIT Sloan Management Review,* 46(2): 71–74.

54. Stakeholder symbiosis. 1998. *Fortune,* March 30: S2.

55. For a definitive, recent discussion of the stakeholder concept, refer to Freeman, R. E., & McVae, J. 2001. A stakeholder approach to strategic management. In Hitt, M. A., Freeman, R. E., & Harrison, J. S. (Eds.). *Handbook of strategic management:* 189–207. Malden, MA: Blackwell.

56. For an insightful discussion on the role of business in society, refer to Handy, op. cit.

57. Stakeholder symbiosis. op. cit., p. S3.

58. Sullivan, C. T. 2005. A stake in the business. *Harvard Business Review,* 83 (9): 57–67.

59. An excellent theoretical discussion on stakeholder activity is Rowley, T. J., & Moldoveanu, M. 2003. When will stakeholder groups act? An interest- and identity-based model of stakeholder group mobilization. *Academy of Management Review,* 28(2): 204–219.

60. Thomas, J. G. 2000. Macroenvironmental forces. In Helms, M. M. (Ed.), *Encyclopedia of management.* (4th ed.): 516–520. Farmington Hills, MI: Gale Group.

61. For a strong advocacy position on the need for corporate values and social responsibility, read Hollender, J. 2004. What matters most: Corporate values and social responsibility. *California Management Review,* 46(4): 111–119.

62. Waddock, S. & Bodwell, C. 2004. Managing responsibility: What can be learned from the quality movement. *California Management Review,* 47(1): 25–37.

63. For a discussion of the role of alliances and collaboration on corporate social responsibility initiatives, refer to Pearce, J. A. II., & Doh, J. P. 2005. The high impact of collaborative social initiatives. *MIT Sloan Management Review,* 46(3): 30–40.

64. Anonymous. 2006. If I did it. *BusinessWeek.* December 18: 108.

65. Bhattacharya, C. B., & Sen, S. 2004, Doing better at doing good: When, why, and how consumers respond to corporate social initiatives. *California Management Review,* 47(1): 9–24.

66. Cone Corporate Citizenship Study, 2002, www.coneinc.com.

67. Refer to www.bsr.org.

68. An insightful discussion of the risks and opportunities associated with global warming, refer to: Lash, J. & Wellington, F. 2007. Competitive advantage on a warming planet. *Harvard Business Review,* 85(3): 94–102.

69. This section draws on Hart, S. L. 1997. Beyond greening: Strategies for a sustainable world. *Harvard Business Review,* 75(1): 66–76, and Berry, M. A. & Rondinelli, D. A. 1998. Proactive corporate environmental management: A new industrial revolution. *Academy of Management Executive,* 12(2): 38–50.

70. Carey, J. 2006. Business on a warmer planet. *BusinessWeek,* July 17: 26–29.

71. Hart, op. cit., p. 67.

72. For a creative perspective on environmental sustainability and competitive advantage as well as ethical implications, read Ehrenfeld, J. R. 2005. The roots of sustainability. *MIT Sloan Management Review,* 46(2): 23–25.

73. McKinsey & Company. 1991. *The corporate response to the environmental challenge.* Summary Report, Amsterdam: McKinsey & Company.

74. Vogel, D. J. 2005. Is there a market for virtue? The business case for corporate social responsibility. *California Management Review,* 47(4): 19–36.

Analyzing the Internal Environment of the Firm

After reading this chapter, you should have a good understanding of:

LO1 How an awareness of strategic goals can help an organization achieve coherence in its strategic direction.

LO2 The primary and support activities of a firm's value chain.

LO3 How value-chain analysis can help managers create value by investigating relationships among activities within the firm and between the firm and its customers and suppliers.

LO4 The usefulness of financial ratio analysis, its inherent limitations, and how to make meaningful comparisons of performance across firms.

LO5 The value of recognizing how the interests of a variety of stakeholders can be interrelated.

Two firms compete in the same industry and both have many strengths in a variety of functional areas: marketing, operations, logistics, and so on. However, one of these firms outperforms the other by a wide margin over a long period of time. How can this be so? This chapter endeavors to answer that question.

We begin with two sections that include frameworks for gaining key insights into a firm's internal environment: We first consider the role of strategic goals. There are three key types of goals: vision, mission, and objectives. Organizations that do well at establishing goals are better positioned for success than those organizations that do not. Second, in value-chain analysis, we divide a firm's activities into a series of value-creating steps. We then explore how individual activities within the firm add value, and also how *interrelationships* among activities within the firm, and between the firm and its suppliers and customers, create value.

In the closing sections, we discuss how to evaluate a firm's performance and make comparisons across firms. We emphasize both the inclusion of financial resources and the interests of multiple stakeholders. Central to our discussion is the concept of the balanced scorecard, which recognizes that the interests of different stakeholders can be interrelated. We also consider how a firm's performance evolves over time and how it compares with industry norms and key competitors.

●˙ LEARNING FROM MISTAKES

In the late 1980s, Goodyear Tire & Rubber Co., then the largest tire company in the world, began an organizationwide initiative to adopt the principles of total quality management (TQM).[1] Like so many other companies that embraced TQM, Goodyear's operations, logistics, procurement, and research and development were reengineered with the objective of producing "defect-free" products. So far, so good? Read on . . .

Unfortunately, sales and distribution, which had always been central to Goodyear's success, were demoted to secondary status because TQM focused almost entirely on the manufacturing process. Not surprisingly, relationships began to sour between manufacturing people and the sales and distribution staff.

Resources to support the highly successful existing U.S. dealer network—which had taken nearly a century to develop and perfect—were reallocated to operations. With fewer resources, Goodyear had little choice but to cannibalize its existing distribution arrangement. Wholesalers became dealers, and vice versa. Everywhere it seemed that multiple sales outlets appeared where there had previously been only one or two Goodyear dealers for years. Thus, Goodyear's control over the sale and distribution of its products began to crumble.

For Goodyear's consumers, this was good news. They could now have Wrangler or American Eagle tires mounted on their cars while they shopped at the mall or purchased dry goods at large, powerful retailers such as Wal-Mart and Sears (where they began selling their tires in the early 1990s). Retailers also came out ahead. Since such new retailers were not exclusive dealers, they placed Goodyear tires next to competing brands—giving their customers more choices. Not surprising, the prices of Goodyear's tires sharply declined. And with a large number of outlets competing for the same customer base, price wars became inevitable.

In the long run, the only loser was Goodyear—and its employees. An erosion of the firm's competitive position and profitability began. Unable to raise its prices through a compromised distribution network, Goodyear faced the inevitable: plant closures. This was done to compensate for steady losses from its ill-conceived dissolution of its dealer network. By early 2003, the company was carrying a huge debt burden and its pension fund was underfunded by $2 billion. What's worse, Goodyear's once-loyal dealers were in open revolt because the company could not even fill the orders from dealers—mainly due to the disconnect between the factories and the distributor network.

Goodyear's problems began when it failed to invest in its valuable resources in its downstream activities—sales and distribution. Instead, it "followed the herd" and became a TQM disciple by focusing its resources on improving its operations, logistics, and research and development activities. Thus, its performance suffered when its key strength began to wither. Without its superb distribution network, the firm was forced to sell its products through mass merchandisers such as Wal-Mart and Sears. Thus, its products became perceived in the eyes of its customers, in essence, as a commodity. Clearly, firms benefit from assessing the internal environment to address what value-creating activities lead to their competitive advantages and develop strategies accordingly. A lack of coherance in strategic direction can undermine a firm's efforts to be successful. Also, over-emphasis on one part of the value chain to the neglect of others may result in a failure to maintain and enhance overall organization effectiveness.*

ENSURING COHERENCE IN STRATEGIC DIRECTION

LO1 How an awareness of strategic goals can help an organization achieve coherence in its strategic direction.

Employees and managers throughout the organization must strive toward common goals and objectives. By specifying desired results, it becomes much easier to move forward. Otherwise, when no one knows what the firm is striving to accomplish, they have no idea of what to work toward. As the old nautical expression puts it, "No wind favors the ship that has no charted course."

Organizations express priorities best through stated goals and objectives that form a *hierarchy of goals,* which includes its vision, mission, and strategic objectives. What visions may lack in specificity, they make up for in their ability to evoke powerful and compelling mental images. On the other hand, strategic objectives tend to be more specific and provide a more direct means of determining if the organization is moving toward broader, overall goals. Visions, as one would expect, also have longer time horizons than either mission statements or strategic objectives. Exhibit 3.1 depicts the hierarchy of goals and its relationship to two attributes: general versus specific and time horizon.

ORGANIZATIONAL VISION

organizational vision
A statement of what an organization ultimately aspires to become.

A **vision** is a goal that is "massively inspiring, overarching, and long term."[2] It represents a destination that is driven by and evokes passion. A vision may or may not succeed; it depends on whether everything else happens according to a firm's strategy. As humorously pointed out by Mark Hurd, Hewlett-Packard's CEO: "Without execution, vision is just another word for hallucination."[3]

---

*As a postscript, the Goodyear story does have the making of a happy ending. In early 2003, Robert Keegan, a former president of Eastman Kodak, replaced 37-year veteran Samir Gibara as chief executive. At the time, Goodyear's stock was struggling around $5 per share (reaching a low of $3.57 on February 3 of that year). Keegan began a restructuring plan to reposition the company as a consumer-products firm rather than a rust belt manufacturer. For years, Goodyear had chased volume, selling low-margin tires to auto manufacturers and replacement tires to the middle of the market. In contrast, under Keegan's leadership the firm began developing expensive tires aimed at performance and luxury-car drivers. Production of low-end tires was being moved offshore to Goodyear plants in lower-wage countries in Latin America, Asia, and Eastern Europe. Says Jonathan Rich, head of North American operations: "We owned the wrong real estate." After a long period of losses for 2001 through 2004, Goodyear turned a net profit of $228 million in 2005. And in the beginning of 2007, its stock was back up to more than $21—far above its level when Keegan took over.

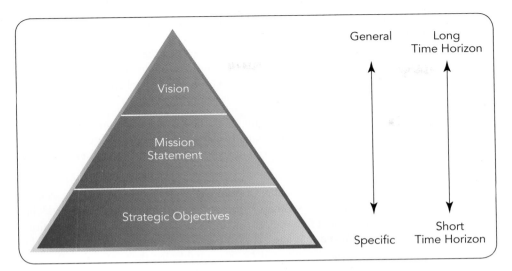

EXHIBIT 3.1   A Hierarchy of Goals

Leaders must develop and implement a vision. In a survey of 1,500 senior leaders, 870 of them CEOs from 20 different countries, respondents were asked what they believed were a leader's key traits. Ninety-eight percent responded that "a strong sense of vision" was the most important. Similarly, when asked about the critical knowledge skills, the leaders cited "strategy formulation to achieve a vision" as the most important skill. In other words, managers need to have not only a vision but also a plan to implement it. Regretably, 90 percent reported a lack of confidence in their own skills and ability to conceive a vision. For example, T. J. Rogers, CEO of Cypress Semiconductor, an electronic chipmaker that faced some difficulties in 1992, lamented that his own shortsightedness had caused the danger: "I did not have the 50,000-foot view, and got caught."[4]

One of the most famous examples of a vision is from Disneyland: "To be the happiest place on earth." Other examples are:

- "Restoring patients to full life." (Medtronic)
- "We want to satisfy all of our customers' financial needs and help them succeed financially." (Wells Fargo)
- "Our vision is to be the world's best quick service restaurant." (McDonald's)

Although such visions cannot be accurately measured by a specific indicator of how well they are being achieved, they do provide a fundamental statement of an organization's values, aspirations, and goals. Such visions go well beyond narrow financial objectives, of course, and strive to capture both the minds and hearts of employees.

The vision statement may also contain a slogan, diagram, or picture—whatever grabs attention.[5] The aim is to capture the essence of the more formal parts of the vision in a few words that are easily remembered, yet that evoke the spirit of the entire vision statement. In its 20-year battle with Xerox, Canon's slogan, or battle cry, was "Beat Xerox." Motorola's slogan is "Total Customer Satisfaction." Outboard Marine Corporation's slogan is "To Take the World Boating." And Chevron strives "To Become Better than the Best."

Clearly, vision statements are not a cure-all. Sometimes they backfire and erode a company's credibility. Visions fail for many reasons, including those discussed in the following paragraphs.[6]

The Walk Doesn't Match the Talk   An idealistic vision can arouse employee enthusiasm. However, that same enthusiasm can be quickly dashed if employees find that senior management's behavior is not consistent with the vision. Often, vision is a sloganeering campaign of new buzzwords and empty platitudes like "devotion to the customer," "teamwork," or "total quality" that aren't consistently backed by management's action.

Irrelevance   Visions created in a vacuum—unrelated to environmental threats or opportunities or an organization's resources and capabilities—often ignore the needs of those who are expected to buy into them. Employees reject visions that are not anchored in reality.

Not the Holy Grail   Managers often search continually for the one elusive solution that will solve their firm's problems—that is, the next holy grail of management. They may have tried other management fads only to find that they fell short of their expectations. However, they remain convinced that one exists. Visions support sound management, but they require everyone to walk the talk and be accountable for their behavior. A vision simply cannot be viewed as a magic cure for an organization's illness.

Too Much Focus Leads to Missed Opportunities   Clearly, one of the benefits of a sound vision statement is that it can focus efforts and excite people. However, the downside is that in directing people and resources toward a grandiose vision, losses can be devastating. Consider Samsung's ambitious venture into automobile manufacturing.

> In 1992, Kun-Hee Lee, chairman of South Korea's Samsung Group, created a bold strategy to become one of the ten largest car makers by 2010. Seduced by the clarity of the vision, Samsung bypassed staged entry through a joint venture or initial supply contract. Instead, Samsung borrowed heavily to build a state-of-the-art research and design facility and erect a greenfield factory—complete with cutting-edge robotics. Samsung Auto suffered operating losses and crushing interest charges from the beginning. And within a few years the business was divested for a fraction of the initial investment.

An Ideal Future Irreconciled with the Present   Although visions are not designed to mirror reality, they must be anchored somehow in it. People have difficulty identifying with a vision that paints a rosy picture of the future but does not account for the often hostile environment in which the firm competes or ignores some of the firm's weaknesses.

MISSION STATEMENTS

mission statement
Statement of the purpose of an organization.

A company's **mission statement** differs from its vision in that it encompasses both the purpose of the company as well as the basis of competition and competitive advantage.

Exhibit 3.2 contains the vision statement and mission statement of WellPoint Health Networks, a giant $57 billion managed health care organization. Note that while the vision statement is broad based, the mission statement is more specific and focused on the means by which the firm will compete. This includes providing branded products that will be tailor-made to customers in order to create long-term customer relationships.

Effective mission statements incorporate the concept of stakeholder management, suggesting that organizations must respond to multiple constituencies if they are to survive and prosper. Customers, employees, suppliers, and owners are the primary stakeholders, but others may also play an important role. Mission statements also have the greatest impact when they reflect an organization's enduring, overarching strategic priorities and competitive positioning. Mission statements also can vary in length and specificity. The two mission statements below illustrate these issues.

EXHIBIT 3.2

Comparing WellPoint Health Network's Vision and Mission

Vision

WellPoint *will redefine our industry:*
Through a new generation of consumer-friendly products that puts individuals back in control of their future.

Mission

The WellPoint companies provide health *security* by offering a *choice* of quality branded health and related financial services *designed* to meet the *changing* expectations of individuals, families, and their sponsors throughout a *lifelong* relationship.

Source: WellPoint Health Network company records.

- To produce superior financial returns for our shareholders as we serve our customers with the highest quality transportation, logistics, and e-commerce. (Federal Express)

- To be the very best in the business. Our game plan is status go . . . we are constantly looking ahead, building on our strengths, and reaching for new goals. In our quest of these goals, we look at the three stars of the Brinker logo and are reminded of the basic values that are the strength of this company . . . People, Quality and Profitability. Everything we do at Brinker must support these core values. We also look at the eight golden flames depicted in our logo, and are reminded of the fire that ignites our mission and makes up the heart and soul of this incredible company. These flames are: Customers, Food, Team, Concepts, Culture, Partners, Community, and Shareholders. As keeper of these flames, we will continue to build on our strengths and work together to be the best in the business. (Brinker International, whose restaurant chains include Chili's and On the Border)[8]

Few mission statements identify profit or any other financial indicator as the sole purpose of the firm. Indeed, many do not even mention profit or shareholder return.[9] Employees of organizations or departments are usually the mission's most important audience. For them, the mission should help to build a common understanding of purpose and commitment to nurture.

Profit maximization not only fails to motivate people but also does not differentiate between organizations. Every corporation wants to maximize profits over the long term. A good mission statement, by addressing each principal theme, must communicate why an organization is special and different. Two studies that linked corporate values and mission statements with financial performance found that the most successful firms mentioned values other than profits. The less successful firms focused almost entirely on profitability.[10] In essence, profit is the metaphorical equivalent of oxygen, food, and water that the body requires. They are not the point of life, but without them, there is no life.

Although vision statements tend to be quite enduring and seldom change, a firm's mission can and should change when competitive conditions dramatically change or the firm is faced with new threats or opportunities. Focus on Strategy 3.1 provides an example of a firm, NextJet, that changed its mission in order to realize new opportunities.

STRATEGIC OBJECTIVES

Thus far, we have discussed both visions and missions. Statements of vision tend to be quite broad and can be described as goals that represents an inspiring, overarching, and emotionally driven destination. Mission statements tend to be more specific and address

NextJet's Change of Mission

The dot-com crash was only the first blow to NextJet, Inc., a Dallas-based business launched in 1999 to ship packages overnight. The bigger blow came with the September 11 terrorist attacks, when passenger airlines were forced to add security and reduce flights. One of NextJet's strengths was its nationwide network of local courier services that got packages to and from airports, all coordinated through their proprietary software that could determine the optimal routing. However, the company's business model fell apart when it could not rely on the airlines to get packages between cities quickly enough to make the added cost for same-day delivery worthwhile.

Rather than give up, NextJet reinvented the business around the idea that its most important asset was the software itself. The company's new mission received almost immediate validation when its software was deployed successfully at United Parcel Service (UPS). NextJet's software provides Atlanta-based UPS with tools for setting online rates and tracking packages. While a lot of same-day business did evaporate when corporations tightened the reins on spending, some things can't wait overnight to be shipped. For example, makers of hospital equipment may need to ship critical parts within a few hours. NextJet's software can help shippers make important decisions in less than a second, finding the fastest and most economical route among air, truck, and courier operations. In addition to UPS, its customers include FedEx, Greyhound, and Menlo Worldwide.

NextJet serves a very large industry segment—Service Parts & Logistics (SPL). The annual expenditures for spare parts in the United States are estimated to be $500 billion. And managers have increased their focus on the importance of effective logistics operations, given its potential impact on a firm's income. After all, whether or not a production line is running can often depend on the quick and effective installation of relatively inexpensive spare parts.

NextJet currently has 50 employees and four offices in the United States, and it seems to be on the right track with its new mission. Although executives at the privately held company will not disclose financial results, they say they are about to complete their third consecutive profitable quarter.

Sources: Goldstein, A. 2002. NextJet is hoping that its software can deliver. *Dallas Morning News,* December 4: 1–3; industry.java.sun.com/javanews/ stories/story2/0, 1072, 34986, 00.html; Nelson, M. G. 2001. NextJet network adds wireless. *Information Week,* April 30: 34; Anonymous. 2004. Who's who in e-logistics. www.americanshipper.com, September; Hudspeth, B., & Jones, J. 2004. Service parts and logistics: Should you in-source or outsource. *3pl line,* www.inboundlogistics.com, October.

strategic objectives
Specific goals that an organization pursues over a short time horizon

questions concerning the organization's reason for being and the basis of its competitive advantage. **Strategic objectives** are used to operationalize the mission statement.[11] That is, they help to provide guidance on how the organization can fulfill or move toward the "higher goals" in the goal hierarchy—the mission and vision. Thus, they are more specific and cover a more well-defined time frame.

Setting objectives demands a yardstick to measure the fulfillment of the objectives.[12] If an objective lacks specificity or measurability, it is not very useful, simply because there is no way of determining whether it is helping the organization move toward its mission and vision.

Exhibit 3.3 lists several firms' strategic objectives, divided into financial and nonfinancial categories. While most of these strategic objectives are directed toward generating greater profits and returns for the owners of the business, others are directed at customers or society at large.

For objectives to be meaningful, they need to satisfy several criteria. They must be:

- *Measurable.* There must be at least one indicator (or yardstick) that measures progress against fulfilling the objective.

- *Specific.* This provides a clear message as to what needs to be accomplished.

- *Appropriate.* It must be consistent with the vision and mission of the organization.

- *Realistic.* It must be an achievable target given the organization's capabilities and opportunities in the environment. In essence, it must be challenging but doable.

- *Timely.* There needs to be a time frame for accomplishing the objective. After all, as the economist John Maynard Keynes once said, "In the long run, we are all dead!"

EXHIBIT 3.3

Strategic Objectives

Strategic Objectives (Financial)

- Increase sales growth 6% to 8% and accelerate core net earnings growth to 13% to 15% per share in each of the next 5 years. (Procter & Gamble)
- Generate Internet-related revenue of $1.5 billion. (AutoNation)
- Increase the contribution of Banking Group earnings from investments, brokerage, and insurance from 16% to 25%. (Wells Fargo)
- Cut corporate overhead costs by $30 million per year. (Fortune Brands)

Strategic Objectives (Nonfinancial)

- We want a majority of our customers, when surveyed, to say they consider Wells Fargo the best financial institution in the community. (Wells Fargo)
- We want to operate 6,000 stores by 2010—up from 3,000 in the year 2000. (Walgreen's)
- We want to be the top-ranked supplier to our customers. (PPG)
- Reduce greenhouse gases by 10 percent (from a 1990 base) by 2010. (BP Amoco)

Sources: Company documents and annual reports.

When objectives satisfy the above criteria, there are many benefits for the organization. First, they help to channel employees throughout the organization toward common goals. This helps the organization concentrate and conserve valuable resources and work collectively in a more timely manner.

Second, challenging objectives can help to motivate and inspire employees throughout the organization to higher levels of commitment and effort. A great deal of research has supported the notion that individuals work harder when they are striving toward specific goals instead of being asked simply to "do their best."

Third, there is always the potential for different parts of an organization to pursue their own goals rather than overall company goals. Although well intentioned, these may work at cross-purposes to the organization as a whole. Meaningful objectives thus help to resolve conflicts when they arise.

Finally, proper objectives provide a yardstick for rewards and incentives. Not only will they lead to higher levels of employee motivation but they will also help to ensure a greater sense of equity or fairness when rewards are allocated.

In summary, care must be taken to ensure consistency throughout the organization in how strategic objectives are implemented. Otherwise, employees and organizational units will be acting at cross purposes, resources will be wasted, and people will become demotivated. Consider how Textron, a $10 billion conglomerate, ensures that its corporate goals are effectively implemented:[13]

> At Textron, each business unit identifies "improvement priorities" that it must act upon to realize the performance outlined in the firm's overall strategic plan. Each improvement priority is translated into action items with clearly defined accountabilities, timetables, and key performance indicators (KPIs) that enable executives to tell how a unit is delivering on a priority. Improvement priorities and action items cascade to every level at the firm—from the management committee (consisting of Textron's top five executives) down to the lowest levels in each of the company's ten business units. Says Lewis Campbell, Textron's CEO: "Everyone needs to know: 'If I have only one hour to work, here's what I'm going to focus on.' Our goal deployment process makes each individual's accountabilities and priorities clear."

As indicated in the above example, organizations have lower-level objectives that are more specific than the strategic objectives that we have focused on in this section. These are often referred to as short-term objectives—essential components of a firm's "action plans" that are critical in implementing a firm's chosen strategy.

VALUE-CHAIN ANALYSIS

LO2 The primary and support activities of a firm's value chain.

value-chain analysis
A strategic assessment of an organization that focuses on value-creating activities.

primary activities
Sequential activities of the value chain that refer to the physical creation of the product or service, its sale and transfer to the buyer, and its service after sale; including inbound logistics, operations, outbound logistics, marketing and sales, and service.

support activities
Activities of the value chain that either add value by themselves or add value through important relationships with both primary activities and other support activities; including procurement, technology development, human resource management, and general administration.

Value-chain analysis is a second key tool to understanding an organization's internal environment. This analysis views the organization as a sequential process of value-creating activities. The approach is useful for understanding the building blocks of competitive advantage. Value-chain analysis was described in Michael Porter's seminal book *Competitive Advantage*.[14] In competitive terms, value is the amount that buyers are willing to pay for what a firm provides them. Value is measured by total revenue, a reflection of the price a firm's product commands and the quantity it can sell. A firm is profitable to the extent that the value it receives exceeds the total costs involved in creating its product or service. Creating value for buyers that exceeds the costs of production (i.e., margin) is a key concept used in analyzing a firm's competitive position.

Porter described two different categories of activities. First, five **primary activities**—inbound logistics, operations, outbound logistics, marketing and sales, and service—contribute to the physical creation of the product or service, its sale and transfer to the buyer, and its service after the sale. Second, **support activities**—procurement, technology development, human resource management, and general administration—either add value by themselves or add value through important relationships with both primary activities and other support activities. Exhibit 3.4 illustrates Porter's value chain.

To get the most out of value-chain analysis, you need to view the concept in its broadest context, without regard to the boundaries of your own organization. That is, place your organization within a more encompassing value chain that includes your firm's suppliers, customers, and alliance partners. Thus, in addition to thoroughly understanding how value

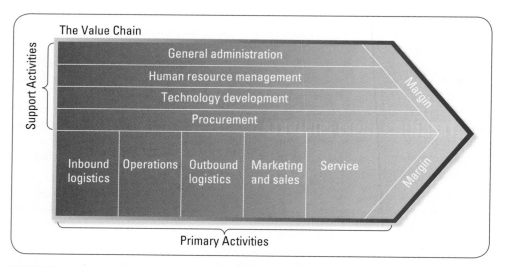

EXHIBIT 3.4   The Value Chain: Primary and Support Activities

is created within the organization, you must become aware of how value is created for other organizations that are involved in the overall supply chain or distribution channel in which your firm participates.[15]

Next, we'll describe and provide examples of each of the primary and support activities. Then, we'll provide examples of how companies add value by means of relationships among activities within the organization as well as activities outside the organization, such as those activities associated with customers and suppliers.[16]

PRIMARY ACTIVITIES

Five generic categories of primary activities are involved in competing in any industry. Each category is divisible into a number of distinct activities that depend on the particular industry and the firm's strategy.[17]

Inbound Logistics   Inbound logistics is primarily associated with receiving, storing, and distributing inputs to the product. It includes material handling, warehousing, inventory control, vehicle scheduling, and returns to suppliers.

Just-in-time (JIT) inventory systems, for example, were designed to achieve efficient inbound logistics. In essence, Toyota epitomizes JIT inventory systems, in which parts deliveries arrive at the assembly plants only hours before they are needed. JIT systems will play a vital role in fulfilling Toyota's commitment to fill a buyer's new car order in just five days.[18] This standard is in sharp contrast to most competitors that require approximately 30 days' notice to build vehicles. Toyota's standard is three times faster than even Honda Motors, considered to be the industry's most efficient in order follow-through. The five days represent the time from the company's receipt of an order to the time the car leaves the assembly plant. Actual delivery may take longer, depending on where a customer lives. How can Toyota achieve such fast turnaround?

- Its 360 key suppliers are now linked to the company by way of computer on a virtual assembly line.

- Suppliers load parts onto trucks in the order in which they will be installed.

- Parts are stacked on trucks in the same place each time to help workers unload them quickly.

- Deliveries are required to meet a rigid schedule with as many as 12 trucks a day and no more than four hours between trucks.

Operations   Operations include all activities associated with transforming inputs into the final product form, such as machining, packaging, assembly, testing, printing, and facility operations.

Creating environmentally friendly manufacturing is one way to use operations to achieve competitive advantage. Shaw Industries (now part of Berkshire Hathaway), a world-class competitor in the floor-covering industry, is well known for its concern for the environment.[19] It has been successful in reducing the expenses associated with the disposal of dangerous chemicals and other waste products from its manufacturing operations. Its environmental endeavors have multiple payoffs. Shaw has received many awards for its recycling efforts—awards that enhance its reputation.

Outbound Logistics   Outbound logistics is associated with collecting, storing, and distributing the product or service to buyers. These activities include finished goods, warehousing, material handling, delivery vehicle operation, order processing, and scheduling.

Campbell Soup uses an electronic network to facilitate its continuous-replenishment program with its most progressive retailers.[20] Each morning, retailers electronically inform Campbell of their product needs and of the level of inventories in their distribution centers. Campbell uses that information to forecast future demand and to determine which products require replenishment (based on the inventory limits previously established with each retailer). Trucks leave Campbell's shipping plant that afternoon and arrive at the retailers' distribution centers the same day. The program cuts the inventories of participating retailers from about a four- to a two-weeks' supply. Campbell Soup achieved this improvement because it slashed delivery time and because it knows the inventories of key retailers and can deploy supplies when they are most needed.

The Campbell Soup example also illustrates the win–win benefits of exemplary value-chain activities. Both the supplier (Campbell) and its buyers (retailers) come out ahead. Since the retailer makes more money on Campbell products delivered through continuous replenishment, it has an incentive to carry a broader line and give the company greater shelf space. After Campbell introduced the program, sales of its products grew twice as fast through participating retailers as through all other retailers. Not surprisingly, supermarket chains love such programs. For example, Wegman's Food Markets in upstate New York has augmented its accounting system to measure and reward suppliers whose products cost the least to stock and sell.

Marketing and Sales   These activities are associated with purchases of products and services by end users and the inducements used to get them to make purchases.[21] They include advertising, promotion, sales force, quoting, channel selection, channel relations, and pricing.[22]

It is not always enough to have a great product.[23] The key is to convince your channel partners that it is in their best interests not only to carry your product but also to market it in a way that is consistent with your strategy. Consider Monsanto's efforts at educating distributors to improve the value proposition of its line of Saflex® windows.[24] The products introduced in the early 1990s had a superior attribute: The window design permitted laminators to form an exceptional type of glass by sandwiching a plastic sheet interlayer between two pieces of glass. This product is not only stronger and offers better ultraviolet protection than regular glass, but also when cracked, it adheres to the plastic sheet—an excellent safety feature for both cars and homes.

Despite these benefits, Monsanto had a hard time convincing laminators and window manufacturers to carry products made with Saflex. According to Melissa Toledo, brand manager at Monsanto, "Saflex was priced at a 30 percent premium above traditional glass, and the various stages in the value chain (distributors and retailers) didn't think there would be a demand for such an expensive glass product." What was Monsanto's solution? Subsequently, it reintroduced Saflex as KeepSafe® and worked to coordinate the product's value propositions. By analyzing the experiences of all of the players in the supply chain, it was able to create marketing programs that helped each build a business aimed at selling its products. Said Toledo, "We want to know how they go about selling those types of products, what challenges they face, and what they think they need to sell our products. This helps us a lot when we try to provide them with these needs." Thus, marketing is often a key element of competitive advantage.[25]

Focus on Strategy 3.2 addresses a vital aspect of marketing—marketing research. We discuss Coach, the high-end producer of leather handbags and other leather products.

At times, a firm's marketing initiatives may become overly aggressive and lead to actions that are both unethical and illegal.[26] For example:

- *Burdines.* This department store chain is under investigation for allegedly adding club memberships to its customers' credit cards without prior approval.

Coach's Effective Marketing Strategy

Coach has put its leather in Lexus cars and Coach insignias on Canon Elph digital camera cases. However, the firm has turned down offers to lend its name to hotels and athletic drinks. It calls the strategy "focus"—and the firm admits that it had a rather stodgy image a decade ago. How things have changed!

Coach, which now has 443 stores, has made a fortune selling stylish but fairly affordable handbags. Revenue has quadrupled since the company went public in 2000. At the time, Coach bags were most often bought by women looking for well-made totes. In the year ending July 1, 2006, sales rose 23% to $2.1 billion, and income before interest and taxes rose 34% to $765 million. The company's stock also hit an all-time high of $46 in January 2007.

A key element of Coach's success is its knowledge of customers' buying habits. It spends $4 million to $5 million a year on market research, including talking to 15,000 women on the phone, in-store or via the Internet or regular mail. Analyzing that information enabled Coach to know that the biggest spenders visit their stores every four to five weeks. Thus, Coach rolls out its new products and store designs to keep pace with this "rhythm."

In addition to market timing, the proprietary information that it gathers provides the basis for market experiments that record the effect of changing such variables as price, features, and offers from competing brands. Based on such data, Coach quickly alters product designs, drops items that test poorly, creates new lines in a wider range of fabrics and colors, changes prices, and tailors merchandise presentation to fit customer demographics at specific stores. Several years ago, Coach had customers preview its Hampton satchel and learned that they would willingly pay $30 more than the company had thought. In the case of another bag, Coach solicited customer feedback on the design and, learning that customers found it "tippy," responded by widening the bag's base.

Sources: Fass, A. 2007. Trading up. *Forbes.* January 29: 48–49; Slywotzky, A. J. & Drzik, J. 2005. Countering the biggest risk of all. *Harvard Business Review,* 83 (4): 78–88; and, Fass. A. 2005. Thank you for spending $300. *Forbes.* January 10: 150.

- *Fleet Mortgage.* This company has been accused of adding insurance fees for dental coverage and home insurance to its customers' mortgage loans without the customers' knowledge.

- *HCI Direct.* Eleven states have accused this direct-mail firm with charging for panty hose samples that customers did not order.

- *Juno Online Services.* The Federal Trade Commission brought charges against this Internet service provider for failing to provide customers with a telephone number to cancel service.

Service   This primary activity includes all actions associated with providing service to enhance or maintain the value of the product, such as installation, repair, training, parts supply, and product adjustment.

Let's see how two retailers are providing exemplary customer service. At Sephora .com, a customer service representative taking a phone call from a repeat customer has instant access to what shade of lipstick she likes best. This will help the rep cross-sell by suggesting a matching shade of lip gloss. CEO Jim Wiggett expects such personalization to build loyalty and boost sales per customer. Nordstrom, the Seattle-based department store chain, goes even a step further. It offers a cyber-assist: A service rep can take control of a customer's Web browser and literally lead her to just the silk scarf that she is looking for. CEO Dan Nordstrom believes that such a capability will close enough additional purchases to pay for the $1 million investment in software.

SUPPORT ACTIVITIES

Support activities in the value chain can be divided into four generic categories, as shown in Exhibit 3.5. As with primary activities, each category of the support activity is divisible into a number of distinct value activities that are specific to a particular industry.

Coach has dramatically improved its competitive position through effective marketing strategies.

For example, technology development's discrete activities may include component design, feature design, field testing, process engineering, and technology selection. Similarly, procurement may be divided into activities such as qualifying new suppliers, purchasing different groups of inputs, and monitoring supplier performance.

Procurement Procurement refers to the function of purchasing inputs used in the firm's value chain, not to the purchased inputs themselves.[27] Purchased inputs include raw materials, supplies, and other consumable items as well as assets such as machinery, laboratory equipment, office equipment, and buildings.[28]

Microsoft has improved its procurement process (and the quality of its suppliers) by providing formal reviews of its suppliers. One of Microsoft's divisions has extended the review process used for employees to its outside suppliers.[29] The employee services group, which is responsible for everything from travel to 401(k) programs to the on-site library, outsources more than 60 percent of the services it provides. Unfortunately, the employee services group was not providing them with enough feedback on how well Microsoft thought they were doing. This was feedback that the suppliers wanted to get and that Microsoft wanted to give. The evaluation system that Microsoft developed helped clarify its expectations to suppliers. An executive noted: "We had one supplier—this was before the new system—that would have scored a 1.2 out of 5. After we started giving this feedback, and the supplier understood our expectations, its performance improved dramatically. Within six months, it scored a 4. If you'd asked me before we began the feedback system, I would have said that was impossible."

Technology Development Every value activity embodies technology.[30] The array of technologies employed in most firms is very broad, ranging from technologies used to prepare documents and transport goods to those embodied in processes and equipment or the product itself. Technology development related to the product and its features supports the entire value chain, while other technology development is associated with particular primary or support activities.

Focus on Strategy 3.3 on page 64 addresses a unique application of technology—using rubber floor mats at a railway station to generate electricity!

Human Resource Management Human resource management consists of activities involved in the recruiting, hiring, training, development, and compensation of all types of personnel.[31] It supports both individual primary and support activities (e.g., hiring of engineers and scientists) and the entire value chain (e.g., negotiations with labor unions).

Like many service companies, JetBlue Airways Corporation is obsessed with hiring superior employees.[32] But they found it difficult to attract college graduates to commit to careers as flight attendants. JetBlue developed a highly innovative recruitment program for flight attendants—a one-year contract that gives them a chance to travel, meet lots of people, and then decide what else they might like to do. They also introduced the idea of training a friend and employee together so that they could share a job. With such employee-friendly initiatives, JetBlue has been very successful in attracting talent.

EXHIBIT 3.5

The Value Chain: Some Factors to Consider in Assessing a Firm's Support Activities

General Administration

- Effective planning systems to attain overall goals and objectives.
- Ability of top management to anticipate and act on key environmental trends and events.
- Ability to obtain low-cost funds for capital expenditures and working capital.
- Excellent relationships with diverse stakeholder groups.
- Ability to coordinate and integrate activities across the "value system."
- High visibility to inculcate organizational culture, reputation, and values.
- Effective information technology to integrate value creating activities.

Human Resource Management

- Effective recruiting, development, and retention mechanisms for employees.
- Quality relations with trade unions.
- Quality work environment to maximize overall employee performance and minimize absenteeism.
- Reward and incentive programs to motivate all employees.

Technology Development

- Effective research and development activities for process and product initiatives.
- Positive collaborative relationships between R&D and other departments.
- State-of-the art facilities and equipment.
- Culture that enhances creativity and innovation.
- Excellent professional qualifications of personnel.
- Ability to meet critical deadlines.

Procurement

- Procurement of raw material inputs to optimize quality and speed, and to minimize the associated costs.
- Development of collaborative "win–win" relationships with suppliers.
- Effective procedures to purchase advertising and media services.
- Analysis and selection of alternate sources of inputs to minimize dependence on one supplier.
- Ability to make proper lease-versus-buy decisions.

Source: Reprinted with the permission of The Free Press, a division of Simon & Schuster Adult Publishing Group, from *Competitive Advantage: Creating and Sustaining Superior Performance* by Michael E. Porter. Copyright © 1985, 1998 by Michael E. Porter. All rights reserved.

Employees often leave a firm because they reach a plateau and begin to look for new opportunities.[33] AT&T strives to retain such people with Resource Link, an in-house temporary service that enables employees with diverse management, technical, or professional skills to market their abilities to different departments for short-term assignments. This enables professionals to broaden their experience base as well as provide a mechanism for other parts of the organization to benefit from new sources of ideas.

Jeffrey Immelt, GE's Chairman, addresses the importance of effective human resource management:[34]

Human resources has to be more than a department. GE recognized early on—50 or 60 years ago—that in a multibusiness company, the common denominators are people and culture. From an employee's first day at GE, she discovers that she's in the people-development business as much as anything else. You'll find that most good companies have the same basic HR processes that we have, but they're discrete. HR at GE is not an agenda item; it is the agenda.

Commuter Power: A New Meaning

How many Japanese commuters does it take to light a bulb? On October 16, 2006, East Japan Railway, or JR East, began testing rubber floor mats that generate electricity when walked on. The mats, which will be at several turnstiles inside Tokyo Station for two months, work by converting vibrations into energy.

Presently, they certainly don't produce much energy: just 100 milliwatts with each commuter's steps.

With about 700,000 commuters entering and leaving Tokyo Station each day, that translates to about 70 kilowatts of power—barely enough to light a 100-watt lightbulb for 10 minutes.

However, officials aren't discouraged. They claim that if the technology gets refined over the years those stomping feet could generate much more energy—providing electricity for a train station's lighting and other needs. "The mats could power machines and signs that don't require much energy," claims JR East spokesman Takaki Nemoto. "But that's far into the future."

Source: Hall, K. 2006. Now that's commuter power. *BusinessWeek*, November 13: 10.

General Administration   General administration consists of a number of activities, including general management, planning, finance, accounting, legal and government affairs, quality management, and information systems. Administration (unlike the other support activities) typically supports the entire value chain and not individual activities.

Although general administration is sometimes viewed only as overhead, it can be a powerful source of competitive advantage. In a telephone operating company, for example, negotiating and maintaining ongoing relations with regulatory bodies can be among the most important activities for competitive advantage. In a similar vein, effective information systems can contribute significantly to cost position, while in some industries top management plays a vital role in dealing with important buyers.[35]

The strong and effective leadership of top executives can also make a significant contribution to an organization's success. As we discussed in Chapter 1, chief executive officers (CEOs) such as Herb Kelleher, Andrew Grove, and Jack Welch have been credited with playing critical roles in the success of Southwest Airlines, Intel, and General Electric, respectively. And Carlos Ghosn is considered one of today's top corporate leaders after his turnaround of Nissan, the Japan-based automobile manufacturer.

Information systems can also play a key role in increasing operating efficiencies and enhancing a firm's performance.[36] Consider Walgreen Co.'s introduction of Intercom Plus, a computer-based prescription management system. Linked by computer to both doctors' offices and third-party payment plans, the system automates telephone refills, store-to-store prescription transfers, and drug reordering. It also provides information on drug interactions and, coupled with revised workflows, frees up pharmacists from administrative tasks to devote more time to patient counseling.

INTERRELATIONSHIPS AMONG VALUE-CHAIN ACTIVITIES WITHIN AND ACROSS ORGANIZATIONS

L03 How value-chain analysis can help managers create value by investigating relationships among activities within the firm and between the firm and its customers and suppliers.

We have defined each of the value-chain activities separately for clarity of presentation. Managers must not ignore, however, the importance of relationships among value-chain activities.[37] There are two levels: (1) interrelationships among activities within the firm and (2) relationships among activities within the firm and with other organizations (e.g., customers and suppliers) that are part of the firm's expanded value chain.[38]

With regard to the first level, recall AT&T's innovative Resource Link program wherein employees who have reached their plateau may apply for temporary positions in other parts of the organization. Clearly, this program has the potential to benefit all

Cardinal Health: Creating Value through the Extended Value Chain

Cardinal Health is a wholesale drug distributor that buys sprays, pills, and capsules from pharmaceutical companies and puts them on the shelves in pharmacies or into the hands of emergency-room nurses. Profitability is a problem in this business, because the company is caught between powerful manufacturers and cost-conscious customers. Cardinal, for example, buys pharmaceuticals from the likes of Pfizer (its biggest supplier) and sells them to the likes of CVS (its largest customer).

Cardinal responded to the profitability challenge by trying to add value for both customers and suppliers. It understood how urgent it was for one of its customer groups (hospitals) to control costs, so it began to offer services to hospital pharmacies. Rather than shipping medications to the hospitals' front door, it "followed the pill" into the hospital and right to the patient's room, offering pharmacy-management services and extending those services to customized surgical kits.

As the knowledgeable intermediary, Cardinal realized it could bring significant value to its suppliers (the pharmaceutical manufacturers) by providing services in drug formulation, testing, manufacturing, and packaging, freeing those companies to concentrate on the discovery of the next round of blockbuster medicines. Cardinal even used its position to develop new services for commercial pharmacies. Cardinal's drug-chain customers depend on third-party payments for most of the prescriptions it fills. It worked with a number of leading chains to develop a system called ScriptLINE that automates the reimbursement process for pharmacies and updates rates daily.

The result of this stream of innovations is a wave of growth and profits. Cardinal, with annual sales of $65 billion, has registered compound annual earnings growth of approximately 20 percent or better for the past 15 years.

The Cardinal Health story is a powerful example of extending the value chain and adding value to the many players involved—from the suppliers to the customers. The company found opportunities in an unpromising business landscape by identifying new customer needs related to the activities that surround the products it sells.

Sources: Slywotzky, A., & Wise, R. 2003. Double digit growth in no-growth times. *Fast Company,* April: 66–70; Stewart, T. 2002. Fueling drug growth during an economic drought. *Business 2.0,* May: 17–21; and Lashinsky, A. 2003. Big man in the "middle." *Fortune,* April 14: 161–162.

activities within the firm's value chain because it creates opportunities for top employees to lend their expertise to all of the organization's value-creating activities.

With regard to the second level, Campbell Soup's use of electronic networks enabled it to improve the efficiency of outbound logistics.[39] However, it also helped Campbell manage the ordering of raw materials more effectively, improve its production scheduling, and help its customers better manage their inbound logistics operations.

An example of how a firm's value-creating activity can enhance customer value is provided by Ciba Specialty Chemicals (which merged with Sandoz in 1996 to form Novartis), a Swiss manufacturer of textile dyes.[40] The firm's research and development experts have created dyes that fix more readily to the fabric and therefore require less salt. How does this innovation add value for Ciba's customers? There are three ways. First, it lowers the outlays for salt. Textile companies using the new dyes are able to reduce their costs for salt by up to 2 percent of revenues, a significant drop in an industry with razor thin profit margins. Second, it reduces manufacturers' costs for water treatment. Used bathwater full of salt and unfixed dye must be treated before it is released into rivers or streams (even in low-income countries where environmental standards are typically lax). Simply put, less salt and less unfixed dye mean lower water-treatment costs. Third, the higher fixation rates of the new dyes make quality control easier, lowering the costs of rework.

We conclude this section with Focus on Strategy 3.4. It addresses how Cardinal Health expertly integrates several value activities to create value for its suppliers and customers.

APPLYING THE VALUE CHAIN TO SERVICE ORGANIZATIONS

The concepts of inbound logistics, operations, and outbound logistics suggest managing the raw materials that might be manufactured into finished products and delivered to customers. However, these three steps do not apply only to manufacturing. They correspond to any transformation process in which inputs are converted through a work process into outputs that add value. For example, accounting is a sort of transformation process that converts daily records of individual transactions into monthly financial reports. In this example, the transaction records are the inputs, accounting is the operation that adds value, and financial statements are the outputs.

What are the "operations," or transformation processes, of service organizations? These could be many different things. At times, the difference between manufacturing and service is in providing a customized solution rather than the kind of mass production that is common in manufacturing. For example, a travel agent adds value by creating an itinerary that includes transportation, accommodations, and activities that are customized to your budget and your dates of travel. A law firm renders services that are specific to a client's needs and circumstances. In both cases, the work process (operation) involves the application of specialized knowledge based on the specifics of a situation (inputs) and the outcome that the client seeks to achieve (outputs).

The application of the value chain to service organizations suggests that the value-adding process may be configured differently depending on the type of business a firm is engaged in. As the preceding discussion on support activities suggests, activities such as procurement and legal services are critical for adding value. Indeed, the activities that may only provide support to one company may be critical to the primary value-adding activity of another firm.

Exhibit 3.6 provides two models of how the value chain might look in service industries. In the retail industry, there are no manufacturing operations. A firm, such as Circuit City, adds value by developing expertise in the procurement of finished goods and by displaying them in their stores in a way that enhances sales. Thus, the value chain makes procurement activities (i.e., partnering with vendors and purchasing goods) a primary rather than a support activity. Operations refer to the task of operating Circuit City's stores.

For an engineering services firm, research and development provides inputs, the transformation process is the engineering itself, and innovative designs and practical solutions

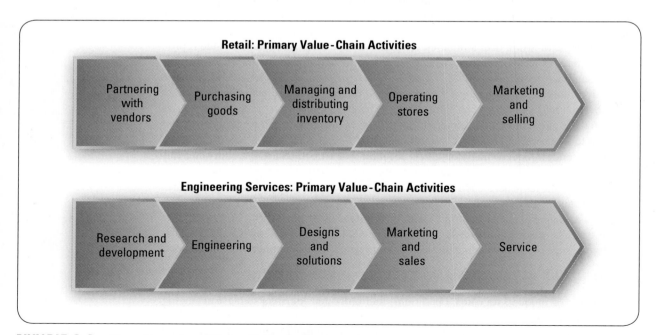

EXHIBIT 3.6   Some Examples of Value Chains in Service Industries

are the outputs. Arthur D. Little, for example, is a large consulting firm with offices in 30 countries. In its technology and innovation management practice, A. D. Little strives to make the best use of the science, technology and knowledge resources available to create value for a wide range of industries and client sectors. This involves activities associated with research and development, engineering, and creating solutions as well as downstream activities such as marketing, sales, and service. These examples suggest that how the primary and support activities of a given firm are configured and deployed will often depend on industry conditions and the extent to which the company is service and/or manufacturing oriented.

EVALUATING FIRM PERFORMANCE: TWO APPROACHES

This section addresses two approaches to use when evaluating a firm's performance. The first is financial ratio analysis, which, generally speaking, identifies how a firm is performing according to its balance sheet, income statement, and market valuation. As we will discuss, when performing a financial ratio analysis, you must take into account the firm's performance from a historical perspective (not just at one point in time) as well as how it compares with both industry norms and key competitors.[41]

The second perspective takes a broader stakeholder view. Firms must satisfy a broad range of stakeholders, including employees, customers, and owners, to ensure their long-term viability. Central to our discussion will be a well-known approach—the balanced scorecard—that has been popularized by Robert Kaplan and David Norton.[42]

FINANCIAL RATIO ANALYSIS

LO4 The usefulness of financial ratio analysis, its inherent limitations, and how to make meaningful comparisons of performance across firms.

The beginning point in analyzing the financial position of a firm is to compute and analyze five different types of financial ratios:

- Short-term solvency or liquidity
- Long-term solvency measures
- Asset management (or turnover)
- Profitability
- Market value

Exhibit 3.7 summarizes each of these five ratios. The Appendix to Chapter 9 (the Case Analysis chapter) provides detailed definitions for and discussions of each of these types of ratios as well as examples of how each is calculated. Refer to pages 207 to 212.

A meaningful ratio analysis must go beyond the calculation and interpretation of financial ratios.[43] It must include an analysis of how ratios change over time as well as how they are interrelated. For example, a firm that takes on too much long-term debt to finance operations will see an immediate impact on its indicators of long-term financial leverage. The additional debt will also have a negative impact on the firm's short-term liquidity ratio (i.e., current and quick ratios) since the firm must pay interest and principal on the additional debt each year until it is retired. Additionally, the interest expenses must be deducted from revenues, reducing the firm's profitability.

A firm's financial position should not be analyzed in isolation. Important reference points are needed. We will address some issues that must be taken into account to make financial analysis more meaningful: historical comparisons, comparisons with industry norms, and comparisons with key competitors.

I. Short-term solvency, or liquidity, ratios

$$\text{Current ratio} = \frac{\text{Current assets}}{\text{Current liabilities}}$$

$$\text{Quick ratio} = \frac{\text{Current assets} - \text{Inventory}}{\text{Current liabilities}}$$

$$\text{Cash ratio} = \frac{\text{Cash}}{\text{Current liabilities}}$$

II. Long-term solvency, or financial leverage, ratios

$$\text{Total debt ratio} = \frac{\text{Total assets} - \text{Total equity}}{\text{Total assets}}$$

$$\text{Debt–equity ratio} = \text{Total debt/Total equity}$$

$$\text{Equity multiplier} = \text{Total assets/Total equity}$$

$$\text{Times interest earned ratio} = \frac{\text{EBIT}}{\text{Interest}}$$

$$\text{Cash coverage ratio} = \frac{\text{EBIT} + \text{Depreciation}}{\text{Interest}}$$

III. Asset utilization, or turnover, ratios

$$\text{Inventory turnover} = \frac{\text{Cost of goods sold}}{\text{Inventory}}$$

$$\text{Days' sales in inventory} = \frac{365 \text{ days}}{\text{Inventory turnover}}$$

$$\text{Receivables turnover} = \frac{\text{Sales}}{\text{Accounts receivable}}$$

$$\text{Days' sales in receivables} = \frac{365 \text{ days}}{\text{Receivables turnover}}$$

$$\text{Total asset turnover} = \frac{\text{Sales}}{\text{Total assets}}$$

$$\text{Capital intensity} = \frac{\text{Total assets}}{\text{Sales}}$$

IV. Profitability ratios

$$\text{Profit margin} = \frac{\text{Net income}}{\text{Sales}}$$

$$\text{Return on assets (ROA)} = \frac{\text{Net income}}{\text{Total assets}}$$

$$\text{Return on equity (ROE)} = \frac{\text{Net income}}{\text{Total equity}}$$

$$\text{ROE} = \frac{\text{Net income}}{\text{Sales}} \times \frac{\text{Sales}}{\text{Assets}} \times \frac{\text{Assets}}{\text{Equity}}$$

V. Market value ratios

$$\text{Price–earnings ratio} = \frac{\text{Price per share}}{\text{Earnings per share}}$$

$$\text{Market-to-book ratio} = \frac{\text{Market value per share}}{\text{Book value per share}}$$

EXHIBIT 3.7   A Summary of Five Types of Financial Ratios

Historical Comparisons   When you evaluate a firm's financial performance, it is very useful to compare its financial position over time. This provides a means of evaluating trends. For example, Microsoft reported revenues of $44.3 billion and net income of $12.6 billion in 2006. Almost all firms—except a few of the largest and most profitable companies in the world—would be very happy with such financial success. These figures reflect an annual growth in revenue and net income of 10 percent and 24 percent, respectively, for the 2004–2006 time period. Clearly, had Microsoft's revenues and net income in 2006 been $35 billion and $10 billion, respectively, it would still be a very large and highly profitable enterprise. However, such performance would have resulted in significant damage to Microsoft's market valuation and reputation—as well as the careers of many executives. Exhibit 3.8 illustrates a 10-year period of return on sales (ROS) for a hypothetical company. As indicated by the dotted trend lines, the rate of growth (or decline) differs substantially over time periods.

Comparison with Industry Norms   When you are evaluating a firm's financial performance, remember also to compare it with industry norms. A firm's current ratio or profitability may appear impressive at first glance. However, it may pale when compared with industry standards or norms.

By comparing your firm with all other firms in your industry, you can assess relative performance. Banks often use such comparisons when evaluating a firm's creditworthiness. Exhibit 3.9 includes a variety of financial ratios for three industries: semiconductors, grocery stores, and skilled-nursing facilities. Why is there such variation among the financial ratios for these three industries? There are several reasons. With regard to the collection period, grocery stores operate mostly on a cash basis, hence a very short collection period. Semiconductor manufacturers sell their output to other manufacturers (e.g., computer makers) on terms such as 2/15 net 45, which means they give a 2 percent discount on bills paid within 15 days and start charging interest after 45 days. Skilled-nursing facilities would also have a longer collection period than grocery stores because they typically rely on payments from insurance companies.

The widespread use of Microsoft's products in offices and homes helps keep the firm highly profitable.

The industry norms for return on sales also highlight some differences among these industries. Grocers, with very slim margins, have a lower return on sales than either skilled-nursing facilities or semiconductor manufacturers. But how might we explain the differences between skilled-nursing facilities and semiconductor manufacturers? Health care facilities, in general, are limited in their pricing structures by Medicare/Medicaid regulations and by insurance reimbursement limits, but semiconductor producers have pricing structures determined by the market. If their products have superior performance, semiconductor manufacturers can charge premium prices.

Comparison with Key Competitors You can gain valuable insights into a firm's financial and competitive position if you make comparisons between a firm and its most direct rivals. Consider Procter & Gamble's ill-fated efforts to enter the highly profitable pharmaceutical industry. Although P&G is a giant in consumer products, its efforts over two decades have produced nominal profits at best. In 1999 P&G spent $380 million

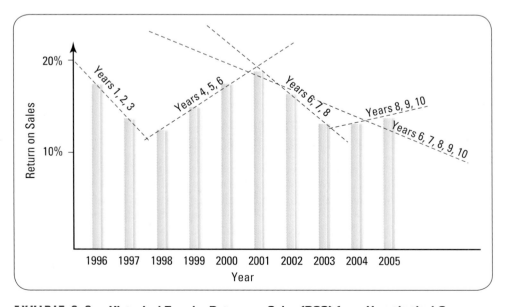

EXHIBIT 3.8 **Historical Trends: Return on Sales (ROS) for a Hypothetical Company**

EXHIBIT 3.9

How Financial Ratios Differ across Industries

Financial Ratio	Semiconductors	Grocery Stores	Skilled-Nursing Facilities
Quick ratio (times)	1.9	0.5	1.1
Current ratio (times)	4.0	1.6	1.6
Total liabilities to net worth (%)	30.7	92.0	163.5
Collection period (days)	49.6	2.9	31.2
Assets to sales (%)	187.8	20.2	101.6
Return on sales (%)	5.8	0.8	1.6

Source: Dun & Bradstreet. *Industry Norms and Key Business Ratios, 2003–2004.* One Year Edition, SIC #2000-3999 (Semiconductors); SIC #5200-5499 (Grocery Stores); SIC #6100-8999 (Skilled-Nursing Facilities). New York: Dun & Bradstreet Credit Services.

Company (or division)	Sales* ($ billions)	R&D Budget ($ billions)
P&G Drug Division	$ 0.8	$0.38
Bristol-Myers Squibb	20.2	1.80
Pfizer	27.4	4.00
Merck	32.7	2.10

Source: Berner, R. 2000. Procter & Gamble: Just say no to drugs. *BusinessWeek*, October 9: 128; data courtesy of Lehman Brothers and Procter & Gamble.

*Data: Lehman Brothers, Procter & Gamble Co.

on R&D in drugs—22 percent of its total corporate R&D budget. However, its drug unit produced only 2 percent of the company's $40 billion sales. Why? While $380 million is hardly a trivial amount of capital, its key competitors dwarf P&G. Consider the drug revenues and R&D budgets of P&G compared to its main rivals as shown in Exhibit 3.10. *BusinessWeek*'s take on P&G's chances in an article entitled "Just Say No to Drugs" was this: "Don't bet on it. P&G may be a giant in detergent and toothpaste, but the consumer-products maker is simply outclassed by the competition."[44]

INTEGRATING FINANCIAL ANALYSIS AND STAKEHOLDER PERSPECTIVES: THE BALANCED SCORECARD

L05 The value of recognizing how the interests of a variety of stakeholders can be interrelated.

It is useful to see how a firm is performing over time in terms of the several ratios. However, such traditional approaches to performance assessments can be a double-edged sword.[45] Many important transactions that managers make—investments in research and development, and employee training and development, and advertising and promotion of key brands—may greatly expand a firm's market potential and create significant long-term shareholder value. But such critical investments are not reflected positively in short-term financial reports. Why? Because financial reports typically measure expenses, not the value created. Thus, managers may be penalized for spending money in the short term to improve their firm's long-term competitive viability!

Now consider the other side of the coin. A manager may be destroying the firm's future value by operating in a way that makes customers dissatisfied, depletes the firm's stock of good products coming out of R&D, or damages the morale of valued employees. Such budget cuts, however, may lead to very good short-term financials. The manager may look good in the short run and even receive credit for improving the firm's performance. In essence, such a manager has mastered "denominator management," whereby decreasing investments makes the return on investment (ROI) ratio larger, even though the actual return remains constant or shrinks.

The Balanced Scorecard: Description and Benefits   To provide a meaningful integration of the many issues that come into evaluating a firm's performance, Kaplan and Norton developed a "balanced scorecard."[46] The **balanced scorecard** is a set of measures that provide top managers with a fast but comprehensive view of the business. In a nutshell, it includes financial measures that reflect the results of actions already taken, but it complements these indicators with operational measures of customer satisfaction, internal processes, and the organization's innovation and improvement activities—operational measures that drive future financial performance.

balanced scorecard
A method of evaluating a firm's performance using performance measures from the customer, internal, innovation and learning, and financial perspectives.

The balanced scorecard enables managers to consider their business from four key perspectives: customer; internal; innovation and learning; and financial. These are briefly described in Exhibit 3.11.

Customer Perspective   Clearly, how a company is performing from its customers' perspective is a top priority for management. The balanced scorecard requires that managers translate their general mission statements on customer service into specific measures that reflect the factors that really matter to customers. For the balanced scorecard to work, managers must articulate goals for four key categories of customer concerns: time, quality, performance and service, and cost. For example, lead time may be measured as the time from the company's receipt of an order to the time it actually delivers the product or service to the customer.

Internal Business Perspective   Although customer-based measures are important, they must be translated into indicators of what the firm must do internally to meet customers' expectations. Excellent customer performance results from processes, decisions, and actions that occur throughout organizations in a coordinated fashion, and managers must focus on those critical internal operations that enable them to satisfy customer needs. The internal measures should reflect business processes that have the greatest impact on customer satisfaction. These include factors that affect cycle time, quality, employee skills, and productivity. Firms also must identify and measure the key resources and capabilities they need to ensure continued strategic success.

Innovation and Learning Perspective   Given the rapid rate of markets, technologies, and global competition, the criteria for success are constantly changing. To survive and prosper, managers must make frequent changes to existing products and services as well as introduce entirely new products with expanded capabilities. A firm's ability to improve, innovate, and learn is tied directly to its value. Simply put, only by developing new products and services, creating greater value for customers, and increasing operating efficiencies can a company penetrate new markets, increase revenues and margins, and enhance shareholder value. A firm's ability to do well from an innovation and learning perspective

EXHIBIT 3.11

The Balanced Scorecard's Four Perspectives

- How do customers see us? (**customer perspective**)
- What must we excel at? (**internal perspective**)
- Can we continue to improve and create value? (**innovation and learning perspective**)
- How do we look to shareholders? (**financial perspective**)

is more dependent on its intangible than tangible assets. Three categories of intangible assets are critically important: human capital (skills, talent, and knowledge), information capital (information systems, networks), and organization capital (culture, leadership).

Financial Perspective Measures of financial performance indicate whether the company's strategy, implementation, and execution are indeed contributing to bottom-line improvement. Typical financial goals include profitability, growth, and shareholder value. Periodic financial statements remind managers that improved quality, response time, productivity, and innovative products benefit the firm only when they result in improved sales, increased market share, reduced operating expenses, or higher asset turnover.[47]

We now provide an example that illustrates the causal relationships among the multiple perspectives in the model. Sears, the huge retailer, found a strong causal relationship between employee attitudes, customer attitudes, and financial outcomes.[48] Through an ongoing study, Sears developed (and continues to refine) what it calls its total performance indicators, or TPI—a set of indicators that shows how well the company is doing with customers, employees, and investors. Sears's quantitative model has shown that a 5.0 percent improvement in employee attitudes leads to a 1.3 percent improvement in customer satisfaction, which in turn will drive a 0.5 percent improvement in revenue. Thus, if a single store improved its employee attitude by 5.0 percent on a survey scale, Sears could predict with confidence that if the revenue growth in the district as a whole were 5.0 percent, the revenue growth in this particular store would be 5.5 percent. Interestingly, Sears's managers consider such numbers as rigorous as any others that they work with every year. The company's accounting firm audits management as closely as it audits the financial statements.

A key implication of the balanced scorecard is that managers do not need to look at their job as primarily balancing stakeholder demands. They need to avoid the following mind-set: "How many units in employee satisfaction do I have to give up to get some additional units of customer satisfaction or profits?" Instead, when done properly, the balanced scorecard provides a win–win approach—a means of simultaneously increasing satisfaction among a wide variety of organizational stakeholders, including employees (at all levels), customers, and stockholders.

Limitations and Potential Downsides of the Balanced Scorecard There is general agreement that there is nothing inherently wrong with the concept of the Balanced Scorecard.[49] The key limitation is that some executives may view it as a "quick fix" that can be easily installed in their organization. However, implementing a balanced metrics system is an evolutionary process. It is not a one-time task that can be quickly checked off as "completed." If managers do not recognize this from the beginning and fail to commit to it long term, the organization will be disappointed with the results. Poor execution becomes the cause of such performance outcomes. And organizational scorecards must be aligned with individuals' scorecards to turn the balanced scorecards into a powerful tool for sustained organizational performance.

In a recent study of 50 Canadian medium and large organizations, the number of users expressing skepticism about scorecard performance was much greater than those claiming positive results. However, the overwhelming perspective was that balanced scorecards can be worthwhile in clarifying an organization's strategy and if this can be accomplished, better results will follow. A few companies stated categorically that scorecards have improved the firm's financial results. For example, one respondent claimed, "We did not meet our financial goals previously, but since implementing our balanced scorecard, we have now met our goals three years running."

On the other hand, a greater number of respondents agreed with the statement, "balanced scorecards don't really work." Some representative comments included: "It became just a number-crunching exercise by accountants after the first year"; "It is just the latest management fad and is already dropping lower on management's list of priorities as all fads eventually do"; and "If scorecards are supposed to be a measurement tool, why is it so hard to measure their results?" Few would argue that there is much work to do before scorecards can become a viable framework for the measurement of sustained strategic performance.

Problems often occur in the Balanced Scorecard implementation efforts when there is an insufficient commitment to learning and the inclusion of employees' personal ambitions. If there is not a set of rules for employees that address continuous process improvement and the personal improvement of individual employees, there will be limited employee buy-in and insufficient cultural change. Thus, many improvements may be temporary and superficial. Often, with scorecards that failed to attain alignment with employee concerns, improvements dissipated very quickly. And in many cases, management's efforts to improve performance were seen as divisive, that is, were viewed by employees as aimed at benefiting senior management compensation, which fostered a "what's in it for me?" attitude among employees. Exhibit 3.12 summarizes some of the primary limitations and potential downsides of the Balanced Scorecard.

EXHIBIT 3.12
Potential Limitations of the Balanced Scorecard

Most agree that the Balanced Scorecard concept is a useful and an appropriate management tool. However, there are many design and implementation issues that may short-circuit its value. Among these are:

- *Lack of a clear strategy.* A Scorecard can be developed without the aid of a strategy. However, it then becomes a key performance indicator or stakeholder system, lacking in many of the attributes offered from a true Balanced Scorecard.

- *Limited or ineffective executive sponsorship.* Although training and education is important, without tenacious leadership and support of a Scorecard project, the effort is most likely doomed.

- *Too much emphasis on financial measures rather than nonfinancial measures.* This leads to measures that do not connect to the drivers of the business and are not relevant to improvement in performance.

- *Poor data on actual performance.* This can negate most of the effort invested in defining performance measures by not being able to monitor actual changes in results from changes in behavior.

- *Inappropriate links of scorecard measures to compensation.* Although linking to compensation can focus managerial and employee attention, exercising it too soon can produce many unintended side-effects such as dysfunctional decision making by managers looking to cash in.

- *Inconsistent or inappropriate terminology.* Everyone must speak the same language if measurement is to be used in guiding change within an organization. Translating strategy into measures becomes even more difficult if everyone cannot agree on (or understand) the same language and terminology.

Sources: Angel, R., & Rampersad, H. 2005. Do scorecards add up? Camagazine.com. may: np; and Niven, P. 2002. *Balanced Scorecard Step by Step: Maximizing Performance and Maintaining Results.* John Wiley & Sons: New York.

SUMMARY

LO1 We examined two key tools for understanding a firm's internal situation. We first discussed the need for consistency among a firm's vision, mission, and strategic objectives. A firm's vision should evoke powerful and compelling mental images that motivate employees to do their best. However, company visions are not very specific. Strategic objectives, or the other hand, are much more specific and are vital to ensuring that the firm is striving toward fulfilling its vision and mission.

LO2, LO3 Second, in conducting a value-chain analysis, we divided the firm into a series of value-creating activities. These include *primary* activities such as inbound logistics, operations, and service as well as *support* activities such as procurement and human resources management. Then we analyzed how each activity adds value as well as how *interrelationships* among value activities in the firm and among the firm and its customers and suppliers add value. Thus, instead of merely determining a firm's strengths and weaknesses per se, analyze them in the overall context of the firm and its relationships with customers and suppliers—the value system.

LO4, LO5 An internal analysis of the firm would not be complete unless one evaluates its performance and make the appropriate comparisons. Determining a firm's performance requires an analysis of its financial situation as well as a review of how well it is satisfying a broad range of stakeholders, including customers, employees, and stockholders. We discussed the concept of the balanced scorecard, in which four perspectives must be addressed: customer, internal business, innovation and learning, and financial. Central to this concept is the idea that the interests of various stakeholders can be interrelated. We provided examples of how indicators of employee satisfaction lead to higher levels of customer satisfaction, which in turn lead to higher levels of financial performance. Thus, improving a firm's performance does not need to involve making trade-offs among different stakeholders. Assessing the firm's performance is also more useful in terms of how it changes over time, compares with industry norms, and compares with key competitors.

SUMMARY REVIEW QUESTIONS

1. Briefly describe the primary and support activities in a firm's value chain.
2. How can managers create value by establishing important relationships among the value-chain activities both within their firm and between the firm and its customers and suppliers?
3. What are the advantages and disadvantages of conducting a financial ratio analysis of a firm?
4. Summarize the concept of the balanced scorecard. What are its main advantages?

KEY TERMS

organizational vision 52
mission statement 54
strategic objectives 56

value-chain analysis 58
primary activities 58

support activities 58
balanced scorecard 71

1. Using published reports, select two CEOs who have recently made public statements regarding a major change in their firm's strategy. Discuss how the successful implementation of such strategies requires changes in the firm's primary and support activities.

2. Select a firm that competes in an industry in which you are interested. Drawing upon published financial reports, complete a financial ratio analysis. Based on changes over time and a comparison with industry norms, evaluate the firm's strengths and weaknesses in terms of its financial position.

3. How might exemplary human resource practices enhance and strengthen a firm's value-chain activities?

4. Using the Internet, look up your university or college. What are some of its key value-creating activities that provide competitive advantages? Why? How are these advantages created?

1. Thomas, A. R., & Wilkinson, T. J. 2006. The outsourcing compulsion. *MIT Sloan Management Review,* 48(1): 10–14; and Fahey, J. 2005. Rolling, rolling, rolling. *Forbes.com.* November 28: np.

2. Lipton, M. 1996. Demystifying the development of an organizational vision. *Sloan Management Review,* 37(4): 83–92.

3. Hardy, Q. 2007. The uncarly. *Forbes,* March 12: 82–90.

4. Quigley, J. V. 1994. Vision: How leaders develop it, share it, and sustain it. *Business Horizons,* September–October: 37–40.

5. Ibid.

6. Lipton, op. cit. Additional pitfalls are addressed in this article.

7. Sull, D. N. 2005. Strategy as active waiting. *Harvard Business Review,* 83(9): 120–130.

8. Company records.

9. Lipton, op. cit.

10. Sexton, D. A., & Van Aukun, P. M. 1985. A longitudinal study of small business strategic planning. *Journal of Small Business Management,* January: 8–15, cited in Lipton, op. cit.

11. For an insightful perspective on the use of strategic objectives, refer to Chatterjee, S. 2005. Core objectives: Clarity in designing strategy. *California Management Review,* 47(2): 33–49.

12. Ibid.

13. Mankins, M. M., & Steele, R. 2005. Turning great strategy into great performance. *Harvard Business Review,* 83(5): 66–73.

14. Our discussion of the value chain will draw on Porter, M. E. 1985. *Competitive advantage:* chap. 2. New York: Free Press.

15. Dyer, J. H. 1996. Specialized supplier networks as a source of competitive advantage: Evidence from the auto industry. *Strategic Management Journal,* 17: 271–291.

16. For an insightful perspective on value-chain analysis, refer to Stabell, C. B., & Fjeldstad, O. D. 1998. Configuring value for competitive advantage: On chains, shops, and networks. *Strategic Management Journal,* 19: 413–437. The authors develop concepts of value chains, value shops, and value networks to extend the value-creation logic across a broad range of industries. Their work builds on the seminal contributions of Porter, 1985, op. cit., and others who have addressed how firms create value through key interrelationships among value-creating activities.

17. Ibid.

18. Maynard, M. 1999. Toyota promises custom order in 5 days. *USA Today,* August 6: B1.

19. Shaw Industries. 1999. Annual report: 14–15.

20. Fisher, M. L. 1997. What is the right supply chain for your product? *Harvard Business Review,* 75(2): 105–116.

21. Jackson, M. 2001. Bringing a dying brand back to life. *Harvard Business Review,* 79(5): 53–61.

22. Anderson, J. C., & Nmarus, J. A. 2003. Selectively pursuing more of your customer's business. *MIT Sloan Management Review,* 44(3): 42–50.

23. An insightful discussion of the role of identity marketing—that is, the myriad labels that people use to express who they are—in successful marketing activities is found in Reed, A., II, & Bolton, L. E.

REFERENCES

2005. The complexity of identify. *MIT Sloan Management Review,* 46(3): 18–22.

24. Berggren, E., & Nacher, T. 2000. Why good ideas go bust. *Management Review,* February: 32–36.

25. For an insightful perspective on creating effective brand portfolios, refer to Hill, S., Ettenson, R., & Tyson, D. 2005. Achieving the ideal brand portfolio. *MIT Sloan Management Review,* 46(2): 85–90.

26. Haddad, C., & Grow, B. 2001. Wait a second—I didn't order that! *BusinessWeek,* July 16: 45.

27. For a scholarly discussion on the procurement of technology components, read Hoetker, G. 2005. How much you know versus how well I know you: Selecting a supplier for a technically innovative component. *Strategic Management Journal,* 26(1): 75–96.

28. For a discussion on criteria to use when screening suppliers for back-office functions, read Feeny, D., Lacity, M., & Willcocks, L. P. 2005. Taking the measure of outsourcing providers. *MIT Sloan Management Review,* 46(3): 41–48.

29. Imperato, G. 1998. How to give good feedback. *Fast Company,* September: 144–156.

30. Bensaou, B. M., & Earl, M. 1998. The right mindset for managing information technology. *Harvard Business Review,* 96(5): 118–128.

31. Ulrich, D. 1998. A new mandate for human resources. *Harvard Business Review,* 96(1): 124–134.

32. Wood, J. 2003. Sharing jobs and working from home: The new face of the airline industry. *AviationCareer. net,* February 21.

33. Follow AT&T's lead in this tactic to retain "plateaued" employees. n.d. *Recruitment & Retention:* 1.

34. Green, S., Hasan, F., Immelt, J. Marks, M., & Meiland, D. 2003. In search of global leaders. *Harvard Business Review,* 81(8): 38–45.

35. For a cautionary note on the use of IT, refer to McAfee, A. 2003. When too much IT knowledge is a dangerous thing. *MIT Sloan Management Review,* 44(2): 83–90.

36. Walgreen Co. 1996. *Information technology and Walgreen's: Opportunities for employment,* January; and Dess, G. G., & Picken, J. C. 1997. *Beyond productivity.* New York: AMACOM.

37. For an interesting perspective on some of the potential downsides of close customer and supplier relationships, refer to Anderson, E.,

& Jap, S. D. 2005. The dark side of close relationships. *MIT Sloan Management Review,* 46(3): 75–82.

38. Day, G. S. 2003. Creating a superior customer-relating capability. *MIT Sloan Management Review,* 44(3): 77–82.

39. To gain insights on the role of electronic technologies in enhancing a firm's connections to outside suppliers and customers, refer to Lawrence, T. B., Morse, E. A., & Fowler, S. W. 2005. Managing your portfolio of connections. *MIT Sloan Management Review,* 46(2): 59–66.

40. Reinhardt, F. L. 1999. Bringing the environment down to earth. *Harvard Business Review,* 77(4): 149–157.

41. Luehrman, T. A. 1997. What's it worth? A general manager's guide to valuation. *Harvard Business Review,* 45(3): 132–142.

42. See, for example, Kaplan, R. S., & Norton, D. P. 1992. The balanced scorecard: Measures that drive performance. *Harvard Business Review,* 69(1): 71–79.

43. Hitt, M. A., Ireland, R. D., & Stadter, G. 1982. Functional importance of company performance: Moderating effects of grand strategy and industry type. *Strategic Management Journal,* 3: 315–330.

44. Berner, R. 2000. Procter & Gamble: Just say no to drugs. *Business Week,* October 9: 128.

45. Kaplan & Norton, op. cit.

46. Ibid.

47. For a discussion of the relative value of growth versus increasing margins, read Mass, N. J. 2005. The relative value of growth. *Harvard Business Review,* 83(4): 102–112.

48. Rucci, A. J., Kirn, S. P., & Quinn, R. T. 1998. The employee-customer-profit chain at Sears. *Harvard Business Review,* 76(1): 82–97.

49. Our discussion draws upon: Angel, R. & Rampersad, H. 2005. Do scorecards add up? *camagazine.com.* May: np.; and, Niven, P. 2002. *Balanced Scorecard Step by Step: Maximizing Performance and Maintaining Results.* John Wiley & Sons: New York.

Analyzing the External Environment

....

After reading this chapter, you should have a good understanding of:

LO1 The impact of the general environment on a firm's strategies and performance.

LO2 How forces in the competitive environment can affect profitability, and how a firm can improve its competitive position by increasing its power vis-à-vis these forces.

LO3 How trends and events in the general environment and forces in the competitive environment are interrelated and affect performance.

LO4 How the Internet and digitally based capabilities are affecting competitive forces and industry profitability.

LO5 The concept of strategic groups and its strategy and performance implications.

....

Strategies are not and should not be developed in a vacuum. They must be responsive to the external business environment. Otherwise, your firm could become, in effect, the best producer of cassette tapes or floppy disks. To avoid such strategic mistakes, firms must become knowledgeable about the business environment. In this chapter, we explain two major elements of the external environment—the general environment and the competitive environment. The general environment consists of five segments— demographic, sociocultural, political/legal, technological, and economic. Trends and events in these segments can have a dramatic impact on your firm.

The competitive environment is closer to home. It consists of five industry-related factors that can dramatically affect the average level of industry profitability. An awareness of these factors is critical in making decisions such as which industries to enter and how to improve your firm's current position within an industry. This is helpful in neutralizing competitive threats and increasing power over customers and suppliers. We also address how industry and competitive practices are being affected by the capabilities provided by Internet technologies. We then place firms within an industry into strategic groups based on similarities in resources and strategies. As we will see, the concept of strategic groups has important implications for the intensity of rivalry and how the effects of a given environmental trend or event differ across groups. In the final part of the chapter, we introduce SWOT analysis. This technique focuses on examining an individual firm's strengths and weaknesses alongside the opportunities and threats presented by the environment in order to begin thinking about strategic alternatives.

LEARNING FROM MISTAKES

Robert Atkins, a cardiologist, was the founder of the original low-carbohydrate, high-protein diet.[1] He wrote several books that popularized his "Atkins diet," including his best-seller, *Dr. Atkins' New Diet Revolution,* that sold over 10 million copies worldwide. As we will see below, in the beer industry, one firm—Anheuser Busch—took quick action and benefited from this popular diet trend. Others, including Coors Brewing, were slow to react—and paid the price.

In September 2002, Anheuser Busch became one of the pioneers in the low-carb category by launching Michelob Ultra. The brand rapidly became the leader, capturing 5.7 percent of the light-beer market by March 2004. The company had jumped on the wave early and rode it during the upsurge of the low-carb trend, which peaked during that year. Clearly, this was an attractive market segment: Beer experts had estimated that about half of the estimated $60 to $70 billion U.S. beer market is from light beer sales as Americans continue to seek out beers that won't add to their waistline.

Coors, in contrast, didn't enter the low-carb market until March 2004—after Michelob Ultra had begun to erode Coors Light's market share. The Coors low-carb brand, Aspen Edge, was too little, too late. By the time Aspen Edge was launched, it faced very stiff competition. In addition to a powerful leader in the segment, Michelob Ultra (which, of course, benefited from Anheuser Busch's deep pockets and marketing prowess), there were already over a dozen other low-carb rivals. These included Rolling Rock which had introduced Rock Green Light, and Miller Brewing which had begun to promote the fact that its staple, Miller Lite, had only 3.2 carbs. Further, there were several imported beers, including Martens Low Carbohydrate, brewed by Brouwerij Martens in Belgium.

Even though Coors invested $30 million in Aspen Edge's launch, its sales peaked at just 0.4 percent of the beer market in July 2004. Then, its market share began to slide and it was discontinued in April 2006.

The sales of printed encyclopedias were decimated by CD-ROMs.

Successful managers must recognize opportunities and threats in their firm's external environment. They must be aware of what's going on outside their company. If they focus exclusively on the efficiency of internal operations, their firm may degenerate into the world's most efficient producer of buggy whips or carbon paper. But if they miscalculate the market, opportunities will be lost—hardly an enviable position for their firm.

In *Competing for the Future,* Gary Hamel and C. K. Prahalad suggest that "every manager carries around in his or her head a set of biases, assumptions, and presuppositions about the structure of the relevant 'industry,' about how one makes money in the industry, about who the competition is and isn't, about who the customers are and aren't, and so on."[2] Environmental analysis requires you to continually question such assumptions. Peter Drucker labeled these interrelated sets of assumptions the "theory of the business."[3] Most would agree that Coors would have benefited from a more rigorous environmental analysis—in particular the growing popularity of low-carb products. By the time Coors took action, the low-carb boom had already peaked.

A firm's strategy may be good at one point in time, but it may go astray when management's frame of reference gets out of touch with the realities of the actual business situation. This results when management's assumptions, premises, or beliefs are incorrect or when internal inconsistencies among them render the overall "theory of the business" invalid. As Warren Buffett, investor extraordinaire, colorfully notes, "Beware of past performance 'proofs.' If history books were the key to riches, the Forbes 400 would consist of librarians." And Arthur Martinez, former chairman of Sears, Roebuck & Co., states, "Today's peacock is tomorrow's feather duster."

In the business world, many peacocks have become feather dusters or at least had their plumage dulled. Consider the high-tech company Novell, which went head-to-head with Microsoft.[4] Novell bought market-share loser WordPerfect to compete with Microsoft Word. The result? A $1.3 billion loss when Novell sold WordPerfect to Corel. And today we may wonder who will be the next Wang, Netscape, or *Encyclopaedia Britannica.*

LO1 The impact of the general environment on a firm's strategies and performance.

general environment
Factors external to an industry, and usually beyond a firm's control, that affect a firm's strategy.

 ## THE GENERAL ENVIRONMENT

The **general environment** is composed of factors that can have dramatic effects on firm strategy. Typically, a firm has little ability to predict trends and events in the general environment and even less ability to control them. When listening to CNBC, for example, you can hear many experts espouse totally different perspectives on what action the Federal Reserve Board may take on short-term interest rates—an action that can have huge effects on the valuation of entire economic sectors. Also, it's difficult to predict future political events such as the ongoing Middle East peace negotiations and tensions on the Korean peninsula. In addition, who would have guessed the Internet's impact on national and global economies in the past decade or two? Such dramatic innovations in information technology (e.g., the Internet) have helped keep inflation in check by lowering the cost of doing business in the United States at the beginning of the 21st century.

We divide the general environment into five segments: demographic, sociocultural, political/legal, technological, and economic. First, we discuss each segment and provide a summary of the segment and examples of how events and trends can impact industries. Second, we address relationships among the general environment segments. Third, we consider how trends and events can vary across industries. Exhibit 4.1 provides examples of key trends and events in each of the segments of the general environment.

EXHIBIT 4.1

**General Environment:
Key Trends and Events**

Demographic

- Aging population
- Rising affluence
- Changes in ethnic composition
- Geographic distribution of population
- Greater disparities in income levels

Sociocultural

- More women in the workforce
- Increase in temporary workers
- Greater concern for fitness
- Greater concern for environment
- Postponement of family formation

Political/Legal

- Tort reform
- Americans with Disabilities Act (ADA) of 1990
- Repeal of Glass-Steagall Act in 1999 (banks may now offer brokerage services)
- Deregulation of utility and other industries
- Increases in federally mandated minimum wages
- Taxation at local, state, federal levels
- Legislation on corporate governance reforms in bookkeeping, stock options, etc. (Sarbanes-Oxley Act of 2002)

Technological

- Genetic engineering
- Emergence of Internet technology
- Computer-aided design/computer-aided manufacturing systems (CAD/CAM)
- Research in synthetic and exotic materials
- Pollution/global warming
- Miniaturization of computing technologies
- Wireless communications
- Nanotechnology

Economic

- Interest rates
- Unemployment rates
- Consumer Price Index
- Trends in GDP
- Changes in stock market valuations

THE DEMOGRAPHIC SEGMENT

Demographics are the most easily understood and quantifiable elements of the general environment. They are at the root of many changes in society. Demographics include elements such as the aging population, rising or declining affluence, changes in ethnic composition, geographic distribution of the population, and disparities in income level.

The impact of a demographic trend, like all segments of the general environment, varies across industries. The aging of the U.S. population has had a positive effect on the health care industry but a negative impact on diaper makers and baby food producers. Rising levels of affluence in many developed countries bode well for brokerage services as well as for upscale pets and supplies. However, these same trends may have an adverse effect on fast-food restaurants because people can afford to dine at higher-priced restaurants. Fast-food restaurants depend on minimum-wage employees to operate efficiently, but the competition for labor intensifies as more attractive employment opportunities become prevalent, thus threatening the employment base for restaurants. Exhibit 4.2 provides other examples of how the impact of environmental trends and events can vary across industries.

EXHIBIT 4.2

The Impact of General Environmental Trends on Various Industries

Segment/Trends and Events	Industry	Positive	Neutral	Negative
Demographic				
Aging population	Health care	✓		
	Baby products			✓
Rising affluence	Brokerage services	✓		
	Fast foods			✓
	Upscale pets and supplies	✓		
Sociocultural				
More women in the workforce	Clothing	✓		
	Baking products (staples)			✓
Greater concern for health and fitness	Home exercise equipment	✓		
	Meat products			✓
Political/legal				
Tort reform	Legal services			✓
	Auto manufacturing	✓		
Americans with Disabilities Act (ADA)	Retail			✓
	Manufacturers of elevators, escalators, and ramps	✓		
Technological				
Genetic engineering	Pharmaceutical	✓		
	Publishing		✓	
Pollution/global warming	Engineering services	✓		
	Petroleum			✓
Economic				
Interest rate increases	Residential construction			✓
	Most common grocery products		✓	

THE SOCIOCULTURAL SEGMENT

Sociocultural forces influence the values, beliefs, and lifestyles of a society. Examples include a higher percentage of women in the workforce, dual-income families, increases in the number of temporary workers, greater concern for healthy diets and physical fitness, greater interest in the environment, and postponement of having children. Such forces enhance sales of products and services in many industries but depress sales in others. The increased number of women in the workforce has increased the need for business clothing merchandise but decreased the demand for baking product staples (since people would have less time to cook from scratch). A greater concern for health and fitness has had differential effects. This trend has helped industries that manufacture exercise equipment and healthful foods but harmed industries that produce unhealthful foods.

The trend toward increased educational attainment by women in the workplace has led to an increase in the number of women in upper management positions. U.S. Department of Education statistics show that women have become the dominant holders of college degrees. Based on figures of a recent graduating class, women with bachelor's degrees will outnumber their male counterparts by 27 percent. By the class of 2006–2007, the gap surged to 38 percent. Additionally, throughout the 1990s the number of women earning MBAs increased by 29 percent compared to only 15 percent for men.[5] Given these educational attainments, it is hardly surprising that companies owned by women have been one of the driving forces of the U.S. economy; these companies (now more than 9 million in number) account for 40 percent of all U.S. businesses and have generated more than $3.6 trillion in annual revenue. In addition, women have a tremendous impact on consumer spending decisions. Not surprisingly, many companies have focused their advertising and promotion efforts on female consumers. Consider, for example, Wilkesboro (North Carolina)–based Lowe's efforts to attract female shoppers:

> Lowe's has found that women prefer to do larger home-improvement projects with a man—be it a boyfriend, husband, or neighbor.[6] As a result, in addition to its "recipe card classes" (that explain various projects that take only one weekend), Lowe's offers co-ed store clinics for projects like sink installation. "Women like to feel they're given the same attention as a male customer," states Lowe's spokespersons Julie Valeant-Yenichek, who points out that most seminar attendees, whether male or female, are inexperienced.
>
> Not surprisingly, Home Depot has recently spent millions of dollars to add softer lighting and brighter signs in 300 stores. Why? It is an effort to match rival Lowe's long-standing appeal to women.

THE POLITICAL/LEGAL SEGMENT

Political processes and legislation influence the environmental regulations with which industries must comply. Some important elements of the political/legal arena include tort reform, the Americans with Disabilities Act (ADA) of 1990, the repeal of the Glass-Steagall Act in 1999 (banks may now offer brokerage services), deregulation of utilities and other industries, and increases in the federally mandated minimum wage.

Government legislation can also have a significant impact on the governance of corporations. The U.S. Congress passed the Sarbanes-Oxley Act in 2002, which greatly increases the accountability of auditors, executives, and corporate lawyers. This act was a response to the widespread perception that existing governance mechanisms have failed to protect the interests of shareholders, employees, and creditors. Perhaps it is not too surprising that Sarbanes-Oxley has also created a tremendous demand for professional accounting services.

THE TECHNOLOGICAL SEGMENT

Developments in technology lead to new products and services and improve how they are produced and delivered to the end user. Innovations can create entirely new industries and alter the boundaries of existing industries. Examples of technological developments and trends are genetic engineering, Internet technology, computer-aided design/computer-aided manufacturing (CAD/CAM), research in artificial and exotic materials, and, on the downside, pollution and global warming. Firms in the petroleum and primary metals industries incur significant expenses to reduce the amount of pollution they produce. Engineering and consulting firms that work with polluting industries derive financial benefits from solving such problems.

Another important technological development is the combination of information technology (IT) and the Internet, which has played a key role in productivity improvement.[7] In the United States, for example, improvement in productivity rates is running at an all-time high. For the 20-year period ending in 1990, U.S. worker productivity grew at less than 1.7 percent annually. In contrast, from 2001 to 2005, it grew at an annual rate of 3.6 percent. In recent years, productivity around the world has also increased by, for example, nearly 6 percent in Taiwan and nearly 10 percent in South Korea. Better productivity means that more work can be done by fewer people.

Nanotechnology is becoming a very promising area of research with many potentially useful applications.[8] Nanotechnology takes place at industry's tiniest stage: one billionth of a meter. Remarkably, this is the size of 10 hydrogen atoms in a row.

Researchers have discovered that matter at such a tiny scale behaves very differently. While some of the science behind this phenomenon is still shrouded in mystery, the commercial potential is coming sharply into focus. Familiar materials—from gold to carbon soot—display startling and useful new properties. Some transmit light or electricity. Others become harder than diamonds or turn into potent chemical catalysts. What's more, researchers have found that a tiny dose of nanoparticles can transform the chemistry and nature of far bigger things, creating everything from stronger fenders to superefficient fuel cells. Exhibit 4.3 lists a few of the potential ways in which nanotechnology could revolutionize industries.

THE ECONOMIC SEGMENT

The economy has an impact on all industries, from suppliers of raw materials to manufacturers of finished goods and services, as well as all organizations in the service, wholesale, retail, government, and nonprofit sectors. Key economic indicators include interest rates, unemployment rates, the Consumer Price Index, the gross domestic product, and net

EXHIBIT 4.3

How Nanotechnology Might Revolutionize Various Industries

- *To fight cancer,* sensors will be able to detect a single cancer cell and will help guide nanoparticles that can burn tumors from the inside out, leaving healthy cells alone.
- *To transform energy,* nano-enhanced solar panels will feed cheap electricity onto superconducting power lines made of carbon nanotubes.
- *To replace silicon,* carbon nanotubes will take over when silicon peters out, leading to far faster chips that need less power than today's.
- *For space travel,* podlike crawlers will carry cargo thousands of miles up a carbon-nanotube cable to a space station for billions less than rocket launches.

Source: Baker, S. & Aston, A. 2004. Universe in a grain of sand. *BusinessWeek,* October 11: 139–140.

disposable income. Interest-rate increases have a negative impact on the residential home construction industry but a negligible (or neutral) effect on industries that produce consumer necessities such as prescription drugs or common grocery items.

Other economic indicators are associated with equity markets. Perhaps the most watched is the Dow Jones Industrial Average (DJIA), which is composed of 30 large industrial firms. When stock market indexes increase, consumers' discretionary income rises and there is often an increased demand for luxury items such as jewelry and automobiles. But when stock valuations decrease, demand for these items shrinks.

Although experts often refer to the state of the economy as good or bad, these labels are overly simplistic. For example, in a "bad" economy, discount retailers such as Dollar General and Wal-Mart tend to prosper. This is because a tough economy leads consumers to be more price conscious.

RELATIONSHIPS AMONG ELEMENTS OF THE GENERAL ENVIRONMENT

In our discussion of the general environment, we see many relationships among the various elements. For example, a demographic trend in the United States, the aging of the population, has important implications for the economic segment (in terms of tax policies to provide benefits to increasing numbers of older citizens). Another example is the emergence of information technology as a means to increase the rate of productivity gains in the United States and other developed countries. Such use of IT results in lower inflation (an important element of the economic segment) and helps offset costs associated with higher labor rates.

Before moving on, let's consider a recent event that has had a strong influence on many segments of the environment—the advent of the Internet. The Internet has been a leading and highly visible component of a broader technological phenomenon—the emergence of digital technology. These technologies are altering the way business is conducted and having an impact on nearly every business domain. Focus on Strategy 4.1 addresses the impact of the Internet and digital technologies on the business environment.

THE COMPETITIVE ENVIRONMENT

In addition to the general environment, managers must also consider the **competitive environment** (also sometimes referred to as the task or industry environment). The nature of competition in an industry, as well as the profitability of a firm, is often more directly influenced by developments in the competitive environment.

The competitive environment consists of many factors that are particularly relevant to a firm's strategy. These include competitors (existing or potential), customers, and suppliers. Potential competitors may include a supplier considering forward integration, such as an automobile manufacturer acquiring a rental car company, or a firm in an entirely new industry introducing a similar product that uses a more efficient technology.

In the following sections, we will discuss key concepts and analytical techniques that managers should use to assess their competitive environments. First, we examine Michael Porter's five-forces model that illustrates how these forces can be used to explain low profitability in an industry.[9] Second, we discuss how the five forces are being affected by the capabilities provided by Internet technologies. Third, we address some of the limitations, or "caveats," with which managers should be familiar when conducting industry analysis. Then, we address the concept of strategic groups. This concept demonstrates that even within an industry it is often useful to group firms on the basis of similarities of their strategies. As we will see, competition tends to be more intense among firms *within* a strategic group than between strategic groups.

LO2   How forces in the competitive environment can affect profitability, and how a firm can improve its competitive position by increasing its power vis-à-vis these forces.

LO3   How trends and events in the general environment and forces in the competitive environment are interrelated and affect performance.

competitive environment
Factors within an industry that affect firms' strategies, including customers, suppliers, competitors, substitutes, and potential new entrants.

The Internet and Digital Technologies: Affecting Many Environmental Segments

The Internet has dramatically changed the way business is conducted in every corner of the globe. According to digital economy visionary Don Tapscott:

> The Net is much more than just another technology development; the Net represents something qualitatively new—an unprecedented, powerful, universal communications medium. Far surpassing radio and television, this medium is digital, infinitely richer, and interactive. . . . Mobile computing devices, broadband access, wireless networks, and computing power embedded in everything from refrigerators to automobiles are converging into a global network that will enable people to use the Net just about anywhere and anytime.

The Internet provides a platform or staging area for the application of numerous technologies, rapid advances in knowledge, and unprecedented levels of global communication and commerce. Even technologies that don't require the Internet to function, such as wireless phones and GPS, rely on the Internet for data transfer and communications.

Growth in Internet usage has surged in recent years both among individual users and businesses. Exhibit 4.4 illustrates

Internet Users (in millions)		
Geographic Region	2005	2010 (estimated)
North America	219,650	259,390
Western Europe	215,734	319,528
Eastern Europe/Russia	70,381	130,888
Asia-Pacific	420,999	745,421
South/Central America	83,724	155,590
Middle East/Africa	64,245	146,624
Total Internet users	1,074,733	1,785,941

EXHIBIT 4.4 **Growth in Internet Activity**

Source: *Computer Industry Almanac.*

(continued)

PORTER'S FIVE-FORCES MODEL OF INDUSTRY COMPETITION

The "five-forces" model developed by Michael E. Porter has been the most commonly used analytical tool for examining the competitive environment. It describes the competitive environment in terms of five basic competitive forces.[10]

1. The threat of new entrants.
2. The bargaining power of buyers.
3. The bargaining power of suppliers.
4. The threat of substitute products and services.
5. The intensity of rivalry among competitors in an industry.

Each of these forces affects a firm's ability to compete in a given market. Together, they determine the profit potential for a particular industry. The model is shown in Exhibit 4.5. As a manager, you should be familiar with the five-forces model for several reasons. It helps you decide whether your firm should remain in or exit an industry. It provides the rationale for increasing or decreasing resource commitments. The model helps you assess how to improve your firm's competitive position with regard to each of the five forces. For example, you can use insights provided by the five-forces model to create higher entry barriers that discourage new rivals from competing with you. Or you may develop strong relationships with your distribution channels. You may decide to find suppliers who satisfy the price/performance criteria needed to make your product or service a top performer.

(continued)

current usage levels as well as worldwide growth trends in Internet use. Business use of the Internet has become nearly ubiquitous throughout the economy. Major corporations all have a Web presence, and many companies use the Internet to interact with key stakeholders. For example, some companies have direct links with suppliers through online procurement systems that automatically reorder inventories and supplies. Companies such as Cisco Systems even interact with their own employees using the Internet to update employment records, such as health care information and benefits.

Small and medium-sized enterprises (SMEs) are also relying on the Internet more than ever. A recent study found that 87 percent of SMEs are receiving monthly revenue from their Web site, and 42 percent derive more than a quarter of their monthly revenue from their Internet presence. According to Joel Kocher, CEO of Interland, "We are getting to the point in most small-business categories where it will soon be safe to say that if you're not online, you're not really serious about being in business."

Despite these advances, the Internet and digital technologies still face numerous challenges. For example, international standards for digital and wireless communications are still in flux. As a result, cell phones and other devices that work in the United States are often useless in many parts of Europe and Asia. And, unlike analog systems, electronic bits of data that are zooming through space can be more easily lost, stolen, or manipulated. However, even with these problems, Internet and digital technologies will continue to be a growing global phenomenon. As Andy Grove, former chairman of Intel, stated, "The world now runs on Internet time."

Sources: Anonymous. 2005. SMBs believe in the Web. *eMarketer.com*, www. emarketer.com, May 16. Downes, L. & Mui, C. 1998. *Unleashing the killer app.* Boston: Harvard Business School Press; Green, H. 2003. Wi-Fi means business. *BusinessWeek,* April 28: 86–92; McGann, R. 2005. Broadband: High speed, high spend. *ClickZ Network,* www.clickz .com, January 24; Tapscott, D. Rethinking strategy in a networked world. *Strategy and Business,* Third Quarter, 2001: 34–41; Yang, C. 2003. Beyond Wi-Fi: A new wireless age. *BusinessWeek,* December 15: 84–88.

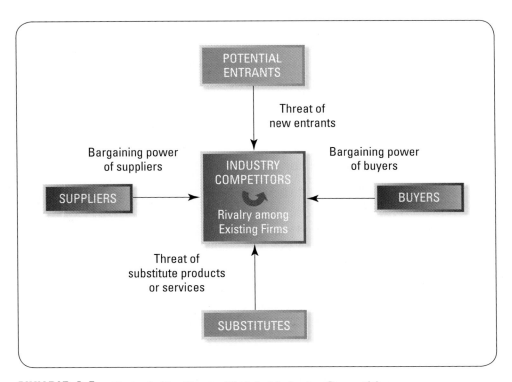

EXHIBIT 4.5   **Porter's Five-Forces Model of Industry Competition**

The Threat of New Entrants The threat of new entrants refers to the possibility that the profits of established firms in the industry may be eroded by new competitors.[11] The extent of the threat depends on existing barriers to entry and the combined reactions from existing competitors. If entry barriers are high and/or the newcomer can anticipate a sharp retaliation from established competitors, the threat of entry is low. These circumstances discourage new competitors. There are six major sources of entry barriers.

Economies of Scale Economies of scale refers to spreading the costs of production over the number of units produced. The cost of a product per unit declines as the absolute volume per period increases. This deters entry by forcing the entrant to come in at a large scale and risk strong reaction from existing firms or come in at a small scale and accept a cost disadvantage. Both are undesirable options.

Product Differentiation When existing competitors have strong brand identification and customer loyalty, differentiation creates a barrier to entry by forcing entrants to spend heavily to overcome existing customer loyalties.

Capital Requirements The need to invest large financial resources to compete creates a barrier to entry, especially if the capital is required for risky or unrecoverable up-front advertising or research and development (R&D).

Switching Costs A barrier to entry is created by the existence of one-time costs that the buyer faces when switching from one supplier's product or service to another.

Access to Distribution Channels The new entrant's need to secure distribution for its product can create a barrier to entry.

Cost Disadvantages Independent of Scale Some existing competitors may have advantages that are independent of size or economies of scale. These derive from:

- Proprietary products
- Favorable access to raw materials
- Government subsidies
- Favorable government policies

In an environment where few, if any, of these entry barriers are present, the threat of new entry is high. For example, if a new firm can launch its business with a low capital investment and operate efficiently despite its small scale of operation, it is likely to be a threat. One company that failed because of low entry barriers in an industry is ProCD.[12] You have probably never heard of this company. It didn't last very long. ProCD provides an example of a firm that failed because it entered an industry with very low entry barriers.

The story begins in 1986 when Nynex (a former Baby Bell company) issued the first electronic phone book, a compact disk containing all listings for the New York City area. It charged $10,000 per copy and sold the CDs to the FBI, IRS, and other large commercial and government organizations. James Bryant, the Nynex executive in charge of the project, smelled a fantastic business opportunity. He quit Nynex and set up his own firm, ProCD, with the ambitious goal of producing an electronic directory covering the entire United States.

As expected, the telephone companies, fearing an attack on their highly profitable Yellow Pages business, refused to license digital copies of their listings to this upstart.

Bryant was not deterred. He traveled to Beijing and hired Chinese workers at $3.50 a day to type every listing from every U.S. telephone book into a database. The result contained more than 70 million phone numbers and was used to create a master disk that enabled ProCD to make hundreds of thousands of copies. Each CD sold for hundreds of dollars and cost less than a dollar each to produce.

It was a profitable business indeed! However, success was fleeting. Competitors such as Digital Directory Assistance and American Business Information quickly launched competing products with the same information. Because customers couldn't tell one product from the next, the players were forced to compete on price alone. Prices for the CD soon plummeted to a few dollars each. A high-priced, high-margin product just months earlier, the CD phone book became little more than a cheap commodity.

The Bargaining Power of Buyers Buyers threaten an industry by forcing down prices, bargaining for higher quality or more services, and playing competitors against each other. These actions erode industry profitability.[13] The power of each large buyer group depends on attributes of the market situation and the importance of purchases from that group compared with the industry's overall business. A buyer group is powerful under the following conditions:

- *It is concentrated or purchases large volumes relative to seller sales.* If a large percentage of a supplier's sales are purchased by a single buyer, the importance of the buyer's business to the supplier increases. Large-volume buyers also are powerful in industries with high fixed costs (e.g., steel manufacturing).

- *The products it purchases from the industry are standard or undifferentiated.* Confident they can always find alternative suppliers, buyers play one company against the other, as in commodity grain products.

- *The buyer faces few switching costs.* Switching costs lock the buyer to particular sellers. Conversely, the buyer's power is enhanced if the seller faces high switching costs.

- *It earns low profits.* Low profits create incentives to lower purchasing costs. On the other hand, highly profitable buyers are generally less price sensitive.

- *The buyers pose a credible threat of backward integration.* If buyers are either partially integrated or pose a credible threat of backward integration, they are typically able to secure bargaining concessions.

- *The industry's product is unimportant to the quality of the buyer's products or services.* When the quality of the buyer's products is not affected by the industry's product, the buyer is more price sensitive.

At times, a firm or set of firms in an industry may increase its buyer power by using the services of a third party. FreeMarkets Online is one such third party.[14] Pittsburgh-based FreeMarkets has developed software enabling large industrial buyers to organize online auctions for qualified suppliers of semistandard parts such as fabricated components, packaging materials, metal stampings, and services. By aggregating buyers, FreeMarkets increases the buyers' bargaining power. The results are impressive. In its first 48 auctions, most participating companies saved over 15 percent; some saved as much as 50 percent.

The Bargaining Power of Suppliers Suppliers can exert bargaining power over participants in an industry by threatening to raise prices or reduce the quality of purchased goods and services. Powerful suppliers can squeeze the profitability of firms in an industry so far that they can't recover the costs of raw material inputs.[15] The factors that make suppliers powerful tend to mirror those that make buyers powerful. A supplier group will be powerful in the following circumstances:

- *The supplier group is dominated by a few companies and is more concentrated (few firms dominate the industry) than the industry it sells to.* Suppliers selling to fragmented industries influence prices, quality, and terms.

- *The supplier group is not obliged to contend with substitute products for sale to the industry.* The power of even large, powerful suppliers can be checked if they compete with substitutes.

- *The industry is not an important customer of the supplier group.* When suppliers sell to several industries and a particular industry does not represent a significant fraction of its sales, suppliers are more prone to exert power.

- *The supplier's product is an important input to the buyer's business.* When such inputs are important to the success of the buyer's manufacturing process or product quality, the bargaining power of suppliers is high.

- *The supplier group's products are differentiated or it has built up switching costs for the buyer.* Differentiation or switching costs facing the buyers cut off their options to play one supplier against another.

- *The supplier group poses a credible threat of forward integration.* This provides a check against the industry's ability to improve the terms by which it purchases.

When considering supplier power, we focus on companies that supply raw materials, equipment, machinery, and associated services. But the supply of labor is also an important input to businesses, and labor's power varies over time and across occupations and industries. Currently, the outlook is not very good for semiskilled and unskilled laborers. Annual wage gains before inflation are taken into account—typically a good measure of workers' bargaining clout in the labor market—wages have remained in the 3 percent range.[16] When the CPI averaged around 2 percent, that provided employees with pay increases that exceeded inflation. With higher consumer prices, however, real wage gains (wage increases above the inflation rate) have been virtually nonexistent recently.

Focus on Strategy 4.2 discusses how catfish farmers were able to enhance their bargaining power vis-à-vis their customers—large agribusiness firms—by banding together to form a cooperative.

The Threat of Substitute Products and Services   All firms within an industry compete with industries producing substitute products and services. Substitutes limit the potential returns of an industry by placing a ceiling on the prices that firms in that industry can profitably charge. The more attractive the price/performance ratio of substitute products, the tighter the lid on an industry's profits.

Identifying substitute products involves searching for other products or services that can perform the same function as the industry's offerings. This is a subtle task, one that leads a manager into businesses seemingly far removed from the industry. For example, the airline industry might not consider video cameras much of a threat. But as digital technology has improved and wireless and other forms of telecommunication have become more efficient, teleconferencing has become a viable substitute for business travel for many executives. That is, the rate of improvement in the price–performance relationship of the substitute product (or service) is high.

Teleconferencing can save both time and money, as IBM found out with its "Manager Jam" idea.[17] Currently, with 319,000 employees scattered around six continents, it is one of the world's largest businesses (including 32,000 managers) and can be a pretty confusing place. The shift to an increasingly mobile workplace means many managers supervise employees they rarely see face-to-face. To enhance coordination, Samuel Palmisano, IBM's new CEO, launched one of his first big initiatives: a two-year program exploring the role of the manager in the 21st century. "Manager Jam," as the project was nicknamed, was a 48-hour real-time Web event in which managers from 50 different countries swapped ideas and strategies for dealing with problems shared by all of them, regardless of geography. Some 8,100 managers logged on to the company's intranet to participate in the discussion forums.

Renewable energy resources are also a promising substitute product and are rapidly becoming more economically competitive with fossil fuels. Focus on Strategy 4.3 addresses this critical issue.

The Intensity of Rivalry among Competitors in an Industry

Rivalry among existing competitors takes the form of jockeying for position. Firms use tactics like price competition, advertising battles, product introductions, and increased customer service or warranties. Rivalry occurs when competitors sense the pressure or act on an opportunity to improve their position.

Some forms of competition, such as price competition, are typically highly destabilizing and are likely to erode the average level of profitability in an industry.[18] Rivals easily match price cuts, an action that lowers profits for all firms. On the other hand, advertising battles expand overall demand or enhance the level of product differentiation for the benefit of all firms in the industry. Rivalry, of course, differs across industries. In some instances it is characterized as warlike, bitter, or cutthroat, whereas in other industries it is referred to as polite and gentlemanly. Intense rivalry is the result of several interacting factors, including the following:

- *Numerous or equally balanced competitors.* When there are many firms in an industry, the likelihood of mavericks is great. Some firms believe they can make moves without being noticed. Even when there are relatively few firms, and they are nearly equal in size and resources, instability results from fighting among companies having the resources for sustained and vigorous retaliation.

- *Slow industry growth.* Slow industry growth turns competition into a fight for market share, since firms seek to expand their sales.

FOCUS ON... STRATEGY 4.3

The Growing Viability of Renewable Resources as Substitutes for Fossil Fuels

Renewable resources currently provide just over 6 percent of total U.S. energy. However, that figure could increase rapidly in the years ahead, according to a joint report issued in September 2006 by the Worldwatch Institute and the Center for Progress, entitled: "American Energy: The Renewable Path to Energy Security."

The report indicates that many of the new technologies that harness renewables are, or soon will be, economically competitive with fossil fuels. Dynamic growth rates are driving down costs and spurring rapid advances in technologies. And since 2000, global wind energy generation has more than tripled; solar cell production has risen six-fold; production of fuel ethanol from crops has more than doubled; and biodiesel production has expanded nearly four-fold. Annual global investment in "new" renewable energy has risen almost six-fold since 1995, with cumulative investment over the period nearly $180 billion. The report claims: "With oil prices soaring, the security risks of petroleum dependence growing, and the environmental costs of today's fuels becoming more apparent, the country faces compelling reasons to put these technologies to use on a larger scale."

A November 2006 study by the RAND Corporation is consistent with the aforementioned report. It asserts that the economy of the United States would likely benefit, rather than be slowed, if the nation attained the goal of supplying 25 percent of its energy needs from renewable sources by 2025. The RAND study also says that while most renewable fuels cannot yet compete with fossil fuels, their costs of production are falling steadily. If the trend continues, America's energy mix by 2025 could be far greener and cleaner—without damaging the economy—than most analysts could have anticipated a few years ago. Such developments would also reduce U.S. dependence on oil, which would mean a substantial start on capping greenhouse-gas emissions, which most scientists link to global warming.

Sources: Clayton, M. 2006. Greener, cleaner . . . and competitive. www.csmonitor.com. December 4; and Anonymous. 2006. Renewables becoming cost-competitive with fossil fuels in the U. S. www.worldwatch.org, September 18.

- *High fixed or storage costs.* High fixed costs create strong pressures for all firms to increase capacity. Excess capacity often leads to escalating price cutting.

- *Lack of differentiation or switching costs.* Where the product or service is perceived as a commodity or near commodity, the buyer's choice is typically based on price and service, resulting in pressures for intense price and service competition. Lack of switching costs, described earlier, has the same effect.

- *Capacity augmented in large increments.* Where economies of scale require that capacity must be added in large increments, capacity additions can be very disruptive to the industry supply/demand balance.

- *High exit barriers.* Exit barriers are economic, strategic, and emotional factors that keep firms competing even though they may be earning low or negative returns on their investments. Some exit barriers are specialized assets, fixed costs of exit, strategic interrelationships (e.g., relationships between the business units and others within a company in terms of image, marketing, shared facilities, and so on), emotional barriers, and government and social pressures (e.g., governmental discouragement of exit out of concern for job loss).

Rivalry between firms is often based solely on price, but it can involve other factors. Take Pfizer's market position in the impotence treatment market. Pfizer was the first pharmaceutical firm to develop a drug that treats impotence called Viagra. Doctors quickly wrote tens of millions of prescriptions, and sales skyrocketed. Pfizer wanted to keep competitors from challenging this lucrative position.

In several countries, the United Kingdom among them, Pfizer faced a lawsuit by Eli Lilly & Co. and Icos Corp. challenging its patent protection. These two pharmaceutical firms recently entered into a joint venture to market Cialis, a drug to compete with Viagra. The U.K. courts agreed and lifted the patent.

This opened the door for Eli Lilly and Icos to proceed with challenging Pfizer's market position. Because Cialis has fewer side effects than Viagra, the drug has the potential to rapidly decrease Pfizer's market share in the United Kingdom if physicians switch prescriptions from Viagra to Cialis. If future patent challenges are successful, Pfizer may see its sales of Viagra erode rapidly. With projected annual sales of Cialis at $1 billion, Pfizer has reason to worry. But Pfizer is hardly standing still. It recently doubled its advertising expenditures on Viagra.

Exhibit 4.6 summarizes our discussion of industry five-forces analysis. It points out how various factors such as economies of scale and capital requirements affect each "force."

EXHIBIT 4.6

Competitive Analysis Checklist

	High	Low
Threat of new entrants is high when:	**High**	**Low**
Economies of scale are		X
Product differentiation is		X
Capital requirements are		X
Switching costs are		X
Incumbent's control of distribution channels is		X
Incumbent's proprietary knowledge is		X
Incumbent's access to raw materials is		X
Incumbent's access to government subsidies is		X
Power of buyers is high when:	**High**	**Low**
Concentration of buyers relative to suppliers is	X	
Switching costs are		X
Product differentiation of suppliers is		X
Threat of backward integration by buyers is	X	
Extent of buyer's profits is		X
Importance of the supplier's input to quality of buyer's final product is		X
Power of suppliers is high when:	**High**	**Low**
Concentration relative to buyer industry is	X	
Availability of substitute products is		X
Importance of customer to the supplier is		X
Differentiation of the supplier's products and services is	X	
Switching costs of the buyer are	X	
Threat of forward integration by the supplier is	X	
Threat of substitute products is high when	**High**	**Low**
The differentiation of the substitute product is	X	
Rate of improvement in price–performance relationship of substitute product is	X	
Intensity of competitive rivalry is high when:	**High**	**Low**
Number of competitors is	X	
Industry growth rate is		X
Fixed costs are	X	
Storage costs are	X	
Product differentiation is		X
Switching costs are		X
Exit barriers are	X	
Strategic stakes are	X	

L04   How the Internet and digitally based capabilities are affecting competitive forces and industry profitability.

HOW THE INTERNET AND DIGITAL TECHNOLOGIES ARE AFFECTING THE FIVE COMPETITIVE FORCES

The Internet and other digital technologies are having a significant impact on nearly every industry. These technologies have fundamentally changed the ways business interact with each other and with consumers. In most cases, these changes have affected industry forces in ways that have created many new strategic challenges. In this section, we will evaluate Michael Porter's five-forces model in terms of the actual use of the Internet and the new technological capabilities that it makes possible.

The Threat of New Entrants   In most industries, the threat of new entrants has increased because digital and Internet-based technologies lower barriers to entry. For example, businesses that reach customers primarily through the Internet may enjoy savings on other traditional expenses such as office rent, sales force salaries, printing, and postage. This may encourage more entrants who, because of the lower start-up expenses, see an opportunity to capture market share by offering a product or performing a service more efficiently than existing competitors. Thus, a new cyber entrant can use the savings provided by the Internet to charge lower prices and compete on price despite the incumbent's scale advantages.

Alternatively, because digital technologies often make it possible for young firms to provide services that are equivalent or superior to an incumbent, a new entrant may be able to serve a market more effectively, with more personalized services and greater attention to product details. A new firm may be able to build a reputation in its niche and charge premium prices. By so doing, it can capture part of an incumbent's business and erode profitability. Consider Voice over Internet Protocol (VoIP), a fast-growing alternative to traditional phone service, which is expected to reach 12.1 million U.S. households by 2009.[19] Savings of 20–30 percent are common for VoIP consumers. This is driving prices down and lowering telecom industry profits. A more sweeping implication is that it threatens the value of the phone line infrastructure that the major carriers have invested in so heavily. Clearly, VoIP represents a major new entrant threat to incumbent phone service providers.

Another potential benefit of Web-based business is access to distribution channels. Manufacturers or distributors that can reach potential outlets for their products more efficiently by means of the Internet may be encouraged to enter markets that were previously closed to them. Such access is not guaranteed, however, because of the strong barriers to entry that may exist in certain industries.[20] Nevertheless, Internet and digital technologies are providing many new entrants with more efficient and lower-cost methods of accessing customers.

The Bargaining Power of Buyers   The Internet and wireless technologies may increase buyer power by providing consumers with more information to make buying decisions and by lowering switching costs. But these technologies may also suppress the power of traditional buyer channels that have concentrated buying power in the hands of a few, giving buyers new ways to access sellers. To sort out these differences, let's first distinguish between two types of buyers: end users and buyer channel intermediaries.

End users, as the name implies, are the final customers in a distribution channel. They are the consumers who actually buy a product and put it to use. Internet sales activity that is labeled "B2C"—that is, business to consumer—is concerned with end users. The Internet is likely to increase the power of these buyers for several reasons. First, a large amount of consumer information is available on the Internet. This gives end users the information

Buyer Power in the Book Industry: The Role of the Internet

The $25 billion book publishing industry illustrates some of the changes brought on by the Internet that have affected buying power among two types of buyers—end users and buyer channel intermediaries. Prior to the Internet, book publishers worked primarily through large distributors. These intermediaries such as Tennessee-based Ingram, one of the largest and most powerful distributors, exercised strong control over the movement of books from publishers to bookstores. This power was especially strong relative to small, independent publishers who often found it difficult to get their books into bookstores and in front of potential customers.

The Internet has significantly changed these relationships. Publishers can now negotiate distribution agreements directly with online retailers such as Amazon and Books-A-Million. Such online bookstores now account for about $4 billion in annual sales. And small publishers can use the Internet to sell directly to end users and publicize new titles, without depending on buyer channel intermediaries to handle their books. By using the Internet to appeal to niche markets, 63,000 small publishers with revenues less than $50 million each generated $14.2 billion in sales in 2005, over half of the industry's total sales.

Sources: Hoynes, M. 2002. Is it the same for book sales? *BookWeb.org*, www.bookweb.org, March 20; www.parapublishing.com; Teague, D. 2005. U.S. book production reaches new high of 195,000 titles in 2004, Fiction soars. *Bowker.com*, www.bowker.com, May 24; and Teicher, C. M. 2007. March of the small presses. *Publishers Weekly*, www.publishersweekly.com, March 26.

they need to shop for quality merchandise and bargain for price concessions. The automobile industry provides an excellent example of this phenomenon. For a small fee, agencies such as Consumers Union (publishers of *Consumer Reports*) will provide customers with detailed information about actual automobile manufacturer costs.[21] This information, available online, can be used to bid down dealers' profits. Second, an end user's switching costs are also potentially much lower because of the Internet. Switching may involve only a few clicks of the mouse to find and view a competing product or service online.

In contrast, the bargaining power of distribution channel buyers may decrease because of the Internet. *Buyer channel intermediaries* are the wholesalers, distributors and retailers who serve as intermediaries between manufacturers and end users. In some industries, they are dominated by powerful players that control who gains access to the latest goods or the best merchandise. The Internet and wireless communications, however, make it much easier and less expensive for businesses to reach customers directly. Thus, the Internet may increase the power of incumbent firms relative to that of traditional buyer channels. Focus on Strategy 4.4 illustrates some of the changes brought on by the Internet that have affected the industry's two types of buyers.

The Bargaining Power of Suppliers   Use of the Internet and digital technologies to speed up and streamline the process of acquiring supplies is already benefiting many sectors of the economy. But the net effect of the Internet on supplier power will depend on the nature of competition in a given industry. As with buyer power, the extent to which the Internet is a benefit or a detriment may also hinge on the supplier's position along the supply chain.

The role of suppliers typically involves providing products or services to other businesses. Thus, the term "B2B"—that is, business-to-business—is often used to refer to businesses that supply or sell to other businesses. The effect of the Internet on the bargaining power of suppliers is a double-edged sword. On the one hand, suppliers may find it difficult to hold onto customers because buyers can do comparative shopping and price negotiations so much faster on the Internet and can turn to other suppliers with a few clicks of the mouse. This is especially damaging to supply-chain intermediaries, such as product distributors, who may not be able to stop suppliers from directly accessing other potential business customers. In addition, one of the greatest threats to supplier power is that the

Internet inhibits the ability of suppliers to offer highly differentiated products or unique services. Most procurement technologies can be imitated by competing suppliers, and the technologies that make it possible to design and customize new products rapidly are being used by all competitors.

On the other hand, several factors may also contribute to stronger supplier power. First, the growth of new Web-based business in general may create more downstream outlets for suppliers to sell to. Second, suppliers may be able to create Web-based purchasing arrangements that make purchasing easier and discourage their customers from switching. Online procurement systems, for example, create a direct link between suppliers and customers that reduces transaction costs and paperwork.[22] Third, the use of proprietary software that links buyers to a supplier's Web site may create a rapid, low-cost ordering capability that discourages the buyer from seeking other sources of supply. Amazon.com, for example, created and patented One-Click purchasing technology that speeds up the ordering process for customers who enroll in the service.[23]

Finally, suppliers will have greater power to the extent that they can reach end users directly without intermediaries. Previously, suppliers often had to work through intermediaries who brought their products or services to market for a fee. But a process known as *disintermediation* is removing the organizations or business process layers responsible for intermediary steps in the value chain of many industries.[24] Just as the Internet is eliminating some business functions, it is creating an opening for new functions. These new activities are entering the value chain by a process known as *reintermediation*—the introduction of new types of intermediaries. Many of these new functions are affecting traditional supply chains. For example, delivery services are enjoying a boom because of the Internet. Many more consumers are choosing to have products delivered to their door rather than going out to pick them up. Electronic delivery of products such as tickets to sporting events and electronic postage stamps is also becoming common.

The Threat of Substitutes   Along with traditional marketplaces, the Internet has created a new marketplace; along with traditional channels, it has become a new channel. In general, therefore, the threat of substitutes is heightened because the Internet introduces new ways to accomplish the same tasks.

Consumers will generally choose to use a product or service until a substitute that meets the same need becomes available at a lower cost. The economies created by Internet technologies have led to the development of numerous substitutes for traditional ways of doing business. For example, a company called Conferenza is offering an alternative way to participate in conferences for people who don't want to spend the time and money to attend. The Web site provides summaries of many conference events, quality ratings using an "event intelligence" score, and schedules of upcoming events.[25]

Another example of substitution is in the realm of electronic storage. With expanded desktop computing, the need to store information electronically has increased dramatically. Until recently, the trend has been to create increasingly larger desktop storage capabilities and techniques for compressing information that create storage efficiencies. But a viable substitute has recently emerged: storing information digitally on the Internet. Companies such as My Docs Online Inc. are providing Web-based storage that firms can access simply by leasing space online. Since these storage places are virtual, they can be accessed anywhere the Web can be accessed. This makes it possible for a traveler to access important documents and files without transporting them physically from place to place. Cyberstorage is not free, but it is still cheaper and more convenient than purchasing and carrying additional disk storage.[26]

The Intensity of Competitive Rivalry Because the Internet creates more tools and means for competing, rivalry among competitors is likely to be more intense. Only those competitors that can use digital technologies and the Web to give themselves a distinct image, create unique product offerings, or provide "faster, smarter, cheaper" services are likely to capture greater profitability with the new technology. Such gains are hard to sustain, however, because in most cases the new technology can be imitated quickly. Thus, the Internet tends to increase rivalry by making it difficult for firms to differentiate themselves and by shifting customer attention to issues of price.

Rivalry is more intense when switching costs are low and product or service differentiation is minimized. Because the Internet makes it possible to shop around with a few clicks of the mouse, it has "commoditized" products that might previously have been regarded as rare or unique. Since the Internet eliminates the importance of location, products that previously had to be sought out in geographically distant outlets are now readily available online. This makes competitors in cyberspace seem more equally balanced, thus intensifying rivalry.

The problem is made worse for marketers by the presence of shopping robots ("bots") and infomediaries that search the Web for the best possible prices. Consumer Web sites like mySimon and PriceSCAN seek out all the Web locations that sell similar products and provide price comparisons.[27] Obviously, this hinders a firm's ability to establish unique characteristics and focuses the consumer exclusively on price. Some shopping infomediaries, such as BizRate and CNET, not only search for the lowest prices on many different products but also rank the customer service quality of different sites that sell similarly priced items.[28] Such infomediary services are good for consumers because they give them the chance to compare services as well as price. For businesses, however, they increase rivalry by consolidating the marketing message that consumers use to make a purchase decision to a few key pieces of information over which the selling company has little control.

Exhibit 4.7 summarizes many of the ways the Internet is affecting industry structure. These influences will also change how companies develop and deploy strategies to generate above-average profits and sustainable competitive advantage.

USING INDUSTRY ANALYSIS: A FEW CAVEATS

For industry analysis to be valuable, a company must collect and evaluate a wide variety of information from many sources. As the trend toward globalization accelerates, information on foreign markets as well as on a wider variety of competitors, suppliers, customers, substitutes, and potential new entrants becomes more critical. Industry analysis helps a firm not only to evaluate the profit potential of an industry, but also to consider various ways to strengthen its position vis-à-vis the five forces. However, we'd like to address a few caveats. First, *managers should not always avoid low profit industries (or low profit segments in profitable industries)*. Such industries can still yield high returns for some players who pursue sound strategies. As examples, consider Paychex, a payroll-processing company, and WellPoint Health Network, a huge health care insurer.[29]

> Paychex, with $1.6 billion in revenues, became successful by serving small businesses. Existing firms had ignored them because they assumed that such businesses could not afford the service. When Paychex's founder, Tom Golisano, failed to convince his bosses at Electronic Accounting Systems that they were missing a great opportunity, he launched the firm. It now serves 550,000 businesses—each employing about 17 employees. Paychex's after-tax-return on sales is a stunning 28 percent.
>
> In 1986, WellPoint Health Network (when it was known as Blue Cross of California) suffered a loss of $160 million. That year, Leonard Schaeffer became CEO and challenged the conventional

EXHIBIT 4.7

How the Internet and Digital Technologies Influence Industry

	Benefits Industry (+)	Disadvantages Industry (−)
Threat of New Entrants		• Lower barriers to entry increases number of new entrants. • Many Internet-based capabilities can be easily imitated.
Bargaining Power of Buyers	• Reduces the power of buyer intermediaries in many distribution channels.	• Switching costs decrease. • Information availability online empowers end users.
Bargaining Power of Suppliers	• Online procurement methods can increase bargaining power over suppliers.	• The Internet gives suppliers access to more customers and makes it easier to reach end users. • Online procurement practices deter competition and reduce differentiating features.
Threat of Substitutes	• Internet-based increases in overall efficiency can expand industry sales.	• Internet-based capabilities create more opportunities for substitution.
Intensity of Rivalry		• Because location is less important, the number of competitors increases. • Differences among competitors are harder to perceive online. • Rivalry tends to focus on price and differentiating features are minimized.

Sources: Bodily, S., & Venkataraman, S. 2004. Not walls, windows: Capturing value in the digital age. *Journal of Business Strategy*, 25(3): 15–25; Lumpkin, G. T., Droege, S. B., & Dess, G. G. 2002. E-commerce strategies: Achieving sustainable competitive advantage and avoiding pitfalls. *Organizational Dynamics*, 30 (Spring): 1–17.

wisdom that individuals and small firms were money losers. (This was certainly "heresy" at the time—the firm was losing $5 million a year insuring 65,000 individuals!) However, by the early 1990s, the health insurer was leading the industry in profitability. The firm has continued to grow and outperform its rivals even during economic downturns. By 2006, its revenues and profits were nearly $60 billion and $3 billion, respectively—each figure representing an *annual* increase of over 35 percent for the most recent five-year period.

Second, five-forces analysis implicitly *assumes a zero-sum game, determining how a firm can enhance its position relative to the forces.* Yet such an approach can often be short-sighted; that is, it can overlook the many potential benefits of developing constructive win–win relationships with suppliers and customers. Establishing long-term mutually beneficial relationships with suppliers improves a firm's ability to implement just-in-time (JIT) inventory systems, which let it manage inventories better and respond quickly to market demands. A recent study found that if a company exploits its powerful position against a supplier, that action may come back to haunt the company.[30] Consider, for example, General Motors's heavy-handed dealings with its suppliers:[31]

Apple's iPod: Relationships with Its Complementors

In 2002, Steve Jobs began his campaign to cajole the major music companies into selling tracks to iPod users through the iTunes Music Store, an online retail site. Most industry executives, after being burned by illegal file-sharing services like Napster and Kazaa, just wanted digital music to disappear. However, Jobs's passionate vision persuaded them to climb on board. He promised to reduce the risks that they faced by offering safeguards against piracy, as well as a hip product (iPod) that would drive sales.

However, Apple had a much stronger bargaining position when its contracts with the music companies came up for renewal in April 2005. By then, iTunes had captured 80% of the market for legal downloads. The music companies, which were receiving between 60 and 70 cents per download, wanted more. Their reasoning: If the iTunes Music Store would only charge $1.50 or $2.00 per track, they could double or triple their revenues and profits. Since Jobs knew that he could sell more iPods if the music was cheap, he was determined to keep the price of a download at 99 cents and to maintain Apple's margins. Given iTunes' dominant position, the music companies had little choice but to relent.

Apple's venture into music has been tremendously successful. For the fiscal year ending September 30, 2006, iPod sales had increased to $7.4 billion and other music-related products and services totaled $1.9 billion. These figures represent increases of 69% and 110%, respectively, over the previous year.

Source: Apple Computer Inc. 10-K, December 29, 2006; and, Yoffie, D. B. & Kwak, M. 2006. With friends like these: The art of managing complementors. *Harvard Business Review,* 84 (9): 88–98.

GM has a reputation for particularly aggressive tactics. Although it is striving to crack down on the most egregious of these, it continues to rank dead last in the annual supplier satisfaction survey. "It's a brutal process," says David E. Cole, who is head of the Center for Automotive Research in Ann Arbor. "There are bodies lying by the side of the road."

Suppliers point to one particularly nasty tactic: shopping their technology out the back door to see if rivals can make it cheaper. In one case, a GM purchasing manager showed a supplier's new brake design to Delphi Corporation. He was fired. However, in a recent survey, parts executives said they tend to bring hot new technology to other carmakers first. This is yet another reason GM finds it hard to compete in an intensely competitive industry.

Third, the five-forces analysis also has been criticized for *being essentially a static analysis.* External forces as well as strategies of individual firms are continually changing the structure of all industries. A key role here is played by **complements**—products or services that have a potential impact on the value of a firm's own products or services. Those who produce complements are usually referred to as complementors.[32] Powerful hardware is of no value to a user unless there is software that runs on it. Similarly, new and better software is possible only if the hardware on which it can be run is available. This is equally true in the video game industry, where the sales of game consoles and video games complement each other. Nintendo's success in the early 1990s was a result of their ability to manage their relationship with their complementors. They built a security chip into the hardware and then licensed the right to develop games to outside firms. These firms paid a royalty to Nintendo for each copy of the game sold. The royalty revenue enabled Nintendo to sell game consoles at close to their cost, thereby increasing their market share, which, in turn, caused more games to be sold and more royalties to be generated.

Despite efforts to create win–win scenarios, conflict among complementors is inevitable.[33] After all, it is naïve to expect that even the closest of partners will do you the favor of abandoning their own interests. And even the most successful partnerships are seldom trouble free. Power is a factor that comes into play—as we see in Focus on Strategy 4.5 with the example of Apple's iPod, an enormously successful product.

complements
Products or services that have an impact on the value of a firm's products or services.

A female employee sits at her desk equipped with both an iMac and an iPod. She works on a spreadsheet, uses iTunes, and listens to an iPod.

LO5 The concept of strategic groups and its strategy and performance implications.

strategic groups
clusters of firms that share similar strategies.

STRATEGIC GROUPS WITHIN INDUSTRIES

In an industry analysis, two assumptions are unassailable: (1) No two firms are totally different, and (2) no two firms are exactly the same. The issue becomes one of identifying groups of firms that are more similar to each other than firms that are not, otherwise known as **strategic groups.**[34] This is important because rivalry tends to be greater among firms that are alike. Strategic groups are clusters of firms that share similar strategies. After all, is Kmart more concerned about Nordstrom or Wal-Mart? Is Mercedes more concerned about Hyundai or BMW? The answers are straightforward.[35]

These examples are not meant to trivialize the strategic groups concept.[36] Classifying an industry into strategic groups involves judgment. If it is useful as an analytical tool, we must exercise caution in deciding what dimensions to use to map these firms. Dimensions include breadth of product and geographic scope, price/quality, degree of vertical integration, type of distribution (e.g., dealers, mass merchandisers, private label), and so on. Dimensions should also be selected to reflect the variety of strategic combinations in an industry. For example, if all firms in an industry have roughly the same level of product differentiation (or R&D intensity), this would not be a good dimension to select.

What value is the strategic groups concept as an analytical tool? *First, strategic groupings help a firm identify barriers to mobility that protect a group from attacks by other groups.*[37] Mobility barriers are factors that deter the movement of firms from one strategic position to another. For example, in the chainsaw industry, the major barriers protecting the high-quality/dealer-oriented group are technology, brand image, and an established network of servicing dealers.

The second value of strategic grouping is that it *helps a firm identify groups whose competitive position may be marginal or tenuous.* We may anticipate that these competitors may exit the industry or try to move into another group. This has been the case in recent years in the retail department store industry, where firms such as JCPenney and Sears have experienced extremely difficult times because they were stuck in the middle, neither an aggressive discount player like Wal-Mart nor a prestigious upscale player like Neiman Marcus.

Third, strategic groupings *help chart the future directions of firms' strategies.* Arrows emanating from each strategic group can represent the direction in which the group (or a firm within the group) seems to be moving. If all strategic groups are moving in a similar direction, this could indicate a high degree of future volatility and intensity of competition. In the automobile industry, for example, the competition in the minivan and sport utility segments has intensified in recent years as many firms have entered those product segments.

Fourth, strategic groups are *helpful in thinking through the implications of each industry trend for the strategic group as a whole.* Is the trend decreasing the viability of a group? If so, in what direction should the strategic group move? Is the trend increasing or decreasing entry barriers in a given group? Will the trend decrease the ability of one group to separate itself from other groups? Such analysis can help in making predictions about industry evolution. A sharp increase in interest rates, for example, would tend to have less impact on providers of higher-priced goods (e.g., Porsches) than on providers of lower-priced goods (e.g., Chevrolet Cobalt). The Chevrolet Cobalt customer base is much more price sensitive.

Exhibit 4.8 provides a strategic grouping of the worldwide automobile industry.[38] The firms in each group are representative; not all firms are included in the mapping. We have

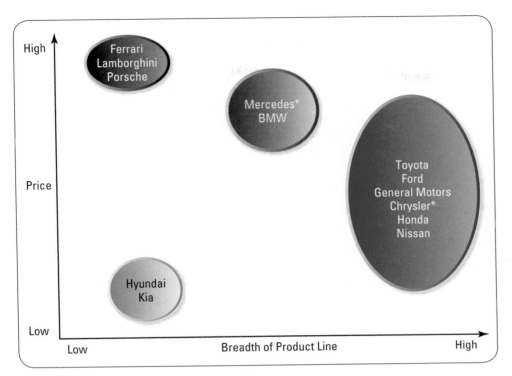

EXHIBIT 4.8   The World Automobile Industry: Strategic Groups

*Chrysler and Mercedes (part of DaimlerChrysler) are separated for purposes of illustration. Note: Members of each strategic group are not inclusive, only illustrative.

identified four strategic groups. In the top left-hand corner are high-end luxury automakers who focus on a very narrow product market. Most of the cars produced by the members of this group cost well over $100,000. Some cost many times that amount. The Ferrari F50 costs roughly $550,000 and the Lamborghini L147 $300,000[39] (in case you were wondering how to spend your employment signing bonus). Players in this market have a very exclusive clientele and face little rivalry from other strategic groups. At the other extreme, in the lower left-hand corner is a strategic group that has low-price/quality attributes and targets a narrow market. These players, Hyundai and Kia, limit competition from other strategic groups by pricing their products very low. The third group (near the middle) consists of firms high in product pricing/quality and average in their product-line breadth. The final group (at the far right) consists of firms with a broad range of products and multiple price points. These firms have entries that compete at both the lower end of the market (e.g., the Ford Focus) and the higher end (e.g., Chevrolet Corvette).

The auto market has been very dynamic and competition has intensified in recent years. Many firms in different strategic groups compete in the same product markets, such as minivans and sport utility vehicles. In the late 1990s Mercedes entered the fray with its M series, and Porsche has a recent entry as well with its Cayenne, a 2004 model. Some players are also going more upscale with their product offerings. Recently, Hyundai introduced its XG300, priced at over $25,000 for a fully loaded model. This brings Hyundai into direct competition with entries from other strategic groups such as Toyota's Camry and Honda's Accord. Hyundai is offering an extensive warranty (10 years, 100,000 miles) in an effort to offset customer perceptions of their lower quality. Perhaps Ford has made the most notable efforts to go upscale. Not content to rely solely on the Lincoln nameplate to attract high-ticket buyers, Ford, like other large players, went on an acquisition binge, purchasing Volvo, Land Rover, Jaguar, and Aston Martin. To further intensify competition, some key automakers are providing offerings in lower-priced segments. Mercedes and BMW, with their C-class and 3-series, respectively, are well-known examples. Such cars, priced in the low $30,000s, compete more directly with products from broad-line manufacturers like Ford, General Motors, and Toyota.

These new products are competing in an industry that has experienced relatively flat unit sales in the first half of this decade.[40] In addition, high-incentive–laden offerings appear to be losing some of their appeal to consumers, and there are higher levels of inventory at dealerships. Further, since manufacturers have maintained, if not increased, production schedules and plant capacity, overall competition should intensify. Don't be surprised, therefore, if rebates and discounting continue on most models. Also on the horizon is the threat of cars from China entering key markets such as the United States.

SWOT ANALYSIS

SWOT analysis
A framework for analyzing a company's internal and external environment, stands for strengths, weaknesses, opportunities, and threats.

In considering the general and competitive environments, our focus was on trends and events that shape an entire industry. With the strategic groups concept, our attention was devoted to the different situations faced by sets of competitors within an industry. We now refine our focus one more step to discuss SWOT analysis, a tool used to examine the situation of an individual company. SWOT stands for strengths, weaknesses, opportunities, and threats. **SWOT analysis** provides a framework for analyzing these four elements of a company's internal and external environment. It provides "raw material"—a basic listing of conditions both inside and surrounding your company.

The **S**trengths and **W**eaknesses portion of SWOT refers to the internal conditions of the firm—where your firm excels (strengths) and where it may be lacking relative to competitors (weaknesses). **O**pportunities and **T**hreats are environmental conditions external to the firm. These could be factors either in the general environment or in the competitive environment. In the general environment, one might experience developments that are beneficial for most companies such as improving economic conditions that cause lower borrowing costs or trends that benefit some companies and harm others. An example is the heightened concern with fitness, which is a threat to some companies (e.g., tobacco) and an opportunity to others (e.g., health clubs). Opportunities and threats are also present in the competitive environment among firms competing for the same customers.

The general idea of SWOT analysis is that a firm's strategy must:

- Build on its strengths.
- Try to remedy the weaknesses or work around them.
- Take advantage of the opportunities presented by the environment.
- Protect the firm from the threats.

Despite its apparent simplicity, the SWOT approach has been immensely popular for a number of reasons. First, it forces managers to consider both internal and external factors simultaneously. Second, its emphasis on identifying opportunities and threats makes firms act proactively rather than reactively. Third, it raises awareness about the role of strategy in creating a match between the environmental conditions and the firm's internal strengths and weaknesses. Thus, SWOT analysis "sets the stage" for determining a firm's strategies. Finally, its conceptual simplicity is achieved without sacrificing analytical rigor.

Managers must analyze the external environment to minimize or eliminate threats and exploit opportunities. We identified two types of environments: the general environment and the competitive environment. The five segments of the general environment are demographic, sociocultural, political/legal, technological, and economic. Trends and events occurring in these segments, such as the aging of the population, higher percentages of women in the workplace, governmental legislation, and increasing (or decreasing) interest rates, can have a dramatic effect on a firm. A given trend or event may have a positive impact on some industries and a negative, neutral, or no impact at all on others.

The competitive environment consists of industry-related factors and has a more direct impact than the general environment. Porter's five-forces model of industry analysis includes the threat of new entrants, buyer power, supplier power, threat of substitutes, and rivalry among competitors. The intensity of these factors determines, in large part, the average expected level of profitability in an industry. A sound awareness of such factors, both individually and in combination, is beneficial not only for deciding what industries to enter but also for assessing how a firm can improve its competitive position. We discuss how many of the changes brought about by the digital economy can be understood in the context of five-forces analysis. The limitations of five-forces analysis include its static nature and its inability to acknowledge the role of complementors. Although we addressed the general environment and competitive environment in separate sections, they are quite interdependent. A given environmental trend or event, such as changes in the ethnic composition of a population or a technological innovation, typically has a much greater impact on some industries than on others.

The concept of strategic groups is also important to the external environment of a firm. No two organizations are completely different nor are they exactly the same. The question is how to group firms in an industry on the basis of similarities in their resources and strategies. The strategic groups concept is valuable for determining mobility barriers across groups, identifying groups with marginal competitive positions, charting the future directions of firm strategies, and assessing the implications of industry trends for the strategic group as a whole.

Finally, SWOT analysis involves a side-by-side comparison of a firm's attributes with the specific external conditions it faces.

LO1

LO2

LO4

LO3

LO5

1. Why must managers be aware of a firm's external environment?
2. Discuss and describe the five elements of the external environment.
3. Select one of these elements and describe some changes relating to it in an industry that interests you.
4. Describe how the five forces can be used to determine the average expected profitability in an industry.
5. What are some of the limitations (or caveats) in using five-forces analysis?
6. Explain how the general environment and industry environment are highly related. How can such interrelationships affect the profitability of a firm or industry?
7. Explain the concept of strategic groups. What are the performance implications?
8. Explain SWOT analysis.

general environment, 80   complements, 99   SWOT Analysis, 102
competitive environment, 85   strategic groups, 100

SUMMARY

SUMMARY REVIEW QUESTIONS

KEY TERMS

1. Imagine yourself as the CEO of a large firm in an industry in which you are interested. Please (1) identify major trends in the general environment, (2) analyze their impact on the firm, and (3) identify major sources of information to monitor these trends. (Use Internet and library resources.)

2. Analyze movements across the strategic groups in the U.S. retail industry. How do these movements within this industry change the nature of competition?

3. What are the major trends in the general environment that have impacted the U.S. pharmaceutical industry?

4. Go to the Internet and look up www.kroger.com. What are some of the five forces driving industry competition that are affecting the profitability of this firm?

REFERENCES

1. Pirovano, T. 2006. Health & wellness trends—the speculation is over. *Retailing Insights,* Spring, 10–15; Anonymous. 2003. Coors goes low carb. November 19: www.realbeer.com: Anonymous. 2004. The "Atkins Effect"—Shrinking waistlines, expanding wallets. January 23: www.frost.com; Lin, J. 2003. Low-carb beer may become the biggest thing since light beer. *Oakland Tribune,* np; Cordova, N. N. 2007. Personal communication. January 12 (Consumer Relations, Coors); and, Day, G. S. & Schoemaker, P. J. H. 2005. Scanning the periphery, *Harvard Business Review,* 83(11): 135–149.

2. Hamel, G., & Prahalad, C. K. 1994. *Competing for the future.* Boston: Harvard Business School Press.

3. Drucker, P. F. 1994. Theory of the business. *Harvard Business Review,* 72: 95–104.

4. The examples of Novell and Silicon Graphics draw on Pickering, C. I. 1998. Sorry . . . Try again next year. *Forbes ASAP,* February 23: 82–83.

5. Challenger, J. 2000. Women's corporate rise has reduced relocations. *Lexington* (KY) *Herald-Leader,* October 29: D1.

6. Tsao, A. 2005. Retooling home improvement. *BusinessWeek.com,* February 14; and, Grow, B. 2004. Who wears the wallet in the family? *BusinessWeek,* August 16:10.

7. Lataif, L. E. 2006. B-Schools and the common good. *BizEd,* March/April: 36–39.

8. Baker, S., & Aston, A. 2005. The business of nanotech. *BusinessWeek,* February 14: 64–71.

9. This discussion draws heavily on Porter, M. E. 1980. *Competitive strategy:* Chapter 1. New York: Free Press.

10 Ibid.

11. For a discussion on the importance of barriers to entry within industries, read Greenwald, B., & Kahn, J. 2005. *Competition demystified: A radically simplified approach to business strategy.* East Rutherford, NJ: Portfolio.

12. The ProCD example draws heavily upon Shapiro, C., & Varian, H. R. 2000. Versioning: The smart way to sell information. *Harvard Business Review,* 78(1): 106–114.

13. Wise, R., & Baumgarter, P. 1999. Go downstream: The new profit imperative in manufacturing. *Harvard Business Review,* 77(5): 133–141.

14. Salman, W. A. 2000. The new economy is stronger than you think. *Harvard Business Review,* 77(6): 99–106.

15. Mudambi, R., & Helper, S. 1998. The "close but adversarial" model of supplier relations in the U.S. auto industry. *Strategic Management Journal,* 19: 775–792.

16. Bernstein, A. 2000. Workers are doing well, but will it last? *BusinessWeek,* October 9: 48.

17. Tischler, L. 2002. IBM: Manager jam. *Fast Company,* October: 48.

18. For an interesting perspective on the intensity of competition in the supermarket industry, refer to Anonymous. 2005. Warfare in the aisles. *The Economist,* April 2: 6–8.

19. McGann, R. 2005. VOIP poised to take flight? *ClickZ.com,* February 23, www.clickz.com.

20. For an interesting perspective on changing features of firm boundaries, refer to Afuah, A. 2003. Redefining firm boundaries in the face of Internet: Are firms really shrinking? *Academy of Management Review,* 28(1): 34–53.

21. www.consumerreports.org.

22. Time to rebuild. 2001. *Economist,* May 19: 55–56.

23. www.amazon.com.

24. For more on the role of the Internet as an electronic intermediary, refer to Carr, N. G. 2000. Hypermediation: Commerce as clickstream. *Harvard Business Review,* 78(1): 46–48.

25. Olofson, C. 2001. The next best thing to being there. *Fast Company,* April: 175; and www.conferenza.com.

26. Lelii, S. R. 2001. Free online storage a thing of the past? *eWEEK,* April 22.

27. www.mysimon.com; and www.pricescan.com.

28. www.cnet.com; and www.bizrate.com.

29. Foust, D. 2007. The best performers. *BusinessWeek,* March 26: 58–95; Rosenblum, D., Tomlinson, D. & Scott, L. 2003. Bottom-feeding for blockbuster businesses. *Harvard Business Review,* 81(3): 52–59; Paychex 2006 Annual Report; and WellPoint Health Network 2005 Annual Report.

30. Kumar, N. 1996. The power of trust in manufacturer–retailer relationship. *Harvard Business Review,* 74(6): 92–110.

31. Welch, D. 2006. Renault-Nissan: Say hello to Bo. *BusinessWeek,* July 31: 56–57.

32. For a scholarly discussion of complementary assets and their relationship to competitive advantage, refer to Stieglitz, N., & Heine, K. 2007. Innovations and the role of complementarities in a strategic theory of the firm. *Strategic Management Journal,* 28(1): 1–15.

33. Yoffie, D. B. & Kwak, M. 2006. With friends like these: The art of managing complementors. *Harvard Business Review,* 84 (9): 88–98.

34. Peteraf, M., & Shanley, M. 1997. Getting to know you: A theory of strategic group identity. *Strategic Management Journal,* 18 (Special Issue): 165–186.

35. An interesting scholarly perspective on strategic groups may be found in Dranove, D., Perteraf, M., & Shanley, M. 1998. Do strategic groups exist? An economic framework for analysis. *Strategic Management Journal,* 19(11): 1029–1044.

36. For an empirical study on strategic groups and predictors of performance, refer to Short, J. C., Ketchen, D. J., Jr., Palmer, T. B., & Hult, T. M. 2007. Firm, strategic group, and industry influences on performance. *Strategic Management Journal,* 28(2): 147–167.

37. This section draws on several sources, including Kerwin, K. R., & Haughton, K. 1997. Can Detroit make cars that baby boomers like? *BusinessWeek,* December 1: 134–148; and Taylor, A., III. 1994. The new golden age of autos. *Fortune,* April 4: 50–66.

38. Csere, C. 2001. Supercar supermarket. *Car and Driver,* January: 118–127.

39. Healey, J. R. 1999. Groomed so as not to marry. *USA Today,* August 6: B1.

40. Smith, J. A. 2005. Auto & Truck Industry. *Value Line,* March 4: 101.

Corporate-Level Strategy

Corporate-level strategy addresses two related issues: (1) what businesses should a corporation compete in, and (2) how can these businesses be managed so they create "synergy"—that is, more value by working together than if they were freestanding units? As we will see, these questions present a key challenge for today's managers. Many diversification efforts fail or, in many cases, provide only marginal returns to shareholders. Thus, determining how to create value through entering new markets, introducing new products, or developing new technologies is a vital issue in strategic management.

We begin by discussing why diversification initiatives, in general, have not yielded the anticipated benefits. Then, in the next three sections of the chapter, we explore the two key alternative approaches: related and unrelated diversification. With related diversification, corporations strive to enter product markets that share some resources and capabilities with their existing business units or increase their market power. Here we suggest four means of creating value: leveraging core competencies, sharing activities, pooled negotiating power, and vertical integration. With unrelated diversification, there are few similarities in the resources and capabilities among the firm's business units, but value can be created in multiple ways. These include restructuring, corporate parenting, and portfolio analysis approaches. Whereas the synergies to be realized with related diversification come from *horizontal relationships* among the business units, the synergies from unrelated diversification are derived from *hierarchical relationships* between the corporate office and the business units.

The last two sections address (1) the various means that corporations can use to achieve diversification and (2) managerial behaviors (e.g., self-interest) that serve to erode shareholder value. We address mergers and acquisitions (M&A), divestitures, joint ventures/ strategic alliances, and internal development. Each of these involves the evaluation of important trade-offs. Detrimental managerial behaviors, often guided by a manager's self-interest, are "growth for growth's sake," egotism, and antitakeover tactics. Some of these behaviors raise ethical issues because managers, in some cases, are not acting in the best interests of a firm's shareholders.

LEARNING FROM MISTAKES

In what *Fortune* magazine claimed was the second biggest merger and acquisition blunder of all time (next only to AOL/Time Warner), Boston Scientific acquired Guidant for $27.3 billion in late 2006. Why did Boston Scientific offer such a huge amount for what at best was a "dubious prize"? In retrospect, this seems like a classic case of the "winner's curse," wherein, in the heat of a bidding war, the winner ends up paying a price that is well above the rest of the market's valuation of the price of an asset. The chances are that the market is right and the winner is wrong.[1] Let's take a brief look at what happened.[2]

On a warm August 2006 evening in Manhattan, the former leaders of medical-device maker Guidant joined their investment bankers in a private room at the tony Bouley restaurant to celebrate the sale of their company to Boston Scientific. Sipping rare Bordeaux, they marveled over the wild bidding war between Boston and rival Johnson & Johnson, which had netted them $27.3 billion, a premium price for their company—at the time reeling from a series of damaging product failures and lawsuits. (Astonishingly, about nine months earlier, on November 15, 2005, J&J and Guidant had agreed on a much lower price of $21.5 billion! But at that point Boston Scientific had entered the fray and a bidding war began.)

Boston Scientific had held its own bash on May 1, 2006, just after the deal had closed (on April 21). Boston investment bankers, Merrill Lynch and Bank of America, organized the feast at the St. Regis Hotel in New York City. However, the day of the event, thunderstorms in the New York area played havoc with the arriving flight schedules. Boston Scientific co-founder Pete Nicholas, CEO Jim Tobin, and CFO Larry Best sat for hours in a drafty hanger on Hanscomb Field in Bedford, Massachusetts, while their lawyers and investment bankers, as well as lower-level executives, partied into the night. The stormy weather turned out to be an omen: while the lawyers and bankers were, of course, well paid for their efforts, the deal turned into to a deluge of bad days for Boston Scientific's top executives.

About two months later, in late June, Boston Scientific issued recalls or warnings on almost 50,000 Guidant cardiac devices and acknowledged that it could take as long as two years to fix its safety problems. Then, on September 21, Boston issued a profit warning that shocked Wall Street, sending its already beaten-down shares plunging another 9.2 percent in a single day.

Since it announced the bid for Guidant on December 2005, Boston's stock had dropped a stunning 46 percent, wiping out $18 billion in shareholder value in a matter of months.

Indeed the deal is arguably the second-worst ever, trailing only the spectacular AOL/Time Warner debacle. "It's like the movie *The Money Pit,*" Matthew Dodds, an analyst at Citigroup, says of Boston's handling of the deal. "Once you've put enough in, you'll go all the way till it's done, regardless of the value."

Boston Scientific is not alone in having a disappointing experience with an acquisition. Many large multinational firms and recent big acquirers have also failed to effectively integrate their acquisitions, paid too high a premium for the target's common stock, or were unable to understand how the acquired firm's assets would fit with their own lines of business. And at times, top executives may not have acted in the best interests of shareholders. That is, the motive for the acquisition may have been to enhance the executives' power and prestige rather than to improve shareholder returns. At times, the only other people who may have benefited were the shareholders of the *acquired* firms—or the investment bankers who advised the acquiring a firms because they collect huge fees upfront regardless of what happens afterward!

Many acquisitions ultimately result in divestiture—an admission that things didn't work out as planned. In fact, some years ago, a writer for *Fortune* magazine lamented, "Studies show that 33 percent to 50 percent of acquisitions are later divested, giving corporate marriages a divorce rate roughly comparable to that of men and women."[3]

L01 How managers can create value through diversification initiatives.

MAKING DIVERSIFICATION WORK: AN OVERVIEW

Not all diversification moves, including those involving mergers and acquisitions, erode performance. For example, acquisitions in the oil industry, such as British Petroleum's purchases of Amoco and Arco, are performing well as is the Exxon-Mobil merger. In the automobile industry, the Renault-Nissan alliance, under CEO Carlos Ghosn's leadership, had led to a quadrupling of its collective market capitalization—from $20.4 billion to $84.9 billion—by the end of 2006.[4] Many leading high-tech firms, such as Microsoft, Cisco Systems, and Intel have dramatically enhanced their revenues, profits, and market values through a wide variety of diversification initiatives, including acquisitions, strategic alliances, and joint ventures, as well as internal development.

So the question becomes: Why do some diversification efforts pay off and others produce disappointing results? Diversification initiatives—whether through mergers and acquisitions, strategic alliances and joint ventures, or internal development—must be justified by the creation of value for shareholders. But this is not always the case. As noted earlier, acquiring firms typically pay high premiums when they acquire a target firm. For example, in 2006 Freeport-McMoRan paid a 30 percent premium to acquire Phelps Dodge in order to create the largest metals and mining concern in the United States. In contrast, you and I, as private investors, can diversify our portfolio of stocks very cheaply. With an intensely competitive online brokerage industry, we can acquire hundreds (or thousands) of shares for a transaction fee of as little as $10.00 or less—a far cry from the 30 to 40 percent (or higher) premiums that corporations typically must pay to acquire companies.

Given the seemingly high inherent downside risks and uncertainties, it might be reasonable to ask why companies should even bother with diversification initiatives. The answer, in a word, is *synergy,* derived from the Greek word *synergos,* which means "working together." This can have two different, but not mutually exclusive, meanings. First, a firm may diversify into *related* businesses. Here, the primary potential benefits to be derived come from *horizontal relationships;* that is, businesses sharing intangible resources (e.g., core competences such as marketing) and tangible resources (e.g., production facilities, distribution channels). Additionally, firms can enhance their market power through pooled negotiating power and vertical integration. For example, Procter & Gamble enjoys many synergies from having businesses that share distribution resources.

Second, a corporation may diversify into *unrelated* businesses. In these instances, the primary potential benefits are derived largely from *hierarchical relationships;* that is, value creation derived from the corporate office. Examples of the latter would include leveraging some of the support activities in the value chain that we discussed in Chapter 3, such as information systems or human resource practices.

Please note that the aforementioned benefits derived from horizontal (related diversification) and hierarchical (related and unrelated diversification) relationships are not mutually exclusive. Many firms that diversify into related areas benefit from information technology expertise in the corporate office. Similarly, firms diversifying into unrelated areas often benefit from the "best practices" of sister businesses even though their products, markets, and technologies may differ dramatically.

Exhibit 5.1 provides an overview of how we will address the various means by which firms create value through both related and unrelated diversification.[5]

RELATED DIVERSIFICATION: ECONOMIES OF SCOPE AND REVENUE ENHANCEMENT

As discussed earlier, **related diversification** enables a firm to benefit from horizontal relationships across different businesses in the diversified corporation by leveraging core competencies and sharing activities (e.g., production facilities and distribution facilities). This enables a corporation to benefit from economies of scope. **Economies of scope** refers to cost savings from leveraging core competencies or sharing related activities among businesses in the corporation. A firm can also enjoy greater revenues if two businesses attain higher levels of sales growth combined than either company could attain independently.

For example, a sporting goods store with one or several locations may acquire retail stores carrying other product lines. This enables it to leverage, or reuse, many of its key resources—favorable reputation, expert staff and management skills, efficient purchasing operations—the basis of its competitive advantage(s), over a larger number of stores.[6] Let's next address how to create value by leveraging core competencies.

LO2 How corporations can use related diversification to achieve synergistic benefits through economies of scope and market power.

related diversification A firm entering a different business in which it can benefit from leveraging core competencies, sharing activities.

economies of scope Cost savings from leveraging core competencies or sharing related activities among businesses in a corporation.

EXHIBIT 5.1

Creating Value through Related and Unrelated Diversification

Source: Reprinted with the permission of the Free Press, a Division of Simon & Schuster Adult Publishing Group, from *Competitive Strategy: Techniques for Analyzing Industries and Competitors* by Micheal E. Porter. Copyright © 1980, 1998 by The Free Press. All rights reserved.

Related Diversification: Economies of Scope

Leveraging core competencies
- 3M leverages its competencies in adhesives technologies to many industries, including automotive, construction, and telecommunications.

Sharing activities
- McKesson, a large distribution company, sells many product lines, such as pharmaceuticals and liquor, through its superwarehouses.

Related Diversification: Market Power

Pooled negotiating power
- The Times Mirror Company increases its power over customers by providing "one-stop shopping" for advertisers to reach customers through multiple media— television and newspapers—in several huge markets such as New York and Chicago.

Vertical integration
- Shaw Industries, a giant carpet manufacturer, increases its control over raw materials by producing much of its own polypropylene fiber, a key input to its manufacturing process.

Unrelated Diversification: Parenting, Restructuring, and Financial Synergies

Corporate restructuring and parenting
- The corporate office of Cooper Industries adds value to its acquired businesses by performing such activities as auditing their manufacturing operations, improving their accounting activities, and centralizing union negotiations.

Portfolio management
- Novartis, formerly Ciba-Geigy, uses portfolio management to improve many key activities, including resource allocation and reward and evaluation systems.

LEVERAGING CORE COMPETENCIES

core competencies
A firm's strategic resources that reflect the collective learning in the organization.

The concept of **core competencies** can be illustrated by the imagery of the diversified corporation as a tree.[7] The trunk and major limbs represent core products; the smaller branches are business units; and the leaves, flowers, and fruit are end products. The core competencies are represented by the root system, which provides nourishment, sustenance, and stability. Managers often misread the strength of competitors by looking only at their end products, just as we can fail to appreciate the strength of a tree by looking only at its leaves. Core competencies may also be viewed as the "glue" that binds existing businesses together or as the engine that fuels new business growth.

Core competencies reflect the collective learning in organizations—how to coordinate diverse production skills, integrate multiple streams of technologies, and market and merchandise diverse products and services. The theoretical knowledge necessary to put a radio on a chip does not in itself assure a company of the skill needed to produce a miniature radio approximately the size of a business card. To accomplish this, Casio, a giant electronic products producer, must synthesize know-how in miniaturization, microprocessor design, material science, and ultrathin precision castings. These are the same skills that it applies in its miniature card calculators, pocket TVs, and digital watches.

For a core competence to create value and provide a viable basis for synergy among the businesses in a corporation, it must meet three criteria.[8]

- *The core competence must enhance competitive advantage(s) by creating superior customer value.* It must enable the business to develop strengths relative to the

Toyota's Diversification into Home Manufacturing

Looking for the biggest Toyota on the market? It's not the Tundra pickups and Sequoia SUVs down at your local dealer. Instead, you'll have to travel to the Toyota factory in Kasugai, a city of 300,000 about three hours west of Tokyo. There, you won't see much in the way of horsepower or acceleration. But they are very roomy—as in multiple bedrooms, a living room, kitchen, bath, and patio.

At Kasugai, Toyota's houses are 85% completed at the plant before being transported by road and built in just six hours. To improve efficiency, Toyota borrows know-how from its fabled Toyota Production System with its principles of just-in-time delivery and *kaizen,* or continuous improvement. Using methods adopted from car production, anticorrosive paint is applied evenly to the houses' steel frames. Just as in all of Toyota's Japan automobile factories, a banner proclaiming "good thinking, good products" hangs from the roof. "We follow the Toyota way in housing," says Senta Morioka, a managing officer at Toyota.

Toyota currently builds about 5,000 prefabricated houses a year. And in 2005, it took a 13% stake in Misawa Homes, another maker of prefabs.

Source: Rowley, I. 2006. Way, way, off-road. *BusinessWeek,* July 17: 36–37.

competition. Every value-chain activity has the potential to provide a viable basis for building on a core competence.[9] At Gillette, for example, scientists developed the Fusion and Mach 3 after the introduction of the tremendously successful Sensor System because of a thorough understanding of several phenomena that underlie shaving. These include the physiology of facial hair and skin, the metallurgy of blade strength and sharpness, the dynamics of a cartridge moving across skin, and the physics of a razor blade severing hair. Such innovations are possible only with an understanding of such phenomena and the ability to combine such technologies into innovative products. Customers have consistently been willing to pay more for such technologically differentiated products.

- ***Different businesses in the corporation must be similar in at least one important way related to the core competence.*** It is not essential that the products or services themselves be similar. Rather, at least one element in the value chain must require similar skills in creating competitive advantage if the corporation is to capitalize on its core competence. At first glance you might think that cars and houses have little in common. However, Focus on Strategy 5.1 discusses how Toyota creates synergies in a business—manufactured homes—that has little to do with its core business, automobiles.

- ***The core competencies must be difficult for competitors to imitate or find substitutes for.*** As we discussed in Chapter 3, competitive advantages will not be sustainable if the competition can easily imitate or substitute them. Similarly, if the skills associated with a firm's core competencies are easily imitated or replicated, they are not a sound basis for sustainable advantages. Consider Sharp Corporation, a $17 billion consumer electronics giant.[10] It has a set of specialized core competencies in optoelectronics technologies that are difficult to replicate and contribute to its competitive advantages in its core businesses. Its most successful technology has been liquid crystal displays (LCDs) that are critical components in nearly all of Sharp's products. Its expertise in this technology enabled Sharp to succeed in videocassette recorders (VCRs) with its innovative LCD viewfinder and led to the creation of its Wizard, a personal electronic organizer.

SHARING ACTIVITIES

As we saw above, leveraging core competencies involves transferring accumulated skills and expertise across business units in a corporation. When carried out effectively, this leads to advantages that can become quite sustainable over time. Corporations also can achieve

Toyota is a world-class automobile producer. This is a Scion, one of its popular products. Toyota has also diversified into many areas, including manufactured homes.

sharing activities
Having activities of two or more businesses' value chains done by one of the businesses.

synergy by **sharing activities** across their business units. These include value-creating activities such as common manufacturing facilities, distribution channels, and sales forces. As we will see, sharing activities can potentially provide two primary payoffs: cost savings and revenue enhancements.

Deriving Cost Savings through Sharing Activities Typically, this is the most common type of synergy and the easiest to estimate. Peter Shaw, head of mergers and acquisitions at the British chemical and pharmaceutical company ICI refers to cost savings as "hard synergies" and contends that the level of certainty of their achievement is quite high. Cost savings come from many sources, including elimination of jobs, facilities, and related expenses that are no longer needed when functions are consolidated, or from economies of scale in purchasing. Cost savings are generally highest when one company acquires another from the same industry in the same country. Shaw Industries, recently acquired by Berkshire Hathaway, is the nation's largest carpet producer. Over the years, it has dominated the competition through a strategy of acquisition which has enabled Shaw, among other things, to consolidate its manufacturing operations in a few, highly efficient plants and to lower costs through higher capacity utilization.

Sharing activities inevitably involve costs that the benefits must outweigh such as the greater coordination required to manage a shared activity. Even more important is the need to compromise on the design or performance of an activity so that it can be shared. For example, a salesperson handling the products of two business units must operate in a way that is usually not what either unit would choose if it were independent. If the compromise erodes the unit's effectiveness, then sharing may reduce rather than enhance competitive advantage.

Enhancing Revenue and Differentiation through Sharing Activities Often an acquiring firm and its target may achieve a higher level of sales growth together than either company could on its own. Shortly after Gillette acquired Duracell, it confirmed its expectation that selling Duracell batteries through Gillette's existing channels for personal care products would increase sales, particularly internationally. Gillette sold Duracell products in 25 new markets in the first year after the acquisition and substantially increased sales in established international markets. Also, a target company's distribution channel can be used to escalate the sales of the acquiring company's product. Such was the case when Gillette acquired Parker Pen. Gillette estimated that it could gain an additional $25 million in sales of its own Waterman pens by taking advantage of Parker's distribution channels.

American Idol: Far More than Just a Television Show

American Idol is one of several of FremantleMedia's (FM) hit television shows. FM is a division of German media giant Bertlesmann, which has approximately $20 billion in revenues. Some of FM's other well-known television shows are *The Apprentice, The Swan,* and at a ripe old age of 48—*The Price Is Right.*

First shown in the United States in June 2002, *American Idol* became a tremendous overnight success. Although the show may be crass and occasionally cruel, it is undeniably brilliant. It's become the ultimate testament to a singular business achievement: FM has become extremely successful at creating truly global programming. In part, that is due to the creative minds at Fremantle; It has some of the best professionals in the business who have a talent for developing shows that appeal to huge populations with different backgrounds and circumstances.

Amazingly, FM, which created *Pop Idol* in Britain in 2001, is now rolling out the show in its 30th country. There's *Belgium Idool, Portugal Idolos, Deutschland Sucht den SuperStar* (Germany), *SuperStar KZ* (Kazakhstan), and of course, the largest and best-known show, *American Idol,* in the United States. *American Idol* is the primary reason that Fremantle's revenue is up 9 percent to more than $1 billion since the show was launched. According to Fremantle's CEO Tony Cohen, "*Idol* has become a national institution in lots of countries." To illustrate, fans cast more than 65 million votes for the *American Idol* finale in May 2004—that is two-thirds as many people as voted in the 2004 U.S. presidential election.

The real key to Fremantle's success is not just adapting its television hits to other countries, but systematically leveraging its core product—television shows—to create multiple revenue streams. In essence, the "Fremantle Way" holds lessons not just for show business but for all business. It enables a company to use its core competence of making products of mass appeal and then to customize them for places with widely varying languages, cultures, and mores. It then milks the hits for every penny through tie-ins, spinoffs, innovative uses of technology, and marketing masterstrokes.

The *Idol* franchise has created a wide variety of new revenue streams for Fremantle's German parent, Bertelsmann. Here's how much *American Idol* has generated in its first two years since its June 2002 launch:

- *Products ($50 million).* Brand extensions range from videogames and fragrances to a planned microphone-shaped soap-on-a-rope. Fremantle receives a licensing fee from manufacturers.
- *TV Licensing ($75 million).* For its rights fee, Fox gets to broadcast the show and, in turn, sell ads and lucrative sponsorships.
- *Compact Discs (CDs) ($130 million).* The most successful performers on the *Idols* shows have sold millions of CDs; more than one-third of the revenue goes to BMG, which, like Fremantle, is an affiliate of Bertelsmann.
- *Concerts ($35 million).* Although artists and their management get the bulk of the take, concerts sell records and merchandise and promote the next *Idol* show.

In addition, Fremantle Licensing Worldwide signed Warner Brothers Publications to produce and distribute *Idol* audition books with CDs for the United States, Canada, United Kingdom, and Australia. The new books/CDs—*Pop Idol* (UK), *Australian Idol,* and *Canadian Idol*—join the *American Idol* book/CD.

Sources: Sloan, P. 2004. The reality factory. *Business 2.0,* August: 74–82; Cooney, J. 2004. In the news. *License!,* March: 48; and, Anonymous. 2005. Fox on top in Feb: NBC languishing at the bottom. www.indiantelevision.com, March 2.

Firms also can enhance the effectiveness of their differentiation strategies by means of sharing activities among business units. A shared order-processing system, for example, may permit new features and services that a buyer will value. Also, sharing can reduce the cost of differentiation. For instance, a shared service network may make more advanced, remote service technology economically feasible.

Focus on Strategy 5.2 discusses how Freemantle Media leverages its hit television show *American Idol* through its core competences and shared activities to create multiple revenue streams.

RELATED DIVERSIFICATION: MARKET POWER

In the previous section, we explained how leveraging core competencies and sharing activities help firms create economies of scale and scope through related diversification. In this section, we discuss how companies achieve related diversification through

market power
firms' abilities to profit through restricting or controlling supply to a market or coordinating with other firms to reduce investment.

market power. We also address the two principal means by which firms achieve synergy through market power: *pooled negotiating power* and *vertical integration*. It is important to recognize that managers have limits on their ability to use market power for diversification, because government regulations can sometimes restrict the ability of a business to gain very large shares of a particular market.

When General Electric announced a $41 billion bid for Honeywell, the European Union stepped in. GE's market clout would have expanded significantly with the deal: GE would have been supplying over one-half the parts needed to build several aircraft engines. The commission's concern, causing them to reject the acquisition, was that GE could use its increased market power to dominate the aircraft engine parts market and crowd out rivals.[11] Thus, while managers need to be aware of the strategic advantages of market power, they must at the same time be aware of regulations and legislation.

POOLED NEGOTIATING POWER

Similar businesses working together or the affiliation of a business with a strong parent can strengthen an organization's bargaining position relative to suppliers and customers and enhance its position vis-à-vis competitors. Compare, for example, the position of an independent food manufacturer with the same business within Nestlé. Being part of Nestlé Corporation provides the business with significant clout—greater bargaining power with suppliers and customers—since it is part of a firm that makes large purchases from suppliers and provides a wide variety of products to its customers. Access to the parent's deep pockets increases the business's strength relative to rivals. Further, the Nestlé unit enjoys greater protection from substitutes and new entrants. Not only would rivals perceive the unit as a more formidable opponent, but the unit's association with Nestlé would also provide greater visibility and improved image.

Consolidating an industry can also increase a firm's market power. This is clearly an emerging trend in the multimedia industry.[12] All of these mergers and acquisitions have a common goal: to control and leverage as many news and entertainment channels as possible. For example, consider the Tribune Company's $8 billion purchase of the Times Mirror Company.

> The merger doubled the size of the Tribune and secured its position among the top tier of major media companies. The enhanced scale and scope helped it to compete more effectively and grow more rapidly in two consolidating industries—newspaper and television broadcasting. The combined company would increase its power over customers by providing a "one-stop shop" for advertisers desiring to reach consumers through multiple media in enormous markets such as Chicago, Los Angeles, and New York. The company has estimated its incremental revenue from national and cross-media advertising will grow from $40 to $50 million in 2001 to $200 million by 2005. The combined company should also increase its power relative to its suppliers. The company's enhanced size is expected to lead to increased efficiencies when purchasing newsprint and other commodities.[13]

VERTICAL INTEGRATION

vertical integration
An expansion or extension of the firm by integrating preceding or successive productive processes.

Vertical integration occurs when a firm becomes its own supplier or distributor. That is, it represents an expansion or extension of the firm by integrating preceding or successive production processes.[14] The firm incorporates more processes toward the original source of raw materials (backward integration) or toward the ultimate consumer (forward integration). For example, an automobile manufacturer might supply its own parts or make its own engines to secure sources of supply. Or it might control its own system of dealerships to ensure retail outlets for its products. Similarly, an oil refinery might secure land leases and develop its own drilling capacity to ensure a constant supply of crude oil. Or it could expand into retail operations by owning or licensing gasoline stations to guarantee customers for its petroleum products.

FOCUS ON... STRATEGY 5.3

Vertical Integration at Shaw Industries

Shaw Industries (now part of Berkshire Hathaway) is an example of a firm that has followed a very successful strategy of vertical integration. By relentlessly pursuing both backward and forward integration, Shaw has become the dominant manufacturer of carpeting products in the United States. According to CEO Robert Shaw, "We want to be involved with as much of the process of making and selling carpets as practical. That way, we're in charge of costs." For example, Shaw acquired Amoco's polypropylene fiber manufacturing facilities in Alabama and Georgia. These new plants provide carpet fibers for internal use and for sale to other manufacturers. With this backward integration,

fully one-quarter of Shaw's carpet fiber needs are now met in-house. In early 1996 Shaw began to integrate forward, acquiring seven floor-covering retailers in a move that suggested a strategy to consolidate the fragmented industry and increase its influence over retail pricing. The accompanying Figure provides a simplified depiction of the stages of vertical integration for Shaw Industries.

Sources: White, J. 2003. Shaw to home in on more with Georgia Tufters deal. *HFN: The Weekly Newspaper for the Home Furnishing Network,* May 5: 32; Shaw Industries. 1993, 2000. Annual reports; and Server, A. 1994. How to escape a price war. *Fortune,* June 13: 88.

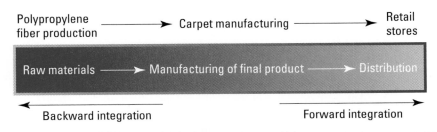

Clearly, vertical integration can be a viable strategy for many firms. Focus on Strategy 5.3 discusses Shaw Industries, a carpet manufacturer that has attained a dominant position in the industry via a strategy of vertical integration. Shaw has successfully implemented strategies of both forward and backward integration.

Benefits and Risks of Vertical Integration Although vertical integration is a means for an organization to reduce its dependence on suppliers or its channels of distribution to end users, it represents a major decision that an organization must carefully consider. The benefits associated with vertical integration—backward or forward—must be carefully weighed against the risks.[15]

The *benefits* of vertical integration include (1) a secure supply of raw materials or distribution channels that cannot be "held hostage" to external markets where costs can fluctuate over time, (2) protection and control over assets and services required to produce and deliver valuable products and services, (3) access to new business opportunities and new forms of technologies, and (4) simplified procurement and administrative procedures since key activities are brought inside the firm, eliminating the need to deal with a wide variety of suppliers and distributors.

Winnebago, the leader in the market for drivable recreational vehicles with a 19.3 percent market share, illustrates some of vertical integration's benefits.[16] The word Winnebago means "big RV" to most Americans. And the firm has a sterling reputation for great quality. The firm's huge northern Iowa factories do everything from extruding aluminum for body parts to molding plastics for water and holding tanks to dashboards. Such vertical integration at the factory may appear to be outdated and expensive, but it guarantees excellent quality. The Recreational Vehicle Dealer Association started giving a quality award in 1996, and Winnebago has won it every year.

The *risks* of vertical integration include (1) the costs and expenses associated with increased overhead and capital expenditures to provide facilities, raw material inputs, and distribution channels inside the organization; (2) a loss of flexibility resulting from the inability to respond quickly to changes in the external environment because of the huge investments in vertical integration activities that generally cannot be easily deployed elsewhere; (3) problems associated with unbalanced capacities or unfilled demand along the value chain; and (4) additional administrative costs associated with managing a more complex set of activities.

In making vertical integration decisions, six issues should be considered.[17]

1. *Is the company satisfied with the quality of the value that its present suppliers and distributors are providing?* If the performance of organizations in the vertical chain—both suppliers and distributors—is satisfactory, it may not, in general, be appropriate for a company to perform these activities themselves. Firms in the athletic footwear industry such as Nike and Reebok have traditionally outsourced the manufacture of their shoes to countries such as China and Indonesia where labor costs are low. Since the strengths of these companies are typically in design and marketing, it would be advisable to continue to outsource production operations and continue to focus on where they can add the most value.

2. *Are there activities in the industry value chain presently being outsourced or performed independently by others that are a viable source of future profits?* Even if a firm is outsourcing value-chain activities to companies that are doing a credible job, it may be missing out on substantial profit opportunities. To illustrate, consider the automobile industry's profit pool. As you may recall from Chapter 3, there is much more potential profit in many downstream activities (e.g., leasing, warranty, insurance, and service) than in the manufacture of automobiles. Not surprising, carmakers such as Ford and General Motors are undertaking forward integration strategies to become bigger players in these high-profit activities.

3. *Is there a high level of stability in the demand for the organization's products?* High demand or sales volatility would not be conducive to a vertical integration strategy. With the high level of fixed costs in plant and equipment as well as operating costs that accompany endeavors toward vertical integration, widely fluctuating sales demand can either strain resources (in times of high demand) or result in unused capacity (in times of low demand). The cycles of "boom and bust" in the automobile industry are a key reason why the manufacturers have increased the amount of outsourced inputs in recent years.

4. *How high is the proportion of additional production capacity actually absorbed by existing products or by the prospects of new and similar products?* The smaller the proportion of production capacity to be absorbed by existing or future products, the lower is the potential for achieving scale economies associated with the increased capacity—either in terms of backward integration (toward the supply of raw materials) or forward integration (toward the end user). Alternatively, if there is excess capacity in the near term, the strategy of vertical integration may be viable if there is the anticipation of future expansion of products.

5. *Does the company have the necessary competencies to execute the vertical integration strategies?* As many companies would attest, successfully executing strategies of vertical integration can be very difficult. For example, Unocal, a major petroleum refiner, which once owned retail gas stations, was slow to capture the potential grocery and merchandise side business that might have resulted from customer

traffic to its service stations. Unocal lacked the competencies to develop a separate retail organization and culture. The company eventually sold the assets and brand to Tosco (now part of Phillips Petroleum).

6. *Will the vertical integration initiative have potential negative impacts on the firm's stakeholders?* Managers must carefully consider the impact that vertical integration may have on existing and future customers, suppliers, and competitors. After Lockheed Martin, a dominant defense contractor, acquired Loral Corporation, an electronics supplier, for $9.1 billion, it had an unpleasant surprise. Loral, as a captive supplier of Lockheed, is now viewed as a rival by many of its previous customers. Thus, before Lockheed Martin can realize any net synergies from this acquisition, it must make up for the substantial business that it has lost.

UNRELATED DIVERSIFICATION: FINANCIAL SYNERGIES AND PARENTING

L03 How corporations can use unrelated diversification to attain synergistic benefits through corporate restructuring, parenting, and portfolio analysis.

With unrelated diversification, unlike related diversification, few benefits are derived from *horizontal relationships*—that is, the leveraging of core competencies or the sharing of activities across business units within a corporation. Instead, potential benefits can be gained from *vertical (or hierarchical) relationships*—the creation of synergies from the interaction of the corporate office with the individual business units. There are two main sources of such synergies. First, the corporate office can contribute to "parenting" and restructuring of (often acquired) businesses. Second, the corporate office can add value by viewing the entire corporation as a family or "portfolio" of businesses and allocating resources to optimize corporate goals of profitability, cash flow, and growth. Additionally, the corporate office enhances value by establishing appropriate human resource practices and financial controls for each of its business units.

CORPORATE PARENTING AND RESTRUCTURING

So far, we have discussed how firms can add value through related diversification by exploring sources of synergy *across* business units. Here, we will discuss how value can be created *within* business units as a result of the expertise and support provided by the corporate office. Thus, we look at these as *hierarchical* sources of synergy.

Parenting The positive contributions of the corporate office have been referred to as the "**parenting** advantage."[18] Many firms have successfully diversified their holdings without strong evidence of the more traditional sources of synergy (i.e., horizontally across business units). Diversified public corporations such as BTR, Emerson Electric, and Hanson and leveraged buyout firms such as Kohlberg, Kravis, Roberts & Company, and Clayton, Dublilier & Rice are a few examples.[19] These parent companies create value through management expertise. How? They improve plans and budgets and provide especially competent central functions such as legal, financial, human resource management, procurement, and the like. Additionally, they help subsidiaries make wise choices in their own acquisitions, divestitures, and new internal development decisions. Such contributions often help business units to substantially increase their revenues and profits. Consider Texas-based Cooper Industries' acquisition of Champion International, the spark plug company, as an example of corporate parenting:[20]

> Cooper applies a distinctive parenting approach designed to help its businesses improve their manufacturing performance. New acquisitions are "Cooperized"—Cooper audits their manufacturing operations; improves their cost accounting systems; makes their planning, budgeting, and human resource

parenting advantage
The positive contributions of the corporate office to a new business as a result of expertise and support provided and not as a result of substantial changes in assets, capital structure, or management.

systems conform with its systems; and centralizes union negotiations. Excess cash is squeezed out through tighter controls and reinvested in productivity enhancements, which improve overall operating efficiency. As one manager observed, "When you get acquired by Cooper, one of the first things that happens is a truckload of policy manuals arrives at your door." Such active parenting has been effective in enhancing the competitive advantages of many kinds of manufacturing businesses.

restructuring
The intervention of the corporate office in a new business that substantially changes the assets, capital structure, and/or management, including selling off parts of the business, changing the management, reducing payroll and unnecessary sources of expenses, changing strategies, and infusing the new business with new technologies, processes, and reward systems.

Restructuring   **Restructuring** is another means by which the corporate office can add substantial value to a business.[21] The central idea can be captured in the real estate phrase "buy low and sell high." Here, the corporate office tries to find either poorly performing firms with unrealized potential or firms in industries on the threshold of significant, positive change. The parent intervenes, often selling off parts of the business; changing the management; reducing payroll and unnecessary sources of expenses; changing strategies; and infusing the company with new technologies, processes, reward systems, and so forth. When the restructuring is complete, the firm can either "sell high" and capture the added value or keep the business in the corporate family and enjoy the financial and competitive benefits of the enhanced performance.[22]

Loews Corporation, a conglomerate with $18 billion in revenues, competes in such industries as oil and gas, tobacco, watches, insurance, and hotels. It provides an exemplary example of how firms can successfully "buy low and sell high" as part of their corporate strategy.[23]

> Energy accounts for 33% of Loews' $30 billion in total assets. In the 1980s it bought six oil tankers for only $5 million each—during a sharp slide in oil prices. The downside was limited. After all these huge hulks could easily have been sold as scrap steel. However, that didn't have to happen. Eight years after Loews purchased the tankers, they sold them for $50 million each.
>
> Loews was also extremely successful with its next energy play: drilling equipment. Although wildcatting for oil is very risky, selling services to wildcatters is not—especially if the assets are bought during a down cycle. Loews did just that. It purchased 10 offshore drilling rigs for $50 million in 1989 and formed Diamond Offshore Drilling. In 1995 Loews received $338 million after taking a 30% piece of this operation public!

For the restructuring strategy to work, the corporate management must have both the insight to detect undervalued companies (otherwise the cost of acquisition would be too high) or businesses competing in industries with a high potential for transformation.[24] Additionally, of course, they must have the requisite skills and resources to turn the businesses around, even if they may be in new and unfamiliar industries.

Restructuring can involve changes in assets, capital structure, or management.

- *Asset restructuring* involves the sale of unproductive assets, or even whole lines of businesses, that are peripheral. In some cases, it may even involve acquisitions that strengthen the core business.

- *Capital restructuring* involves changing the debt-equity mix, or the mix between different classes of debt or equity. Although the substitution of equity with debt is more common in buyout situations, occasionally the parent may provide additional equity capital.

- *Management restructuring* typically involves changes in the composition of the top management team, organizational structure, and reporting relationships. Tight financial control, rewards based strictly on meeting short- to medium-term performance goals, and reduction in the number of middle-level managers are common steps in management restructuring. In some cases, parental intervention may even result in changes in strategy as well as infusion of new technologies and processes.

Hanson, plc, a British conglomerate, made numerous such acquisitions in the United States in the 1980s, often selling these firms at significant profits after a few years of successful restructuring efforts. Hanson's acquisition and subsequent restructuring of the SCM group is a classic example of the restructuring strategy. Hanson acquired SCM, a diversified manufacturer of industrial and consumer products (including Smith-Corona typewriters, Glidden paints, and Durkee Famous Foods), for $930 million in 1986 after a bitter takeover battle. In the next few months, Hanson sold SCM's paper and pulp operations for $160 million, the chemical division for $30 million, Glidden paints for $580 million, and Durkee Famous Foods for $120 million, virtually recovering the entire original investment. In addition, Hanson also sold the SCM headquarters in New York for $36 million and reduced the headquarters staff by 250. They still retained several profitable divisions, including the titanium dioxide operations and managed them with tight financial controls that led to increased returns.[25]

PORTFOLIO MANAGEMENT

During the 1970s and early 1980s, several leading consulting firms developed the concept of **portfolio management** to achieve a better understanding of the competitive position of an overall portfolio (or family) of businesses, to suggest strategic alternatives for each of the businesses, and to identify priorities for the allocation of resources. Several studies have reported widespread use of these techniques among American firms.[26]

portfolio management
A method of (1) assessing the competitive position of a portfolio of businesses within a corporation, (2) suggesting strategic alternatives for each business, and (3) identifying priorities for the allocation of resources across the businesses.

Description and Potential Benefits   The key purpose of portfolio models was to assist a firm in achieving a balanced portfolio of businesses.[27] This consists of businesses whose profitability, growth, and cash flow characteristics complements each other and adds up to a satisfactory overall corporate performance. Imbalance, for example, could be caused either by excessive cash generation with too few growth opportunities or by insufficient cash generation to fund the growth requirements in the portfolio. Monsanto, for example, used portfolio planning to restructure its portfolio, divesting low-growth commodity chemicals businesses and acquiring businesses in higher-growth industries such as biotechnology.

The Boston Consulting Group's (BCG) growth/share matrix is among the best known of these approaches.[28] In the BCG approach, each of the firm's strategic business units (SBUs) is plotted on a two-dimensional grid in which the axes are relative market share and industry growth rate. The grid is broken into four quadrants. Exhibit 5.2 depicts the BCG matrix. Following are a few clarifications:

1. Each circle represents one of the corporation's business units. The size of the circle represents the relative size of the business unit in terms of revenues.

2. Relative market share, measured by the ratio of the business unit's size to that of its largest competitor, is plotted along the horizontal axis.

3. Market share is central to the BCG matrix. This is because high relative market share leads to unit cost reduction due to experience and learning curve effects and, consequently, superior competitive position.

Each of the four quadrants of the grid has different implications for the SBUs that fall into the category:

- *Stars* are SBUs competing in high-growth industries with relatively high market shares. These firms have long-term growth potential and should continue to receive substantial investment funding.

- *Question Marks* are SBUs competing in high-growth industries but having relatively weak market shares. Resources should be invested in them to enhance their competitive positions.

- *Cash Cows* are SBUs with high market shares in low-growth industries. These units have limited long-run potential but represent a source of current cash flows to fund investments in "stars" and "question marks."

EXHIBIT 5.2
The Boston Consulting Group (BCG) Portfolio Matrix

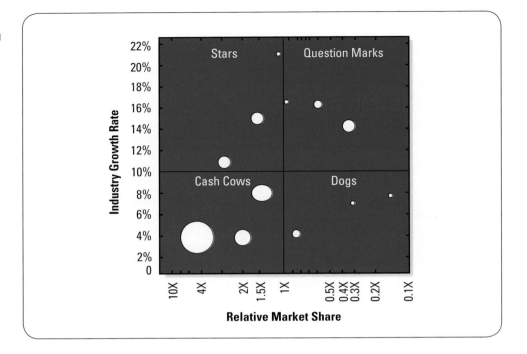

- *Dogs* are SBUs with weak market shares in low-growth industries. Because they have weak positions and limited potential, most analysts recommend that they be divested.

In using portfolio strategy approaches, a corporation tries to create synergies and shareholder value in a number of ways.[29] Since the businesses are unrelated, synergies that develop are those that result from the actions of the corporate office with the individual units (i.e., hierarchical relationships) instead of among business units (i.e., horizontal relationships). First, portfolio analysis provides a snapshot of the businesses in a corporation's portfolio. Therefore, the corporation is in a better position to allocate resources among the business units according to prescribed criteria (e.g., use cash flows from the "cash cows" to fund promising "stars"). Second, the expertise and analytical resources in the corporate office provide guidance in determining what firms may be attractive (or unattractive) acquisitions. Third, the corporate office is able to provide financial resources to the business units on favorable terms that reflect the corporation's overall ability to raise funds. Fourth, the corporate office can provide high-quality review and coaching for the individual businesses. Fifth, portfolio analysis provides a basis for developing strategic goals and reward/evaluation systems for business managers. For example, managers of cash cows would have lower targets for revenue growth than managers of stars, but the former would have higher threshold levels of profit targets on proposed projects than the managers of star businesses. Compensation systems would also reflect such realities. Cash cows understandably would be rewarded more on the basis of cash that their businesses generate than would managers of star businesses. Similarly, managers of star businesses would be held to higher standards for revenue growth than managers of cash cow businesses.

To see how companies can benefit from portfolio approaches, consider Ciba-Geigy.

> In 1994 Ciba-Geigy adopted portfolio planning approaches to help it manage its business units, which competed in a wide variety of industries, including chemicals, dyes, pharmaceuticals, crop protection, and animal health.[30] It placed each business unit in a category corresponding to the BCG matrix. The business unit's goals, compensation programs, personnel selection, and resource allocation were strongly associated with the category within which the business was placed. For example, business units classified as "cash cows" had much higher hurdles for obtaining financial resources (from the corporate office) for expansion than "question marks" since the latter were businesses for which Ciba-Geigy had high hopes for accelerated future growth and profitability. Additionally, the compensation of a business unit manager in a cash cow would be strongly associated with its success in generating cash to fund other businesses, whereas a manager of a question mark business would be rewarded on his or her ability to increase revenue growth and market share. The portfolio planning approaches appear to be working. In 2006, Ciba-Geigy's (now Novartis) revenues and net income stood at $26 billion and $8 billion, respectively. This represents a 22 percent increase in revenues and a most impressive 40 percent growth in net income over the past two years.

Limitations Despite the potential benefits of portfolio models, there are also some notable downsides. First, they compare SBUs on only two dimensions, making the implicit but erroneous assumption that (1) those are the only factors that really matter and (2) every unit can be accurately compared on that basis. Second, the approach views each SBU as a stand-alone entity, ignoring common core business practices and value-creating activities that may hold promise for synergies across business units. Third, unless care is exercised, the process becomes largely mechanical, substituting an oversimplified graphical model for the important contributions of the CEO's (and other corporate managers's) experience and judgment. Fourth, the reliance on "strict rules" regarding resource allocation across SBUs can be detrimental to a firm's long-term viability. For example, according to one study, over one-half of all the businesses that should have been cash users (based on the BCG matrix) were instead cash providers.[31]

To see what can go wrong, consider Cabot Corporation.

> Cabot Corporation supplies carbon black for the rubber, electronics, and plastics industries. Following the BCG matrix, Cabot moved away from its cash cow, carbon black, and diversified into stars such as ceramics and semiconductors in a seemingly overaggressive effort to create more revenue growth for the corporation. Predictably, Cabot's return on assets declined as the firm shifted away from its core competence to unrelated areas. The portfolio model failed by pointing the company in the wrong direction in an effort to spur growth— away from their core business. Recognizing its mistake, Cabot Corporation returned to its mainstay carbon black manufacturing and divested unrelated businesses. Today the company is a leader in its field with $2.5 billion in 2006 revenues.[32]

CAVEAT: IS RISK REDUCTION A VIABLE GOAL OF DIVERSIFICATION?

Analysts and academics have suggested that one of the purposes of diversification is to reduce the risk that is inherent in a firm's variability in revenues and profits over time. In essence, the argument is that if a firm enters new products or markets that are affected differently by seasonal or economic cycles, its performance over time will be more stable. For example, a firm manufacturing lawn mowers may diversify into snow blowers to even out its annual sales. Or a firm manufacturing a luxury line of household furniture may introduce a lower-priced line since affluent and lower-income customers are affected differently by economic cycles.

At first glance the above reasoning may make sense, but there are some problems with it. First, a firm's stockholders can diversify their portfolios at a much lower cost than can a corporation. As we have noted in this chapter, individuals can purchase their shares with almost no premium (e.g., only a small commission is paid to a discount broker), and they don't have to worry about integrating the acquisition into their portfolio. Second,

"Cows" in the BCG matrix as well as "live" cows need nourishment to be productive. Corporations will falter if they "milk" their cows excessively and fail to invest in these business units.

economic cycles as well as their impact on a given industry (or firm) are difficult to predict with any degree of accuracy.

Notwithstanding the above, some firms have benefited from diversification by lowering the variability (or risk) in their performance over time. Consider Emerson Electronic.

> Emerson Electronic is a $16 billion manufacturer that has enjoyed an incredible run—43 consecutive years of earnings growth![33] It produces a wide variety of products, including measurement devices for heavy industry, temperature controls for heating and ventilation systems, and power tools sold at Home Depot. Recently, many analysts questioned Emerson's purchase of companies that sell power systems to the volatile telecommunications industry. Why? This industry is expected to experience, at best, minimal growth. However, CEO David Farr maintained that such assets could be acquired inexpensively because of the aggregate decline in demand in this industry. Additionally, he argued that the other business units, such as the sales of valves and regulators to the now-booming oil and natural gas companies, were able to pick up the slack. Therefore, while net profits in the electrical equipment sector (Emerson's core business) sharply decreased, Emerson's overall corporate profits increased 1.7 percent.

In summary, risk reduction in and of itself is rarely viable as a means to create shareholder value. It must be undertaken with a view of a firm's overall diversification strategy.

LO4 The various means of engaging in diversification—mergers and acquisitions, joint ventures/strategic alliances, and internal development.

THE MEANS TO ACHIEVE DIVERSIFICATION

In the prior two sections, we have addressed the types of diversification (e.g., related and unrelated) that a firm may undertake to achieve synergies and create value for its shareholders. In this section, we address the means by which a firm can go about achieving these desired benefits.

MERGERS AND ACQUISITIONS

mergers
The combining of two or more firms into one new legal entity.

acquisition
The incorporation of one firm into another through purchase.

The rate of **mergers** and **acquisitions** (M&A) had dropped off beginning in 2001. This trend was largely a result of a recession, corporate scandals, and a declining stock market. However, the situation has changed dramatically. Recently, several large mergers and acquisitions were announced. These include:[34]

- Mittal Steel's acquisition of Arcelor for $33 billion.
- Freeport-McMoRan's acquisition of Phelps Dodge for $26 billion.
- BellSouth's acquisition of AT&T for $86.0 billion.

- Sprint's merger with Nextel for $39 billion.

- Johnson & Johnson's $25 billion acquisition of medical device maker Guidant.

- Exelon's acquisition of Public Service Enterprise Group for $12 billion.

- Procter & Gamble's purchase of Gillette for $57 billion.

- Kmart Holding Corp.'s acquisition of Sears, Roebuck & Co. for $11 billion.

Motives and Benefits Growth through mergers and acquisitions has played a critical role in the success of many corporations in a wide variety of high-technology and knowledge-intensive industries. Here, market and technology changes can occur very quickly and unpredictably.[35] Speed—speed to market, speed to positioning, and speed to becoming a viable company—is critical in such industries. For example, Alex Mandl, then AT&T's president, was responsible for the acquisition of McCaw Cellular. Although many industry experts felt the price was too steep, he believed that cellular technology was a critical asset for the telecommunications business and that it would have been extremely difficult to build that business from the ground up. Mandl claimed, "The plain fact is that acquiring is much faster than building."[36]

As we discussed earlier in the chapter, mergers and acquisitions also can be a means of *obtaining valuable resources that can help an organization expand its product offerings and services.* For example, Cisco Systems, a dominant player in networking equipment, acquired more than 70 companies over a recent seven-year period.[37] This provides Cisco with access to the latest in networking equipment. Then it uses its excellent sales force to market the new technology to its corporate customers and telephone companies. Cisco also provides strong incentives to the staff of acquired companies to stay on. In order to realize the greatest value from its acquisitions, Cisco also has learned to integrate acquired companies efficiently and effectively.[38]

Mergers and acquisitions also can *provide the opportunity for firms to attain the three bases of synergy that were addressed earlier in the chapter—leveraging core competencies, sharing activities, and building market power.* Consider Procter & Gamble's $57 billion acquisition of Gillette.[39] First, it helps Procter & Gamble to leverage its core competencies in marketing and product positioning in the area of grooming and personal care brands. For example, P&G has experience in repositioning brands such as Old Spice in this market (which recently passed Gillette's Right Guard brand to become No. 1 in the deodorant market). Gillette has very strong brands in razors and blades. Thus, P&G's marketing expertise enhances its market position. Second, there are opportunities to share value-creating activities. Gillette will benefit from P&G's stronger distribution network in developing countries where the potential growth rate for the industry's products remains higher than in the United States, Europe, or Japan. Consider the insight of A. F. Lafley, P&G's CEO:

> When I was in Asia in the 90s, we had already gone beyond the top 500 cities in China. Today, we're way down into the rural areas. So we add three, four, five Gillette brands, and we don't even have to add a salesperson.

Finally, the addition of Gillette increases P&G's market power. In recent years, the growth of powerful global retailers such as Wal-Mart, Carrefour, and Costco has eroded much of the consumer goods industry's pricing power. A central part of P&G's recent strategy has been to focus its resources on enhancing its core brands. Today, 16 of its brands (each with revenues of over $1 billion) account for $30 billion of the firm's $51.4 billion in total revenues. Gillette, with $10.5 billion in total revenues, adds five brands which also have revenues of over $1 billion. P&G anticipates that its growing stable of "superbrands" will help it to weather the industry's tough pricing environment and enhance its power relative to large, powerful retailers such as Wal-Mart and Target.

Potential Limitations As noted in the previous section, mergers and acquisitions provide a firm with many potential benefits. However, at the same time, there are many potential drawbacks or limitations to such corporate activity.[40]

First, *the takeover premium that is paid for an acquisition is very high.* Two times out of three, the stock price of the acquiring company falls once the deal is made public. Since the acquiring firm often pays a 30 percent to 40 percent premium for the target company, the acquirer must create synergies and scale economies that result in sales and market gains exceeding the premium price. Firms paying higher premiums set the performance hurdle even higher. For example, Household International paid an 82 percent premium to buy Beneficial, and Conseco paid an 83 percent premium to acquire Green Tree Financial. Historically, paying a high premium over the stock price has been a largely unprofitable strategy.

Second, *competing firms often can imitate any advantages realized or copy synergies that result from the M&A.* Thus, a firm can often see its advantages quickly evaporate if it plans to achieve competitive advantage through M&A activity. Unless the advantages are sustainable and difficult to copy, investors will not be willing to pay a high premium for the stock. Similarly, the time value of money must be factored into the stock price. M&A costs are paid up front. Conversely, firms pay for research and development, ongoing marketing, and capacity expansion over time. This stretches out the payments needed to gain new competencies. The M&A argument is that a large initial investment is worthwhile because it creates long-term advantages. However, stock analysts want to see immediate results from such a large cash outlay. If the acquired firm does not produce results quickly, investors often sell the stock, driving the price down.

Third, *managers' credibility and ego can sometimes get in the way of sound business decisions.* If the M&A does not perform as planned, managers who pushed for the deal find that their reputation may be at stake. Sometimes, this can lead these managers to protect their credibility by funneling more money, or escalating their commitment, into an inevitably doomed operation. Further, when a merger fails and a firm tries to unload the acquisition, managers often find that they must sell at a huge discount. These problems further compound the costs and weaken the stock price.

Fourth, *there can be many cultural issues that may doom the intended benefits from M&A endeavors.* Consider, for example, the insights of Joanne Lawrence, who played an important role as vice president and director of communications and investor relations at SmithKline Beecham, in the merger between SmithKline and the Beecham Group, a diversified consumer-oriented group headquartered in the United Kingdom.[41]

> The key to a strategic merger is to create a new culture. This was a mammoth challenge during the SmithKline Beecham merger. We were working at so many different cultural levels, it was dizzying. We had two national cultures to blend—American and British—that compounded the challenge of selling the merger in two different markets with two different shareholder bases. There were also two different business cultures: One was very strong, scientific, and academic; the other was much more commercially oriented. And then we had to consider within both companies the individual businesses, each of which has its own little culture.[42]

Divestment: The Other Side of the "M&A Coin" When firms acquire other businesses it typically generates quite a bit of "press" in business publications such as *The Wall Street Journal, BusinessWeek,* and *Fortune.* It makes for exciting news and one thing is for sure—large acquiring firms automatically improve their standing in the Fortune 500 rankings (since they are based solely on total revenues). However, managers must also carefully consider the strategic implications of exiting businesses.

Divestment, the exit of a business from a firm's portfolio, is quite common. One study found that large, prestigious U.S. companies had divested more acquisitions than they had kept.[43] Well-known divestitures in business history include (1) Novell's purchase of WordPerfect for stock valued at $1.4 billion and later sold to Corel for $124 million, and (2) Quaker Oats' unloading of the Snapple Beverage Company to Triarc for only $300 million in 1997—three years after it had bought it for $1.8 billion! Also, in 2007, DaimlerChrysler sold most of the ownership of Chrysler, which it had acquired a decade earlier.[44]

Divesting a business can accomplish many different objectives.* As the examples above demonstrate, it can be used to help a firm reverse an earlier acquisition that didn't work out as planned. Often, this is simply to help "cut their losses." Other objectives include: (1) enabling managers to focus their efforts more directly on the firm's core businesses;[45] (2) providing the firm with more resources to spend on more attractive alternatives; and (3) raising cash to help fund existing businesses.

In summary, divesting can enhance a firm's competitive position only to the extent that it reduces its tangible costs (e.g., maintenance, investments, etc.) or intangible costs (e.g., opportunity costs, managerial attention) without sacrificing a current competitive advantage or the seeds of future advantages.[46] To be effective, divesting requires a thorough understanding of a business unit's current ability and future potential to contribute to a firm's value creation. However, since such decisions involve a great deal of uncertainty, it is very difficult to make such evaluations. In addition, because of managerial self-interest and organizational inertia, firms often delay divestments of underperforming businesses.

STRATEGIC ALLIANCES AND JOINT VENTURES

A **strategic alliance** is a cooperative relationship between two (or more) firms. Alliances may be either informal or formal, that is, involving a written contract. **Joint ventures** represent a special case of alliances wherein two (or more) firms contribute equity to form a new legal entity.

Strategic alliances and joint ventures are assuming an increasingly prominent role in the strategy of leading firms, both large and small.[47] Such cooperative relationships have many potential advantages. Among these are entering new markets, reducing manufacturing (or other) costs in the value chain, and developing and diffusing new technologies.[48]

Entering New Markets Often a company that has a successful product or service wants to introduce it into a new market. However, it may not have the requisite marketing expertise because it does not understand customer needs, know how to promote the product, or have access to the proper distribution channels.

The partnerships formed between Time Warner, Inc., and three African American–owned cable companies in New York City are examples of joint ventures created to serve a domestic market. Time Warner built a 185,000-home cable system in the city and asked the three cable companies to operate it. Time Warner supplied the product, and the cable companies supplied the knowledge of the community and the know-how to market the cable

divestment
The exit of a business from a firm's portfolio.

strategic alliance
A cooperative relationship between two or more firms.

joint ventures
New entities formed within a strategic alliance in which two or more firms, the parents, contribute equity to form the new legal entity.

---

*Firms can divest their businesses in a number of ways. Sell-offs, Spin-offs, equity carve-outs, asset sales/dissolution, and split-ups are some modes of divestment. In a sell-off, the divesting firm privately negotiates with a third party to divest a unit/subsidiary for cash/stock. In a spin-off, a parent company distributes shares of the unit/subsidiary being divested pro-rata to its existing shareholders and a new company is formed. Equity carve-outs are similar to spin-offs except that shares in the unit/subsidiary being divested are offered to new shareholders. Dissolution involves sale of redundant assets, not necessarily as an entire unit/subsidiary as in sell-offs, but a few bits at a time. A split-up, on the other hand, is an instance of divestiture where the parent company is split into two or more new companies and the parent ceases to exist. Shares in the parent company are exchanged for shares in new companies and the exact distribution varies case by case.

system. Joining with the local companies enabled Time Warner to win the acceptance of the cable customers and to benefit from an improved image in the black community.

Reducing Manufacturing (or Other) Costs in the Value Chain   Strategic alliances (or joint ventures) often enable firms to pool capital, value-creating activities, or facilities in order to reduce costs. For example, Molson Companies and Carling O'Keefe Breweries in Canada formed a joint venture to merge their brewing operations. Although Molson had a modern and efficient brewery in Montreal, Carling's was outdated. However, Carling had the better facilities in Toronto. In addition, Molson's Toronto brewery was located on the waterfront and had substantial real estate value. Overall, the synergies gained by using their combined facilities more efficiently added $150 million of pretax earnings during the initial year of the venture. Economies of scale were realized and facilities were better utilized.

Developing and Diffusing New Technologies   Strategic alliances also may be used to build jointly on the technological expertise of two or more companies in order to develop products technologically beyond the capability of the companies acting independently. STMicroelectronics (ST) is a high-tech company based in Geneva, Switzerland, that has thrived—largely due to the success of its strategic alliances.[49] The firm develops and manufactures computer chips for a variety of applications such as mobile phones, set-top boxes, smart cards, and flash memories. In 1995 it teamed up with Hewlett-Packard to develop powerful new processors for various digital applications that are now nearing completion. Another example was its strategic alliance with Nokia to develop a chip that would give Nokia's phones a longer battery life. Here, ST produced a chip that tripled standby time to 60 hours—a breakthough that gave Nokia a huge advantage in the marketplace.

The firm's CEO, Pasquale Pistorio, was among the first in the industry to form R&D alliances with other companies. Now ST's top 12 customers, including HP, Nokia, and Nortel, account for 45 percent of revenues. According to Pistorio, "Alliances are in our DNA." Such relationships help ST keep better-than-average growth rates, even in difficult times. That's because close partners are less likely to defect to other suppliers. ST's financial results are most impressive. During 2000 its revenues grew 55 percent—nearly double the industry average.

Despite their promise, many alliances and joint ventures fail to meet expectations for a variety of reasons. First, without the proper partner, a firm should never consider undertaking an alliance, even for the best of reasons. Each partner should bring the desired complementary strengths to the partnership. Ideally, the strengths contributed by the partners are unique; thus synergies created can be more easily sustained and defended over the longer term. The goal must be to develop synergies between the contributions of the partners, resulting in a win–win situation for both. Moreover, the partners must be compatible and willing to trust each other. Unfortunately, often little attention is given to nurturing the close working relationships and interpersonal connections that bring together the partnering organizations. The human or people factors are not carefully considered or, at worst, they are dismissed as an unimportant consideration.

INTERNAL DEVELOPMENT

Firms can also diversify by means of corporate entrepreneurship and new venture development. Sony and the Minnesota Mining & Manufacturing Co. (3M), for example, are known for their dedication to innovation, R&D, and cutting-edge technologies. 3M has developed its entire corporate culture to support its ongoing policy of generating at least

The Ritz-Carlton Leadership Center: A Successful Internal Venture

Companies worldwide often strive to be the "Ritz-Carlton" of their industries. Ritz-Carlton, the large luxury hotel chain, is the only service company to have won the prestigious Malcolm Baldrige National Quality Award twice—in 1992 and 1999 (one year after being acquired by Marriott). It also has placed first in guest satisfaction among luxury hotels in the most recent J. D. Power & Associates hotel survey.

Until a few years ago, being "Ritz-Carlton-like" was just a motivational simile. However, in 2000, the company launched the Ritz-Carlton Leadership Center, where it offers 12 leadership development programs for its employees and seven benchmarking seminars and workshops to outside companies. It also conducts 35 off-site presentations on such topics as "Creating a Dynamic Employee Orientation," and "The Key to Retaining and Selecting Talented Employees." (Incidentally, Ritz-Carlton's annual turnover rate among nonmanagement employees is 25 percent— roughly half the average rate for U.S. luxury hotels.)

Within its first four years of operation, 800 different companies from such industries as health care, banking and finance, hospitality, and the automotive industries have participated in the Leadership Center's programs. And to date it has generated over $2 million in revenues. Ken Yancey, CEO of the nonprofit small-business consultancy, Score, says the concepts he learned, like "the three steps of service," apply directly to his business. "Hotels are about service to a client," he says. "And we are too."

To give a few specifics on one of the Leadership Center's programs, consider its "Legendary Service I" course. The topics that are covered include empowerment, using customer recognition to boost loyalty, and Ritz-Carlton's approach to quality. The course lasts two days and costs $2,000 per attendee. Well-known companies that have participated include Microsoft, Morgan Stanley, and Starbucks.

Sources: McDonald, D. 2004. Roll out the blue carpet. *Business 2.0*, May: 53; and Johnson, G. 2003. Nine tactics to take your corporate university from good to GREAT. *Training*, July/August: 38–41.

25 percent of total sales from products created within the most recent four-year period. During the 1990s, 3M exceeded this goal by achieving about 30 percent of sales per year from new internally developed products.

The luxury hotel chain Ritz-Carlton has long been recognized for its exemplary service. In fact, it is the only service company ever to win two Malcolm Baldrige National Quality Awards. It has built on this capability by developing a highly successful internal venture to offer leadership development programs—both to its employees as well as to outside companies. We address this internal venture in Focus on Strategy 5.4.

Compared to mergers and acquisitions, firms that engage in internal development are able to capture the value created by their own innovative activities without having to "share the wealth" with alliance partners or face the difficulties associated with combining activities across the value chains of several companies or merging corporate cultures. Another advantage is that firms can often develop new products or services at a relatively lower cost and thus rely on their own resources rather than turning to external funding. There are also potential disadvantages. Internal development may be time consuming; thus, firms may forfeit the benefits of speed that growth through mergers or acquisitions can provide. This may be especially important among high-tech or knowledge-based organizations in fast-paced environments where being an early mover is critical. Thus, firms that choose to diversify through internal development must develop capabilities that allow them to move quickly from initial opportunity recognition to market introduction.

HOW MANAGERIAL MOTIVES CAN ERODE VALUE CREATION

L05 Managerial behaviors that can erode the creation of value.

Thus far in the chapter we have implicitly assumed that CEOs and top executives are "rational beings"; that is, they act in the best interests of shareholders to maximize long-term shareholder value. In the real world, however, this is not the case. Frequently, they may act in their own self-interest. Next, we address some managerial motives that can

Cornelius Vanderbilt: Going to Great Lengths to Correct a Wrong!

Cornelius Vanderbilt's legendary ruthlessness set a bar for many titans to come. Back in 1853, the Commodore took his first vacation, an extended voyage to Europe aboard his yacht. He was in for a big surprise when he returned. Two of his associates had taken the power of attorney that he had left them and sold his interest in his steamship concern, Accessory Transit Company, to themselves.

"Gentlemen," he wrote, in a classic battle cry, "you have undertaken to cheat me. I won't sue you, for the law is too slow. I'll ruin you." He converted his yacht to a passenger ship to compete with them and added other vessels. He started a new line, appropriately named *Opposition*. Before long, he bought his way back in and regained control of the company.

Source: McGregor, J. 2007. Sweet revenge. *BusinessWeek*, January 22: 64–70.

serve to erode, rather than enhance, value creation. These include "growth for growth's sake," excessive egotism, and the creation of a wide variety of antitakeover tactics.

GROWTH FOR GROWTH'S SAKE

There are huge incentives for executives to increase the size of their firm, and many of these are hardly consistent with increasing shareholder wealth. Top managers, including the CEO, of larger firms typically enjoy more prestige, higher rankings for their companies on the Fortune 500 list (which is based on revenues, not profits), greater incomes, more job security, and so on. There is also the excitement and associated recognition of making a major acquisition. As noted by Harvard's Michael Porter, "There's a tremendous allure to mergers and acquisitions. It's the big play, the dramatic gesture. With one stroke of the pen you can add billions to size, get a front-page story, and create excitement in markets."[50]

At times, executives' overemphasis on growth can result in a plethora of ethical lapses, which can have disastrous outcomes for their companies. A good example (of bad practice) is Joseph Bernardino's leadership at Andersen Worldwide. Bernardino had a chance early on to take a hard line on ethics and quality in the wake of earlier scandals at clients such as Waste Management and Sunbeam. Instead, according to former executives, he put too much emphasis on revenue growth. Consequently, the firm's reputation quickly eroded when it audited and signed off on the highly flawed financial statements of such infamous firms as Enron, Global Crossing, and WorldCom. WorldCom, in fact, is recognized as the biggest financial fraud of all time. Bernardino ultimately resigned in disgrace in March 2002, and his firm was dissolved later that year.[51]

EGOTISM

Most would agree that there is nothing wrong with ego, per se. After all, a healthy ego helps make a leader confident, clearheaded, and able to cope with change. CEOs, by their very nature, are typically fiercely competitive people in the office as well as on the tennis court or golf course. However, sometimes when pride is at stake, individuals will go to great lengths to win. Such behavior, of course, is not a new phenomenon. We discuss the case of Cornelius Vanderbilt, one of the original American moguls, in Focus on Strategy 5.5.

The business press has included many stories of how egotism and greed have infiltrated organizations. Some incidents are considered rather astonishing, such as Tyco's former (and now convicted) CEO Dennis Kozlowski's well-chronicled purchase of a $6,000 shower curtain and vodka-spewing, full-size replica of Michaelangelo's David.[52] Other well-known examples of power grabs and extraordinary consumption of compensation and perks include executives at Enron, the Rigas family who were convicted of defrauding Adelphia of roughly $1 billion, former CEO Bernie Ebbers's $408 million loan from WorldCom, and so on.

Poison Pills: How Antitakeover Strategies Can Raise Ethical Issues

Poison pills are almost always good for managers but not always so good for shareholders. They present managers with an ethical dilemma: How can they balance their own interests with their fiduciary responsibility to shareholders?

Here's how poison pills work. In the event of a takeover bid, existing shareholders have the option to buy additional shares of stock at a discount to the current market price. This action is typically triggered when a new shareholder rapidly accumulates more than a set percentage of ownership (usually 20 percent) through stock purchases. When this happens, managers fear that the voting rights and increased proportional ownership of the new shareholder might be a ploy to make a takeover play.

To protect existing shareholders, stock is offered at a discount, but only to existing shareholders. As the existing owners buy the discounted stock, the stock is diluted (i.e., there are now more shares, each with a lower value). If there has been a takeover offer at a set price per share, the overall price for the company immediately goes up since there are now more shares. This assures stockholders of receiving a fair price for the company.

Sounds good, but here's the problem. Executives on the company's board of directors retain the right to allow the stock discount. The discounted stock price for existing shareholders may or may not be activated when a takeover is imminent. This brings in the issue of motive: Why did the board enact the poison pill provision in the first place? At times, it may have been simply to protect the existing shareholders. At other times, it may have been to protect the interests of those on the board of directors. In other words, the board may have enacted the rule not to protect shareholders, but to protect their own jobs.

When the board receives a takeover offer, the offering company will be aware of the poison pill provision. This gives negotiating power to board members of the takeover target. They may include as part of the negotiation that the new company keep them as members of the board. In exchange, the board members would not enact the discounted share price; existing stockholders would lose, but the jobs of the board members would be protected.

When a company offers poison pill provisions to shareholders, the shareholders should keep in mind that things are not always as they seem. The motives may reflect concern for shareholders. But on the other hand . . .

Sources: Vicente, J. P. 2001. Toxic treatment: Poison pills proliferate as Internet firms worry they've become easy marks. *Red Herring*, May 1 and 15: 195; Chakraborty, A., & Baum, C. F. 1998. Poison pills, optimal contracting and the market for corporate control: Evidence from Fortune 500 firms. *International Journal of Finance*, 10(3): 1120–1138; Sundaramurthy, C. 1996. Corporate governance within the context of antitakeover provisions. *Strategic Management Journal*, 17: 377–394.

ANTITAKEOVER TACTICS

Unfriendly or hostile takeovers can occur when a company's stock becomes undervalued. A competing organization can buy the outstanding stock of a takeover candidate in sufficient quantity to become a large shareholder. Then it makes a tender offer to gain full control of the company. If the shareholders accept the offer, the hostile firm buys the target company and either fires the target firm's management team or strips them of their power. For this reason, antitakeover tactics are common. Three of these are greenmail, golden parachutes, and poison pills.[53]

The first, *greenmail,* is an effort by the target firm to prevent an impending takeover. When a hostile firm buys a large block of outstanding target company stock and the target firm's management feels that a tender offer is impending, they offer to buy the stock back from the hostile company at a higher price than the unfriendly company paid for it. The positive side is that this often prevents a hostile takeover. On the downside, the same price is not offered to preexisting shareholders. However, it protects the jobs of the target firm's management.

The second strategy is a *golden parachute.* A golden parachute is a prearranged contract with managers specifying that, in the event of a hostile takeover, the target firm's managers will be paid a significant severance package. Although top managers lose their jobs, the golden parachute provisions protect their income.

Focus on Strategy 5.6 illustrates how "poison pills" are used to prevent takeovers. *Poison pills* are means by which a company can give shareholders certain rights in the event of a takeover by another firm. Poison pills are also known as *shareholder rights plans.*

As you can easily see, antitakeover tactics often raise interesting ethical issues.

LO1   A key challenge for today's managers is to create "synergy" when engaging in diversification activities. As we discussed in this chapter, corporate managers do not, in general, have a very good track record in creating value in such endeavors when it comes to mergers and acquisitions. Among the factors that serve to erode shareholder values are paying an excessive premium for the target firm, failing to integrate the activities of the newly acquired businesses into the corporate family, and undertaking diversification initiatives that are too easily imitated by the competition.

LO2   We addressed two major types of corporate-level strategy: related and unrelated diversification. With *related diversification* the corporation strives to enter into areas in which key resources and capabilities of the corporation can be shared or leveraged. Synergies come from horizontal relationships between business units. Cost savings and enhanced revenues can be derived from two major sources. First, economies of scope can be achieved from the leveraging of core competencies and the sharing of activities. Second, market power can be attained from greater, or pooled, negotiating power and from vertical integration.

LO3   When firms undergo *unrelated diversification* they enter product markets that are dissimilar to their present businesses. Thus, there is generally little opportunity to either leverage core competencies or share activities across business units. Here, synergies are created from vertical relationships between the corporate office and the individual business units. With unrelated diversification, the primary ways to create value are corporate restructuring and parenting, as well as the use of portfolio analysis techniques.

LO4   Corporations have three primary means of diversifying their product markets—mergers and acquisitions, joint ventures/strategic alliances, and internal development. There are key trade-offs associated with each of these. For example, mergers and acquisitions are typically the quickest means to enter new markets and provide the corporation with a high level of control over the acquired business. However, with the expensive premiums that often need to be paid to the shareholders of the target firm and the challenges associated with integrating acquisitions, they can also be quite expensive. Not surprisingly, many poorly performing acquisitions are subsequently divested. At times, however, divestitures can help firms to refocus their efforts and generate resources. Strategic alliances and joint ventures between two or more firms, on the other hand, may be a means of reducing risk since they involve the sharing and combining of resources. But such joint initiatives also provide a firm with less control (than it would have with an acquisition) since governance is shared between two independent entities. Also, there is a limit to the potential upside for each partner because returns must be shared as well. Finally, with internal development, a firm is able to capture all of the value from its initiatives (as opposed to sharing it with a merger or alliance partner). However, diversification by means of internal development can be very time-consuming—a disadvantage that becomes even more important in fast-paced competitive environments.

LO5   Finally, some managerial behaviors may serve to erode shareholder returns. Among these are "growth for growth's sake," egotism, and antitakeover tactics. Some of these—particularly antitakeover tactics—also raise ethical considerations because the managers of the firm are not acting in the best interests of the shareholders.

1.   Discuss how managers can create value for their firm through diversification efforts.

2.   What are some of the reasons that many diversification efforts fail to achieve desired outcomes?

3.   How can companies benefit from related diversification? Unrelated diversification? What are some of the key concepts that can explain such success?

4.   What are some of the important ways in which a firm can restructure a business?

5.   Discuss some of the various means that firms can use to diversify. What are the pros and cons associated with each of these?

6.   Discuss some of the actions that managers may engage in to erode shareholder value.

1. What were some of the largest mergers and acquisitions over the last two years? What was the rationale for these actions? Do you think they will be successful? Explain.

2. Discuss some examples from business practice in which an executive's actions appear to be in his or her self-interest rather than serving the corporation's well-being.

3. Discuss some of the challenges that managers must overcome in making strategic alliances successful. What are some strategic alliances with which you are familiar? Were they successful or not? Explain.

4. Use the Internet and select a company that has recently undertaken diversification into new product markets. What do you feel were some of the reasons for this diversification (e.g., leveraging core competencies, sharing infrastructures)?

1. For a detailed discussion of the phenomenon of the winner's curse, refer to Thaler, R. H. 1992. *The winner's curse.* The Free Press: New York.

2. This example draws upon Tully, S. 2006. The (second) worst deal ever. *Fortune,* October 2006: 102–119; and Levenson, E. 2006. Buyer's remorse. *Fortune,* October 16: 12.

3. Pare, T. P. 1994. The new merger boom. *Fortune,* November 28: 96.

4. Ghosn, C. 2006. Inside the alliance: The win–win nature of a unique business mode. Address to the Detroit Economic Club , November 16.

5. Our framework draws upon a variety of sources, including Goold, M., & Campbell, A. 1998. Desperately seeking synergy. *Harvard Business Review,* 76(5): 131–143; Porter, M. E. 1987. From advantage to corporate strategy. *Harvard Business Review,* 65(3): 43–59; and Hitt, M. A., Ireland, R. D., & Hoskisson, R. E. 2001. *Strategic management: competitiveness and globalization* (4th ed.). Cincinnati, OH: South-Western.

6. Collis, D. J., & Montgomery, C. A. 1987. *Corporate strategy: Resources and the scope of the firm.* New York: McGraw-Hill.

7. This imagery of the corporation as a tree and related discussion draws on Prahalad, C. K., & Hamel, G. 1990. The core competence of the corporation. *Harvard Business Review,* 68(3): 79–91. Parts of this section also draw on Picken, J. C., & Dess, G. G. 1997. *Mission critical:* chap. 5. Burr Ridge, IL: Irwin Professional Publishing.

8. This section draws on Prahalad & Hamel, op. cit.; and Porter, op. cit.

9. A recent study that investigates the relationship between a firm's technology resources, diversification, and performance can be found in Miller, D. J. 2004. Firms' technological resources and the performance effects of diversification. A longitudinal study. *Strategic Management Journal,* 25: 1097–1119.

10. Collis & Montgomery, op. cit.

11. Hill, A., & Hargreaves, D. 2001. Turbulent times for GE–Honeywell deal. *Financial Times,* February 28: 26.

12. Lowry, T. 2001. Media. *BusinessWeek,* January 8: 100–101.

13. The Tribune Company. 1999. *Annual report.*

14. This section draws on Hrebiniak, L. G., & Joyce, W. F. 1984. *Implementing strategy.* New York: MacMillan; and Oster, S. M. 1994. *Modern competitive analysis.* New York: Oxford University Press.

15. The discussion of the benefits and costs of vertical integration draws on Hax, A. C., & Majluf, N. S. 1991. *The strategy concept and process: A pragmatic approach:* 139. Englewood Cliffs, NJ: Prentice Hall.

16. Fahey, J. 2005. Gray winds. *Forbes.* January 10: 143.

17. This discussion draws on Oster, op. cit.; and Harrigan, K. 1986. Matching vertical integration strategies to competitive conditions. *Strategic Management Journal,* 7(6): 535–556.

18. Campbell, A., Goold, M., & Alexander, M. 1995. Corporate strategy: The quest for parenting advantage. *Harvard Business Review,* 73(2): 120–132; and Picken & Dess, op. cit.

19. Anslinger, P. A., & Copeland, T. E. 1996. Growth through acquisition: A fresh look. *Harvard Business Review,* 74(1): 126–135.

20. Campbell et al., op. cit.

21. This section draws on Porter, op. cit.; and Hambrick, D. C. 1985. Turnaround strategies. In Guth, W. D. (Ed.). *Handbook of business strategy:* 10-1–10-32. Boston: Warren, Gorham & Lamont.

22. There is an important delineation between companies that are operated for a long-term profit and those that are bought and sold for short-term gains. The latter are sometimes referred to as "holding companies" and are generally more concerned about financial issues than strategic issues.

23. Lenzner, R. 2007. High on Loews. *Forbes,* February 26: 98–102.

24. Casico. W. F. 2002. Strategies for responsible restructuring. *Academy of Management Executive,* 16(3): 80–91; and Singh, H. 1993. Challenges in researching corporate restructuring. *Journal of Management Studies,* 30(1): 147–172.

25. Cusack, M. 1987. *Hanson Trust: A review of the company and its prospects.* London: Hoare Govett.

26. Hax & Majluf, op. cit. By 1979, 45 percent of Fortune 500 companies employed some form of portfolio analysis, according to Haspelagh, P. 1982. Portfolio planning: Uses and limits. *Harvard Busines Review,* 60: 58–73. A later study conducted in 1993 found that over 40 percent of the respondents used portfolio analysis techniques, but the level of usage was expected to increase to more than 60 percent in the near future: Rigby, D. K. 1994. Managing the management tools. *Planning Review,* September–October: 20–24.

27. Goold, M., & Luchs, K. 1993. Why diversify? Four decades of management thinking. *Academy of Management Executive,* 7(3): 7–25.

28. Other approaches include the industry attractiveness–business strength matrix developed jointly by General Electric and McKinsey and Company, the life-cycle matrix developed by Arthur D. Little, and the profitability matrix proposed by Marakon. For an extensive review, refer to Hax & Majluf, op. cit.: 182–194.

29. Porter, op. cit.: 49–52.

30. Collis, D. J. 1995. Portfolio planning at Ciba-Geigy and the Newport investment proposal. Harvard Business School Case No. 9-795-040. Novartis AG was created in 1996 by the merger of Ciba-Geigy and Sandoz.

31. Buzzell, R. D., & Gale, B. T. 1987. *The PIMS principles: linking strategy to performance.* New York: Free Press; and Miller, A., & Dess, G. G. 1996. *Strategic management,* (2nd ed.). New York: McGraw-Hill.

32. Picken & Dess, op. cit.; Cabot Corporation. 2001. 10-Q filing, Securities and Exchange Commission, May 14.

33. Koudsi, S. 2001. Remedies for an economic hangover. *Fortune,* June 25: 130–139.

34. Coy, P., Thornton, E., Arndt, M., & Grow, B. 2005. Shake, rattle, and merge. *BusinessWeek,* January 10: 32–35; and Anonymous. 2005. Love is in the air. *Economist* , February 5: 9.

35. For an interesting study of the relationship between mergers and a firm's product-market strategies, refer to Krisnan, R. A., Joshi, S., & Krishnan, H. 2004. The influence of mergers on firms' product-mix strategies. *Strategic Management Journal,* 25: 587–611.

36. Carey, D., moderator. 2000. A CEO roundtable on making mergers succeed. *Harvard Business Review,* 78(3): 146.

37. Shinal, J. 2001. Can Mike Volpi make Cisco sizzle again? *BusinessWeek,* February 26: 102–104; Kambil, A. Eselius, E. D., & Monteiro, K. A. 2000. Fast venturing: The quick way to start Web businesses. *Sloan Management Review,* 41(4): 55–67; and Elstrom, P. 2001. Sorry, Cisco: The old answers won't work. *BusinessWeek,* April 30: 39.

38. Like many high-tech firms during the economic slump that began in mid-2000, Cisco Systems has experienced declining performance.

On April 16, 2001, it announced that its revenues for the quarter closing April 30 would drop 5 percent from a year earlier—and a stunning 30 percent from the previous three months—to about $4.7 billion. Furthermore, Cisco announced that it would lay off 8,500 employees and take an enormous $2.5 billion charge to write down inventory. By late October 2002, its stock was trading at around $10, down significantly from its 52-week high of $70. Elstrom, op. cit.: 39.

39. Coy et al., op. cit.; Anonymous. 2005. The rise of the superbrands. *Economist.* February 5: 63–65; and Sellers, P. 2005. It was a no-brainer. *Fortune,* February 21: 96–102.

40. This discussion draws upon Rappaport, A., & Sirower, M. L. 1999. Stock or cash? The trade-offs for buyers and sellers in mergers and acquisitions. *Harvard Business Review,* 77(6): 147–158; and Lipin, S., & Deogun, N. 2000. Big mergers of 90s prove disappointing to shareholders. *The Wall Street Journal,* October 30: C1.

41. Mouio, A. (Ed.). 1998. Unit of one. *Fast Company,* September: 82.

42. Ibid.

43. Porter, M. E. 1987. From competitive advantage to corporate strategy. *Harvard Business Review,* 65 (3): 43.

44. This was originally termed a "merger of equals." However, as noted in *The Economist* and elsewhere, it has turned out to be "just another disastrous car-industry takeover." For an interesting, recent discussion, see: Anonymous. 2007. Dis-assembly. *The Economist.* February 17: 63–64.

45. The divestiture of a business which is undertaken in order to enable managers to better focus on its core business has been termed "downscoping." Refer to Hitt, M. A., Harrison, J. S. & Ireland, R. D. 2001. *Mergers and acquisitions: A guide to creating value for stakeholders.* Oxford Press: New York.

46. Sirmon, D. G., Hitt, M. A., & Ireland, R. D. 2007. Managing firm resources in dynamic environments to create value: Looking inside the black box. *Academy of Management Review,* 32 (1): 273–292.

47. For scholarly perspectives on the role of learning in creating value in strategic alliances, refer to Anard, B. N., & Khanna, T. 2000. Do firms learn to create value? *Strategic Management Journal,* 12(3): 295–317; and Vermeulen, F., & Barkema, H. P. 2001. Learning through acquisitions. *Academy of Management Journal,* 44(3): 457–476.

48. This section draws on Hutt, M. D., Stafford, E. R., Walker, B. A., & Reingen, P. H. 2000. Case study: Defining the strategic alliance. *Sloan Management Review,* 41(2): 51–62; and Walters, B. A., Peters, S., & Dess, G. G. 1994. Strategic alliances and joint ventures: Making them work. *Business Horizons,* 4: 5–10.

49. Edmondson, G., & Reinhardt, A. 2001. From niche player to Goliath. *BusinessWeek,* March 12: 94–96.

50. Porter, op. cit.: 43–59.

51. *BusinessWeek.* 2003. The fallen. January 13: 80–82.

52. Polek, D. 2002. The rise and fall of Dennis Kozlowski. *Business-Week,* December 23: 64–77.

53. This section draws on Weston, J. F., Besley, S., & Brigham, E. F. 1996. *Essentials of managerial finance* (11th ed.): 18–20. Fort Worth, TX: Dryden Press, Harcourt Brace.

Business-Level Strategy

After reading this chapter, you should have a good understanding of:

LO1   The central role of competitive advantage in the study of strategic management.

LO2   The three generic strategies: overall cost leadership, differentiation, and focus.

LO3   How the successful attainment of generic strategies can improve a firm's relative power vis-à-vis the five forces that determine an industry's average profitability.

LO4   The pitfalls managers must avoid in striving to attain generic strategies.

LO5   How firms can effectively combine the generic strategies of overall cost leadership and differentiation.

How firms compete with each other and how they attain and sustain competitive advantages go to the heart of strategic management. In short, the key issue becomes: Why do some firms outperform others and enjoy such advantages over time? This subject, business-level strategy, is the focus of Chapter 6.

The chapter draws on Michael Porter's framework of generic strategies. He identifies three strategies—overall cost leadership, differentiation, and focus—that firms may apply to outperform their rivals in an industry. We begin by describing each of these strategies and provide examples of firms that have successfully attained them as a means of outperforming competitors in their industry. Next, we address how these strategies help a firm develop a favorable position vis-à-vis the "five forces" (Chapter 4). We then suggest some of the pitfalls that managers must avoid if they are to successfully pursue these generic strategies and discuss the conditions under which firms may effectively combine generic strategies to outperform rivals.

LEARNING FROM MISTAKES

Few companies have been as successful as Starbucks. What began in 1985 as a small coffee shop in Seattle's Pike Place Market has emerged as a megabrand, with almost $8 billion in revenues and more than 13,000 retail outlets worldwide. By early 2007, Starbucks' market capitalization was approaching that of Ford and General Motors *combined*.[1] And by doing what? By selling cups of consistently brewed—if richly priced—coffee. But even hugely successful companies can stumble.

Starbucks' strategy is driven by innovation—a promise that is implicit in its well-known and complicated menu. To spur growth, Starbucks places a tremendous amount of effort and expense in developing new products. Also, it continually researches various metrics to tease out customer attitudes about new beverages.

However, Starbucks found that there was an unexpected cost to such complex, innovative offerings. Such added complexity increased the time required to serve customers. And not too surprisingly, demand for its labor-intensive customized drinks declined.

According to Starbucks' research, a "highly satisfied customer" spent $4.42 on average during each visit and visited an average of 7.2 times a month. In contrast, although "unsatisfied customers" spent about the same amount per visit ($3.88), they averaged only about half (3.9) as many visits each month. Further, the company's research found that 75 percent of customers valued friendly, fast, convenient service, while only 15 percent considered new, innovative beverages to be highly important. Clearly, although innovation is a key part of Starbucks' strategy, it loses its value if customers must wait too long. As one would expect, Starbucks promptly took corrective action. It streamlined its artisan approach to making drinks by automating and standardizing various elements of the latte manufacturing process. Further, the firm spent $40 million adding staff to cut wait times. It also introduced the Starbucks Card to speed payment. The result: 85 percent of customers were served within three minutes compared to the prior 54 percent, and customer satisfaction levels increased 20 percent.

Because all firms endeavor to enjoy above-average profits, the question of how management should go about achieving this is a core issue in strategic management. Organizations that have created sustainable competitive advantages don't rely too much on a single strength—as Starbucks apparently did with its overemphasis on innovation. Instead they strive for well-rounded strategies that recognize the trade-offs associated with their competitive positions. Trade-offs occur when activities are incompatible (e.g., innovation and fast customer service).[2] Managers who recognize trade-offs in their strategies and activities enhance the chance that their firm's advantages will endure.

Starbucks' competitive advantage is based on the unique "Starbucks experience"—a superior product served by a knowledgeable salesperson in a friendly social environment with short wait times. It is this uniqueness that enables the company to charge a premium price.

 LO1 The central role of competitive advantage in the study of strategic management.

TYPES OF COMPETITIVE ADVANTAGE AND SUSTAINABILITY

Michael Porter presented three generic strategies that a firm can use to overcome the external environment's five forces and achieve competitive advantage.[3] Each of Porter's generic strategies has the potential to allow a firm to outperform rivals in its industry. The first, *overall cost leadership,* is based on creating a low-cost-position. Here, a firm must manage the relationships throughout the value chain and lower costs throughout the entire chain. On the other hand, *differentiation* requires a firm to create products and/or services that are unique and valued. Here, the primary emphasis is on "nonprice" attributes for which customers will gladly pay a premium, such as Starbucks' coffee. Finally, with a *focus* strategy, firms must direct their attention (or "focus") toward narrow product lines, buyer segments, or targeted geographic markets and they must attain advantages either through differentiation or cost leadership. Whereas the overall cost leadership and differentiation strategies strive to attain advantages industrywide, focusers build their strategy with a narrow target market in mind. Exhibit 6.1 illustrates these three strategies on two dimensions: competitive advantage and strategic target.

LO2 The three generic strategies: overall cost leadership, differentiation, and focus.

overall cost leadership strategy
A strategy based on appeal to the industrywide market based on low cost products or services.

OVERALL COST LEADERSHIP

The first generic strategy is **overall low cost leadership.** Overall low cost leadership requires a tight set of interrelated tactics that include:

- Aggressive construction of efficient-scale facilities.
- Vigorous pursuit of cost reductions from experience.

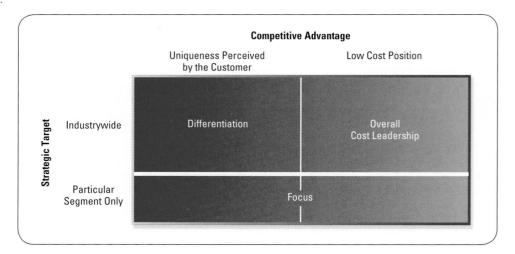

EXHIBIT 6.1   Three Generic Strategies

Source: Reprinted with the permission of The Free Press, a division of Simon & Schuster Adult Publishing Group, from *Competitive Strategy: Techniques for Analyzing Industries and Competitors* by Michael E. Porter. Copyright © 1980, 1998 by The Free Press. All rights reserved.

- Tight cost and overhead control.

- Avoidance of marginal customer accounts.

- Cost minimization in all activities in the firm's value chain, such as R&D, service, sales force, and advertising.

An important concept related to an overall cost leadership strategy is the experience curve, which refers to how business "learns" how to lower costs as it gains experience with production processes. That is, with experience, unit costs of production decline as output increases in most industries.

To generate above-average performance, a firm following an overall low cost leadership position must attain **competitive parity** on the basis of differentiation relative to competitors. In other words, a firm achieving parity is similar to its competitors, or "on par," with respect to differentiated products.[4] Competitive parity on the basis of differentiation permits a cost leader to translate cost advantages directly into higher profits than can be attained by competitors. Thus, the cost leader earns above-average returns.[5]

The failure to attain parity on the basis of differentiation can be illustrated with an example from the automobile industry—the ill-fated Yugo. Below is an excerpt from a speech by J. W. Marriott, Jr., Chairman of the Marriott Corporation:[6]

competitive parity
A firm's achievement of similarity, or being "on par," with competitors with respect to low cost, differentiation, or other strategic product characteristics.

> . . . money is a big thing. But it's not the only thing. In the 1980s, a new automobile reached North America from behind the Iron Curtain. It was called the Yugo, and its main attraction was price. About $3,000 each. But the only way they caught on was as the butt of jokes. Remember the guy who told his mechanic, "I want a gas cap for my Yugo." "OK," the mechanic replied, "that sounds like a fair trade."
>
> Yugo was offering a lousy value proposition. The cars literally fell apart before your eyes. And the lesson was simple. Price is just one component of value. No matter how good the price, the most cost-sensitive consumer won't buy a bad product.

Next, we discuss two examples of how firms have enhanced a cost leadership position.

While other managed care providers were having a string of weak years, WellPoint, based in Thousand Oaks, California, enjoyed an annual profit growth of over 50 percent to $3.1 billion over the past three years.[7] Chairman Leonard Schaeffer credits the company's focus on innovation for both expanding revenues and cutting costs. Recently, for example, WellPoint asked the Food and Drug Administration (FDA) to make the allergy drug Claritin available over the counter. Surprisingly, this may be the first time that an insurer has approached the FDA with this type of request. Schaeffer claimed, "They were kind of stunned," but the FDA agreed to consider the request. It was a smart move for WellPoint. If approved as an over-the-counter drug, Claritin would reduce patient visits to doctors and eliminate the need for prescriptions—two reimbursable expenses for which WellPoint would otherwise be responsible.

Stephen Sanger, CEO of General Mills, recently came up with an idea that helped his firm cut costs.[8] To improve productivity, he sent technicians to watch pit crews during a NASCAR race. That experience inspired the techies to figure out how to reduce the time it takes to switch a plant line from five hours to 20 minutes. This provided an important lesson: Many interesting benchmarking examples can take place far outside of an industry. Often, process improvements involve identifying the best practices in other industries and adapting them for implementation in your own firm. After all, when firms benchmark competitors in their own industry, the end result is often copying and playing catch-up.

Focus on Strategy 6.1 discusses Ryanair—a firm that has developed a very unique overall cost leadership strategy. One might say that it "one-upped" Southwest Airlines!

Ryanair: A Highly Effective Overall Cost Leadership Strategy

Michael O'Leary, CEO of Ryanair Holdings PLC, makes no apologies for his penny-pinching. Want to check luggage? You'll pay up to $9.50 per bag for the privilege. Expecting free drinks and snacks? You'll be disappointed. Even a bottle of water will cost you $3.40. And it is not just the passengers who are affected. Flight crews buy their own uniforms, and staff at Ryanair's Spartan Dublin Airport headquarters must supply their own pens. After a customer sued Ryanair for charging $34 for the use of a wheelchair, the company added a 63-cent "wheelchair levy" to every ticket!

U.S. low-fare carriers have taken the opposite approach from Ryanair's by adding perks such as leather seats, live television, and business class. "All of the low-cost carriers' costs have gotten a little out of control," says Tim Sieber, general manager of The Boyd Group, an Evergreen, Colorado, aviation consultant. Clearly, Ryanair hasn't followed its industry peers.

Ryanair has been extremely successful. For 2006, its revenues were $2.1 billion—only one-seventh the size of British Airways (BA). However, its operating margins are 22.7%—three times as large as BA's. Not too surprising, Ryanair's market capitalization of nearly $14 billion (in early 2007) is more than that of British Airways ($12.5 billion)—and incidentally, even more than Southwest Airlines ($12.1 billion). The latter, of course, has been the industry role model for low-cost strategies.

What is O'Leary's secret? He thinks like a retailer and charges for every little thing. Imagine the seat as a cell phone: It comes free, or nearly free, but its owner winds up spending on all sorts of services.

However, what O'Leary loses in seat revenue he more than makes up by turning both his planes and the Ryanair Web site into stores brimming with irresistible goodies, even as he charges for such "perks" as priority boarding and assigned seating.

Sounds outrageous? Probably so, but the strategy is clearly working. Although its average fare is $53, compared with $92 for Southwest Airlines, Ryanair's net margins are, at 18%, more than double the 7% achieved by Southwest. Says Nick van den Brul, an aviation analyst: "Ryanair is Wal-Mart with wings." And a good summary comment by O'Leary: "You want luxury? Go somewhere else."

A few other Ryanair practices:

- Flight attendants sell digital cameras ($137.50) and iPocket MP3 players ($165). Soon-to-come: onboard gaming and cell-phone service.
- The seats don't recline, and seat-back pockets have been removed to cut cleaning time and speed turnaround of the planes. There's no entertainment; seat-back trays will soon carry ads.
- Ryanair sells more than 98 percent of its tickets online. Its Web site offers insurance, hotels, car rentals, and more—even online bingo.

Sources: Capell, K. 2006. "Wal-Mart with Wings," *BusinessWeek,* November 27: 44–45; Kumar, N. 2006. Strategies to fight low-cost rivals. *Harvard Business Review,* 84 (12): 104–113; and *Ryanair Annual Report,* 2006.

LO3 How the successful attainment of generic strategies can improve a firm's relative power vis-à-vis the five forces that determine an industry's average profitability.

Overall Low Cost Leadership: Improving Competitive Position vis-à-vis the Five Forces An overall low-cost position enables a firm to achieve above-average returns despite strong competition. It protects a firm against rivalry from competitors, because lower costs allow a firm to earn returns even if its competitors eroded their profits through intense rivalry. A low-cost position also protects firms against powerful buyers. Buyers can exert power to drive down prices only to the level of the next most efficient producer. Also, a low-cost position provides more flexibility to cope with demands from powerful suppliers for input cost increases. The factors that lead to a low-cost position also provide substantial entry barriers from economies of scale and cost advantages. Finally, a low-cost position puts the firm in a favorable position with respect to substitute products introduced by new and existing competitors.

A few examples will illustrate these points. Ryanair's close attention to costs helps to protect them from buyer power and intense rivalry from competitors. Thus, they are able to drive down costs and enjoy relatively high power over their customers. By increasing its productivity and lowering unit costs, General Mills (and its competitors in that industry) enjoy greater scale economies and erect higher entry barriers for others who want to enter the industry. Finally, as competitors such as WellPoint lower costs through means such as petitioning the FDA to make certain drugs available over the counter, they become less vulnerable to substitutes such as Internet-based competitors.

Potential Pitfalls of Overall Cost Leadership Strategies
These are:

L04 The pitfalls managers must avoid in striving to attain generic strategies.

- *Too much focus on one or a few value-chain activities.* Would you consider a person to be astute if he cancelled his newspaper subscription and quit eating out to save money, but then "maxed out" several credit cards, requiring him to pay hundreds of dollars a month in interest charges? Of course not. Similarly, firms need to pay attention to all activities in the value chain. Too often managers make big cuts in operating expenses, but don't question year-to-year spending on capital projects. Or managers may decide to cut selling and marketing expenses but ignore manufacturing expenses. Managers should explore *all* value-chain activities, including relationships among them, as candidates for cost reductions.

- *All rivals share a common input or raw material.* Here, firms are vulnerable to price increases in the factors of production. Since they're competing on costs, they are less able to pass on price increases, because customers can take their business to rivals who have lower prices. Consider the hardship experienced by fertilizer producers in early 2001 when energy prices spiked.[9] A quadrupling of prices to $10 per thousand cubic feet of natural gas forced firms to shut down nearly half of their production capacity. Why? Natural gas accounts for over 70 percent of the fertilizer's cost. According to Betty-Ann Hegge, senior vice president of Potash Corporation of Saskatchewan, Inc., North America's second largest producer, "Many companies are not even covering their cash costs at these prices."

- *The strategy is imitated too easily.* One of the common pitfalls of a cost leadership strategy is that a firm's strategy may consist of value-creating activities that are easy to imitate. Such was the case with online brokers in recent years.[10] As of early 2001, there were about 140 online brokers, hardly symbolic of an industry where imitation is extremely difficult. But according to Henry McVey, financial services analyst at Morgan Stanley, "We think you need five to ten" online brokers.

  What are some of the dynamics? First, although online brokers were geared up to handle 1.2 million trades a day, volume had shrunk to about 834,000—a 30 percent drop. Thus, competition for business intensified. Second, when the stock market is down, many investors trust their instincts less and seek professional guidance from brokerages that offer differentiated services. Eric Rajendra of A. T. Kearney, an international consulting company, claimed, "The current (online broker) model is inadequate for the pressures the industry is facing now."

- *A lack of parity on differentiation.* As noted earlier, firms striving to attain cost leadership advantages must obtain a level of parity on differentiation. Organizations providing online degree programs to adults working full-time may offer low prices. However, they may not be successful unless they can offer instruction that is perceived as comparable to traditional providers. For them, parity can be achieved on differentiation dimensions such as reputation and quality and through signaling mechanisms such as national and regional accreditation agencies.

- *Erosion of cost advantages when the pricing information available to customers increases.* This is becoming a more significant challenge as the Internet dramatically increases both the quantity and volume of information available to consumers about pricing and cost structures. Life insurance firms offering whole life insurance provide an interesting example.[11] One study found that for each 10 percent increase in consumer use of the Internet, there is a corresponding reduction in insurance prices to consumers of 3 to 5 percent. Recently, the nationwide savings (or, alternatively, reduced revenues to providers) was between $115 and $125 million annually.

Through effective advertising, Intel strives to further differentiate its products. This advertisement touts Apple's use of its processors in their newest line of computers. An Apple store is behind the ad.

LO2 The three generic strategies: overall cost leadership, differentiation, and focus.

differentiation strategy
A strategy based on creating differences in the firm's product or service offering by creating something that is perceived as unique and valued by customers.

DIFFERENTIATION

As the name implies, a **differentiation strategy** consists of creating differences in the firm's product or service offering by creating something that is perceived *industrywide* as unique and valued by customers. Differentiation can take many forms:

- Prestige or brand image (Adam's Mark hotels, BMW automobiles).
- Technology (Martin guitars, Marantz stereo components, North Face camping equipment).
- Innovation (Medtronic medical equipment, Nokia cellular phones).
- Features (Cannondale mountain bikes, Honda Goldwing motorcycles).
- Customer service (Nordstrom department stores, Sears lawn equipment retailing).
- Dealer network (Lexus automobiles, Caterpillar earth-moving equipment).

Firms may differentiate themselves along several different dimensions at once. For example, BMW is known for its high prestige, superior engineering, and high-quality automobiles. And, Harley-Davidson differentiates on image and dealer services.

Firms achieve and sustain differentiation advantages and attain above-average performance when their price premiums exceed the extra costs incurred in being unique. For example, both BMW and Harley-Davidson must increase consumer costs to offset added marketing expenses. Thus, a differentiator will always seek out ways of distinguishing itself from similar competitors to justify price premiums greater than the costs incurred by differentiating. Clearly, a differentiator cannot ignore costs. After all, its premium prices would be eroded by a markedly inferior cost position. Therefore, it must attain a level of cost *parity* relative to competitors. Differentiators can do this by reducing costs in all areas that do not affect differentiation. Porsche, for example, invests heavily in engine design—an area in which its customers demand excellence—but it is less concerned and spends fewer resources in the design of the instrument panel or the arrangement of switches on the radio.[12]

Many companies successfully follow a differentiation strategy.[13] For example, FedEx's CEO and founder, Fred Smith, claims that the key to his firm's success is innovation.[14] He contends his management team didn't understand their real goal when they started the firm in 1971: "We thought that we were selling the transportation of goods; in fact, we were selling peace of mind." To that end, they now provide each driver with a handheld computer and a transmitting device that makes it possible for customers to track their packages right from their desktop PCs.

Focus on Strategy 6.2 discusses how three firms have been successful through effective differentiation strategies. Similar to Starbucks, these firms have taken commodity-type products and converted them to high-priced goods.

Differentiation: Improving Competitive Position vis-à-vis the Five Forces Differentiation provides protection against rivalry since brand loyalty lowers customer sensitivity to price and raises customer switching costs. By increasing a firm's margins, differentiation also avoids the need for a low-cost position. Higher entry barriers result because of customer loyalty and the firm's ability to provide uniqueness in its products or services. Differentiation also provides higher margins that enable a firm to deal with supplier power. And it reduces buyer power, because buyers lack comparable alternatives and are therefore less price sensitive. Supplier power is also decreased because there is a certain amount of prestige associated with being the supplier to a producer of highly differentiated products and services. Last, differentiation enhances customer loyalty, thus reducing the threat from substitutes.

LO3 How the successful attainment of generic strategies can improve a firm's relative power vis-à-vis the five forces that determine an industry's average profitability.

Our examples illustrate these points. Lexus has enjoyed enhanced power over buyers because its top J. D. Power ranking makes buyers more willing to pay a premium price. This lessens rivalry, since buyers become less price-sensitive. The prestige associated with its brand name also lowers supplier power since margins are high. Suppliers would probably desire to be associated with prestige brands, thus lessening their incentives to drive up prices. Finally, the loyalty and "peace of mind" associated with a service provider such as FedEx makes such a firm less vulnerable to rivalry or substitute products and services.

Potential Pitfalls of Differentiation Strategies These include:

LO4 The pitfalls managers must avoid in striving to attain generic strategies.

- *Uniqueness that is not valuable.* A differentiation strategy must provide unique bundles of products and/or services that customers value highly. It's not enough just to be "different." An example is Gibson's Dobro bass guitar. Gibson came up with a unique idea: Design and build an acoustic bass guitar with sufficient sound volume so that amplification wasn't necessary. The problem with other acoustic bass guitars was that they did not project enough volume because of the low-frequency bass notes. By adding a resonator plate on the body of the traditional acoustic bass, Gibson increased the sound volume. Gibson believed this product would serve a particular niche market—bluegrass and folk artists who played in small group "jams" with other acoustic musicians. Unfortunately, Gibson soon discovered that its targeted market was content with their existing options: an upright bass amplified with a microphone or an acoustic electric guitar. Thus, Gibson developed a unique product, but it was not perceived as valuable by its potential customers.[15]

- *Too much differentiation.* Firms may strive for quality or service that is higher than customers desire. Thus, they become vulnerable to competitors who provide an appropriate level of quality at a lower price. For example, consider the expensive Mercedes-Benz S-Class, which ranges in price between $75,000 and $125,000.[16] *Consumer Reports* described it as "sumptuous," "quiet and luxurious," and a "delight to drive." The magazine also considered it to be the least reliable sedan available in the United States. According to David Champion, who runs their testing program, the problems are electronic. "The engineers have gone a little wild," he says. "They've put every bell and whistle that they think of, and sometimes they don't have the attention to detail to make these systems work." Some features: a computer-driven suspension that reduces body roll as the vehicle whips around a corner; cruise control that automatically slows the car down if it gets too close to another car; and seats that are adjustable 14 ways and that are ventilated by a system that uses eight fans.

- *Too high a price premium.* This pitfall is quite similar to too much differentiation. Customers may desire the product, but they are repelled by the price premium. For example, Duracell (a division of Gillette) recently charged too much for batteries.[17] The firm tried to sell consumers on its superior quality products, but the mass market wasn't convinced. Why? The price differential was simply too high. At a CVS drugstore just one block from Gillette's headquarters, a four-pack of Energizer AA batteries was on sale at $2.99 compared with a Duracell four-pack at $4.59. Duracell's market share dropped 2 percent in a recent two-year period and its profits declined over 30 percent. Clearly, the price/performance proposition Duracell offered customers was not accepted.

- *Differentiation that is easily imitated.* As we noted in Chapter 3, resources that are easily imitated cannot lead to sustainable advantages. Similarly, firms may strive for, and even attain, a differentiation strategy that is successful for a time. However, the advantages are eroded through imitation. In Focus on . . . Strategy 6.2 we discussed Cereality's innovative differentiation strategy of offering a wide variety of cereals.[18] As one would expect, once their idea proved successful, competitors entered the market because much of the initial risk had already been taken. Rivals include an Iowa City restaurant named the Cereal Cabinet, the Cereal Bowl in Miami; and Bowls: A Cereal Joint in Gainesville, Florida. Says David Roth, one of Cereality's founders: "With any good business idea, you're faced with people who see you've cracked the code and who try to cash in on it."

- *Dilution of brand identification through product-line extensions.* Firms may erode their quality brand image by adding products or services with lower prices and less quality. Although this can increase short-term revenues, it may be detrimental in the long run. Consider Gucci.[19] In the 1980s Gucci wanted to capitalize on its prestigious brand name by launching an aggressive strategy of revenue growth. It added a set of lower-priced canvas goods to its product line. It also pushed goods heavily into department stores and duty-free channels and allowed its name to appear on a host of licensed items such as watches, eyeglasses, and perfumes. In the short term, this strategy worked. Sales soared. However, the strategy carried a high price. Gucci's indiscriminate approach to expanding its products and channels tarnished its sterling brand. Sales of its high-end goods (with higher profit margins) fell, causing profits to decline.

• *Perceptions of differentiation may vary between buyers and sellers.* The issue here is that "beauty is in the eye of the beholder." Companies must realize that although they may perceive their products and services as differentiated, their customers may view them as commodities. Indeed, in today's marketplace, many products and services have been reduced to commodities.[20] Thus, a firm could overprice its offerings and lose margins altogether if it has to lower prices to reflect market realities.

FOCUS

A **focus strategy** is based on the choice of a narrow competitive scope within an industry. A firm following this strategy selects a segment or group of segments and tailors its strategy to serve them. The essence of focus is the exploitation of a particular market niche. As you might expect, narrow focus itself (like merely "being different" as a differentiator) is simply not sufficient for above-average performance. The focus strategy, as indicated in Exhibit 6.1, has two variants. In a cost focus, a firm strives to create a cost advantage in its target segment. In a differentiation focus, a firm seeks to differentiate in its target market. Both variants of the focus strategy rely on providing better service than broad-based competitors who are trying to serve the focuser's target segment. Cost focus exploits differences in cost behavior in some segments, while differentiation focus exploits the special needs of buyers in other segments.

Let's look at examples of two firms that have successfully implemented focus strategies. Network Appliance (NA) has developed a more cost-effective way to store and distribute computer files.[21] Its larger rival, EMC, makes mainframe-style products priced over $1 million that store files and accommodate Internet traffic. NA makes devices that cost under $200,000 for particular storage jobs such as caching (temporary storage) of Internet content. Focusing on such narrow segments has certainly paid off for NA; it has posted a remarkable 20 straight quarters of revenue growth.

Bessemer Trust competes in the private banking industry. A differentiation focuser, it targets families with a minimum of $5 million in assets, who desire both capital preservation and wealth accumulation. In other words, these are not people who want to put all their "eggs in a dot-com basket." Bessemer configures its activities for highly personalized service by assigning one account officer for every 14 families. Meetings are more likely to be held at a client's ranch or yacht than in Bessemer's office. Bessemer offers a wide range of customized services, such as investment management, estate administration, oversight of oil and gas investments, and accounting for race horses and aircraft. Despite the industry's most generous compensation of account officers and the highest personnel cost as a percentage of operating expenses, Bessemer's focused differentiation strategy is estimated to yield the highest return on equity in the industry.

Focus: Improving Competitive Position vis-à-vis the Five Forces Focus requires that a firm either have a low-cost position with its strategic target, high differentiation, or both. As we discussed with regard to cost and differentiation strategies, these positions provide defenses against each competitive force. Focus is also used to select niches that are least vulnerable to substitutes or where competitors are weakest.

LO2 The three generic strategies: overall cost leadership, differentiation, and focus.

focus strategy
A strategy based on appeal to a narrow market segment within an industry.

LO3 How the successful attainment of generic strategies can improve a firm's relative power vis-à-vis the five forces that determine an industry's average profitability.

As the market for organic products grows, longtime organic food makers such as Nature's Path are facing increased competition from traditional food makers, including General Mills and Nestlé.

Let's look at our examples to illustrate some of these points. First, Bessemer Trust experienced less rivalry and lower buyer bargaining power by providing products and services to a targeted market segment that was less price-sensitive. New rivals would have difficulty attracting customers away from Bessemer based only on lower prices. Similarly, the brand image and quality that this brand evoked heightened rivals' entry barriers. Additionally, we could reasonably speculate that Bessemer Trust enjoyed some protection against substitute products and services because of their relatively high reputation, brand image, and customer loyalty. With regard to the strategy of cost focus, Network Appliances, the successful rival to EMC in the computer storage industry, was better able to absorb pricing increases from suppliers as a result of its lower cost structure, reducing supplier power.

Potential Pitfalls of Focus Strategies These include:

- *Erosion of cost advantages within the narrow segment.* The advantages of a cost focus strategy may be fleeting if the cost advantages are eroded over time. For example, Dell's pioneering direct selling model in the personal computer industry, while still the industry standard, is constantly being challenged and eroded by rivals such as Hewlett-Packard as they gain experience with Dell's distribution method. Similarly, other firms have seen their profit margins drop as competitors enter their product segment.

- *Even product and service offerings that are highly focused are subject to competition from new entrants and from imitation.* Some firms adopting a focus strategy may enjoy temporary advantages because they select a small niche with few rivals. However, their advantages may be short-lived. A notable example is the multitude of dot-com firms that specialize in very narrow segments such as pet supplies, ethnic foods, and vintage automobile accessories. The entry barriers tend to be low, there is little buyer loyalty, and competition becomes intense. And since the marketing strategies and technologies employed by most rivals are largely nonproprietary, imitation is easy. Over time, revenues fall, profits margins are squeezed, and only the strongest players survive the shakeout.

- *Focusers can become too focused to satisfy buyer needs.* Some firms attempting to attain competitive advantages through a focus strategy may have too narrow a product or service. Examples include many retail firms. Hardware chains such as Ace and True Value are losing market share to rivals such as Lowe's and Home Depot who offer a full line of home and garden equipment and accessories. And given the enormous purchasing power of the national chains, it would be difficult for such specialty retailers to attain parity on costs.

COMBINATION STRATEGIES: INTEGRATING OVERALL LOW COST AND DIFFERENTIATION

There has been ample evidence—in the popular press and in research studies—about the strategic benefits of combining generic strategies. Perhaps the primary benefit to firms that integrate low cost and differentiation strategies is that it is generally harder for rivals to duplicate or imitate. This strategy enables a firm to provide two types of value to customers: differentiated attributes (e.g., high quality, brand identification, reputation) and lower prices (because of the firm's lower costs in value-creating activities). The goal becomes one of providing unique value to customers in an efficient manner.[22] Some firms are able to attain both types of advantages simultaneously. For example, superior quality can lead to lower costs because of less need for rework in manufacturing, fewer warranty claims, a reduced need for customer service personnel to resolve customer complaints, and so forth. Thus, the benefits of combining advantages can be additive, instead of merely involving trade-offs. Next, we consider three approaches to combining overall low cost and differentiation.

Automated and Flexible Manufacturing Systems Given the advances in manufacturing technologies such as CAD/CAM (computer aided design and computer aided manufacturing) as well as information technologies, many firms have been able to manufacture unique products in relatively small quantities at lower costs—a concept known as "mass customization."[23]

Let's consider Andersen Windows of Bayport, Minnesota—a $1 billion manufacturer of windows for the building industry. Until about 20 years ago, Andersen was a mass producer, in small batches, of a variety of standard windows. However, to meet changing customer needs, Andersen kept adding to its product line. The result was catalogs of ever-increasing size and a bewildering set of choices for both homeowners and contractors. Over a 6-year period, the number of products tripled, price quotes took several hours, and the error rate increased. This not only damaged the company's reputation, but also added to its manufacturing expenses.

To bring about a major change, Andersen developed an interactive computer version of its paper catalogs that it sold to distributors and retailers. Salespersons can now customize each window to meet the customer's needs, check the design for structural soundness, and provide a price quote. The system is virtually error free, customers get exactly what they want, and the time to develop the design and furnish a quotation has been cut by 75 percent. Each showroom computer is connected to the factory, and customers are assigned a code number that permits them to track the order. The manufacturing system has been developed to use some common finished parts, but it also allows considerable variation in the final products. Despite its huge investment, Andersen has been able to lower costs, enhance quality and variety, and improve its response time to customers.

Below are some other examples of how flexible production systems have enabled firms to successfully engage in mass customization for their customers:[24]

- At *Nikeid.com,* customers can design an athletic or casual shoe to their specifications online, selecting almost every element of the shoe from the material of the sole to the color of the shoelace.

- *Eleuria* sells custom perfumes. Each product is created in response to a user profile constructed from responses to a survey about habits and preferences. Eleuria provides a sample at modest cost to verify fit.

- *Lands' End* offers customized shirts and pants. Consumers specify style parameters, measurements, and fabrics through the company's Web site. These settings are saved so that returning users can easily order a duplicate item.

- *Cannondale* permits consumers to specify the parameters that define a road bike frame, including custom colors and inscriptions. The user specifies the parameters on the company's Web site and then arranges for delivery through a dealer.

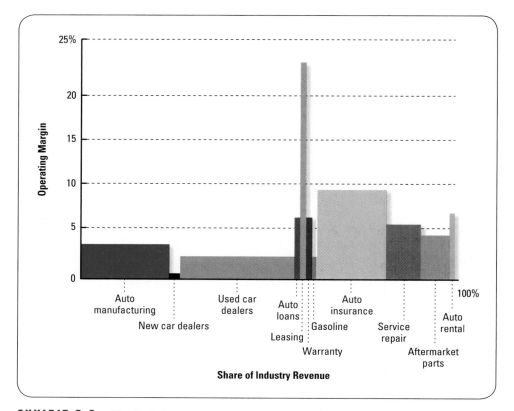

EXHIBIT 6.2 **The U.S. Automobile Industry's Profit Pool**

Source: Adapted and reprinted by permission of *Harvard Business Review*, Exhibit from "Profit Pools: A Fresh Look at Strategy," by O. Gadiesh and J. L. Gilbert, May–June 1999. Copyright © 1999 by the Harvard Business School Publishing Corporation. All rights reserved.

Exploiting the Profit Pool Concept for Competitive Advantage A profit pool can be defined as the total profits in an industry at all points along the industry's value chain.[25] Although the concept is relatively straightforward, the structure of the profit pool can be complex. The potential pool of profits will be deeper in some segments of the value chain than in others, and the depths will vary within an individual segment. Segment profitability may vary widely by customer group, product category, geographic market, or distribution channel. Additionally, the pattern of profit concentration in an industry is very often different from the pattern of revenue generation.

Consider the automobile industry profit pool in Exhibit 6.2. Here we see little relationship between the generation of revenues and capturing of profits. While manufacturing generates most of the revenue, this value activity is far smaller profitwise than other value activities such as financing and extended warranty operations. So while a car manufacturer may be under tremendous pressure to produce cars efficiently, much of the profit (at least proportionately) can be captured in the aforementioned downstream operations. Thus, a carmaker would be ill-advised to focus solely on manufacturing and leave downstream operations to others through outsourcing.

Coordinating the "Extended" Value Chain by Way of Information Technology Many firms have achieved success by integrating activities throughout the "extended value chain" by using information technology to link their own value chain with the value chains of their customers and suppliers. This approach enables a firm to add value not only through its own value-creating activities, but also for its customers and suppliers.

Such a strategy often necessitates redefining the industry's value chain. A number of years ago, Wal-Mart took a close look at its industry's value chain and decided to reframe the competitive challenge.[26] Although its competitors were primarily focused on retailing—merchandising and promotion—Wal-Mart determined that it was not so much in the retailing industry as in the transportation logistics and communications industries. Here, linkages in the extended value chain became central. That became Wal-Mart's chosen battleground. By redefining the rules of competition that played to its strengths, Wal-Mart has attained competitive advantages and dominates its industry.

Integrated Overall Low-Cost and Differentiation Strategies: Improving Competitive Position vis-à-vis the Five Forces

Firms that successfully integrate both differentiation and cost advantages create an enviable position. For example, Wal-Mart's integration of information systems, logistics, and transportation helps it to drive down costs and provide outstanding product selection. This dominant competitive position serves to erect high entry barriers to potential competitors that have neither the financial nor physical resources to compete head-to-head. Wal-Mart's size—$316 billion in 2006 sales—provides the chain with enormous bargaining power over suppliers. Its low pricing and wide selection reduce the power of buyers (its customers), because there are relatively few competitors that can provide a comparable cost/value proposition. This reduces the possibility of intense head-to-head rivalry, such as protracted price wars. Finally, Wal-Mart's overall value proposition makes potential substitute products (e.g., Internet competitors) a less viable threat.

Pitfalls of Integrated Overall Cost Leadership and Differentiation Strategies   These include:

- *Firms that fail to attain both strategies may end up with neither and become "stuck in the middle."* A key issue in strategic management is the creation of competitive advantages that enable a firm to enjoy above-average returns. Some firms may become "stuck in the middle" if they try to attain both cost and differentiation advantages. An example that we are all familiar with would be the "Big 3" U.S. automobile makers. They are plagued by very expensive "legacy costs" associated with pension and health care obligations. And they suffer from long-term customer perceptions of mediocre quality—inferior to their European and Japanese rivals. The troubling quality perceptions persist despite the fact that the "Big 3" have attained approximate parity with their Japanese and European competitors in recent J. D. Power surveys.

- *Underestimating the challenges and expenses associated with coordinating value-creating activities in the extended value chain.* Successfully integrating activities across a firm's value chain with the value chain of suppliers and customers involves a significant investment in financial and human resources. Managers must not underestimate the expenses linked to technology investment, managerial time and commitment, and the involvement and investment required by the firm's customers and suppliers. The firm must be confident that it can generate a sufficient scale of operations and revenues to justify all associated expenses.

- *Miscalculating sources of revenue and profit pools in the firm's industry.* Firms may fail to accurately assess sources of revenue and profits in their value chain. This can occur for several reasons. For example, a manager may be biased due to his or her functional area background, work experiences, and educational background. If the manager's background is in engineering, he or she might perceive that proportionately greater revenue and margins were being created in manufacturing, product, and process design than a person whose background is in a "downstream" value-chain activity such as marketing and sales. Or politics could make managers "fudge" the numbers to favor their area of operations. This would make them responsible for a greater proportion of the firm's profits, thus improving their bargaining position.

A related problem is directing an overwhelming amount of managerial time, attention, and resources to value-creating activities that produce the greatest margins—to the detriment of other important, albeit less profitable, activities. For example, a car manufacturer may focus too much on downstream activities, such as warranty fulfillment and financing operations, to the detriment of differentiation and cost of the cars themselves.

SUMMARY

LO1   How and why firms outperform each other goes to the heart of strategic management. In this chapter, we identified three generic strategies and discussed how firms are able not only to attain advantages over competitors, but also to sustain such advantages over time. Why do some advantages become long-lasting while others are quickly imitated by competitors?

LO2, LO3   The three generic strategies—overall cost leadership, differentiation, and focus—form the core of this chapter. We began by providing a brief description of each generic strategy (or competitive advantage) and furnished examples of firms that have successfully implemented these strategies. Successful generic strategies invariably enhance a firm's position vis-à-vis the five forces of that industry—a point that we stressed and illustrated with examples. However, as we pointed out, there are pitfalls to each of the generic strategies. Thus, the sustainability of a firm's advantage is always challenged because of imitation or substitution by new or existing rivals. Such competitor moves erode a firm's advantage over time.

LO4, LO5   We also discussed the viability of combining (or integrating) overall cost leadership and generic differentiation strategies. If successful, such integration can enable a firm to enjoy superior performance and improve its competitive position. However, this is challenging, and managers must be aware of the potential downside risks associated with such an initiative.

SUMMARY REVIEW QUESTIONS

1. Explain why the concept of competitive advantage is central to the study of strategic management.

2. Briefly describe the three generic strategies—overall cost leadership, differentiation, and focus.

3. Explain the relationship between the three generic strategies and the five forces that determine the average profitability within an industry.

4. Describe some of the pitfalls associated with each of the three generic strategies.

5. Can firms combine the generic strategies of overall cost leadership and differentiation? Why or why not?

KEY TERMS

overall low cost leadership
  strategy, 136

competitive parity, 137
differentiation strategy, 140

focus strategy, 143

1. Go to the Internet and look up www.walmart.com. Has this firm been able to combine overall cost leadership and differentiation strategies?

2. Choose a firm with which you are familiar in your local business community. Is the firm successful in following one (or more) generic strategies? Why or why not? What do you think are some of the challenges it faces in implementing these strategies in an effective manner?

3. Think of a firm that has attained a differentiation focus or cost focus strategy. Are their advantages sustainable? Why? Why not? (*Hint:* Consider its position vis-à-vis Porter's five forces.)

4. Think of a firm that successfully achieved a combination overall cost leadership and differentiation strategy. What can be learned from this example? Are these advantages sustainable? Why? Why not? (*Hint:* Consider its competitive position vis-à-vis Porter's five forces.)

1. The Starbucks example draws upon the following sources: Crane, M. 2007. How to run a restaurant: Best role model. www.forbes.com, February 2: np; McGovern, G. J., Court, D., Quelch, J. A., & Crawford, B. 2004. Bringing customers into the boardroom. *Harvard Business Review,* 82(11): 70–80; Gottfrendson, M., & Aspinall, K. 2005. Innovation and complexity. *Harvard Business Review,* 83(11): 62–71; and Francis, D. 2005. The secret of successful marketing. *Financial Post,* November 25: FP2.

2. For a seminal discussion on competitive advantage and the importance of recognizing trade-offs, refer to Porter, M. 1996. What is strategy? *Harvard Business Review,* 74(6): 61–78.

3. For a recent perspective by Porter on competitive strategy, refer to Porter, M. E. 1996. What is strategy? *Harvard Business Review,* 74(6): 61–78.

4. For a scholarly discussion and analysis of the concept of competitive parity, refer to Powell, T. C. 2003. Varieties of competitive parity. *Strategic Management Journal,* 24(1): 61–86.

5. Rao, A. R., Bergen, M. E., & Davis, S. 2000. How to fight a price war. *Harvard Business Review,* 78(2): 107–120.

6. Marriot, J. W. Jr. Our competitive strength: Human capital. A speech given to the Detroit Economic Club on October 2, 2000.

7. Whalen, C. J., Pascual, A. M., Lowery, T., & Muller, J. 2001. The top 25 managers. *BusinessWeek,* January 8: 63.

8. Ibid.

9. Symonds, W. C., Arndt, M., Palmer, A. T., Weintraub, A., & Holmes, S. 2001. Trying to break the choke hold. *BusinessWeek,* January 22: 38–39.

10. Thornton, E., 2001, Why e-brokers are broker and broker. *BusinessWeek,* January 22: 94.

11. Koretz, G. 2001. E-commerce: The buyer wins. *BusinessWeek,* January 8: 30.

12. Taylor, A., III. 2001. Can you believe Porsche is putting its badge on this car? *Fortune,* February 19: 168–172.

13. Ward, S., Light, L., & Goldstine, J. 1999. What high-tech managers need to know about brands. *Harvard Business Review,* 77(4): 85–95.

14. Rosenfeld, J. 2000. Unit of one. *Fast Company,* April: 98.

15. The authors would like to thank Scott Droege, a faculty member at Western Kentucky University, for providing this example.

16. Flint, J. 2004. Stop the nerds. *Forbes,* July 5: 80; and, Fahey, E. 2004. Over-engineering 101. *Forbes,* December 13: 62.

17. Symonds, W. C. 2000. Can Gillette regain its voltage? *BusinessWeek,* October 16: 102–104.

18. Caplan, J. 2006. In a real crunch. *Inside Business,* July: A37–A38.

19. Gadiesh, O., & Gilbert, J. L. 1998. Profit pools: A fresh look at strategy. *Harvard Business Review,* 76(3): 139–158.

20. Colvin, G. 2000. Beware: You could soon be selling soybeans. *Fortune,* November 13: 80.

21. Whalen et al., op. cit.: 63.

22. Gilmore, J. H., & Pine, B. J., II. 1997. The four faces of customization. *Harvard Business Review,* 75(1): 91–101.

23. Ibid. For interesting insights on mass customization, refer to Cattani, K., Dahan, E., & Schmidt, G. 2005. Offshoring versus "spackling." *MIT Sloan Management Review,* 46(3): 6–7.

24. Randall, T., Terwiesch, C., & Ulrich, K. T. 2005. Principles for user design of customized products. *California Management Review,* 47(4): 68–85.

25. Gadiesh & Gilbert, op. cit.: 139–158.

26. This example draws on Dess, G. G., & Picken, J. C 1997. *Mission Critical.* Burr Ridge, IL: Irwin.

Creating Effective Organizational Designs

After reading this chapter, you should have a good understanding of:

LO1   The importance of organizational structure and the concept of the "boundaryless" organization in implementing strategies.

LO2   Each of the traditional types of organizational structure: simple, functional, divisional, and matrix.

LO3   The relative advantages and disadvantages of traditional organizational structures.

LO4   The different types of boundaryless organizations—barrier-free, modular, and virtual—and their relative advantages and disadvantages.

To implement strategies successfully, firms must have appropriate organizational structures. These include the processes and integrating mechanisms necessary to ensure that boundaries among internal activities and external parties, such as suppliers, customers, and alliance partners, are flexible and permeable. A firm's performance will suffer if its managers don't carefully consider both of these organizational design attributes.

In the first section, we address the different types of traditional structures—simple, functional, divisional, and matrix—and their relative advantages and disadvantages.

The second section discusses the concept of the "boundaryless" organization. We do *not* argue that organizations should have no internal and external boundaries. Instead, we suggest that in rapidly changing and unpredictable environments, organizations must strive to make their internal and external boundaries both flexible and permeable. We suggest three different types of boundaryless organizations: barrier-free, modular, and virtual.

LEARNING FROM MISTAKES

As 2007 began, Airbus's A380 double-decker jet was two years behind schedule, sending about $6 billion in potential profits down the drain.[1] What is the root of Airbus's problem? Let's take a look.

Airbus factories in Germany and France were using incompatible design software. Engineers in Hamburg were drawing on a two-dimensional computer program, while their counterparts in Toulouse were working in 3-D. Thus, wiring produced in Hamburg didn't fit properly into the plane on the assembly line in Toulouse. As noted by Hans Weber, CEO of San Diego–based consultant Tecop International: "The various Airbus locations had their own legacy software, methods, procedures, and Airbus never succeeded in unifying all those efforts." (There are 348 *miles* of bundled wiring in each A380.)

The A380 fiasco became one of the costliest blunders in the history of commercial aviation, and it plunged Airbus into crisis. Chief Executive Christian Streiff quit in October 2006 after only three months on the job. He clashed with Airbus's parent, European Aeronautic Defense & Space Company, over how to sort out the mess. EADS will probably wind up taking a $6 billion hit to its profit—measured by the expected loss in earnings from production delays—over the next four years. Further, the resulting cash crunch could slow Airbus's plans to develop a new mid-size wide-body challenge to Boeing's highly successful 787 Dreamliner. Through September 2006, Airbus fell far behind Boeing on total aircraft orders, logging only 226 versus 723 for its U.S. rival.

What went wrong? The software debacle exposes a salient flaw in Airbus. Although it likes to project a seamless, pan-European image, Airbus is terribly balkanized. Its factories in Germany, France, Britain, and Spain cling to traditional operating methods and harbor cross-border jealousies. As Strieff told the French newspaper *Le Figaro* in an interview, "It is still, in part, a juxtaposition of four companies."

Each of those four companies comes, as one would expect, with a government attached. In essence, constant political meddling is the price Airbus must pay for the billions of dollars in low-interest government loans that have helped it launch new designs. Politicians have a powerful weapon with which to exert influence in order to spread work across Airbus's 16 European factories. As noted by *Washington Post* writer Steven Pearlstein: ". . . it's about the pigheadedness of . . . partners who care less about how many planes Airbus sells than how the work is divided between the countries." Such attitudes sap efficiency and increase the risk of production glitches. Eric Chaney, Morgan Stanley's chief

European economist, asserts: "The fairy tale has turned into a nightmare that even the fiercest Euro-skeptics wouldn't have imagined possible."

There is, however, good news in all of this—for Boeing. The delays on the Airbus A380 have created a sort of virtuous cycle. First, they force air transport companies to switch freighter orders, as both International Lease Finance and FedEx did. Second, the delays in the passenger version of the A380 mean potential customers have to keep older planes, such as Boeing 747-400s, in passenger service longer, instead of converting them into cargo haulers—a much cheaper option than buying new. So, fewer used jets lying around mean more demand for the new cargo jets—which Boeing is happy to sell.

One of the central concepts in this chapter is the importance of boundaryless organizations. That is, successful organizations create permeable boundaries among the internal activities as well as between the organization and its external customers, suppliers, and alliance partners. We introduced this idea in Chapter 3 in our discussion of the value-chain concept, which consists of several primary (e.g., inbound logistics, marketing and sales) and support activities (e.g., procurement, human resource management). Clearly, the underlying cause of Airbus's problem is its inability to establish close and effective working relationships between its various factories operating in four countries. Frequently, managers (and politicians) are seemingly more focused on national interests instead of what is best for Airbus shareholders.

The most important implication of this chapter is that today's managers are faced with two ongoing and vital activities in structuring and designing their organizations. First, they must decide on the most appropriate type of organizational structure. Second, they need to assess what mechanisms, processes, and techniques are most helpful in enhancing the permeability of both internal and external boundaries.

⚫ TRADITIONAL FORMS OF ORGANIZATIONAL STRUCTURE

Organizational structure refers to the formalized patterns of interactions that link a firm's tasks, technologies, and people.[2] Structures help to ensure that resources are used effectively in accomplishing an organization's mission. Structure provides a means of balancing two conflicting forces: a need for the division of tasks into meaningful groupings and the need to integrate such groupings in order to ensure efficiency and effectiveness. Structure identifies the executive, managerial, and administrative organization of a firm and indicates responsibilities and hierarchical relationships. It also influences the flow of information as well as the context and nature of human interactions.

Most organizations begin very small and either die or remain small. Those few that survive and prosper embark on strategies designed to increase the overall scope of operations and enable them to enter new product-market domains. Such growth places additional pressure on executives to control and coordinate the firm's increasing size and diversity. The most appropriate type of structure depends on the nature and magnitude of growth in a firm. Next, we address various types of structural forms, their advantages and disadvantages, and their relationships to the strategies that organizations undertake.

SIMPLE STRUCTURE

The **simple organizational structure** is the oldest, and most common, organizational form. Most organizations are very small and have a single or very narrow product line in which the owner-manager (or top executive) makes most of the decisions. In effect, the owner-manager controls all activities, and the staff serves as an extension of the top executive.

Advantages   The simple structure is highly informal and the coordination of tasks is accomplished by direct supervision. Decision making is highly centralized, there is little specialization of tasks, few rules and regulations, and an informal evaluation and reward system. Although the owner-manager is intimately involved in almost all phases of the business, another manager is often employed to oversee day-to-day operations.

Disadvantages   A simple structure may often foster creativity and individualism because there are generally few rules and regulations. However, such "informality" may lead to problems. Employees may not clearly understand their responsibilities, which can lead to conflict and confusion. Employees also may take advantage of the lack of regulations and act in their own self-interest. Such actions can erode motivation and satisfaction as well as lead to the possible misuse of organizational resources. Further, small organizations have flat structures that limit opportunities for upward mobility. Without the potential for future advancement, recruiting and retaining talent may become very difficult.

FUNCTIONAL STRUCTURE

When an organization is very small, it is not necessary to have a variety of formal arrangements and groupings of activities. However, as firms grow, excessive demands may be placed on the owner-manager in order to obtain and process all of the information necessary to run the business. Chances are the owner will not be skilled in all specialties (e.g., accounting, engineering, production, marketing). Thus, he or she will need to hire specialists in the various functional areas. Such growth in the overall scope and complexity of the business necessitates a functional structure wherein the major functions of the firm are grouped internally. The coordination and integration of the functional areas becomes one of the most important responsibilities of the top executive. Exhibit 7.1 presents a diagram of a **functional organizational structure.**

Functional structures are generally found in organizations in which there is a single or closely related product or service, high production volume, and some vertical integration. Initially, firms tend to expand the overall scope of their operations by penetrating existing markets, introducing similar products in additional markets, or increasing the level of vertical integration. Such expansion activities clearly increase the scope and complexity of the operations. Fortunately, the functional structure provides for a high level of centralization that helps to ensure integration and control over the related product-market activities or multiple primary activities (from inbound logistics to operations to marketing, sales, and service) in the value chain (addressed in Chapter 3).

L03   The relative advantages and disadvantages of traditional organizational structures.

functional organization structure
An organizational form in which the major functions of the firm, such as production, marketing, R&D, and accounting, are grouped internally.

EXHIBIT 7.1   *Functional Organizational Structure*

Parkdale Mills: A Successful Functional Organizational Structure

For more than 80 years, Parkdale Mills, with approximately $1 billion in revenues, has been the industry leader in the production of cotton and cotton blend yarns. Their expertise comes by concentrating on a single product line, perfecting processes, and welcoming innovation. According to CEO Andy Warlick, "I think we've probably spent more than any two competitors combined on new equipment and robotics. We do this because we have to compete in a global market where a lot of the competition has a lower wage structure and gets subsidies that we don't receive, so we really have to focus on consistency and cost control." Yarn making is generally considered to be a commodity business, and Parkdale is the industry's low-cost producer.

Tasks are highly standardized and authority is centralized with Duke Kimbrell, founder and chairman, and CEO Andy Warlick. The firm operates a bare-bones staff with a small staff of top executives. Kimbrell and Warlick are considered shrewd about the cotton market, technology, customer loyalty, and incentive pay.

Sources: Stewart, C. 2003. The perfect yarn. *The Manufacturer.com,* July 31; www.parkdalemills.com; Berman, P. 1987. The fast track isn't always the best track. *Forbes,* November 2: 60–64; and personal communication with Duke Kimbrell, March 11, 2005.

Focus on Strategy 7.1 provides an example of an effective functional organization structure—Parkdale Mills.

LO3 The relative advantages and disadvantages of traditional organizational structures.

Advantages By bringing together specialists into functional departments, a firm is able to enhance its coordination and control within each of the functional areas. The structure also ensures that decision making will be centralized at the top. This enhances the organizational-level (as opposed to functional area) perspective across the various functions in the organization. In addition, the functional structure provides for a more efficient use of managerial and technical talent because functional area expertise is pooled in a single department (e.g., marketing) instead of being spread across a variety of product-market areas. Finally, career paths and professional development in specialized areas are facilitated.

Disadvantages There also are some significant disadvantages associated with the functional structure. First, the differences in values and orientations among functional areas may impede communication and coordination. Edgar Schein has argued that shared assumptions, often based on similar backgrounds and experiences of members, form around functional units in an organization. This leads to what are often called "stove pipes" or "silos," in which departments view themselves as isolated, self-contained units with little need for interaction and coordination with other departments. This erodes communication because functional groups may have not only different goals but also differing meanings of words and concepts. According to Schein:

> The word "marketing" will mean product development to the engineer, studying customers through market research to the product manager, merchandising to the salesperson, and constant change in design to the manufacturing manager. When they try to work together, they will often attribute disagreements to personalities and fail to notice the deeper, shared assumptions that color how each function thinks.[3]

Such narrow orientations also may lead to short-term thinking based largely upon what is best for the functional area, not the entire organization. For example, in a manufacturing firm, sales may want to offer a wide range of customized products to appeal to the firm's customers; research and development may overdesign products and components to achieve technical elegance; and manufacturing may favor no-frills products that can be produced at low cost by means of long production runs. In addition, functional structures may overburden top executives because conflicts have a tendency to be "pushed up" to the top of the organization since there are no managers who are responsible for the specific product lines.

Finally, functional structures make it difficult to establish uniform performance standards across the entire organization. Whereas it may be relatively easy to evaluate production managers on the basis of production volume and cost control, establishing performance measures for engineering, research and development, and accounting is difficult.

DIVISIONAL STRUCTURE

The **divisional organizational structure** (sometimes called the multidivisional structure or M-Form) is organized around products, projects, or markets. Each of the divisions, in turn, includes its own functional specialists who are typically organized into departments. A divisional structure encompasses a set of relatively autonomous units governed by a central corporate office. The operating divisions are relatively independent and consist of products and services that are different from those of the other divisions. Operational decision making in a large business places excessive demands on the firm's top management. In order to attend to broader, longer-term issues, top managers must delegate decision making to lower-level managers. Thus, divisional executives play a key role. In conjunction with corporate-level executives, they help to determine the product-market and financial objectives for the division as well as their division's contribution to overall corporate performance. The rewards are based largely on measures of financial performance such as net income and revenue. Exhibit 7.2 illustrates a divisional structure.

General Motors was among the earliest firms to adopt the divisional organizational structure.[4] In the 1920s the company formed five major product divisions (Cadillac, Buick, Oldsmobile, Pontiac, and Chevrolet) as well as several industrial divisions. Since then, many firms have discovered that as they diversified into new product-market activities, functional structures—with their emphasis on single functional departments—were unable to manage the increased complexity of the entire business.

divisional organization structure
An organizational form in which products, projects, or product markets are grouped internally.

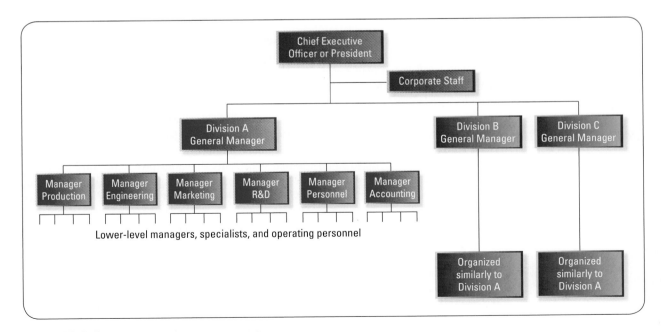

EXHIBIT 7.2 **Divisional Organizational Structure**

Brinker International Changes to a Divisional Organizational Structure

Although Brinker International had a traditional functional structure, changes in its competitive outlook forced management to take a closer look at the organizational design of the firm. The firm controls a variety of restaurant chains and bakeries, including Wildfire, Big Bowl, and Chili's.

With all these interests under one corporate roof, management of these disparate entities became difficult. The fragmented $330 billion restaurant and bakery industry caters to highly focused market niches. The original functional design of the Brinker chain had some disadvantages as the company grew. With areas separated by function, it became hard to focus efforts on a single restaurant chain. The diverse markets served by the bakeries and restaurants began to lose their focus.

As a result, Brinker International changed to a divisional structure. This allowed the company to consolidate individuals who worked with a single restaurant or bakery chain into a separate division. Brinker referred to these as concept teams, with each concept team responsible for the operation of a single line of business. This focused effort streamlined the company's ability to concentrate on the market niche served by each of its restaurants and bakeries.

Source: CEO interview: Ronald A. McDougall, Brinker International. 1999. *Wall Street Transcript,* January 20: 1–4.

LO3 The relative advantages and disadvantages of traditional organizational structures.

Advantages By creating separate divisions to manage individual product markets, there is a separation of strategic and operating control. That is, divisional managers can focus their efforts on improving operations in the product markets for which they are responsible, and corporate officers can devote their time to overall strategic issues for the entire corporation. The focus on a division's products and markets—by the divisional executives—provides the corporation with an enhanced ability to respond quickly to important changes in the external environment. Because there are functional departments within each division of the corporation, the problems associated with sharing resources across functional departments are minimized. Finally, because there are multiple levels of general managers (that is, executives responsible for integrating and coordinating all functional areas), the development of general management talent is enhanced. Focus on Strategy 7.2 discusses the rationale behind Brinker Corporation's change in structure from functional to divisional.

Disadvantages A divisional structure also has potential disadvantages. First, it can be very expensive; that is, there can be increased costs due to the duplication of personnel, operations, and investment because each division must staff multiple functional departments. There also can be dysfunctional competition among divisions because each division tends to become concerned solely about its own operations. Further, divisional managers are often evaluated on common measures such as return on assets and sales growth. Thus, if goals are conflicting, there can be a sense of a "zero-sum" game that discourages sharing ideas and resources among the divisions for the common good of the corporation.

Another potential disadvantage is that with many divisions providing different products and services, there is the chance that differences in image and quality may occur across divisions. For example, one division may offer no-frills products of lower quality that may erode the brand reputation of another division that has top quality, highly differentiated offerings. Finally, because each division is evaluated in terms of financial measures such as return on investment and revenue growth, there is often an urge to focus on short-term performance. For example, if corporate management uses quarterly profits as the key performance indicator, divisional management may tend to put significant emphasis on "making the numbers" and minimizing activities, such as advertising, maintenance, and capital investments, which would detract from short-term performance measures.

Before moving on, we'll discuss two variations of the divisional form of organizational structure: the strategic business unit (SBU) and holding company structures.

Strategic Business Unit (SBU) Structure   Highly diversified corporations such as ConAgra, a $12 billion food producer, may consist of dozens of different divisions. If ConAgra were to use a purely divisional structure, it would be nearly impossible for the corporate office to plan and coordinate activities because the span of control would be too large. Instead, to attain synergies, ConAgra has put its diverse businesses into three primary SBUs: food service (restaurants), retail (grocery stores), and agricultural products.

With a **strategic business unit (SBU) structure,** divisions with similar products, markets, and/or technologies are grouped into homogenous groups in order to achieve some synergies. These include those discussed in Chapter 5 for related diversification, such as leveraging core competencies, sharing infrastructures, and market power. Generally speaking, the more related businesses are within a corporation, the fewer SBUs will be required. Each of the SBUs in the corporation operates as a profit center.

Advantages   The major advantage of the SBU structure is that it makes the task of planning and control by the corporate office more manageable. Also, with greater decentralization of authority, individual businesses can react more quickly to important changes in the environment than if all divisions had to report directly to the corporate office.

Disadvantages   There are also some disadvantages to the SBU structure. Because the divisions are grouped into SBUs, it may become difficult to achieve synergies across SBUs. That is, if divisions that are included in different SBUs have potential sources of synergy, it may become difficult for them to be realized. The additional level of management increases the number of personnel and overhead expenses, while the additional hierarchical level removes the corporate office further from the individual divisions. Thus, the corporate office may become unaware of key developments that could have a major impact on the corporation.

Holding Company Structure   The **holding company structure** (sometimes referred to as a *conglomerate*) is also a variation of the divisional structure. Whereas the SBU structure is often used when similarities exist between the individual businesses (or divisions), the holding company structure is appropriate when the businesses in a corporation's portfolio do not have much in common. Thus, the potential for synergies is limited.

Holding company structures are most appropriate for firms with a strategy of unrelated diversification. Companies such as Hanson Trust, ITT, and the CP group of Thailand have used holding company structures to implement their unrelated diversification strategies. Because there are few similarities across the businesses, the corporate offices in these companies provide a great deal of autonomy to operating divisions and rely on financial controls and incentive programs to obtain high levels of performance from the individual businesses. Corporate staffs at these firms tend to be small because of their limited involvement in the overall operation of their various businesses.

Advantages   An important advantage of the holding company structure is the cost savings associated with fewer personnel and the lower overhead resulting from a small corporate office and fewer hierarchical levels. In addition, the autonomy of the holding company structure increases the motivational level of divisional executives and enables them to respond quickly to market opportunities and threats.

Disadvantages   The primary disadvantage of the holding company structure is the inherent lack of control and dependence that corporate-level executives have on divisional executives. Major problems could arise if key divisional executives leave the firm, because

strategic business unit (SBU) structure
An organizational form in which product, project, or product market divisions are grouped into homogeneous units.

LO3   The relative advantages and disadvantages of traditional organizational structures.

holding company structure
An organizational form that is a variation of the divisional organizational structure in which the divisions have a high degree of autonomy both from other divisions and from corporate headquarters.

LO3   The relative advantages and disadvantages of traditional organizational structures.

the corporate office has very little "bench strength"—that is, additional managerial talent ready to quickly fill key positions. And if problems arise in a division, it may become very difficult to turn around individual businesses because of limited staff support in the corporate office.

MATRIX STRUCTURE

matrix organization structure
An organizational form in which there are multiple lines of authority and some individuals report to at least two managers.

At times, managers may find that none of the structures that we have described above fully meet their needs. One approach that tries to overcome the inadequacies inherent in the other structures is the **matrix structure.** It is, in effect, a combination of the functional and divisional structures. Most commonly, functional departments are combined with product groups on a project basis. For example, a product group may want to develop a new addition to its line; for this project, it obtains personnel from functional departments such as marketing, production, and engineering. These personnel work under the manager of the product group for the duration of the project, which can vary from a few weeks to an open-ended period of time. The individuals who work in a matrix organization become responsible to two managers: the project manager and the manager of their functional area. Exhibit 7.3 illustrates a matrix structure.

In addition to the product-function matrix, other bases may be related in a matrix. Some large multinational corporations rely on a matrix structure to combine product groups and geographical units. Product managers have global responsibility for the development, manufacturing, and distribution of their own line, while managers of geographical regions have responsibility for the profitability of the businesses in their regions.

Dell Computer relies on the matrix concept—with its dual reporting responsibility—in order to enhance accountability as well as develop general managers. According to former CEO Kevin Rollins:[5]

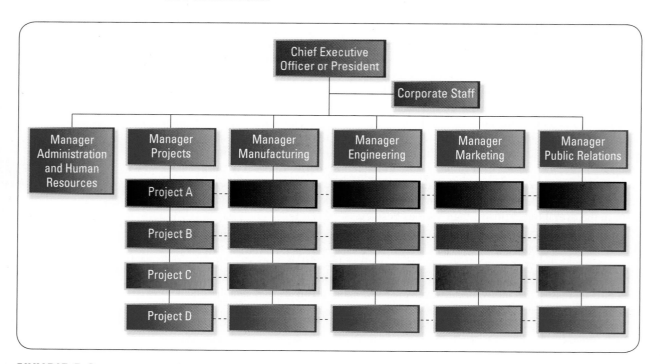

EXHIBIT 7.3 **Matrix Organizational Structure**

We're organized in a matrix of sales regions and product groups. Then we break each of those groups down to a pretty fine level of subproducts and sales subsegments. Dell has more P&L managers, and smaller business units, than most companies its size. This not only increases accountability to the customer, it helps train general managers by moving them from smaller to larger businesses as their skills develop.

Our matrix organization has a third level—our business councils. For example, we have a small-business sales group in each country, along with product development people who become very familiar with what small-business customers buy. In addition, we have our worldwide small-business council made up of all our small-business GMs and product managers. Everyone in these councils sees everyone else's P&L, so it provides another set of checks and balances.

Advantages A primary advantage of the matrix structure is that it facilitates the use of specialized personnel, equipment, and facilities. Instead of duplicating functions, as would be the case in a divisional structure based on products, the resources are shared. Individuals with high expertise can divide their time among multiple projects. Such resource sharing and collaboration enable a firm to use resources more efficiently and to respond more quickly and effectively to changes in the competitive environment. In addition, the flexibility inherent in a matrix structure provides professionals with a broader range of responsibility. Such experience enables them to develop their skills and competencies.

LO3 The relative advantages and disadvantages of traditional organizational structures.

Disadvantages Matrix structures have many potential disadvantages. The dual-reporting structures can result in uncertainty and lead to intense power struggles and conflict over the allocation of personnel and other resources. Additionally, working relationships become more complicated. This may result in excessive reliance on group processes and teamwork, along with a diffusion of responsibility, which in turn may erode timely decision making. Exhibit 7.4 briefly summarizes the advantages and disadvantages of the functional, divisional, and matrix organizational structures.

HOW AN ORGANIZATION'S STRUCTURE CAN INFLUENCE STRATEGY FORMULATION

Discussions of the relationship between strategy and structure usually strongly imply that structure follows strategy. That is, the strategy that a firm chooses (e.g., related diversification) dictates such structural elements as the division of tasks, the need for integration of activities, and authority relationships within the organization. However, an existing structure can influence strategy formulation. For example, once a firm's structure is in place, it is very difficult and expensive to change. Executives may not be able to modify their duties and responsibilities greatly, or may not welcome the disruption associated with a transfer to a new location. Further, there are costs associated with hiring, training, and replacing executive, managerial, and operating personnel. Thus, strategy cannot be formulated without considering structural elements.

The type of organizational structure can also strongly influence a firm's strategy, day-to-day operations, and performance.[6] We discussed Brinker International's move to a divisional structure in order to organize its restaurant groups into different units to focus on market niches. This new structure should enable the firm to adapt to change more rapidly and innovate more effectively with the various restaurant brands.

⦿ BOUNDARYLESS ORGANIZATIONAL DESIGNS

LO4 The different types of boundaryless organizations—barrier-free, modular, and virtual—and their relative advantages and disadvantages.

The term *boundaryless* may bring to mind a chaotic organizational reality in which "anything goes." This is not the case. As Jack Welch, GE's former CEO, has suggested,

IBIT 7.4

Functional, Divisional, and Matrix Organizational Structures: Advantages and Disadvantages

LO3   The relative advantages and disadvantages of traditional organizational structures.

Functional Structure

Advantages	Disadvantages
• Pooling of specialists enhances coordination and control.	• Differences in functional area orientation impede communication and coordination.
• Centralized decision making enhances an organizational perspective across functions.	• Tendency for specialists to develop short-term perspective and narrow functional orientation.
• Efficient use of managerial and technical talent.	• Functional area conflicts may overburden top-level decision makers.
• Facilitates career paths and professional development in specialized areas.	• Difficult to establish uniform performance standards.

Divisional Structure

Advantages	Disadvantages
• Increases strategic and operational control, permitting corporate-level executives to address strategic issues.	• Increased costs incurred through duplication of personnel, operations, and investment.
• Quick response to environmental changes.	• Dysfunctional competition among divisions may detract from overall corporate performance.
• Increases focus on products and markets.	• Difficult to maintain uniform corporate image.
• Minimizes problems associated with sharing resources across functional areas.	• Overemphasis on short-term performance.
• Facilitates development of general managers.	

Matrix Structure

Advantages	Disadvantages
• Increases market responsiveness through collaboration and synergies among professional colleagues.	• Dual-reporting relationships can result in uncertainty regarding accountability.
• Allows more efficient utilization of resources.	• Intense power struggles may lead to increased levels of conflict.
• Improves flexibility, coordination, and communication.	• Working relationships may be more complicated and human resources duplicated.
• Increases professional development through a broader range of responsibility.	• Excessive reliance on group processes and teamwork may impede timely decision making.

boundaryless organizational designs

Organizations in which the boundaries, including vertical, horizontal, external, and geographic boundaries, are permeable.

boundaryless does not imply that all internal and external boundaries vanish completely. Although boundaries may continue to exist in some form, they become more open and permeable. Focus on Strategy 7.3 discusses four types of boundaries and provides examples of how organizations have made them more permeable.

We are not suggesting that **boundaryless organizational designs** replace the traditional forms of organizational structure, but rather that they should complement them. For example, Sharp Corp. has implemented a functional structure to attain economies of scale

Boundary Types

There are primarily four types of boundaries that place limits on organizations. In today's dynamic business environment, different types of boundaries are needed to foster high degrees of interaction with outside influences and varying levels of permeability.

1. *Vertical boundaries between levels in the organization's hierarchy.* SmithKline Beecham asks employees at different hierarchical levels to brainstorm ideas for managing clinical trial data. The ideas are incorporated into action plans that significantly cut the new product approval time of its breakthrough pharmaceuticals. This would not have been possible if the barriers between levels of individuals in the organization had been too high.

2. *Horizontal boundaries between functional areas.* Fidelity Investments makes the functional barriers more porous and flexible among divisions, such as marketing, operations, and customer service, in order to offer customers a more integrated experience when conducting business with the company. Customers can take their questions to one person, reducing the chance that customers will "get the runaround" from employees who feel customer service is not their responsibility. At Fidelity, customer service is everyone's business, regardless of functional area.

3. *External boundaries between the firm and its customers, suppliers, and regulators.* GE Lighting, by working closely with retailers, functions throughout the value chain as a single operation. This allows GE to track point-of-sale purchases, giving it better control over inventory management.

4. *Geographic boundaries between locations, cultures, and markets.* The global nature of today's business environment spurred PricewaterhouseCoopers to use a global groupware system. This allows the company to instantly connect to its 26 worldwide offices.

Source: Ashkenas, R. 1997. The organization's new clothes. In Hesselbein, F., Goldsmith, M., and Beckhard, R. (Eds.). *The organization of the future:* 104–106. San Francisco: Jossey Bass.

---

with its applied research and manufacturing skills. However, to bring about this key objective, Sharp has relied on several integrating mechanisms and processes.

> To prevent functional groups from becoming vertical chimneys that obstruct product development, Sharp's product managers have responsibility—but not authority—for coordinating the entire set of value-chain activities. And the company convenes enormous numbers of cross-unit and corporate committees to ensure that shared activities, including the corporate R&D unit and sales forces, are optimally configured and allocated among the different product lines. Sharp invests in such time-intensive coordination to minimize the inevitable conflicts that arise when units share important activities.[7]

We will discuss three approaches to making boundaries more permeable. These approaches help to facilitate the widespread sharing of knowledge and information across both the internal and external boundaries of the organization. We'll begin with the *barrier-free* type, which involves making all organizational boundaries—internal and external—more permeable. We'll place particular emphasis on team concepts, because teams are a central building block for implementing the boundaryless organization. In the next two sections, we will address the *modular* and *virtual* types of organizations. These forms focus on the need to create seamless relationships with customers and suppliers. While the modular type emphasizes the outsourcing of noncore activities, the virtual (or network) organization focuses on alliances among independent entities formed to exploit specific market opportunities.

THE BARRIER-FREE ORGANIZATION

The "boundary" mind-set is ingrained deeply into bureaucracies. It is evidenced by such clichés as "That's not my job" and "I'm here from corporate to help." In the traditional company, boundaries are clearly delineated in the design of a structure. Their basic advantage

Teams are a central building block for creating boundary-less organizations.

is that the roles of managers and employees are simple, clear, well-defined, and long-lived. A major shortcoming was pointed out to the authors during an interview with a high-tech executive: "Structure tends to be divisive; it leads to territorial fights."

Today such structures are being replaced by fluid, ambiguous, and deliberately ill-defined tasks and roles. Just because work roles are no longer clearly defined, however, does not mean that differences in skills, authority, and talent disappear.

A **barrier-free organization** enables a firm to bridge real differences in culture, function, and goals to find common ground that facilitates information sharing and other forms of cooperative behavior. Eliminating the multiple boundaries that stifle productivity and innovation can enhance the potential of the entire organization.

Focus on Strategy 7.4 describes how United Technologies Corporation used the boundaryless concept to develop a revolutionary product, Pure Cycle.

Creating Permeable Internal Boundaries

For barrier-free organizations to work effectively, the level of trust and shared interests among all parts of the organization must be raised. Similarly, the organization needs to develop among its employees the skill level needed to work in a more democratic organization. Barrier-free organizations also require a shift from investments in high-potential individuals to investments in leveraging the talents of all individuals.

Teams can be an important aspect of barrier-free structures. Jeffrey Pfeffer, author of several insightful books, including *The Human Equation,* suggests that teams have three primary advantages.[8] First, teams substitute peer-based control for hierarchical control of work activities. In essence, employees control themselves, reducing the time and energy management needs to devote to supervision.

Second, teams frequently develop more creative solutions to problems because they encourage the sharing of the tacit knowledge held by individuals. Brainstorming, or group problem solving, involves the pooling of ideas and expertise to enhance the chances that at least one group member will think of a way to solve the problems at hand.

Third, by substituting peer control for hierarchical control, teams permit the removal of layers of hierarchy and absorption of administrative tasks previously performed by specialists. This avoids the costs of having people whose sole job is to watch the people who watch other people do the work. As Norman Augustine humorously pointed out in *Augustine's Laws,* "If a sufficient number of management layers are superimposed on top of each other, it can be assured that disaster is not left to chance!"[9]

Developing Effective Relationships with External Constituencies

In barrier-free organizations, managers must also create flexible, porous organizational boundaries and establish communication flows and mutually beneficial relationships with internal (e.g., employees) and external (e.g., customers) constituencies. Michael Dell, founder and CEO of Dell Computer, is a strong believer in fostering close relationships with his customers. In an interview, he explained:

> We're not going to be just your PC vendor anymore. We're going to be your IT department for PCs. Boeing, for example, has 100,000 Dell PCs, and we have 30 people that live at Boeing, and if you look at the things we're doing for them or for other customers, we don't look like a supplier, we look more like Boeing's PC department. We become intimately involved in planning their PC needs and the configuration of their network.

United Technologies Corporation's PureCycle: An Effective Use of the Boundaryless Concept

United Technologies Corporation is a giant manufacturing conglomerate which has been on a roll. Revenues and profits for 2006 were $48 billion and $3.7 billion, respectively, which represent an annual increase of over 15 percent over the most recent four-year period.

Like many diversified firms, UTC faced a challenge in developing synergies across business units. UTC's wide variety of products include Carrier heating and air conditioning; Hamilton Sundstrand aerospace systems and industrial products; Otis elevators and escalators; Pratt & Whitney aircraft engines; Sikorsky helicopters; UTC Fire & Security systems; and UTC Power fuel cells. Overall, UTC spends a huge amount of money on research—about 3.5% of total revenues.

Historically, UTC's culture placed a high value on decentralized decision making, with each unit operating almost entirely independently of the others. Such an approach may have motivational benefits and help units focus their efforts. However, it leads to "silo business units" and prevents the corporation from generating innovations in the white spaces between business units.

This approach to business troubled UTC senior vice president John Cassidy and Carl Nett, director of the firm's corporate research center, UTRC. The center is staffed with nearly 500 scientists, engineers, and staff who are charged with "bringing future technologies to the point of product insertion." They both believed that tremendous potential for growth existed in the junctures between the business units. However, such collaboration was not consistent with the history, work practices, and cultural norms at UTC. In fact, Cassidy felt that integrating expertise and talent across business units was an "unnatural act."

What to do? In 2002, the two executives invited top technical talent from each unit to several brainstorming sessions. The goal was to bring together a diverse set of talented professionals to create and service new markets.

Early on, a potential winner emerged from the intersection of cooling, heating, and power. Engineers from Carrier, Pratt & Whitney, and UTRC recognized that using cooling and heating equipment could transform an innovative power generation concept into a revolutionary product. Called PureCycle, the product contained virtually no new components. However, it offered a breakthrough value proposition: Customers could convert waste heat to electricity at rates substantially below those of utilities. The product held great promise because U.S. industrial plants emit roughly as much waste heat as a 50-gigawatt power plant generates (enough to run most major U.S. cities).

In retrospect, engineers involved in the PureCycle project find it hard to believe that nobody had previously thought of the idea. Thierry Jomard, a former Carrier engineer who transferred to UTRC to head the effort, explains: "Carrier people are trained to think in terms of using heat exchange to produce cold air—that's the output that counts: the compressor is just there to move the fluid. Pratt & Whitney engineers, on the other hand, are power people. The outcome they are about is power, and they use turbines to get it." It wasn't until they began their collaboration that anyone recognized the opportunities before them.

Sources: www.utc.com; 2005 *UTC Annual Report;* Davidson, A. 2007. Conglomerates: United Technologies. *Forbes,* January 8: 96; and Cross, R., Liedtka, J. & Weiss, L. 2005. A practical guide to social networks. *Harvard Business Review,* 83 (3): 92–101.

It's not that we make these decisions by ourselves. They're certainly using their own people to get the best answer for the company. But the people working on PCs together, from both Dell and Boeing, understand the needs in a very intimate way. They're right there living it and breathing it, as opposed to the typical vendor who says, "Here are your computers. See you later."[10]

Thus far, we have argued that barrier-free organizations create successful relationships between both internal and external constituencies. However, there is one additional constituency—competitors—with whom some organizations have benefited as they developed cooperative relationships.

For example, after years of seeing its empty trucks return from warehouses back to production facilities after deliveries, General Mills teamed up with 16 of its competitors. They formed an e-commerce business to help the firms find carriers with empty cargo trailers to piggyback freight loads to distributors near the production facilities.[11] This increases revenue for all network members and reduces fuel costs.

Risks, Challenges, and Potential Downsides Despite its potential benefits, many firms find that creating and managing a barrier-free organization can be frustrating.[12] For example, Puritan-Bennett Corporation, a Lenexa, Kansas, manufacturer of respiratory equipment, found that its product development time more than doubled after it adopted team management. Roger J. Dolida, director of R&D, attributed this failure to a lack of top management commitment, high turnover among team members, and infrequent meetings. Often, managers trained in rigid hierarchies find it difficult to make the transition to the more democratic, participative style that teamwork requires.

Christopher Barnes, now a consultant with PricewaterhouseCoopers in Atlanta, previously worked as an industrial engineer for Challenger Electrical Distribution (a subsidiary of Westinghouse, now part of CBS) at a plant in Jackson, Mississippi, which produced circuit-breaker boxes. His assignment was to lead a team of workers from the plant's troubled final-assembly operation with the mission: "Make things better." Not surprisingly, that vague notion set the team up for failure.

After a year of futility, the team was disbanded. In retrospect, Barnes identified several reasons for the debacle: (1) limited personal credibility—he was viewed as an "outsider"; (2) a lack of commitment to the team—everyone involved was forced to be on the team; (3) poor communications—nobody was told why the team was important; (4) limited autonomy—line managers refused to give up control over team members; and (5) misaligned incentives—the culture rewarded individual performance over team performance. Barnes's experience has implications for all types of teams, whether they are composed of managerial, professional, clerical, or production personnel.[13] The pros and cons of barrier-free structures are summarized in Exhibit 7.5.

THE MODULAR ORGANIZATION

As Charles Handy, author of *The Age of Unreason,* has noted:

> Organizations have realized that, while it may be convenient to have everyone around all the time, having all of your workforce's time at your command is an extravagant way of marshaling the necessary resources. It is cheaper to keep them outside the organization, employed by themselves or by specialist contractors, and to buy their services when you need them.[14]

modular organization
An organization in which nonvital functions are outsourced, which uses the knowledge and expertise of outside suppliers, while retaining strategic control.

Consistent with Handy's vision, the **modular organization** outsources nonvital functions, tapping into the knowledge and expertise of "best in class" suppliers, but retains strategic control. Outsiders may be used to manufacture parts, handle logistics, or perform accounting activities. As we discussed in Chapter 3, the value chain can be used to identify the key primary and support activities performed by a firm to create value. The key question becomes: Which activities do we keep "in-house" and which activities do we outsource

EXHIBIT 7.5

Pros and Cons of Barrier-Free Structures

Pros	Cons
• Leverages the talents of all employees.	• Difficult to overcome political and authority boundaries inside and outside the organization.
• Enhances cooperation, coordination, and information sharing among functions, divisions, SBUs, and external constituencies.	• Lacks strong leadership and common vision, which can lead to coordination problems.
• Enables a quicker response to market changes through a single-goal focus.	• Time-consuming and difficult-to-manage democratic processes.
• Can lead to coordinated win–win initiatives with key suppliers, customers, and alliance partners.	• Lacks high levels of trust, which can impede performance.

to suppliers?[15] The organization becomes a central hub surrounded by networks of outside suppliers and specialists and, much like Lego blocks, parts can be added or taken away. Both manufacturing and service units may be modular.

Apparel is an industry in which the modular type has been widely adopted. Nike and Reebok, for example, concentrate on their strengths: designing and marketing high-tech, fashionable footwear. Nike has few production facilities and Reebok owns no plants. These two companies contract virtually all their footwear production to suppliers in China, Vietnam, and other countries with low-cost labor. Avoiding large investments in fixed assets helps them derive large profits on minor sales increases. Thus, Nike and Reebok can keep pace with changing tastes in the marketplace because their suppliers have become expert at rapidly retooling to produce new products.

Adidas is one of many athletic shoe companies that have outsourced most of their production to low cost labor countries such as China and Vietnam.

In a modular company, outsourcing the noncore functions offers three advantages.

1. A firm can decrease overall costs, stimulate new product development by hiring suppliers whose talent may be superior to that of in-house personnel, avoid idle capacity, reduce inventories, and avoid being locked into a particular technology.

2. Outsourcing enables a company to focus scarce resources on the areas where it holds a competitive advantage. These benefits can translate into more funding for research and development, hiring the best engineers, and providing continuous training for sales and service staff.

3. By enabling an organization to tap into the knowledge and expertise of its specialized supply-chain partners, it adds critical skills and accelerates organizational learning.[16]

The modular type enables a company to leverage relatively small amounts of capital and a small management team to achieve seemingly unattainable strategic objectives.[17] Freed from the need to make big investments in fixed assets, the modular company can grow rapidly. Certain preconditions are necessary before the modular approach can be successful. First, the company must work closely with suppliers to ensure that the interests of each party are being fulfilled. Companies need to find loyal, reliable vendors who can be trusted with trade secrets. They also need assurances that suppliers will dedicate their financial, physical, and human resources to satisfy strategic objectives such as lowering costs or being first to market.

Second, the modular company must be sure that it selects the proper competencies to keep in-house. For Nike and Reebok, the core competencies are design and marketing, not shoe manufacturing; for Honda, the core competence is engine technology. These firms are unlikely to outsource any activity that involves their core competence. An organization must avoid outsourcing components that may compromise its long-term competitive advantages.

Strategic Risks of Outsourcing While adopting the modular form clearly has some advantages, managers must also weigh associated risks. The main strategic concerns are (1) loss of critical skills or developing the wrong skills, (2) loss of cross-functional skills, and (3) loss of control over a supplier.[18]

Too much outsourcing can result in a firm "giving away" too much skill and control. Outsourcing relieves companies of the requirement to maintain skill levels needed to manufacture essential components. Over time, these skills that were once part of the knowledge base of the company disappear. At one time, semiconductor chips seemed like a simple technology to outsource. But now, they have become a critical component of a wide variety of products. Companies that have outsourced the manufacture of these chips run the risk of losing the ability to manufacture them as the technology escalates. Thus, they become more dependent upon their suppliers.

Cross-functional skills refer to the skills acquired through the interaction of individuals in various departments within a company. Often, such interaction assists a department in solving problems as employees interface with others across functional units. However, if a firm outsources key functional responsibilities, such as manufacturing, communication across departments can become more difficult. This is because a firm and its employees must now integrate their activities with a new, outside supplier. This typically brings about new challenges in the coordination of joint efforts.

Another drawback occurs when the outsourced products give suppliers too much power over the manufacturer. Suppliers that are key to a manufacturer's success can, in essence, hold the manufacturer "hostage." Nike manages this potential problem by sending full-time "product expatriates" to work at the plants of its suppliers. Also, Nike often brings top members of supplier management and technical teams to its headquarters. This way, Nike keeps close tabs on the pulse of new developments, builds rapport and trust with suppliers, and develops long-term relationships to prevent hostage situations. Exhibit 7.6 summarizes the pros and cons of modular structures.

THE VIRTUAL ORGANIZATION

In contrast to the "self-reliant" thinking that guided traditional organizational designs, the strategic challenge today has become doing more with less and looking outside the firm for opportunities and solutions to problems. The "virtual organization" provides a new means of leveraging resources and exploiting opportunities.

virtual organization
A continually evolving network of independent companies that are linked together to share skills, costs, and access to one another's markets.

The **virtual organization** can be viewed as a continually evolving network of independent companies—suppliers, customers, even competitors—linked together to share skills, costs, and access to one another's markets.[19] The members of a virtual organization, by pooling and sharing the knowledge and expertise of each of the component organizations, simultaneously "know" more and can "do" more than any one member of the group

EXHIBIT 7.6

Pros and Cons of Modular Structures

Pros	Cons
• Directs a firm's managerial and technical talent to the most critical activities.	• Inhibits common vision through reliance on outsiders.
• Maintains full strategic control over most critical activities—core competencies.	• Diminishes future competitive advantages if critical technologies or other competences are outsourced.
• Achieves "best in class" performance at each link in the value chain.	• Increases the difficulty of bringing back into the firm activities that now add value due to market shifts.
• Leverages core competencies by outsourcing with smaller capital commitment.	• Leads to an erosion of cross-functional skills.
• Encourages information sharing and accelerates organizational learning.	• Decreases operational control and potential loss of control over a supplier.

Collaborative Relationships in Biotechnology

Collaboration in biotechnology has benefited a variety of firms. Amgen collaborates with a number of smaller firms including ARRIS, Environgen, Glycomex, and Interneuron, among others. The companies work on joint marketing projects and bring R&D scientists together to explore opportunities for new pharmaceutical product development. In exchange for the expertise of the scientists and marketers at the smaller companies, Amgen provides financial clout and technical assistance when new-product opportunities are identified.

Another biotech company that utilizes collaborative relationships with competitors is Biogen. This large pharmaceutical firm once outsourced clinical testing of its new drugs. But now, the company brings experts from other firms to Biogen laboratories to work with their scientists.

Chiron, one of the largest pharmaceutical firms, with over 7,500 employees, makes extensive use of collaborative efforts with its competitors. The company currently collaborates with over 1,400 companies, tapping into the knowledge base of R&D experts with a wide variety of skill and expertise in the field. Chiron considers this network one of its core competencies.

Source: Powell, W. W. 1998. Learning from collaboration: Knowledge and networks in the biotechnology and pharmaceutical industries. *California Management Review,* 40 (3): 228–240; Williams, E., & Langreth, R. 2001. A biotech wonder grows up. *Forbes,* September 3: 118.

could do alone. By working closely together, each gains in the long run from individual and organizational learning. The term *virtual,* meaning "being in effect but not actually so," is commonly used in the computer industry. A computer's ability to appear to have more storage capacity than it really possesses is called virtual memory. Similarly, by assembling resources from a variety of entities, a virtual organization may seem to have more capabilities than it really possesses.[20]

The virtual organization is a grouping of units from different organizations that have joined in an alliance to exploit complementary skills in pursuing common strategic objectives. A case in point is Lockheed Martin's use of specialized coalitions between and among three entities—the company, academia, and government—to enhance competitiveness. According to former CEO Norman Augustine:

> The underlying beauty of this approach is that it forces us to reach outward. No matter what your size, you have to look broadly for new ideas, new approaches, new products. Lockheed Martin used this approach in a surprising manner when it set out during the height of the Cold War to make stealth aircraft and missiles. The technical idea came from research done at the Institute of Radio Engineering in Moscow in the 1960s that was published, and publicized, quite openly in the academic media.
>
> Despite the great contrasts among government, academia and private business, we have found ways to work together that have produced very positive results, not the least of which is our ability to compete on a global scale.[21]

Virtual organizations need not be permanent and participating firms may be involved in multiple alliances. Virtual organizations may involve different firms performing complementary value activities, or different firms involved jointly in the same value activities, such as production, R&D, and distribution. The percentage of activities that are jointly performed with partners may vary significantly from alliance to alliance.[22]

How does the virtual type of structure differ from the modular type? Unlike the modular type, in which the focal firm maintains full strategic control, the virtual organization is characterized by participating firms that give up part of their control and accept interdependent destinies. Participating firms pursue a collective strategy that enables them to cope with uncertainty through cooperative efforts. The benefit is that, just as virtual memory increases storage capacity, the virtual organizations enhance the capacity or competitive advantage of participating firms. Focus on Strategy 7.5 addresses the variety of collaborative relationships in the biotechnology industry.

Each company (as Strategy Spotlight 7.5 illustrates) that links up with others to create a virtual organization contributes only what it considers its core competencies. It will mix and match what it does best with the best of other firms by identifying its critical capabilities and the necessary links to other capabilities.

Challenges and Risks   Despite their many advantages, such alliances often fail to meet expectations. For example, the alliance between IBM and Microsoft soured in early 1991 when Microsoft began shipping Windows in direct competition to OS/2, which they had jointly developed. The runaway success of Windows frustrated IBM's ability to set an industry standard. In retaliation, IBM entered into an alliance with Microsoft's archrival, Novell, to develop network software to compete with Microsoft's LAN Manager.

The virtual organization demands a unique set of managerial skills. Managers must build relationships with other companies, negotiate win–win deals for all parties involved, find the right partners with compatible goals and values, and provide the right balance of freedom and control. In addition, information systems must be designed and integrated to facilitate communication with current and potential partners.

Managers must be clear about the strategic objectives while forming alliances. Some objectives are time bound, and those alliances need to be dissolved once the objective is fulfilled. Some alliances may have relatively long-term objectives and will need to be clearly monitored and nurtured to produce mutual commitment and avoid bitter fights for control. The highly dynamic personal computer industry, for example, is characterized by multiple temporary alliances among hardware, operating systems, and software producers. But alliances in the more stable automobile industry, such as those involving Nissan and Renault as well as Mazda and Ford, have long-term objectives and tend to be relatively stable. Exhibit 7.7 summarizes the advantages and disadvantages of the virtual form.

BOUNDARYLESS ORGANIZATIONS: MAKING THEM WORK

Designing an organization that simultaneously supports the requirements of an organization's strategy, is consistent with the demands of the environment, and can be effectively implemented by the people around the manager is a tall order for any manager.[23] The most

EXHIBIT 7.7

Pros and Cons of Virtual Structures

Pros	Cons
• Enables the sharing of costs and skills.	• Harder to determine where one company ends and another begins, due to close interdependencies among players.
• Enhances access to global markets.	
• Increases market responsiveness.	• Leads to potential loss of operational control among partners.
• Creates a "best of everything" organization since each partner brings core competencies to the alliance.	• Results in loss of strategic control over emerging technology.
• Encourages both individual and organizational knowledge sharing and accelerates organizational learning.	• Requires new and difficult-to-acquire managerial skills.

Source: Miles, R. E., & Snow, C. C. 1986. Organizations: New concepts for new forms. *California Management Review,* Spring: 62–73; Miles & Snow. 1999. Causes of failure in network organizations. *California Management Review,* Summer: 53–72; and Bahrami, H. 1991. The emerging flexible organization: Perspectives from Silicon Valley. *California Management Review,* Summer: 33–52.

Technical Computer Graphics' Boundaryless Organization

The Technical Computer Graphics (TCG) group manufactures items such as handheld bar code readers and scanning software. The company uses 13 "alliances," or small project teams, employing a total of 200 employees. Each team is responsible for either specific customers or specific products. Alliance teams share a common infrastructure, but they can develop new business opportunities without approval from upper management. Projects often emerge from listening to what customers need.

TCG uses a "triangulation approach"—alliances that include customers, suppliers, and other alliances. Suppliers and customers who provide funding are involved at the outset of the project. The alliances recognize that attaining the initial customer funding is crucial; it stimulates them to focus on what customers have to say. With an emphasis on speed, new products come to market quickly, providing the firm and its partners with tangible benefits. Sometimes another alliance acts as either the customer or the supplier and provides funding.

While each alliance is independent, it shares financial concern for other alliance teams. When a new business opportunity is discovered, an alliance draws on technical expertise from the other alliances. The purpose is not only to acquire additional knowledge, but also to share accumulated learning. There's no benefit to hoarding information: Learning gained from one software project might prove especially valuable to one under way in another alliance. This technological diffusion of information produces products that quickly reach the market.

TCG's formal structure is designed to ensure that such knowledge diffusion occurs. The company's culture is structured to encourage this as well. The TCG culture attracts both the entrepreneur and the team-oriented person at the same time. Working with multiple stakeholders through TCG's triangulation model forces employees to listen to the customers and respond quickly. Because the customer matters more than the functional title, teams lend expertise to each other in return for sharing the gains realized from supplying value to the customer.

Source: Snow, C. 1997. Twenty-first century organizations: Implications for a new marketing paradigm. *Journal of the Academy of Marketing Science,* Winter: 72–74; Allred, B. Snow, C. & Miles, R. 1996. Characteristics of managerial careers of the 21st century. *Academy of Management Executive,* November: 17–27; Herzog, V. L. 2001. Trust building on corporate collaborative teams. *Project Management Journal,* March: 28–41.

effective solution is usually a combination of organizational types. That is, a firm may outsource many parts of its value chain to reduce costs and increase quality, engage simultaneously in multiple alliances to take advantage of technological developments or penetrate new markets, and break down barriers within the organization to enhance flexibility. In Focus on Strategy 7.6, we see how an innovative firm, Technical Computer Graphics, combines both barrier-free and virtual organizational forms.

When an organization faces external pressures, resource scarcity, and declining performance, it tends to become more internally focused, rather than directing its efforts toward managing and enhancing relationships with existing and potential external stakeholders. We believe that this may be the most opportune time for managers to carefully analyze their value-chain activities and evaluate the potential for adopting elements of modular, virtual, and barrier-free organizational types.

Regardless of the form of organization ultimately chosen, achieving the coordination and integration necessary to maximize the potential of an organization's human capital involves much more than just creating a new structure. Techniques and processes to ensure the coordination and integration of an organization's key value-chain activities are critical. Teams are key building blocks of the new organizational forms, and teamwork requires new and flexible approaches to coordination and integration.

Often managers trained in rigid hierarchies find it difficult to make the transition to the more democratic, participative style that teamwork requires. As Douglas K. Smith, coauthor of *The Wisdom of Teams,* pointed out, "A completely diverse group must agree on a goal, put the notion of individual accountability aside and figure out how to work with each other. Most of all, they must learn that if the team fails, it's everyone's fault."[24] Within the framework of an appropriate organizational design, managers must select a mix and balance of tools and techniques to facilitate the effective coordination and integration of key activities. Some of the factors that must be considered include:

- Common culture and shared values.
- Horizontal organizational structures.
- Horizontal systems and processes.
- Communications and information technologies.
- Human resource practices.

Common Culture and Shared Values   Shared goals, mutual objectives, and a high degree of trust are essential to the success of boundaryless organizations. It is neither feasible nor desirable to attempt to "control" suppliers, customers, or alliance partners in the traditional sense. In the fluid and flexible environments of the new organizational architectures, common cultures, shared values, and carefully aligned incentives are often less expensive to implement and are often a more effective means of strategic control than rules, boundaries, and formal procedures.

Horizontal Organizational Structures   Horizontal organizational structures, which group similar or related business units under common management control, facilitate sharing resources and infrastructures to exploit synergies among operating units and help to create a sense of common purpose. Consistency in training and the development of similar structures across business units facilitates job rotation and cross training and enhances understanding of common problems and opportunities. Cross-functional teams and interdivisional committees and task groups represent important opportunities to improve understanding and foster cooperation among operating units.

Horizontal Systems and Processes   Organizational systems, policies, and procedures are the traditional mechanisms for achieving integration among functional units. Too often, however, existing policies and procedures do little more than institutionalize the barriers that exist from years of managing within the framework of the traditional model. The concept of business reengineering focuses primarily on these internal processes and procedures. Beginning with an understanding of basic business processes in the context of "a collection of activities that takes one or more kinds of input and creates an output that is of value to the customer," Michael Hammer and James Champy's 1993 best-selling *Reengineering the Corporation* outlined a methodology for redesigning internal systems and procedures that has been embraced, in its various forms, by many organizations.[25] Proponents claim that successful reengineering lowers costs, reduces inventories and cycle times, improves quality, speeds response times, and enhances organizational flexibility. Others advocate similar benefits through the reduction of cycle times, total quality management, and the like.

Communications and Information Technologies   Improved communications through the effective use of information technologies can play an important role in bridging gaps and breaking down barriers between organizations. Electronic mail and videoconferencing can improve lateral communications across long distances and multiple time zones and circumvent many of the barriers of the traditional model. Information technology can be a powerful ally in the redesign and streamlining of internal business processes and in improving coordination and integration between suppliers and customers. Internet technologies have eliminated the paperwork of purchase order and invoice documentation in many buyer–supplier relationships, enabling cooperating organizations to reduce inventories, shorten delivery cycles, and reduce operating costs. Today, information technology must be viewed more as a prime component of an organization's overall strategy than simply in terms of its more traditional role as administrative support.

Human Resource Practices   Change, whether in structure, process, or procedure, always involves and impacts the human dimension of organizations. The attraction, development, and retention of human capital are vital to value creation. As boundaryless structures are implemented, processes are reengineered, and organizations become increasingly dependent on sophisticated information technologies, the skills of workers and managers alike must be upgraded to realize the full benefits.

Successful organizations must ensure that they have the proper type of organizational structure. Furthermore, they must incorporate the necessary integration and processes so that the internal and external boundaries of their firms are flexible and permeable. This is increasingly important as the environments of firms become more complex, rapidly changing, and unpredictable.   **L01**

In the first section of the chapter, we addressed the different types of organizational structure—simple, functional, divisional (including two variations—strategic business unit and holding company), and matrix as well as their relative advantages and disadvantages.   **L02, L03**

The second section of the chapter introduced the concept of the boundaryless organization. We did not suggest that the concept of the boundaryless organization replaces the traditional forms of organizational structure. Rather, it should complement them. This is necessary to cope with the increasing complexity and change in the competitive environment. We addressed three types of boundaryless organizations. The barrier-free type focuses on the need for the internal and external boundaries of a firm to be more flexible and permeable. The modular type emphasizes the strategic outsourcing of noncore activities. The virtual type centers on the strategic benefits of alliances and the forming of network organizations. We discussed both the advantages and disadvantages of each type of boundaryless organization and suggested some techniques and processes that are necessary to successfully implement them. These are common culture and values, horizontal organizational structures, horizontal systems and processes, communications and information technologies, and human resource practices.   **L04**

1. Why is it important for managers to carefully consider the type of organizational structure that they use to implement their strategies?

2. What are the relative advantages and disadvantages of the types of organizational structure—simple, functional, divisional, matrix—discussed in the chapter?

3. Briefly describe the three different types of boundaryless organizations: barrier-free, modular, and virtual.

4. What are some of the key attributes of effective groups? Ineffective groups?

5. What are the advantages and disadvantages of the three types of boundaryless organizations: barrier-free, modular, and virtual?

simple organization
 structure, 152
functional organization
 structure, 153
divisional organization
 structure, 155

strategic business unit (SBU)
 structure, 157
holding company
 structure, 157
matrix organization
 structure, 158

boundaryless organizational
 designs, 160
barrier-free organization, 162
modular organization, 164
virtual organization, 166

APPLICATION QUESTIONS EXERCISES

1. Select an organization that competes in an industry in which you are particularly interested. Go on the Internet and determine what type of organizational structure this organization has. In your view, is it consistent with the strategy that it has chosen to implement? Why or why not?

2. Choose an article from *BusinessWeek, Fortune, Forbes, Fast Company,* or any other well-known publication that deals with a corporation that has undergone a significant change in its strategic direction. What are the implications for the structure of this organization?

3. Go on the Internet and look up some of the public statements or speeches of an executive in a major corporation about a significant initiative such as entering into a joint venture or launching a new product line. What do you feel are the implications for making the internal and external barriers of the firm more flexible and permeable? Does the executive discuss processes, procedures, integrating mechanisms, or cultural issues that should serve this purpose? Or are other issues discussed that enable a firm to become more boundaryless?

4. Look up a recent article in the publications listed in question 2 above that addresses a firm's involvement in outsourcing (modular organization) or in strategic alliance or network organizations (virtual organization). Was the firm successful or unsuccessful in this endeavor? Why or why not?

REFERENCES

1. Tomanio, J., Burke, D. & Morser, B. 2007. Missed connections. *Fortune*, March 5: 103–108; Schwartz, N. D. 2007. Big plane, big problems. *Fortune,* March 5: 95–98; Anonymous. 2007. Hard landing. *The Economist.* February 17: 68; Pearlstein, S. 2006. Political winds are pushing Airbus. www.washingtonpost.com, October 11: D01; Holmes, S. 2007. The secret weapon of Boeing. *BusinessWeek,* January 8: 34; Matlack, C. 2006. Wayward Airbus. *BusinessWeek,* October 23: 46–48; and Matlack, C. 2006. Airbus: First, blame the software. *BusinessWeek,* October 5: np.

2. This introductory discussion draws upon Hall, R. H. 2002. *Organizations: Structures, processes, and outcomes* (8th ed.). Upper Saddle River, NJ: Prentice Hall; and Duncan, R. E. 1979. What is the right organization structure? Decision-tree analysis provides the right answer. *Organizational Dynamics,* 7(3): 59–80. For an insightful discussion of strategy-structure relationships in the organization theory and strategic management literatures, refer to Keats, B., & O'Neill, H. M. 2001. Organization structure: Looking through a strategy lens. In Hitt, M. A., Freeman, R. E., & Harrison, J. S. 2001. *The Blackwell handbook of strategic management:* 520–542. Malden, MA: Blackwell.

3. Schein, E. H. 1996. Three cultures of management: The key to organizational learning. *Sloan Management Review,* 38(1): 9–20.

4. For a thorough and seminal discussion of the evolution toward the divisional form of organizational structure in the United States, refer to Chandler, A. D. 1962. *Strategy and Structure.* Cambridge, MA: MIT Press. A rigorous empirical study of the strategy and structure relationship is found in Rumelt, R. P. 1974. *Strategy, structure, and economic performance.* Cambridge, MA: Harvard Business School Press.

5. Dell, M. & Rollins, K. 2005. Execution without excuses. *Harvard Business Review,* 83(3): 102–111.

6. Many authors have argued that a firm's structure can influence a firm's strategy and performance. These include Amburgey, T. L., & Dacin, T. 1995. As the left foot follows the right? The dynamics of strategic and structural change. *Academy of Management Journal,* 37: 1427–1452; Dawn, K., & Amburgey, T. L. 1991. Organizational inertia and momentum: A dynamic model of strategic change. *Academy of Management Journal,* 34: 591–612; Fredrickson, J. W. 1986. The strategic decision process and organization structure. *Academy of Management Review,* 11: 280–297; Hall, D. J., & Saias, M. A. 1980. Strategy follows structure! *Strategic Management Journal,* 1: 149–164; and Burgelman, R. A. 1983. A model of the interaction of strategic behavior, corporate context, and the concept of strategy. *Academy of Management Review,* 8: 61–70.

7. Collis, D. J., & Montgomery, C. A. 1998. Creating corporate advantage. *Harvard Business Review,* 76(3): 70–83.

8. Pfeffer, J. 1998. *The human equation: Building profits by putting people first.* Cambridge, MA: Harvard Business School Press.

9. Augustine, N. R. 1983. *Augustine's laws.* New York: Viking Press.

10. Magretta, J. 1998. The power of virtual integration: An interview with Dell Computer's Michael Dell. *Harvard Business Review,* 76(2): 75.

11. Forster, J. 2001. Networking for cash. *BusinessWeek,* January 8: 129.

12. Dess, G. G., Rasheed, A. M. A., McLaughlin, K. J., & Priem, R. 1995. The new corporate architecture. *Academy of Management Executive,* 9(3): 7–20.

13. Barnes, C. 1998. A fatal case. *Fast Company,* February–March: 173.

14. Handy, C. 1989. *The age of unreason.* Boston: Harvard Business School Press; Ramstead, E. 1997. APC maker's low-tech formula: Start with the box. *Wall Street Journal,* December 29: B1; Mussberg, W. 1997. Thin screen PCs are looking good but still fall flat. *The Wall Street Journal,* January 2: 9; Brown, E. 1997. Monorail: Low cost PCs. *Fortune,* July 7: 106–108; and Young, M. 1996. Ex-Compaq executives start new company. *Computer Reseller News,* November 11: 181.

15. For a discussion of some of the downsides of outsourcing, refer to Rossetti, C., & Choi, T. Y. 2005. On the dark side of strategic

sourcing: Experiences from the aerospace industry. *Academy of Management Executive,* 19(1): 46–60.

16. Quinn, J. B. 1992. *Intelligent enterprise: A knowledge and service based paradigm for industry.* New York: Free Press.

17. For an insightful perspective on outsourcing and its role in developing capabilities, read Gottfredson, M., Puryear, R., & Phillips, C. 2005. Strategic sourcing: From periphery to the core. *Harvard Business Review,* 83(4): 132–139.

18. This discussion draws upon Quinn, J. B., & Hilmer, F. C. 1994. Strategic outsourcing. *Sloan Management Review,* 35(4): 43–55.

19. Doz, Y., & Hamel, G. 1998. *Alliance advantage: The art of creating value through partnering.* Boston: Harvard Business School Press.

20. Barringer, B. R., & Harrison, J. S. 2000. Walking a tightrope: Creating value through interorganizational alliances. *Journal of Management,* 26: 367–403.

21. Davis, E. 1997. Interview: Norman Augustine. *Management Review,* November: 14.

22. One contemporary example of virtual organizations is R&D consortia. For an insightful discussion, refer to Sakaibara, M. 2002. Formation of R&D consortia: Industry and company effects. *Strategic Management Journal,* 23(11): 1033–1050.

23. This section draws upon Dess, G. G., & Picken, J. C. 1997. *Mission critical.* Burr Ridge, IL: Irwin Professional Publishing.

24. Katzenbach, J. R., & Smith, D. K. 1994. *The wisdom of teams: Creating the high performance organization.* New York: HarperBusiness.

25. Hammer, M., & Champy, J. 1993. *Reengineering the corporation: A manifesto for business revolution.* New York: HarperCollins.

Strategic Control

After reading this chapter, you should have a good understanding of:

LO1 The value of effective strategic control systems in strategy implementation.

LO2 The key difference between "traditional" and "contemporary" control systems.

LO3 The imperative for "contemporary" control systems in today's complex and rapidly changing competitive and general environments.

LO4 The benefits of having the proper balance among the three levers of behavioral control: culture, rewards and incentives, and boundaries.

Organizations must have effective strategic controls if they are to successfully implement their strategies. These include systems that exercise both informational control and behavioral control.

In this chapter, we address the need to have effective informational control, contrasting two approaches to informational control. The first approach, which we call "traditional," is highly sequential. Goals and objectives are set, then implemented, and after a set period of time, performance is compared to the desired standards. In contrast, the second approach, termed "contemporary," is much more interactive. Here, the internal and external environments are continually monitored, and managers determine whether the strategy itself needs to be modified. Today the contemporary approach is required, given the rapidly changing conditions in virtually all industries.

Next, we discuss behavioral control. Here the firm must strive to maintain a proper balance among culture, rewards, and boundaries. We also argue that organizations which have strong, positive cultures and reward systems can rely less on boundaries such as rules, regulations, and procedures. When individuals in the firm internalize goals and strategies, there is less need for monitoring behavior, and efforts are focused more on important organizational goals and objectives.

° LEARNING FROM MISTAKES

Incentives are designed to boost productivity and help a company achieve its goals.[1] This works as long as the incentives are designed with organizational goals in mind. Problems can arise quickly when incentives are not designed in a way that aligns the goals of employees with those of the firm.

Consider the case of Lantech, a $100 million company headquartered in Louisville, Kentucky, that had to face this problem. The firm has a dominant position in a market that it pioneered—stretch wrapping equipment that encases pallet loads of products (such as Kellogg's Corn Flakes) in clear plastic film for shipment to customers.

Lantech wanted to increase the productivity of its workers, and the obvious way seemed to be to reward high-performing divisions with productivity incentives. Each of the firm's manufacturing divisions was offered a productivity bonus that could increase the pay of each employee in the division by 10 percent.

Unfortunately, the results weren't exactly what Lantech's managers had in mind. The bonus was based on each division's productivity, and because one measure of productivity is the ratio of costs to revenues, employees began to devise ways to decrease costs in their division. But rather than *cutting* costs, employees focused their efforts on *shifting* costs.

Production at Lantech required mutual cooperation between divisions; each division relied on the others for parts and engineering expertise. However, the incentive plan inadvertently encouraged workers to assign costs to other divisions while claiming revenue for themselves. Workers argued over who was responsible for shared costs, with no division wanting to accept its fair share. But, needless to say, they were all willing to claim responsibility for revenues. It got to the point that one division wanted to assign a greater percentage of toilet paper costs to another division with a higher number of employees of a certain gender, arguing that one gender used more toilet paper than the other!

Chairman Pat Lancaster claimed that he spent 95 percent of his time resolving arguments after he had initiated this new incentive plan. He claimed that, "The bonuses moved managers in the direction of favoring short-term profit over long-term customer satisfaction. They were so busy fighting over who was going to pay for what that they couldn't make decisions that were good for the customers as a whole." And CEO Jim Lancaster, his son, said that the new system caused "so much secrecy, politicking, and sucking noise that you wouldn't believe it."

It should come as no surprise that the plan was eliminated after just a short period. In its place, Lantech offered a profit-sharing plan where employees benefited only if the entire firm performed well. The bottom line is that incentive plans must align the employees' desire for extra income with the firm's need for profits.

In this chapter, we will focus on how organizations can develop and use effective strategic control.[2] We explore two central aspects of strategic control: (1) *informational control,* which is the ability to respond effectively to environmental change, and (2) *behavioral control,* which is the appropriate balance and alignment among a firm's culture, rewards, and boundaries.

LO1   The value of effective strategic control systems in strategy implementation.

ENSURING INFORMATIONAL CONTROL: RESPONDING EFFECTIVELY TO ENVIRONMENTAL CHANGE

In this section we will discuss two broad types of control systems. The first one, which we label "traditional," is based largely on a feedback approach; that is, there is little or no action taken to revise strategies, goals, and objectives until the end of the time period in question, usually a quarter or a month. The second one, which we call "contemporary," emphasizes the importance of continually monitoring the environment (both internal and external) for trends and events that signal the need to make modifications to a firm's strategies, goals, and objectives. As both general and competitive environments become more unpredictable and complex, the need for contemporary systems increases.

LO2   The key difference between "traditional" and "contemporary" control systems.

A TRADITIONAL APPROACH TO STRATEGIC CONTROL

traditional approach to strategic control
A sequential method of organizational control in which (1) strategies are formulated and top management sets goals, (2) strategies are implemented, and (3) performance is measured against the predetermined goal set.

The **traditional approach to strategic control** is sequential: (1) strategies are formulated and top management sets goals, (2) strategies are implemented, and (3) performance is measured against the predetermined goal set, as illustrated in Exhibit 8.1.

Control is based on a feedback loop from performance measurement to strategy formulation. This process typically involves lengthy time lags, often tied to a firm's annual planning cycle. It is most appropriate when the environment is stable and relatively simple, goals and objectives can be measured with a high level of certainty, and there is little need for complex measures of performance. Sales quotas, operating budgets, production schedules, and similar quantitative control mechanisms are typical. The appropriateness of the business strategy or standards of performance is seldom questioned.[3]

The idea that well-managed companies should move forward in accordance with detailed and precise plans has come under attack.[4] James Brian Quinn of Dartmouth College has argued that grand designs with precise and carefully integrated plans seldom work. Rather, most strategic change proceeds incrementally—one step at a time. Leaders should introduce some sense of direction, some logic in incremental steps.[5]

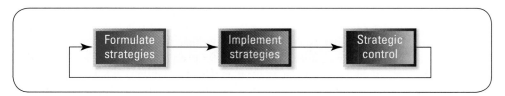

EXHIBIT 8.1   **Traditional Approach to Strategic Control**

When the Tech Bubble Burst

We can learn some lessons from fallen stars. Cisco Systems, Inc., once the invincible momentum stock adored by Wall Street, came crashing down just as we were beginning the 21st century. What went wrong?

Problems started when Cisco announced a $2.2 billion inventory write-off; Wall Street severely punished the stock as a result. With all of its experience, why didn't Cisco see the problems coming? Cisco made a common mistake: It projected the past into the future.

Past demand had been vigorous, but customers were requiring less and less of the firm's products. And financing was cheap—it was no problem for a company like Cisco to find capital to finance ongoing operations even when things didn't look so bright on the horizon. Overtaken by its own success, Cisco failed to see the slowdown in customer demand. John Sterman at MIT sums up the situation: "If you were in the pasta business, you want to know how much pasta people are cooking and eating, not how much they're buying, and certainly not how much supermarkets and distributors are ordering from the factory." Consumers ultimately determine demand; Cisco missed this important point and inaccurately forecast new sales orders. When the orders didn't materialize, a stockpile of inventory sat on the shelves while Wall Street annulled the short-lived marriage between investors and their beloved Cisco.

In contrast, Siebel Systems, Inc., kept its eye on the future. The company rewarded its sales force for providing accurate information concerning future demand. Salespeople receive commissions not only for sales, but also for forecast information. Haim Mendelson at Stanford University remarked that this provides the company "with a deep understanding of what customers are going to do."

Sources: Weber, J. 2001. Management lessons from the bust. *BusinessWeek*, August 27: 104–112; Morrison, S. 2001. Positive sales news takes the sting out of Cisco revamp. *Financial Times Online*, August 26; Reuters. 2001. Siebel sees economic rebound late 2002: August 20.

Similarly, McGill University's Henry Mintzberg has written about leaders "crafting" a strategy.[6] Drawing on the parallel between the potter at her wheel and the strategist, Mintzberg pointed out that the potter begins work with some general idea of the artifact she wishes to create, but the details of design—even possibilities for a different design—emerge as the work progresses. For businesses facing complex and turbulent business environments, the craftsperson's method seems more appropriate than that provided by the traditional, more rational, planner. The former helps us deal with the uncertainty about how a design will work out in practice and allows for a creative element.

Mintzberg's argument, like Quinn's, questions the value of rigid planning and goal-setting processes. Fixed strategic goals also become dysfunctional for firms competing in highly unpredictable competitive environments. Here, strategies need to change frequently and opportunistically. An inflexible commitment to predetermined goals and milestones can prevent the very adaptability that is required of a good strategy.

Even organizations that have been extremely successful in the past can become complacent or fail to adapt their goals and strategies to the new conditions. An example of such a firm is Cisco Systems, whose market value at one time approached an astonishing $600 billion, but as of early 2007 was about $160 billion. Cisco has minimized the potential for such problems in the future by improving its informational control systems. Other firms such as Siebel Systems (now part of Oracle) have been more successful in anticipating change and have made proper corrections to their strategies. We discuss these firms in Focus on Strategy 8.1.

Without doubt, the traditional "feedback" approach to strategic control has some important limitations. Is there another, better, way?

A CONTEMPORARY APPROACH TO STRATEGIC CONTROL

LO3 The imperative for "contemporary" control systems in today's complex and rapidly changing competitive and general environments.

Adapting to and anticipating both internal and external environmental change is an integral part of strategic control. The relationships among strategy formulation, implementation,

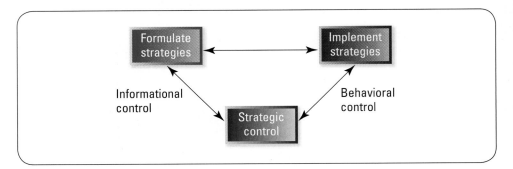

EXHIBIT 8.2 **Contemporary Approach to Strategic Control**

and control are highly interactive, as suggested by Exhibit 8.2. The exhibit also illustrates two different types of strategic control: informational control and behavioral control. **Informational control** is primarily concerned with whether or not the organization is "doing the right things." **Behavioral control,** on the other hand, asks if the organization is "doing things right" in the implementation of its strategy. Both the informational and behavioral components of strategic control are necessary, but not sufficient, conditions for success. That is, what good is a well-conceived strategy that cannot be implemented? Or, alternatively, what use is an energetic and committed workforce if it is focused on the wrong strategic target?

John Weston is the former CEO of ADP Corporation, the largest payroll and taxfiling processor in the world. He captures the essence of contemporary control systems.

> At ADP, 39 plus 1 adds up to more than 40 plus 0. The 40-plus-0 employee is the harried worker who at 40 hours a week just tries to keep up with what's in the "in" basket. He tries to do whatever he thinks he's supposed to do. Because he works with his head down, he takes zero hours to think about what he's doing, why he's doing it, and how he's doing it. Does he need to do it in the first place? On the other hand, the 39-plus-1 employee takes at least 1 of those 40 hours to think about what he's doing and why he's doing it. That's why the other 39 hours are far more productive.[7]

Informational control deals with the internal environment as well as the external strategic context. It addresses the assumptions and premises that provide the foundation for an organization's strategy. The key question becomes: Do the organization's goals and strategies still "fit" within the context of the current strategic environment? Depending on the type of business, such assumptions may relate to changes in technology, customer tastes, government regulation, and industry competition.

This involves two key issues. First, managers must scan and monitor the external environment, as we discussed in Chapter 4. Recall, for example, the failure of Coors to anticipate and act on the trend toward low-carb beer. Also, conditions can change in the internal environment of the firm, as we discussed in Chapter 3, requiring changes in the strategic direction of the firm. These may include, for example, the resignation of key executives or delays in the completion of major production facilities.

In the contemporary approach, information control is part of an ongoing process of organizational learning that continuously updates and challenges the assumptions that underlie the organization's strategy. Here the organization's assumptions, premises, goals, and strategies are continuously monitored, tested, and reviewed. The benefits of continuous monitoring are evident—time lags are dramatically shortened, changes in the competitive environment are detected earlier, and the organization's ability to respond with speed and flexibility is enhanced.

informational control
A method of organizational control in which a firm gathers and analyzes information from the internal and external environment in order to obtain the best fit between the organization's goals and strategies and the strategic environment.

behavioral control
A method of organizational control in which a firm influences the actions of employees through culture, rewards, and boundaries.

A key question becomes: How is this done? Contemporary control systems must have four characteristics to be effective.[8]

1. They must focus on constantly changing information that top managers identify as having potential strategic importance.

2. The information is important enough to demand frequent and regular attention from operating managers at all levels of the organization.

3. The data and information generated by the control system are best interpreted and discussed in face-to-face meetings of superiors, subordinates, and peers.

4. The contemporary control system is a key catalyst for an ongoing debate about underlying data, assumptions, and action plans.

An executive's decision to use the control system interactively—in other words, to invest the time and attention to review and evaluate new information—sends a clear signal to the organization about what is important. The dialogue and debate that emerge from such an interactive process can often lead to new strategies and innovations.

Focus on Strategy 8.2 discusses how executives at *USA Today,* Gannett Co.'s daily newspaper, review information delivered each Friday.

Let's now turn our attention to behavioral control.

ATTAINING BEHAVIORAL CONTROL: BALANCING CULTURE, REWARDS, AND BOUNDARIES

LO4 The benefits of having the proper balance among the three levers of behavioral control: culture, rewards and incentives, and boundaries.

Behavioral control is focused on implementation—doing things right. Effectively implementing strategy requires manipulating three key control "levers": culture, rewards, and boundaries. These three levers are illustrated in Exhibit 8.3. Furthermore, there are two compelling reasons for an increased emphasis on culture and rewards in implementing a system of behavioral controls.

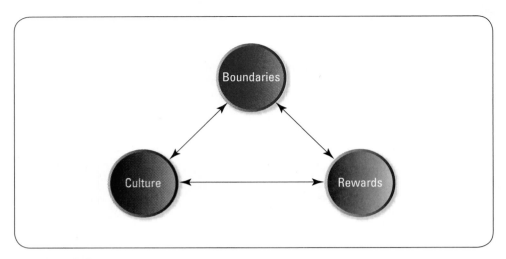

EXHIBIT 8.3   Essential Elements of Behavioral Control

First, the competitive environment is increasingly complex and unpredictable, demanding both flexibility and quick response to its challenges. As firms simultaneously downsize and face the need for increased coordination across organizational boundaries, a control system based primarily on rigid strategies and rules and regulations is dysfunctional. Thus, the use of rewards and culture to align individual and organizational goals becomes increasingly important.

Second, the implicit long-term contract between the organization and its key employees has been eroded.[9] Today's younger managers have been conditioned to see themselves as "free agents" and view a career as a series of opportunistic challenges. As managers are advised to "specialize, market yourself, and have work, if not a job," the importance of culture and rewards in building organizational loyalty claims greater importance.

Each of the three levers—culture, rewards, and boundaries—must work in a balanced and consistent manner. Let's consider the role of each.

BUILDING A STRONG AND EFFECTIVE CULTURE

organizational culture
A system of shared values and beliefs that shapes a company's people, organizational structures, and control systems to produce behavioral norms.

What is culture? Consistent with our discussion in Chapter 3, **organizational culture** is a system of shared values (what is important) and beliefs (how things work) that shape a company's people, organizational structures, and control systems to produce behavioral norms (the way we do things around here). How important is culture? Very. Over the years, numerous best sellers, such as *Theory Z, Corporate Cultures, In Search of Excellence, and Good to Great,*[10] have emphasized the powerful influence of culture on what goes on within organizations and how they perform.

Collins and Porras argued in *Built to Last* that the key factor in sustained exceptional performance is a cultlike culture.[11] You can't touch it, you can't write it down, but it's there, in every organization, and its influence is pervasive. It can work for you or against you.[12] Effective leaders understand its importance and strive to shape and use it as one of their important levers of strategic control.[13]

The Role of Culture   Culture wears many different hats, each woven from the fabric of those values that sustain the organization's primary source of competitive advantage. Some examples are:

- Federal Express and Southwest Airlines focus on customer service.

- Lexus (a division of Toyota) and Hewlett-Packard emphasize product quality.

- Newell Rubbermaid and 3M place a high value on innovation.

- Nucor (steel) and Emerson Electric are concerned, above all, with operational efficiency.

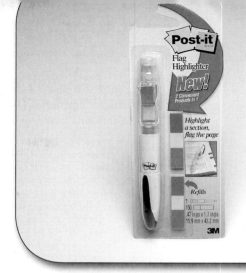

3M is well known for its innovative culture. Above is a yellow 3M Post-it Highlighter Package.

Culture sets implicit boundaries—that is, unwritten standards of acceptable behavior—in dress, ethical matters, and the way an organization conducts its business.[14] By creating a framework of shared values, culture encourages individual identification with the organization and its objectives. Thus, culture acts as a means of reducing monitoring costs.[15]

Sustaining an Effective Culture Powerful organizational cultures just don't happen overnight, and they don't remain in place without a strong commitment—both in terms of words and deeds—by leaders throughout the organization. A viable and productive organizational culture can be strengthened and sustained. However, it cannot be "built" or "assembled"; instead, it must be cultivated, encouraged, and "fertilized."

Storytelling is one way effective cultures are maintained. Many are familiar with the story of how Art Fry's failure to develop a strong adhesive led to 3M's enormously successful Post-it Notes. Perhaps less familiar is the story of Francis G. Okie.[16] In 1922 Okie came up with the idea of selling sandpaper to men as a replacement for razor blades. The idea obviously didn't pan out, but Okie was allowed to remain at 3M. Interestingly, the technology developed by Okie led 3M to develop its first blockbuster product: a waterproof sandpaper that became a staple of the automobile industry. Such stories foster the importance of risk taking, experimentation, freedom to fail, and of course innovation—all vital elements of 3M's culture.

Rallies or "pep talks" by top executives also serve to reinforce a firm's culture. The late Sam Walton was well known for his pep rallies at local Wal-Mart stores. Four times a year, the founders of Home Depot—CEO Bernard Marcus and Arthur Blank—used to don orange aprons and stage Breakfast with Bernie and Arthur, a 6:30 a.m. pep rally, broadcast live over the firm's closed-circuit TV network to most of its 45,000 employees.[17]

Southwest Airlines' "Culture Committee" is a unique vehicle designed to perpetuate the company's highly successful culture. The following excerpt from an internal company publication describes its objectives:

> The goal of the Committee is simple—to ensure that our unique Corporate Culture stays alive. . . . Culture Committee members represent all regions and departments across our system and they are selected based upon their exemplary display of the "Positively Outrageous Service" that won us the first-ever Triple Crown; their continual exhibition of the "Southwest Spirit" to our Customers and to their fellow workers; and their high energy level, boundless enthusiasm, unique creativity, and constant demonstration of teamwork and love for their fellow workers.[18]

MOTIVATING WITH REWARDS AND INCENTIVES

Reward and incentive systems represent a powerful means of influencing an organization's culture, focusing efforts on high-priority tasks, and motivating individual and collective task performance.[19] Just as culture deals with influencing beliefs, behaviors, and attitudes of people within an organization, the reward system—by specifying who gets rewarded and why—is an effective motivator and control mechanism.[20] Consider how John Thompson, CEO of the $1 billion software security firm Symantec, distributes financial rewards based on contribution:[21]

> When Thompson arrived at Symantec, any executive who was promoted to vice president automatically received a BMW. Senior management's bonuses were paid quarterly and were heavily skewed toward cash—not stock. Thompson says: "So if the stock didn't do well, they didn't care. We now have a stock option plan that is broad based but not universal. One of the things we recognized early on was that if we were going to grow at the rate that we were growing, we had to be more selective in who we gave options to so as not to dilute the value of our stock. And the first thing we did was identify a range of employees who were valuable to the company but didn't need equity to come to work, and we focused their compensation around cash bonuses. Then we increased the equity we gave to the engineers and other people that were critical to our long-term success." By paying the two groups of people in a different manner, the new compensation scheme recognizes their distinctive importance.

The Potential Downside   Generally speaking, people in organizations act rationally, motivated by their personal best interest.[22] However, the collective sum of individual behaviors of an organization's employees does not always result in what is best for the organization; that is, individual rationality is no guarantee of organizational rationality.

As corporations grow and evolve, they often develop different business units with multiple reward systems. They may differ based on industry contexts, business situations, stage of product life cycles, and so on. Thus, subcultures within organizations may reflect differences among an organization's functional areas, products, services, and divisions. To the extent that reward systems reinforce such behavioral norms, attitudes, and belief systems, cohesiveness is reduced; important information is hoarded rather than shared, individuals begin working at cross-purposes, and they lose sight of over-all goals.

Such conflicts are commonplace in many organizations. For example, sales and marketing personnel promise unrealistically quick delivery times to bring in business, much to the dismay of operations and logistics; overengineering by R&D creates headaches for manufacturing; and so on. Conflicts also arise across divisions when divisional profits become a key compensation criterion. As ill will and anger escalate, personal relationships and performance may suffer.

Creating Effective Reward and Incentive Programs   To be effective, incentive and reward systems need to reinforce basic core values and enhance cohesion and commitment to goals and objectives. They also must not be at odds with the organization's overall mission and purpose.[23]

At General Mills, a manager's interest in the overall performance of his or her unit is ensured by tying half of a manager's annual bonus to business-unit results and half to individual performance.[24] For example, if a manager simply matches a rival manufacturer's performance, his or her salary is roughly 5 percent lower. However, if a manager's product ranks in the industry's top 10 percent in earnings growth and return on capital, the manager's total pay can rise to nearly 30 percent beyond the industry norm.

Effective reward and incentive systems share a number of common characteristics. For example, the perception that a plan is "fair and equitable" is critically important. Similarly, the firm must have the flexibility to respond to changing requirements as its direction and objectives change. In recent years many companies have begun to place more emphasis on growth. Emerson Electric is one company that has shifted its emphasis from cost cutting to growth. To ensure that changes take hold, the management compensation formula has been changed from a largely bottom-line focus to one that emphasizes growth, new products, acquisitions, and international expansion. Discussions about profits are handled separately, and a culture of risk taking is encouraged.[25]

EXHIBIT 8.4

**Characteristics of
Effective Reward and
Evaluation Systems**

- Objectives are clear, well understood, and broadly accepted.
- Rewards are clearly linked to performance and desired behaviors.
- Performance measures are clear and highly visible.
- Feedback is prompt, clear, and unambiguous.
- The compensation "system" is perceived as fair and equitable.
- The structure is flexible; it can adapt to changing circumstances.

Exhibit 8.4 summarizes some of the attributes of effective reward and evaluation systems.

SETTING BOUNDARIES AND CONSTRAINTS

In an ideal world, a strong culture and effective rewards should be sufficient to ensure that all individuals and subunits work toward the common goals and objectives of the whole organization.[26] In practice, however, this is not usually the case. Counterproductive behavior can arise because of motivated self-interest, lack of a clear understanding of goals and objectives, or outright malfeasance. Boundaries and constraints, when used properly, can serve many useful purposes for organizations, including:

- Focusing individual efforts on strategic priorities.
- Providing short-term objectives and action plans to channel efforts.
- Improving efficiency and effectiveness.
- Minimizing improper and unethical conduct.

Focusing Efforts on Strategic Priorities   Boundaries and constraints play a valuable role in focusing a company's strategic priorities. A well-known example of a strategic boundary is Jack Welch's (former CEO of General Electric) demand that any business in the corporate portfolio be ranked first or second in its industry. Similarly, Eli Lilly has reduced its research efforts to five broad areas of disease, down from eight or nine a decade ago.[27] This concentration of effort and resources provides the firm with greater strategic focus and the potential for stronger competitive advantages in the remaining areas.

Norman Augustine, Lockheed Martin's former chairman, provided four criteria for selecting candidates for diversification into "closely related" businesses.[28] They must (1) be high tech, (2) be systems-oriented, (3) deal with large customers (either corporations or government) as opposed to consumers, and (4) be in growth businesses. Augustine said, "We have found that if we can meet most of those standards, then we can move into adjacent markets and grow."

Boundaries also have a place in the nonprofit sector. For example, a British relief organization uses a system to monitor strategic boundaries by maintaining a list of companies whose contributions it will neither solicit nor accept. Such boundaries clearly go beyond simply taking the moral high road. Rather, they are essential for maintaining legitimacy with existing and potential benefactors.

Providing Short-Term Objectives and Action Plans   Short-term objectives and action plans represent boundaries that help to allocate resources in an optimal manner and to channel the efforts of employees at all levels throughout the

Developing Meaningful Action Plans: Aircraft Interior Products, Inc.

MSA Aircraft Interior Products, Inc., is a manufacturing firm based in San Antonio, Texas, that was founded in 1983 by Mike Spraggins and Robert Plenge. The firm fulfills a small but highly profitable niche in the aviation industry with two key products. The Accordia line consists of patented, lightweight, self-contained window-shade assemblies. MSA's interior cabin shells are state-of-the-art assemblies that include window panels, side panels, headliners, and suspension system structures. MSA's products have been installed on a variety of aircraft, such as the Gulfstream series; the Cessna Citation; and Boeing's 727, 737, 757, and 707.

Much of MSA's success can be attributed to carefully articulated action plans consistent with the firm's mission and objectives. During the past five years, MSA has increased its sales at an annual rate of 15 to 18 percent. It has also succeeded in adding many prestigious companies to its customer base. Below are excerpts from MSA's mission statement and objectives as well as the action plans to achieve a 20 percent annual increase in sales.

Mission Statement

- Be recognized as an innovative and reliable supplier of quality interior products for the high-end, personalized transportation segments of the aviation, marine, and automotive industries.

- Design, develop, and manufacture interior fixtures and components that provide exceptional value to the customer through the development of innovative designs in a manner that permits decorative design flexibility while retaining the superior functionality, reliability, and maintainability of well-engineered, factory-produced products.
- Grow, be profitable, and provide a fair return, commensurate with the degree of risk, for owners and stockholders.

Objectives

1. Achieve sustained and profitable growth over the next three years:
   - 20 percent annual growth in revenues
   - 12 percent pretax profit margins
   - 18 percent return on shareholder's equity

2. Expand the company's revenues through the development and introduction of two or more new products capable of generating revenues in excess of $8 million a year by 2010.

3. Continue to aggressively expand market opportunities and applications for the Accordia line of window-shade assemblies, with the objective of sustaining or exceeding a 20 percent annual growth rate for at least the next three years.

   Exhibit 8.5 details an "Action Plan" for Objective 3.

   (continued)

organization.[29] To be effective, short-term objectives must have several attributes. They should:

- Be specific and measurable.
- Include a specific time horizon for their attainment.
- Be achievable, yet challenging enough to motivate managers who must strive to accomplish them.

Research has found that performance is enhanced when individuals are encouraged to attain specific, difficult, yet achievable, goals (as opposed to vague "do your best" goals).[30]

Short-term objectives must provide proper direction and at the same time provide enough flexibility for the firm to keep pace with and anticipate changes in the external environment. Such changes might include new government regulations, a competitor introducing a substitute product, or changes in consumer taste. Additionally, unexpected events within a firm may require a firm to make important adjustments in both strategic and short-term objectives. For example, the emergence of new industries can have a drastic effect on the demand for products and services in more traditional industries.

Along with short-term objectives, action plans are critical to the implementation of chosen strategies. Unless action plans are specific, there may be little assurance that managers have thought through all of the resource requirements for implementing their strategies. In addition, unless plans are specific, managers may not understand what needs to be

(continued)

Description	Primary Responsibility	Target Date
1. Develop and implement 2008 marketing plan, including specific plans for addressing Falcon 20 retrofit programs and expanded sales of cabin shells.	R. H. Plenge (V.P. Marketing)	December 15, 2007
2. Negotiate new supplier agreement with Gulfstream Aerospace.	M. Spraggins (President)	March 1, 2008
3. Continue and complete the development of the UltraSlim window and have a fully tested and documented design ready for production at a manufacturing cost of less than $900 per unit.	D. R. Pearson (V.P. Operations)	June 15, 2008
4. Develop a window design suitable for L-1011 and similar wide-body aircraft and have a fully tested and documented design ready for production at a manufacturing cost comparable to the current Boeing window.	D. R. Pearson (V.P. Operations)	September 15, 2008

EXHIBIT 8.5   Action Plan for Objective Number 3

MSA's action plans are supported by detailed month-by-month budgets and strong financial incentives for its executives. Budgets are prepared by each individual department and include all revenue and cost items. Managers are motivated by their participation in a profit-sharing program, and the firm's two founders each receive a bonus equal to 3 percent of total sales.

Source: For purposes of confidentiality, some of the information presented in this spotlight has been disguised. We would like to thank company management and Joseph Picken, consultant, for providing us with the information used in this application.

implemented or have a clear time frame for completion. This is essential for the scheduling of key activities that must be implemented. Finally, individual managers must be held accountable for the implementation of action plans. This helps to provide the necessary motivation and "sense of ownership" to implement action plans on a timely basis. Focus on Strategy 8.3 illustrates how action plans fit into the mission statement and objectives of a small manufacturer of aircraft interior components. Here, Exhibit 8.5 provides details of an "action plan" to fulfill one of the firm's objectives.

Improving Operational Efficiency and Effectiveness   Rule-based controls are most appropriate in organizations with the following characteristics:

- Environments are stable and predictable.
- Employees are largely unskilled and interchangeable.
- Consistency in product and service is critical.
- The risk of malfeasance is extremely high (e.g., in banking or casino operations), and controls must be implemented to guard against improper conduct.[31]

For example, McDonald's Corp. has extensive rules and regulations that regulate the operation of its franchises.[32] Its policy manual states, "Cooks must turn, never flip, hamburgers. If they haven't been purchased, Big Macs must be discarded in 10 minutes after being cooked and French fries in 7 minutes. Cashiers must make eye contact with and smile at every customer."

The process of cooking a hamburger at McDonald's is carefully specified to ensure the consistency of taste and appearance.

Guidelines can also be effective in setting spending limits and the range of discretion for employees and managers, such as the $2,500 limit that hotelier Ritz-Carlton uses to empower employees to placate dissatisfied customers. Regulations also can be initiated to improve the use of an employee's time at work.[33] Computer Associates restricts the use of e-mail during the hours of 10 a.m. to noon and 2 p.m. to 4 p.m. each day.[34]

Minimizing Improper and Unethical Conduct Guidelines can be useful in specifying proper relationships with a company's customers and suppliers.[35] For example, many companies have explicit rules regarding commercial practices, including the prohibition of any form of payment, bribe, or kickback. Cadbury Schweppes has followed a rather simple but effective step in controlling the use of bribes by specifying that all payments, no matter how unusual, are recorded on the company's books. Its chairman, Sir Adrian Cadbury, contended that such a practice causes managers to pause and consider whether a payment is simply a bribe or a necessary and standard cost of doing business.[36] Consulting companies, too, typically have strong rules and regulations directed at protecting client confidentiality and conflicts of interest.

Regulations backed up with strong sanctions can also help an organization avoid conducting business in an unethical manner. In the wake of the corporate scandals of the early 21st century and the passing of the Sarbanes-Oxley Act (which, among other things, provides for stiffer penalties for financial reporting misdeeds), many chief financial officers (CFOs) have taken steps to ensure ethical behavior in the preparation of financial statements. For example, Home Depot's CFO, Carol B. Tome, strengthened the firm's code of ethics and developed stricter guidelines. Now all 25 of her subordinates must sign personal statements that all of their financial statements are correct—just as she and her CEO have to do now according to the congressional legislation.[37]

BEHAVIORAL CONTROL IN ORGANIZATIONS: SITUATIONAL FACTORS

We have discussed the behavioral dimension of control. Here, the focus is on ensuring that the behavior of individuals at all levels of an organization is directed toward achieving organizational goals and objectives. The three fundamental types of control are culture, rewards and incentives, and boundaries and constraints. An organization may pursue one or a combination of them on the basis of a variety of internal and external factors.

Not all organizations place the same emphasis on each type of control.[38] For example, in high-technology firms engaged in basic research, members may work under high levels of autonomy. Here, an individual's performance is generally quite difficult to measure accurately because of the long lead times involved in research and development activities. Thus, internalized norms and values become very important.

When the measurement of an individual's output or performance is quite straightforward, control depends primarily on granting or withholding rewards. Frequently, a sales manager's compensation is in the form of a commission and bonus tied directly to his or

EXHIBIT 8.6

Organizational Control: Alternative Approaches

Approach	Some Situational Factors
Culture: A system of unwritten rules that forms an internalized influence over behavior.	• Often found in professional organizations. • Associated with high autonomy. • Norms are the basis for behavior.
Rules: Written and explicit guidelines that provide external constraints on behavior.	• Associated with standardized output. • Tasks are generally repetitive and routine. • Little need for innovation or creative activity.
Rewards: The use of performance-based incentive systems to motivate.	• Measurement of output and performance is rather straightforward. • Most appropriate in organizations pursuing unrelated diversification strategies. • Rewards may be used to reinforce other means of control.

her sales volume, which is relatively easy to determine. Here, behavior is influenced more strongly by the attractiveness of the compensation than by the norms and values implicit in the organization's culture. Furthermore, the measurability of output precludes the need for an elaborate system of rules to control behavior.

Control in bureaucratic organizations is dependent on members following a highly formalized set of rules and regulations. In such situations, most activities are routine and the desired behavior can be specified in a detailed manner because there is generally little need for innovative or creative activity. For example, managing an assembly plant requires strict adherence to many rules as well as exacting sequences of assembly operations. In the public sector, the Department of Motor Vehicles in most states must follow clearly prescribed procedures when issuing or renewing driver licenses.

Exhibit 8.6 provides alternative approaches to behavioral control and some of the situational factors associated with them.

EVOLVING FROM BOUNDARIES TO REWARDS AND CULTURE

In most environments, organizations should strive to provide a system of rewards and incentives, coupled with a culture strong enough that boundaries become internalized. This reduces the need for external controls such as rules and regulations. We suggest several ways to move in this direction.

First, hire the right people—individuals who already identify with the organization's dominant values and have attributes consistent with them. Microsoft's David Pritchard is well aware of the consequences of failing to hire properly:

> If I hire a bunch of bozos, it will hurt us, because it takes time to get rid of them. They start infiltrating the organization and then they themselves start hiring people of lower quality. At Microsoft, we are always looking for people who are better than we are.

Second, training plays a key role. For example, in elite military units such as the Green Berets and Navy SEALs, the training regimen so thoroughly internalizes the culture that individuals, in effect, lose their identity. The group becomes the overriding concern and focal point of their energies. At firms such as FedEx, training not only builds skills, but also plays a significant role in building a strong culture on the foundation of the organization's dominant values.

Third, managerial role models are vital. When he led Intel Andy Grove did not need (or want) a large number of bureaucratic rules to determine who is responsible for what, who is supposed to talk to whom, and who gets to fly first class (no one does). He encouraged openness by not having many of the trappings of success—he worked in a cubicle like all the other professionals. Can you imagine any new manager asking whether or not he can fly first class? Grove's personal example eliminates such a need.

Fourth, reward systems must be clearly aligned with the organizational goals and objectives. Where do you think rules and regulations are more important in controlling behavior—Home Depot, with its generous bonus and stock option plan, or Kmart, which does not provide the same level of rewards and incentives?

SUMMARY

LO1 For firms to be successful, they must practice effective strategic control and corporate governance. Without such controls, the firm will not be able to achieve competitive advantages and outperform rivals in the marketplace.

LO2, LO3 We began the chapter with the key role of informational control. We contrasted two types of control systems: what we termed "traditional" and "contemporary" information control systems. Whereas traditional control systems may have their place in placid, simple competitive environments, there are fewer of those in today's economy. Instead, we advocate the contemporary approach wherein the internal and external environment are constantly monitored so that when surprises emerge, the firm can modify its strategies, goals, and objectives.

LO4 Behavioral controls are also a vital part of effective control systems. We argue that firms must develop the proper balance between culture, rewards and incentives, and boundaries and constraints. Where there are strong and positive cultures and rewards, employees tend to internalize the organization's strategies and objectives. This permits a firm to spend fewer resources on monitoring behavior, and assures the firm that the efforts and initiatives of employees are more consistent with the overall objectives of the organization.

SUMMARY REVIEW QUESTIONS

1. Why are effective strategic control systems so important in today's economy?

2. What are the main advantages of "contemporary" control systems over "traditional" control systems? What are the main differences between these two systems?

3. Why is it important to have a balance between the three elements of behavioral control—culture, rewards and incentives, and boundaries?

4. Discuss the relationship between types of organizations and their primary means of behavioral control.

5. Boundaries become less important as a firm develops a strong culture and reward system. Explain.

6. Why is it important to avoid a "one best way" mentality concerning control systems? What are the consequences of applying the same type of control system to all types of environments?

KEY TERMS

traditional approach to strategic control, 176

informational control, 178
behavioral control, 178

organizational culture, 180

APPLICATION QUESTIONS EXERCISES

1. The problems of many firms may be attributed to a "traditional" control system that failed to continuously monitor the environment and make necessary changes in their strategy and objectives. What companies are you familiar with that responded appropriately (or inappropriately) to environmental change?

2. How can a strong, positive culture enhance a firm's competitive advantage? How can a weak, negative culture erode competitive advantages? Explain and provide examples.

3. Use the Internet to research a firm that has an excellent culture and/or reward and incentive system. What are this firm's main financial and nonfinancial benefits?

REFERENCES

1. Limperis, J. 2004. Frame of mind. *The Manufacturer.com,* October 31; Cavanaugh, M. 2001. When the wheels start turning. *Business First,* March 9: B3; Nulty, P. 1995. Incentive plans can be crippling. *Fortune,* November 13: 235; and Lancaster, P. R. 1994. Incentive pay isn't good for your company. *Inc.,* September: 23–24.

2. This chapter draws upon Picken, J. C., & Dess, G. G. 1997. *Mission critical.* Burr Ridge, IL: Irwin Professional Publishing.

3. Simons, R. 1995. Control in an age of empowerment. *Harvard Business Review,* 73: 80–88. This chapter draws on this source in the discussion of informational control.

4. Goold, M., & Quinn, J. B. 1990. The paradox of strategic controls. *Strategic Management Journal,* 11: 43–57.

5. Quinn, J. B. 1980. *Strategies for change.* Homewood, IL: Richard D. Irwin.

6. Mintzberg, H. 1987. Crafting strategy. *Harvard Business Review,* 65: 66–75.

7. Weston, J. S. 1992. Soft stuff matters. *Financial Executive,* July–August: 52–53.

8. This discussion of control systems draws upon Simons, op. cit.

9. For an interesting perspective on this issue and how a downturn in the economy can reduce the tendency toward "free agency" by managers and professionals, refer to Morris, B. 2001. White collar blues. *Fortune,* July 23: 98–110.

10. Ouchi, W. 1981. *Theory Z.* Reading, MA: Addison-Wesley; Deal, T. E., & Kennedy, A. A. 1982. *Corporate cultures.* Reading, MA: Addison-Wesley; Peters, T. J., & Waterman, R. H. 1982. *In search of excellence.* New York: Random House; Collins, J. 2001. *Good to great.* New York: HarperCollins.

11. Collins, J. C., & Porras, J. I. 1994. *Built to last: Successful habits of visionary companies.* New York: HarperBusiness.

12. Lee, J., & Miller, D. 1999. People matter: Commitment to employees, strategy, and performance in Korean firms. *Strategic Management Journal,* 6: 579–594.

13. For an insightful discussion of IKEA's unique culture, see Kling, K., & Goteman, I. 2003. IKEA CEO Anders Dahlvig on international growth and IKEA's unique corporate culture and brand identity. *Academy of Management Executive,* 17(1): 31–37.

14. For a discussion of how professionals inculcate values, refer to Uhl-Bien, M., & Graen, G. B. 1998. Individual self-management: Analysis of professionals' self-managing activities in functional and cross-functional work teams. *Academy of Management Journal,* 41(3): 340–350.

15. A perspective on how antisocial behavior can erode a firm's culture can be found in Robinson, S. L., & O'Leary-Kelly, A. M. 1998. Monkey see, monkey do: The influence of work groups on the antisocial behavior of employees. *Academy of Management Journal,* 41(6): 658–672.

16. Mitchell, R. 1989. Masters of innovation. *BusinessWeek,* April 10: 58–63.

17. Sellers, P. 1993. Companies that serve you best. *Fortune,* May 31: 88.

18. Southwest Airlines Culture Committee. 1993. *Luv Lines* (company publication), March–April: 17–18; for an interesting perspective on the "downside" of strong "cultlike" organizational cultures, refer to Arnott, D. A. 2000. *Corporate cults.* New York: AMACOM.

19. Kerr, J., & Slocum, J. W., Jr. 1987. Managing corporate culture through reward systems. *Academy of Management Executive,* 1(2): 99–107.

20. For a unique perspective on leader challenges in managing wealthy professionals, refer to Wetlaufer, S. 2000. Who wants to manage a millionaire? *Harvard Business Review,* 78(4): 53–60.

21. Neilson, G. L., Pasternack, B. A., & Van Nuys, K. E. 2005. The passive-aggressive organization. *Harvard Business Review,* 83 (10): 82–95.

22. These next two subsections draw upon Dess, G. G., & Picken, J. C. 1997. *Beyond Productivity.* New York: AMACOM.

23. For a discussion of the benefits of stock options as executive compensation, refer to Hall, B. J. 2000. What you need to know about stock options. *Harvard Business Review,* 78(2): 121–129.

24. Tully, S. 1993. Your paycheck gets exciting. *Fortune,* November 13: 89.

25. Zellner, W., Hof, R. D., Brandt, R., Baker, S., & Greising, D. 1995. Go-go goliaths. *BusinessWeek,* February 13: 64–70.

26. This section draws on Dess & Picken, op. cit.: chap. 5.

27. Simons, op. cit.

REFERENCES

28. Davis, E. 1997. Interview: Norman Augustine. *Management Review,* November: 11.

29. This section draws upon Dess, G. G., & Miller, A. 1993. *Strategic management.* New York: McGraw-Hill.

30. For a good review of the goal-setting literature, refer to Locke, E. A., & Latham, G. P. 1990. *A theory of goal setting and task performance.* Englewood Cliffs, NJ: Prentice Hall.

31. For an interesting perspective on the use of rules and regulations that is counter to this industry's (software) norms, refer to Fryer, B. 2001. Tom Siebel of Siebel Systems: High tech the old fashioned way. *Harvard Business Review,* 79(3): 118–130.

32. Thompson, A. A., Jr., & Strickland, A. J., III. 1998. *Strategic management: Concepts and cases* (10th ed.): 313. New York: McGraw-Hill.

33. Ibid.

34. Teitelbaum, R. 1997. Tough guys finish first. *Fortune,* July 21: 82–84.

35. Weaver, G. R., Trevino, L. K., & Cochran, P. L. 1999. Corporate ethics programs as control systems: Influences of executive commitment and environmental factors. *Academy of Management Journal,* 42(1): 41–57.

36. Cadbury, S. A. 1987. Ethical managers make their own rules. *Harvard Business Review,* 65: 3, 69–73.

37. Weber, J. 2003. CFOs on the hot seat. *BusinessWeek,* March 17: 66–70.

38. William Ouchi has written extensively about the use of clan control (which is viewed as an alternate to bureaucratic or market control). Here, a powerful culture results in people aligning their individual interests with those of the firm. Refer to Ouchi, op. cit. This section also draws on Hall, R. H. 2002. *Organizations: Structures, processes, and outcomes* (8th ed.). Upper Saddle River, NJ: Prentice Hall.

Analyzing Strategic Management Cases

chapter objectives

After reading this chapter, you should have a good understanding of:

LO1 How analyzing strategic management cases can help develop the ability to differentiate, speculate, and integrate when evaluating complex business problems.

LO2 The steps involved in conducting a strategic management case analysis.

LO3 How to use financial analysis to assess a company's current situation and future prospects.

LO4 How to get the most out of case analysis.

Case analysis is one of the most effective ways to learn strategic management. It provides a complement to other methods of instruction by asking you to use the tools and techniques of strategic management to deal with an actual business situation. Strategy cases include detailed descriptions of management challenges faced by executives and business owners. By studying the background and analyzing the strategic predicaments posed by a case, you first see that the circumstances businesses confront are often difficult and complex. Then you are asked what decisions you would make to address the situation in the case and how the actions you recommend will affect the company. Thus, the processes of analysis, formulation, and implementation that have been addressed by this textbook can be applied in a real-life situation.

WHY ANALYZE STRATEGIC MANAGEMENT CASES?

It is often said that the key to finding good answers is to ask good questions. Strategic managers and business leaders are required to evaluate options, make choices, and find solutions to the challenges they face every day. To do so, they must learn to ask the right questions. The study of strategic management poses the same challenge. The process of analyzing, decision making, and implementing strategic actions raises many good questions.

- Why do some firms succeed and others fail?
- Why are some companies higher performers than others?
- What information is needed in the strategic planning process?
- How do competing values and beliefs affect strategic decision making?
- What skills and capabilities are needed to implement a strategy effectively?

How does a student of strategic management answer these questions? By strategic case analysis. **Case analysis** simulates the real-world experience that strategic managers and company leaders face as they try to determine how best to run their companies. It places students in the middle of an actual situation and challenges them to figure out what to do.[1]

Asking the right questions is just the beginning of case analysis. In the previous chapters we have discussed issues and challenges that managers face and provided analytical frameworks for understanding the situation. But once the analysis is complete, decisions have to be made. Case analysis forces you to choose among different options and set forth a plan of action based on your choices. But even then the job is not done. Strategic case analysis also requires that you address how you will implement the plan and the implications of choosing one course of action over another.

A strategic management case is a detailed description of a challenging situation faced by an organization.[2] It usually includes a chronology of events and extensive support materials, such as financial statements, product lists, and transcripts of interviews with employees. Although names or locations are sometimes changed to provide anonymity, cases usually report the facts of a situation as authentically as possible.

One of the main reasons to analyze strategic management cases is to develop an ability to evaluate business situations critically. In case analysis, memorizing key terms and conceptual frameworks is not enough. To analyze a case, it is important that you go beyond textbook prescriptions and quick answers. It requires you to look deeply into the information that is provided and root out the essential issues and causes of a company's problems.

LO1 How analyzing strategic management cases can help develop the ability to differentiate, speculate, and integrate when evaluating complex business problems.

case analysis
A method of learning complex strategic management concepts such as environmental analysis, the process of decision making, and implementing strategic actions through placing students in the middle of an actual situation and challenging them to figure out what to do.

The types of skills that are required to prepare an effective strategic case analysis can benefit you in actual business situations. Case analysis adds to the overall learning experience by helping you acquire or improve skills that may not be taught in a typical lecture course. Three capabilities that can be learned by conducting case analysis are especially useful to strategic managers—the ability to differentiate, speculate, and integrate.[3] Here's how case analysis can enhance those skills.

1. *Differentiate.* Effective strategic management requires that many different elements of a situation be evaluated at once. This is also true in case analysis. When analyzing cases, it is important to isolate critical facts, evaluate whether assumptions are useful or faulty, and distinguish between good and bad information. Differentiating between the factors that are influencing the situation presented by a case is necessary for making a good analysis. Strategic management also involves understanding that problems are often complex and multilayered. This applies to case analysis as well. Ask whether the case deals with operational, business-level, or corporate issues. Do the problems stem from weaknesses in the internal value chain or threats in the external environment? Dig deep. Being too quick to accept the easiest or least controversial answer will usually fail to get to the heart of the problem.

2. *Speculate.* Strategic managers need to be able to use their imagination to envision an explanation or solution that might not readily be apparent. The same is true with case analysis. Being able to imagine different scenarios or contemplate the outcome of a decision can aid the analysis. Managers also have to deal with uncertainty since most decisions are made without complete knowledge of the circumstances. This is also true in case analysis. Case materials often seem to be missing data or the information provided is contradictory. The ability to speculate about details that are unknown or the consequences of an action can be helpful.

3. *Integrate.* Strategy involves looking at the big picture and having an organization-wide perspective. Strategic case analysis is no different. Even though the chapters in this textbook divide the material into various topics that may apply to different parts of an organization, all of this information must be integrated into one set of recommendations that will affect the whole company. A strategic manager needs to comprehend how all the factors that influence the organization will interact. This also applies to case analysis. Changes made in one part of the organization affect other parts. Thus, a holistic perspective that integrates the impact of various decisions and environmental influences on all parts of the organization is needed.

In business, these three activities sometimes "compete" with each other for your attention. For example, some decision makers may have a natural ability to differentiate among elements of a problem but are not able to integrate them very well. Others have enough innate creativity to imagine solutions or fill in the blanks when information is missing. But they may have a difficult time when faced with hard numbers or cold facts. Even so, each of these skills is important. The mark of a good strategic manager is the ability to simultaneously make distinctions and envision the whole, and to imagine a future scenario while staying focused on the present. Thus, another reason to conduct case analysis is to help you develop and exercise your ability to differentiate, speculate, and integrate.

Case analysis takes the student through the whole cycle of activity that a manager would face. Beyond the textbook descriptions of concepts and examples, case analysis asks you to "walk a mile in the shoes" of the strategic decision maker and learn to evaluate situations critically. Executives and owners must make decisions every day with limited information and a swirl of business activity going on around them.

HOW TO CONDUCT A CASE ANALYSIS

LO2   The steps involved in conducting a strategic management case analysis.

The process of analyzing strategic management cases involves several steps. In this section we will review the mechanics of preparing a case analysis. Before beginning, there are two things to keep in mind that will clarify your understanding of the process and make the results of the process more meaningful.

First, unless you prepare for a case discussion, there is little you can gain from the discussion and even less that you can offer. Effective strategic managers don't enter into problem-solving situations without doing some homework—investigating the situation, analyzing and researching possible solutions, and sometimes gathering the advice of others. Good problem solving often requires that decision makers be immersed in the facts, options, and implications surrounding the problem. In case analysis, this means reading and thoroughly comprehending the case materials before trying to make an analysis.

The second point is related to the first. To get the most out of a case analysis you must place yourself "inside" the case—that is, think like an actual participant in the case situation. However, there are several positions you can take. These are discussed in the following paragraphs:

- *Strategic decision maker.* This is the position of the senior executive responsible for resolving the situation described in the case. It may be the CEO, the business owner, or a strategic manager in a key executive position.
- *Board of directors.* Because the board of directors represents the owners of a corporation, it has a responsibility to step in when a management crisis threatens the company. As a board member, you may be in a unique position to solve problems.
- *Outside consultant.* Either the board or top management may decide to bring in outsiders. Consultants often have an advantage because they can look at a situation objectively. But they also may be at a disadvantage because they have no power to enforce changes.

Before beginning the analysis, it may be helpful to envision yourself assuming one of these roles. Then, as you study and analyze the case materials, you can make a diagnosis and recommend solutions in a way that is consistent with your position. Try different perspectives. You may find that your view of the situation changes depending on the role you play. As an outside consultant, for example, it may be easy for you to conclude that certain individuals should be replaced in order to solve a problem presented in the case. However, if you take the role of the CEO who knows the individuals and the challenges they have been facing, you may be reluctant to fire them and will seek another solution instead.

The idea of assuming a particular role is similar to the real world in various ways. In your career, you may work in an organization where outside accountants, bankers, lawyers, or other professionals are advising you about how to resolve business situations or improve your practices. Their perspective will be different from yours but it is useful to understand things from their point of view. Conversely, you may work as a member of the audit team of an accounting firm or the loan committee of a bank. In those situations, it would be helpful if you understood the situation from the perspective of the business leader who

Using a Business Plan Framework to Analyze Strategic Cases

Established businesses often have to change what they are doing in order to improve their competitive position or sometimes simply to survive. To make the changes effectively, businesses usually need a plan. Business plans are no longer just for entrepreneurs. The kind of market analysis, decision making, and action planning that is considered standard practice among new ventures can also benefit going concerns that want to make changes, seize an opportunity, or head in a new direction.

The best business plans, however, are not those loaded with decades of month-by-month financial projections or that depend on rigid adherence to a schedule of events that is impossible to predict. The good ones are focused on four factors that are critical to new-venture success. These same factors are important in case analysis as well because they get to the heart of many of the problems found in strategic cases.

1. **The People.** "When I receive a business plan, I always read the résumé section first," says Harvard Professor William Sahlman. The people questions that are critically important to investors include: What are their skills? How much experience do they have? What is their reputation? Have they worked together as a team? These same questions also may be used in case analysis to evaluate the role of individuals in the strategic case.

2. **The Opportunity.** Business opportunities come in many forms. They are not limited to new ventures. The chance to enter new markets, introduce new products, or merge with a competitor provide many of the challenges that are found in strategic management cases. What are the consequences of such actions? Will the proposed changes affect the firm's business concept? What factors might

stand in the way of success? The same issues are also present in most strategic cases.

3. **The Context.** Things happen in contexts that cannot be controlled by a firm's managers. This is particularly true of the general environment where social trends, economic changes, or events such as the September 11, 2001, terrorist attacks can change business overnight. When evaluating strategic cases, ask: Is the company aware of the impact of context on the business? What will it do if the context changes? Can it influence the context in a way that favors the company?

4. **Risk and Reward.** With a new venture, the entrepreneurs and investors take the risks and get the rewards. In strategic cases, the risks and rewards often extend to many other stakeholders, such as employees, customers, and suppliers. When analyzing a case, ask: Are the managers making choices that will pay off in the future? Are the rewards evenly distributed? Will some stakeholders be put at risk if the situation in the case changes? What if the situation remains the same? Could that be even riskier?

Whether a business is growing or shrinking, large or small, industrial or service oriented, the issues of people, opportunities, context, and risks and rewards will have a large impact on its performance. Therefore, you should always consider these four factors when evaluating strategic management cases.

Sources: Wasserman, E. 2003. A simple plan. *MBA Jungle,* February: 50–55; DeKluyver, C. A. 2000. *Strategic thinking: An executive perspective.* Upper Saddle River, NJ: Prentice Hall; Sahlman, W. A. 1997. How to write a great business plan. *Harvard Business Review,* 75(4): 98–108.

must weigh your views against all the other advice that he or she receives. Case analysis can help develop an ability to appreciate such multiple perspectives.

One of the most challenging roles to play in business is as a business founder or owner. For small businesses or entrepreneurial start-ups, the founder may wear all hats at once—key decision maker, primary stockholder, and CEO. Hiring an outside consultant may not be an option. However, the issues faced by young firms and established firms are often not that different, especially when it comes to formulating a plan of action. Business plans that entrepreneurial firms use to raise money or propose a business expansion typically revolve around a few key issues that must be addressed no matter what the size or age of the business. Focus on Strategy 9.1 reviews business planning issues that are most important to consider when evaluating any case, especially from the perspective of the business founder or owner.

Next we will review five steps to follow when conducting a strategic management case analysis: becoming familiar with the material, identifying the problems, analyzing the strategic issues using the tools and insights of strategic management, proposing alternative solutions, and making recommendations.[4]

BECOME FAMILIAR WITH THE MATERIAL

Written cases often include a lot of material. They may be complex and include detailed financials or long passages. Even so, to understand a case and its implications, you must become familiar with its content. Sometimes key information is not immediately apparent. It may be contained in the footnotes to an exhibit or an interview with a lower-level employee. In other cases the important points may be difficult to grasp because the subject matter is so unfamiliar. When you approach a strategic case try the following technique to enhance comprehension:

- Read quickly through the case one time to get an overall sense of the material.
- Use the initial read-through to assess possible links to strategic concepts.
- Read through the case again, in depth. Make written notes as you read.
- Evaluate how strategic concepts might inform key decisions or suggest alternative solutions.
- After formulating an initial recommendation, thumb through the case again quickly to help assess the consequences of the actions you propose.

IDENTIFY PROBLEMS

When conducting case analysis, one of your most important tasks is to identify the problem. Earlier we noted that one of the main reasons to conduct case analysis was to find solutions. But you cannot find a solution unless you know the problem. Another saying you may have heard is, "A good diagnosis is half the cure." In other words, once you have determined what the problem is, you are well on your way to identifying a reasonable solution.

Some cases have more than one problem. But the problems are usually related. For a hypothetical example, consider the following: Company A was losing customers to a new competitor. Upon analysis, it was determined that the competitor had a 50 percent faster delivery time even though its product was of lower quality. The managers of company A could not understand why customers would settle for an inferior product. It turns out that no one was marketing to company A's customers that its product was superior. A second problem was that falling sales resulted in cuts in company A's sales force. Thus, there were two related problems: inferior delivery technology and insufficient sales effort.

When trying to determine the problem, avoid getting hung up on symptoms. Zero in on the problem. For example, in the company A example above, the symptom was losing customers. But the problems were an underfunded, understaffed sales force combined with an outdated delivery technology. Try to see beyond the immediate symptoms to the more fundamental problems.

Another tip when preparing a case analysis is to articulate the problem.[5] Writing down a problem statement gives you a reference point to turn to as you proceed through the case analysis. This is important because the process of formulating strategies or evaluating implementation methods may lead you away from the initial problem. Make sure your recommendation actually addresses the problems you have identified.

One more thing about identifying problems: Sometimes problems are not apparent until *after* you do the analysis. In some cases the problem will be presented plainly, perhaps in the opening paragraph or on the last page of the case. But in other cases the problem does not emerge until after the issues in the case have been analyzed. We turn next to the subject of strategic case analysis.

CONDUCT STRATEGIC ANALYSES

This textbook has presented numerous analytical tools (e.g., five-forces analysis and value-chain analysis), contingency frameworks (e.g., when to use related rather than unrelated diversification strategies), and other techniques that can be used to evaluate strategic situations. The previous eight chapters have addressed practices that are common in strategic management, but only so much can be learned by studying the practices and concepts. The best way to understand these methods is to apply them by conducting analyses of specific cases.

The first step is to determine which strategic issues are involved. Is there a problem in the company's competitive environment? Or is it an internal problem? If it is internal, does it have to do with organizational structure? Strategic controls? Uses of technology? Or perhaps the company has overworked its employees or underutilized its intellectual capital. Has the company mishandled a merger? Chosen the wrong diversification strategy? Botched a new product introduction? Each of these issues is linked to one or more of the concepts discussed earlier in the text. Determine what strategic issues are associated with the problems you have identified. Remember also that most real-life case situations involve issues that are highly interrelated. Even in cases where there is only one major problem, the strategic processes required to solve it may involve several parts of the organization.

Once you have identified the issues that apply to the case, conduct the analysis. For example, you may need to conduct a five-forces analysis or dissect the company's competitive strategy. Perhaps you need to evaluate whether its resources are rare, valuable, difficult to imitate, or difficult to substitute. Perhaps the international entry mode needs to be reevaluated because of changing conditions in the host country. Employee empowerment techniques may need to be improved to enhance organizational learning. Whatever the case, all the strategic concepts introduced in the text include insights for assessing their effectiveness. Determining how well a company is doing these things is central to the case analysis process.

Financial ratio analysis is one of the primary tools used to conduct case analysis. The Appendix at the end of this chapter includes a discussion and examples of the financial ratios that are often used to evaluate a company's performance and financial well-being. Exhibit 9.1 provides a summary of the financial ratios presented in the Appendix to this Chapter 9.1.

In this part of the overall strategic analysis process, it is also important to test your own assumptions about the case.[6] First, what assumptions are you making about the case materials? It may be that you have interpreted the case content differently than your team members or classmates. Being clear about these assumptions will be important in determining how to analyze the case. Second, what assumptions have you made about the best way to resolve the problems? Ask yourself why you have chosen one type of analysis over another. This process of assumption checking can also help determine if you have gotten to the heart of the problem or are still just dealing with symptoms.

As mentioned earlier, sometimes the critical diagnosis in a case can only be made after the analysis is conducted. However, by the end of this stage in the process, you should know the problems and have completed a thorough analysis of them. You can now move to the next step: finding solutions.

PROPOSE ALTERNATIVE SOLUTIONS

It is important to remember that in strategic management case analysis, there is rarely one right answer or one best way. Even when members of a class or a team agree on what the problem is, they may not agree upon how to solve the problem. Therefore, it is helpful to consider several different solutions.

LO3 How to use financial analysis to assess a company's current situation and future prospects.

financial ratio analysis
A method of evaluating a company's performance and financial well-being through ratios of accounting values, including short term solvency, long term solvency, asset utilization, profitability, and market value ratios.

EXHIBIT 9.1

Summary of Financial Ratio Analysis Techniques

Ratio	What It Measures
Short-term solvency, or liquidity, ratios:	
Current ratio	Ability to use assets to pay off liabilities.
Quick ratio	Ability to use liquid assets to pay off liabilities quickly.
Cash ratio	Ability to pay off liabilities with cash on hand.
Long-term solvency, or financial leverage, ratios:	
Total debt ratio	How much of a company's total assets are financed by debt.
Debt-equity ratio	Compares how much a company is financed by debt with how much it is financed by equity.
Equity multiplier	How much debt is being used to finance assets.
Times interest earned ratio	How well a company has its interest obligations covered.
Cash coverage ratio	A company's ability to generate cash from operations.
Asset utilization, or turnover, ratios:	
Inventory turnover	How many times each year a company sells its entire inventory.
Days' sales in inventory	How many days on average inventory is on hand before it is sold.
Receivables turnover	How frequently each year a company collects on its credit sales.
Days' sales in receivables	How many days on average it takes to collect on credit sales (average collection period).
Total asset turnover	How much of sales is generated for every dollar in assets.
Capital intensity	The dollar investment in assets needed to generate $1 in sales.
Profitability ratios:	
Profit margin	How much profit is generated by every dollar of sales.
Return on assets (ROA)	How effectively assets are being used to generate a return.
Return on equity (ROE)	How effectively amounts invested in the business by its owners are being used to generate a return.
Market value ratios:	
Price-earnings ratio	How much investors are willing to pay per dollar of current earnings.
Market-to-book ratio	Compares market value of the company's investments to the cost of those investments.

After conducting strategic analysis and identifying the problem, develop a list of options. What are the possible solutions? What are the alternatives? First, generate a list of all the options you can think of without prejudging any one of them. Remember that not all cases call for dramatic decisions or sweeping changes. Some companies just need to make small adjustments. In fact, "Do nothing" may be a reasonable alternative in some cases. Although that is rare, it might be useful to consider what will happen if the company does nothing. This point illustrates the purpose of developing alternatives: to evaluate what will happen if a company chooses one solution over another.

Thus, during this step of a case analysis, you will evaluate choices and the implications of those choices. One aspect of any business that is likely to be highlighted in this part of the analysis is strategy implementation. Ask how the choices made will be implemented. It may be that what seems like an obvious choice for solving a problem creates an even bigger problem when implemented. But remember also that no strategy or strategic "fix" is going to work if it cannot be implemented. Once a list of alternatives is generated, ask:

- Can the company afford it? How will it affect the bottom line?
- Is the solution likely to evoke a competitive response?
- Will employees throughout the company accept the changes? What impact will the solution have on morale?
- How will the decision affect other stakeholders? Will customers, suppliers, and others buy into it?
- How does this solution fit with the company's vison, mission, and objectives?
- Will the culture or values of the company be changed by the solution? Is it a positive change?

The point of this step in the case analysis process is to find a solution that both solves the problem and is realistic. A consideration of the implications of various alternative solutions will generally lead you to a final recommendation that is more thoughtful and complete.

MAKE RECOMMENDATIONS

The basic aim of case analysis is to find solutions. Your analysis is not complete until you have recommended a course of action. In this step the task is to make a set of recommendations that your analysis supports. Describe exactly what needs to be done. Explain why this course of action will solve the problem. The recommendation should also include suggestions for how best to implement the proposed solution because the recommended actions and their implications for the performance and future of the firm are interrelated.

Recall that the solution you propose must solve the problem you identified. This point cannot be overemphasized; too often students make recommendations that treat only symptoms or fail to tackle the central problems in the case. Make a logical argument that shows how the problem led to the analysis and the analysis led to the recommendations you are proposing. Remember, an analysis is not an end in itself; it is useful only if it leads to a solution.

The actions you propose should describe the very next steps that the company needs to take. Don't say, for example, "If the company does more market research, then I would recommend the following course of action. . . ." Instead, make conducting the research part of your recommendation. Taking the example a step further, if you also want to suggest subsequent actions that may be different *depending* on the outcome of the market research, that's OK. But don't make your initial recommendation conditional on actions the company may or may not take.

EXHIBIT 9.2   Preparing an Oral Case Presentation

Rule	Description
Organize your thoughts.	Begin by becoming familiar with the material. If you are working with a team, compare notes about the key points of the case and share insights that other team members may have gleaned from tables and exhibits. Then make an outline. This is one of the best ways to organize the flow and content of the presentation.
Emphasize strategic analysis.	The purpose of case analysis is to diagnose problems and find solutions. In the process, you may need to unravel the case material as presented and reconfigure it in a fashion that can be more effectively analyzed. Present the material in a way that lends itself to analysis—don't simply restate what is in the case. This involves three major categories with the following emphasis:

	Background/Problem Statement	10–20%
	Strategic Analysis/Options	60–75%
	Recommendations/Action Plan	10–20%

	As you can see, the emphasis of your presentation should be on analysis. This will probably require you to reorganize the material so that the tools of strategic analysis can be applied.
Be logical and consistent.	A presentation that is rambling and hard to follow may confuse the listener and fail to evoke a good discussion. Present your arguments and explanations in a logical sequence. Support your claims with facts. Include financial analysis where appropriate. Be sure that the solutions you recommend address the problems you have identified.
Defend your position.	Usually an oral presentation is followed by a class discussion. Anticipate what others might disagree with and be prepared to defend your views. This means being aware of the choices you made and the implications of your recommendations. Be clear about your assumptions. Be able to expand on your analysis.
Share presentation responsibilities.	Strategic management case analyses are often conducted by teams. Each member of the team should have a clear role in the oral presentation, preferably a speaking role. It's also important to coordinate the different parts of the presentation into a logical, smooth-flowing whole. How well a team works together is usually very apparent during an oral presentation.

In summary, case analysis can be a very rewarding process but, as you might imagine, it can also be frustrating and challenging. If you will follow the steps described above, you will address the different elements of a thorough analysis. This approach can give your analysis a solid footing. Then, even if there are differences of opinion about how to interpret the facts, analyze the situation, or solve the problems, you can feel confident that you have not missed any important steps in finding the best course of action.

Students are often asked to prepare oral presentations of the information in a case and their analysis of the best remedies. This is frequently assigned as a group project. Or you may be called upon in class to present your ideas about the circumstances or solutions for a case the class is discussing. Exhibit 9.2 provides some tips for preparing an oral case presentation.

L04 How to get the most out of case analysis.

HOW TO GET THE MOST FROM CASE ANALYSIS

One of the reasons case analysis is so enriching as a learning tool is that it draws on many resources and skills besides just what is in the textbook. This is especially true in the study of strategy. Why? Because strategic management itself is a highly integrative task that draws on many areas of specialization at several levels, from the individual to the whole of society. Therefore, to get the most out of case analysis, expand your horizons beyond the concepts in this text and seek insights from your own reservoir of knowledge. Here are some tips for how to do that.[7]

- *Keep an open mind.* Like any good discussion, a case analysis discussion often evokes strong opinions and high emotions. But it's the variety of perspectives that makes case analysis so valuable: Many viewpoints usually lead to a more complete analysis. Therefore, avoid letting an emotional response to another person's style or opinion keep you from hearing what he or she has to say. Once you evaluate what is said, you may disagree with it or dismiss it as faulty. But unless you keep an open mind in the first place, you may miss the importance of the other person's contribution. Also, people often place a higher value on the opinions of those they consider to be good listeners.

- *Take a stand for what you believe.* Although it is vital to keep an open mind, it is also important to state your views proactively. Don't try to figure out what your friends or the instructor wants to hear. Analyze the case from the perspective of your own background and belief system. For example, perhaps you feel that a decision is unethical or that the managers in a case have misinterpreted the facts. Don't be afraid to assert that in the discussion. For one thing, when a person takes a strong stand, it often encourages others to evaluate the issues more closely. This can lead to a more thorough investigation and a more meaningful class discussion.

- *Draw on your personal experience.* You may have experiences from work or as a customer that shed light on some of the issues in a case. Even though one of the purposes of case analysis is to apply the analytical tools from this text, you may be able to add to the discussion by drawing on your outside experiences and background. Of course, you need to guard against carrying that to extremes. In other words, don't think that your perspective is the only viewpoint that matters! Simply recognize that firsthand experience usually represents a welcome contribution to the overall quality of case discussions.

- *Participate and persuade.* People who speak their mind can often influence the views of others. But to do so, you have to be prepared and convincing. Being persuasive is more than being loud or long-winded. It involves understanding all sides of an argument and being able to overcome objections to your own point of view. These efforts can make a case discussion more lively. And they parallel what happens in the real world; in business, people frequently share their opinions and attempt to persuade others to see things their way.

- *Be concise and to the point.* In the previous point, we encouraged you to speak up and "sell" your ideas to others in a case discussion. But you must be clear about what you are selling. Make your arguments in a way that is explicit and direct. Zero in on the most important points. Be brief. Don't try to make a lot of points at once by jumping around between topics. Avoid trying to explain the whole case situation at once.

Effectively working in teams is a critical skill—both in the classroom and in business organizations.

Remember, other students usually resent classmates who go on and on, take up a lot of "airtime," or repeat themselves unnecessarily. The best way to avoid this is to stay focused and be specific.

- *Think out of the box.* It's OK to be a little provocative; sometimes that is the consequence of taking a stand on issues. But it may be equally important to be imaginative and creative when making a recommendation or determining how to implement a solution. Albert Einstein once stated, "Imagination is more important than knowledge." The reason is that managing strategically requires more than memorizing concepts. Strategic management insights must be applied to each case differently—just knowing the principles is not enough. Imagination and out-of-the-box thinking help to apply strategic knowledge in novel and unique ways.

- *Learn from the insights of others.* Before you make up your mind about a case, hear what other students have to say. Get a second opinion, and a third, and so forth. Of course, in a situation where you have to put your analysis in writing, you may not be able to learn from others ahead of time. But in a case discussion, observe how various students attack the issues and engage in problem solving. Such observation skills also may be a key to finding answers within the case. For example, people tend to believe authority figures, so they would place a higher value on what a company president says. In some cases, however, the statements of middle managers may represent a point of view that is even more helpful for finding a solution to the problems presented by the case.

- *Apply insights from other case analyses.* Throughout the text, we have used examples of actual businesses to illustrate strategy concepts. The aim has been to show you how firms think about and deal with business problems. During the course, you may be asked to conduct several case analyses as part of the learning experience. Once you have performed a few case analyses, you will see how the concepts from the text apply in real-life business situations. Incorporate the insights learned from the text examples and your own previous case discussions into each new case that you analyze.

- *Critically analyze your own performance.* Performance appraisals are a standard part of many workplace situations. They are used to determine promotions, raises, and work assignments. In some organizations, everyone from the top executive down is subject to such reviews. Even in situations where the owner or CEO is not evaluated by others, they often find it useful to ask themselves regularly, Am I being effective? The same can be applied to your performance in a case analysis situation. Ask yourself, Were my comments insightful? Did I make a good contribution? How might I improve next time? Use the same criteria on yourself that you use to evaluate others. What grade would you give yourself? This technique will not only make you more fair in your assessment of others but also will indicate how your own performance can improve.

- *Conduct outside research.* Many times, you can enhance your understanding of a case situation by investigating sources outside the case materials. For example, you may want to study an industry more closely or research a company's close competitors. Recent moves such as mergers and acquisitions or product introductions may be reported in the business press. The company itself may provide useful information on its Web site or in its annual reports. Such information can usually spur additional discussion and enrich the case analysis. It is best to check with your instructor in advance to be sure this kind of additional research is encouraged. Bringing in outside research may conflict with the instructor's learning objectives. If your instructor encourages outside research, good Web sites to consult include:

www.annualreports.com and www.carol.co.uk

These Web sites offer annual reports from a wide variety of firms based in the United States and Europe.

www.sec.gov

The Securities Exchange Commission's Web site provides access to financial documents such as 10-kg that publicly traded companies must file on a regular basis.

www.hoovers.com

Hoover's Online provides information on companies, industries, and executives.

finance.yahoo.com

This Web site links to information on U.S. markets, world markets, data sources, financial ratios for companies, investment editorials, and business news.

Several of the points suggested above for how to get the most out of case analysis apply only to an open discussion of a case, like that in a classroom setting. Exhibit 9.3 provides some additional guidelines for preparing a written case analysis.

EXHIBIT 9.3

Preparing a Written Case Analysis

Rule	Description
Be thorough.	Many of the ideas presented in Exhibit 9.2 about oral presentations also apply to written case analysis. However, a written analysis typically has to be more complete. This means writing out the problem statement and articulating assumptions. It is also important to provide support for your arguments and reference case materials or other facts more specifically.
Coordinate team efforts.	Written cases are often prepared by small groups. Within a group, just as in a class discussion, you may disagree about the diagnosis or the recommended plan of action. This can be healthy if it leads to a richer understanding of the case material. But before committing your ideas to writing, make sure you have coordinated your responses. Don't prepare a written analysis that appears contradictory or looks like a patchwork of disconnected thoughts.
Avoid restating the obvious.	There is no reason to restate material that everyone is familiar with already, namely, the case content. It is too easy for students to use up space in a written analysis with a recapitulation of the details of the case—this accomplishes very little. Stay focused on the key points. Only restate the information that is most central to your analysis.
Present information graphically.	Tables, graphs, and other exhibits are usually one of the best ways to present factual material that supports your arguments. For example, financial calculations such as break-even analysis, sensitivity analysis, or return on investment are best presented graphically. Even qualitative information such as product lists or rosters of employees can be summarized effectively and viewed quickly by using a table or graph.
Exercise quality control.	When presenting a case analysis in writing, it is especially important to use good grammar, avoid misspelling words, and eliminate typos and other visual distractions. Mistakes that can be glossed over in an oral presentation or class discussion are often highlighted when they appear in writing. Make your written presentation appear as professional as possible. Don't let the appearance of your written case keep the reader from recognizing the importance and quality of your analysis.

SUMMARY

L01   Strategic management case analysis provides an effective method of learning how companies analyze problems, make decisions, and resolve challenges. Strategic cases include detailed accounts of actual business situations. The purpose of analyzing such cases is to gain exposure to a wide variety of organizational and managerial situations. By putting yourself in the place of a strategic decision maker, you can gain an appreciation of the difficulty and complexity of many strategic situations. In the process you can learn how to ask good strategic questions and enhance your analytical skills. Presenting case analyses can also help develop oral and written communication skills.

L02, L03, L04   In this chapter we have discussed the importance of strategic case analysis and described the five steps involved in conducting a case analysis: becoming familiar with the material, identifying problems, analyzing strategic issues, proposing alternative solutions, and making recommendations. We have also discussed how to get the most from case analysis and how financial analysis can provide insight into a company's current situation and future prospects.

KEY TERMS

case analysis 193

financial ratio analysis 198

REFERENCES

1. The material in this chapter is based on several sources, including Barnes, L. A., Nelson, A. J., & Christensen, C. R. 1994. *Teaching and the case method: Text, cases and readings.* Boston: Harvard Business School Press; Guth, W. D. 1985. Central concepts of business unit and corporate strategy. In W. D. Guth (Ed.). *Handbook of business strategy:* 1–9. Boston: Warren, Gorham & Lamont; Lundberg, C. C., & Enz, C. 1993. A framework for student case preparation. *Case Research Journal,* 13 (Summer): 129–140; and Ronstadt, R. 1980. *The art of case analysis: A guide to the diagnosis of business situations.* Dover, MA: Lord Publishing.

2. Edge, A. G., & Coleman, D. R. 1986. *The guide to case analysis and reporting* (3rd ed.). Honolulu, HI: System Logistics.

3. Morris, E. 1987. Vision and strategy: A focus for the future. *Journal of Business Strategy* 8: 51–58.

4. This section is based on Lundberg & Enz, op. cit., and Ronstadt, op. cit.

5. The importance of problem definition was emphasized in Mintzberg, H., Raisinghani, D., & Theoret, A. 1976. The structure of "unstructured" decision processes. *Administrative Science Quarterly,* 21(2): 246–275.

6. Drucker, P. F. 1994. The theory of the business. *Harvard Business Review,* 72(5): 95–104.

7. This section draws on Edge & Coleman, op. cit.

L04
How to get
the most
out of case
analysis.

•° APPENDIX TO CHAPTER 9

Financial Ratio Analysis

Standard Financial Statements

One obvious thing we might want to do with a company's financial statements is to compare them to those of other, similar companies. We would immediately have a problem, however. It's almost impossible to directly compare the financial statements for two companies because of differences in size.

For example, Oracle and IBM are obviously serious rivals in the computer software market, but IBM is much larger (in terms of assets), so it is difficult to compare them directly. For that matter, it's difficult to even compare financial statements from different points in time for the same company if the company's size has changed. The size problem is compounded if we try to compare IBM and, say, SAP (of Germany). If SAP's financial statements are denominated in German marks, then we have a size *and* a currency difference.

To start making comparisons, one obvious thing we might try to do is to somehow standardize the financial statements. One very common and useful way of doing this is to work with percentages instead of total dollars. The resulting financial statements are called *common-size statements*. We consider these next.

Common-Size Balance Sheets

For easy reference, Prufrock Corporation's 2004 and 2005 balance sheets are provided in Exhibit 9A.1. Using these, we construct common-size balance sheets by expressing each item as a percentage of total assets. Prufrock's 2004 and 2005 common-size balance sheets are shown in Exhibit 9A.2.

Notice that some of the totals don't check exactly because of rounding errors. Also notice that the total change has to be zero since the beginning and ending numbers must add up to 100 percent.

In this form, financial statements are relatively easy to read and compare. For example, just looking at the two balance sheets for Prufrock, we see that current assets were 19.7 percent of total assets in 2005, up from 19.1 percent in 2004. Current liabilities declined from 16.0 percent to 15.1 percent of total liabilities and equity over that same time. Similarly, total equity rose from 68.1 percent of total liabilities and equity to 72.2 percent.

Overall, Prufrock's liquidity, as measured by current assets compared to current liabilities, increased over the year. Simultaneously, Prufrock's indebtedness diminished as a percentage of total assets. We might be tempted to conclude that the balance sheet has grown "stronger."

Source: Adapted from Rows, S. A., Westerfield, R. W., & Jordan, B. D. 1999. *Essentials of Corporate Finance* (2nd ed.). chap. 3. New York: McGraw-Hill. 1999.

EXHIBIT 9A.1

Prufrock Corporation

Balance Sheets as of December 31, 2004 and 2005 ($ in millions)

	2004	2005
Assets		
Current assets		
Cash	$ 84	$ 98
Accounts receivable	165	188
Inventory	393	422
Total	$ 642	$ 708
Fixed assets		
Net plant and equipment	$2,731	$2,880
Total assets	$3,373	$3,588
Liabilities and Owners' Equity		
Current liabilities		
Accounts payable	$ 312	$ 344
Notes payable	231	196
Total	$ 543	$ 540
Long-term debt	$ 531	$ 457
Owners' equity		
Common stock and paid-in surplus	$ 500	$ 550
Retained earnings	1,799	2,041
Total	$2,299	$2,591
Total liabilities and owners' equity	$3,373	$3,588

Common-Size Income Statements

A useful way of standardizing the income statement, shown in Exhibit 9A.3, is to express each item as a percentage of total sales, as illustrated for Prufrock in Exhibit 9A.4.

This income statement tells us what happens to each dollar in sales. For Prufrock, interest expense eats up $.061 out of every sales dollar and taxes take another $.081. When all is said and done, $.157 of each dollar flows through to the bottom line (net income), and that amount is split into $.105 retained in the business and $.052 paid out in dividends.

These percentages are very useful in comparisons. For example, a relevant figure is the cost percentage. For Prufrock, $.582 of each $1.00 in sales goes to pay for goods sold. It would be interesting to compute the same percentage for Prufrock's main competitors to see how Prufrock stacks up in terms of cost control.

EXHIBIT 9A.2

Prufrock Corporation

Common-Size Balance Sheets as of December 31, 2004 and 2005 (%)

	2004	2005	Change
Assets			
Current assets			
Cash	2.5%	2.7%	+ .2%
Accounts receivable	4.9	5.2	+ .3
Inventory	11.7	11.8	+ .1
Total	19.1	19.7	+ .6
Fixed assets			
Net plant and equipment	80.9	80.3	– .6
Total assets	100.0%	100.0%	.0%
Liabilities and Owners' Equity			
Current liabilities			
Accounts payable	9.2%	9.6%	+ .4%
Notes payable	6.8	5.5	–1.3
Total	16.0	15.1	– .9
Long-term debt	15.7	12.7	–3.0
Owners' equity			
Common stock and paid-in surplus	14.8	15.3	+ .5
Retained earnings	53.3	56.9	+3.6
Total	68.1	72.2	+4.1
Total liabilities and owners' equities	100.0%	100.0%	.0%

Note: Numbers may not add up to 100.0% due to rounding.

EXHIBIT 9A.3

Prufrock Corporation

2005 Income Statement($ in millions)

Sales		$2,311
Cost of goods sold		1,344
Depreciation		276
Earnings before interest and taxes		$ 691
Interest paid		141
Taxable income		$ 550
Taxes (34%)		187
Net income		$ 363
Dividends	$ 121	
Addition to retained earnings	242	

EXHIBIT 9A.4

Prufrock Corporation

2005 Common-Size Income Statement (%)

Sales		100.0%
Cost of goods sold		58.2
Depreciation		11.9
Earnings before interest and taxes		29.9
Interest paid		6.1
Taxable income		23.8
Taxes (34%)		8.1
Net income		15.7%
Dividends	5.2%	
Addition to retained earnings	10.5	

Ratio Analysis

Another way of avoiding the problems involved in comparing companies of different sizes is to calculate and compare *financial ratios*. Such ratios are ways of comparing and investigating the relationships between different pieces of financial information. We cover some of the more common ratios next, but there are many others that we don't touch on.

One problem with ratios is that different people and different sources frequently don't compute them in exactly the same way, and this leads to much confusion. The specific definitions we use here may or may not be the same as others you have seen or will see elsewhere. If you ever use ratios as a tool for analysis, you should be careful to document how you calculate each one, and, if you are comparing your numbers to those of another source, be sure you know how its numbers are computed.

For each of the ratios we discuss, several questions come to mind:

1. How is it computed?
2. What is it intended to measure, and why might we be interested?
3. What is the unit of measurement?
4. What might a high or low value be telling us? How might such values be misleading?
5. How could this measure be improved?

Financial ratios are traditionally grouped into the following categories:

1. Short-term solvency, or liquidity, ratios.
2. Long-term solvency, or financial leverage, ratios.
3. Asset management, or turnover, ratios.
4. Profitability ratios.
5. Market value ratios.

We will consider each of these in turn. In calculating these numbers for Prufrock, we will use the ending balance sheet (2005) figures unless we explicitly say otherwise. The numbers for the various ratios come from the income statement and the balance sheet.

Short-Term Solvency, or Liquidity, Measures

As the name suggests, short-term solvency ratios as a group are intended to provide information about a firm's liquidity, and these ratios are sometimes called *liquidity measures.* The primary concern is the firm's ability to pay its bills over the short run without undue stress. Consequently, these ratios focus on current assets and current liabilities.

For obvious reasons, liquidity ratios are particularly interesting to short-term creditors. Since financial managers are constantly working with banks and other short-term lenders, an understanding of these ratios is essential.

One advantage of looking at current assets and liabilities is that their book values and market values are likely to be similar. Often (though not always), these assets and liabilities just don't live long enough for the two to get seriously out of step. On the other hand, like any type of near cash, current assets and liabilities can and do change fairly rapidly, so today's amounts may not be a reliable guide to the future.

Current Ratio One of the best-known and most widely used ratios is the *current ratio.* As you might guess, the current ratio is defined as:

$$\text{Current ratio} = \frac{\text{Current assets}}{\text{Current liabilities}}$$

For Prufrock, the 2005 current ratio is:

$$\text{Current ratio} = \frac{\$708}{\$540} = 1.31 \text{ times}$$

Because current assets and liabilities are, in principle, converted to cash over the following 12 months, the current ratio is a measure of short-term liquidity. The unit of measurement is either dollars or times. So, we could say Prufrock has $1.31 in current assets for every $1 in current liabilities, or we could say Prufrock has its current liabilities covered 1.31 times over.

To a creditor, particularly a short-term creditor such as a supplier, the higher the current ratio, the better. To the firm, a high current ratio indicates liquidity, but it also may indicate an inefficient use of cash and other short-term assets. Absent some extraordinary circumstances, we would expect to see a current ratio of at least 1, because a current ratio of less than 1 would mean that net working capital (current assets less current liabilities) is negative. This would be unusual in a healthy firm, at least for most types of businesses.

The current ratio, like any ratio, is affected by various types of transactions. For example, suppose the firm borrows over the long term to raise money. The short-run effect would be an increase in cash from the issue proceeds and an increase in long-term debt. Current liabilities would not be affected, so the current ratio would rise.

Finally, note that an apparently low current ratio may not be a bad sign for a company with a large reserve of untapped borrowing power.

Quick (or Acid-Test) Ratio Inventory is often the least liquid current asset. It's also the one for which the book values are least reliable as measures of market value, since the quality of the inventory isn't considered. Some of the inventory may later turn out to be damaged, obsolete, or lost.

More to the point, relatively large inventories are often a sign of short-term trouble. The firm may have overestimated sales and overbought or overproduced as a result. In this case, the firm may have a substantial portion of its liquidity tied up in slow-moving inventory.

To further evaluate liquidity, the *quick,* or *acid-test, ratio* is computed just like the current ratio, except inventory is omitted:

$$\text{Quick ratio} = \frac{\text{Current assets} - \text{Inventory}}{\text{Current liabilities}}$$

Notice that using cash to buy inventory does not affect the current ratio, but it reduces the quick ratio. Again, the idea is that inventory is relatively illiquid compared to cash.

For Prufrock, this ratio in 2005 was:

$$\text{Quick ratio} = \frac{\$708 - 422}{\$540} = .53 \text{ times}$$

The quick ratio here tells a somewhat different story than the current ratio, because inventory accounts for more than half of Prufrock's current assets. To exaggerate the point, if this inventory consisted of, say, unsold nuclear power plants, then this would be a cause for concern.

Cash Ratio A very short-term creditor might be interested in the *cash ratio:*

$$\text{Cash ratio} = \frac{\text{Cash}}{\text{Current liabilities}}$$

You can verify that this works out to be .18 times for Prufrock.

Long-Term Solvency Measures

Long-term solvency ratios are intended to address the firm's long-run ability to meet its obligations, or, more generally, its financial leverage. These ratios are sometimes called *financial leverage ratios* or just *leverage ratios.* We consider three commonly used measures and some variations.

Total Debt Ratio   The *total debt ratio* takes into account all debts of all maturities to all creditors. It can be defined in several ways, the easiest of which is:

$$\text{Total debt ratio} = \frac{\text{Total assets} - \text{Total equity}}{\text{Total assets}}$$

$$= \frac{\$3{,}588 - 2{,}591}{\$3{,}588} = .28 \text{ times}$$

In this case, an analyst might say that Prufrock uses 28 percent debt.[1] Whether this is high or low or whether it even makes any difference depends on whether or not capital structure matters.

Prufrock has $.28 in debt for every $1 in assets. Therefore, there is $.72 in equity ($1 − .28) for every $.28 in debt. With this in mind, we can define two useful variations on the total debt ratio, the *debt-equity ratio* and the *equity multiplier:*

$$\text{Debt-equity ratio} = \text{Total debt/Total equity}$$
$$= \$.28/\$.72 = .39 \text{ times}$$
$$\text{Equity multiplier} = \text{Total assets/Total equity}$$
$$= \$1/\$.72 = 1.39 \text{ times}$$

The fact that the equity multiplier is 1 plus the debt-equity ratio is not a coincidence:

$$\text{Equity multiplier} = \text{Total assets/Total equity} = \$1/\$.72 = 1.39$$
$$= (\text{Total equity} + \text{Total debt})/\text{Total equity}$$
$$= 1 + \text{Debt-equity ratio} = 1.39 \text{ times}$$

The thing to notice here is that given any one of these three ratios, you can immediately calculate the other two, so they all say exactly the same thing.

Times Interest Earned   Another common measure of long-term solvency is the *times interest earned (TIE) ratio.* Once again, there are several possible (and common) definitions, but we'll stick with the most traditional:

$$\text{Times interest earned ratio} = \frac{\text{EBIT}}{\text{Interest}}$$

$$= \frac{\$691}{\$141} = 4.9 \text{ times}$$

As the name suggests, this ratio measures how well a company has its interest obligations covered, and it is often called the interest coverage ratio. For Prufrock, the interest bill is covered 4.9 times over.

Cash Coverage   A problem with the TIE ratio is that it is based on earnings before interest and taxes (EBIT), which is not really a measure of cash available to pay interest. The reason is that depreciation, a noncash expense, has been deducted. Since interest is most definitely a cash outflow (to creditors), one way to define the *cash coverage ratio* is:

$$\text{Cash coverage ratio} = \frac{\text{EBIT} + \text{Depreciation}}{\text{Interest}}$$

$$= \frac{\$691 + 276}{\$141} = \frac{\$967}{\$141} = 6.9 \text{ times}$$

---

[1]Total equity here includes preferred stock, if there is any. An equivalent numerator in this ratio would be (Current liabilities + Long-term debt).

The numerator here, EBIT plus depreciation, is often abbreviated EBDIT (earnings before depreciation, interest, and taxes). It is a basic measure of the firm's ability to generate cash from operations, and it is frequently used as a measure of cash flow available to meet financial obligations.

Asset Management, or Turnover, Measures

We next turn our attention to the efficiency with which Prufrock uses its assets. The measures in this section are sometimes called *asset utilization ratios.* The specific ratios we discuss can all be interpreted as measures of turnover. What they are intended to describe is how efficiently, or intensively, a firm uses its assets to generate sales. We first look at two important current assets: inventory and receivables.

Inventory Turnover and Days' Sales in Inventory   During the year, Prufrock had a cost of goods sold of $1,344. Inventory at the end of the year was $422. With these numbers, *inventory turnover* can be calculated as:

$$\text{Inventory turnover} = \frac{\text{Cost of goods sold}}{\text{Inventory}}$$

$$= \frac{\$1{,}344}{\$422} = 3.2 \text{ times}$$

In a sense, we sold off, or turned over, the entire inventory 3.2 times. As long as we are not running out of stock and thereby forgoing sales, the higher this ratio is, the more efficiently we are managing inventory.

If we know that we turned our inventory over 3.2 times during the year, then we can immediately figure out how long it took us to turn it over on average. The result is the average *days' sales in inventory:*

$$\text{Days' sales in inventory} = \frac{365 \text{ days}}{\text{Inventory turnover}}$$

$$= \frac{365}{3.2} = 114 \text{ days}$$

This tells us that, on average, inventory sits 114 days before it is sold. Alternatively, assuming we used the most recent inventory and cost figures, it will take about 114 days to work off our current inventory.

For example, we frequently hear things like "Majestic Motors has a 60 days' supply of cars." This means that, at current daily sales, it would take 60 days to deplete the available inventory. We could also say that Majestic has 60 days of sales in inventory.

Receivables Turnover and Days' Sales in Receivables   Our inventory measures give some indication of how fast we can sell products. We now look at how fast we collect on those sales. The *receivables turnover* is defined in the same way as inventory turnover:

$$\text{Receivables turnover} = \frac{\text{Sales}}{\text{Accounts receivable}}$$

$$= \frac{\$2{,}311}{\$188} = 12.3 \text{ times}$$

Loosely speaking, we collected our outstanding credit accounts and reloaned the money 12.3 times during the year.[2]

This ratio makes more sense if we convert it to days, so the *days' sales in receivables* is:

$$\text{Days' sales in receivables} = \frac{365 \text{ days}}{\text{Receivables turnover}}$$

$$= \frac{365}{12.35} = 30 \text{ days}$$

Therefore, on average, we collect on our credit sales in 30 days. For obvious reasons, this ratio is very frequently called the *average collection period (ACP)*.

Also note that if we are using the most recent figures, we can also say that we have 30 days' worth of sales currently uncollected.

Total Asset Turnover   Moving away from specific accounts like inventory or receivables, we can consider an important "big picture" ratio, the *total asset turnover ratio.* As the name suggests, total asset turnover is:

$$\text{Total asset turnover} = \frac{\text{Sales}}{\text{Total assets}}$$

$$= \frac{\$2,311}{\$3,588} = .64 \text{ times}$$

In other words, for every dollar in assets, we generated \$.64 in sales.

A closely related ratio, the *capital intensity ratio,* is simply the reciprocal of (i.e., 1 divided by) total asset turnover. It can be interpreted as the dollar investment in assets needed to generate \$1 in sales. High values correspond to capital intensive industries (e.g., public utilities). For Prufrock, total asset turnover is .64, so, if we flip this over, we get that capital intensity is \$1/.64 = \$1.56. That is, it takes Prufrock \$1.56 in assets to create \$1 in sales.

Profitability Measures

The three measures we discuss in this section are probably the best known and most widely used of all financial ratios. In one form or another, they are intended to measure how efficiently the firm uses its assets and how efficiently the firm manages its operations. The focus in this group is on the bottom line, net income.

Profit Margin   Companies pay a great deal of attention to their *profit margin:*

$$\text{Profit margin} = \frac{\text{Net income}}{\text{Sales}}$$

$$= \frac{\$363}{\$2,311} = 15.7\%$$

This tells us that Prufrock, in an accounting sense, generates a little less than 16 cents in profit for every dollar in sales.

All other things being equal, a relatively high profit margin is obviously desirable. This situation corresponds to low expense ratios relative to sales. However, we hasten to add that other things are often not equal.

For example, lowering our sales price will usually increase unit volume, but will normally cause profit margins to shrink. Total profit (or, more importantly, operating cash flow) may go up or down; so the fact that margins are smaller isn't necessarily bad. After all, isn't it possible that, as the saying goes, "Our prices are so low that we lose money on everything we sell, but we make it up in volume!"[3]

Return on Assets   *Return on assets (ROA)* is a measure of profit per dollar of assets. It can be defined several ways, but the most common is:

$$\text{Return on assets} = \frac{\text{Net income}}{\text{Total equity}}$$

$$= \frac{\$363}{\$3,588} = 10.12\%$$

Return on Equity   *Return on equity (ROE)* is a measure of how the stockholders fared during the year. Since benefiting shareholders is our goal, ROE is, in an accounting sense, the true bottom-line measure of performance. ROE is usually measured as:

$$\text{Return on equity} = \frac{\text{Net income}}{\text{Total assets}}$$

$$= \frac{\$363}{\$2,591} = 14\%$$

For every dollar in equity, therefore, Prufrock generated 14 cents in profit, but, again, this is only correct in accounting terms.

Because ROA and ROE are such commonly cited numbers, we stress that it is important to remember they are accounting rates of return. For this reason, these measures should properly be called *return on book assets* and *return on book equity.* In addition, ROE is sometimes called *return on net worth.* Whatever it's called, it would be inappropriate to compare the results to, for example, an interest rate observed in the financial markets.

The fact that ROE exceeds ROA reflects Prufrock's use of financial leverage. We will examine the relationship between these two measures in more detail below.

Market Value Measures

Our final group of measures is based, in part, on information not necessarily contained in financial statements—the market price per share of the stock. Obviously, these measures can only be calculated directly for publicly traded companies.

We assume that Prufrock has 33 million shares outstanding and the stock sold for \$88 per share at the end of the year. If we recall that Prufrock's net income was \$363 million, then we can calculate that its earnings per share were:

$$\text{EPS} = \frac{\text{Net income}}{\text{Shares outstanding}} = \frac{\$363}{33} = \$11$$

Price-Earnings Ratio   The first of our market value measures, the *price-earnings,* or PE, *ratio* (or multiple), is defined as:

---

[2]Here we have implicitly assumed that all sales are credit sales. If they were not, then we would simply use total credit sales in these calculations, not total sales.

[3]No, it's not; margins can be small, but they do need to be positive!

$$\text{PE ratio} = \frac{\text{Price per share}}{\text{Earnings per share}}$$

$$= \frac{\$85}{\$11} = 8 \text{ times}$$

In the vernacular, we would say that Prufrock shares sell for eight times earnings, or we might say that Prufrock shares have, or "carry," a PE multiple of 8.

Since the PE ratio measures how much investors are willing to pay per dollar of current earnings, higher PEs are often taken to mean that the firm has significant prospects for future growth. Of course, if a firm had no or almost no earnings, its PE would probably be quite large; so, as always, be careful when interpreting this ratio.

Market-to-Book Ratio   A second commonly quoted measure is the *market-to-book ratio:*

$$\text{Market-to-book ratio} = \frac{\text{Market value per share}}{\text{Book value per share}}$$

$$= \frac{\$88}{(\$2,591/33)} = \frac{\$88}{\$78.5} = 1.12 \text{ times}$$

Notice that book value per share is total equity (not just common stock) divided by the number of shares outstanding.

Since book value per share is an accounting number, it reflects historical costs. In a loose sense, the market-to-book ratio therefore compares the market value of the firm's investments to their cost. A value less than 1 could mean that the firm has not been successful overall in creating value for its stockholders.

Conclusion

This completes our definition of some common ratios. Exhibit 9A.5 summarizes the ratios we've discussed.

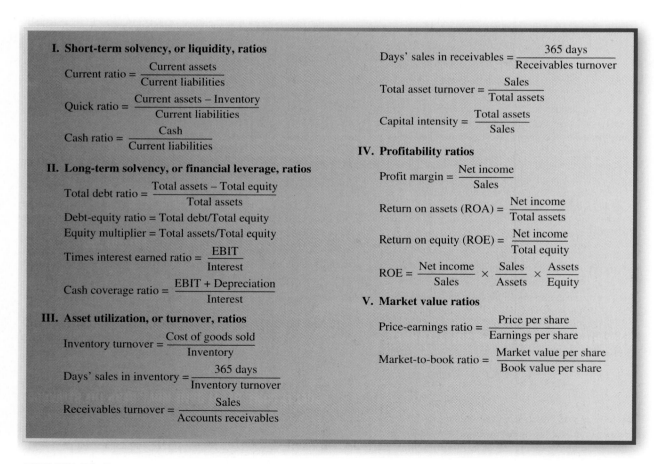

I. Short-term solvency, or liquidity, ratios

$$\text{Current ratio} = \frac{\text{Current assets}}{\text{Current liabilities}}$$

$$\text{Quick ratio} = \frac{\text{Current assets} - \text{Inventory}}{\text{Current liabilities}}$$

$$\text{Cash ratio} = \frac{\text{Cash}}{\text{Current liabilities}}$$

II. Long-term solvency, or financial leverage, ratios

$$\text{Total debt ratio} = \frac{\text{Total assets} - \text{Total equity}}{\text{Total assets}}$$

$$\text{Debt-equity ratio} = \text{Total debt/Total equity}$$

$$\text{Equity multiplier} = \text{Total assets/Total equity}$$

$$\text{Times interest earned ratio} = \frac{\text{EBIT}}{\text{Interest}}$$

$$\text{Cash coverage ratio} = \frac{\text{EBIT} + \text{Depreciation}}{\text{Interest}}$$

III. Asset utilization, or turnover, ratios

$$\text{Inventory turnover} = \frac{\text{Cost of goods sold}}{\text{Inventory}}$$

$$\text{Days' sales in inventory} = \frac{365 \text{ days}}{\text{Inventory turnover}}$$

$$\text{Receivables turnover} = \frac{\text{Sales}}{\text{Accounts receivable}}$$

$$\text{Days' sales in receivables} = \frac{365 \text{ days}}{\text{Receivables turnover}}$$

$$\text{Total asset turnover} = \frac{\text{Sales}}{\text{Total assets}}$$

$$\text{Capital intensity} = \frac{\text{Total assets}}{\text{Sales}}$$

IV. Profitability ratios

$$\text{Profit margin} = \frac{\text{Net income}}{\text{Sales}}$$

$$\text{Return on assets (ROA)} = \frac{\text{Net income}}{\text{Total assets}}$$

$$\text{Return on equity (ROE)} = \frac{\text{Net income}}{\text{Total equity}}$$

$$\text{ROE} = \frac{\text{Net income}}{\text{Sales}} \times \frac{\text{Sales}}{\text{Assets}} \times \frac{\text{Assets}}{\text{Equity}}$$

V. Market value ratios

$$\text{Price-earnings ratio} = \frac{\text{Price per share}}{\text{Earnings per share}}$$

$$\text{Market-to-book ratio} = \frac{\text{Market value per share}}{\text{Book value per share}}$$

EXHIBIT 9A.5   **Summary of Financial Ratios**

CASE 1   Enron: On the Side of the Angels

"We're on the side of angels. We're taking on the entrenched monopolies. In every business we've been in, we're the good guys."

—**Jeffrey Skilling**, President and CEO,
Enron Corporation

On the day he was elected CEO, Enron's president, Jeffrey Skilling, was pictured on the front cover of the February 12, 2001 edition of *BusinessWeek* dressed in a black turtleneck and holding an electrified orb in his right hand, appearing more sorcerer than executive. Enron was charging into the deregulated energy markets. Skilling defended Enron's activities, saying;

> We're on the side of angels. We're taking on the entrenched monopolies. In every business we're in, we're the good guys.[1]

By August 2001, the charge would be over and Skilling would resign after only six months as CEO. In September 2000, Enron's stock price was in the $85 to $90 region; by November 2001 it had declined to less than a dollar. In January 2002, John Clifford Baxter, an Enron executive, died, an apparent suicide. Timothy Belden, an Enron trader in the California markets, would plead guilty to conspiracy to manipulate markets in the California energy market[2] and another, John Forney, would be arrested for conspiracy and wire fraud in the same California market.[3] The angels, it seems, had come back to earth.

FROM PIPELINES TO COMMODITY TRADER

In June 1984, the board of Houston Natural Gas (HNG), a natural gas distribution firm, hired Kenneth Lay as Chair and CEO. His first task was to defend HNG from a take-over bid by refocusing HNG on its core business. In a 1990 speech, Lay characterized his leadership:

> In carrying out that assignment, between June 1984 and January 1985, $632 million of non-natural gas operations were sold and $1.2 billion of natural gas operations were purchased. As one director was heard to quip at the time, the Board gave me unlimited authority, and I exceeded it.[4]

Lay created Enron, a natural gas and oil company, in 1986, through the merger of HNG with InterNorth, a natural gas pipeline company and other acquisitions.[5] Lay, the merger's architect and Enron's first CEO, appeared to be one of the few individuals who recognized the opportunities of deregulation in the United States. and privatization abroad. By the early 1990s, Enron owned an interest in a 4,100 mile pipeline in Argentina, and commenced its power marketing business worldwide.

In 1994, *Fortune* ranked Enron first in a new category, pipelines, and 39th overall as one of "America's Most Admired Companies." By 1996 Enron had climbed to 22nd overall. In the 1990s, Enron busily expanded its business structure into other areas, such as energy generation, broadband, and financial markets. Yet Enron maintained its dominance of the pipeline industry's ranking and was ranked in the top 20 firms overall through February 2001. In that year, *Fortune* named Enron the most innovative firm in the United States for the second consecutive year. It first won the category in 1997. From 1994 to 2001 the firm steadily climbed in *Fortune*'s "America's Most Admired Company" list. Its stock price rose as dramatically: on December 31, 1996, Enron's stock listed at $21\frac{7}{16}$ (adjusted for a 1999 split), and on December 31, 2000, its price was $83\frac{1}{8}$. In the entry foyer, a huge banner was placed, reading, "World's Leading Company."[6] Skilling's license plate, which had once read "WLEC" (World's Leading Energy Company) changed to "WMM" (We Make Markets).[7]

Throughout 2001, as Enron's stock declined, its rankings dropped from first to last in its industry. Enron was ranked 523 (of 530) in wise use of corporate assets and quality of management and 521 in fiscal soundness.

"GET IT DONE. GET IT DONE NOW. REAP THE REWARDS."

Lay built a management team, not of gas and energy people, but primarily of MBAs. Rebecca Mark, an energy professional who rose from part-time trader to president of Enron International and Azurix Water, characterized Enron employees as ex-military, Harvard Business School, and ex-entrepreneurship types. A *Fortune* article described the employees as "aggressive, well-compensated traders."[8] Enron had developed from an oil and gas exploration and pipeline company to a derivatives trading company. In its office tower, the executive offices on the seventh floor overlooked the sixth floor, an expansive derivatives trading operation.[9]

Enron's management saw creativity and human capital as the real resource behind its future growth. In the 1999 Annual Report Letter to Shareholders, Lay wrote:

> Creativity is a fragile commodity. Put a creative person in a bureaucratic atmosphere, and the creative output will die. We support employees with the most innovative culture possible, where people are measured not by how many mistakes they make, but how often they try.[10]

Every employee received a copy of the *Code of Ethics*, and with it a memo from Lay dated July 1, 2000, that read in part:

> As officers and employees of Enron Corp. . . . we are responsible for conducting the business affairs of the Company in accordance with all applicable laws and in a moral and honest manner. . . . An employee shall not conduct himself or herself in a manner, which directly or indirectly would be detrimental to the best interests of the Company or in a manner which would bring the employee financial gain separately derived as a direct consequence of his or her employment with the Company. . . . We want to be proud of Enron and to know that it enjoys a reputation for fairness and honesty that is respected. . . . **Let's keep that reputation high.**[6]

---

*This case was prepared from published materials by Professors Donald Schepers and Naomi A. Gardberg from Baruch College, City University of New York, to provide a basis for class discussion. Copyright © 2003 by the *Journal of Business and Applied Management.* Reprinted with permission of the *Journal of Business and Applied Management.* Readers may find the two Appendices at the end of the case helpful in reading the case. Appendix A is a timeline of major events in this case. Appendix B is a glossary of various financial terms used in the case.

In April 2002 Lay described Enron's culture:

> One of our greatest successes at Enron was creating a culture, an environment, where people could try to achieve their God-given potential. But certainly I wanted it to be a highly moral and highly ethical environment. I have done the best job I can of following that everywhere I have been.[11]

Skilling put his own mark on Enron's culture. Extravagance was celebrated. At one meeting, Mark rode onto the stage with another executive on a Harley. At another, an adult elephant was brought in. One executive arrived at an employee gathering with a tractor-trailer full of expensive sports cars. The floors of the parking garage were marked by words to remind employees of valued attributes: bold, innovative, smart, united, ambitious, accomplished, resourceful, creative, confident, adventurous, adaptable, and undaunted.[6]

Two realities of life existed at Enron: stock price and the Peer Review Committee (PRC).[12] Nothing else mattered. Michael J. Miller, a manager in Enron's failed high-speed Internet service venture described the atmosphere as "Get it done. Get it done now. Reap the rewards." An acrylic paperweight from the legal department stated its mission as "To provide prompt and first-rate legal service to Enron on a proactive and cost-effective basis."[13] Below that was "Translation: We do big, complex, and risky deals without blowing up Enron." Employees were rewarded for earnings that could be quickly booked, regardless of the long-term consequences. Two of the Enron executives who closed the deal on the doomed Dabhol power project in India received bonuses in the range of $50 million just for closing the deal.[14]

Like many dot-coms in the 1990s, Enron had a high reward structure. More than 2000 Enron employees were millionaires. Employees received free laptops and hand-held devices, expensive ergonomic chairs and lunches at Houston's finest restaurants. Enron's Board of Directors was also well compensated. Chosen by management, Enron directors received cash and stock worth $300,000 a year.[14]

Recruitment took place both in long, intense interviews and visits to topless bars and strip clubs.[6] Once past an initial interview, candidates were invited to a "Super Saturday" session of 8, 50-minute interviews. Offers would go out within a few days, and candidates that declined would be offered signing bonuses or other financial inducements.[12]

Central to Enron's human resource policy was Skilling's PRC, or what became known as the "rank and yank" process.[6] Every six months, each person would choose five individuals (four plus the immediate supervisor) to provide feedback on his or her performance. This feedback went to the PRC's ratings meeting where employees were rated on a scale from 1 (excellent) to 5 (worst performing). The PRC took place behind closed doors, but in plain sight, since interior walls on the trading floors were glass. The picture of the individual being discussed would appear on a slide show, visible to all on the floor, while management discussed the evaluations. The PRC was a forced ranking system, where 15 percent of those reviewed had to receive 5s. These would then be "redeployed,"

meaning they had to search for a job in the organization or find themselves unemployed.

On the trading floor, men rated women as potential calendar models. When one of the "candidates" would walk onto the floor, someone would yell the name of the month to alert others of her presence.[6] Gambling was also prevalent. One year, the NCAA basketball pool supposedly reached almost $90,000.[15]

This culture spilled out of the doors and into Enron's relationships with others. On one occasion, Andy Fastow, the Chief Financial Officer (CFO), was asked by a Citigroup banker if he understood the equations on the whiteboard in the conference room next to his office. Fastow replied, "I pulled them out of a book to intimidate people."[16]

Analysts who listened to the quarterly earnings report conference calls would be derided if they had questions about the details. During the April 17, 2001, conference call, Skilling had finished presenting the numbers and was responding to questions when Richard Grubman, a managing director of Highlands Capital Management, asked about Enron's balance sheet and cash-flow statement after earnings. Enron had failed to provide either. When Grubman commented that Enron was the only financial institution that never provided such statements for these calls, Skilling shot back, "Well, thank you very much. We appreciate that, [expletive]."[6]

ENRON AND THE CAPITAL MARKETS

Prior to his employment at Enron, Skilling served as consultant to Enron for McKinsey & Co. In 1989, Enron launched GasBank at Skilling's urging for the purpose of hedging risk for natural gas producers and wholesale suppliers.[12] Both parties could arrange forward contracts (contracts to purchase or sell commodities at a future date) at set prices, and Enron would sell financial derivative contracts to sell the risk of the forward contracts to other interested investors. In 1990, Enron became a market maker, a financial clearinghouse, for natural gas, selling swaps and futures on the New York Mercantile Exchange. In that same year, Lay hired Skilling as CEO of Enron Gas Services (EGS), and Skilling hired Fastow as CFO. EGS was ultimately renamed Enron Capital and Trade Resources (ECT).

ECT provided financial and risk management services for Enron and its trading partners. The process, asset securitization, involves selling the rights to future cash flow streams. Corporations, such as mortgage companies, would take their risky investments and sell them to another financial institution, such as an investment bank. The investment bank, in turn, would bundle a number of such investments together, separate the cash flows by level of risk, and put the result into securities they would then sell. In the case of mortgage-backed securities, investment banks might offer two securities, one based on the principal and the second on the interest payments. Each would have a different yield, based on the level of risk. Asset securitization is attractive to the originating corporation on two counts: it transfers risk of default to the investment bank and lowers cost of capital by providing immediate cash inflow.

ECT fulfilled two functions. First, it provided asset securitization services for Enron's natural gas and oil entities, making those entities much more profitable. Second, it moved Enron further toward Lay's vision of the company as a market maker for a variety of commodities. With the attainment of risk management and capital flow-through, Enron could in principle trade anything. Through the 1990s, Enron was rapidly becoming a commodities market based in Houston. Even weather risk was commoditized and traded.[6] This was supplemented with what Skilling would term "asset-lite": the hard assets Enron originally controlled in such deals would be sold, in many cases to special-purpose entities (SPEs) that were created by Enron.

Two Critical Elements: Mark-to-Market and the SPEs

Enron funded its growth as a financial services firm using very sophisticated financial practices, mark-to-market accounting, and SPEs. Originally termed mark-to-model, the mark-to-market accounting method was intended to assist investors in obtaining some reference point in valuing a security. A model was constructed using a number of assumptions, and the security was then valued using that model. In reality, these prices were generated by computers, not by market process. Enron relied on this procedure to establish prices (sometimes unrealistically high) in its new commodities (for example, weather) where there were no reference prices.[9]

The second mechanism Enron used was the creation of special-purpose entities. SPEs are financial devices designed to give companies greater flexibility in finance and risk management. There are two requirements for SPEs to be legitimate: first, there must be a 3 percent outside equity position; and second, the outside capital must clearly be at risk.

Fastow set up a number of SPEs for Enron. Among the more famous were partnerships named Chewco, JEDI, LJM1, and LJM2, and four investments named Raptors. In 1993, Joint Energy Development Investment (JEDI), a $500 million partnership between Enron and the California Public Employees Retirement System (CalPERS), was the first SPE created. This partnership would continue until 1997, when CalPERS sold its position to Chewco, another SPE created specifically by Enron to purchase the CalPERS shares in JEDI. Enron hoped that this buyout would then encourage CalPERS to invest in JEDI II, a proposed $1 billion venture.

SPEs would be used to solve Enron's financial problems. Enron not only brokered commodities contracts, but actually bought and sold natural gas. High default risk on Enron's part would ruin the swap business. SPEs provided Enron the opportunity to continually move debt from its balance sheet, keeping its high credit rating and its swap business.

As Enron expanded the use of SPEs, new investors were required to satisfy the SEC requirement of 3 percent outside equity investment. Fastow and Michael Kopper (managing director, Enron Global Finance, and a direct report to Fastow) established the "Friends of Enron." These "friends" were actually relatives or friends of Enron's executives. Fastow and Kopper funneled monies through these people to finance the "outside equity" in the SPEs.

Enron's need for a high credit rating drove the creation of over 3,000 SPEs to keep debt off the balance sheet.[9] Maturing markets meant decreasing profits, but profits were necessary to continue Enron's trading mechanism. The only way to create more profits was to open new commodity markets, exploit them quickly, and then create newer markets. The SPEs were critical to this strategy, keeping debt from the books and providing capital. Enron's stock price soared dramatically, unburdened by the debt that was accumulating in the SPEs.

The SPEs presented Enron with the opportunity to disguise debt and loss as revenue, but did not necessarily result in cash flow.[9] Enron would establish an SPE by issuing Enron stock to collateralize the SPE, and then engage other entities such as banks to invest in the SPE. Enron would then "sell" the SPE deal that it had set up to handle in return for either cash or a promissory note, which Enron would then book as revenue. In one case, it was a forward contract on shares of an Internet company in which Enron had invested. Another case was "dark fiber," that is, fiber optic cable that was already laid but as yet unusable. In both cases, Enron had a "make whole" contract with the SPE, ensuring that the SPE would not lose money. However, even as the dot-com bubble burst, the shares in the Internet company declined, and the value of the dark fiber likewise dropped, Enron was able to shield its balance sheet from these losses.

Constructed on Enron stock, these SPE arrangements contained triggers, that is, valuation points where these deals would need infusions of either more Enron stock or other collateral. For example, in an SPE named Osprey, if Enron's stock fell below $59.78, Enron was obligated to either issue new stock or provide cash sufficient to bring the value of Osprey up to cover its debt obligations.[17] In another instance, Enron's stock price decline forced restructuring of four SPEs named Raptor I, II, III, and IV in December 2000, and then requiring an additional infusion of stock in the first quarter of 2001 to shore up their falling credit capacity. By the end of the restructuring, Raptors II and IV owed an additional $260 million to Enron.[18]

The Investment Bank Connection

Enron's need for a high credit rating influenced its relationships with investment banks as well. In return for its business, Enron sought short-term deals that allowed it to disguise loans as sales revenue, and in turn unload (for brief periods of time) unprofitable entities from Enron's balance sheet. Between 1992 and 2001, Enron borrowed $8 billion from Citigroup and J. P. Morgan Chase & Co. in transactions that had the appearance of gas trades rather than loans, understating Enron's debt by $4 billion, and overstating its $3.2 billion cash flow from operations by 50 percent.[19] An independent bank examiner, Neal Batson, found that Enron had recorded profit of $1.4 billion through similar transactions with six investment banks.[20]

The Enron Control System

> Our philosophy is not to stand in the way of our employees, so we don't insist on hierarchical approval. We do, however, keep a keen eye on how prudent they are, and rigorously evaluate and control the risk involved in each of our activities.[10]

The Enron culture was not without its system of checks and balances, particularly in the financial dealings. The Board turned to those checks and balances when approving the deals with the SPEs, as well as Fastow's role in the various SPEs. It was the task of Risk Assessment and Control (RAC) to examine each deal and perform due diligence. RAC had the responsibility to oversee and approve all deals in which Enron engaged, over 400 each year. Each deal was accompanied by a Deal Approval Sheet (DASH) assembled by the business unit responsible for the deal. Each DASH had a description of the deal, origination information, economic data, a cash-flow model, risk components, financial approval sheet, and authorization page.[6] Corporate policy required approval from the relevant business unit, legal department, RAC, and senior management. Many of the DASH forms for SPEs had incomplete authorizations. In particular, Skilling's signature is blank on many of the DASH forms associated with the LJM deals.[18]

As the number of deals with LJM increased, a separate LJM approval sheet was added as a control procedure. This approval sheet was printed with check marks already in the boxes. No third-party documentation was required to substantiate claims made on the document. Conclusions were used as questions ("Was this transaction done strictly on an arm's-length basis?"), while others revealed low standards ("Was Enron advised by any third party that this transaction was not fair, from a financial perspective, to Enron?").[18]

Enron formed 20 deals with LJM1 and LJM2. In setting up the LJM entities, the Board had waived Enron's Code of Ethics and allowed Fastow to be named general partner, with a $1 million investment in LJM1 alone. When Fastow presented the option of creating the LJM entities to the Board, he portrayed them as alternative purchasers for Enron assets, providing perhaps better valuations for assets Enron was in the process of selling. In fact, there were no alternative buyers for most of what was sold to the SPEs.

The Board made two critical assumptions. First, it assumed that, since the operational results of each division were at stake, each division would therefore aggressively market assets. Second, it assumed that Andersen's counsel on the LJM deals would be independent. The Board relied on the reviews by Richard Causey (Chief Accounting Officer) and Richard Buy (Chief Risk Officer) as a first level of control. In addition, the Board's Audit and Finance committees were assigned the task of reviewing all the previous year's transactions. The Board also required Skilling to review and approve all LJM transactions, as well as to review Fastow's economic interest in Enron and LJM.

Skilling, as COO and later CEO, did not sign many of the DASH forms for the LJM transactions. No evidence exists that Skilling knew how much money Fastow was making through LJM. Skilling, in one note, simply said that Fastow's first duty was to Enron because he received more compensation through salary and options than he might be making through LJM.

Neither stockholders nor analysts found it easy to monitor Enron's overall performance. Information on the financial dealings, particularly those with the SPEs, was difficult to find. The information on the SPE deals was disclosed either through proxy statements or in footnotes on the 10-Ks and 10-Qs. At one level, accounting standards required adequate information for management to assert the related-party transactions were at least comparable with those that would have taken place with unrelated parties. Second, details were often omitted. In the 2000 10-K, Enron stated, "Enron paid $123 million to purchase share-settled options from the [Raptor] entities on 21.7 million shares of Enron common stock." What Enron had actually purchased were put options, thereby betting that its stock would decline.[18]

THREE INTERNATIONAL DEALS

Rebecca Mark served as president of Enron Development Corporation. The power plant at Dabhol, India, was one of her achievements, though its overall value to Enron faded over time. Mark finalized the $3 billion deal in 1995, partnering Enron with General Electric and Bechtel (Enron's share was 65 percent; GE and Bechtel each owned 10 percent). The remaining 15 percent was owned by the state of Maharashtra electric utility. In addition to the partners, four lenders (the Industrial Development Bank of India, Citibank, Bank of America, and the Overseas Private Investment Corporation, a U.S. government agency) lent $2 billion.[21]

The Dabhol plant was troubled from the beginning with local and state authorities. The Clinton administration, at Lay's request, sent Ron Brown, secretary of commerce, to India in 1995 to keep the deal afloat. During construction, there were reports of human rights violations by guards.[22] Enron distanced itself from such instances, noting that it was only leasing the property, though it also paid the guards.

There were local benefits. Roads were constructed, and the local economy benefited both from increasing levels of employment and consumption. But when the plant opened in 1999, opposition exploded as energy bills rose as much as 400 percent. Maharashtra annulled its contract, and the plant was shuttered.

Mark also negotiated the Cuiaba project in Brazil. Enron had a 65 percent share in a gas-fired power generating plant and its associated pipelines. Construction exceeded the budget by over $120 million and showed no signs of profit. In 1999, LJM1 bought a 13 percent interest in the project for $11.3 million, enabling Enron to shield the associated debts from its balance sheet. In addition, the sale allowed Enron to mark to market a related power supply contract. With the sale and recognition of this contract, Enron booked a total of $65 million profit in the last half of 1999. Enron had a secret agreement with LJM1 to buy the interest back, should it be necessary for LJM1's profit. This buyback occurred in 2001, for $13.725 million.[23]

Azurix was a 1998 spin-off from Enron. Mark was named chair and CEO, with the mandate to create deals in the water supply industry. Enron's strategy was to assert itself as an international market maker in water. With Azurix divorced from Enron, these deals could be done under Enron oversight without the debt accruing to the balance sheet. Azurix went public in 1999, amassing $695 million in capital in the process.[12]

In 1999, Azurix acquired Wessex Water in the UK for $2.4 billion in cash and $482 million in debt.[24] Following that, Azurix bought the rights to an Argentinian water utility. These two acquisitions quickly undid Azurix, Mark, and any remaining Enron strategy involving hard assets. The Argentinian utility was plagued with contaminated water and labor union issues. The British government reduced the price Wessex could charge for its water. Mark was forced to resign in the summer of 2000, and she left Enron. Wessex Water was sold in 2002 to YTL Power International, a Malaysian firm, for $777 million in cash, with YTL also assuming $991 million in Wessex debt.[24]

It Comes Undone

Six months after taking the reins as CEO on February 12, 2001, Skilling abruptly resigned effective August 14, 2001. His 15 years at Enron were over, but Enron would haunt him long after. Skilling cited "personal reasons" as the cause, but there was widespread speculation that more was behind it.

Exhibit 1 provides a quick glance at Enron's profit and loss from 1998 to 2000. The declining gross margin indicates that Enron's nonderivatives business was losing money. Any profitability was coming from derivatives. In fact, Enron's derivative profits were roughly equivalent to Goldman Sachs, Inc.'s annual net revenue.[9]

In the Raptor restructurings from late 2000 to early 2001, a series of promissory notes from the Raptors had been recorded as increases in shareholders' equity, eventually totaling $1 billion. In August 2001, Andersen accountants declared that Raptors I, II, and IV were improperly accounted for, and revisions were required. On November 8, 2001, Lay announced a $1.2 billion

reduction to shareholders' equity, with the additional $200 million write-down resulting from a difference in contracts between the Raptors and Enron. In addition to the $1.2 billion write-down in shareholders' equity, Enron consolidated the SPEs back to 1997. Hence, the balance sheets of Chewco, JEDI, and LJM were now part of Enron's balance sheet. These adjustments reduced Enron's income by $591 million, and increased its debt by just less than $2.6 billion. And some feared that the restatements were insufficient.

In the midst of this restructuring, Milberg Weiss Bershad Hynes & Lerach, LLP filed a class-action suit on behalf of Enron shareholders on October 22, 2001. As part of its filing the lawsuit disclosed the names and amounts of stock sold by Enron insiders, both senior management and directors (see Exhibit 2).[6]

During this time, Enron's one hope was a proposed merger with Dynegy, a corporation once viewed by Enron employees as an insignificant competitor. This merger also died of the same problems that had plagued Enron: fear of what was not disclosed. The merger was announced on November 9, the day after the restatements. On November 28, Standard & Poor's downgraded Enron debt to junk status, Dynegy declared the merger dead, and Enron's share price dropped from $3.69 at opening to $0.61 at close. On December 2, 2001, Enron filed for Chapter 11 bankruptcy protection. Jeff McMahon (Executive Vice President, Finance, and Treasurer, Enron Corp.) was named president and CEO following Ken Lay's resignation on January 23, 2002. McMahon would in turn resign in April 2002.

THE AFTERSHOCKS
Criminal Actions

In addition to a number of Congressional hearings, the Enron bankruptcy also brought criminal actions by the government. David Duncan, Arthur Andersen's lead auditor for Enron, pleaded guilty to obstruction of justice in April 2002 for document shredding in connection with the Enron account. Kopper pleaded guilty in August 2002 to conspiracy to commit wire fraud and money laundering, losing almost approximately $12 million that he admitted he had improperly acquired through

EXHIBIT 1
(in $ millions)   Enron Corp. and Subsidiaries 2000 Consolidated Income Statement

	2000	1999	1998
Nonderivative revenues	$93,557	$34,774	$27,215
Nonderivative expenses	94,517	34,761	26,381
Nonderivatives gross margin	(960)	13	834
Gain (loss) from derivatives	7,232	5,338	4,045
Other expenses	(4,319)	(4,549)	(3,501)
Operating income	1,953	802	1,378

Source: Testimony of Frank Partnoy in Hearings before the United States Senate Committee on Governmental Affairs, January 24, 2002.

EXHIBIT 2   Senior Management and Board of Director Members Accused of Insider Trading

Senior Management and Board Members	Proceeds from Enron Stock Traded between October 1998 and November 2001
J. Clifford Baxter[a]	$ 34,734,854
Robert A. Belfer[b]	$111,941,200
Norman P. Blake Jr.[b]	$ 1,705,328
Richard B. Buy[a]	$ 10,656,595
Richard A. Causey[a]	$ 13,386,896
James V. Derrick Jr.[a]	$ 12,563,928
John H. Duncan[b]	$ 2,009,700
Andrew S. Fastow[a]	$ 33,675,004
Mark A. Frevert[a]	$ 54,831,220
Wendy L. Gramm[b]	$ 278,892
Kevin P. Hannon[a]	"Unknown but substantial"
Ken L. Harrison[a]	$ 75,416,636
Joseph M. Hirko[a]	$ 35,168,721
Stanley C. Horton[a]	$ 47,371,361
Robert K. Jaedicke[b]	$ 841,438
Steven J. Kean[a]	$ 5,166,414
Mark E. Koenig[a]	$ 9,110,466
Kenneth L. Lay[a,b]	$184,494,426
Rebecca P. Mark[a,b]	$ 82,536,737
Michael S. McConnell[a]	$ 2,506,311
Jeffrey McMahon[a]	$ 2,739,226
Cindy K. Olson[a]	$ 6,505,870
Lou L. Pai[a]	$270,276,065
Kenneth D. Rice[a]	$ 76,825,145
Jeffrey K. Skilling[a,b]	$ 70,687,199
Joseph W. Sutton[a]	$ 42,231,283
Lawrence Greg Whalley[a]	"Unknown but substantial"

[a]Employee, Enron Corp.

[b]Member, Enron Board of Directors

Source: Cruver, B. 2002. *Anatomy of greed: The unshredded truth from an Enron insider.* New York: Carroll and Graf Publishers: 132–133.

various SPE deals. Fastow was indicted in October 2002 on 78 counts for his role at Enron and in the various SPEs, and his accounts were frozen. On January 13, 2004, Fastow pled guilty to two counts, one for covering up financial problems and one for defrauding the company, and was sentenced to 10 years in a federal prison.[25] His wife, Lea, pled guilty to one count of tax fraud and received a 1-year sentence. On February 21, 2004, Jeff Skilling and Rick Causey were indicted for their roles, and on July 7, 2004,[26] Ken Lay was indicted for his.[25]

The Retirement Vanishes

Enron had been a significant holding in many large funds, particularly pension funds that sought to invest by industry segment. Enron employees' 401(k)s were primarily Enron, and they were barred from selling their shares until they turned 55. Many were solely invested in Enron. As late as the summer of 2001, Ken Lay was predicting that Enron would regain much of its loss in stock price. His e-mail announcing the resignation of Skilling as CEO, and his own resumption of that post, ends with this:

> Our performance has never been stronger; our business model has never been more robust; our growth has never been more certain; and most importantly, we have never had a better nor deeper pool of talent throughout the company. We have the finest organization in American business today. Together, we will make Enron the world's leading company.[12]

At the same time, however, Lay was busy selling much of his Enron stock. During 2001, Lay is reported to have sold $70 million in Enron shares. For almost an entire year, he was selling between 3,000 and 4,000 shares each work-day.[27] He sold some shares back to the company to repay a loan from Enron. By doing so, he not only disposed of the stock, but also circumvented disclosure laws that would have required him to report insider stock sales.

The pension funds of every state were invested, to some extent, in Enron stock. The estimated loss to these funds was $1.5 billion. Florida lost $328 million, California $142 million, and Georgia $122 million.[28]

The Accounting Profession

Fallout spread throughout the accounting profession as well, as reports of inadequate oversight continued throughout the fall of Enron. In the fall of 2001, the Houston office of Arthur Andersen shredded documents associated with the Enron account. Nancy Temple, a lawyer associated with Arthur Andersen's Chicago offices, e-mailed David Duncan, the lead Enron auditor for Andersen, a reminder of the corporate policy on memo retention leading to massive document shredding efforts at Andersen's Houston offices. Duncan later pleaded guilty to criminal obstruction of justice, and Temple was named by a grand jury as one of four or five "corrupt persuaders" who encouraged the destruction of documents.[29] Andersen itself was stripped of its license to audit public corporations in the U.S. and ceased to do business.

A major feature of the Sarbanes-Oxley Act was aimed at the conflicts that some thought brought about Enron: the mix of consulting and audit business. Andersen had both audit and consulting relationships with Enron, earning $52 million in

2001, split almost equally between consulting and audit fees. Enron was Andersen's largest client.[9] Audit firms would no longer be allowed to offer consulting services to audit clients. In addition, a number of other services were also proscribed, such as actuarial services, expert witnessing, and investment banking services, to name a few. In short, many of the services rendered by audit firms in attempts to generate extra revenue are now banned.

The Charity Fallout

Enron and its executives were very generous to not only their hometown of Houston but to educational institutions nationwide and the favorite causes of its board members. Initiatives included sponsorship of Enron Field (home to the Houston Astros), college scholarships, United Way, and university endowments.

Enron also generously contributed to the causes of several of its directors.[30] For instance, when the president of M.D. Andersen Cancer Center, John Mendelsohn, became an Enron director and member of its audit committee, Enron and Lay donated $332,150 to the center. Of $60,000 donated to a think tank at George Mason University, $45,000 was contributed after Wendy Lee Gramm (wife of then Senator Phil Gramm, R-TX, and an associate of the center), became an Enron board member. Concerned with an appearance of conflict of interest and a threat to independence, the U.S. House of Representatives passed a bill dubbed the "Enron Bill" to require disclosure of certain contributions and noncash gifts to organizations associated with board members.

Conclusion

This case is still writing its own ending. Many of the stakeholders will never recover from their losses. Criminal actions have resulted in some going to jail, and others being indicted and waiting for trial. Two of the investment banks, Citigroup and J. P. Morgan Chase, have settled investor lawsuits for $2.575 billion and $2.2 billion, respectively. Other investment banks still face civil actions.[31] And federal lawmakers are debating the cost of some provisions of the Sarbanes-Oxley Act. This case will evolve for years to come.

Appendix A Enron Timeline

1984	Ken Lay becomes CEO of Houston Natural Gas (HNG).
1985	HNG merges with Internorth. Lay becomes CEO of the new company.
1986	Company changes name to Enron, and moves to Lay's hometown, Houston.
1990	Skilling leaves McKinsey & Co. to join Enron as executive officer of Enron Gas Services. Skilling hires Andrew Fastow from banking industry.
1991	Enron adopts mark-to-market accounting strategy, reporting income and value of assets at their replacement cost. Fastow forms first legitimate SPEs.
1993	Deregulation of worldwide energy markets. Enron begins marketing power and forms first SPE, JEDI, with CalPERS to invest in natural gas projects.
1994	As deregulation in the U.S. grows, Enron begins trading electricity.
1996	Enron commences construction of the Dabhol power plant in India. Lay promotes Skilling to Enron's president and COO.
1997	Enron buys first electric utility, Portland General Electric. Fastow promoted to head new finance department. Enron applies energy-trading model to new commodities markets such as weather derivatives, coal, pulp and paper, and bandwidth capacity. Chewco (another SPE) created to purchase CalPERS' shares of JEDI1 so that CalPERS could participate in a larger partnership, JEDI2. Chewco never meets the 3 percent outside ownership and is never a legitimate SPE.
1998	Fastow named CFO. Enron begins power trading in Argentina, becoming first power marketer, and gains control of Brazilian utility. Enron acquires UK utility Wessex Water and forms Azurix, a global water business. It then takes Azurix public, retaining a 69 percent stake. Enron trades most of Enron Oil & Gas for cash and its properties in India and China.
1999	New Houston Astros baseball stadium named Enron Field. Skilling and Fastow present LJM partnerships to board of directors.
2000	
February	*Fortune* names Enron "the most innovative company in America" for the fifth consecutive year.
April	Enron creates the first Raptor SPE.
August	Rebecca Mark resigns due to poor results at Azurix and tension with Skilling. Stock hits all-time high of $90 and revenue surpasses $100 billion making it the seventh largest company in the Fortune 500.
2001	
February	Lay steps down as CEO. President and COO Skilling replaces Lay as CEO.
August	Skilling resigns and Lay becomes CEO again. Sherron Watkins, an Enron accountant, sends anonymous memo to Lay warning of potential accounting scandal.
September	Arthur Andersen compels Enron to change an aggressive accounting action, causing a $1.2 billion reduction in Enron's equity.
October	SEC launches investigation of Enron's off-balance-sheet partnerships. Enron changes its 401(k) pension plan administrator, preventing employees from selling Enron stock for 30 days. Fastow is put on leave. Enron establishes special committee to investigate third-party transactions to be known as the Powers Report. Enron's stock drops to $11.
November	Enron strikes deal with Dynegy, its largest energy-industry rival. Dynegy backs out of the deal once more details of Enron's finances are available. Enron trades at less than $1 per share.
December	Enron files for Chapter 11 bankruptcy protection and lays off 4,000 employees.
2002	
January	Watkins's memo leaked to Congress. U.S. Justice Department launches a criminal investigation into Enron's fall. Enron fires Arthur Andersen LLP. Enron sells its energy trading business to

(continued)

(continued)

UBS's investment banking unit. Sells Wessex Water to a Malaysian firm, and shuts down its broadband unit. Lay resigns, and McMahon becomes CEO. Former Enron Vice Chairman Cliff Baxter is found dead as government investigation deepens.

February	Skilling testifies before Congress. Lay pleads the Fifth Amendment. Watkins testifies before Congress about her memo to Lay.
April	Andersen lays off 7,000 employees. McMahon resigns as of June 1.
August	Kopper pleads guilty to money laundering and wire-fraud conspiracy. Cooperates with authorities.
October	Fastow indicted on 78 counts of federal fraud, conspiracy, and money laundering.

2003

May	Federal prosecutors file new charges against Fastow and two others. Indicted Fastow's wife and seven other former Enron officials for fraud and other criminal investigations.

2004

January	Fastow pleads guilty on two counts and receives 10 years in federal prison. Lea Fastow pleads guilty to one count of tax fraud and receives a 1-year sentence.
February	Skilling and Causey indicted on 42 counts, including securities fraud, wire fraud, and insider trading.
July	Lay indicted on 11 counts, including wire and bank fraud, as well as making false statements.

Appendix B   Glossary of Terms

Adjustments	A deduction made to financial statements to charge off a loss, as with a bad debt.
Asset-lite	Enron jargon for short-term or noncapital-intensive assets.
CalPERS	California Public Employees Retirement System
DASH	Deal Approval Sheet
Derivative	A financial instrument whose characteristics and value depend upon the characteristics and value of an underlier, typically a commodity, bond, equity or currency.
Downgrade	A negative change in an analyst's ratings for a security.
Hedge	An investment made in order to reduce the risk of adverse price movements in a security, by taking an offsetting position in a related security.
Insider stock sales	Selling of a company's stock by individual directors, executives or other employees.
JEDI	Joint Energy Development Investment—an Enron SPE
Mark-to-Market	Recording the price or value of a security, portfolio, or account on a daily basis to calculate profits and losses or to confirm that margin requirements are being met.
Off-balance sheet	Financing from sources other than debt and equity offerings, such as joint ventures, R&D partnerships, and operating leases.
Options	The right, but not the obligation, to buy (for a call option) or sell (for a put option) a specific amount of a given stock, commodity, currency, index, or debt, at a specified price (the strike price) during a specified period of time.
Premium	The amount by which a bond or stock sells above its par value.
Privatization	The process of moving from a government-controlled system to a privately run, for-profit system.
Put options	An option contract that gives the holder the right to sell a certain quantity of an underlying security to the writer of the option, at a specified price (strike price) up to a specified date (expiration date); also called *put*.
RAC	Risk Assessment & Control, an Enron department.

Rank and Yank   Employee jargon for Enron's employee review process.

Securitization   The process of aggregating similar instruments, such as loans or mortgages, into a negotiable security.

SPEs   Special Purpose Entities

Write-down   Make a downward adjustment in the accounting value of an asset.

Yields   The annual rate of return on an investment, expressed as a percentage.

Endnotes

1. *BusinessWeek Online,* February 12, 2001.

2. Eichenwald, K. 2002. A powerful, flawed witness against Enron. *New York Times,* October 21: C1.

3. Eichenwald, K. 2003. Ex-trader at Enron is charged in California power case. *New York Times,* June 4: C6.

4. Lay, K. 1990. The Enron story. Speech delivered on October 9, 1990 in New York to Newcomen Society of the United States.

5. A more detailed history of the origin of Enron can be found at www.hoovers.com.

6. Cruver, B. 2002. *Anatomy of greed: The unshredded truth from an Enron insider.* New York: Carroll & Graf Publishers.

7. Preston, R., & Koller, M. 2000. Enron feels the power. *Internetweekonline:* October 30.

8. O'Reilly, B. 1997. The secrets of America's most admired corporations: New ideas, new products. *Fortune,* 135(4): 60–64.

9. Testimony of Frank Partnoy in Hearings before the United States Senate Committee on Governmental Affairs, January 24, 2002.

10. 1999 Annual Report, Enron Corp.

11. Grulye, B., & Smith, R. 2002. Anatomy of a fall: Keys to success left Kenneth Lay open to disaster—From rural Missouri to helm of Enron to ignominy—Trust and willfull optimism—"The American dream is alive." *The Wall Street Journal,* April 26: A1.

12. Fusaro, P. C., & Miller, R. M. 2002. *What went wrong at Enron: Everyone's guide to the largest bankruptcy in U.S. History.* Hoboken, NJ: John Wiley & Sons.

13. Schwartz, J. 2002. As Enron purged its ranks, dissent was swept away. *New York Times,* February 4.

14. Levin, C. 2002. After Enron: Government's role and corporate cultures. *Mid-American Journal of Business,* 17(2): 7–10.

15. Banerjee, N., Berboza, D., & Warren, A. 2002. Enron's many strands: Corporate culture; at Enron, lavish excess often came before success. *New York Times,* February 26: C1.

16. Raghavan, A., Kranhold, K., & Barriounuevo, A. 2002. Full speed ahead: How Enron bosses created a culture of pushing limits—Fastow and others challenged staff, badgered bankers; Porsches, Ferraris were big—A chart to "intimidate people." *The Wall Street Journal,* August 26: A1

17. Note 8, Q3 SEC filing, 2001.

18. Report of Investigation by the Special Investigative Committee of the Board of Directors of Enron Corp. (the Powers Report).

19. Reason, CFO.com, 2002.

20. Berger, E., & Fowler, T. 2002. The fall of Enron; Enron masked loans as sales, report says; deals inflated bottom line by $1.4 billion. *Houston Chronicle,* September 22: A1.

21. Rai, S. 2002. Seeking ways to sell Enron's plant in India. *New York Times,* April 11: W1.

22. Kolker, C., & Fowler, T. 2002. The fall of Enron; roots of discontent; dead Enron power plant affecting environment, economy and livelihoods in India. *Houston Chronicle,* August 4: B1.

23. Criminal Complaint, United States Securities and Exchange Commission v. Andrew S. Fastow, October 1, 2002, #s 15–22.

24. Goldberg, L. 2002. Enron's Azurix to well Wessex Water at a loss. *Houston Chronicle,* March 26: B4.

25 Eichenwald, K. 2004. Enron ex-chief indicted by U.S. in fraud case. *New York Times,* July 8: A1.

26. Carr, R. 2004. Former Enron chief indicted. *Atlanta Constitution,* February 20: 1A.

27. Flood, M., & Fowler, T. 2002. The fall of Enron; grand jurors eye Lay; $70 million in stock sales focus of probe. *Houston Chronicle,* October 24: A1.

28. Healy, B. 2002. Shared pain: Bay State isn't alone in taking a hit from Enron. *Boston Globe,* September 10: C1.

29. Fowler, T. 2002. Andersen attorney may be next. *Houston Chronicle,* June 27: B1.

30. Weber, J., & McNamee, M. 2002. Boardroom charity: Reforms don't go far enough. *BusinessWeek,* June 10: 128.

31. Creswell, J. 2005. J.P. Morgan Chase to pay Enron investors $2.2 billion. *New York Times,* June 15: C1.

CASE 2   QVC

On March 22, 2007, QVC, one of the world's largest multimedia retailers, shipped its billionth package in the United States. It was shipped to Mary Pew in Canton, Michigan, who received a 24-hour shopping spree and a $10,000 gift card from QVC for being its billionth customer. The firm also offered special prices with free shipping and handling on selected products that were featured each hour on its television home shopping channel throughout the day. "This is our chance to acknowledge the millions of loyal customers who have made this milestone possible," said the firm's new president and CEO Mike George.[1]

Since it was launched in 1986, QVC has rapidly grown to become the largest television shopping network. Although it entered the market a couple of years after rival Home Shopping Network, the channel has managed to build a leading position. By 2006, its reach had extended to over 95 percent of all U.S. cable homes as well as over 25 million satellite homes. It shipped over 140 million packages during 2006 to customers around the world, resulting in almost $7.1 billion in sales and an over $1 billion operating profit (see Exhibits 1 and 2). Its sales were made to over 10 million customers, who watched its shows across the United States, the UK, Germany, and Japan (see Exhibit 3). Almost a fifth of these represented new customers who had shopped with QVC for the first time.

The success of QVC is largely driven by its popular television home shopping shows that feature a wide variety of eye-catching products, many of which are unique to the channel. It organizes product searches in cities all over the United States to continuously find new offerings that can be pitched to customers. During these events, the firm has to screen hundreds of products to select those that it will offer. In one of its recent searches, QVC had to evaluate the appeal of products such as nail clippers that catch clippings, bicycle seats built for bigger bottoms, and novelty items shaped like coffins.

Thousands of entrepreneurs have used QVC's product searches over the years to try to sell their products on the popular home shopping channel. A chance to display their offerings

*This case was developed by Professor Jamal Shamsie, Michigan State University with the assistance of Professor Alan B. Eisner, Pace University. Material has been drawn from published sources to be used for class discussion. © 2007 Jamal Shamsie & Alan B. Eisner.

EXHIBIT 1   Sales Growth ($)

2006	7.1 billion
2004	5.7 billion
2001	3.8 billion
1998	2.4 billion
1995	1.6 billion
1992	0.9 billion
1989	0.2 billion
Source: QVC, Liberty Media.	

EXHIBIT 2   Income Statement

	Years Ended December 31		
	2006	2005	2004
	(Amounts in $ Millions)		
Net Revenue	$7,074	6,501	5,687
Cost of Sales	(4,426)	(4,112)	(3,594)
Gross Profit	2,648	2,389	2,093
Operating Expenses*	(579)	(570)	(497)
S, G, & A Expenses	(413)	(397)	(366)
Operating Cash Flow	1,656	1,422	1,230
Stock Compensation	(50)	(52)	(33)
Depreciation & Amortization**	(476)	(449)	(437)
Operating Income	$1,130	$ 921	$760

*Operating expenses consist of commissions and license fees, order processing and customer service, credit card processing fees, and provision for doubtful accounts.

**Depreciation & amortization includes amortization of intangible assets recorded in connection with the purchase of QVC by Liberty Media.

Source: Liberty Media, QVC.

EXHIBIT 3   Geographical Revenue Breakdown

	Years Ended December 31		
	2006	2005	2004
	(Amounts in $ Millions)		
U.S.	$4,983	4,640	4,141
UK	612	554	487
Germany	848	781	643
Japan	631	526	416

Homes

	Years Ended December 31		
	2006	2005	2004
	(Amounts in Millions)		
U.S.	90.7	90.0	88.4
UK	19.4	17.8	15.6
Germany	37.9	37.4	35.7
Japan	18.7	16.7	14.7

Source: Liberty Media, QVC.

to QVC's national TV audience can transform a one-person operation into a multibillion-dollar business. "The vendors who are our success stories for this past decade have done over $1 billion in sales on QVC over the past ten years," said Marilyn Montross, the channel's director of vendor relations.[2]

Early in 2007, QVC partnered with Oprah Winfrey on a Search for the Next Big Idea. Oprah invited hopeful entrepreneurs to pitch their creative products during one of three national trade shows that QVC was sponsoring in Chicago, Los Angeles, and Philadelphia during March 2007. Up to 10 finalists from these events would get the opportunity to present their invention on *The Oprah Winfrey Show* and the studio audience would vote for their favorite. The winning invention would eventually be featured on QVC's home shopping network. A QVC publicist remarked about the use of such stunts to find products: "It's the *American Idol* of retailing."[3]

PURSUING A LEADING POSITION

QVC was founded by Joseph Segel in June 1986 and began broadcasting by November of the same year. In early 1986, Segel had tuned into the Home Shopping Network, which had been launched just two years earlier. He had not been particularly impressed with the crude programming and the down-market products of the firm. But Segel was convinced that another televised shopping network would have the potential to attract a large enough client base. He also felt that such an enterprise should be able to produce significant profits because the operating expenses for a shopping network could be kept relatively low.

Over the next few months, Segel raised $30 million in start-up capital, hired several seasoned television executives, and launched his own shopping network. Operating out of headquarters that were located in West Chester, Pennsylvania, QVC offered 24-hour-a-day, seven-day-a-week television home shopping to consumers. By the end of its first year of operation, QVC had managed to extend its reach to 13 million homes by satellite and cable systems. 700,000 viewers had already become customers, resulting in the shipping of 3 million orders. Its sales had already topped $100 million, and the firm was actually able to show a small profit.

Segel attributed the instant success of his company to the potential offered by television shopping. "Television's combination of sight, sound and motion is the best way to sell a product. It is more effective than presenting a product in print or just putting the product on a store shelf," he stated. "The cost-efficiency comes from the cable distribution system. It is far more economical than direct mail, print advertising, or traditional retail store distribution."[4]

In the fall of 1988, Segel acquired the manufacturing facilities, proprietary technology, and trademark rights of the Diamonique Corporation, which produced a wide range of simulated gemstones and jewelry that could be sold on QVC's shows. Over the next couple of years, Segel expanded QVC by acquiring its competitors such as the Cable Value Network Shopping channel.

By 1993, QVC had overtaken Home Shopping Network to become the leading televised shopping channel in terms of sales and profits. Its reach extended to over 80 percent of all cable homes and to 3 million satellite dishes. Segel retired during the same year, passing control of the company to Barry Diller. Since then, QVC's sales have continued to grow at a substantial rate. As a result, it has consistently widened the gap between its sales and those of Home Shopping Network, which has remained its closest competitor.

ACHIEVING EFFICIENCY IN OPERATIONS

Over the years, QVC has managed to establish itself as the world's preeminent virtual shopping mall that never closes. Its televised shopping channel has become a place where customers around the world can, and do, shop at any hour at the rate of more than five customers per second. It sells a wide variety of products, using a combination of description and demonstration by live program hosts. Each of the products is presented by QVC in a format where it is attractively modeled and carefully explained by the hosts of the show and by representatives from the vendor. QVC works hard to develop descriptions for each of their offerings that have been carefully crafted to resonate with its viewing audience. If necessary, complete on-air instructions are also provided for the use of every product that it sells.

In addition, most of the products are offered on regularly scheduled shows, each of which is focused on a particular type of product and a well-defined market (see Exhibit 4). Each of these shows typically lasts for one hour and is based on a theme such as "Now You're Cooking" or "Cleaning Solutions." QVC has enticed celebrities such as clothing designers or book authors to appear live on special program segments to sell their own products. On some occasions, customers are able to call in and have on-air conversations with program hosts and visiting celebrities.

Over the past year, QVC has been trying to capitalize on the growing success of reality-based television shows. It has begun to incorporate some of the concepts from these popular shows into its shopping programs. In one of its recently introduced shows, *Room for Improvement,* the shopping channel has carried out an extensive renovation of a bedroom and a kitchen for a family. Products that were featured on the show sold well. In another show, Finola Hughes, who sells jewelry on QVC, plans to focus on the elaborate makeover of an individual participant.

QVC's themed programs are telecast live 24 hours a day, seven days a week, to over 90 million households in the United States and 160 million homes worldwide. The shopping channel transmits its programming live from its central production facilities in Pennsylvania through uplinks to a satellite. Of all the orders placed with QVC, more than 90 percent are shipped within 48 hours from one of their distribution centers. Paul Day, a logistics manager for QVC, explained how they can ensure the fast delivery to their customers: "The whole supply chain has to be working, from how the buyers buy and set up dates

EXHIBIT 4   **QVC Programming Typical Weekly Schedule**

Eastern Standard Time	Monday	Tuesday	Wednesday	Thursday	Friday	Saturday	Sunday
7–8 AM	The QVC MORNING SHOW	THE QVC MORNING SHOW	THE QVC MORNING SHOW	THE QVC MORNING SHOW	THE QVC MORNING SHOW	Select Comfort Sleep Number	AM STYLE
8–9 AM	The QVC MORNING SHOW	THE QVC MORNING SHOW	THE QVC MORNING SHOW	THE QVC MORNING SHOW	FASHION FRIDAY	AM STYLE	AM STYLE
9–10 AM	PATRICIA WEXLER, MD DERMATOLOGY	SPRING SPOTLIGHT	NutriSystem Nourish Weight-Loss Program	SUSAN GRAVER STYLE	SLEEP SOLUTIONS	AM STYLE	AM STYLE
10–11 AM	CITIKNITS	BATH SHOP	FINE JEWELRY COLLECTION	ORGANIZE IT ALL	TRAVELING WITH KIDS	CREATING KEEPSAKES	
11 AM–12 PM	HOME STYLE	DENIM & CO	ELLIOTT LUCCA HANDBAGS	WHITE MOUNTAIN FOOTWEAR	IMPERIAL GOLD	MAGAZINE PAPER CRAFTING	MODERN SOUL KNITWEAR
12–1 PM	BEAUTY BEAT	NOW YOU'RE COOKING	14K GOLD JEWELRY	EATING SMART	IMPERIAL GOLD	BY POPULAR DEMAND	DIALOGUES THE NEW LANGUAGE OF STYLE
1–2 PM	LINEN CLOSET	LINEA BY LOUIS DELL'OLIO	B.O.C. FOOTWEAR	BY POPULAR DEMAND	THE FAMILY ROOM	RATIO & GARDEN	LINEA BY LOUIS DELL'OLIO
2–3 PM	OUTDOOR ENTERTAINING	LINEA BY LOUIS DELL'OLIO	QON ASLETT'S CLEANING SECRETS	NINA LEONARD COLLECTION FASHION	BIRKENSTOCK COLLECTIONS	SMASHBOX COSMETICS	SUMMER FUN FASHION
3–4 PM	DENIM & CO	EPIPHANY PLATINUM	PROACTIV SOLUTION SKIN CARE	NINA LEONARD COLLECTION FASHION	INSTANT FLOWER GARDEN	ANNA GRIFFIN ELEGANT CRAFTING	CITIKNITS
4–5 PM	QVC SAMPLER	CLAD SILVER & DIAMONIQUE JEWELRY	In-Home Care	AUTO SHOP	AROUND THE HOUSE	CREATING KEEPSAKES MAGAZINE–PAPER CRAFTING	STATEMENTS ON STYLE
5–6 PM	ETIENNE AIGNER	FOCUS ON FASHION	JEWELRY SHOWCASE	PATRICIA WANG JADE STUDIO	AROUND THE HOUSE	SCRAPBOOKING DAY CELEBRATION	DENIM & CO
6–7 PM	HOME STYLE	KITCHEN IDEAS	NutriSystem Nourish Weight-Loss Program	QVC SAMPLER	KITCHEN IDEAS	Select Comfort Sleep Number	DENIM & CO
7–8 PM	PATRICIA WEXLER, MD DERMATOLOGY	LINEA BY LOUIS DELL'OLIO	KEEP IT CLEAN	MADE FOR iPOD	ELECTRONICS TODAY	SATURDAY NIGHT BEAUTY	SUSAN GRAVER STYLE

Source: QVC.

on their orders to how we receive the orders."[5] The distribution centers have a combined floor space of 4.6 million square feet, which is equivalent to the size of 103 football fields.

In order to make it easier for viewers to purchase products that they may see on their home shopping channel, QVC also provides a credit program to allow customers to pay for goods over a period of several months. Everything it sells is also backed by a 30-day unconditional money-back guarantee. Furthermore, QVC does not impose any hidden charges, such as a restocking fee, for any returned merchandise. These policies help the home shopping channel to attract customers for products that they can view but are not able to either touch or feel.

SEARCHING FOR PROFITABLE PRODUCTS

More than 100 experienced, informed buyers comb the world on a regular basis to search for new products to launch on QVC. The shopping channel concentrates on unique products that can be demonstrated on live television. Furthermore, the price of these products must be high enough for viewers to justify the additional shipping and handling charge. Over the course of a typical year, QVC carries more than 50,000 products. Almost 1,700 items are typically offered in any given week, of which about 15 percent, or 250, are new products for the network. QVC's suppliers range from some of the world's biggest companies to small entrepreneurial enterprises.

All new products must, however, pass through stringent tests that are carried out by QVC's in-house Quality Assurance Lab. In many cases, this inspection process is carried out manually by the firm's employees. Only 15 percent of the products pass the firm's rigorous quality inspection on first try and as many as a third are never offered to the public because they fail altogether. Everyone at QVC works hard to make sure that every item works as it should before it is shipped and that its packaging will protect it during the shipping process. "Nothing ships unless it is quality-inspected first," said Day. "Since our product is going business-to-consumer, there's no way to fix or change a product-related problem."[6]

About a third of QVC's sales come from broadly available national brands. The firm has been able to build trust among its customers in large part through the offering of these well-known brands. QVC also relies upon promotional campaigns with a variety of existing firms for another third of its sales. It has made deals with firms ranging from Dell, Target, and Bath & Body Works for special limited time promotional offerings. But QVC has been most successful with products that are exclusively sold on QVC or not readily available through other distribution channels. Although such products account for another third of its sales, the firm has been able to earn higher margins with these proprietary products, many of which come from firms that are either start-ups or new entrants into the U.S. market.

Apart from searching for exclusive products, QVC has also been trying to move away from some product categories, such as home appliances and electronic gadgets, which offer lower margins. It has been gradually expanding into many new product categories that have higher margins such as cosmetics, apparel, food, and toys. Several of these new categories have also displayed the strongest rates of growth in sales for the shopping channel over the past couple of years.

The shopping channel has been turning to products by various fashion designers such as Arnold Scassi, Heidi Klum, and Dana Buchman. Many designers have been attracted to QVC because of its access to a much broader market. More recently, the firm has been offering apparel, jewelry, and accessories by exclusive designers that have been specifically created for the mass market. In late 2004, QVC contracted with Marc Bouwer to develop an M collection to be sold exclusively on its home shopping channel. Bouwer's initial products included a $50 kimono blouse, $50 matte jersey pants with side slits, and a $149 silk dress with a ruffled front. "Where else can you sell thousands of units in virtually minutes?" Bouwer asked.[7]

EXPANDING ON THE CUSTOMER BASE

By 2005, QVC's shopping channel had penetrated almost all of the cable television and broadcast satellite homes in the United States. The firm was still trying to increase sales by making it easier for customers to buy its products by adding features such as an interactive service that would allow them to purchase whatever it is offering on its shopping channel with the single click of a remote. QVC is also relying on the reasonably strong reputation that surveys have indicated it has established among a large majority of its current consumers. By its initials alone, QVC had promised that it would deliver quality, value, and convenience to its viewers. More than three-quarters of the shopping channel's customers have given it a score of seven out of seven for trustworthiness. This has led most of its customers to demonstrate a strong tendency to purchase often from the channel and to recommend it to their friends.

QVC has also been trying to enter new markets by offering its shopping channel to customers outside North America. Over the last decade, QVC has expanded to the UK, Germany, and Japan, giving it access to almost 70 million new households in these three countries. Partly as a result of this expansion into new markets, a large part of the shopping network's strong growth in sales over the past few years has come from the regular addition of new customers. In a typical month, QVC can gain as many as 200,000 new customers worldwide, and many of them stay on to become repeat customers. The firm's total customer base is approaching 45 million customers who are spread over a few different countries.

QVC has also benefited from the growing percentage of women entering the workforce, resulting in a significant increase in dual-income families. Although the firm's current customer base does span several socioeconomic groups, it is led by young professional families who have above average disposable income. They also enjoy various forms of thrill-seeking activities and rank shopping relatively high as a leisure activity when compared to the typical consumer.

In 1995, QVC launched its own retail Web site to complement its television home shopping channel. Called iQVC, the 24-hour service has provided the firm access to more than 100 million households in the United States that have Internet connections. The Web site has also allowed the firm to perform well with some product categories that have not done as well on the television channel. For example, its Books, Movies and Music link offers more than 500,000 books, 100,000 movies, and 150,000 compact discs. During 2006, QVC was able to generate $1 billion of sales on its Internet operations.

Recently, QVC has also been adding branded video-on-demand channels through a partnership with AOL. This includes the AOL Video portal's first live streaming channel. The live stream of QVC's broadcast will carry the shopping channel's live 24/7 format. Another QVC On Demand channel will include more than 400 clips of video content from various daily shows and events that will be updated continuously. "QVC is looking for new ways to be everywhere consumers want to shop," said Bob Myears, Senior Vice President of QVC.com. "Launching streaming video on AOL will allow more e-commerce consumers to experience QVC and our innovative product offerings."[8]

POSITIONING FOR FUTURE GROWTH

Over the last year, QVC has been deploying aggressive marketing campaigns to create more publicity for the firm. Jeff Charney, its newly appointed marketing director, challenged employees to a competition in which the individual that attracted the most attention while wearing a QVC T-shirt would win $10,000. Before the contest ended in September 2006, the firm had 725 entries, with employees who wore the T-shirt engaging in activities ranging from forming an aerial Q while skydiving to recording a musical that drew 5,000 viewers on YouTube.

During 2003, John Malone placed a value of $14.1 billion on QVC when he purchased the firm. It was clear that Malone felt that the home shopping network would continue to grow in spite of the development of competing forms of home shopping. Over the years, QVC's sales have actually grown to match that of Internet giant Amazon.com. But while the Internet firm has been struggling to show strong profits, QVC has been generating tons of cash. Furthermore, QVC certainly looks like it is well positioned with its shopping channel, its Web site, and streaming videos for continued growth in sales from a vast assortment of merchandise.

In fact, since the launching of its Web site, QVC has taken steps to become an innovative practitioner of electronic retailing. Its Web site has moved well beyond its initial capabilities, when it simply offered supplementary information on the products that were featured on the television shopping channel. The recent introduction of the interactive service for the shopping channel represents one of the first launches of on-screen interactivity, the kind in which viewers can interact with television content simply through the remote control. Looking towards the future, QVC is already focusing on new avenues for growth, such as those that might be offered through retailing on the mobile telephone.

Regular technological developments may, in fact, allow QVC to continue to offer much higher margin products to both existing and new markets. Doug Rose, the vice president of merchandising brand development, claims that interactivity in all aspects of the firm's business, including its television shopping channel, will only become more pronounced in the future, making it easier for customers to act on what they see. QVC believes that it still has a lot of room to grow, since only about 2 percent to 3 percent of its television viewers currently purchase at any given time.

"I was at an anniversary for employees last month, and they were showing clips of what QVC looked like 10 years ago," Rose said. "I was just stunned at how, by my reckoning, it looked so primitive. I fully expect that in 10 years, I'll be looking at clips of what we are doing now and think, 'How primitive.' So much has changed here, and yet we are taking baby steps. We're very much in our infancy."[9]

Endnotes

1. QVC. Talk about a special delivery: QVC ships its billionth package. Press Release, March 22, 2007.

2. Feldstein, M. J. 2005. Investors, entrepreneurs vie for QVC appearance. *Knight Ridder Tribune Business News,* February 11:1.

3. Kilgannon, C. 2006. Oh, to be discovered by the folks at QVC. *New York Times,* November 15: 9.

4. QVC Annual Report, 1987–1988.

5. Gilligan, E. 2004. The show must go on. *Journal of Commerce,* April 12: 1.

6. *Journal of Commerce,* April 12, 2004, p. 1.

7. Feitelberg, R. 2004. Bouwer prime for QVC. *WWD,* November 23: 8.

8. QVC, AOL and QVC launch first live streaming channel on AOL video. Press Release, January 17, 2007.

9. Duff, M. 2005. QVC Turns up the volume. *DSN Retailing Today,* March 14: 2.

CASE 3   JetBlue Airlines: Is the Blue Fading?

No other airline bore the brunt of bad weather as JetBlue did during Valentine's Day 2007 (See Exhibit 1). With hundreds of passengers stranded in the airports for more than $10\frac{1}{2}$ hours, about half of its 500 daily flights canceled due to snow and ice, and over another 1,100 flights canceled due to the snowball effect of the Valentine's Day disaster, the otherwise dream airline company—JetBlue—is being called into question with respect to its operational efficacy. In a major effort to protect its brand image and public relations, the company spent about $14 million for refunds and chartering other airplanes to fly its passengers and earmarked another $16 million in future free flights for the affected customers. David Neeleman, the CEO of JetBlue, apologized publicly and promised that such an event would not repeat ever again.[1]

Within a week's time, Morgan Stanley and others had downgraded JetBlue shares citing an estimated cost of $25 million to $30 million in pretax profits. William Greene, a Morgan Stanley analyst wrote in a research report that the stock is "dead money for now"(see Exhibit 2 for stock performance). In embarking on the repair measures, David Neeleman announced a Customer Bill of Rights. The bill included promises such as notifying customers about delays and cancellations, as well as deplaning passengers from flights ground-delayed for five hours. "This is a

big wake-up call for JetBlue," said Neeleman, adding "If there's a silver lining, it is the fact that our airline is going to be stronger and even better prepared to serve our customers."

However, the wake-up call seems to have come otherwise. Within less than three months from the meltdown, Neeleman was pushed out from being the CEO in May 2007. Dave Barger, the chief operating officer and an airline veteran, took his place. Neeleman has been the chief executive since 1998, but now will continue as the chairman. Some experts opine that JetBlue was already heading towards a leadership change even before the operations meltdown in February 2007. "That might have been the final straw but they were moving in that direction already," said Neidl, who downgraded his recommendation to neutral after its April 2007 earnings report. "JetBlue has reached a certain size where they need tough, experienced managers." Neeleman said he agreed with the decision to make a management change. "When you're a founder and an entrepreneur and you get mired in the operation, it's not good for anybody. This is a much better structure for us going forward. That was the board's recommendation, and I said, 'Great, let's do it'." So is a change in management going to fix the problems at JetBlue? Or is the problem deeper?[2]

THE U.S. AIRLINE INDUSTRY[3]

Deregulation of the U.S. airline industry in 1978 ushered in competition in the previously protected industry. Several low-cost, low-fare operators entered the competitive landscape that

*This case study was prepared by Naga Lakshmi Damaraju of The Ohio State University, Alan B. Eisner, Pace University, and Gregory G. Dess of the University of Texas at Dallas. All rights reserved to the authors. This case study has been developed purely from secondary sources. The purpose of the case is to stimulate class discussion rather than illustrating effective or ineffective handling of a business situation.

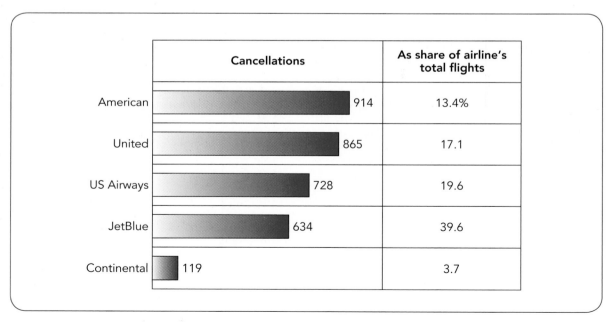

	Cancellations	As share of airline's total flights
American	914	13.4%
United	865	17.1
US Airways	728	19.6
JetBlue	634	39.6
Continental	119	3.7

EXHIBIT 1   **Flight Cancellations Feb. 13–15, 2007, due to Severe Weather**

Source: FlightStats.

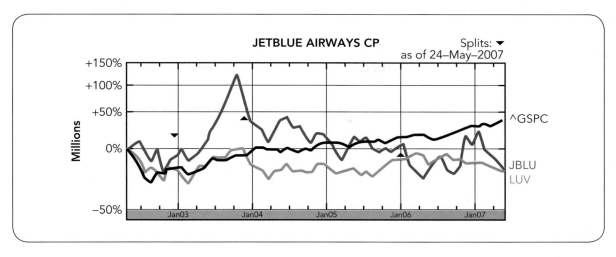

EXHIBIT 2   **JetBlue's Stock Performance vs. Southwest vs. S&P 500**

Source: http://finance.yahoo.com/.

Southwest pioneered. In 1971 Southwest initiated service as a regional carrier, but by 1990 it became a major airline when its revenues crossed the $1 billion mark.[4] The Southwest model was based on operating a single-type aircraft fleet with high utilization, a simplified fare structure with single-class seating, and high productivity from its human and physical assets. On the other hand, the "hub-and-spoke" system, increased labor costs, and increases in multitype aircraft fleets bloated the cost structure of the major airlines. There are three primary segments in the airline industry: major airlines, regional airlines, and low-fare airlines. Major U.S. airlines, as defined by the Department of Transportation, are those with annual revenues of over $1 billion. Eleven passenger airlines belong to this category, the largest of which include American Airlines, Continental Airlines, Delta Air Lines, Northwest Airlines, and United Airlines. These airlines offer scheduled flights to most large cities within the United States and abroad and also serve numerous smaller cities. Most major airlines adopted the hub-and-spoke route system. In this system, the operations are concentrated in a limited number of hub cities while other destinations are served by providing one-stop or connecting service through the hub. As of the beginning of 2007, there are 16 major airlines. Regional airlines typically operate smaller aircraft on lower-volume routes than major airlines. Unlike the low-fare airlines, the regional airlines do not have an independent route system. They typically enter into relationships with major airlines and carry their passengers on the "spoke"—that is, between a hub or larger city and a smaller city. There are five regional major U.S. airlines as of 2007. The low-fare airlines, on the other hand, operate from "point to point" and have their own route system. The target segment of low-fare airlines is fare-conscious leisure and business travelers who might otherwise have used alternative forms of transportation or not traveled at all. Low-fare airlines

stimulated demand in this segment and also have been successful in weaning business travelers from the major airlines. There are four major low-cost U.S. airlines. The main bases of competition in the airline industry are fare pricing, customer service, routes served, flight schedules, types of aircraft, safety record and reputation, code-sharing relationships, in-flight entertainment systems, and frequent flyer programs.

The economic downturn in the late 1990s and the terrorist attacks on the World Trade Center and the Pentagon on September 11, 2001, severely affected the airline industry. The demand for air travel dropped significantly and led to a reduction in traffic and revenue. Security concerns, security costs, and liquidity concerns increased. Lower fares and also increased capacity of the low-cost airlines created a very unprofitable environment for traditional network. Most of the traditional network airlines, since 2001, have filed for bankruptcy or undergone financial restructuring, mergers and/or consolidations. With these restructurings, many of them are able to significantly reduce labor costs, restructure debt, and have generally gained a more competitive cost structure. The major airlines are able to provide innovative offerings similar to those of low-cost airlines while still maintaining their alliances, frequent flier programs, and expansive route networks. The gap between low-cost airlines and traditional network airlines has been diminishing quite drastically. In 2005 and 2006, the industry experienced further consolidation and this could result in further rationalized route structures and lower operating costs, which could lead to aggressive competition in the future.[5]

NEELEMAN AND JETBLUE[6]

Born in São Paulo, Brazil, and brought up in Salt Lake City, David Neeleman dropped out of the University of Utah after his freshman year to move back to Brazil and become a missionary.

After two years of missionary work, he made his modest beginning in establishing his own business by renting out condominiums in Hawaii. He then established his own travel agency and began chartering flights from Salt Lake City to the islands to bring in prospective clients for his rental services. Neeleman's sales prowess caught the attention of June Morris, who owned one of Utah's largest corporate travel agencies. Soon after, in 1984, Neeleman and Morris launched the Utah-based "Morris Air," a charter operation. Morris Air was closely modeled after Southwest Airlines, the legendary discount airlines in the United States. Neeleman considered Herb Kelleher, Southwest's founder, his idol. He studied everything Kelleher accomplished and tried to do it better, which meant keeping costs low and turning planes around quickly, among a host of other operational and strategic activities/choices. While following the Southwest model, Neeleman brought his own innovations into the business. He pioneered the use of "at-home reservation agents"—routing calls to agents' homes to save money on office rent and infrastructure expense. He also developed the first electronic ticketing system in the airline industry. By 1992 Morris Air had grown into a regularly scheduled airline and was ready for an initial public offering (IPO) when Southwest, impressed by Morris's low costs and high revenue, bought the company for $129 million. Neeleman became the executive vice president of Southwest. However, Neeleman could not adjust to Southwest's pace of doing things. By 1994, he was at odds with the top executives and left after signing a five-year noncompete agreement. In the interim between leaving Southwest and establishing JetBlue, Neeleman developed the electronic ticketing system he initiated at Morris Air into one of the world's simplest airline reservation systems: Open Skies. He sold Open Skies to Hewlett-Packard in 1999. During the same period, he was also a consultant to a low-fare Canadian start-up airline, WestJet Airlines.[7] After the completion of the noncompete agreement with Southwest Airlines in 1999, Neeleman launched his own airline. He raised about $130 million of capital in a span of two weeks, an unprecedented amount for a start-up airline.[8] Weston Presidio Capital and Chase Capital, venture capital firms that

backed Neeleman's prior ventures, were return investors, and financier George Soros was also brought into the deal. "David's a winner; I knew anything David touched would turn to gold," said Michael Lazarus of Weston Presidio Capital, which had earlier funded Morris Air. "We were intrigued with his ideas about a low-cost airline."[9] With such strong support from venture capitalists, JetBlue began as the highest funded start-up airline in U.S. aviation history.

JetBlue commenced operations in August 2000, with John F. Kennedy International Airport (JFK) as its primary base of operations. In 2001 JetBlue extended its operations to the West Coast from its base at Long Beach Municipal Airport, which served the Los Angeles area. In 2002 the company went public and was listed on the Nasdaq as JBLU. JetBlue had expected to sell 5.5 million shares at about $24 to $26 in its initial public offering. Instead, it sold 5.87 million shares at $27 per share through its lead underwriters Morgan Stanley and Merrill Lynch. The shares closed at $47, up by $18, on the first day of trading. Jet Blue's stock offering was one of the hottest IPOs of the year.[10] Jet Blue was established with the goal of being a leading low-fare passenger airline that offered customers a differentiated product and high-quality customer service. It was positioned as a low-cost, low-fare airline providing quality customer service on point-to-point routes. JetBlue had a geographically diversified flight schedule that included both short-haul and long-haul routes. The mission of the company, according to David Neeleman, was "to bring humanity back to air travel." The airline focused on underserved markets and large metropolitan areas that had high average fares in order to stimulate demand. The "JetBlue effect" aspired to create fares going down, traffic going up, and JetBlue ending up with a big chunk of business (Exhibit 3).

JetBlue was committed to keeping its costs low. To achieve this objective, the company originally operated a single-type aircraft fleet comprising Airbus A320 planes as opposed to the more popular but costly Boeing 737. The A320s had 162 seats compared to 132 seats in the Boeing 737. According to JetBlue, the A320 was thus cheaper to maintain and also was more

EXHIBIT 3   **The JetBlue Effect**

Route	Increase in Daily Passengers %	Decrease in Average Fare %	JetBlue's Share of Local Traffic %
New York to Miami/Ft. Lauderdale	14%	17% (to $121.50)	23.1%
New York to Los Angeles Basin	2	26 (to $219.31)	18.0
New York to Buffalo	94	40 (to $86.09)	61.2

Figures as of second quarter, 2003.

Source: Data from Back Aviation Solutions: adapted from W. Zellner. 2004. Is JetBlue's flight plan flawed? *BusinessWeek*, February 16.

EXHIBIT 4   **JetBlue's Growth**

Year	Destinations	Employees	Operating Aircraft		
			Owned	Leased	Total
2000	12	1,174	4	6	10
2001	18	2,361	9	12	21
2002	20	4,011	21	16	37
2003	21	5,433	29	24	53
2004	30	7,211	44	25	69
2005	33	9,021	61	31	92
2006	49	10,377	70	49	119

Source: JetBlue SEC filings 2006.

fuel-efficient. Since all of JetBlue's planes were new, the costs of maintenance were also lower. In addition, the single type of aircraft kept training costs low and increased manpower utilization. JetBlue was the first to introduce the "paperless cockpit" in which pilots, equipped with laptops, had ready access to flight manuals that were constantly updated at headquarters. As a result, pilots could quickly calculate the weight and balance and take-off performance of the aircraft instead of having to download and print the manuals for making the calculations. The paperless cockpit thus ensured faster take-offs by reducing paperwork and helped in achieving quicker turnarounds and higher aircraft utilization.[11] There were no meals served on the planes, and pilots even had to be ready, if need be, to do the cleanup work on the plane to keep the time the aircraft was on the ground as short as possible. This was further helped by the airline's choice of less congested airports.[12] Innovation was everywhere; for example, there were no paper tickets to lose and no mileage statements to mail to frequent fliers. With friendly, customer service–oriented employees, new aircraft, roomy leather seats with 36 channels of free LiveTV, 100 channels of free XM satellite radio and movie channel offerings from FOXInflight, and wider legroom (one row of seats was removed from its A320 aircraft to create additional space), JetBlue promises its customers a distincitive flying experience, the "JetBlue Experience." With virtually no incidents of passengers being denied boarding; high completion factors (99.6 percent as compared to other major airlines which are at 98.3 percent); lowest incidence of delayed, mishandled or lost bags; and third lowest customer complaints, the company was indeed setting standards for low-cost operations in the industry. The company was voted the best domestic airline in the Conde Nast Traveler's Readers' Choice Awards for the fifth consecutive year and was rated the World's Best Domestic Airline by readers of *Travel + Leisure Magazine* in 2006. In addition, it also earned the Passenger Service Award from *Air Transport World*.[13]

EXPANSION AND GROWTH

Within a span of seven years of its existence, JetBlue grew to serve more than 50 destinations in 21 states, Puerto Rico, Mexico, and the Carribean. Service to about 17 new destinations began in 2006 (see Exhibit 4). In March 2007, JetBlue added services from White Plains, New York to Florida and in April 2007, it expanded services from Boston to San Diego and the Caribbean Island of Aruba. Also in summer 2007, it plans to double its services from Salt Lake City and to launch new services from this destination to San Diego and San Francisco.[14]

On the other hand, the clear divergence from its original model can be seen. From operating a single aircraft type, which was the basis of having low training costs, flexibility in manpower management, etc., the airline moved to include a second type of aircraft, the Embraer 190. The company is still not comfortable operating this type of plane. Also, JetBlue acquired LiveTV, LLC, in 2002 for $41 million in cash and the retirement of $39 million of LiveTV debt.[15] The acquisition does not necessarily represent an extension of JetBlue's core competence. Further, the company is embarking on other paths where it does not necessarily have prior experience. On February 6, 2007, *USA Today* announced that JetBlue plans to enter into an alliance with Aer Lingus, an Irish flag carrier. The alliance is expected to facilitate easy transfers to both airlines' customers but will not allow either airline to sell seats on the other airline, unlike traditional codeshare alliances, meaning customers must make individual reservations with both carriers.[16] On February 14, 2007, the first codeshare agreement with Cape Air was announced. Under this agreement, JetBlue passengers from Boston's Logan Airport will be carried to Cape Air's destinations throughout Cape Cod and the surrounding islands. Under this agreement, customers on both airlines will be able to purchase seats on both airlines under one reservation.

EXHIBIT 5   Statements of Operations Data[17]

Statements of Operations Data (in $ millions, except per share data)	Year Ended December 31				
	2006	2005	2004	2003	2002
Operating revenues	2,363	1,701	1,265	998	635
Operating expenses: Salaries, wages, and benefits	553	428	337	267	162
Aircraft fuel	752	488	255	147	76
Landing fees and other rents	158	112	92	70	44
Depreciation and amortization	151	115	77	51	27
Aircraft rent	103	74	70	60	41
Sales and marketing	104	81	63	54	44
Maintenance materials and repairs	87	64	45	23	9
Other operating expenses	328	291	215	159	127
Total operating expenses	2,236	1,653	1,154	831	530
Operating income	127	48	111	167	105
Government compensation	—	—	—	23	—
Other income (expense)	−118	−72	−36	−16	−10
Income (loss) before income taxes	9	−24	75	174	95
Income tax expense (benefit)	10	−4	29	71	40
Net income (loss)	−1	−20	46	103	55
Earnings (loss) per common share					
Basic	—	−0.13	0.3	0.71	0.49
Diluted	—	−0.13	0.28	0.64	0.37
Other Financial Data					
Operating margin %	5.4	2.8	8.8	16.8	16.5
Pre-tax margin %	0.4	−1.4	5.9	17.4	15
Ratio of earnings to fixed charges	—	—	1.6	3.1	2.7
Net cash provided by operating activities	274	170	199	287	217
Net cash used in investing activities	−1,307	−1,276	−720	−987	−880
Net cash provided by financing activities	1,037	1,093	437	789	657

On the other hand, high fuel prices, the competitive pricing environment, and other cost increases, are making it increasingly difficult to fund JetBlue's growth profitability. The airline suffered its first ever losses after its IPO in 2005. It posted net loss of $1 million and $20 million for the years ending December 31, 2006 and 2005, respectively, with the primary reasons being rising fuel costs (see Exhibit 5 and Exhibit 6). In 2006, the company modified its growth plans by reducing the number of Airbus A320 aircraft and Embraer 190 aircraft to be delivered through 2010 and by selling five Airbus A320

aircraft. In its 10-k for 2006, the company also stated it will reduce its future growth plans from previously announced levels. As much touted as its unique culture is, in 2006, the IAM (International Association of Machinists) attempted to unionize JetBlue's ramp service workers. Though the union organizing petition was dismissed by the National Mediation Board because fewer than 35 percent of eligible employees supported an election, unionization is a possibility going forward.[18] What all this means to JetBlue's cultural fabric remains yet to be seen.

EXHIBIT 6   **Operating Statistics (Unaudited)**[19]

Operating Statistics (Unaudited)*					
	Year Ended December 31				
	2006	**2005**	**2004**	**2003**	**2002**
Revenue passengers (thousands)	18,565	14,729	11,783	9,012	5,752
Revenue passenger miles (millions)	23,320	20,200	15,730	11,527	6,836
Available seat miles (ASMs) (millions)	28,594	23,703	18,911	13,639	8,240
Load factor %	81.6	85.2	83.2	84.5	83
Breakeven load factor (%)*	81.4	86.1	77.9	72.6	71.5
Aircraft utilization (hours per day)	12.7	13.4	13.4	13	12.9
Average fare ($)	119.73	110.03	103.49	107.09	106.95
Yield per passenger mile (cents)	9.53	8.02	7.75	8.37	9
Passenger revenue per ASM (cents)	7.77	6.84	6.45	7.08	7.47
Operating revenue per ASM (cents)	8.26	7.18	6.69	7.32	7.71
Operating expense per ASM (cents)	7.82	6.98	6.1	6.09	6.43
Operating expense per ASM, excluding fuel (cents)	5.19	4.92	4.75	5.01	5.51
Airline operating expense per ASM (cents)*	7.76	6.91	6.04	6.08	6.43
Departures	159,152	112,009	90,532	66,920	44,144
Average stage length (miles)	1,186	1,358	1,339	1,272	1,152
Average number of operating aircraft during period	106.5	77.5	60.6	44	27
Average fuel cost per gallon ($)	1.99	1.61	1.06	0.85	0.72
Fuel gallons consumed (millions)	377	303	241	173	106
Percent of sales through jetblue.com during period	79.1	77.5	75.4	73	63
Full-time equivalent employees at period end*	9,265	8,326	6,413	4,892	3,572

*This excludes results of employees and operations of LiveTV LLC that are unrelated to the airline operations.

Note: See Case Appendix for a glossary of terms used.

THE OPERATIONS MELTDOWN AND BEYOND[20]

Valentine's Day 2007 is perhaps the nightmare in JetBlue's hitherto glorious history for more than one reason. The event not only destroyed JetBlue's reputation for customer friendliness and cost Neeleman his job, but it also exposed the critical weaknesses in the systems at the airline that keep the operations going.

There was trouble in the Midwest for several days before the Valentine's Day storm reached the East Coast. Unlike the blowing snow and frigid temperatures that were occurring in cities like Chicago, the storm turned into freezing rain and sleet slamming the mid-Atlantic region, causing havoc on major highways, and virtually shutting down airports. Most other airlines cancelled dozens of flights in preparation for the storm. However, JetBlue management opted to wait it out. With its policy to do whatever it can to ensure a flight is completed, even if it means waiting for several hours, the airline sent outbound flights to the runway at John F. Kennedy airport in New York at about 8 a.m. This was to ensure that they were ready to take off as soon as the weather let up. But instead of letting up, the weather only deteriorated further. The federal aviation guidelines do not allow planes to take off in ice pellet conditions, and so soon planes and equipment were literally freezing to the tarmac. By about 3 p.m., with no hope of getting planes off the ground, the airline began calling in buses to bring passengers back to the terminal. However, the damage was done by then. Airport terminals, more so in the JFK hub, were filled with passengers still expecting to get on flights, and compounding the problem, they were now being joined by hundreds of infuriated passengers getting off planes. "Things spiraled out of control. We did a horrible job," said Neeleman in a conference call early the next week. "We got ourselves into a situation where we were doing rolling cancellations instead of a massive cancellation. Communications broke down, we weren't able to reach out to passengers and they continued to arrive at the airports . . . it had a cascading effect." The chaotic situation could not be brought under control for another week.

A number of shortcomings in the company's information systems were responsible for this debacle, according to Charles Mees, the new CIO who joined the company a few months before the event. The reservation system, for example, was not expanded enough to meet the extreme customer call volume. As the seriousness of the Valentine's Day situation became apparent, managers with JetBlue's Salt Lake City–based reservation office began calling in off-duty agents to assist with the expected high volume of calls. These agents otherwise primarily work from their homes, using an Internet-based communications system to tap into the company's Navitaire Open Skies reservation system (headquarted in Minneapolis, Navitaire hosts the reservation system for JetBlue and about another dozen discount airlines). The passengers who were bumped off or arrived at JFK and other East Coast airports to find their JetBlue flights had been cancelled had only one option to rebook their flights: call the JetBlue reservation office. JetBlue customers did not have an option to rebook their flights via its Web site using airport kiosks. The company has been working on the online rebooking issue since December 2006 but the new feature was not yet ready to be rolled out by February 2007. As a result, the Salt Lake City reservation agents were suddenly flooded with calls from irate passengers looking to get on another flight or to find out compensation possibilities. With Mees's emergency call to Navitaire, the system could be boosted to accommodate up to 950 agents at one time (up 300 from the original 650), but then it hit a wall. Even with the boosted capacity, there was difficulty finding enough bodies to staff the phones. Off-duty crews and airport personnel volunteered for the task, but they were not trained in how to use the system.

Also in a mess was the baggage-handling mechanism. As passengers struggled through to get reservations, their bags piled up in huge mounds at airports. Very interestingly, JetBlue did not have a computerized system in place for recording and tracking lost bags. Since the airline hardly ever cancelled flights, if there were bags left over at the end of a flight, airport personnel figured out ownership by looking up a passenger's record. However, such a process became totally unmanageable with massive cancellations happening. The airline had entered into an agreement earlier with Lufthansa in 2003 to purchase a system called BagScan, but the system was never implemented. Mees admits, "We didn't prioritize it—probably because it is

so focused on the SAP Project." JetBlue was growing fast and needed increased capabilities in the SAP ERP system to handle its human resources functions.

There were other systems headaches to deal with. JetBlue uses several applications from Sabre Airline solutions of Southlake, Texas, as part of its core operations infrastructure. This is in addition to the Navitaire reservation system. The application Sabre Flight control suite provides the airline utilities to manage, schedule, and track its planes and crews, while Sabre's Dispatch Manager is used to develop actual flight plans. Another application, Flite Trac, within the Flight Control Suite, interfaces with the Navitaire reservation system. This application provides real-time information to managers on factors such as flight status; fuel information; passenger lists; and the original, revised, estimated, and actual arrival times. Sabre CrewTrac is another application that tracks crew assignments, ensures legal requirements are met, and provides pilots and flight attendants with access to their schedules via a secure Web portal. During this disastrous event, there was a glitch between these Sabre applications and Navitaire's SkySolver that JetBlue uses to figure out the best way to emerge from flight disruptions.

Neeleman said, "We had so many people in the company who wanted to help who weren't trained to help. We had an emergency control center full of people who didn't know what to do. I had flight attendants sitting in hotel rooms for three days who couldn't get hold of us. I had pilots e-mailing me saying, 'I'm available, what do I do?'" Mees says he does not have an idea why the information could not be transferred or why the system incompatibility could not be discovered beforehand. He, of course, added that there were other day-to-day priorities to manage. "In the heat of battle at any rapidly growing company, you're always trying to address your most immediate needs," Mees said. "But you've got to continually remind yourself that you have to take a step back and look at the things that aren't right in front of you—find out what the tipping points are—before they can impact you."

Southwest by contrast handled the Valentine's Day weather disaster with ease by simply canceling most services during this period. It looked as if JetBlue had completely missed out on this obvious solution (see Exhibit 7 for direct competitor comparison).

The airline's reputation was hitting rock-bottom. Apart from announcing huge compensation to customers as refunds and future flights, which were to cost the airline about $30 million, Neeleman quickly announced the new Customer Bill of Rights. This Customer Bill of Rights basically outlined self-imposed penalties for JetBlue and major rewards for its passengers if the airline experienced operational problems and could not adjust to weather-related cancellations within a "reasonable" amount of time. For example, the bill contained provisions for notifying customers of delays prior to scheduled departure, cancellations and diversions, and their causes. It also promises that the airline will take necessary action to deplane customers if an aircraft is ground-delayed for five hours. Further, if a flight landed and

EXHIBIT 7   **Direct Competitor Comparison**

	JetBlue	AMR Corp	Southwest	UAL Corp	Delta Airlines	Major Airlines
Market Capitalization	1.89B	6.22B	11.16B	3.76B	3.60B	3.81B
Employees	8,393	86,600	32,664	55,000	51,300	49.96K
Quarterly Revenue Growth (yoy)	24.10%	1.60%	8.90%	−2.10%	11.40%	8.90%
Revenue	2.48B	22.65B	9.27B	19.25B	17.60B	17.60B
Gross Margin	30.88%	28.13%	62.99%	15.06%	18.14%	28.13%
EBITDA	311.00M	2.57B	1.36B	1.53B	1.98B	1.53B
Operating Margins	5.12%	5.27%	8.28%	2.43%	4.04%	4.38%
Net Income	9.00M	404.00M	531.00M	86.00M	−4.26B	275.57M
EPS	0.051	1.5	0.652	0.738	−21.606	1.5
P/E	208.04	17.24	21.92	45.18	N/A	15.3

Source: http://finance.yahoo.com/ as of May 2007.

was unable to taxi in to a gate right away, customers were to receive compensation between $25 to the full-amount of their one-way fare (in vouchers redeemable towards a future JetBlue flight), depending on the extent of delay.

All these announcements and even a public apology could, of course, not restore things to normalcy. Neeleman was pushed out as CEO on May 10, 2007. While this move is being framed as having been an already impending management change in view of JetBlue's outgrowing its status as an entrepreneurial venture, is JetBlue standing on thinner ice than was thought earlier?

Endnotes

1. Bachman, J. 2007. JetBlue's fiasco could improve flying. *Business-Week Online Edition,* http://www.businessweek.com/bwdaily/dnflash/content/feb2007/db20070221_ 957314_page_2.htm.

2. http://money.cnn.com/2007/05/10/news/companies/jetblue/index.htm.

3. This section draws heavily from the SEC filings of JetBlue for the year 2007. Other sources include: Zellner, W. 2003. Look who's buzzing the discounters. *BusinessWeek,* November 24; Zellner, W. 2004. Folks are finally packing their bags. *BusinessWeek,* January 12; and a joint study by Kearney, A. T., & the Society of British Aerospace Companies, The emerging airline industry, www.atkearney. com/shared_res/pdf/Emerging_Airline_Industry_S.pdf.

4. www.southwest.com/about_swa/airborne.html.

5. JetBlue SEC filings, 2006.

6. This section draws heavily from Gajilan, A. T. 2004. The amazing JetBlue. Fortune Small Business, www.fortune/ smallbusiness/articles/0.15114,444298-2,00.html.

7. Brazilian-American Chamber of Commerce of Florida. 2004. *Chamber News,* 2004 Excellence Award, www.brazilchamber.org/news/chambernews/ ExcellenceAward2004.htm.

8. JetBlue Airways Corporation, *International directory of company histories,* http://galenet.galegroup.com.

9. Gajilan, 2004. Op. cit. DiCarlo, L. 2001. Management and trends, Jet Blue skies. *Forbes.com,* January 31, www.forbes.com/2001/01/31/0131jetblue.html.

10. JetBlue IPO soars. 2002. *CNNmoney,* April 12, http://money.cnn.com/2002/04/12/markets/ipo/jetblue/.

11. WEBSMART50. 2003. *BusinessWeek,* November 24: 92.

12. Interview with David Neeleman by Willow Bay of CNN Business Unusual. 2002. Aired June 23; www.cnn.com/ TRANSCRIPTS/0206/23/bun.00.html.

13. JetBlue SEC filings, 2006.

14. From the company's press releases, www.jetblue.com.

15. From the company's press releases, www.jetblue.com.

16. JetBlue, Aer Lingus to forge world's first international discount alliance. February 6, 2007.

17. JetBlue SEC filings, 2006.

18. Schlangenstein, M. 2006. No union vote for JetBlue. *Bloomberg News.* July 19, http://findarticles.com/p/articles/mi_qn4188/is_20060719/ai_n16541848.

19. JetBlue SEC filings, 2006.

20. This section draws heavily from the following sources: Bartholomew, D., & Duvall, M. 2007. What really happened at JetBlue?, http://www.baselinemag.com/article2/0,1397,2111614,00.asp; Bailey, J. 2007. Long delays hurt image of JetBlue. *The New York Times,* p. 1.

Appendix   Glossary of Key Terms Used

aircraft utilization—The average number of block hours operated per day per aircraft for the total fleet of aircraft.

available seat miles—The number of seats available for passengers multiplied by the number of miles the seats are flown.

average fare—The average one-way fare paid per flight segment by a revenue passenger.

average stage length—Average number of miles flown per flight.

breakeven load factor—The passenger load factor that will result in operating revenues being equal to operating expenses, assuming constant revenue per passenger mile and expenses.

load factor—The percentage of aircraft seating capacity that is actually utilized (revenue passenger miles divided by available seat miles).

operating expense per available seat mile—Operating expenses divided by available seat miles.

operating revenue per available seat mile—Operating revenues divided by available seat miles.

passenger revenue per available seat mile—Passenger revenue divided by available seat miles.

revenue passenger miles—The number of miles flown by revenue passengers.

revenue passengers—The total number of paying passengers flown on all flight segments.

yield per passenger mile—The average amount one passenger pays to fly one mile.

Source: JetBlue. SEC filings, 2006.

CASE 4   Johnson & Johnson

On April 17, 2007, health care products maker Johnson & Johnson projected that its sales and profits for the current year would not be significantly affected by the decline in sales over safety concerns about its drug-coated stents. But the firm's growth in earnings had begun to fall over the last couple of years, after it had managed to deliver well over 10 percent growth each year for the previous two decades. In response to this slower growth rate, J&J's stock struggled to maintain its value, a sharp contrast to the spark that had driven its value up twentyfold since the mid-1980s.

Most of the growth for J&J has clearly been driven by the acquisitions that it has made over the years, mostly of small firms that were working on promising new products. Over the past decade, the firm made more than 60 acquisitions with a combined value that exceeds $30 billion. But the firm recently lost out to Boston Scientific in its long struggle to acquire Guidant Corporation. The acquisition would have been the largest that the firm would have made in its 120-year-old history, giving J&J a strong presence in the fast growing market for devices that stabilize heart rhythms.

William C. Weldon, chairman and chief executive officer, realizes that it is getting much harder for J&J to maintain its growth rate through a reliance on acquisitions. During 2006, the firm's biggest acquisition was the $16.6 billion purchase of consumer products from Pfizer. Although these products show greater consistency in sales growth, they provide much lower margins. But it has become increasingly difficult to spot smaller firms with promising drugs and to avoid running up against other firms that are looking to make the same kinds of deals. "You get to a point where finding acquisitions that fit the mold and make a contribution becomes increasingly difficult," warned UBS Warburg analyst David Lothson.[1]

Weldon recently told investors that his firm would search for other avenues for growth: "We'll come at it from a variety of different ways, to accelerate top- and bottom-line growth."[2] In particular, he has been trying to squeeze out more growth from J&J's existing businesses. Weldon also wants to decrease his firm's reliance on pharmaceuticals, which have consistently accounted for almost half of the firm's revenues and operating profits. Like the rest of the pharmaceutical industry, J&J has been looking at declining revenues from its best-selling drugs because of expiring patents and growing competition.

Given the scope of the businesses that J&J manages, Weldon has felt that the best opportunities may come from increased collaboration between its different units. The firm has the ability to develop new products by combining its strengths across pharmaceutical products, medical devices and diagnostics, and consumer products. But Weldon is also aware that the success of J&J has been based on the relative autonomy and independence that it has accorded its various business units. Any push

*This case was developed by Professor Jamal Shamsie, Michigan State University with the assistance of Professor Alan B. Eisner, Pace University. Material has been drawn from published sources to be used for class discussion. Copyright © 2007 Jamal Shamsie & Alan B. Eisner.

for greater collaboration must build upon the entrepreneurial spirit that has been built over the years through this type of organization.

CREATING AUTONOMOUS BUSINESS UNITS

As it has grown, J&J has developed into an astonishingly complex enterprise, made up of over 200 different businesses organized into three different divisions. The most widely known of these is the division that makes consumer products such as Band-Aid adhesive strips, Aveeno skin-care lotions and various baby products. But most of J&J's recent growth has come from its pharmaceutical products and from its medical devices and diagnostics. With revenues exceeding $50 billion, J&J has already become one of the largest health care companies in the United States (see Exhibits 1 and 2). Its competitors in this field are well aware of J&J's rare combination of scientific expertise and marketing savvy that have helped it to gain a leading position.

To a large extent, however, J&J's success across its three divisions and many different businesses has hinged on its unique structure and culture. Each of its far-flung business units has operated pretty much as an independent enterprise (see Exhibit 3). The firm has been able to turn itself into a powerhouse precisely because each of the businesses that it either buys or starts has always been granted near-total autonomy. That independence has fostered an entrepreneurial attitude that has kept J&J intensely competitive as others around it have faltered. The relative autonomy that is accorded to the business units provides the firm with the ability to respond swiftly to emerging opportunities.

In other words, the business units have been given considerable freedom to set their own strategies. Besides developing their strategies, these units are allowed to plan for their own resources. Many of the businesses even have their own finance and human resources departments. While this degree of decentralization makes for relatively high overhead costs, none of the executives that have run J&J, Weldon included, has ever thought that this was too high a price to pay. "The company really operates more like a mutual fund than anything else," commented Pat Dorsey, director of equity research at Morningstar.[3]

In spite of the benefits that J&J has derived from giving its various enterprises considerable autonomy, there is a growing feeling that they can no longer operate in near isolation. Weldon has begun to realize, as do most others in the industry, that some of the most important breakthroughs in 21st century medicine are likely to come from the ability to apply scientific advances in one discipline to another. J&J should therefore be in a strong position to exploit new opportunities by drawing on the diverse skills of its various business units across the three divisions.

PUSHING FOR SYNERGIES

Weldon strongly believed that J&J was perfectly positioned to profit from this shift toward combining drugs, devices, and diagnostics, since few companies could match its reach and strength

EXHIBIT 1   **Income Statements**

Annual Income Statement	12/31/2006	01/01/2006	01/02/2005	12/28/2003	12/29/2002
			(in $ Millions)		
Sales to customers	53,324	50,514	47,348	41,862	36,298
Cost of products sold	15,057	13,954	13,422	12,176	10,447
Gross profit	38,267	36,560	33,926	29,686	25,851
Selling, marketing, & administrative expenses	17,433	16,877	15,860	14,131	12,216
Research expense	7,125	6,312	5,203	4,684	3,957
Purchased in-process research & development expenses	559	362	18	918	189
Interest income	829	487	195	177	256
Interest expense, net of portion capitalized	63	54	187	207	160
Other income (expense), net	671	214	(15)	385	(294)
Total income (expenses), net	23,680	22,904	21,088	19,378	16,560
Earnings before taxes—U.S.	8,110	7,381	7,895	—	—
Earnings before taxes—international	6,477	6,275	4,943	—	—
Earnings before provision for taxes on income	14,587	13,656	12,838	10,308	9,291
U.S. taxes—current	3,625	2,181	3,654	2,934	2,042
International taxes—current	1,077	1,110	1,173	897	726
Total current taxes	4,702	3,291	4,827	3,831	2,768
U.S. taxes (benefit)—deferred	(726)	228	(70)	(409)	20
International taxes (benefit)—deferred	(442)	(274)	(428)	(311)	(94)
Total deferred taxes (benefit)	(1,168)	(46)	(498)	(720)	(74)
Provision for taxes on income	3,534	3,245	4,329	3,111	2,694
Net earnings	11,053	10,411	8,509	7,197	6,597
Weighted average shares outstanding—basic	2,936.4	2,973.9	2,968.4	2,968.1	2,998.3
Weighted average shares outstanding—diluted	2,961	3,012.5	3,003.5	3,008.1	3,054.1
Year-end shares outstanding	2,893.23	2,974.478	2,971.023	2,967.973	2,968.295
Net earnings per share–basic	3.76	3.5	2.87	2.42	2.2
Net earnings per share–diluted	3.73	3.46	2.84	2.4	2.16
Dividends per common share	1.455	1.275	1.095	0.925	0.795
Total number of employees	122,200	115,600	109,900	110,600	108,300
Number of common stockholders	176,808	181,031	187,840	187,708	—

Source: J&J, Mergentonline.com.

EXHIBIT 2   **Balance Sheets**

	12/31/2006	01/01/2006	01/02/2005	12/28/2003	12/29/2002
			(in $ Millions)		
Cash & cash equivalents	4,083	16,055	9,203	5,377	2,894
Marketable securities	1	83	3,681	4,146	4,581
Accounts receivable, trade, gross	8,872	7,174	7,037	6,766	5,590
Less: allowance for doubtful accounts	160	164	206	192	191
Accounts receivable, trade, net	8,712	7,010	6,831	6,574	5,399
Raw materials & supplies	980	931	964	966	835
Goods in process	1,253	1,073	1,113	981	803
Finished goods	2,656	1,955	1,667	1,641	1,665
Inventories	4,889	3,959	3,744	3,588	3,303
Deferred taxes on income	2,094	1,845	1,737	1,526	1,419
Prepaid expenses & other receivables	3,196	2,442	2,124	1,784	1,670
Total current assets	22,975	31,394	27,320	22,995	19,266
Marketable securities, noncurrent	16	20	46	84	121
Land & land improvements	611	502	515	594	472
Buildings & building equipment	7,347	5,875	5,907	5,219	4,364
Machinery & equipment	13,108	10,835	10,455	9,558	7,869
Construction in progress	2,962	2,504	1,787	1,681	1,609
Property, plant & equipment, cost	24,028	19,716	18,664	17,052	14,314
Less: accumulated depreciation	10,984	8,886	8,228	7,206	5,604
Property, plant & equipment, net	13,044	10,830	10,436	9,846	8,710
Intangible assets, net	15,348	6,185	11,842	11,539	9,246
Goodwill, net	13,340	5,990	—	—	—
Deferred taxes on income	3,210	385	551	692	236
Other assets	2,623	3,221	3,122	3,107	2,977
Total assets	70,556	58,025	53,317	48,263	40,556
Loans & notes payable	4,579	668	280	1,139	2,117
Accounts payable	5,691	4,315	5,227	4,966	3,621
Accrued liabilities	4,587	3,529	3,523	2,639	3,820
Accrued rebates, returns, & promotions	2,189	2,017	2,297	2,308	—
Accrued salaries, wages, & commissions	1,391	1,166	1,094	1,452	1,181
Accrued taxes on income	724	940	1,506	944	710
Total current liabilities	19,161	12,635	13,927	13,448	11,449
Convertible subordinated debentures	182	202	737	—	—
Debentures	1,250	1,250	1,250	—	1733

(continued)

EXHIBIT 2   **Balance Sheets** *(continued)*

	12/31/2006	01/01/2006	01/02/2005	12/28/2003	12/29/2002
			(in $ Millions)		
Notes	591	578	596	—	166
Long-term debt	2,023	2,030	2,583	—	2,099
Less: current portion	9	13	18	—	77
Total long-term debt	2,014	2,017	2,565	2,955	2,022
Deferred tax on income	1,319	211	403	780	643
Pension benefits	2,380	1,264	1,109	—	643
Postretirement benefits	2,009	1,157	1,071	—	907
Postemployment benefits	781	322	244	—	193
Deferred compensation	631	511	397	—	335
Employee-related obligations	5,584	3,065	2,631	2,262	1,967
Other liabilities	3,160	2,226	1,978	1,949	1,778
Total liabilities	31,238	20,154	21,504	—	—
Common stock	3,120	3,120	3,120	3,120	3,120
Note receivable from employee stock ownership	—	—	(11)	(18)	(25)
Foreign currency translations	(158)	(520)	(105)	(373)	—
Unrealized gains (losses) on securities	61	70	86	27	—
Pension liability adjustments	(2,030)	(320)	(346)	(64)	—
Gains (losses) on derivative hedging	9	15	(150)	(180)	—
Accumulated other comprehensive income (loss)	(2,118)	(755)	(515)	(590)	(842)
Retained earnings (accumulated deficit)	49,290	41,471	35,223	30,503	26,571
Total equity before treasury stock	50,292	43,836	37,817	33,015	28,824
Less: common stock held in treasury, at cost	10,974	5,965	6,004	6,146	6,127
Total shareholders' equity (deficit)	39,318	37,871	31,813	26,869	22,697

Source: J&J, Mergentonline.com.

in these basic areas. According to Weldon, "There is a convergence that will allow us to do things we haven't done before." [4] Indeed, J&J has top-notch products in each of those categories (see Exhibit 4). It has been boosting its research and development budget by more than 10 percent annually for the past few years, which puts it among the top spenders. It now spends about 13 percent of its sales, or $6.5 billion, on over 9,000 scientists working in research laboratories around the world.

Weldon believed however, that J&J could profit from this convergence by finding ways to make its fiercely independent businesses work together. Through pushing these units to pool their resources, Weldon believed that the firm could become one of the few that may actually be able to attain that often-promised, rarely delivered idea of synergy. Some of the firm's new products, such as the new Cyper drug-coated stent, had clearly resulted from the collaborative efforts and

EXHIBIT 3   **Segment Information**

Johnson & Johnson is made up of over 200 different companies, many of which it has acquired over the years. These individual companies have been assigned to three different divisions:

Pharmaceuticals

Share of Firm's 2006 Sales: 44%

Share of Firm's 2001 Sales: 46%

Share of Firm's 2006 Operating Profits: 46%

Share of Firm's 2001 Operating Profits: 63%

Medical Devices

Share of Firm's 2006 Sales: 38%

Share of Firm's 2001 Sales: 35%

Share of Firm's 2006 Operating Profits: 43%

Share of Firm's 2001 Operating Profits: 25%

Consumer Products

Share of Firm's 2006 Sales: 18%

Share of Firm's 2001 Sales: 20%

Share of Firm's 2006 Operating Profits: 11%

Share of Firm's 2001 Operating Profits: 12%

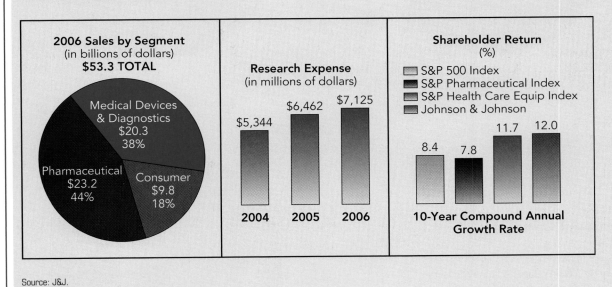

2006 Sales by Segment
(in billions of dollars)
$53.3 TOTAL

Medical Devices & Diagnostics $20.3 38%

Pharmaceutical $23.2 44%

Consumer $9.8 18%

Research Expense
(in millions of dollars)

$5,344 $6,462 $7,125

2004   2005   2006

Shareholder Return
(%)

- S&P 500 Index
- S&P Pharmaceutical Index
- S&P Health Care Equip Index
- Johnson & Johnson

8.4   7.8   11.7   12.0

10-Year Compound Annual Growth Rate

Source: J&J.

sharing of ideas between its various far-flung divisions (see Exhibit 5).

Weldon's vision for the new J&J may well have emerged from the steps that he took to reshape the pharmaceutical operation shortly after he took it over in 1998. At the time, J&J's drug business had been making solid gains as a result of popular products such as the anemia drug Procrit and the anti-psychotic medication Risperdal. But Weldon did expect that regulatory

EXHIBIT 4   **Key Brands**

Pharmaceuticals

Risperdal for schizophrenia
Procrit for anemia
Remicade for rheumatoid arthritis
Topamix for epilepsy

Medical Devices

Depuy orthopedic joint reconstruction products
Cordis Cypher stents
Ethicon endo surgery products
Lifescan diabetic testing products

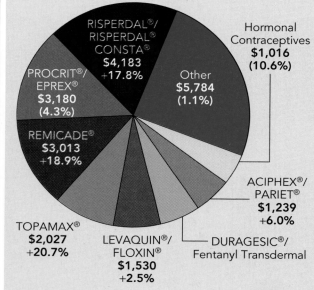

Pharmaceutical Segment Sales
Sales by Major Product
2006 Sales: $23,267 million Growth Rate: 4.2%
(in millions of dollars)

RISPERDAL®/ RISPERDAL® CONSTA® $4,183 +17.8%
PROCRIT®/ EPREX® $3,180 (4.3%)
REMICADE® $3,013 +18.9%
TOPAMAX® $2,027 +20.7%
LEVAQUIN®/ FLOXIN® $1,530 +2.5%
DURAGESIC®/ Fentanyl Transdermal
ACIPHEX®/ PARIET® $1,239 +6.0%
Other $5,784 (1.1%)
Hormonal Contraceptives $1,016 (10.6%)

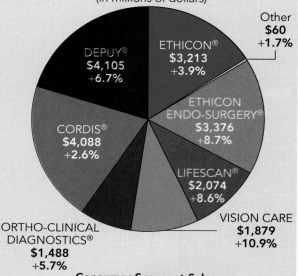

Medical Devices & Diagnostics Segment Sales
Sales by Major Franchise
2006 Sales: $20,283 million Growth Rate: 6.2%
(in millions of dollars)

DEPUY® $4,105 +6.7%
ETHICON® $3,213 +3.9%
Other $60 +1.7%
ETHICON ENDO-SURGERY® $3,376 +8.7%
CORDIS® $4,088 +2.6%
LIFESCAN® $2,074 +8.6%
VISION CARE $1,879 +10.9%
ORTHO-CLINICAL DIAGNOSTICS® $1,488 +5.7%

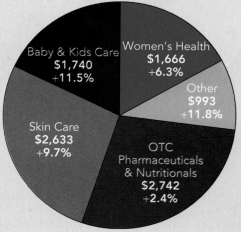

Consumer Segment Sales
Sales by Major Franchise
2006 Sales: $9,774 million Growth Rate: 7.5%
(in millions of dollars)

Baby & Kids Care $1,740 +11.5%
Women's Health $1,666 +6.3%
Other $993 +11.8%
Skin Care $2,633 +9.7%
OTC Pharmaceuticals & Nutritionals $2,742 +2.4%

Consumer Products

Tylenol pain killers
Splenda sweetners
Johnson & Johnson baby care products
Stay Free women's health products

Source: J&J 2006 Annual Report.

EXHIBIT 5   **Synergies at J&J**

Improved Drugs

J&J's pharmaceutical operation is working with the company's drug-delivery operation, Alza, to come up with a new formulation of the epilepsy drug Topamax. The drug has been shown to also promote weight loss, and this would make it a more tolerable obesity treatment.

New Medical Tests

A new diagnostic unit is working with data generated by drug researchers; they could, for example, develop a gene-based test to identify patients most likely to respond to experimental cancer treatments.

Cutting-edge Consumer Products

In 2002, J&J rolled out the new Band-Aid Brand Liquid Bandage, a liquid coating that is applied to cuts on hard-to-cover areas like fingers and knuckles. The product is based on a material used in a wound-closing product sold by J&J's hospital-products company, Ethicon.

Source: Barrett, Amy, "Staying on Top," *BusinessWeek*, May 5, 2003, p. 60.

hurdles and competitive challenges would cut into the revenues and profits that his firm could derive from pharmaceuticals.

Consequently, Weldon felt that J&J should try to increase its efforts to develop new drugs that might become blockbusters. Towards this end, he created a new post to oversee all of the pharmaceutical division's R&D efforts. He also formed a divisional committee that brought together executives from R&D with those from sales and marketing to decide which projects to green-light. Up until then, the R&D group had made these critical decisions on their own without the involvement of any other departments.

But Weldon felt that his firm could further increase its new product development and reduce its dependence upon drugs through interaction between the business units that lie across its pharmaceutical, medical devices, and consumer products divisions. Such a push for communication and coordination would allow J&J to develop the synergy that Weldon was seeking. But any effort to get the different business units to collaborate must not quash the entrepreneurial spirit that has spearheaded most of the growth of the firm to date. Jerry Caccott, managing director of consulting firm Strategic Decisions Group, emphasized that cultivating those alliances "would be challenging in any organization, but particularly in an organization that has been so successful because of its decentralized culture."[5]

SHIFTING THE COMPANY CULTURE

Weldon, like every other leader in the company's history, has worked his way up through the ranks. His long tenure within the firm has turned him into a true believer in the J&J system. He certainly does not want to undermine the entrepreneurial spirit that has resulted from the autonomy that has been given to each of the businesses. Consequently, even though Weldon may talk incessantly about synergy and convergence, he has been cautious in the actual steps he has taken to push J&J's units to collaborate with each other.

For the most part, Weldon has confined himself to the development of new systems to foster better communication and more frequent collaboration among J&J's disparate operations. Among other things, he has worked with James T. Lenehan, vice chairman and president of J&J, to set up groups that draw people from across the firm to focus their efforts on specific diseases. Each of the groups is expected to report every six months on potential strategies and projects.

Although most of the changes that Weldon has instituted at J&J are not likely to yield real results for some time, there is already some evidence that this new collaboration is working. Perhaps the most promising result of this approach has been J&J's drug-coated stent, called Cypher. The highly successful new addition to the firm's lineup was a result of the efforts of teams that combined people from the drug business with others from the device business. They collaborated on manufacturing the stent, which props open arteries after angioplasty. Weldon claims that if J&J had not been able to bring together people with different types of expertise, it could not have developed the stent without getting assistance from outside the firm.

Even the company's fabled consumer brands have been starting to show growth as a result of increased collaboration between the consumer products and pharmaceutical divisions. Its new liquid Band-Aid is based on a material used in a wound-closing product sold by one of J&J's hospital-supply businesses. And J&J has used its prescription antifungal treatment, Nizoral, to develop a dandruff shampoo. In fact, products that have developed in large part out of such a form of cross-fertilization have allowed the firm's consumer business to grow by 2 to 3 percent per year over the last four years.

Some of the projects that J&J is currently working on could produce even more significant results. Researchers working on genomic studies in the firm's labs were building a massive data-base using gene patterns that correlate to a certain disease or to someone's likely response to a particular drug. Weldon encouraged them to share this data with the various business units. As a result, the diagnostics team has been working on a test that the researchers in the pharmaceutical division could use to predict which patients would benefit from an experimental cancer therapy.

MAINTAINING THE PRESSURE

Even as Weldon moves carefully to encourage collaboration between the business units, he has continued to push for the highest possible levels of performance. Those who know him well would say that he is compulsively competitive. As Weldon has been known to state on more than one occasion, "It's no fun to be second."[6] He is such an intense athlete that he was just a sprint away from ruining his knee altogether when he finally decided to give up playing basketball.

Weldon is not discouraged by setbacks, such as J&J has been facing in its pharmaceutical business. At this point, several of J&J's important drugs are under assault from competitors. The recent expiry of the patent on the firms' blockbuster pain drug, Duragesic, has resulted in a significant drop in its sales. Its well-known anemia drug Procit has been dealing with rising competition and with growing safety concerns. Furthermore, a new anti-psychosis drug, called Invega, recently launched to replace a best-selling older drug, Risperdal, has shown lackluster sales in its first few months. Attempts to launch other new drugs have run into regulatory hurdles with the Food and Drug Administration. "We are seeing increasing risk aversion among regulators, influenced by growing political sentiment for risk-free medicine," explained Weldon.[7]

Weldon is confident that the various divisions will find ways to deal with the challenges that they face. According to Vice Chairman Christine A. Poon, who leads the firm's pharmaceutical group, "We'll deal with these external challenges as we have always."[8] In fact, sales of schizophrenia drug Risperdal and rheumatoid-arthritis drug Remicade have continued to show growth, even as their patents are set to expire and they are facing growing competition. And despite a drop in sales arising out of safety concerns, J&J's Cypher drug stent continues to be a market leader.

For the most part, Weldon is also letting his managers make their own decisions on the teams where they are working with each other on various projects. He usually does like to get briefed once a month on the progress that is being made on these projects. Beyond that, Weldon claims that he likes to trust his people. "They are the experts who know the marketplace, know the hospitals, and know the cardiologists," Weldon said about the team that has been working on the Cypher stent. "I have the utmost confidence in them."[9]

Even as Weldon tries to let his managers handle their own affairs, he clearly expects them to seek results with the same tenacity that he displayed in his climb to the top. As he rose through the ranks at J&J, Weldon became famous for setting near-impossible goals for his people and holding them to it. And for those executives who may fall short, Weldon does not usually have any difficulty in making it clear that he does not like to be disappointed. When a new J&J drug business, Centocor Incorporated, failed to meet the aggressive sales goals it was set for 2000, Weldon was at its headquarters before the week was out. Everyone at the firm knew they could not allow their performance to fall below the targeted level for the next year.

IS THERE A CURE AHEAD?

Weldon realizes that J&J may face a few challenges over the next couple of years as it tries to find new blockbusters to replace those that are likely to show less growth potential. In both its medical devices and its pharmaceuticals businesses, the firm is confronting growing safety concerns, higher levels of competition and greater pricing uncertainty. Consequently, the firm may have to accept lower growth rates over the short term. "We don't commit to double-digit growth every single year, but we do have this goal of delivering that kind of growth over long periods of time," said Poon.[10]

J&J is in the final stages of acquiring the consumer health care unit of Pfizer, which will result in the addition of more familiar brands such as Listerine mouthwash and Visine eye drops. The purchase of Pfizer's brands will continue to reduce the firm's dependence on the volatile pharmaceuticals business and boost the share of consumer products to almost 25 percent of total sales. Commenting on the acquisition, Weldon explained: "It took some risk out because it doesn't have the volatility of others, but it also just enhances our opportunities as we go further into the future."[11]

But it is becoming much more difficult to find promising acquisitions that do not command a high price. Without reliance on acquisitions for its growth, Weldon will need to draw on all of his competitive spirit to maintain J&J's growth trajectory. He recently announced that the firm has at least 10 new drugs in the late stages of development, some of which could become blockbusters. These would compete for a share of promising markets such as for thinning blood and for treating hepatitis. Above all, Weldon has high hopes for more products that will be developed as a result of his efforts to get different business units across different divisions of J&J to work together. Cross-divisional teams have been working on possible new treatments for diabetes and for stroke.

But it is clear that as Weldon searches for various avenues to maintain J&J's growth record, he must find ways to encourage its businesses to work more closely together than they have ever done in the past. The firm can tap into many more opportunities when it tries to bring together the various skills that it has managed to develop across different divisions. At the same time, he is acutely aware that much of the firm's success has resulted from the relative autonomy that it has granted to each of its business units. Weldon knows that even as he strives to push for more collaborative effort, he does not want to threaten the entrepreneurial spirit that has served J&J so well.

Endnotes

1. Barrett, A. 2003. Staying on top. *BusinessWeek,* May 5: 61

2. Bowe, C. 2006. J&J reveals its guidant motive. *Financial Times,* January 25: 17.

3. Preston, H. H. 2005. Drug giant provides a model of consistency. *Herald Tribune,* March 12–13: 12.

4. *BusinessWeek.* 2003. May 5: 62.

5. *BusinessWeek.* 2003. May 5: 62.

6. *BusinessWeek.* 2003. May 5: 62.

7. Hensley, S. 2006 J&J's Drug sales hurt revenue. *The Wall Street Journal,* January 25: A3.

8. Barrett, A. 2004. Toughing out the drought. *BusinessWeek,* January 26: 85.

9. *BusinessWeek.* 2003. May 5: 66.

10. Weintraub, A. 2007. Under the weather at J&J. *BusinessWeek,* April 23: 82.

11. Johnson, J&J's consumer play paces growth. *The Wall Street Journal,* January 24: A3.

CASE 5   Yahoo!

Terry Semel, who had headed Yahoo! since 2001, resigned from his position as CEO after shareholders expressed dissatisfaction with his performance at the annual shareholders meeting on June 12, 2007. In particular, shareholders complained about the

*This case was developed by Professor Jamal Shamsie, Michigan State University with the assistance of Professor Alan B. Eisner, Pace University. Material has been drawn from published sources to be used for class discussion. Copyright © 2007 Jamal Shamsie & Alan B. Eisner.

$71.7 million that the former Hollywood mogul received in 2006, putting him at the top of the list of highest-paid CEOs among Standard & Poor's 500 companies. Semel's compensation drew a strong reaction from shareholders because the shares of Yahoo! have dropped 10 percent over the last year, and its revenue growth has fallen in each of the last four quarters (see Exhibits 1 and 2).

Yahoo! has trailed Google in revenues and profits largely because it has not been able to match its rival in crucial areas

EXHIBIT 1   Income Statements

	2006	2005	2004	2003	2002
	(in $ millions)				
Revenue	6,425.68	5,257.67	3,574.52	1,625.1	953.07
Total Revenue	**6,425.68**	**5,257.67**	**3,574.52**	**1,625.1**	**953.07**
Cost of Revenue, Total	2,669.1	2,096.2	1,342.34	370.09	162.88
Gross Profit	**3,756.58**	**3,161.47**	**2,232.18**	**1,255.01**	**790.19**
Selling/General/Administrative Expenses, Total	2,002.49	1,397.41	1,072.92	709.67	539.05
Research & Development	688.34	547.14	368.76	207.29	141.77
Depreciation/Amortization	124.79	109.2	101.92	42.39	21.19
Interest Expense (Income), Net Operating	0.0	0.0	0.0	0.0	0.0
Unusual Expense (Income)	0.0	0.0	0.0	0.0	0.0
Other Operating Expenses, Total	0.0	0.0	0.0	0.0	0.0
Operating Income	**940.97**	**1,107.73**	**688.58**	**295.67**	**88.19**
Interest Income (Expense), Net Nonoperating	139.78	1,092.45	475.96	45.98	87.69
Gain (Loss) on Sale of Assets	15.16	337.97	0.0	0.0	0.0
Other, Net	2.09	5.44	20.49	1.53	2.35
Income Before Tax	**1,098.0**	**2,543.58**	**1,185.02**	**343.17**	**178.23**
Income Tax—Total	458.01	767.82	437.97	147.02	71.29
Income After Tax	**639.99**	**1,775.77**	**747.06**	**196.15**	**106.94**
Minority Interest	−0.71	−7.78	−2.5	−5.92	0.0
Equity In Affiliates	112.11	128.24	94.99	47.65	0.0
U.S. GAAP Adjustment	0.0	0.0	0.0	0.0	0.0
Net Income Before Extra Items	**751.39**	**1,896.23**	**839.55**	**237.88**	**106.94**
Total Extraordinary Items	0.0	0.0	0.0	0.0	−64.12
Accounting Change	0.0	0.0	0.0	0.0	−64.12
Net Income	**751.39**	**1,896.23**	**839.55**	**237.88**	**42.82**

Source: Yahoo!

EXHIBIT 2   **Balance Sheets**

	2006	2005	2004	2003	2002
			(in $ millions)		
Assets					
Cash and Short-Term Investments	2,601.4	2,560.83	3,511.98	1,309.52	774.18
Cash & Equivalents	1,569.87	1,429.69	823.72	415.89	310.97
Short-Term Investments	1,031.53	1,131.14	2,688.25	893.63	463.2
Total Receivables, Net	930.96	721.72	479.99	282.42	113.61
Accounts Receivable–Trade, Net	930.96	721.72	479.99	282.42	113.61
Accounts Receivable–Trade, Gross	969.16	763.58	514.21	314.38	137.46
Provision for Doubtful Accounts	−38.2	−41.86	−34.22	−31.96	−23.85
Total Inventory	0.0	0.0	0.0	0.0	0.0
Prepaid Expenses	68.81	70.71	72.62	50.99	82.22
Other Current Assets, Total	148.97	96.27	25.89	78.79	0.0
Total Current Assets	**3,750.14**	**3,449.53**	**4,090.48**	**1,721.71**	**970.0**
Property/Plant/Equipment, Total–Net	955.3	648.9	531.7	449.51	371.27
Goodwill, Net	2,968.56	2,895.56	2,550.96	1,805.56	415.23
Intangibles, Net	405.82	534.62	480.67	445.64	96.25
Long-Term Investments	2,873.12	3,200.34	1,295.37	1,447.63	763.41
Note Receivable–Long Term	0.0	0.0	0.0	0.0	0.0
Other Long-Term Assets, Total	560.67	102.9	229.04	61.6	174.02
Other Assets, Total	0.0	0.0	0.0	0.0	0.0
Total Assets	**11,513.61**	**10,831.83**	**9,178.2**	**5,931.65**	**2,790.18**
Liabilities and Shareholders' Equity					
Accounts Payable	109.13	70.29	48.21	31.89	18.74
Payable/Accrued	0.0	0.0	0.0	0.0	0.0
Accrued Expenses	1,035.12	826.64	657.2	483.63	257.58
Notes Payable/Short-Term Debt	0.0	0.0	0.0	0.0	0.0
Current Port. of LT Debt/Capital Leases	0.0	0.0	0.0	0.0	0.0
Other Current Liabilities, Total	329.74	307.13	475.3	192.28	135.5
Total Current Liabilities	**1,473.99**	**1,204.05**	**1,180.71**	**707.8**	**411.81**
Total Long Term Debt	749.92	750.0	750.0	750.0	0.0
Long-Term Debt	749.92	750.0	750.0	750.0	0.0
Deferred Income Tax	19.2	243.58	35.77	72.37	0.0
Minority Interest	8.06	0.0	44.27	37.48	31.56
Other Liabilities, Total	101.83	67.8	66.01	0.52	84.54
Total Liabilities	**2,353.0**	**2,265.42**	**2,076.76**	**1,568.16**	**527.91**
Common Stock	1.49	1.47	1.42	1.35	0.61
Additional Paid-In Capital	8,615.92	6,417.86	5,682.88	4,340.51	2,430.22
Retained Earnings (Accumulated Deficit)	3,717.56	2,966.17	1,069.94	230.39	−7.49
Treasury Stock–Common	−3,324.86	−547.72	−159.99	−159.99	−159.99
Other Equity, Total	150.51	−271.36	507.2	−48.78	−1.08
Total Equity	**9,160.61**	**8,566.42**	**7,101.45**	**4,363.49**	**2,262.27**
Total Liabilities & Shareholders' Equity	**11,513.61**	**10,831.83**	**9,178.2**	**5,931.65**	**2,790.18**
Total Common Shares Outstanding	1,360.25	1,430.16	1,383.58	1,321.41	1,189.72

Source: Yahoo!

of Web search and related advertising. Semel had shaken up his firm's management in December and launched its much-delayed search advertising system known as Project Panama in February. The new system had promised to deliver more targeted ads with search results, an area in which Google's technology holds a big edge. "Our goal is to create an advertising platform that takes advantage of Yahoo!, which has the largest network of both users and content in the world," said CEO Terry S. Semel.[1]

The eagerly awaited Panama, on which the firm has been working for the past 18 months, was expected to allow Yahoo! to close the gap with Google in the search for search advertising dollars. But Tim Cadogan, vice president for Yahoo! Search Marketing, had been worried about high expectations. "Panama is a foundation for us to start sewing together all our advertising assets," he said. "I don't think it gets us ahead. It gets us to a place where we can compete more effectively."[2]

Semel was persuaded by Yahoo! cofounder Jerry Yang to come out of retirement in 2001 to take over the floundering firm. Advertising revenues at the Internet icon had been plummeting, leading to a precipitous decline in its stock value. When he took over, Semel articulated a basic strategy to build the Yahoo! Web site into a digital form of Disneyland, a souped-up theme park for the Internet Age. His goal has been to build the Yahoo! site into a self-contained world of irresistible offerings that would grab and keep surfers glued to it for hours at a time. By imposing such a strong sense of direction, he managed to craft one of the most remarkable revivals of a beleaguered dot-com.

In spite of his significant accomplishments, Semel had been under considerable pressure to build on opportunities for the future growth of Yahoo!. He had failed to clinch some crucial deals, including one with Facebook, one of the hottest social-networking Web sites. Morale among the firm's employees had begun to sag as some of the top talent had been defecting to the developing competition. More critically, Yahoo! had begun to show slower growth in display advertising, which had long represented one of its key strengths. All of these developments had led Ellen Siminoff, a former Yahoo! executive, to state, "Panama is very important to Yahoo!, but it is not the only thing they need to focus on."[3]

REMAKING THE CULTURE

Like many other Internet firms, Yahoo! began by attracting visitors by developing a site that would offer a variety of services for free. Those who logged on were able to obtain, among other things, the latest stock quotes and news headlines. The firm relied on online advertising for as much as 90 percent of its revenue. Yahoo! founders Koogle and Yang were confident that advertisers would continue to pay in order to reach its younger and technologically savy surfers. In fact, the firm had made little effort to reach out to clients or to try to build any long-term relationships with them.

By the spring of 2001, Yahoo!'s advertising revenue was falling precipitously, its stock was losing most of its value, and

some observers were questioning the firm's business model. With the collapse of the dot-com advertisers, the firm's revenue was down by almost a third from the previous year. Its stock had fallen below an all-time low of $15, having lost more than two-thirds of its value from just two years earlier. Semel was asked to help turn Yahoo! around, but he agreed to take on the task only after the firm's admired cofounder Timothy Koogle had agreed to step down as chairman.

When Semel took over, the changes that he set about making may not have been evident to the casual observer. Visitors to Yahoo!'s headquarters could still see the purple cow in the lobby, be confronted with acres of cubicles, and meet workers clad in jeans. But Semel's style was in stark contrast to the relaxed, laid-back approach of Koogle. He immediately started to work on replacing Yahoo!'s freewheeling culture with a much more deliberate sense of order. Semel moved swiftly to chop down the 44 business units he inherited to 5, stripping many executives of pet projects. He did not care much for the firms's "cubicles only" policy, finally locating his own office in a cube adjacent to a conference room so he could make phone calls in private.

Semel even changed Yahoo!'s old freewheeling approach to decision making. When Koogle was in charge, executives would brainstorm for hours, often following hunches with new initiatives. Under Semel, managers have been required to make formal presentations to bring up their new ideas in weekly meetings of a group called the Product Council. Championed by Semel and his chief operating officer, Daniel Rosensweig, the Product Council has typically included nine managers from all corners of the company. The group sizes up business plans to make sure all new projects bring benefits to Yahoo!'s existing businesses.

"We need to work within a framework," said Semel. "If it's a free-for-all . . . we won't take advantage of the strengths of our company."[4] With the focus and discipline that he imposed on the firm, Semel made some progress in getting Yahoo! to grow again. Most of the employees, who had been anxious to see the value of their stock rise again, began to support Semel in his efforts to remake Yahoo!. "People don't always agree with the direction they're getting, but they're happy the direction is there," said a Yahoo! manager who requested anonymity.[5]

RETHINKING THE BUSINESS MODEL

Semel began turning Yahoo! around by wooing traditional advertisers, making gestures to advertising agencies that it had angered with its arrogance during the boom. He tried to attract back the business of big advertisers by using technology that allowed the Web site to move beyond static banner advertising, offering eye-catching animation, videos, and other rich-media formats. As a result of these efforts, Yahoo! was able to show a significant increase in its advertising revenues benefiting in part from the gradual resurgence in online advertising (see Exhibit 3).

Semel also used the deal-making skills that made him a legend in the movie business to land crucial acquisitions and partnerships that would allow Yahoo! to tap into new sources of

EXHIBIT 3   Breakdown of Revenues

	Advertising	Fees
	(in $ millions)	
2006	5,627	798
2005	4,594	664
2004	3,127	447
2003	1,322	303
	U.S.	Foreign
2006	4,366	2,060
2005	3,668	1,590
2004	2,653	921
2003	1,355	270

Source: Yahoo!

advertising revenue (see Exhibit 4). His biggest was a $1.8 billion deal for Overture Services, whose "pay per click" lets advertisers buy placement next to search results. The move allowed Yahoo! to move away from its reliance on Google for search capabilities, which Semel saw as a growing rival. It was

EXHIBIT 4   Significant Acquisitions

2006	Flickr
	Photo sharing
	Del.icio.us
	Social book marking
2005	Verdisoft
	Software development
2004	Musicmatch
	Personalized music
	Kelkoo
	Online consumer shopping
2003	Overture
	Search advertising
	Inktomi
	Search

Source: Yahoo!

also expected to provide Yahoo! with a substantial new stream of revenue from a new form of search-related advertising.

But Semel did not want Yahoo! to rely primarily on advertising revenues. He has been trying to add services that consumers would be willing to pay for. The strategy has been slow to put into place. When Semel took over, he was shocked to find out that Yahoo! did not have the technology in place to handle surging demand for paid services such as online personals, say two former executives. He had to crack down on the firm to whip it into shape to handle the addition of such premium services.

With the capabilities in place, Semel also began making acquisitions that would allow Yahoo! to offer more premium services. One of the first of these was the buyout of HotJobs .com in 2002, which moved the firm into the online job-hunting business. Semel followed up with the acquisition of online music service Musicmatch Inc., hoping to bring more subscribers into the Yahoo! fold. Over the last year, the firm has acquired more promising firms such as Flickr, a photo-sharing site, and Del.icio.us, a bookmark-sharing site (see Exhibit 5 for key Yahoo! offerings).

By making such smart deals, Semel built Yahoo! into a site that can offer surfers many different services, with several of them requiring the customer to pay a small fee. The idea has been to coax Web surfers to spend hard cash on everything from digital music and online games to job listings and premium e-mail accounts with loads of extra storage. Semel hoped that the contribution from such paid services would continue to rise over the next few years, allowing the firm to rely less heavily on advertising. He talked about the opportunities that would be provided by premium services: "We planted a lot of seeds . . . and some are beginning to grow."[6]

BUILDING A THEME PARK

In order to build upon the foundation that he has already laid, Semel envisions building Yahoo! into a digital Disneyland, a souped-up theme park for the Internet Age. The idea is that Web surfers logging on to Yahoo!'s site, like customers squeezing through the turnstiles in Anaheim, should find themselves in a self-contained world full of irresistible offerings. Instead of Yahoo! being an impartial tour guide to the Web, it should be able to entice surfers to stay inside its walls as long as possible.

This vision for Yahoo! represents a drastic change from the model that had been developed by its original founders. Koogle had let his executives develop various offerings that operated relatively independently. Managers had built up their own niches around the main Yahoo! site. No one had thought about developing the portal as a whole, much less how the various bits and pieces could work together. "Managers would beg, borrow, and steal from the network to help their own properties," said Greg Coleman, Yahoo!'s executive vice president for media and sales.[7]

Semel pushed to stitch it all together. He demanded that Yahoo!'s myriad offerings from e-mail accounts to stock quotes to job listings interact with each other. Semel calls this concept "network optimization" and regards this as a key goal for the

EXHIBIT 5   **Key Yahoo! Offerings**

Search

Yahoo! Search

Yahoo! Local

Yahoo! Yellow Pages

Yahoo! Maps

Marketplace

Yahoo! Shopping

Yahoo! Real Estate

Yahoo! Travel

Yahoo! Personals

Yahoo! HotJobs

Information & Entertainment

My Yahoo!

Yahoo! News

Yahoo! Finance

Yahoo! Sports

Yahoo! Music

Yahoo! Movies

Yahoo! Games

Communications

Yahoo! Mail

Yahoo! Messenger

Yahoo! Photos

Yahoo! Mobile

Source: Yahoo!

EXHIBIT 6   **Search Site Rankings**

October 2006 Share of U.S. Search Audience	
Google	45.4%
Yahoo!	28.2%
MSN	11.7%
Ask Jeeves	5.8%
AOL	5.4%
All Others	3.5%

Source: comScore Media Metrix.

music and interactive games, are data hogs that appeal mostly to surfers who have high-speed links. Furthermore, since broadband is always on, many of Yahoo!'s customers are more likely to be be lingering in Semel's theme park for hours on end, day after day. "The more time you spend on Yahoo!, the more apt you are to sample both free and paid services," he said.[8]

SEARCHING FOR A FOCUS

In spite of Semel's efforts to tightly control the growth of Yahoo! into new areas, the push to develop a digital theme park has led some analysts to question whether the firm has spread itself too thin (see Exhibit 6). Few people inside Yahoo! question its goal of providing a broad range of services that can attract an audience that can be sold to advertisers. But Brad Garlinghouse, a senior Yahoo! vice president, who once shaved a "Y" in the back of his head, has argued that the firm needs to focus on a few areas. This would allow the Web site to make heavier investments in activities in which it thinks it can excel and move away from others that it does not regard as essential.

In particular, there has been some concern about Yahoo!'s lack of relative success in new areas that are likely to fuel future growth. The firm ran into problems with its move into video programming. It recruited some talent from Hollywood to develop new video-focused Web sites, but dropped the idea because of considerable internal resistance. Subsequently, the media group and the search group fought with each other to offer a service for users to upload their own video clips. The delay allowed YouTube, a start-up, to dominate the market.

Yahoo! took the early lead in social networking with the 2005 acquisition of Flickr, a popular photo-sharing site. Since then, however, its efforts have been overshadowed by the acquisition of MySpace by News Corporation and YouTube by Google. Rob Norman, a WPP Group executive, claimed that these represented opportunities that Semel failed to pursue: "Yahoo! had every single asset you would have needed to do those bigger, faster, and sooner than anyone else."[9] Meanwhile, Yahoo! has failed to make much headway with Yahoo! 360, its

firm. To make this concept work, every initiative should not only make money but also feed Yahoo!'s other businesses. Most of the focus of the Product Council meetings had been on the painstaking job of establishing these interconnections between the various services that were offered on the site.

With these constraints, it has become much harder for new projects to get approved. Semel was determined to have any new offerings tied in with what was already being offered on Yahoo! He claimed this made them easier for customers to find, increasing their chances of success. Although many different ideas are always under consideration, only a few are eventually offered by Yahoo!.

A key element of Semel's strategy to build Yahoo! into a digital theme park also rested on his ability to push customers into broadband. Lots of the services that he banked on, such as own social networking site. Semel then began looking at a deal to buy Facebook, a social networking site that is popular among college students.

Semel recently acknowledged that Yahoo! needed to sharpen its focus on key areas. "We've got to get back to basics and again zero in on a few key priorities," he recently stated. "I am not satisfied with our current financial performance and we intend to improve it."[10] The areas that Yahoo! expects to focus on include search and display advertising, video clips, and social media. It is expected that services for individuals such as online dating and services for small businesses such as Web hosting are likely to be dropped.

Garlinghouse believes that efforts to focus the firm would result in more focused responsibilities and speedier decision making. Yahoo!'s attempts to offer a wide variety of services have led to a proliferation of new executive hires, which have contributed to a growth of conflict between various business units. There was a push to create managerial positions to take charge of each of the areas that the firm wanted to develop. He was considering replacing the current "matrix" structure that involved many executives with the appointment of managers who would take responsibility for bottom-line results in their respective areas.

BACK TO THE FUTURE?

Although Semel resigned from his position as chief executive, he did agree to stay on as nonexecutive chairman of the board. This allowed the firm to deal with the shareholder concerns about his hefty compensation. But many analysts believed that Semel did deserve to be rewarded for pulling off a stunning revival of a floundering firm by cutting costs, imposing discipline, and making deals. At the same time, Yahoo!'s growth in revenues and profits has fallen further and further behind those of Google. Semel had argued that Yahoo! is more of an all-round media company that competes in searches with Google, in e-mail with Microsoft, in instant messaging with AOL, in news with CNN, and in social networking with MySpace.

Above all, Semel had been well aware that Yahoo! was not the only player with aspirations to becoming a digital theme park. Given the scope of its ambitions, critics have argued that Semel should have moved more aggressively to close the deals that are necessary to make sure that Yahoo! holds on to its status as the world's most popular Web site. "When you become Yahoo!'s size, you become a little complacent, a little fat and happy," said Youssef H. Squali, an analyst for Jefferies and Company.[11] An outside advisor to the firm believes that the firm had fallen behind because it took too much time to make decisions as a result of Semel's low-risk, nonconfrontational nature. At the same time, some people who are close to the company have argued that its decision not to buy high-flying start-up businesses such as MySpace or YouTube represented sound financial management that is likely to pay off in the long run.

With Semel's departure, Jerry Yang, one of the two founders who had continued to serve on the board, took over the job on a temporary basis. Unlike his predecessor, Yang may be able to

EXHIBIT 7   **Direct Competitor Comparison**

	Yahoo!	Google
Market Cap:	38.51B	155.38B
Employees:	11,400	10,674
Quarterly Revenue Growth:	6.70%	62.60%
Revenue:	6.53B	12.02B
Gross Margin:	60.01%	60.29%
EBITDA:	2.05B	5.23B
Operating Margins:	13.92%	33.62%
Net Income:	733.96M	3.49B

Source: Yahoo! Finance.

use his technical background to turn around the morale, which has been dropping as a result of the departure of some of the firm's top talent. He may also be much better at challenging the engineers and bringing in new ones. Yang may also be better at clinching deals with some of the entrepreneurial start-ups that Yahoo! needs to acquire in order to keep growing.

In spite of the slower growth, few observers would question the ability of Yahoo! to survive and grow even in a more intensely competitive environment. They believe that Semel has already managed to build Yahoo! into a brand that will be able to hold its own against formidable rivals. It is expected that under Yang, the firm will be able to move on to tackle the other challenges that it faces. "We are a healthy paranoid company," said Dan Rosenweig, the firm's chief operating officer. "We are appropriately focused on the fact that this is a fluid market, but we're a company born out of competition."[12]

Endnotes

1. Chmielewski, D. C. 2007. Yahoo's ad system is almost ready. *Los Angeles Times,* January 24: C1.
2. Helft, M. 2007. A long-delayed ad system has Yahoo crossing its fingers. *New York Times,* February 5, 2007: C3.
3. *New York Times,* February 5, 2007: C3.
4. Elgin, B., & Grover R. 2003. Yahoo!: Act two. *BusinessWeek,* June 2: 74.
5. *BusinessWeek,* June 2, 2003: 74.
6. *BusinessWeek,* June 2, 2003: 72.
7. *BusinessWeek,* June 2, 2003: 74.
8. *BusinessWeek,* June 2, 2003: 72.
9. Delaney, K. J. 2006. As Yahoo falters, executive's memo calls for overhaul. *The Wall Street Journal,* November 18–19: A7.
10. *The Wall Street Journal,* November 18–19, 2006: A7.
11. Hansell, S. 2006. At Yahoo, all is not well. *New York Times,* October 11: C7.
12. Zeller, T. Jr., 2005. Yahoo's profit soars in quarter on ad spending and investments. *New York Times,* January 19: C5.

CASE 6   World Wrestling Entertainment

On Sunday, April 1, 2007, 80,103 people from 24 countries and all 50 states packed the cavernous Ford Field stadium in Detroit for WrestleMania, the annual pop culture spectacular that is hosted by World Wrestling Entertainment (WWE). Among the attractions was a marquee matchup pitting Bobby Lashley, fighting on behalf of Donald Trump, against Umaga, fighting on behalf of WWE co-founder and Chairman Vince McMahon, in the Battle of the Billionaires. Fans packed the venue from ringside to the rafters, even as the show was being delivered by satellite to millions more in over 110 countries. Kurt Schneider, Executive Vice President of Marketing, proclaimed, "Ford Field shook to the very core of its foundation with the thunderous noise from the record setting crowd."[1]

The drawing power of the annual event indicated that WWE had clearly moved out of a slump that it had to endure between 2001 and 2005. During the 1990s, WWE's potent mix of shaved, pierced, and pumped-up muscled hunks; buxom, scantily clad, and sometimes cosmetically enhanced beauties; and body-bashing clashes of good versus evil had resulted in an empire that claimed over 35 million fans. Furthermore, the vast majority of these fans were males between the ages of 12 and 34, the demographic segment that makes most advertisers drool. And these guys had driven up WWE's revenues by their insatiable appetite for tickets, broadcasts, and merchandise.

By the end of 1999, the husband-and-wife team of Vince and Linda McMahon used WWE's surge in popularity to raise $170 million through an initial public offering. But the firm's failure with a football league, which folded after just one season, was followed by a drop in revenues from its core wrestling businesses. Its attendance began to drop off at its live shows, and advertising revenues for its television shows started to decline. WWE struggled with its efforts to build new wrestling stars and to introduce new characters into its shows.

Since 2005, however, things finally seem to be turning around for WWE (see Exhibits 1 and 2). Vince and Linda have turned pro wrestling into a perpetual traveling road show that makes more than 2 million fans pass through turnstiles worldwide. Its wrestling shows attract more than 15 million television viewers every week, making them a fixture among the top-rated cable programs. WWE sold more than 4 million DVDs during the last year and signed pacts with 100 different licensees to sell merchandise such as video games, toys, and trading cards (see Exhibits 3 to 5).

WWE was also drawing on its wrestling roots to build up a stronger ad-supported Internet presence, selling merchandise and offering video programming. Even bolder was the firm's expansion into feature film production with its wrestling super-stars. "We continue to see the distribution of our creative content through various emerging channels," stated WWE's President and CEO Linda McMahon.[2] According to a recent ranking of popular Web searches, WWE was drawing considerable attention.

It had the fourth most online buzz, trailing only top television hits such as *American Idol* and *Dancing with the Stars.*

DEVELOPING A WRESTLING EMPIRE

Most of the success of the WWE can be attributed to the persistent efforts of Vince McMahon. He was a self-described juvenile delinquent who went to military school as a teenager to avoid being sent to a reformatory institution. Around 1970, Vince joined his father's wrestling company, Capital Wrestling Corporation. He did on-air commentary, developed scripts, and otherwise promoted wrestling matches. Vince bought Capital Wrestling from his father in 1982, eventually renaming it World Wrestling Federation (WWF). At that time, wrestling was managed by regional fiefdoms where everyone avoided encroaching on anyone else's territory. Vince began to change all that by paying local television stations around the country to broadcast his matches. His aggressive pursuit of audiences across the country gradually squeezed out most of the other rivals. "I banked on the fact that they were behind the times, and they were," said McMahon.[3]

Soon after, Vince broke another taboo by admitting to the public that wrestling matches were scripted. Although he had made this admission in order to avoid the scrutiny of state athletic commissions, wrestling fans appreciated the honesty. The WWF began to draw in more fans through the elaborate story lines and the captivating characters of its wrestling matches. The firm turned wrestlers such as Hulk Hogan and Andre the Giant into mainstream icons of pop culture. By the late 1980s, the WWF's *Raw is War* had become a top-rated show on cable and the firm had also begun to offer pay-per-view shows.

Vince faced his most formidable competition after 1988, when Ted Turner brought out World Championship Wrestling (WCW), one of the few major rivals that was still operating. He spent millions luring away WWF stars such as Hulk Hogan and Macho Man Randy Savage. He used these stars to launch a show on his own TNT channel to go up against WWF's major show, *Raw is War.* Although Turner's new show caused a temporary dip in the ratings for WWF's shows, Vince fought back with pumped-up scripts, mouthy muscle-men, and Lycra-clad women. "Ted Turner decided to come after me and all of my talent," growled Vince, "and now he's where he should be. . . ."[4]

In 2001, Vince was finally able to acquire WCW from Turner's parent firm AOL Time Warner for a bargain price of $5 million. Because of the manner in which he eliminated most of his rivals, Vince has earned a reputation for being as aggressive and ambitious as any character in the ring. Paul MacArthur, publisher of *Wrestling Perspective,* an industry newsletter praised his accomplishments: "McMahon understands the wrestling business better than anyone else. He's considered by most in the business to be brilliant."[5]

In 2002, WWF was also hit by a ruling from a British court that stated that their original WWF acronym belonged to the World Wildlife Fund. The firm had to undergo a major branding transition, changing its well-known name and triple logo from WWF back to WWE. Although the change in name was

*This case was developed by Professor Jamal Shamsie, Michigan State University with the assistance of Professor Alan B. Eisner, Pace University. Material has been drawn from published sources to be used for class discussion. Copyright © 2007 Jamal Shamsie & Alan B. Eisner.

EXHIBIT 1   **Income Statements**

	12/31/2006	04/30/2006	04/30/2005
	(in $ thousands)		
Net revenues	262,937	400,051	366,431
Cost of revenues	157,094	227,172	213,289
Selling, general, & administrative expenses	61,043	87,173	86,874
Depreciation & amortization	5,557	10,472	11,874
Stock compensation costs	—	4,694	4,101
Operating income (loss)	39,243	70,540	50,293
Investment income	6,440	7,390	5,362
Interest expense	421	587	642
Other income (loss)	884	553	1,346
Income before income taxes	46,146	77,896	56,359
Current federal income taxes	11,514	22,595	10,443
Current state & local income taxes	278	7,232	1,623
Current foreign income taxes	295	2,718	5,325
Deferred federal income taxes	2,167	(2,139)	2,183
Deferred state & local income taxes	275	478	(993)
Provision for income taxes	14,529	30,884	18,581
Income (loss) from continuing operations	31,617	47,012	37,778
Income (loss) from discontinued operations	—	35	1,369
Net income (loss)	31,617	47,047	39,147
Year end shares outstanding	70,997.479	70,556.998	68,880.655
Dividend per share	0.36	0.72	0.36
Total number of employees	560	460	433
Number of class A common stockholders	11,794	11,374	11,282
Number of class B common stockholders	3	3	3

Source: Mergentonline.com.

costly, it did not seem to have hurt the firm in the long run. "Their product is really the entertainment. It's the stars. It's the bodies," said Larry McNaughton, managing director and principal of CoreBrand, a branding consultancy.[6] Linda stated that the new name might have actually been beneficial for the firm. "Our new name puts the emphasis on the 'E' for entertainment," she commented.[7]

CREATING A SCRIPT FOR SUCCESS

Since the day he took over the firm, Vince worked to change the entire focus of the wrestling shows. He looked to television soap operas for enhancing the entertainment value of his live events. Vince reduced the amount of actual wrestling and

replaced it with wacky, yet somewhat compelling, story lines. He began to develop interesting characters and create compelling story lines by employing techniques that were quite similar to those being used by many successful television shows. There was a great deal of reliance on the "good versus evil" or the "settling the score" themes in the development of the plots for his wrestling matches. The plots and subplots ended up providing viewers with a mix of romance, sex, sports, comedy, and violence against a backdrop of pyrotechnics.

Over time, the scripts for the matches became tighter, with increasingly intricate story lines, plots, and dialogue. All the details of every match were worked out well in advance, leaving the wrestlers themselves to decide only the manner in which

EXHIBIT 2   **Balance Sheets**

	12/31/2006	04/30/2006	04/30/2005
	(in $ thousands)		
Cash & cash equivalents	86,267	175,203	56,568
Short-term investments	161,889	105,655	201,487
Accounts receivable	—	71,515	65,188
Allowance for doubtful accounts	—	3,740	3,287
Accounts receivable, net	52,113	67,775	61,901
Inventory, net	3,049	1,788	1,057
Prepaid expenses & other current assets	13,334	11,140	15,191
Assets of discontinued operations	469	457	544
Total current assets	317,121	362,018	336,748
Land, buildings, & improvements	56,084	55,957	51,958
Equipment	45,752	44,788	42,511
Corporate aircraft	20,829	20,710	20,710
Vehicles	634	518	542
Property & equipment, gross	123,299	121,973	115,721
Less: accumulated depreciation & amortization	55,327	54,403	49,083
Property & equipment, net	67,972	67,570	66,638
Feature film production assets	53,560	36,094	28,771
Intangible assets, gross	11,012	—	—
Less: accumulated amortization—intangible assets	7,684	—	—
Intangible assets, net	3,328	1,461	2,608
Other assets	11,304	12,247	6,640
Total assets	453,285	479,390	441,405
Current portion of long-term debt	862	817	756
Accounts payable	14,909	19,826	15,669
Accrued pay-per-view event costs	5,228	7,500	5,691
Accrued income taxes	—	7,418	—
Accrued talent royalties	—	714	368
Accrued payroll related costs	5,403	9,176	6,038
Accrued television costs	—	1,487	1,958
Accrued legal & professional fees	2,051	3,254	1,007
Accrued home video production & distribution	5,144	3,121	2,013
Accrued publishing print & distribution	—	625	580
Accrued other expenses	7,709	2,722	3,496
Accrued expenses & other current liabilities	25,535	36,017	21,151
Deferred income	20,166	19,874	20,843
Liabilities of discontinued operations	302	294	254
Total current liabilities	61,774	76,828	58,673
Long-term debt	5,800	6,381	7,198
Class A common stock	233	227	210
Class B common stock	477	479	479
Additional paid-in capital	286,985	277,693	254,716
Accumulated other comprehensive income (loss)	666	355	(908)
Retained earnings (accumulated deficit)	97,350	117,427	121,037
Total stockholders' equity	385,711	396,181	375,534

Source: Mergentonline.com.

EXHIBIT 3   **Breakdown of Net Revenues**

	December 31, 2006	April 30, 2006	April 30, 2005
	(in $ millions)		
Live & televised entertainment	183.0	290.8	299.5
Consumer products	59.2	86.4	53.9
Digital media	20.7	22.9	13.0
WWE films	—	—	—
Total	262.9	400.1	366.4

Source: WWE.

EXHIBIT 4   **Breakdown of Operating Income**

	December 31, 2006	April 30, 2006	April 30, 2005
	(in $ millions)		
Live & televised entertainment	57.0	93.9	100.6
Consumer products	26.9	46.4	26.9
Digital media	3.8	2.9	1.2
WWE films	(1.1)	(1.3)	(1.0)

Source: WWE.

EXHIBIT 5   **Percentage Breakdown of Net Revenues**

	December 31, 2006	April 30, 2006	April 30, 2005
Live & televised entertainment			
Live events	20%	19%	22%
Venue merchandise sales	5%	4%	3%
Television	22%	20%	21%
Pay per view	20%	24%	23%
Video on demand	1%	—	—
Consumer products			
Licensing	6%	8%	6%
Home video	13%	11%	6%
Magazine publishing	3%	3%	3%
Digital media	3%	2%	2%
WWE films	—	—	—

Source: WWE.

they would dispatch their opponents to the mat. Vince's use of characters was well thought out and he began to refer to his wrestlers as "athletic performers" who were selected on the basis of their acting ability in addition to their physical stamina. Vince also ensured that his firm owned the rights to the characters that were played by his wrestlers. This would allow him to continue to exploit the characters that he developed for his television shows, even after the wrestler that played that character had left his firm.

By the late 1990s Vince had two weekly shows on television. Besides *Raw,* the original flagship program on the USA cable channel, WWE had added a *Smackdown!* show on the UPN broadcast channel. He developed a continuous storyline using the same characters so that his audience would be driven to both the shows. But the acquisition of the WCW resulted in a significant increase in the number of wrestling stars under contract. Trying to incorporate more than 150 characters into the story lines for WWE's shows proved to be a challenging task. At the same time, the move of *Raw* to Spike TV channel resulted in a loss of viewers.

In October 2005, WWE signed a new agreement with NBC that moved *Raw* back to the USA channel and gave the firm a new show called *ECW: Extreme Championship Wrestling* on the SCI FI channel. Because of the greater coverage of these cable channels, the firm has seen a significant rise in viewers. Its other show *Smackdown* is now carried by the new expanded CW channel, which resulted from the recent combination of the UPN network with the WB network. The shows are also attracting new viewers because of the growth in popularity of a new breed of characters such as John Cena and Chris Benoit.

MANAGING A ROAD SHOW

A typical work week for the WWE can be grueling for the McMahons, for the talent, and for the crew. The organization is now putting on more than 300 live shows a year requiring everyone to be on the road most days of the week. The touring crew includes over 200 crew members, including stage hands. All of WWE's live events, including those that are used for its two longstanding weekly shows *Raw* and *Smackdown!* as well as the newer ones, are held in different cities. Consequently, the crew is always packing up a dozen 18-wheelers and driving hundreds of miles to get from one performance to the next. Since there are no repeats of any WWE shows, the live performances must be held all year round.

In fact, the live shows form the core of all of WWE's businesses (see Exhibit 6). They give the firm a big advantage in the entertainment world. Most of the crowd shows up wearing WWE merchandise and screams throughout the show. Vince and his crew pay special attention to the response of the audience to different parts of the show. They claim that these live events provide them with a real-time assessment of the popularity of their storylines and characters. The script for each performance is not set until the day of the show and sometimes changes are made even in the middle of a show. Vince boasted:

"We're in contact with the public more than any entertainment company in the world."[8]

Although the live shows usually fill up, the attendance fee—running on average around $35—barely covers the cost of the production. But these live performances provide content for nine hours of original television programming as well as for the growing list of pay-per-view offerings. Much of the footage from these live shows is also being used on the WWE Web site, which is the growth engine for its new digital media business. Finally, the shows create strong demand for WWE merchandise ranging from home videos and magazines to video games and toys.

The whole endeavor is managed not only by Vince, but by all of his family. Vince's efforts notwithstanding, the development of the WWE has turned into a family affair. While the slick and highly toned Vince could be regarded as the creative muscle behind the growing sports entertainment empire, his wife Linda began to quietly manage its day-to-day operation. Throughout its existence, she helped to balance the books, do the deals, and handle the details that were necessary for the growth and development of the WWE franchise.

One of Vince and Linda's greatest pleasures has been to see their kids also move into the business. Their son, Shane, heads wwe.com, the firm's streaming-media site and their daughter Stephanie, has been part of the creative writing team. "This business is my heart and soul and passion and always has been," Stephanie commented.[9] The family's devotion lies behind much of the success of WWE. "If they are out there giving 110 percent, it's a lot easier to get it from everyone else," said wrestler Steve Blackman.[10]

PURSUING NEW OPPORTUNITIES

In 1999, shortly after going public, WWF (as it was called then) launched an eight-team football league called the XFL. Promising full competitive sport unlike the heavily-scripted wrestling matches, Vince tried to make the XFL a faster-paced, more fan-friendly form of football than the NFL's brand. Vince was able to partner with NBC, which was looking for a lower-priced alternative to the NFL televised games. The XFL kicked off with great fanfare in February 2001. Although the games drew good attendance, television ratings dropped steeply after the first week. The football venture folded after just one season, resulting in a $57 million loss for WWF. Both Vince and Linda insist that the venture could have paid off if it had been given enough time. Vince commented; "I think our pals at the NFL went out of their way to make sure this was not a successful venture."[11]

Since then, the firm has tried to seek out growth opportunities that are driven by its core wrestling business. With more characters at their disposal and different characters being used in each of their shows, WWE has been ramping up the number of live shows, including more in overseas locations. During 2006, the firm staged over 40 live events outside the United States in far-flung locations such as the U.K., Spain, Panama, the Philippines, and New Zealand. An increase in the number of

EXHIBIT 6   **Wrestlemania's Five Best Bouts**

Andre the Giant vs. Hulk Hogan

WrestleMania III, March 29, 1987

- **The Lowdown:** A record crowd of 93,173 witnessed Andre the Giant, undefeated for 15 years, versus Hulk Hogan, wrestling's golden boy.
- **The Payoff:** Hogan body-slammed the 500-pound Giant, becoming the sport's biggest star and jump-starting wrestling's first big boom.

The Rock vs. Stone Cold Steve Austin

WrestleMania X-7, April 1, 2001

- **The Lowdown:** The two biggest stars of wrestling's modern era went toe-to-toe in the culmination of a two-year-long feud.
- **The Payoff:** Good-guy Austin aligned with "evil" WWE owner Vince McMahon and decimated the Rock to win the title in front of a shocked crowd.

Hulk Hogan vs. The Ultimate Warrior

WrestleMania VI, April 1, 1990

- **The Lowdown:** The most divisive feud ever—fan favorite Hulk Hogan defended his title against up-and-coming phenom the Ultimate Warrior.
- **The Payoff:** Half the crowd went into cardiac arrest (the other half were in tears) when Hogan missed his patented leg drop and the Warrior won.

Bret Hart. vs. Shawn Michaels

WrestleMania XII, March 31, 1996

- **The Lowdown:** Two men who didn't like each other outside the ring locked up in a 60-minute Iron Man match for the title.
- **The Payoff:** After an hour, neither man had scored a pinfall. Finally, Michaels, aka the Heartbreak Kid, pinned Hart in overtime to win the belt.

Kurt Angle vs. Brock Lesnar

WrestleMania XIX, March 30, 2003

- **The Lowdown:** Olympic medalist Angle squared off against former NCAA wrestling champ Lesnar in a punishing bout.
- **The Payoff:** The 295-pound Lesnar landed on his head after attempting a high-flying attack. But he recovered to pin Angle and capture the championship.

Source: *TV Guide*. 2004. March 13.

shows around the globe is also helping to boost the worldwide revenues that the firm is able to generate from its merchandise.

There has also been considerable excitement generated by the launch of WWE 24/7, a subscriber video-on-demand service. The new service allows the firm to distribute for a fee about 40 hours of content each month consisting of highlights from old shows as well as exclusive new programming. The service is being expanded to various cable companies reaching a growing number of VOD enabled homes. Within a year of its launch, WWE 24/7 has shown considerable growth, generating over $1.5 million in revenue.

WWE is also pushing into a new area of digital media, building an e-commerce site that offers the widest range of the firm's merchandise. The site also offers a wide range of content, including live broadcasts, transactional video footage, and original programming. In a recent tally, WWE.com was attracting more than 16 million unique users each month. The firm has barely tapped into the online ad market, with digital media revenue accounting for less than 10 percent of its total revenue. "The real value creation and growth will come from monetizing the presence on the Internet, where the company has a fanatic and loyal fan base," said Bobby Melnick, general partner with

Terrier Partners, a New York money management firm that owns WWE stock.[12]

Finally, WWE has also become involved with movie production using its wrestling stars, releasing two films during 2006. *See No Evil,* a horror thriller starring Kane, was released by Lions Gate, and John Cena's action adventure *The Marine* was released by Twentieth Century Fox. Though the films generated a small revenue in theaters, Linda believes that their movies will earn a profit from home video markets, distribution on premium channels, and offerings on pay-per-view. In fact, *The Marine* debuted in January 2007 as the top DVD rental.

POISED FOR A RESURGENCE?

In spite of the growth of WWE in many directions, Wrestle-Mania remains the pinnacle. An annual event that began at New York's Madison Square Garden in 1985, Wrestle-Mania is now an almost weeklong celebration of everything wrestling. No wrestler becomes a true star until his performance is featured at WrestleMania, and any true fan must make the pilgrimage at least once in his or her life.

Besides the hoopla that is created through each of the stagings of WrestleMania, Vince and his crew have been using the new WWE name to try to recreate the buzz that had surrounded his firm during the 1990s before it hit some serious bumps. The firm has used a new advertising campaign with the message "Get the 'F' out." Linda rejects any suggestion that the fortunes of WWE may be driven by a fad that is unlikely to last. She maintains that the interest in their shows will survive in spite of growing competition from newer sources of entertainment such as reality-based television shows.

Furthermore, Vince and Linda McMahon claim that their attempts to diversify were never meant to convey any loss of interest in wrestling. In fact, they believed that it was their experience with staging wrestling shows over the years that had provided them with the foundation to move into other areas of entertainment. After all, it was their ability to use wrestling to create a form of mass entertainment that had made the WWE such a phenomenal success. In response to critics who question the value of wrestling matches whose outcomes are rigged, James F. Byrne, senior vice president for marketing, stated: "Wrestling is 100 percent entertainment. There's no such thing as fake entertainment."[13]

Although WWE stock has failed to show much appreciation, the firm has boosted its dividend three times in the past five years. Analysts have noted that the firm has little debt and considerable cash flow, making it a relatively good investment over the longer term. "For long-term investors, WWE is very interesting," remarked Michael Kelman, an analyst with Susquehanna Financial Group.[14] "We make money when we are not hot," explained Vince. "When we are hot, it's off the charts."[15]

"Those who understand don't need an explanation. Those who need an explanation will never understand."

—**Marty,** a 19-year-old wrestling addict quoted in *Fortune,* October 6, 2000.

Endnotes

1. WWE. Wrestlemania blows away attendance record at Ford Field. Press Release, April 1, 2007.
2. WWE. World Wrestling Entertainment, Inc. Reports Q3 Results. Press Release, February 23, 2005.
3. McLean, B. 2000. Inside the world's weirdest family business. *Fortune,* October 16: 298.
4. Bradley, D. 2000. Wrestling's real grudge match. *BusinessWeek,* January 24: 164.
5. Mooradian, D. 2001. WWF gets a grip after acquisition. *Amusement Business,* June 4: 20.
6. Oestricher, D., & Steinberg, B. 2002. WW . . . E it is, after fight for F nets new name. *The Wall Street Journal,* May 7: B2.
7. Finnigan, D. 2002. Down but not out, WWE is using a rebranding effort to gain strength. *Brandweek,* June 3: 12.
8. *Fortune,* October 16, 2000: 304.
9. *Fortune,* October 16, 2000: 302.
10. *Fortune,* October 16, 2000: 302.
11. Bradley, D. 2004. Rousing itself off the mat? *BusinessWeek,* February 2: 73.
12. La Monica, P. R. 2007. Wrestling's "Trump" card. CNN Money.com, March 30, 2007.
13. Wyatt, E. 1999. Pro wrestling tries to pin down a share value. *New York Times,* August 4: c11.
14. CNN Money.com, March 30, 2007.
15. *BusinessWeek,* February 2, 2004: 74.

CASE 7 The Casino Industry

Driven by the steady growth in gaming revenues, Las Vegas is experiencing another building boom as construction cranes share air space with towering casino resorts. Ever since the mobster Bugsy Siegel opened the first of the modern day casinos in 1946, firms have competed against each other by building more expensive and extravagant casino resorts. But even Las Vegas has never witnessed the kind of expansion that is clearly evident in the spring of 2007. "This is the most outrageous, over-the-top expansion," said legendry casino mogul Steve Wynn.[1] His Wynn Resort represented the one of the most expensive casino resorts ever built when it was launched in 2005.

Topping the list of new projects is the City Center, being built at an expense of more than $7 billion by MGM Mirage, which owns the neighboring Bellagio along with several other well-known casinos in Las Vegas. The project is already becoming known as the most expensive privately financed project in American history. Even competitors marvel at the scope of this minicity bordering the Las Vegas Strip, which will feature six towering buildings that will reach as high as 61 stories. Covering 67 acres, City Center will include a 4,000-room hotel, 2,700 condominium units, a sprawling convention center, and a half million square feet of retail space. "We think it will be the hub of Las Vegas," said MGM Mirage CEO Terry Lanni.[2]

Furthermore, progress on the City Center is being matched by the gradual rise of several other glamorous new resorts all over Las Vegas. Boyd Gaming has started to develop a casino called Echelon Place on the former site of Stardust, which was demolished in March 2007. At $4.4 billion, the 5,000-room Echelon Place will be far more expensive than the previous record for a single casino, which was set when Wynn built his $2.7 billion resort. Other casinos are also building expensive additions to their properties. Las Vegas Sands is completing a 3,025-room resort called the Palazzo adjacent to its Venetian casino. And Steve Wynn is constructing Encore at Wynn Las Vegas, next to his recently opened resort.

Fueling this construction frenzy is the high occupancy rates at most of the Las Vegas casino resorts, as the city attracted just under 39 million visitors in 2006—an 86 percent increase over the 21 million who visited the city in 1990 (see Exhibit 1). The growth has occurred even as American Indian casinos and other gambling outposts have mushroomed across more than 30 states. With the growth in the acceptance and popularity of various forms of gaming, Las Vegas continues to attract people who want to enjoy the experience that it offers (see Exhibit 2).

With more hotel rooms than any other city in the United States, there is much speculation about the number of casinos that Las Vegas can keep adding. But David G. Schwartz, director of the Center for Gambling Research at the University of Nevada–Las Vegas, shrugs off these questions. "People

*This case was developed by Professor Jamal Shamsie, Michigan State University with the assistance of Professor Alan B. Eisner, Pace University. Material has been drawn from published sources to be used for class discussion. Copyright © 2007 Jamal Shamsie & Alan B. Eisner.

EXHIBIT 1   Las Vegas Visitors

	(in $ millions)
2006	39.0
2005	38.6
2004	37.4
2003	35.5
2002	35.1
2001	35.0
2000	35.8
1999	33.8
1998	30.6
1997	30.5
1996	29.6
1995	29.0

Source: Las Vegas Convention & Visitors Authority.

have been predicting dating back to 1955 that Las Vegas will reach a saturation point. But me, I wouldn't bet against casino growth."[3]

RIDING THE GROWTH WAVE

Although some form of gambling can be traced back to colonial times, the recent advent of casinos can be traced back to the legalization of gaming in Nevada in 1931. For many years, this was the only state in which casinos were allowed. As a result, Nevada still retains its status as the state with the highest revenues from casinos, with gambling revenues rising to almost $12 billion in 2006. After New Jersey passed laws in 1976 to allow gambling in Atlantic City, this allowed the large population on the East Coast easier access to casinos. However, the further growth of casinos has only been possible since 1988, as more and more states have begun to legalize the operation of casinos because of their ability to help generate more commercial activity and create more jobs, in large part through the growth of tourism.

The greatest growth has come in the form of water-borne casinos operating in six states that have allowed casinos to develop at waterfronts such as rivers and lakes. As of 2006, about 70 such casinos generated almost $11 billion in revenues. Several of the casinos along the Gulf Coast were destroyed or severely damaged by Hurricane Katrina. To encourage casinos to rebuild, Mississippi lawmakers passed a law in 2005 allowing casinos to operate up to 800 feet from the shore, which gives them a stronger foundation to withstand future hurricanes. Most of the damaged casinos in the area had reopened by early 2007.

EXHIBIT 2   **U.S. Casino Industry Gaming Revenues***

	2006	2005	2004	2003	2002	2001	2000
				Revenues (in $ millions)			
Nevada, total	12,622	11,649	10,562	9,625	9,447	9,469	9,600
Las Vegas Strip	6,688	6,034	5,334	4,760	4,654	4,704	4,806
Atlantic City, total	5,218	5,018	4,807	4,489	4,382	4,303	4,301
Western towns, total	867	839	804	768	786	735	685
Deadwood, SD	85	84	78	70	66	58	53
Colorado	782	755	726	698	720	677	632
Other land-based, total	1,641	1,458	1,509	1,412	1,400	1,257	989
New Orleans	338	229	320	282	275	250	245
Detroit	1,303	1,229	1,189	1,130	1,125	1,007	744
Riverboats, total	11,237	10,640	10,626	10,232	10,156	9,714	9,038
Iowa	814	747	727	694	656	615	598
Illinois	1,924	1,799	1,717	1,710	1,832	1,784	1,658
Mississippi	2,570	2,472	2,777	2,700	2,717	2,701	2,649
Louisiana	1,853	1,676	1,562	1,566	1,610	1,633	1,447
Missouri	1,592	1,532	1,473	1,332	1,279	1,138	997
Indiana	2,484	2,414	2,370	2,230	2,062	1,843	1,689
Native American casinos	25,700	22,600	16,700	15,055	13,290	11,400	9,700
Total	57,285	52,204	45,008	41,581	39,461	36,877	34,313

*Gaming revenues include the amount of money won by casinos from various gaming activities such as slot machines, table games, and sports betting.

Sources: *Casino Journal's* National Gaming Summary; Standard & Poor's estimates.

As casinos have spread to more states, there has also been a growing tendency to regard casino gambling as an acceptable form of entertainment for a night out. Although casinos have tended to draw players from all demographic segments, a recent national survey found that their median age was 47 and their median household income was around $50,000. On the whole, casino gamblers tended to be better educated and more affluent than those who bought lottery tickets. In fact, the bigger casinos attracted a high-roller segment, which could stake millions of dollars and included players from all over the world. Many of the casinos work hard to obtain the business of this market segment, despite the risk that the sustained winning streak of a single player could significantly weaken the earnings for a particular quarter.

The growth of casino gambling has also been driven by the significantly better payouts that they give players compared with other forms of gambling. Based on industry estimates, casinos typically keep less than $5 of every $100 that is wagered. This compares favorably with racetrack betting which holds back over $20 of every $100 that is wagered and with state-run lotteries that usually keep about $45 of every $100 that is spent on tickets. Such comparisons can be somewhat misleading, however, because winnings are put back into play in casinos much faster than they are in other forms of gaming. This provides a casino with more opportunities to win from a customer, largely offsetting its lower retention rate.

Finally, most of the growth in casino revenues has come from the growing popularity of slot machines. Coin-operated slot machines typically account for more than 60 percent of all casino gaming revenues. A major reason for their popularity is that it is easier for prospective gamblers to feed a slot machine than to learn the nuances of various table games. New slot machines tend to be based on familiar games such as Monopoly or TV shows such as *Star Trek, The Munsters,* or *Wheel of Fortune.* With the advent of new technology, these slot machines are being replaced by electronic gaming devices that have video screens instead of spinning wheels, buttons to push instead of handles to pull, and prepaid tickets rather than coins for payment.

BETTING ON A FEW LOCATIONS

Although casinos have spread across much of the country, two cities have dominated the casino business. Both Las Vegas and Atlantic City have seen a spectacular growth in casino gaming revenues over the years (see Exhibit 3). Although Las Vegas has far more hotel casinos, each of the dozen casinos in Atlantic City typically generate much higher revenues. By 2006, these two locations accounted for almost a quarter of the total revenues generated by all forms of casinos throughout the United States.

Las Vegas clearly acts a magnet for the overnight casino gamblers, offering more than 150,000 hotel rooms and many choices for fine dining, great shopping, and top-notch entertainment. It is linked by air to many major cities both in the United States and around the world. During the 1990s, Las Vegas tried to become more receptive to families, with attractions such as circus performances, animal reserves, and pirate battles. But the city has been very successful with its recent return to its sinful roots with a stronger focus on topless shows, hot night clubs, and other adult offerings that have been highlighted by the new advertising slogan "What happens in Vegas, stays in Vegas." Paul Cappelli, who creates advertising messages, believes that Las Vegas lost its way with the effort to become family friendly. "People don't see Vegas as Jellystone Park. They don't want to go there with a picnic basket," he explained.[4]

For the most part, Las Vegas has continued to show a consistent pattern of visitor growth. "We still compete with Orlando and New York," said Terry Jicinsky, head of marketing for the Las Vegas Convention and Visitors Authority. "But based on overnight visitors, we're the top destination in North America."[5] In order to accommodate this growth, several of the major resorts such as Bellagio and Mandalay Bay did add new wings during 2003 and 2004, leading to the opening of Steve Wynn's brand new casino resort in the spring of 2005. Even some of the older properties have been remodeled. Caesars Palace has been given an expensive renovation and expanded to include a new Colosseum and a new Roman Plaza. According to Tom Graves, stock analyst at Standard & Poor's, "There's a perception among gamblers that Las Vegas is still the foremost gaming market."[6]

By comparison, Atlantic City cannot compete with Las Vegas in terms of the broad range of dining, shopping, and entertainment choices. It does, however, offer a beach and a boardwalk along which its dozen large casino hotels are lined. Atlantic City attracts gamblers from various cities in the Northeast, many of whom arrive by charter bus and stay for less than a day. Atlantic City officials point out that one-quarter of the nation's population lives sufficiently close so that they can drive there on just one tank of gas.

The opening of the much-ballyhooed Borgata Hotel Casino in 2003 started a drive to make Atlantic City much more competitive with Las Vegas. As the first new casino to open in the city in 13 years, the Borgata was at the center of a $2 billion makeover of Atlantic City that might make it a hotter destination. "There's no question that this is a Las Vegas–style megaresort," said Bob Boughner, the CEO of the Borgata.[7] Two of the town's older casinos are adding expensive new wings to accommodate more overnight visitors. Other casino hotels such as Caesars, Trump Plaza, and Hilton have also added outdoor bars on the beach that have helped to turn the waterfront into one big party zone. "Bogata is the catalyst for a new Atlantic City," said Mike Epifanio, the editor of *Atlantic City Weekly*. "There's been a major change of thinking in town."[8]

RAISING THE STAKES

The gradual rise in the number of casinos, including those on riverboats, has led each of them to compete more heavily with each other to entice gamblers. Casinos have had to continuously strive to offer more in order to stand out and gain attention. This is most evident in Las Vegas and Atlantic City, the two destinations where most of the largest casinos are located next to each other. Potential gamblers have more choices when they visit either of these cities than they have anywhere else.

In Las Vegas, each of the casinos has tried to deal with this competition by differentiating itself in several different ways. A large number of them have tried to differentiate on the basis of a special theme that characterizes their casino, such as a medieval castle, a pirate ship, or a movie studio. Others have tried to incorporate into their casinos the look and feel of specific foreign destinations. Luxor's pyramids and columns evoke ancient Egypt, Mandalay Bay borrows looks from the Pacific Rim, and the Venetian's plazas and canals recreate the Italian resort.

Aside from ramping up the appeal of their particular properties, most casinos must also offer incentives to keep their customers from moving over to competing casinos. These incentives can be particularly helpful in retaining those high rollers who come often and spend large amounts of money.

EXHIBIT 3   **Comparitive Statistics**

	Las Vegas	Atlantic City
Gambling legalized	1931	1976
Annual visitors	39 million	34 million
Average stay	3.4 days	1.5 days
Number of casinos	190	12
Casino revenue	$6.2 billion	$5.3 billion
Hotel rooms	133,000	16,000
Largest hotel	MGM Grand	Borgata
	5,035 rooms	2,002 rooms

Sources: Nevada Casino Control Board, Las Vegas News Bureau, New Jersey Casino Control Commission, Atlantic City Convention & Visitors Bureau.

Casinos try to maintain their business by providing complimentary rooms, food, beverages, shows, and other perks each year that are worth billions of dollars. Gamblers could also earn various types of rewards through the loyalty programs that the casinos offer, with the specific rewards being tied to the amount that they bet on the slot machines and at the tables.

Some of the larger casinos in Las Vegas were also trying to fend off competition by growing through mergers and acquisitions. In 2004, Harrah's announced that it was buying casino rival Caesars, allowing it to become the nation's leading operator of casinos, with several properties in both Las Vegas and Atlantic City. This deal came just a month after MGM Mirage had stated that it was buying the Mandalay Resort Group, allowing it to double the number of casinos it held on the Las Vegas Strip. Firms that own several casinos can also pitch each of their properties to a different market and allow all of their customers to earn rewards on the firm's loyalty program by gambling at any of these properties (see Exhibit 4).

Such a trend toward consolidation, however, does not seem to make a serious dent in smaller firms that operate just one or two resorts that appeal to particular types of customers. Wynn's new casino hotel was expected to attract up to 8 million customers each year, which represents about 60 percent of the annual attendance of Disneyland. Las Vegas Sands has also been drawing hordes of visitors to the luxury suites that it offers in its opulent Venetian Resort. In fact, the recently opened 455-room Palms Hotel Casino has already become one of the hottest and most profitable properties in Las Vegas. "There will always be a market for a person who doesn't feel comfortable in a big casino setting," said George Maloof, a co-owner of the Palms Resort.[9]

RESPONDING TO GROWING THREATS

Even though the traditional casinos had been working hard to maintain and build upon their sizable market, they are facing growing competition from a variety of sources. Foremost among these was the rise in the number of Native American casinos. The Indian Gaming and Recreation Act of 1988 authorized Native Americans to offer gaming on tribal lands as a way to encourage their self-sufficiency. Of the approximately 550 Native American tribes in the United States, more than 200 have negotiated agreements with states to allow gaming on tribal land. Native American casinos are exempt from federal regulations and are not required to pay any taxes on their revenues, but they generally pay a percentage of their winnings to the state in which they are located.

Estimates from the National Indian Gaming Commission indicate that in fiscal 2006, Native American casinos generated over $19 billion in gaming revenues, representing almost 60 percent of the total gaming revenues that were generated outside Nevada and Atlantic City. At two high-volume casinos in southern Connecticut, one owned by the Mashantucket Pequot tribe and the other by the Mohegan tribe, total gaming revenues

were expected to exceed $2.5 billion in 2006. About 70 percent of the growth in U.S. gaming revenues over the past five years has come from all Native American casinos.

The impact of Native American casinos over the traditional casino industry was likely to increase over the next few years. Several states were reaching agreements to allow the introduction or expansion of Native American casinos because of the additional revenues that they can provide. This had created fears that the growth of these Native American casinos were likely to draw gamblers away from the other types of casinos. In particular, the growth of these casinos in states such as California and New York may reduce the number of gamblers that make trips to gambling destinations such as Las Vegas and Atlantic City.

The casino industry was also facing growing competition as a result of the move to introduce gaming machines at racetracks. Several states were passing legislation that would allow racetracks to raise their revenues by providing slot machines to their visitors. The introduction of gaming machines at racetracks—sometimes referred to as "racinos"—had being growing in popularity in the six states where they are presently allowed. According to the American Gaming Association, gaming activity at these racetracks has shown considerable growth over the last five years.

Finally, all casinos were closely observing the growth of gambling on the Internet. Although the United States has introduced legislation to ban Internet gambling, some 2,000 offshore sites generated about $12 billion in revenue in 2005. Electronic payment systems have made it possible for gamblers in the United States to make bets on these sites without cash, checks, or credit cards. Most casino operators believe that Internet gambling could represent both a threat and an opportunity for them. Placing bets through home computers offers convenience for prospective gamblers and a potentially low-cost business model for firms that already operate casinos. It is widely believed that gambling on the Internet might eventually be legalized, regulated, and taxed. "We frankly find attempts at prohibition to be very short-sighted," said Alan Feldman, senior vice-president of MGM Mirage in Las Vegas.[10]

GAMBLING ON THE FUTURE

Even as the competition from both rivals and substitutes continues to grow, all of the firms in the casino industry have little choice but to keep spending in order to survive and grow. In many cases, the heavy spending can burden the firm with large amounts of debt that must be serviced through profits from the casino. The debt can be harder to manage if demand for casino gambling does not stay strong and even show some growth. A few casinos in Las Vegas and Atlantic City have run into financial problems, forcing some of them to close. Most recently, Alladin, one of the recent additions to the Las Vegas Strip, was sold off to a partnership of Planet Hollywood and Starwood Resorts.

EXHIBIT 4   **Leading Casino Operators**

Harrah's Entertainment

2006 Revenue: $9.67 billion

2006 Income: $535.8 million

Was purchased by a private equity firm in early 2007. Operates 36 casinos across the United States, including 12 riverboats. Also operates 4 casinos on Indian reservations. Runs several upscale casinos such as Bellagio, Caesars Palace, Ballys, Paris, Flamingo, Harrah's, and Rio in Las Vegas. Also planning overseas expansion into Spain and Bahamas.

MGM Mirage

2006 Revenue: $7.18 billion

2006 Income: $648.3 million

Operates 19 casinos throughout the country. Most of its casinos in Las Vegas, such as MGM Grand, Bellagio, New York New York, Mirage, Treasure Island, Luxor, and Monte Carlo, cater to the high end of the market. Developing the City Center project in Las Vegas. Also operates casinos on the Gulf coast and in Detroit. Overseas, is developing MGM Grand Macau.

Boyd Gaming

2006 Revenues: $2.28 billion

2006 Income: $116.8 million

Operates 16 casinos in various states around the United States. Las Vegas properties that target the middle income segment include Barbary Coast, Orleans, and Sam's Town. Is developing a higher end casino Echelon Place in Las Vegas. Runs the newly opened Borgata in Atlantic City.

Las Vegas Sands

2006 Revenues: $2.24 billion

2006 Income: $442.0 million

Operates the Venetian and will open the sister casino Palazzo in Las Vegas. Also developing several casinos in Macau, spearheaded by the Venetian Macau and developing a casino in Singapore.

Penn National Gaming

2006 Revenues: $2.24 billion

2004 Income: $327.1 million

In 2005, merged with Argosy Gaming. Operates 11 mid-priced casinos spread across the United States, including 5 riverboats spread over different states. No properties in Las Vegas or Atlantic City. Also operates several racetracks.

Wynn Resorts

2006 Revenues: $1.43 billion

2006 Income: $628.7 million

Operates the higher end Wynn Resort and will shortly open sister Encore casino, both in Las Vegas. Also expanding overseas with the Wynn Macau.

Station Casinos

2006 Revenues: $1.34 billion

2006 Income: $110.2 million

Operates 9 mid-priced casinos in Las Vegas area. Leading casinos are Palace Station, Sunset Station, and Boulder Station.

Aztar Corporation

2006 Revenues: $1.10 billion*

2006 Income: $225.0 million*

Was acquired by private equity firm in early 2007. Operates 13 mid-market casinos including 2 riverboats. Runs the Tropicana in both Las Vegas and Atlantic City.

Trump Entertainment Resorts

2006 Revenues: $1.03 billion

2006 Income: $(18.5) million

Operates 3 casinos in Atlantic City, a riverboat in Indiana and an overseas casino. Atlantic City properties consist of Trump Taj Mahal, Trump Plaza, and Trump Marina.

Ameristar Casinos

2006 Revenues: $1.00 billion

2006 Income: $59.6 million

Operates 7 mid-priced casinos across the United States including a couple of riverboats. No properties in Las Vegas or Atlantic City.

Isle of Capri Casinos

2006 Revenues: $988 million

2006 Income: $19.0 million

Operates 13 riverboat casinos across the United States.

*Estimated figures.

Most of the gaming firms nevertheless believed that the industry was certain to grow well into the future. Their optimism was based on the growing number of aging boomers who are entering the empty-nest phase of their free-spending lives. Las Vegas had shifted its image away from being family-friendly and was catering to this lucrative segment that is likely to spend more of their money on gambling. But it was still not clear how gaming revenues might be affected by any significant increases in gas prices, which would make travel more expensive and reduce disposable income.

Furthermore, there were questions about the possible impact of the proliferation of casinos around the country and the availability of Internet gambling on the revenue growth of gaming centers such as Las Vegas and Atlantic City. Some observers believe that the spread of gaming had created a bigger market for the casino resorts in these locations. People who gain a taste for gambling would eventually want to visit Las Vegas or Atlantic City in order to get a feel of the real thing. "I suppose one day Las Vegas will reach its limit," said Anthony Curtis, president of LasVegasAdvisor.com, a local travel site. "But that day is nowhere in sight."[11]

Endnotes

1. Rivlan, G. 2007. Too many hotels aren't enough. *New York Times,* April 24: C1.
2. Woodyard, C. 2004. MGM Mirage plans hotel-condo complex that would be Las Vegas "hub." *USA Today,* November 11: B3.
3. *New York Times,* April 24, 2007: C10.
4. McCarthy, M. 2005. Vegas goes back to naughty roots; ads trumpet return to adult playground. *USA Today,* April 11: B6.
5. *USA Today,* April 11, 2005: B6.
6. Chris Woodyard, C., & Krantz, M. 2004. Latest Vegas marriage: Harrah's, Caesar's tie knot; $5 billion deal marks strategy to reach more gamblers. *USA Today,* July 16: B1.
7. Sloan, G. 2003. Atlantic City bets on glitz: Down-at-the-heels resort rolls the dice, wagering a cool $2 billion that it will one day rival Las Vegas. *USA Today,* August 29: D1.
8. *USA Today,* August 29, 2003: D1.
9. Palmeri, C. 2004. Little guys with big plans for Vegas. *BusinessWeek,* August 2: 49.
10. Woellert, L. 2004. Can online betting change its luck? *BusinessWeek,* December 20: 67.
11. *New York Times,* April 24, 2007: C10.

CASE 8 Claire's Stores: Competing Betwixt and Between

In the fall of 2006, Marla and Bonnie Schaefer, co-chairwomen and co-CEOs of Claire's Stores, Inc. (CLE), faced several challenges. Since their promotion to coleadership of the company after their father's stroke and subsequent retirement in 2002, they had done well, nearly doubling profits in the first two years of their tenure,[1] but analysts were beginning to wonder whether this growth could be sustained. In 2005, when net income increases began to slow, Marla Schaefer, considered the more visionary of the two sisters, responded, "You can post double-digit increases when you are building a business but at some point you mature and level off. Our goal is to keep the business healthy, keep inventories in line and keep moving forward. We always want to be ready for the next hot item. We don't run the business for Wall Street. We run it for our shareholders and employees and customers."[2]

Claire's Stores had been enviable because of its unique niche in the specialty retail sector. With no direct competitors for its "tween" and teen shoppers, ages 7 to 17, who were looking for low-price but trendy jewelry, hair ornaments, cosmetics, and fashion accessories, Claire's was able to grow steadily, albeit cautiously, both in the United States and abroad. With low overhead and high margins, partly due to an efficient distribution system, the real key to success seemed to be effective merchandising—both anticipating and creating trends and keeping inventories fluid, updated, and well priced. The average selling price hadn't varied much from the $4.00 level in almost 10 years. As one market researcher said in 2005, "Claire's has carved out a niche that does not have much to do with economic times. It's about merchandising, and they've got the merchandise that teens want."[3]

However, in retail it was never good to get complacent. Discounters such as Wal-Mart and Target were devoting increasingly more square footage to accessories,[4] and were debuting celebrity merchandise by Mary Kate and Ashley Olsen and Hillary Duff, among others, who were of major appeal to Claire's Stores' main demographic.[5] Claire's was also able to sign these teen designers to deals for jewelry, cosmetics, and signature accessories, but the celebrity draw was traditionally short-lived. In addition, the big-box players such as Target could use their size and "fashion-forward" merchandising to further appeal to Claire's target market, but with lower price points.[6] When asked about competition from other teen-targeted retailers like Abercrombie & Fitch, Marla bluntly replied, "We have always had competition, and we always will have competition. In fact, I call it stealth competition because it seems to come from all sides. Even malls love to open accessory kiosks right in front of our stores. But we do it bigger and better."[7]

Claire's Stores had steadily increased its store presence in malls across the United States, growing from a total of 1,167 U.S.

stores in 1995 to 2,106 in 2006, but there wasn't much room for real estate growth, with available mall space in short supply, and it was possible the core stores had reached market saturation. At that point, retailers usually considered brand extension, with spin-offs targeting slightly different demographics to retain growth. Claire's had acquired the Afterthoughts chain from Woolworth's in 1999 and revamped it, calling it Icing by Claire's, as a way to reach out beyond the teen market to customers aged 17 to 27, but, as of 2006, sales per square foot had not met expectations, and planned expansion had been slow, partly out of fear that the concept might cannibalize Claire's Stores sales.[8]

In addition, the older consumer, especially women from 25 to 40, a potential market for Claire's, expected a certain level of service and store design that might have required more experimentation before Claire's could get it right. As one market researcher said, "A woman will know within the first 7 to 12 seconds of entering a store whether she will buy or not. She is a very visual consumer who makes up her mind quickly. She's driven by a combination of factors: the look of the product, how it's displayed, will it be easy for her to make a purchase decision, and somehow a lot of things resonate within her before she buys."[9] If Claire's decided to try to reach out to this market with the Icing concept, further differentiation of Icing by Claire's from Claire's Stores might require a different look and feel to the store shopping experience.

As Claire's Stores had steadily increased its presence in malls across the United States and in Puerto Rico, it had also embarked on a steady international expansion. Starting in late 1994, Claire's had entered into a joint venture in Japan with AEON, Co. Ltd., and then, in 1995, opened 45 new stores in Canada. Claire's continued to expand into the U.K. by acquiring 48 Bows & Bangles stores in 1996. In 1998, Claire's acquired Bijoux One, a 53-store chain covering Switzerland, Austria, and Germany, and in 2000 acquired Cleopatre's 42 stores in France. Additional stores were opened in Belgium, Holland, and Spain. In 2000, Claire's also made its first venture into franchising, in Kuwait, the United Arab Emirates, and Saudi Arabia, followed in 2004 with merchandising agreements in South Africa (see Exhibit 1). Entering the fall season of 2006, Claire's Stores, Inc. had continued to post growth numbers worldwide (see Exhibits 2A, 2B, 2C and 3).

With the European stores about half the size of the average 1,200 square foot ones in the United States, yet sales per square foot almost twice as much, international expansion appeared to be the best strategy. However, the Schaefer sisters seemed to be cautious. As Bonnie Schaefer said, "We like to be methodical, and we don't want to go into any venture recklessly with our own company or others. We do take a modest approach, and it has worked well for us so far."[10] With overall revenue growth slowing for Claire's in 2006, and same-store September sales up only 1 percent compared to 8 percent in 2005, analysts were getting frustrated. In 2006 one said, "The whole issue in the U.S. is there is no unit growth for Icing or Claire's.

*This case was prepared by Professor Pauline Assenza of Manhattanville College, Professor Alan B. Eisner of Pace University and Professor Ron Heimler, LIM—The College for the Business of Fashion. This case was primarily based upon library research as well as interviews and was developed for class discussion rather than to illustrate either effective or ineffective handling of an administrative situation. Copyright © 2007 Pauline Assenza, Alan B. Eisner, and Ron Heimler.

EXHIBIT 1   **Claire's Store Growth 1992–2006**

Claire's Stores Consolidated Store Growth Fiscal 1992–2006*

FYE	Number of Stores**	Sales per Square Foot	Sales per Store	Inventory Turns	Return on Sales
2006	3,050	477	$475,000	2.9	12.60%
2005	2,984	476	$468,000	2.9	11.40%
2004	2,935	413	$415,000	3	10.20%
2003	2,912	370	$357,000	3	7.80%
2002	2,875	339	$326,000	2.9	4.53%
2001	2,873	347	$332,000	2.5	7.22%
2000	2,887	379	$365,000	3.4	12.27%
1999	1,941	348	$340,000	2.6	11.36%
1998	1,725	328	$314,000	2.9	11.70%
1997	1,560	320	$301,000	3	10.31%
1996	1,359	296	$273,000	3.1	8.70%
1995	1,232	294	$263,000	3.2	7.70%
1994	1,087	293	$265,000	3.3	8.40%
1993	1,038	269	$244,000	3.1	5.90%
1992	995	279	$248,000	2.3	2.20%

*From continuing operations.

**Excludes franchised stores.

FY 2006 Store Locations*

North America	2,106	Holland	10
Austria	28	Japan	172
Belgium	1	Spain	15
France	201	Switzerland	53
Germany	17	U.K./Ireland	447

*In addition, 84 Claire's Stores operate under various licensing and merchandising agreements throughout the Middle East in Kuwait and Saudia Arabia with seven located in South Africa.

Source: Claire's Stores.

The company has played around with a number of new concepts, but to really have a super premium or superior model, you need a growth vehicle, and they don't have one queued up. That's the big negative here."[11]

For a specialty retailer targeting an age demographic, paying attention to trends and adjusting store concepts accordingly was crucial. According to Philadelphia-based marketing consultancy Twentysomething Inc., there were 38 million young people between the ages of 11 and 19 in the United States at the beginning of 2006, with an estimated buying power of almost $2,000 per capita per year. As one retailer said, "Where are all these folks going to go when they get tired of shopping in teenage land?" To make matters more complicated, reconfiguring to chase the twentysomething market may not have been a good long-term strategy because there was a smaller generation behind it—only about 27.6 million 6- to 12-year-olds in the United

EXHIBIT 2   **Claire's Stores Financials**

2A Claire's Stores, Inc. Annual Balance Sheet (in U.S. $ millions)					
Period Ended	**1/28/2006**	**1/29/2005**	**1/31/2004**	**2/1/2003**	**2/2/2002**
Assets					
Cash	431.12	191.01	224.63	195.48	99.91
Marketable Securities	N/A	134.61	N/A	N/A	1.56
Receivables	10.33	N/A	N/A	N/A	N/A
Total Inventories	118.52	110.07	92.5	88.33	78.6
Raw Materials	5.11	N/A	N/A	N/A	N/A
Finished Goods	113.41	110.07	92.5	88.33	78.6
Other Current Assets	38.05	57.64	42.9	37.79	34.35
Total Current Assets	**598.01**	**493.33**	**360.02**	**321.61**	**214.42**
Net, Property, Plant & Equipment	222.72	204.53	187.4	174.48	163.97
Property, Plant & Equipment	509.31	467.89	432.19	385.81	341.97
Accumulated Depreciation	286.6	263.37	244.79	211.33	178
Interest and Advance to Subsidiaries	5.1	3.2	N/A	N/A	N/A
Intangibles	254.81	253.54	242.15	227.45	211.37
Deposits & Other Assets	10.06	11.54	16.35	14.59	21.81
Total Assets	**1,090.70**	**966.13**	**805.92**	**738.13**	**611.58**
Liabilities					
Accounts Payable	50.24	41.99	48.94	43.19	30.87
Current Long-Term Debt	N/A	N/A	N/A	40.92	21.04
Accrued Expense	74.44	94.34	65.24	43.76	25.82
Income Taxes	36.71	30.6	29.15	13.15	4.8
Other Current Liabilities	18.06	N/A	N/A	N/A	N/A
Total Current Liabilities	**179.45**	**166.94**	**143.33**	**141.01**	**82.54**
Deferred Charges/Inc.	42.94	43.5	30.15	25.87	14.75
Long-Term Debt	N/A	N/A	N/A	70	110.1
Total Liabilities	**222.38**	**210.44**	**173.47**	**236.88**	**207.39**
Shareholder Equity					
Common Stock	4.97	4.95	4.95	2.44	2.44
Capital Surplus	63.32	50.48	49.39	32.83	29.87
Retained Earnings	781.68	672.22	558	458.76	389.04
Treasury Stock	N/A	N/A	N/A	N/A	0.45
Total Shareholders' Equity	**868.32**	**755.69**	**632.45**	**501.25**	**404.19**
Total Liabilities & Shareholders' Equity	**1,090.70**	**966.13**	**805.92**	**738.13**	**611.58**

Source: Data Provided by Thomson Financial.

(continued)

EXHIBIT 2 **Claire's Stores Financials (continued)**

2B Claire's Stores, Inc. Annual Income Statement
(in U.S. $ millions except for per share items)

Period Ended	1/28/2006	1/29/2005	1/31/2004	2/1/2003	2/2/2002
Net Sales	1,369.75	1,279.41	1,132.83	1,001.54	918.74
Cost of Goods Sold	625.87	587.69	524.46	486.86	473.79
Gross Profit	**743.89**	**691.72**	**608.38**	**514.68**	**444.95**
SG & A Expense	498.46	475.75	385.45	351.39	328.79
Non-Operating Income	14.24	5.86	−45.94	−38.73	−41.15
Interest Expense	N/A	0.19	2.56	4.44	10.42
Income Before Taxes	**259.67**	**221.64**	**174.42**	**120.12**	**64.6**
Provision for Income Taxes	87.33	75.38	59.38	42.14	23.47
Extra Items & Discount Operations	N/A	−3.14	N/A	−0.24	−21.54
Net Income	**172.34**	**143.12**	**115.04**	**77.74**	**19.58**

Source: Data Provided by Thomson Financial.

2C Claire's Stores, Inc. Annual Cash Flow
(in U.S. $ millions)

Period Ended	1/28/2006	1/29/2005	1/31/2004	2/1/2003	2/2/2002
Net Income (Loss)	172.34	146.26	115.04	77.98	41.13
Depreciation/Amortization	50.13	46.01	42.66	38.62	43.78
Net Increase (Decrease) in Assets/Liabilities	16.09	−0.89	37.08	56.74	8.62
Cash Flow from Discount Operations	N/A	N/A	N/A	0.35	20.58
Other Adjustments—Net	4.29	7.91	9.63	−6.45	−5.11
Net Cash Flow from Operating	**242.86**	**199.29**	**204.41**	**167.24**	**108.99**
Increase (Decrease) in Property Plant & Equipment	−73.44	−63.57	−50.09	−45.5	−45.06
Increase (Decrease) in Securities Invest.	134.61	−134.61	N/A	1.56	−1.56
Other Cash Flow from Investing	−9.06	−7.46	−8.62	−7.19	−11.11
Net Cash Flow from Investing	**52.11**	**−205.64**	**−58.71**	**−51.12**	**−57.73**
Issue (Repayment) of Debt	N/A	N/A	−85.93	−20.23	−51.49
Increase (Decrease) in Borrowing	N/A	N/A	−25	N/A	N/A
Dividends, Other Distribution	−62.89	−28.91	−13.34	−7.58	−7.57
Net Cash Flow from Financing	**−58**	**−28.14**	**−113.98**	**−24.83**	**−59.02**
Effect of Exchange Rate on Cash	3.14	0.86	−2.57	4.29	−4.2
Cash or Equivalents at Year Start	191.01	224.63	195.48	N/A	N/A
Cash or Equivalents at Year End	431.12	191.01	224.63	N/A	N/A
Net Change in Cash or Equivalent	**240.12**	**−33.62**	**29.15**	**95.57**	**−11.95**

Source: Claire's Stores.

Data Provided by Thomson Financial.

EXHIBIT 3   **Claire's Stores Key Historical Statistics**

	1995	1998	2006
Store Profile			
Average Square Feet	900	960	1,150 U.S./600 Int'l
Total Stores	1,214	1,752	3,050
U.S. & Puerto Rico	1,167	1,495	2,106
Canada	45	102	Included in U.S.
Japan*	2	54	172
Other International	0	101 (England)	772**
Net Income	$23.9M	$58.2M	$172.3M
Gross Profit	53.9%	53.3%	54.3%
Total Sales	$301.4M	$500.2M	$1,370B
U.S. Sales	N/A	$445.2M	$964M (includes Canada)
International Sales	N/A	$10.8M	$405.7M
Average Unit Selling Price	$4.00	$4.00	$4.40
Accessories Sales	35%	51.6%	42% U.S./55% Int'l
Jewelry Sales	65%	48.4%0	58% U.S./45% Int'l

*Japanese stores are operated under a joint venture arrangement with Jusco Co., Ltd.

**Includes 84 stores licensed in the Middle East under an agreement with Al Shaya Co., Ltd., a Kuwaiti company, and 7 stores in South Africa licensed to the House of Busby Limited.

Accessories sales include hair ornaments, totes and bags, trend gifts, and apparel. Jewelry sales include ear-piercing services.

Source: Claire's Stores.

States as of 2006.[12] The number of Americans ages 25 to 34 was expected to rise to 5.2 percent of the population by 2010, but those ages 12 to 18 were forecasted to fall by 3.3 percent.[13]

Based on these numbers, Claire's Stores' major target market was shrinking. Other specialty retailers of apparel such as Abercrombie & Fitch, Aeropostale, and American Eagle Outfitters were creating new stores as brand extensions to try to capture the 18- to 40-year-olds. Given this trend, the success of Icing by Claire seemed increasingly important for long-term growth. With the shortage of desirable U.S. real estate, an option for Claire's might have been acquisition of a related concept retailer, as when it bought Afterthoughts, but this had not always worked well in the past. The boys and men's apparel store Mr. Rags, acquired in 1998, never performed for Claire's, and was sold off in 2002. When asked in 2005 about this potential strategy, Marla Schaefer said, "Over the course of 30 years we have made acquisitions that have not been in our core capabilities, and we have learned lessons from that, which is stick to your knitting, do what you do best, and excel at it. That's what we intend to continue doing."[14]

In 2005 Claire's tested a concept, Claire's Club, targeted at children age 0 to 6, but results had not been up to expectations, and the idea was not expanded. This young target demographic caused Claire's problems for another reason. In 2006 a Minneapolis 4-year-old died of lead poisoning from swallowing a piece of a charm bracelet (not from Claire's). This prompted Maryland and California to take action requiring U.S. retailers and distributors to dramatically reduce the levels of lead in costume jewelry, particularly when sold to children.[15] The Baltimore health department found a ring sold at Claire's Stores to contain more than 100 times the level of lead acceptable under federal regulations, and Claire's removed the ring from Baltimore stores, but kept it for sale in stores elsewhere, pending in-house testing. Marisa Jacobs, Claire's Corporate Communications VP, stated that the chance of the jewelry injuring a child was a "remote possibility." Wal-Mart, notified of problems with one of their items, also a ring, pulled the product from its stores nationwide. The Baltimore Health Commissioner said that Wal-Mart's response was exactly right, and that "it is a mistake" for Claire's not to pull all its products off the shelves right away.[16]

One other larger issue that affected Claire's Stores' potential growth was the scarcity of retail talent "in the wings." Given the consolidation of retailing since 1995, training programs had been cut, and executives tended to cycle from one related company to another.[17] Given the uncertainty preceding the Schaefer sisters' promotion at Claire's, succession planning was a concern. Both Marla and Bonnie appeared resistant to any outsider, and had said someone "would need at least a year to learn the business" in order to succeed in an executive role at Claire's.[18] This might have been expected, given that their father had run the business for over 40 years. Rowland Schaefer had not been able to relinquish control easily, going through five Claire's presidents from 1991 to 2000.[19] If the company was to remain a family firm, Marla and Bonnie had to work to keep the business in the family long enough for Marla's two daughters, teenagers in 2006, to have the same experience, should they be interested.

In the Annual Report for the fiscal year ending January 28, 2006, Marla and Bonnie Schaefer had laid out a "strategic roadmap" for the next five years. In it they mentioned the need for international expansion into new countries, continued astute merchandising, upgrading and enhancement of operational and information technology, more reliance on data mining for market research and management decision making, and depth of management. In the closing remarks they said, "We will be expanding our talent pool to ensure that we are appropriately staffed at all levels of the organization. Depth of management is critically important as Claire's continues to move into new forms of business and expands its global reach."[20]

In 2005, when asked why investors should be interested in Claire's Stores, Marla Schaefer responded, "I think it's a great concept with enormous expansion possibilities throughout much of the world. We have a healthy balance sheet. We generate an enormous amount of cash. We have a great demographic with disposable income who also loves to shop. We've got enormous brand name recognition, and we are steady. We've been in business over 30 years, and we have not yet had a year that was not profitable. So I think that says it all."[21] Merriam-Webster's Online Dictionary defines "betwixt and between" as "neither one thing nor the other."[22] Claire's Stores was not the normal specialty retailer, nor did it have the normal management structure. It had successfully captured the attention of the "tweens," and was "betwixt" the apparel and the high-end accessories retailers. Were these strengths or weaknesses? Were the Schaefer sisters too sure of themselves, would their formula for success falter due to caution or complacency? What would it take to keep the business growing?

In early December 2006, Claire's Stores announced it was putting itself up for sale, but with no guarantee it could find a buyer. Like other publicly-traded firms in this time frame, CLE had reached out to private equity firms for some relief from public scrutiny in a tightening sales market. Sales through November 2006 had slowed to an average of 2.6 percent, down from the 6 percent in the same period in 2005. Profit was also lower than previously, partly because of currency factors and lower demand in Europe and a shift of sales from jewelry to accessories, with accompanying lower margins. Claire's did have a healthy balance sheet, as Marla had said, with no debt, and a working capital at the end of Fiscal 2006 of $418.6 million, which made it attractive to potential buyers. As of December 2006, between Marla and Bonnie Schaefer and their father, they held 9.3 percent of the company's common shares, and controlled 32 percent of the votes.[23]

INDUSTRY OVERVIEW

The specialty retail industry had traditionally been volatile. Specialty retailers offered products within a single category, often to a specifically segmented target market. Unlike department stores that sold many different types of products for a one-stop shopping experience, specialty retailers could focus on one type of item and offer many varieties of that item. Wal-Mart and JC Penney were examples of the department store. Gap, Best-Buy, Barnes & Noble, and Toys "R" Us were examples of retailers who specialized in one general product category, sometimes offered to only one market segment: Gap offered clothing, Best-Buy offered electronics, Barnes & Noble offered books, and Toys "R" Us offered toys and gifts specifically for children. At the extreme end of the specialty market were the mall kiosks and carts, sometimes only seasonal, which often offered a way for entrepreneurs to test a narrowly focused concept prior to a more extensive sales and marketing investment.

The major advantage for any specialty retailer was the reduced cost in merchandising and distribution, sometimes using only one or two suppliers, and the associated ability to change inventory quickly with little to no adaptation needed in the physical layout of the selling space. The major disadvantage was that the single product category required the retailer to keep on top of trends in the category, since lost sales in one area could not be recouped by a shift of interest to another entirely different product area in the store. As a comparison, at Wal-Mart or JC Penney, if interest in apparel, for instance, was down in any particular sales cycle, new housewares or toys offerings may have been able to offset the temporary loss.

Within the specialty environment, companies might also do specialty branding to a more closely focused target market. For instance, as of 2006, Gap had created Forth & Towne to appeal to a more upscale, sophisticated female customer, augmenting Gap's existing apparel brands of Banana Republic, Old Navy, and the online shoe store Piperlime, launched in 2006. Another major player, Limited Brands (formerly known as The Limited, Inc.), as of 2006 operated Victoria's Secret (lingerie), Express (contemporary clothing for men and women), Bath & Body Works (fragrances, bath items), The Limited (general apparel), C.O. Bigelow (a specialty pharmacy), The White Barn Candle Co. (home fragrances), and Henri Bendel (upscale women's apparel). More focused specialty retailers in 2006 included the Charming Shoppes holding company, operating women's clothing stores for niche sizes such as Lane Bryant, Fashion Bug,

EXHIBIT 4   **Specialty Retailers Changing Hands as of 2006**

Brand Name	First Established	Formerly Owned/ Acquired By	Now Owned By	Fiscal 2005 Total Sales	Comments
Abercrombie & Fitch	1892	The Limited, Inc, in 1988	Abercrombie & Fitch Co., as of 1996	$2.78B	"Casual luxury" preppy image
Lane Bryant	1904	The Limited, Inc., in 1982	Charming Shoppes, as of 2001	$2.76B	Number one in women's plus-size apparel
Lerner New York	1918	The Limited, Inc. in 1985	New York & Company, as of 2002	$1.13B	Moderately priced women's apparel
Limited Too	1987 as a younger girls/infants version of The Limited	The Limited, Inc. in 1987	Tween Brands, Inc. 2006, also operates Justice, girl's sportswear	$0.758B	Apparel & lifestyle products to girls 7–14

Note: In Fiscal 2005, Gap had total sales of $16.02B; Limited Brands, Inc. had total sales of $9.7B. Gap, Limited Brands, Abercrombie & Fitch, and Charming Shoppes were numbers one through four on the *Woman's Wear Daily* list of the Top 20 publicly traded specialty retailers in 2005. Claire's was number 11. (From Gustke, C. 2006. High volume specialists: Top 20 publicly traded specialty retailers ranked by most recent annual volume. *Women's Wear Daily*, 192 (12): 12.

Catherine's (all three for plus-sizes), and Petit Sophisticates. A major international presence in the United States since 2000, H&M (Hennes & Mauritz, AB, a Swedish public company) expanded significantly worldwide into Dubai, Kuwait, and China in 2006. H&M, known for inexpensive yet fashionable men's and women's clothing, bought out the Gap's German holdings in 2004 and had been aggressively marketing itself, fairly successfully, in North America.

Both acquisitions and spin-offs were common in this apparel, accessories, and home fashion specialty retail category. Well-known names such as Abercrombie & Fitch, Lane Bryant, Lerner New York, and The Limited Too all had changed hands over the years, sometimes in order to capitalize on the ability to concentrate merchandising and marketing on a specific category and market segment (see Exhibit 4).

As of 2007, the top specialty retailers targeting teenagers included apparel, gifts and accessories brands Limited Too and Justice (owned by Tween Brands, Inc.), and Club Libby Lu, an "experience-based" store for girls aged 6 to 12, a wholly owned subsidiary of Saks, Inc. Where Limited Too and Justice sold mainly apparel, Club Libby Lu sold cosmetics, bath products, and ear piercing, all supporting a palette of pinks and purples, accented by glitter and sparkle, and provided a clublike environment where girls could purchase a "makeover" kit used to create pretend characters such as a rock star or princess, create their own spa package to use to hold home parties, or select a furry stuffed "pooch" companion to take home in a couture carrier. Their celebrity tween cosmetic line, "Pink Twinkle," is the creation of Ashley Tisdale, Disney actress and pop star.[24]

Club Libby Lu was created by former Claire's Stores executive Mary Drolet in 2000 and was acquired by Saks, Inc. in 2003. The store held group activities like birthday parties in its predominately pink interior and offered membership in the VIP ("Very Important Princess") club. Responding to this very specific targeting, one reporter commented, "Besides encouraging kids to be egotistical brats, Libby Lu and other kiddie stores like Monkey Dooz reinforce annoying stereotypes—as opposed to legitimate sexual differences—and transform children into tiny grotesques destined for an adulthood as gender-polarized as their parents. Do all little girls long to be pretty in pink?"[25]

Regardless of the effect of this kind of specialty targeting, the tween market (children between ages 8 to 12) was large and potentially lucrative. As industry research revealed, "Children 11 and older don't consider themselves children anymore . . . by treating pre-adolescents as independent, mature consumers, marketers have been very successful in removing the gatekeepers (parents) from the picture."[26] Data showed that 86 percent of the time the choice of brand was made by the tween rather than the parent, even though in most instances, the parent paid.[27] Cosmetics was one of the areas predicted to grow, and Target had created a brand, "Dottie Loves," in 2005 that included accessories, apparel, glittery cosmetics, and pink costumes, but the line was quickly discontinued by 2006, highlighting the fleeting nature of this type of specific merchandising. For those continuing to target these tweens, at least one analyst in late 2006 believed that Tween Brands, Inc., with its Limited Too and Justice apparel brands, had "no direct specialty retail competitor" and had "the ability to become the category killer in the tween market across all income brackets," with opportunities during 2007 "to increase its operating margin to 15% or more."[28]

CLAIRE'S BACKGROUND

The profile of Claire's Stores, Inc. in 2007 was almost certainly due to the vision of Rowland Schaefer, who bought Harry Camp & Co. in 1960 and subsequently turned that firm, a seller of wigs, handbags, and accessories from leased department store counters, into Fashion Tress, Inc., a manufacturer of wigs and accessories distributed worldwide. Fashion Tress went public in over-the-counter trading in 1961, and in 1973 Schaefer renamed it FT Industries, Inc. after he purchased Claire's Boutiques, Inc., a small specialty chain with 60 stores in the Chicago area. After realizing that the Claire's name had some brand significance, Schaefer changed the company name to Claire's Stores, Inc. in 1983, and the common stock was listed on the New York Stock Exchange in 1985.

Starting in 1994, Claire's embarked on expansion outside North America, with the initiation of a joint venture with Japan's Jusco Co., Ltd., a member of the AEON Group. The first store opened in Tokyo in November 1994 and by 2006 included 172 locations. In 1995, Claire's purchased Bow Bangles Holding, Ltd., a Birmingham, England–based chain of 71 accessories stores, eventually rebranding them as Claire's Accessories. Further major European expansion continued. In 1998, Claire's acquired Bijoux One, a 53-store chain covering Switzerland, Austria, and Germany, and in 2000 acquired 42 Cleopatre stores in France.

Starting in 1993, Rowland Schaeffer had steadily bought up rival small accessories businesses, including Topkapi, Dara Michelle, L'cessory, Accessory Place, and The Icings, a major acquisition in 1996. Various forays into related businesses included "trend gift" stores such as Arcadio; Art Explorion; E. 57th, which sold T-shirts, unframed posters, calendars and stationery products, and a mail-order apparel and accessories catalog operation under the trade name "just nikki." Starting in 1995, the "trend gift" stores were either closed or converted into accessory stores, and the catalog business was allowed to close. In 1998, Claire's acquired a unisex teenage apparel chain operating under the trade name Mr. Rags from Lux Corporation. The concept never really worked for Claire's, and Mr. Rags was sold off in 2002. Claire's had acquired the Afterthoughts chain of 768 stores from Woolworth's in 1999, incorporating that into the existing Icing stores, renaming this Icing by Claire's as a brand extension targeting older teens and young women.

OPERATIONAL INFORMATION

Claire's Stores experienced the traditional retail seasonal sales cycle, with peak periods during Christmas, Easter, and back-to-school time frames. Stores were predominately located in enclosed shopping malls using company-designed displays in such a way that merchandise could be adjusted and rotated easily, and allowed presentation of a wide variety of items in a relatively small space. The low square footage combined with the normally small merchandise size allowed for high sales per square foot, even at an average unit retail price of $4.40 in 2006.

Merchandise was sourced from importers primarily located in Asia and was distributed from the central warehouse in Illinois for North America and Puerto Rico and from Birmingham, England, for stores in the U.K., Ireland, France, Holland, and Belgium. Additional distribution facilities in Zurich, Switzerland, and Vienna, Austria, served stores in Switzerland, Austria, Germany, and Spain. Merchandise was typically delivered to stores three to five times a week. Over the years, Claire's had been able to use its increasing buying power to negotiate lower prices from vendors, resulting in correspondingly higher mark-ups and resulting margins, especially on jewelry items.

To a large extent, similar to most specialty retail operations, Claire's success was dependent on merchandising—anticipating the fashion trends and being able to respond to changes and switch out merchandise without having to take inventory loss. Active management of merchandising was accomplished through constant product testing and assessment of the effectiveness of store displays. Significant investment in management information systems, begun in earnest in 1997 and continuing through 2006, allowed for efficient decision making and effective utilization of inventory distribution systems. The emphasis in 2007 was on conversion of all international information systems to a single, unified platform so merchandise decisions could be made with centralized control.

Claire's had always been known for astute money management—significant cash on hand and the ability to generate cash flow from operations and available funds under its credit line. Under the Schaefers, Claire's also was able to keep debt to a minimum and in 2006 had no debt at all.

IMPERATIVES AND CHALLENGES

At Claire's Stores, Inc., Marla Schaefer, located in New York City, identified herself as the visionary, and had a background in merchandising. Bonnie Schaefer, located at the company's headquarters in Pembroke Pines, Florida, was the operations and real estate expert and international strategist. They said they worked well together, and although at least one consultant believed that manager-duos can be a key to success, some worried whether the Schaefer sisters would be able to continue to balance each other's strengths and weaknesses, especially if the company was going to grow under their leadership.[29] If their strategic vision was just a hold-over from their father, they risked being replaced.

The Schaefer sisters' task may have been made easier because they had no real direct competitors as of 2007. Even the competitors selected by financial analysts didn't consistently measure up to Claire's operational numbers (see Exhibits 5 & 6). However, Claire's continued to be under the scrutiny of the public investment community. Certainly there were demographic, technological, economic, and social trends that would

EXHIBIT 5   **Claire's Stores Direct Competitor Comparison**

(from http://finance.yahoo.com/q/co?s=CLE as of 2006)					
	CLE	**Pvt1**	**TWB**	**WTSLA**	**Industry**
Market Cap:	2.66B	N/A	1.29B	467.84M	1.83B
Employees:	7,560	N/A	2,800	1,735	5,06K
Quarterly Revenue Growth (yoy):	7.40%	N/A	19.90%	2.50%	14.10%
Revenue (ttm):	1.40B	640.00M1	819.53M	525.35M	1.94B
Gross Margin (ttm):	53.65%	N/A	38.14%	45.25%	46.24%
EBITDA (ttm):	299.20M	N/A	123.12M	73.81M	255.94M
Oper Margins (ttm):	17.36%	N/A	11.10%	13.58%	10.42%
Net Income (ttm):	172.85M	N/A	60.68M	−18.55M	94.57M
EPS (ttm):	1.743	N/A	1.808	−0.312	1.51
P/E (ttm):	16.04	N/A	21.69	N/A	20.92
PEG (5-yr expected):	1.08	N/A	0.81	0.39	1.07
P/S (ttm):	1.92	N/A	1.59	0.89	1.37

Pvt 1 = Forever 21, Inc. (privately help)

TWB = Tween Brands, Inc.

WTSLA = Wet Seal Inc.

Industry = Apparel Stores

Tween Brands, Inc., founded in 1987, operates as specialty retailer for tween girls in the United States. It primarily operates two specialty retailing concepts under Limited Too and Justice brand names. The company's product portfolio comprises apparel, such as jeanswear and bottoms, knit tops and T-shirts, graphic T-shirts, dresses, and outerwear; accessories, including jewelry, hair ornaments, hats, key chains, wallets, backpacks, purses, watches, and legwear; footwear, such as slippers, sandals, boots, and shoes; lifestyle products comprising bedroom furnishings, music, small electronics, stationary, candy, and party favors; personal care products, which include cosmetics and toiletries; and add-ons, such as underwear, sleepwear, and swimwear for girls aged 7 to 14 years. It also offers these products through its Web site, www.limitedtoo .com. As of July 10, 2006, the company operated 565 Limited Too stores in 46 states and Puerto Rico and 111 Justice stores in the United States. The company also licenses approximately 19 Limited Too stores in the Kingdom of Saudi Arabia, Kuwait, the United Arab Emirates, and Qatar.

The Wet Seal, Inc. and its subsidiaries operate as a specialty retailer of apparel and accessory items designed for female consumers in the United States. The company operates two mall-based chains of retail stores under the names Wet Seal and Arden B. The Wet Seal targets the fashion-conscious junior customer by providing brand name and company-developed apparel and accessories. The Arden B. stores delivers a feminine, contemporary, sophisticated wardrobe of branded fashion separates and accessories. The company also provides Wet Seal online, a Web-based store located at www.wetseal.com, as well as at www.ardenb.com, which offers Arden B. apparel and accessories. As of April 10, 2006, it operated 400 retail stores in 46 states, Puerto Rico, and Washington DC, including 308 Wet Seal stores and 92 Arden B. stores. The company, formerly known as Lorne's, was founded in 1962 by Lorne Huycke and is headquartered in Foothill Ranch, California.

You don't have to be over 21 to shop at **Forever 21**'s stores—you just need your wallet. The company operates about 390 mainly mall-based U.S. stores in the United States and Canada under the Forever 21, Forever XXI, and For Love 21 banners. The stores offer cheap and chic fashions and accessories for women and junior girls. Its trendy clothes are priced 2 percent lower than its competitors. Most of the retailer's apparel is private label and is made in Southern California. Forever XXI stores are larger than classic Forever 21 shops and offer men's and women's fashions, as well as lingerie, footwear, cosmetic items, and other accessories. Owner and CEO Don Chang and his wife founded the company as Fashion 21 in 1984.

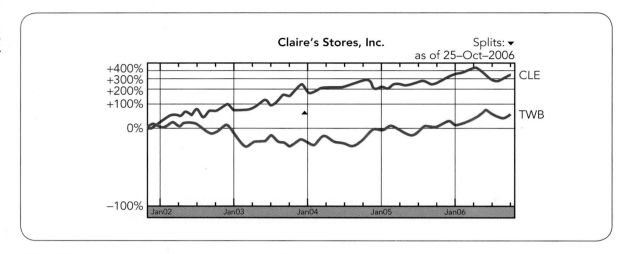

EXHIBIT 6   **Claire's Stores (CLE) Stock Price vs. Tween Brands (TWB) (Competitor)**

be important to address going forward from 2007, both in the United States and internationally.

Regarding management depth in Claire's upper ranks, changing demographics in 2006 predicted a future shortage of entry-level retail employees. In retail, managers tended to rotate from retailer to retailer, recycling talent within the industry. Since Claire's preferred to "grow their own," they had to create relationships with prospective employees. Claire's Stores was a member of the DECA Association of Marketing Students National Advisory Board, offered scholarships to DECA students employed in its stores, and created internships in various retail-related career tracks.[30] The Annual Report of 2006 seemed to indicate this was a strategy that would take time to mature.

Well developed over 40 years, Claire's operational mechanisms seemed to be a major source of their strength. The Schaefer sisters were emphasizing the upgrading of management information systems and appeared to give the same level of attention to their marketing and sales. Marla said she believed Claire's had "practically 100 percent name recognition" among its core demographic, and that anyone "who has female children knows exactly what Claire's is."[31] Claire's appeared to be continuing to utilize a strategy that might be sustainable over time, although not at the growth levels of the past, but this strategy assumed no direct pressure from creative players like Target, Abercrombie & Fitch, or the combined might of Limited Brands. Claire's corporate strategy seemed to be, as Marla said, to "stick to the knitting." Unlike many of their fellow specialty retailers, they didn't pursue more diversification, seeming content to know that Rowland Schaefer had already tested those waters, for instance with the Mr. Rags apparel line. Limited Brands, however, with its diversified holdings, received positive marks going into the holiday shopping season of 2006,

especially after seeing its first quarter earnings increase by 56 percent.[32]

International expansion seemed to be of primary importance for Claire's Stores going into 2007, with their revised franchising and merchandising strategies. Bonnie Schaefer seemed to prefer building new stores rather than acquiring existing ones and seemed to believe in importing North American "best practices" to the stores abroad, to gain operational efficiencies.[33] Sometimes this didn't translate well to other cultures. In their 2006 10K Filing, the Schaefer's identified their strategy as one of organic growth—entering into agreements with "unaffiliated third parties who are familiar with the local retail environment and have sufficient retail experience to operate stores in accordance with our business model."[34] Analysts were cautious to see if Claire's entry and operational strategies would be appropriate for their new chosen foreign markets. For reaching beyond the physical store front, Claire's Stores had a consumer Web site at www.claires.com, but it was not a shopping site.

Given that Claire's Stores was a publicly traded family firm with ownership in 2006 still heavily in family hands and most investors of the institutional variety, Claire's might have to make sure they have succession planning systems that allow top nonfamily executives to move forward. Although Claire's had a good "corporate governance quotient," better than 61 percent of other retailers,[35] governance of family businesses was always troublesome during transitions.[36] If the Schaefer sisters modeled themselves after their father, it would have been hard for them to relinquish control, yet as they expanded into more international locations and considered implications of U.S. stagnation, they had to have considered different possible operational configurations. As always, challenges remained regarding how to spur new growth during 2007 and beyond, especially if the company was taken private in a leveraged buyout.

Endnotes

1. Foust, D. 2006. A sister act that's wowing them. *BusinessWeek Online,* 3/13/2006, from http://www.businessweek.com.

2. LeClaire, J. 2005. Sitting pretty: Claire's Stores is raking in a pretty penny with value-priced fashion jewelry. Can the company keep up with Wall Street's expectations? *South Florida CEO,* July, from http://www.findarticles.com/p/articles/mi_m0OQD/is_6_9/ai_n14841842.

3. LeClaire, op. cit.

4. Little, M. 2006. Fashionably profitable: With an estimated $30 spent annually on women's fashion accessories, stores are taking notice. *Knight Ridder Tribune Business News,* June 4: 1.

5. Celebrity merchandising aims at the young; the Olsen twins' success led other stars to try to cash in on the teen and preteen market. *Los Angeles Times* (Home Edition), 7/11/2006: C8.

6. Owen, E. 2006. Claire's Stores reaps big market in accessories for young shoppers. *The Wall Street Journal* (Eastern Edition), April 12.

7. LeClaire, op. cit.

8. Owen, op. cit.

9. Baker, S. 2006. The apparel industry's top seven mega-trends: Management briefing: Smart retailers and brands give consumers more options, more often. *Just–Style,* October: 6.

10. Owen, op. cit.

11. Owen, op. cit.

12. Kang, S. 2006. Chasing Generation Y: Retailers scramble to serve a glut of twentysomethings. *The Wall Street Journal* (Eastern Edition), September 1: A11.

13. Barbaro, M. 2006. New clothing chain caters to the 25-to-40 buyer. *New York Times* (Late Edition–East Coast), September 5: C1.

14. CEO interview: Marla Schaefer—Claire's Stores Inc. *The Wall Street Transcript Corporation,* March 14: 1.

15. Attorney General Lockyer announces court approves settlement with Wal-Mart to reduce lead in costume jewelry. *U.S. Fed News Service,* Including U.S. State News (Dateline Sacramento, CA), 4/20/2006.

16. Emery, C. 2006. City plans to ban tainted jewelry: U.S. fails to protect children from lead, health chief says. *Knight Ridder Tribune Business News,* August 15: 1.

17. Gustke, C., & Poggi, J. 2006. Biggest earners; the top 20 apparel retail executives of publicly held U.S. companies with the highest compensation packages from 2005. *Woman's Wear Daily,* 192 (39): 12.

18. Foust, op. cit.

19. Fakler, J. T. 2000. Claire's Stores ring up sales but lose another president. *Business Journal,* 21 (6): A27.

20. Claire's Stores, Inc. Annual Report Fiscal Year Ended January 28, 2006, from http://www.clairestores.com/phoenix.zhtml?c=68915&p=irol-report2006.

21. *The Wall Street Transcript Corporation,* op. cit.

22. http://www.m-w.com.

23. Cimilluca, D. 2006. Claire's hires Goldman, contacts potential buyers, people say. *Bloomberg News,* 12/1/06, http://www.bloomberg.com/apps/news?pid=20601103&sid=ajMDL8B_NEvI&refer=news.

24. "High School Musical" star Ashley Tisdale adds panache to new tween cosmetic line from Club Libby Lu. July 13, 2006, from http://www.cllublibbylu.com/news.aspx?cat1=7.

25. Chonin, N. 2006. Nothin' but a Tween thang. *San Francisco Chronicle,* July 23, from http://66.35.240.8/cgi-bin/article.cgi?file=/chronicle/archive/2006/07/23/PKGDOILVQU1.DTL&type=printable.

26. Special issues for tweens and teens, retrieved 12/9/06 from http://www.media-awareness.ca/english/parents/marketing/issues_teens_marketing.cfm.

27. Clack, E. 2004. What a tween wants . . . now, *Children's Business,* 4/01/04, http://www.reachadvisors.com/childrensbusinessarticle2.html.

28. RTTNews, 2006. Management reshuffles—weekly recap. November 24, from *Quote.com,* http://new.quote.com/news/story.action?id=RTT611241030000462.

29. Pounds, M. H. 2006. South Florida Sun-Sentinel Business Strategies column. *Knight Ridder Tribune Business News,* March 1: 1.

30. From http://www.clairestores.com/phoenix.zhtml?c=68915&p=irol-commitment.

31. *The Wall Street Transcript Corporation,* op. cit.

32. Halpern, S. 2006. Stock picking pros favor specialty retail and apparel. *MarketWatch: The Stock Advisors.com,* December 4, http://www.marketwatch.com/News/Story/Story.aspx?guid=%7B9F8A2608-3D44-4775-88B6-42A68F71D7FB%7D&siteid=yhoo&dist=.

33. Q2 2007 Claire's Stores, Inc. earnings conference call. *Fair Disclosure Wire,* 8/17/2006.

34. Claire's Stores 10K Filing, 4/12/06, p. 12, from http://www.clairestores.com/phoenix.zhtml?c=68915&p=irolsec&secCat01v1_rs=31&secCat01v1_rc=10.

35. From http://finance.yahoo.com/q/pr?s=CLE.

36. Loyalka, M. D. 2006. Family-biz circle: The boomer handoff. *BusinessWeek Online,* February 14, http://www.businessweek.com/smallbiz/content/feb2006/sb20060213_147073.htm?chan=careers_careers_career+information.

CASE 9   Nintendo's Wii

When Nintendo released the Wii video game console, it was already in the midst of a very competitive market. The previous generation of video game consoles consisted of the Sega Dreamcast, Sony PlayStation 2, Nintendo GameCube, and Microsoft Xbox. These systems were all released between 1999 and 2001 in the United States, and although the GameCube sold more systems than the Sega Dreamcast, it fell into third place behind the PlayStation 2 and the Xbox. The PlayStation 2 sold more than 115 million units worldwide, more than twice the combined unit sales of the GameCube and Xbox (21 million and 24 million, respectively). The next generation of video game consoles was about to become even more competitive.

Not only did Nintendo sit behind Sony and Microsoft in terms of overall sales, but it derived most of its revenue from the video game business. Sony had more than 158,000 employees and its 2006 revenues were over $63 billion. Microsoft had more than 70,000 employees and its 2006 revenues were $44 billion. Nintendo was founded in 1889 but had only roughly 3,000 employees and 2006 revenues of $4.5 billion. Thus, Nintendo sat in the middle of two potentially dominating firms. Yet Nintendo was in the lead in video console sales growth and second in overall units sold to Microsoft, which had shipped its product a year ahead of Nintendo and Sony.

BACKGROUND

Although Nintendo dates back to 1889 as a playing card maker, Nintendo's first video game systems were developed in 1979 and were known as TV Game 15 and TV Game 6.[1] In 1980 Nintendo developed the first portable LCD video game with a microprocessor. In 1985 Nintendo created the Nintendo Entertainment System (NES), an 8-bit video game console. The original NES was very successful, as its graphics were superior to any home-based console that was available at the time, and as a result more than 60 million units were sold worldwide.[2] The NES set the bar for subsequent consoles in platform design, as well as accepting games that were manufactured by third-party developers. As competitors began developing a 16-bit devices, such as Sega's Genesis system or NEC's PC Engine, Nintendo knew that it had to respond and develop its own 16-bit system.

The Super Nintendo Entertainment System (SNES) was developed to stay current with the competitors. The Super Nintendo was released in 1991 and when purchased came with one game, Super Mario World. This was the successor to the previous Mario Brothers games that were played on the original 8-bit NES. In 1996 Nintendo released Nintendo 64, which caused the popularity of the Super Nintendo to decline. The Nintendo 64 is Nintendo's third generation video game console and was named after the 64-bit processor. The retail price of the Nintendo 64 was $199.

The Nintendo 64, like its predecessors, used cartridges to play its games, but at the time, the competing systems of Sony and Sega were using CDs for game storage. Cartridges could store 64 megabytes of data, while CDs could store around 700 megabytes of data. Also, CDs were much cheaper to manufacture, distribute, and create, thus many game developers that traditionally supported Nintendo platforms began creating games that would support the other platforms to increase profits.[3] At the time, the average cost of producing a Nintendo 64 cartridge was cited as $25 per cartridge versus 10 cents per CD. Therefore game producers passed these higher expenses to the consumer, which explains why Nintendo 64 games tended to sell for higher prices than Sony PlayStation games. While most Sony PlayStation games rarely exceeded $50, Nintendo 64 titles could reach $70.[4] Third-party developers naturally switched to the systems that used a less expensive CD platform (such as the PlayStation).

In 2001 Nintendo released its GameCube, which was part of the sixth generation era of video game systems. These systems include Sony's PlayStation 2, Microsoft's Xbox, and Sega's Dreamcast. Although the GameCube no longer used cartridges, it began producing its games using a proprietary optical-disc technology. This technology, while similar in appearance to CDs, was actually several inches smaller in diameter and was unable to be played using a standard CD player.

Mr. Genyo Takeda, General Manager of Integrated Research and Development for Nintendo, explained that innovation and creativity were fostered by giving several different development teams "free rein to couple a dedicated controller or peripheral with a GameCube title, and then see whether or not the end result was marketable. This project gave rise not only to the Donkey Kong Bongos and the Dancing Stage Mario Mix Action Pad, but also to a number of ideas and designs that would find their way into the Wii Remote."[5]

As of 2007, Nintendo's revenues and income were on attractive upward trajectories (see Exhibits 1 and 2). Exhibit 3 shows that Nintendo's stock price was soaring relative to its larger competitions.

THE LAUNCH OF THE WII

In 2006 Nintendo released its direct successor to the Game-Cube, the Wii (pronounced *we*). There have been many reasons cited as to why the name Wii was chosen, but perhaps the most compelling reason was "'Wii' sounds like 'we,' which emphasizes that the console was for everyone. Wii could be remembered easily by people around the world, no matter what language they spoke. No confusion."[6] Initially the system was known by its code name, Revolution, but later the name was changed to Wii. Nintendo stated that it wanted to make the Wii a system that would make anyone who tried it talk to their friends and neighbors about it.[7]

The Wii was created to establish a new standard in game control, using an innovative and unprecedented interface, the Wii Remote.[8] The Wii Remote was what made the Wii a unique home console. The remote acted as the primary controller for the Wii.

*This case was prepared by graduate student Eshai J. Gorshein and Professor Alan B. Eisner of Pace University. This case was based solely upon library research and was developed for class discussion rather than to illustrate either effective or ineffective handling of an administrative situation. Copyright © 2007 Alan B. Eisner.

EXHIBIT 1   **Income Statements**

(in millions of Japanese Yen except for per share items)	2007 03/31/07	2006 03/31/06	2005 03/31/05	2004 03/31/04	2003 03/31/03
Total Revenue	966,534	509,249	515,292	514,805	504,135
Cost of Revenue, Total	568,722	294,133	298,115	307,233	308,525
Selling/Gen/Admin. Expense	171,787	21,837	16,366	16,014	20,448
Labor & Related Expense	—	15,131	13,402	12,716	11,693
Advertising Expense	—	55,442	53,756	53,488	46,227
Sell/General/Admin. Expenses, Total	171,787	92,410	83,524	82,218	78,368
Research & Development	—	30,588	20,505	15,820	14,590
Depreciation/Amortization	—	1,764	1,621	1,846	2,526
Restructuring Charge	—	—	—	—	0
Impair-Assets Held for Sale	335	1,383	1,612	510	864
Other Unusual Expense (Income)	(338)	(3,610)	(1,735)	(2,575)	(117)
Unusual Expense (Income)	(3)	(2,227)	(123)	(2,065)	747
Total Operating Expense	740,506	416,668	403,642	405,052	404,756
Operating Income	226,028	92,581	111,650	109,753	99,379
Interest Expense, Net Nonoperating	—	(1)	0	0	(1)
Interest Income, Nonoperating	33,987	22,497	13,510	8,999	15,942
Investment Income, Nonoperating	26,632	49,017	18,336	(67,876)	(3,615)
Inter/Invest Inc, Nonoperating	60,619	71,514	31,846	(58,877)	12,327
Interest Income (Expense), Net Nonoperating	60,619	71,513	31,846	(58,877)	12,326
Gain (Loss) on Sale of Assets	(132)	(20)	(13)	761	(59)
Other, Net	3,087	2,398	1,924	1,335	1,677
Net Income before Taxes	289,602	166,472	145,407	52,972	113,323
Provision for Income Taxes	115,347	68,138	57,962	19,692	45,973
Net Income after Taxes	174,255	98,334	87,445	33,280	67,350
Minority Interest	37	46	(24)	(79)	(74)
Net Income before Extra Items	174,292	98,380	87,421	33,201	67,276
Net Income	174,292	98,380	87,421	33,201	67,276

Source: reuters.com.

Due to its motion sensor capabilities it allowed the user to interact and manipulate objects on the screen by moving and pointing the remote in various directions.[9] It was the size of a traditional remote control, and was "limited only by the game designer's imagination."[10] For example, in a game of tennis it served as the racket when the user swung his or her arm, or in a shooting game it served as the user's gun. Not only did the remote serve as a controller but it also had a built-in speaker and a rumble feature for even greater tactile feedback and game involvement.

The Wii remote came with an arm strap that could be tied to the user's wrist to avoid the remote flying away when being used. The remote was powered by two AA batteries, which could power the remote for approximately 30 to 60 hours.[11] Exhibit 4 shows the Wii and Wii Remote.

The second part of the Wii remote innovation was the Wii Nunchuk. The Nunchuk was designed to perfectly fit the user's hand, and connected to the remote at its expansion port. The Nunchuk had the same motion-sensing capabilities that the

EXHIBIT 2   **Balance Sheets**

(in millions of Japanese Yen except for per share items)	2007 03/31/07	2006 03/31/06	2005 03/31/05	2004 03/31/04	2003 03/31/03
Cash & Equivalents	962,197	812,064	826,653	767,270	748,650
Short-Term Investments	115,971	64,287	20,485	17,375	8,266
Cash and Short-Term Investments	1,078,168	876,351	847,138	784,645	756,916
Trade Accounts Receivable, Gross	89,666	43,826	51,143	28,493	49,085
Provision for Doubtful Accounts	(1,886)	(1,514)	(1,880)	(3,028)	(5,463)
Total Receivables, Net	87,780	42,312	49,263	25,465	43,622
Total Inventory	88,609	30,835	49,758	30,955	104,524
Deferred Income Tax	35,631	24,170	19,513	24,911	31,158
Other Current Assets	104,483	45,061	28,217	24,784	33,088
Other Current Assets, Total	140,114	69,231	47,730	49,695	64,246
Total Current Assets	1,394,671	1,018,729	993,889	890,760	969,308
Land/Improvements	32,595	32,604	32,069	31,925	33,134
Construction in Progress	217	41	410	0	7
Property/Plant/Equipment Net	57,597	55,968	54,417	55,083	59,367
Intangibles, Net	505	319	354	245	225
Long-Term Investments	92,412	60,213	73,393	53,866	38,551
Other Long-Term Assets	15,991	15,156	277	883	3,352
Total Assets	1,575,590	1,160,699	1,132,485	1,010,026	1,085,515
Accounts Payable	301,080	83,817	111,045	57,945	96,475
Accrued Expenses	1,779	1,732	1,650	1,712	1,672
Notes Payable/Short-Term Debt	—	0	0	0	0
Income Taxes Payable	90,013	53,040	51,951	11,165	38,913
Other Current Liabilities	75,563	43,684	40,801	42,423	48,988
Other Current Liabilities, Total	165,576	96,724	92,752	53,588	87,901
Total Current Liabilities	468,435	182,273	205,447	113,245	186,048
Total Long-Term Debt	—	0	0	0	0
Total Debt	—	0	0	0	0
Minority Interest	138	176	222	232	153
Pension Benefits–Underfunded	4,443	3,299	4,890	5,701	8,810
Other LT Liabilities	698	861	461	602	135
Other Liabilities, Total	5,141	4,160	5,351	6,303	8,945
Total Liabilities	473,714	186,609	211,020	119,780	195,146
Common Stock	10,065	10,065	10,065	10,065	10,065
Additional Paid-In Capital	11,586	11,585	11,584	11,584	11,584
Retained Earnings (Accumulated Deficit)	1,220,293	1,096,073	1,032,834	964,524	950,262
Treasury Stock–Common	(155,396)	(155,112)	(129,896)	(86,898)	(81,521)
Unrealized Gain (Loss)	8,898	10,717	7,194	6,650	2,254
Other Equity, Total	6,432	762	(10,315)	(15,677)	(2,275)
Total Equity	1,101,878	974,090	921,466	890,248	890,369
Total Liabilities & Shareholders' Equity	1,575,592	1,160,699	1,132,486	1,010,028	1,085,515
Total Common Shares Outstanding	128	128	130	134	134
Treasury Shares–Common Primary Issue	14	14	12	8	7

Source: reuters.com.

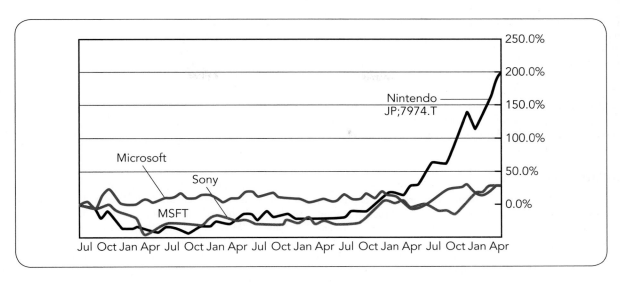

EXHIBIT 3   **Stock Chart of Nintendo, Microsoft, and Sony, 2003–2007**

Source: reuters.com.

EXHIBIT 4   **Wii Game Console and Remote**

remote has, but it also had an analog stick to help the user move his or her characters. In addition to the analog stick, the Nunchuk had two buttons that gave the user quick access to other game functions. Thus the Nunchuk offered some of the benefits of a standard game controller coupled with the high-technology motion sensors of the remote. Users could hold a Nunchuk in one hand and the Wii remote in the other while playing the Wii Sports Boxing game and be transformed into the boxing ring with on-screen opponent. The game controls were intuitive for jabs and punches; however, a missed block did not hurt as much as if one were really in the boxing ring.

The ambidextrous nature of the Wii controllers was something seldom seen in other game controllers; the Wii controllers permitted the user to hold the remote and Nunchuk whichever way felt most comfortable.[12]

FEATURES

In addition to the Wii Remote there were other features unique to the Wii. One of these features was the Wii Menu, which was the first screen that appeared on the television when the Wii was turned on. According to Nintendo, the Wii Menu easily integrates itself into the everyday lives of its users.[13]

The menu displayed several different icons, one of them the Mii Channel (pronounced *me*). This channel gave the users the ability to create and personalize a 3-D caricature of themselves. Another icon was the Everybody Votes Channel, which permitted individuals to vote in national and worldwide polls on a variety of topics. There was also a News Channel that gave the individual up-to-date breaking news from around the world organized into a variety of topics. The Forecast Channel was another icon displayed on the Wii Menu. This allowed the individual to view weather reports from anywhere around the world.

Users had the ability to download older Nintendo games from the Wii Shopping Channel. A Wii Message Board allowed users to leave messages on the Wii for other users of the same console, or reminders for themselves. An Internet Channel allowed individuals to surf the Internet from their Wii. There was a Photo Channel that allowed the user to view photos stored on a standard SD memory card. And lastly there was a Disc Channel that gave the user the ability to play Wii games or Nintendo GameCube discs.[14] The Wii was backward compatible with the Nintendo Game-Cube's games, memory cards, and controllers.

ONLINE CAPABILITIES

Nintendo's Wii was the first Nintendo console that had online capabilities. The Wii could connect to the Internet in several different ways. The Wii could connect to the Internet via a standard wireless protocol—a consumer's home high speed Internet hookup (usually from a cable TV service or telephone company DSL). Another way the Wii could connect to the Internet was via the Nintendo DS, which had wireless capability built in. The Wii could also be connected to the Internet via an optional wired USB–Ethernet adapter.

According to Nintendo of America's president and COO, Reggie Fils-Aime, the Wii would "offer online-enabled games that consumers will not have to pay a subscription fee for. They'll be able to play right out of the box. . . . It will not have any hidden fees or costs."[15] However as of mid-2007, no such games existed. So far the only consoles to allow an individual to play games interactively with other users online were the competing products: Microsoft Xbox 360 and Sony PlayStation 3.

The Wii was released in North America on November 19, 2006, and sales as of March 3, 2007 were in excess of 2 million units (see Exhibit 5).[16]

However, although these numbers may seem quite large, Nintendo had been experiencing production problems with the Wii. Nintendo had been unable to meet demand during 2007. In an interview on the Web site Game Theory, Perrin Kapaln, Nintendo vice president of marketing and corporate affairs, suggested that shortages were expected for some time. "We are at absolute maximum production and doing everything we can . . . but demand continues to be really high."[17]

EXHIBIT 5 Wii Units Sold

Region	Units Sold	First Available
North America	2,083,880	11/19/06
Japan	2,014,310	12/2/06
Europe	2,000,000	12/8/06
Australia	68,000	12/7/06
Total	**6,166,190**	

DEMOGRAPHICS

According to Nintendo, one of the key differences between the Wii and the competitors' systems was the broad audience that the Wii targeted.[18] Many of the Wii games were able to be played by people of all ages, and were easier to control than the complicated controllers of the Sony PlayStation 3 or Microsoft Xbox 360. Nintendo's TV commercials for the Wii showed people of all ages and different social classes playing the Wii. According to Nintendo, the Wii remote allowed people of all ages to enjoy its use. Nintendo wanted to create a controller that was "as inviting as it was sophisticated."[19] Nintendo's goal was to create games that everyone could play, a system that would appeal to women and people who had never played video games in the past. Shigeru Miyamoto, a senior director at Nintendo explained, "Most of the game business is going down a similar path toward hyperrealistic graphics which recreate sports or movies. . . . We want to put a little more art into it in a way that casual consumers can enjoy the game."[20] The Wii offered something for both the advanced gamer and the person who had never played a video game before. The advanced gamer would enjoy the remote's unique features, whereas the novice gamer could use the remote as his or her hand and wouldn't need elaborate instructions on how to play a new game straight out of the box. Although the Nintendo games were easily played by a greater range of ages, the graphics were undoubtedly a relative weakness of the product.

Although Nintendo had been able to target a large range of age groups, it seemed to lack the lineup of games offered by other systems. Nintendo had focused on its proprietary Mario Brothers series games, as well as low graphic, low complexity games that could be played by a wide range of age levels. PlayStation 3's top-selling game was *Resistance: Fall of Man,* which had won many awards, but more importantly had a rating of *Mature* (a rating given by The Entertainment Software Rating Board), which meant that it was suitable for audiences of 17 and older only. Xbox's best-selling game was *Gears of War,* which also had a rating of *Mature.* The Wii's best-selling games were *The Legend of Zelda: Twilight Princess,* which had a rating of *Teen,* which meant it's suitable for ages 13 and up, and *Wii Sports,* which was rated *Everyone,* suitable for all audiences. One of the Wii's shortcomings was obviously its graphics.[21] It was widely believed that the Wii had 2.5 times the power of the GameCube, but hardly enough to compete with the Xbox 360 or PlayStation 3.

Although Nintendo hoped to target people of all ages, it has long been seen as a system that makes video games for children, as evident from its Mario, Zelda, and Donkey Kong series. It was going to be difficult for Nintendo to position itself as a console for gamers of all ages and tastes.

GAINING THE INTEREST OF GAME DEVELOPERS

As evident from the history of game consoles, game developers have tried to make games more and more complex with each new generation of systems. This means that more money was

EXHIBIT 6   **Game Systems Comparison**

	Nintendo	Sony	Microsoft
Console Name	Wii	PlayStation 3	Xbox 360
Game Format	12 cm Wii Optical Disc	Blu-ray Disc, DVD-Rom, CD-Rom	HD DVD, DVD, DVD-DL
Hard Drive	None	20GB or 60GB	20GB or 120GB
Price	$249	$599 (60GB)	$299 core, $399 premium, or $479 elite
Ethernet	Wi-fi standard	Wi-fi optional	Wi-fi optional
Online Services	WiiConnect24 Wii Channels, no online game play yet	PlayStation Network, has online game play	Xbox live, has online game play
Controller	Wii remote (wireless, motion sensing)	Max 7 SIXAXIS (wireless)	Wired or wireless
Backward Compatibility	Yes (Nintendo GameCube)	Yes (PlayStation 2)	Yes (certain Xbox games)
Game Count	235	150[22]	270

Sources: Company reports and author estimates.

invested in the production of each subsequent generation of games. Because game developers were spending more money on developing games, they were at great financial risk if games did not succeed. Thus, many developers felt more secure in simply creating sequels to existing games, which in turn restricted innovation. The Wii's innovative controller, the Wii remote, required a rethinking and reengineering of the human interface for game developers and programmers. Another issue with developing games for the Wii was that its graphics were not quite as good as those of the PlayStation 3 and Xbox 360, and therefore game developers were required to be more creative and develop special Wii editions of their games.

Many game developers use virtual machine software in developing new games. It was believed that game developers could develop games for the Wii and then make them for other platforms based on the same programming, thereby reducing production costs. However, while the Wii remote distinguished itself from its competitors, it created a hurdle for developers. When a developer created a game for the PlayStation 3, she could create the same game for the Xbox 360 and vice versa, whereas when a developer created a game for the Wii, it required significant rework to deploy the title for the other platforms. Converting a title from the Xbox 360 or PlayStation 3 also required significant work to modify the game to incorporate code for the Wii Remote's special features.

THE COMPETITION

The launches of the Wii and the PlayStation 3 in November of 2006 were the beginning of the battle for market share in the fierce competition of the seventh generation of video game

consoles (see Exhibit 6). Although the Xbox 360 was released a year earlier, Microsoft intended to relaunch the Xbox 360 after some minor enhancements.

The price of $299 for the Wii included the Wii Remote, the Nunchuk attachment, the sensor bar, and the Wii Sports software title. The Wii sports title included tennis, baseball, golf, bowling, and boxing games. This retail price was much less than the prices of the PlayStation 3 and Xbox 360, possibly due to the fact that the Wii did not have as advanced a central processor unit or a high definition video player.

XBOX 360

The Xbox 360 by Microsoft was released in November 2005, giving it a year lead over Nintendo and Sony's new systems. The Xbox 360 came in three different versions: Elite ($479 retail), Premium System ($399 retail) and Core System ($299 retail).

Although such prices were quite expensive to the retail consumer, in reality Microsoft was losing money on each sale. Take, for example, Microsoft's cost of producing the Premium System. It cost Microsoft $470 before assembly, and an additional $55 for the cost of the cables, power cord, and controllers, bringing Microsoft's cost to $526. Thus, Microsoft was losing $126 on the sale of each system. This was not only the case with the Xbox 360, but also with its predecessor, the Xbox. There too Microsoft was selling a system for $299 that cost Microsoft $323 to produce. Microsoft believed that through the sale of games and accessories it would turn a profit during 2007.[23]

One of the important features of the Xbox 360 was Xbox Live. According to Microsoft, Xbox Live was the "premier online gaming and entertainment service that enables you to connect your Xbox to the Internet and play games online."[24] This feature allowed individuals to play online against other users from all around the world. Thus Microsoft had created a community of individuals who were able to communicate with one another by voice chats and/or playing against each other in a video game. It even allowed users to "see what their friends are up to at any time" and to look not only at their friend's list but also their friend's friend's list.[25] Another service offered by Xbox Live was the Xbox Live Marketplace, which enabled users to download movies, game trailers, game demos, and arcade games. It is estimated that more than 70 percent of connected Xbox users were downloading content from the Xbox Live Marketplace, totaling more than 4 million members.[26] According to Microsoft there were more than 12 million downloads in less than a year and, due to this popularity, major publishers and other independent gamers had submitted more than 1,000 Xbox Live games.[27] Similar to the Wii, the Xbox 360 has a dashboard that showed up when the system is powered up. This gave the user the ability to either play DVDs or games.

The Xbox 360 had the capability to play High Definition DVDs.[28] The CPU of the Xbox 360 was a custom triple core PowerPC–based design manufactured by IBM, known as the Xenon. The Xbox 360 played all its games in 5.1-channel Dolby Digital surround sound, and along with the HD display, the Xbox 360 could truly display excellent picture and sound quality. However, a consumer who did not have a high-definition–enabled television set was not able to enjoy the high definition features of the system. The Xbox 360 played all its games on dual-layer DVDs which could store up to 8.5 GB per disc, but also had the ability to play many other formats.[29] The system had an Ethernet port and three USB ports but could also connect to the Internet via a wireless network.

Microsoft began production of the Xbox 360 only 69 days prior to the launch date.[30] This resulted in Microsoft being unable to supply enough systems to meet the initial demand, and therefore many potential customers were not able to purchase a console at launch.[31] However, according to Bill Gates, Microsoft had over 10 million units out in the market by the time Sony and Nintendo launched their systems.[32]

SONY PLAYSTATION 3

The PlayStation 3 was Sony's seventh-generation video game console. The PlayStation 3 had many advanced features including a Cell Broadband Engine 64-bit processor that features a main power-processing element and up to eight parallel processing elements. This was a multiprocessing unit that provided advanced support for graphics-intense games. Another notable feature of the PlayStation 3 was its ability to play Blu-Ray Discs. Blu-Ray was a form of high-definition video, which enabled game developers to create games of higher sophistication.[33] Another key feature of the PlayStation 3 was the SIXAXIS wireless controller. This controller had sensors that could determine when a player maneuvered or angled his or her controller to allow game play to become a "natural extension of

EXHIBIT 7   **PlayStation 3 Units Sold During First Six Months**

Region	Units Sold	First Available
North America	1,370,300	11/17/06
Japan	870,492[34]	11/17/06
Europe	920,000	3/23/07
Australia	27,000[35]	3/23/07
Total	More than 3.25 million[36]	

the player's body."[37] Although this was a more advanced remote than a standard wired remote, it lacked the true motion-sensing capabilities of the Wii Remote in its first version.[38]

The PlayStation 3 could play music CDs, connect to the Internet, copy CDs directly to its hard drive, play Blu-Ray Discs and DVDs, connect to a digital camera, view photos, and more. However, a consumer who did not have a high-definition–enabled television set was not able to enjoy the high-definition features of the system.

Sales in North America were initially strong and tapered off rapidly with 1.3 million units sold during the first six months of sales (see Exhibit 7).[39] The United Kingdom also saw record-breaking sales of PlayStation 3 with more than 165,000 units (through heavy preordering) in its first two days on the shelves,[40] although the total European sales for the first six months of availability were only 920,000 units.[41] Sony CEO Howard Stringer attributed the slowing sales to a lack of software titles and said that Sony expects at least 380 new PlayStation 3 games to hit the market by 2008.[42]

Part of the PlayStation Network's success was the ability to play games online. This allowed individuals to play other players who might be located in other parts of the world. The PlayStation Network allowed users to download games, view movie and game trailers, and text message and chat with friends. Users were also able to browse the Internet and open up to six windows at once.[43]

Since the launch of the PlayStation 3, there had been mixed reports about it. On the positive note, it was once called the "most important home entertainment device since the TV."[44] Also, MSN stated that the PlayStation 3 was a "versatile and impressive piece of home-entertainment equipment that lives up to the hype . . . the PS3 is well worth its hefty price tag." [45] However, *PC WORLD* magazine ranked the PlayStation 3 eighth out of The Top 20 Tech Screw-ups of 2006.[46]

SUPPLY AND DEMAND

When the Xbox 360 hit stores in November 2005, thousands of video game fans waited outside stores (some even in freezing weather) to be the first to purchase the console. And although the console quickly sold out, it became available several months later and there have not been problems purchasing one since. The same held true with the release of the PlayStation 3. Although it quickly sold out in stores, it was available thereafter, and anyone willing to spend the money is able to purchase it. However, Nintendo fans have had problems finding a Wii to purchase since its launch in November of 2006. Lucky customers might walk into a retailer at the moment the latest Wii shipment has arrived or wait in lines for hours for the privilege of paying the retail price of only $249. The unlucky customers have to search various auction sites such as eBay and pay premiums of double to triple the retail price.

There has been a great deal of speculation regarding the production problems with the Wii. Several analysts have argued that lack of availability of the Wii was a marketing ploy to create hype and increase demand. However, others have hypothesized that Nintendo was having production problems and was unable to meet the huge demand for the Wii. Billy Pidgeon, program manager for IDC's Consumers Markets, claimed that consumers would have a difficult time purchasing the Wii through late 2008. Pidgeon stated that he believed that the Wii would continue to be a successful force in the gaming industry, and that Nintendo needed to start shipping out more consoles. Furthermore, he said that he didn't believe "supply will meet demand for the Wii until 2009."[47]

The supply problem was confirmed by Nintendo CEO Satoru Iwata during a company financial briefing and later on a Web site question and answer session in May of 2007. CEO Iwata said that "we are currently facing product shortages . . . we have been running short of inventories, and [the retailers] are getting after us."[48] Iwata said further, "Making a significant volume of the high-tech hardware, and making an additional volume, is not an easy task at all. "In fact, when we clear one bottleneck for a production increase, we will face another one."[49]

As evident from Exhibit 5 there are 235 games for the Wii. This number indicates that the Wii is obviously a successful system—one that has drawn a good amount of interest from game developers and gamers around the world. The production problem then is augmented because there is great interest in the Wii. However, if Nintendo did not meet the hardware demand, game developers might simply begin developing software for systems that were available to consumers.

CEO Iwata claimed that "shipments will increase and that we are trying to increase the shipments in order to comply with the needs of patiently waiting customers" as well as the number of software titles available for the system from Nintendo and third-party software developers.[50] However the question remained as to whether Nintendo's Iwata could manage to keep the Wii momentum rolling into the next generation of gaming systems.

Endnotes

1. Nintendo Annual Report 2006.
2. http://www.nintendo.com/systemsclassic?type=nes.
3. Bacani, C. & Mutsuko, M. 1997. Nintendo's new 64-bit platform sets off a scramble for market share. *AsiaWeek,* April 18, http://www.asiaweek.com/asiaweek/97/0418/cs1.html.
4. Biggest blunders. *GamePro,* May 2005: 45.
5. http://wii.nintendo.com/iwata_asks_vol2_p1.jsp.
6. Carless, S. 2006. Nintendo announces new revolution name—Wii. *gamasutra.com,* April 27, http://www.gamasutra.com/php-bin/news_index.php?story=9075.
7. Nintendo exec talks Wii Online, marketing. August 17, 2006, www.cnet.com.
8. Nintendo Annual Report 2006.
9. http://arstec hnica.com/news.ars/post/20060615-7067.html.
10. http://wii.nintendo.com/controller.jsp.
11. http://wii.ign.com/articles/718/718946p1.html.
12. http://wii.nintendo.com/controller.jsp.
13. See http://wii.Nintendo.com.
14. See http://wii.nintendo.com.
15. Surette, T. 2006. Nintendo exec talks Wii online, marketing *GameSpot.com.* August 17, http://www.cnet.com.au/games/wii/0,239036428,240091920,00.htm.
16. Nintendo Consolidated Financial Statements, 1/25/2007.
17. http://livenintendo.com/2007/04/12/more-supply-problems-for-the-wii.
18. http://www.marketingvox.com/archives/2007/01/26/nintendo-wii-to-provide-ap-news-on-free-channel/.
19. http://wii.nintendo.com/controller.jsp.
20. En garde! Fight foes using a controller like a sword, *New York Times,* October 30, 2006, http://www.nytimes.com/2006/10/30/technology/30nintendo.html?ex=1319864400&en=135a11a72ad4a4f7&ei=5088&partner=rssnyt&emc=rss.
21. http://www.pcmag.com/article2/0,1895,2058406,00.asp.
22. Layne, N., & Hamada K. 2007. Sony promises more games to boost PS3 demand. June 21, *reuters.com,* http://www. reuters.com/article/technologyNews/idUST28081120070621?sp=true.
23. Microsoft's red-ink game, *BusinessWeek Online,* 11/22/2005. http://businessweek.com/technology/content/nov2005/tc20051122_410710.htm.
24. www.Xbox.com/en-US.
25. http://www.xbox.com/en-US/live/globalcommunity/fosteringcommunity.htm.
26. http://news.teamxbox.com/xbox/12028/Latest-Xbox-Live-Facts-and-Stats/.
27. Ibid.
28. http://arstechnica.com/news.ars/post/20061030-8108.html.
29. http://www.xbox.com/en-AU/support/xbox360/manuals/xbox-360specs.htm.
30. http://money.cnn.com/2006/07/05/commentary/column_gaming/index.htm?section=money_latest.
31. http://news.bbc.co.uk/2/hi/technology/4491804.stm.
32. http://www.microsoft.com/presspass/press/2006/may06/05-09E32006BriefingPR.mspx.
33. www.us.playstation.com/PS3/About/BluRay.
34. http://www.gamasutra.com/php-bin/news_index.php?story=12408.
35. http://au.ps3.ign.com/articles/778/778530p1.html.

36. Author estimates of units sold, approximately 5.5 million units shipped, but 3.25 million sold.

37. http://www.us.playstation.com/PS3/About/WirelessController.

38. http://www.scei.co.jp/corporate/release/pdf/060509be.pdf.

39. http://www.cbsnews.com/stories/2007/01/07/ap/business/main D8MGN9J80.shtml.

40. http://news.bbc.co.uk/1/hi/technology/6499841.stm.

41. http://news.bbc.co.uk/2/hi/technology/6499841.stm.

42. Layne, N., & Hamada, K. 2007. Sony promises more games to boost PS3 demand, June 21, *reuters.com,* http://www. reuters.com/article/technologyNews/idUST28081120070621?sp=true.

43. http://www.us.playstation.com/PS3/Network.

44. http://www.n4g.com/tech/News-35187.aspx.

45. http://tech.uk.msn.com/features/article.aspx?cp-documentid= 4370234.

46. http://www.pcworld.com/article/id,128265-page,4-c,industrynews/ article.html.

47. http://news.teamxbox.com/xbox/13335/Analyst-Supply-Wont-Meet-Demand-for-the-Wii-Until-2009/.

48. *Nintendo Investor Relations* Web site, http://www.nintendo.co.jp/ir/en/library/events/070427qa/02.html.

49. Boyes, E. 2007. Nintendo: Wii have a supply problem. *CNET.News .com,* http://news.com.com/Nintendo+Wii+have+a+supply+problem/2100-1043_3-6181842.html

50. *Nintendo Investor Relations* Web site, http://www.nintendo.co.jp/ir/en/library/events/070427qa/02.html.

CASE 10 Ford Motor Company on the Edge?

Ford Motor Company was setting records, but, unfortunately, not encouraging ones. Although Ford's F-series pickups and the new Edge crossover vehicle were selling well, it had not been enough to stem the losses. The new crossover vehicle, the Ford Edge, was on track to sell 100,000 units in 2007, normally a success story. However, each Edge unit sold was less profitable than the larger sport utility vehicles (SUV) that they typically replaced, according to Ron Pinelli of industry research firm Auto-data Corporation. Ford's chief sales analyst, George Pipas, said that the company was "retaining Ford buyers who were in traditional SUVs that are moving into another category."[1]

On January 25, 2007, the struggling automaker posted a full-year net loss of $12.7 billion for 2006, the largest single-year loss in the company's history.[2] Ford's attempts at restructuring have been under way since 2001; however, it has been projected that the situation will not turn around until at least 2009.[3] In an attempt to stem the downward slide at Ford, and perhaps to jump-start a turnaround, Alan Mulally was elected as President and Chief Executive Officer of Ford on September 5, 2006. Mulally, former head of commercial airplanes at Boeing, was expected to steer the struggling automaker out of the problems of falling market share and serious financial losses (see Exhibit 1).

WHY WOULD FORD INVITE IN AN OUTSIDER?

The Ford empire had been around for over a century and the company had not gone outside its ranks for a top executive since hiring Ernest Breech away from General Motors Corporation in 1946[4] (see Exhibit 2.) Since taking the CEO position in 2001, Bill Ford had tried several times to find a qualified successor, "going after such industry luminaries as Renault-Nissan CEO, Carlos Ghosn, and DaimlerChrysler Chairman, Dieter Zetsche."[5] Now Mulally had been selected and was expected to accomplish "nothing less than undoing a strongly entrenched management system put into place by Henry Ford II almost 40 years ago"— a system of regional fiefdoms around the world that has sapped the company's ability to compete in today's global industry and one that Chairman Bill Ford couldn't or wouldn't unwind.[6]

It had become more common to hire a CEO from outside the family or board. According to Joseph Bower from Harvard Business School, around one-third of the time for the firms comprising the S&P 500, and around 40 percent of the time when companies were struggling with problems in operations or financial distress, an outsider was appointed as CEO. The reasons may be to get a fresh point of view or to get the support of the board. "Results suggest that forced turnover followed by outsider succession, on average, improves firm performance."[7] Bill Ford claimed that to undertake major changes in Ford's dysfunctional culture, an outsider was more qualified than even the most proficient auto industry insider.[8]

An outsider CEO might also help restore faith in Ford management among investors, who had been discontented with the Ford family's high dividends and extravagant lifestyle. The Ford family controlled about 40 percent of the company's voting shares through their ownership of all its Class B stock and holdings of common stock. The class B family shares had almost the same market value as that of common stock, but the voting rights of the family shares are exceptionally high by industry standards (see Exhibits 3 and 4). The dividend stream had been an annuity, which over the years had helped various family members to own a football team, fund museums and philanthropic causes, and even promote the Hare Krishna movement. Given that the company was experiencing serious financial problems, these activities had raised stockholder dissent, as the annual retained earnings in the past were dissipated as dividends instead of reinvested in firm operations or acquisitions to increase the net value of the firm.

MULALLY—THE NEW SAVIOR

Alan Mulally came from a metal-bending business, like auto-making, that is influenced by global competition, has a unionized workforce, and was subject to complex regulations and rapidly changing technologies.[9] Although he is not an auto guy, he had a proven record in an industry that faces similar issues as the automobile industry, and a lot of his expertise and management techniques were highly transferable. In his own words "Everybody says, well, I'm not a car guy, so you couldn't make a contribution here. But I'm a product (guy) and I'm a designer."[10]

Prior to joining Ford, Mulally served as executive vice president of The Boeing Company, and as president and chief executive officer of Boeing Commercial Airplanes. In those roles, he was responsible for The Boeing Company's entire commercial airplane programs and related services.[11] The advanced technology 777, which Mulally led the development of in the early 1990s, is now the most popular twin-engine jet in its class and was a testimony for Mulally's product and technology ingenuity. Under his leadership, Boeing regained its market leadership from Airbus. The appointment of Mulally at Ford had been seen by the market as a move to utilize his experience and success in managing manufacturing and assembly lines to help shape the future of Ford.

Bill Ford praised Mulally as "an outstanding leader and a man of great character."[12] He noted that Mulally had applied many of the lessons from Ford's success in developing the Taurus to Boeing's creation of the revolutionary Boeing 777 airliner. "Clearly, the challenges Boeing faced in recent years have many parallels to our own," said Bill Ford about Mulally's appropriateness for the top position at Ford.[13] In his e-mail to Ford employees announcing the appointment of Mulally, Bill Ford wrote, "Alan has deep experience in customer satisfaction, manufacturing, supplier relations and labor relations, all of which have applications to the challenges of Ford. He also has the personality and team-building skills that will help guide our Company in the right direction."[14]

*This case study was prepared by Professor Helaine J. Korn of Baruch College, City University of New York, Ms. Naga Lakshmi Damaraju of The Ohio State University, and Professor Alan B. Eisner of Pace University. The purpose of the case is to stimulate class discussion rather than to illustrate effective or ineffective handling of a business situation. Copyright © 2007 Helaine Korn, Naga Damaraju, & Alan Eisner.

EXHIBIT 1   **Income Statements**

Ford Motor Company and Subsidiaries
For the Years Ended December 31,
(in $ millions, except per share amounts)

	2006	2005	2004
Automotive			
Sales	$143,307	$153,474	$147,119
Costs and expenses			
Cost of sales	148,869	144,924	135,755
Selling, administrative and other expenses	12,359	12,738	11,564
Total costs and expenses	161,228	157,662	147,319
Operating income/(loss)	(17,921)	(4,188)	(200)
Interest expense	995	1,220	1,221
Interest income and other nonoperating income/(expense), net	1,478	1,249	988
Equity in net income/(loss) of affiliated companies	421	285	255
Income/(loss) before income taxes—Automotive	(17,017)	(3,874)	(178)
Financial Services			
Revenues	16,816	23,422	25,197
Costs and expenses			
Interest expense	7,788	7,197	7,250
Depreciation	5,295	5,854	6,618
Operating and other expenses	1,526	6,030	5,830
Provision for credit and insurance losses	241	483	1,212
Total costs and expenses	14,850	19,564	20,910
Gain on sale of Hertz (Note 19)	—	1,095	—
Income/(loss) before income taxes—Financial Services	1,966	4,953	4,287
Total Company			
Income/(loss) before income taxes	(15,051)	1,079	4,109
Provision for/(benefit from) income taxes (Note 18)	(2,646)	(845)	643
Income/(loss) before minority interests	(12,405)	1,924	3,466
Minority interests in net income/(loss) of subsidiaries	210	280	282
Income/(loss) from continuing operations	(12,615)	1,644	3,184
Income/(loss) from discontinued operations (Note 19)	2	47	(146)
Income/(loss) before cumulative effects of changes in accounting principles	(12,613)	1,691	3,038
Cumulative effects of changes in accounting principles (Note 27)	—	(251)	—
Net income/(loss)	$ (12,613)	$ 1,440	$ 3,038
Average number of shares of Common and Class B Stock outstanding	1,879	1,846	1,830
Amounts Per Share of Common and Class B Stock Basic income/(loss)			
Income/(loss) from continuing operations	$ (6.72)	$ 0.89	$ 1.74
Income/(loss) from discontinued operations	—	0.03	(0.08)
Cumulative effects of changes in accounting principles	—	(0.14)	—
Net income/(loss)	$ (6.72)	$ 0.78	$ 1.66
Diluted Income/(loss)			
Income/(loss) from continuing operations	$ (6.72)	$ 0.87	$ 1.59
Income/(loss) from discontinued operations	—	0.02	(0.07)
Cumulative effects of changes in accounting principles	—	(0.12)	—
Net income/(loss)	$ (6.72)	$ 0.77	$ 1.52
Cash dividends	$ 0.25	$ 0.40	$ 0.40

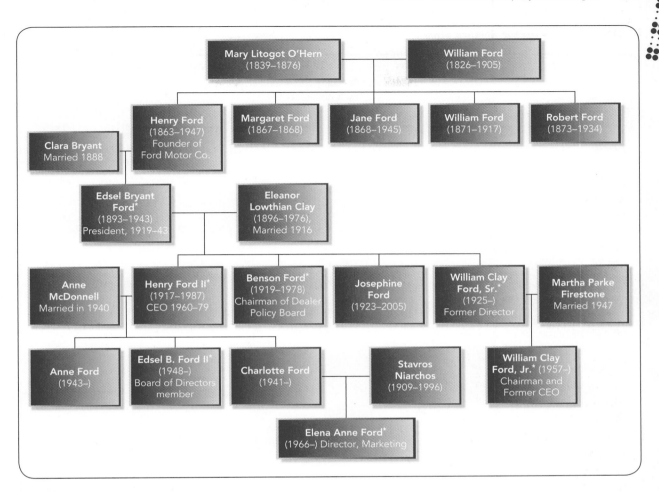

EXHIBIT 2   Ford Family Tree

*Ford Family members who have worked at Ford Motor Co.

Note: Family tree includes descendants; of Henry Ford who worked at Ford Motor Co. and their children.

Sources: Benson Ford Research Center; WSJ research; Wildpedia.

Nonetheless, when Mulally took over the steering wheel, Ford was already poised to make significant structural changes as the company announced details of its accelerated "Way Forward" plan. Moreover, the company seemed to indicate that Mulally's appointment would not change the timelines and decisions associated with those restructuring actions, according to analyst Himanshu Patel of J.P. Morgan. This indicated that in spite of the appointment of Mulally as CEO, much of the decision making still remains with Bill Ford, who said he would remain "extremely active" in the business.

WHAT CHANGES HAS THE NEW CEO BROUGHT IN?

In his effort to set Ford in the right direction, Mulally flew to Japan in January 2007 to meet with top executives of Ford's toughest competitor, Toyota, to seek their advice.[15] This was a huge break from the Ford tradition, and only an outsider CEO would have the courage and imagination to openly try to learn from foreign competitors.

Mulally has set his own priorities for fixing Ford: "At the top of the list, I would put dealing with reality."[16] In early 2007, Mulally signaled that "the bigger-is-better worldview that has defined Ford for decades was being replaced with a new approach: Less is More."[17] Ford needed to pay more attention to cutting costs and transforming the way it did business than to traditional measurements like market share.[18] The vision was to have a smaller and more profitable Ford. There were echoes in Detroit of Mulally's smaller-is-better thinking. G.M. was in the middle of its own revamping plan and Chrysler was also preparing a plan of cutbacks.[19] "Less is More" could be a new trend in the auto industry.

Mulally's cutback plan builds on the 14 plant closures and 30,000-plus job cuts announced by Ford in January 2007. Ford's

EXHIBIT 3   **Sector Balance Sheets**

Ford Motor Company and Subsidiaries (in $ millions)		
	December 31, 2006	December 31, 2005
Assets		
Automotive		
Cash and cash equivalents	$ 16,020	$ 13,388
Marketable securities (Note 3)	11,310	6,860
Loaned securities (Note 3)	5,256	3,461
Total cash marketable and loaned securities	32,586	23,709
Receivables, less allowances of $196 and $298	3,878	3,075
Inventories (Note 8)	11,578	10,271
Deferred income taxes	1,569	1,249
Other current assets	7,714	8,177
Total current assets	57,325	46,481
Equity in net assets of affiliated companies	2,029	1,756
Net property (Note 10)	38,236	40,348
Deferred income taxes	14,880	10,999
Goodwill and other net intangible assets (Note 12)	6,920	5,928
Assets of discontinued/held-for-sale operations	—	5
Other assets	3,244	8,308
Total Automotive assets	122,634	113,825
Financial Services		
Cash and cash equivalents	12,874	15,018
Marketable securities (Note 3)	10,162	3,812
Finance receivables, net (Note 4)	110,767	111,436
Net investment in operating leases (Note 5)	26,606	22,951
Retained interest in sold receivables (Note 7)	990	1,420
Goodwill and other intangible assets (Note 12)	17	17
Other assets	6,167	7,457
Receivable from Automotive (Note 1)	1,467	83
Total Financial Services assets	169,060	162,194
Intersector elimination	(1,467)	(83)
Total assets	$290,217	$276,936
Liabilities and Stockholders' Equity		
Automotive		
Trade payables	$ 17,069	$ 16,637
Other payables	4,893	4,222
Accrued liabilities and deferred revenue (Note 14)	28,995	28,829
Deferred income taxes	3,139	804
Debt payable within one year (Note 15)	1,499	978
Current payable to Financial Services (Note 1)	640	83
Total current liabilities	56,235	51,553
		(continued)

EXHIBIT 3   **Sector Balance Sheets (continued)**

Ford Motor Company and Subsidiaries (in $ millions)	December 31, 2006	December 31, 2005
Long-term debt (Note 15)	28,514	16,900
Other liabilities (Note 14)	49,398	38,639
Deferred income taxes	441	586
Noncurrent payable to Financial Services (Note 1)	827	—
Total Automotive liabilities	135,415	107,678
Financial Services		
Payables	1,587	2,051
Debt (Note 15)	142,036	135,400
Deferred income taxes	10,827	10,747
Other liabilities and deferred income	4,125	5,579
Total Financial Services liabilities	158,575	153,777
Minority Interests	1,159	1,122
Stockholders' equity		
Capital stock (Note 20)		
Common Stock, par value $0.01 per share (1,837 million shares issued, 6,000 million shares authorized)	18	18
Class B Stock, par value $0.01 per share (71 million shares issued; 530 million shares authorized)	1	1
Capital in excess of par value of stock	4,562	4,872
Accumulated other comprehensive income/(loss)	(7,846)	(3,680)
Treasury stock	(183)	(833)
Retained earnings/(Accumulated deficit)	(17)	13,064
Total stockholders' equity	(3,465)	13,442
Intersector elimination	(1,487)	(83)
Total liabilities and stockholders' equity	**$290,217**	**$275,936**

new plan added two more North American plants to the closure list and targets $5 billion in cost cuts by the end of 2008, but pushed back a target for North American profitability by one year to 2009.[20] The company targeted seven vehicle manufacturing sites for closure and plans to have an optimum capacity at that point. At the same time, it also plans to increase the plant utilization and production levels in each production unit, while focusing more on larger, more fuel-efficient vehicles. The overall strategy seemed to be towards restructuring as a tool to obtain operating profitability at lower volume and with a changing mix of products that better appeals to the market.

Mulally also refocused the company on the Ford brand when he announced a formal review of Volvo in July 2007 as the first steps to putting the division up for sale. Volvo had been acquired eight years earlier to be part of the Premier Automotive Group of Ford among Jaguar, Aston Martin, and Land Rover.[21] However, Volvo's primary selling point of superior safety had been challenged as other manufacturers made advances in safety technologies in their own brands. Ford was also reviewing bids for Jaguar and Land Rover, both of which had lost money in four out of the last five years. Mulally said that the "real opportunity going forward is to integrate and leverage our Ford assets around the world," and decide on the best mix of brands in the company's portfolio.[22]

Since his appointment, Mulally had made some structural and procedural changes in the company. For instance, instead of discussing business plans monthly or semiannually as they used to do at Ford, executives now met with Mulally weekly. The in-depth sessions were a contrast to executives' previous efforts to explain away bad news, said Donat R. Leclair, Ford's

EXHIBIT 4   **Sector Statements of Cash Flows**

Ford Motor Company and Subsidiaries
For the Years Ended December 31,
(in $ millions)

	2006		2005		2004	
	Automotive	**Financial Services**	**Automotive**	**Financial Services**	**Automotive**	**Financial Services**
Cash flows from operating activities of continuing operations						
Net cash flows from operating activities (Note 21)	$ (4,185)	$ 7,318	$ 5,433	$ 6,912	$ 6,963	$ 7,963
Cash flows from investing activities of continuing operations						
Capital expenditures	(6,809)	(39)	(7,123)	(394)	(6,280)	(458)
Acquisitions of retail and other finance receivables and operating leases	—	(59,793)	—	(54,024)	—	(63,284)
Collections of retail and other finance receivables and operating leases	—	41,867	—	48,245	—	51,220
Net (increase)/decrease in wholesale receivables	—	6,113	—	4,751	—	2,882
Net acquisitions of daily rental vehicles	—	—	—	(1,988)	—	(2,492)
Purchases of securities	(4,068)	(19,610)	(5,714)	(6,169)	(7,590)	(4,177)
Sales and maturities of securities	4,865	13,591	5,106	3,629	7,615	9,033
Proceeds from sales of retail and other finance receivables and operating leases	—	5,120	—	17,288	—	6,481
Proceeds from sale of wholesale receivables	—	—	—	3,739	—	3,957
Proceeds from sale of businesses	56	—	280	7,657	125	412
Cash paid for acquisitions	—	—	(2,031)	—	(30)	—
Transfer of cash balances upon disposition of discontinued held-for-sale operations	(4)	—	—	(1,255)	(26)	(13)
Investing activity from Financial Services	1,185	—	8,407	—	4,361	—
Investing activity to Financial Services	(1,400)	—	—	—	—	—
Other	18	307	387	1,462	107	2,185
Net cash (used in) provided by investing activities	(6,157)	(12,444)	(688)	22,941	(1,718)	5,746
Cash flows from financing activities of continuing operations						
Cash dividends	(468)	—	(738)	—	(733)	—
Sales of Common Stock	431	—	895	—	21	—

(continued)

EXHIBIT 4   **Sector Statements of Cash Flows** *(continued)*

	2006 Automotive	2006 Financial Services	2005 Automotive	2005 Financial Services	2004 Automotive	2004 Financial Services
Ford Motor Company and Subsidiaries *For the Years Ended December 31, (in $ millions)*						
Purchases of Common Stock	(183)	—	(570)	—	(172)	—
Changes in short-term debt	414	(6,239)	(115)	(8,598)	(342)	5,227
Proceeds from issuance of other debt	12,254	46,004	385	24,174	469	21,754
Principal payments on other debt	(758)	(35,843)	(758)	(35,322)	(2,564)	(33,436)
Financing activity from Automotive	—	1,400	—	—	—	—
Financing activity to Automotive	—	(1,185)	—	(8,407)	—	(4,361)
Other	(147)	(192)	(177)	24	(39)	(97)
Net cash (used in/provided by financing activities	11,543	3,945	(1,078)	(28,129)	(3,360)	(10,913)
Effect of exchange rate changes on cash	104	360	(23)	(473)	117	388
Net change in intersector receivables/ payables and other liabilities	1,321	(1,321)	(394)	394	1,258	(1,258)
Net increase (decrease) in cash and cash equivalents from continuing operations	2,626	(2,144)	3,250	1,645	3,260	1,926
Cash from discontinued operations						
Cash flows from operating activities of discontinued operations	2	—	(16)	71	(149)	464
Cash flows from investing activities of discontinued operations	—	—	17	(66)	137	(457)
Cash flows from financing activities of discontinued operations	—	—	—	—	—	—
Net increase/(decrease) in cash and cash equivalents	$ 2,628	$ (2,144)	$ 3,251	$ 1,650	$ 3,248	$ 1,933
Cash and cash equivalents at January 1	$ 13,388	$15,018	$10,139	$ 12,689	$ 6,853	$10,819
Cash and cash equivalents of discontinued/ held-for-sale operations at January 1	4	—	2	679	40	616
Net increase (decrease) in cash and cash equivalents	2,628	(2,144)	3,251	1,650	3,248	1,933
Less cash and cash equivalents of discontinued held-for-sale operations at December 31	—	—	(4)	—	(2)	(679)
Cash and cash equivalents at December 31	$ 16,020	$12,874	$13,388	$ 15,018	$10,139	$12,689

chief financial officer. "The difference I see now is that we're actually committed to hitting the numbers. Before, it was a culture of trying to explain why we were off the plan. The more eloquently you could explain why you were off the plan, the more easy it was to change the plan."[23]

Mulally also did some senior executive reorganization at Ford and many of the newly appointed would report to him directly, including a global head of product development. In addition, the head of worldwide purchasing, the chief of quality and advanced manufacturing, the head of information technology, the chief technical officer, and the leaders of Ford's European division, its Asia, Pacific, and Africa units and its Americas unit would all report directly to him.[24]

ABOUT THE FORD MOTOR COMPANY

Ford Motor had been sinking since 1999, when profits had reached a remarkable $7.2 billion ($5.86 per share) and pretax income was $11 billion. At that time people even speculated that Ford would soon overtake General Motors as the world's number one automobile manufacturer (see Exhibits 5-7). But soon Toyota, through its innovative technology, management philosophy of continuous improvement, and cost arbitrage due to its presence in multiple geographical locations, took over the

giants—GM and Ford. Compounding this were Ford's internal organizational problems and a failed diversification strategy led by Jacques Nasser, the CEO at that time, and Ford's market share began to drop—from 25 percent in 1999 to 18 percent in 2006, with major blows to market share in the light vehicle segment.

Moreover, in 2006, Chevrolet outsold the Ford division for the first time since 1986. Despite an extensive mechanical update, the much-improved Ford Explorer, which had been the world's best-selling sport utility vehicle, fell behind the dated Chevy TrailBlazer in sales. It did not help that the new Explorer looked just like the model it replaced. The long-neglected Ranger, which had been the top-selling small pickup, fell behind both Toyota Motor and Chevrolet, and despite 20 years of trying, the company has never been able to build a competitive minivan. Ford's most successful vehicles were the F-series pickup trucks (see Exhibit 8).

The company was also experiencing serious financial problems. Ford's turnaround plan aims to cut $5 billion in costs by the end of 2008 by slashing 10,000 white-collar workers and offering buyouts to all of its 75,000 unionized employees. The loss, including restructuring costs, was Ford's largest quarterly loss since the first quarter of 1992, when the company lost $6.7 billion due mainly to accounting changes. Ford said special charges for the third quarter of 2006 totaled $5.26 billion

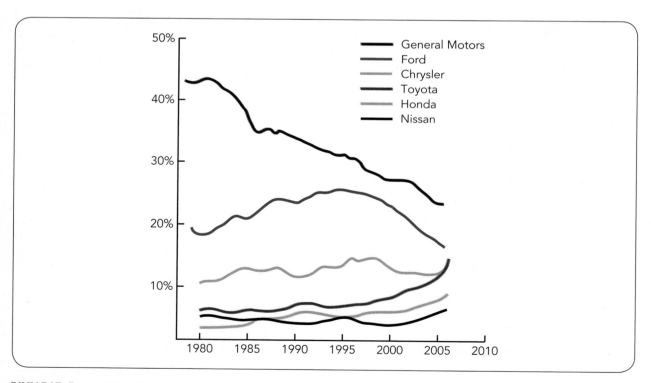

EXHIBIT 5 **U.S. Market Share**

Source: Autodata.

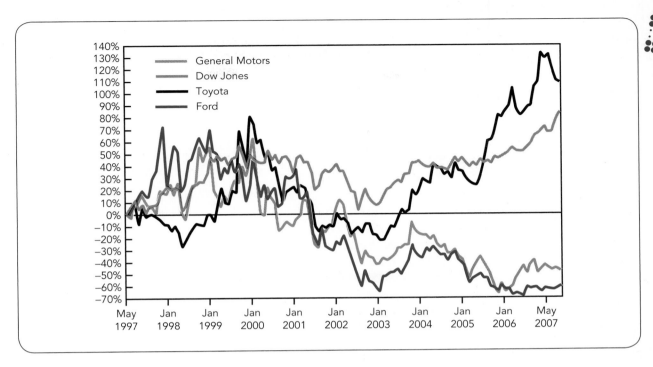

EXHIBIT 6   **Ford 10-Year Stock Price History**

before taxes. The charges included $2.2 billion to revalue assets in North America and $1.6 billion to decrease the value of Jaguar and Land Rover assets.

AUTOMOBILE INDUSTRY IN THE UNITED STATES

The automotive industry in the United States was a highly competitive, cyclical business. The number of cars and trucks sold to retail buyers or "industry demand" varied substantially from year to year depending on "general economic situations, the cost of purchasing and operating cars and trucks, the availability of credit and fuel." Because cars and trucks are durable items, consumers could wait to replace them; industry demand reflected this factor (see Exhibit 9).

Competition in the United States intensified in the last few decades with Japanese carmakers gaining a foothold in the market. To counter the foreign problem, Japanese companies had set up production facilities in the United States and gained acceptance from American consumers. Production quality and lean production were judged to be the major weapons that Japanese carmakers used to gain an advantage over American carmakers. "The Toyota Motor Company of Japan issued a 2007 forecast that would make it first in global sales, ahead of General Motors, which has been the world's biggest auto company since 1931. Toyota, which had not even built its first automobile back then, expects to sell 9.34 million vehicles next year. That would exceed the 9.2 million vehicles that GM expects to sell worldwide this year."[25] For American consumers, Toyota vehicles

have been "a better value proposition" than Detroit's products, said Mulally, who was the first Detroit leader who readily said he was an avid student of Toyota.[26]

While there was a glut in the U.S. automobile market, the markets of Asia, Central and South America, and central and Eastern Europe all showed increasing promise for automobiles, and the automobile industry entered into an era of "global motorization."

CHALLENGES MULALLY FACES

Mulally was faced with a lot of challenges. He had considerable experience dealing with manufacturing and labor relations issues, but he did not have much background in finance. Given the cash drain at Ford due to restructuring costs and product development, and the B+ junk credit rating of Ford stock, cash was crucial to keep the company afloat and Mulally's abilities would be tested.[27]

"Mulally's fearlessness was well suited to pushing through projects at Boeing, but its suitability to Ford's culture remains to be seen. Like every new leader, he will have to move with confidence in his early days, but as an industry outsider, he will have to take care to avoid violating the long-standing industry norms."[28]

"Mulally's approach to management and communication hasn't been seen before in the halls of Ford, which have historically been the atmosphere of a kingdom with competing dukes."[29] Mulally was still in the honeymoon period but already clashes had surfaced between his management style and the "Ford way."

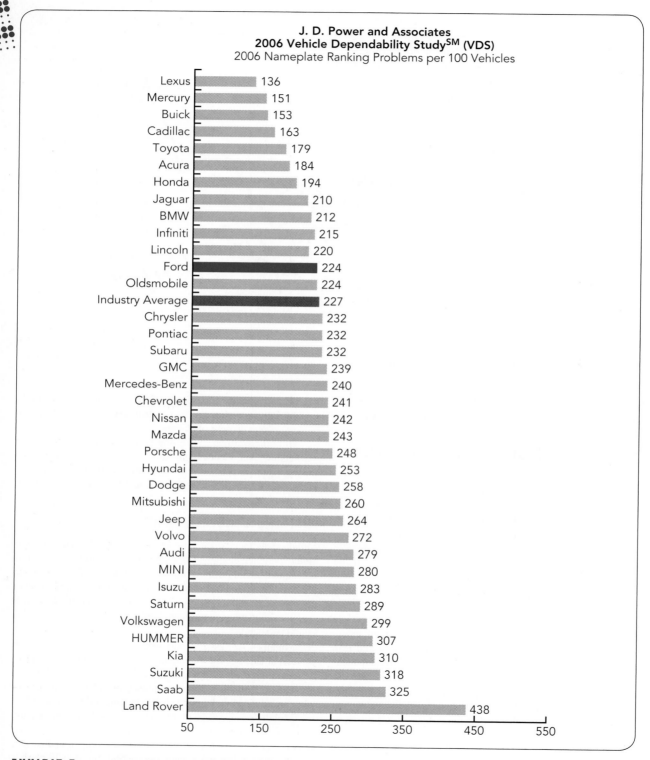

J. D. Power and Associates
2006 Vehicle Dependability Study^{SM} (VDS)
2006 Nameplate Ranking Problems per 100 Vehicles

Nameplate	Problems
Lexus	136
Mercury	151
Buick	153
Cadillac	163
Toyota	179
Acura	184
Honda	194
Jaguar	210
BMW	212
Infiniti	215
Lincoln	220
Ford	224
Oldsmobile	224
Industry Average	227
Chrysler	232
Pontiac	232
Subaru	232
GMC	239
Mercedes-Benz	240
Chevrolet	241
Nissan	242
Mazda	243
Porsche	248
Hyundai	253
Dodge	258
Mitsubishi	260
Jeep	264
Volvo	272
Audi	279
MINI	280
Isuzu	283
Saturn	289
Volkswagen	299
HUMMER	307
Kia	310
Suzuki	318
Saab	325
Land Rover	438

EXHIBIT 7   **2006 Vehicle Dependability Rankings**

Source: J. D. Power and Associates 2006 Vehicle Dependability Study.^{SM}

EXHIBIT 8   **Top-Selling Vehicles of 2006**

1. Ford F-Series (includes F-150, F-250 Super Duty, and F-350 Super Duty)—796,039
2. Chevrolet Silverado (includes 1500, 1500 Classic, 1500 SS Classic, 1500HD Classic, 2500HD, 2500HD Classic, 3500HD, 3500 Classic—636,069
3. Toyota Camry and Camry Solara—448,445
4. Dodge Ram (includes 1500, 2500 and 3500)—364,177
5. Honda Accord—354,441
6. Toyota Corolla—318,123
7. Honda Civic—316,638
8. Chevrolet Impala—289,868
9. Nissan Altima—232,457
10. Chevrolet Cobalt—211,449

Source: *Automotive News* and Edmunds.com, http://www.edmunds.com/reviews/list/top10/120637/article.html.

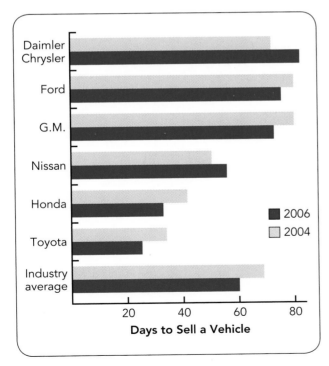

EXHIBIT 9   **Dealer Turnover**

Source: Ward's AutoInfoBank.

Mulally busied himself breaking down a global structure in which Ford Europe, Ford Asia, Ford North America, Ford Australia, and Ford South America had long created redundancies of efforts, products, engineering platforms, engines, and the like as a way of perpetuating each division's independence.[30] Since the initial purpose of having an outsider CEO was to break the dysfunctional Ford culture, these clashes were expected and generally viewed as constructive.

However, the clashes also had their drawbacks. Unable to accept the Mulally management approach, some senior executives left Ford. International chief of the company, Mark A. Schulz, was one of them. "He had decided to retire this year after working for more than three decades at the company. Mr. Schulz is just the latest in a string of senior executives to leave since Mulally took over. Ford's second-ranking North American executive, its North American manufacturing chief and its chief of staff also all announced their departures after Mulally's hiring."[31] Ford had lost some of its most experienced leaders because of the outsider CEO.

Despite his rich experience and proven success in turning around the manufacturing operations at Boeing, Mulally was still not completely qualified or accepted as an auto guy. "He recently had to ask what the name of the auto industry's lobby group is (Alliance of Automobile Manufacturers) and what NADA stands for (National Automobile Dealers Assn., which he will address in a keynote speech in February)."[32] He had to learn the business and its unique terms on the fly. Speaking the auto language was still critical for an outsider CEO to be accepted in a giant company like Ford, which had a long and distinct tradition of promoting insider leaders.

Nonetheless, Mulally was confident that his years of experience running a big manufacturer and his technical background had prepared him for the challenges facing Ford.[33]

LOOKING AHEAD

The year-end earnings report was not without some good news. Ford was out to cut operating costs by $5 billion by 2008. Mulally said that the more he learned about Ford's global operations, the more opportunities he saw to overshoot that target.[34] Maybe Mulally's smaller-is-better strategy was the lifesaver for Ford. Only time would tell whether bringing in an outsider was a good move for Ford and, more specifically, whether Alan Mulally was the right outsider for the job.

Endnotes

1. Bunkley, Nick. 2007. A crossover helps Ford, but not enough to hold its no. 2 spot. *New York Times*. May 2. www. nytimes.com.
2. Kiley, D. 2007. The record year Ford hopes to shake off. *BusinessWeek Online*. January 26. www.businessweek.com.
3. Kiley, D. 2007. Can this man save Ford? *BusinessWeek Online*. January 19. www.businessweek.com.
4. Knowles, F. 2006. Boeing exec flies the coop: Ford hires Mulally to turn things. *Chicago Sun-Times*. September 6.
5. Welch D., Kiley D., & Holmes S. 2006. Alan Mulally: A plan to make Ford fly. *BusinessWeek*

6. Kiley, D. 2007. Mulally: Ford's most important new model. *Business-Week Online*. January 9. www.businessweek.com.

7. Rakesh, K . 1998. The changing of the guard: Causes, process and consequences of CEO turnover.

8. Berfield, S. 2006. The best leaders. *BusinessWeek Online*. December 18. www.businessweek.com.

9. Levin, D. 2006. Mulally's hire by Ford may be too late. *Bloomberg.com*.

10. Crain, K. 2006. Mulally wants fewer platforms, fewer dealers. *New York Times*. November 20.

11. Ford Motor Company, http://media.ford.com/article_display.cfm?article_id=24203.

12. Ford Motor Company, http://media.ford.com/article_display.cfm?article_id=24203.

13. Ford Motor Company, http://media.ford.com/article_display.cfm?article_id=24203.

14. Ford Motor Company, http://media.ford.com/article_display.cfm?article_id=24203.

15. Maynard, M. 2007. Ford chief sees small as virtue and necessity. *New York Times*. January, 25. http://www.nytimes.com.

16. Maynard, M. 2007. Ford chief sees small as virtue and necessity. *New York Times*. January, 25. http://www.nytimes.com.

17. Maynard, M. 2007. Ford chief sees small as virtue and necessity. *New York Times*. January, 25. http://www.nytimes.com.

18. Maynard, M. 2006. Ford expects to fall soon to no. 3 spot. *New York Times*. December 21. http://www.nytimes.com.

19. Maynard, M. 2007. Ford chief sees small as virtue and necessity. *New York Times*. January, 25. http://www.nytimes.com.

20. Stoll, John. 2006. Ford looks to reshape business model, executive says. *Dow Jones Newswires*. September 18.

21. Maynard, Micheline. 2007. Ford seeks a future by going backward. *New York Times*. July, 17: C1.

22. Bunkley, Nick and Maynard, Micheline. 2007. Ford breaks string of losing quarters, but says respite will be brief. *New York Times*. July, 27: C3.

23. Maynard, Micheline. 2007. Ford chief sees small as virtue and necessity. *New York Times*. January, 25. http://www. nytimes.com.

24. Bloomberg News. 2006. Ford reorganizes executives. *New York Times*. December 15. http://www.nytimes.com.

25. Maynard, M., & Fackler, M. 2006. Toyota is poised to supplant GM as world's largest carmaker. *New York Times*. December 22. http://www.nytimes.com.

26. Maynard, M., & Fackler, Martin 2006. Toyota is poised to supplant GM as world's largest carmaker. *New York Times*. December 22. http://www.nytimes.com.

27. Welch D., Kiley D., & Holmes S. 2006. Alan Mulally: A plan to make Ford fly. *BusinessWeek*.

28. Welch D., Kiley D., & Holmes S. 2006. Alan Mulally: A plan to make ford fly. *BusinessWeek*.

29. Kiley, D. 2007. Mulally: Ford's most important new model. *Business-Week Online*. January 9. www.businessweek.com.

30. Kiley, D. 2007. The record year Ford hopes to shake off. *Business-Week Online*. January 26. www.businessweek.com.

31. Bloomberg News. 2006. Ford reorganizes executives. *New York Times*. December 15. http://www.nytimes.com.

32. Kiley, D. 2007. Mulally: Ford's most important new model. *BusinessWeek Online*. January 9. www.businessweek.com.

33. Maynard, M. 2007. Ford chief sees small as virtue and necessity. *New York Times*. January, 25. http://www.nytimes.com.

34. Kiley, D. 2007. The record year Ford hopes to shake off. *BusinessWeek Online*. January 26. www.businessweek.com.

Indexes

Name Index

A

B

C